D1228671

MOTHERS
IN THE
FATHERLAND

MOTHERS IN THE FATHERLAND

WOMEN, THE FAMILY, AND NAZI POLITICS

CLAUDIA KOONZ

ST. MARTIN'S PRESS
NEW YORK

MIDDLE ISLAND PUBLIC LIBRARY

Grateful acknowledgment is made for permission to reprint from the following:

Sylvia Plath, *The Collected Poems*, ed. by Ted Hughes. Copyright © 1981 by Harper and Row Publishers Inc. Reprinted by permission of Harper and Row Publishers Inc.

Harold Poor, *Kurt Tucholsky and the Ordeal of Germany: 1914–1935.* Copyright © 1968 by Harold Poor. Published by Scribner and Sons, Co. 1968. Permission to reprint granted by the author.

A. J. Ryder, *Twentieth Century Germany.* Copyright © 1973 by A. J. Ryder. Reprinted by permission of Columbia University Press.

MOTHERS IN THE FATHERLAND. Copyright © 1987 by Claudia Koonz. All rights reserved. Printed in the United States of America. No part of this book may be used or reproduced in any manner whatsoever without written permission except in the case of brief quotations embodied in critical articles or reviews. For information, address St. Martin's Press, 175 Fifth Avenue, New York, N.Y. 10010.

Design by Beth Tondreau

Library of Congress Cataloging-in-Publication Data

Koonz, Claudia.
Mothers in the fatherland.

1. Women—Germany—History—20th century. 2. Family—Germany—History—20th century. 3. Germany—Social conditions—1918-1933. 4. Germany—Social conditions—1933-1945. 5. National socialism. I. Title.
HQ1623.K66   1986   306'.0943   86-13815
ISBN 0-312-54933-4

First Edition
10 9 8 7 6 5 4 3 2 1

For my parents,
Oliver W. and Edna Kingston Koonz

What is past is not dead; it is not even past. We cut ourselves off from it; we preferred to be strangers.
—Christa Wolf, *Model Childhood*

CONTENTS

ACKNOWLEDGMENTS

From the very beginning of my study of women in Nazi Germany, I knew that I would depend upon the close collaboration of archivists, colleagues, and friends. The scarcity of published documents and secondary works in the mid-1970s meant that before even beginning this undertaking I needed the advice of dozens of curators at state, local, church, and organizational archives. From the very first, too, I received vital feedback from other historians who shared their specialized knowledge about sources and also forced me to relate information about women to the wider perspectives of the history of inter-war Germany. Gathering information about so dismal a period becomes depressing. The historical figures I admired were nearly always killed and the women Nazis I deplored virtually always thrived, even after 1945. Without the friends who helped me think through my responses to the unrelieved tragedy of the Nazi period, I might have succumbed either to a professional callousness that blotted out empathy or despaired completely and abandoned the project altogether.

I have looked forward to writing this acknowledgment as a tribute to the many individuals who helped me out in so many ways. My first thanks go to colleagues who encouraged me to begin my forays into archives from the Nazi period. Renate Bridenthal, Rudolf Binion, Hannah Papaneck, Fritz Ringer, Carl Schorske, and Joan Scott read and commented on my earliest proposals for this research in the mid-1970s. More recently, the late Warren Susman, John Gillis, Peter Gay, Charles S. Meier, and Ismar Schorsch helped me to rethink my conclusions and consider new dimensions of my findings.

Without substantial aid I could never have completed extensive archival research in Germany. Most of all, the College of the Holy Cross has supported me with not only a sabbatical year, but a one-semester Faculty Fellowship, unlimited computer time and a VAX terminal, and generous annual grants to defray expenses for travel, interviewing, and Xeroxing. The German Marshall Foundation and the Rockefeller Foundation each granted me yearlong fellowships to pursue research and writing. The National Endowment for the Humanities awarded me a Travel-to-Collections grant so I could carry on interviews with Jewish Germans living in Germany.

Because the success of this study depended upon my discovering little-known source material, I want to acknowledge my special debt to the dozens of staff members of archives in Germany, France, England, and the United States who gave so generously of their time and shared their immense knowledge of their respective collections. Agnes Peterson early on directed my attention to the valuable autobiographical essays in the Abel Collection at the Hoover Institution for War, Revolution and Peace at Stanford University. I continued my search for individual records at the Berlin Document Center, where Herr Pix and William Simon patiently provided me with files and new "leads." In my search for background information and periodicals, Frau Lorenz at the German Institute for Social Questions in Berlin provided me with hours of thoughtful assistance. In the process, she allowed me access to the papers of Helene Lange Collection. Frau Rasch at the library of the Verband Weiblicher Angestellte in Berlin allowed me to spend days reading in the organization's extensive periodical collection.

Dr. Rumschöttel at the Munich State Archives opened up to me the extraordinary collection of women's papers and memos in the Ministry of Education and National Socialist Teachers' Union (NSLB) files. For material on women in the early part of the century, I am grateful for the guidance of Dr. Cecile Lowenthal-Hess of the Geheimes Staatsarchiv Preussischer Kulturbesitz, Dr. Eberhard Heyl of the Bavarian Hauptstaatsarchiv IV, and Herr Teichmann of the Siemens Archives in Munich. Elke Frölich at the Institute for Contemporary History shared with me her study of police files and gave me valuable guidelines to the Institute collections. Frau Brigitte Emmer helped me out with procedures and catalogues. Blanche Wiesen Cook called my attention to the Robbins papers at the Roosevelt Library.

Dr. Neugebauer shared with me his extensive knowledge of the Federal Military Archive in Freiburg holdings related to women's participation in wartime labor mobilization. Herr Scharmann supplied me with relevant information about the Federal Archives in Koblenz. At the Munich State Archives, Fräulein Booms brought me files and explained procedures. The staff of the North Rhineland Westphalian Gestapo Archives in Düsseldorf supplied me with access to organizational files in their collections. In the Nuremberg State Archives, Frau B. Bauerschäfer guided me through the indices related to local and regional government. Frau Pietrowski introduced me to the Lower Saxony Hauptstaatsarchiv in Pattensen. At the Hessian State Archives Herr Helfer and Frau Dr. Löwenstein explained the holdings and suggested I investigate the extensive Nazi Party membership applications. At the Kalkum branch of the Düsseldorf State Archives, Herr Reuter patiently supplied dozens and dozens of folios on local and regional social history.

Herr Wolfgang Strecker clarified the extraordinarily rich organizational records of Catholic organizations at the Deutscher Caritasverband Archives in Freiburg, and Herr Dr. Hans-Josef Wollasch allowed me access to the social work and educational library at the Caritas Fachhochschule in Freiburg. In the Archbishopric Archives in Freiburg, Frau Ulrike Dehn spent hours with me pouring through catalogues and files related to women, Archbishop Gröber, and local educational organizations. At the office of the League of Catholic Women Teachers in Essen, Frau Dr. Pflug and Frau Emmerich gave unstintingly of their time to share with me their collection of teachers' autobiographies from the Nazi period. Maria Prym and Frau Klöpper made me feel at home by not only allowing me to read in their collection at the Catholic Women's League in Cologne, but also by their willingness to discuss their organization's history.

In Berlin two wonderful collections and their personnel sustained me through several months of research into Protestant women's organizations. Frau Helge Tonges on several occasions explained the holdings of the Protestant National Archives in Berlin and over the years has provided me with much vital information on women's organizations. Hans-Jochen Kaiser has for a decade shared with me his writings and his extensive knowledge about Protestant women's organizations under Nazism. At the Protestant Archives in Karlsruhe, Frau Sakdowski invited me to use the excellent collection related to the Neuland Organization and Protestant associations. I want especially to thank Dr. Helmut Tlasko, Herr Deppe, Frau Dohmke, Frau Schwetlinski, Frau Pohl, and Frau Erdmann, whose good humor and efficiency made working at the Diakonisches Werk Archives in Berlin so rewarding.

The staff of the Bibliothèque de Documentation Internationale Contemporaine, at the University of Paris, Nanterre, has sustained me with their efficiency, knowledge, and good humor. Working at the Centre de documentation Juives Contemporaine in Paris inspired me with awe at the collections and with a strong sense of continuity with the past they describe. Dr. Monika Richarz, of the Germania Judaica in Cologne, prodded me forward with sharp questions and suggestions for further reading. Michael Riff, Frank Mecklenberg, Sybil Milton, and Allan Divack have for years helped me in my research and made the days I have spent at the Leo Baeck Institute among the highlights of my archival searches. Dr. Fred Grubel introduced me to a network of scholars researching the history of Jewish organizations in Nazi Germany. Marion Kaplan told me about dozens of files and articles and asked me vexing questions that made me rethink my assumptions about Jewish women in Nazi Germany. My search for photos was aided by Fräulein Ledder at the Ullstein Photo Service, Frau Klausener at Prussian Picture Archives, and Frau Dr. Mahnke at the Prussian State Library in Berlin. The Peter Hammar Press generously mailed the only copy in its possession of the photo of Hitler with the mother of a Nazi martyr, which I used as the last illustration in this book.

To Rabbi Stanley Davids and the members of Temple Emanuel in Worcester who lived in Germany before 1939, I am grateful for their willingness to explore painful memories. Lilli Kretzmir's retrospective wisdom and sharp questions opened up new dilemmas and insights into how it felt to be betrayed not only by one's "Fatherland" but also most of one's neighbors and friends. Dr. Robert Salomon shared his extraordinary knowledge of Jewish history and, together with his wife Johanna Salomon, Charlotte Blaschke, Ilse Rothschild, Annie Bader, Magda Meyersohn, Harold Rogers, Helen Sachse, and Ilse Wischnia, participated in a collective exploration of the years they had spent in Germany. Elisabeth do Pazo's honesty made me aware of the moral ambiguities of resistance.

My deepest gratitude goes to a host of friend-colleagues. Joyce Engelson, my editor at St. Martin's during the early stages of this book, gave me her precise reactions to every chapter and invariably sent me back to the drawing board. Just two of her many terse questions, "What about Jewish women?" and "Did no women resist?" resulted in over a year of additional research, thinking, and writing. I owe much to her enthusiasm, unfailing good judgment, and patient determination. Thomas Dunne gave his thoughtful commentary on the final version. As the manuscript took its final form, Betsy Williams, with steady nerves and good humor, guided it across the finish line, and Amelie Littell carefully checked the result as it arrived.

Lois Brynes and Serena Hilsinger unfailingly offered me their comments and hospitality, especially during the weeks when I almost lived in front of the word processor screen in my office. In Munich Eva Kollmar Krell and Eberhardt Kollmar held "debriefing" sessions after long days in the archives, and in Berlin Gudrun Schwarz, Karin Hausen, Annemarie Tröger, Gisela Bock, Dagmar Schultz, Ursula Kirchner, and Elisabeth Meyer-Renschhausen offered their hospitality and conversation. Max and Miriam Awerbuch drew me into spirited discussions about life among Jews in Israel, Berlin, and the United States. My colleagues at the College of the Holy Cross gave me sharp criticisms and good-humored encouragement at every stage. Especially I want to thank Ross Beales, Robert L. Brandfon, Randall K. Burkett, Ann Flynn, Karen Gottschang, William Green, Anthony J. Kuzniewski, Theresa M. Mc-Bride, and James F. Powers for their collegial support. Rachel S. Degutis, aided by Paula McGrail, answered dozens of bibliographical inquiries. Barbara Puddister found every missing book. Rev. Joseph F. Pomeroy and Ellen Keohane helped out with all word processing crises.

Bonnie Anderson read the penultimate draft and returned it full of marginal comments and pages of valuable notes. To Mary Ellen Capek, Temma Kaplan, and Harriet Lutzky I am grateful for questions and detailed reactions on the chapters they read. In an important sense, my largest debt is to Charlotte Sheedy, who was the first person to urge me to expand my focus beyond women Nazis and to address the panorama of German women as Catholics, Protestants, Jews, and resisters. Since our initial conversations in 1980, she has piloted this manuscript through the publishing process, given me unsparing feedback, and cheered my way.

Each time I completed a chapter, I gritted my teeth and distributed it to nine friend-colleagues who I knew would dissect it, call for more evidence, dispute its fundamental thesis, and suggest at least ten alternative organizational approaches. The relentless cross-questioning and spirited discussions that resulted were the high points of my work on this manuscript. Thank you, Bonnie Anderson, Renate Bridenthal, Jane Caplan, Atina Grossman, Amy Hackett, Deborah Hertz, Marion Kaplan, Molly Nolan, and Joan Reuterschan. Françoise Basch perused every chapter, unfailingly welcomed me in Paris after archival forays to Germany, and constantly warned me about the difference between *tout comprendre* and *tout pardonner*.

PREFACE

As I waited for Gertrud Scholtz-Klink to walk through the door of a cluttered editorial office in the prosperous suburb of a quaint German university town, I tried to imagine how she might have changed in the forty years since I had lost her trail in the archives. In the early 1940s, American historian Mary Beard had been awestruck at the power of this woman, whom she had described as "spectacular and utterly ruthless."

> By 1941 she [Gertrud Scholtz-Klink] was governing some thirty million German women and tightening her grip on some twenty million other women in lands occupied by German troops. The dictatorial authority of this "Lady *Führer über Alles*" was vividly described by Peter Engelmann. . . . "Frau Klink," wrote Engelmann, "rules the lives of women in all things. She tells them how many children they must have, and when; what they shall wear, what they shall cook and how. What they shall say, laughing to their husbands and sons marching to war. How they shall behave, smiling, when their men are killed. Here is the responsibility for the home spirit, the core of national morale."[1]

She had impressed William Shirer, on the other hand, as "particularly obnoxious and vapid."[2] This woman was about to walk through the door, and I wondered again what I would say, what I might learn. What had brought me here?

Curiosity? Of course. But I also felt a sleuthlike need to follow up on every clue related to the role of women in Nazi Germany. I had already gathered evidence from books and archives on women who embraced Nazism and joined the Party, on Catholics and Protestants who expressed reservations but welcomed the arrival of an authoritarian state in 1933, on women who opposed Hitler, and finally on Jewish women who defended themselves against incremental and ultimately lethal danger. This was not, as my friends and colleagues were quick to point out, "happy history."

"How," my friends asked, "can you live with such a depressing topic?" Like all historians, I had a ready-made response. " 'Those who don't know their history are condemned to repeat it.' " Was that a feeble excuse? Americans today see no swastikas on their political horizons. Uniformed, goose-stepping militarism surely died out after the advent of missiles and guerrillas. Still, underneath the unique and dated style of Nazism lurked a more universal appeal—the longing to return to simpler times, to restore lost values, to join a moral crusade. What needs drove those millions of "good Germans" willingly into dictatorship, war, and genocide? Did those needs exist in other nations at other times? Could what Susan Sontag has called "the drama of the leader and the chorus" continue to play a role after the demise of the fascist hero?[3] During the Great Depression, Germans rallied to one-man-one-party rule, uniforms, flags and rifles, mass rallies, racial hatred, and appeals to national glory. What would happen in other countries if small businessmen, housewives, artisans, white-collar workers, and students felt betrayed by an alien political establishment, a fraying welfare net, and chronic economic dislocations?

I thought back on the years I had spent in Germany during the late 1950s and early 1960s—to innumerable hitchhiking conversations, when I stumbled onto my own interview format with my standard opener, "What wonderful highways you have here."

"You like our autobahn?"

"Oh, yes, it seems very fast, and scenic, too."

"You would never guess who built it." I never once gave into the temptation to say, "You bet I would!"

And we would slide into conversation about the glorious 1930s, when a dynamic leader pulled his nation out of the Depression (more successfully than "your" Roosevelt) and inspired people with a new idealism. I don't know if a random sample of Germans stopped to pick up foreign hitchhikers. I asked why they gave rides to students, and they invariably told me that they had begun the practice during the war years, when sharing seemed more important than privacy. After the war in the days before Eurail passes, kindly European drivers routinely gave students not only lifts to the next town but allowed them an intimate glimpse into their values and culture. In my case, hundreds of Germans shared with me their memories of a Nazism without genocide, racism, or war. They recalled a social world of close families, sports activities and vacations, a strong community spirit, high moral standards, and economic security. Men and women looked back with fondness, sad only about the war—that is, the defeat, not the brilliant military victories before the Battle of Stalingrad. Since visions of Hitler as evil incarnate had colored my childhood, I wondered that people would be so open in their defense of the Nazi state. Especially I asked the women with whom I spoke how they had felt about so militaristic a regime. "Politics, police, the army—all those bad things—they were men's concerns," they answered. History recorded the "bad things"; memory preserved a benign face of fascism.

Fifteen years later I returned to the question of women's participation in the Third Reich and realized that I would have to find the documents because so little had been published about women. The endeavor led me to search for memos, orders, letters, and articles, by and about one Gertrud Scholtz-Klink, the chief of the Women's Bureau under Hitler. Never had it occurred to me that one day she would emerge from the historical shadows, take on human form and speak. Political scientists meet their subjects; but normally historians study dead leaders. One day in 1980 I noticed Scholtz-Klink's book, *The Woman in the Third Reich*, in a feminist bookstore in Berlin, and picked it up. Upon leafing through it, it became clear the the contents were speeches and articles written by Scholtz-Klink and her staff during the 1930s. The dust jacket announced the collection as "a pioneering work of supreme importance" and a testimonial to Scholtz-Klink's "extraordinary achievements as well as great suffering during fateful bitter times." The publicity promises that Scholtz-Klink's writings will demonstrate how women "came naturally to form the 'biological middle point' " of a new society, driven by "nationalist and racial powers. . . . Without the courage, power and steadfastness of women, girls, and mothers in the Third Reich, the Germany of today would be unthinkable." Such a book, I thought to myself, in a women's bookstore. Although its essays carried a deeply anti-feminist message, the bookstore stocked it because its author was female. Richard Evans' excellent history of German feminism, by contrast, had been ruled out because its author was male. Biology still counted more than opinion in Berlin. My ideological doubts subsided, however, as the historian in me realized that Scholtz-Klink might still be alive. Not really expecting a reply, I wrote a polite note to the publisher and forgot about it. She would of course refuse my request to speak with her, but then I could include a footnote saying I had tried.

One day as I returned from a research trip, I found a letter addressed in a familiar hand. The postmark, Tübingen, meant nothing to me; I knew no one who lived there. Then I felt a chill travel up my spine. How many times had I seen that regular, graceful hand at the end of letters and documents. *"Sehr geehrte Frau Dr. Koonz,"* the letter began. I had always met my subjects through their records; now a ghost rose out of the archival mist and addressed me. The leader of millions of Nazi women under Hitler had decided to talk to me. What did she want? What did I want from her?

When I embarked on this research project, the paradox of the topic

riveted my attention. In the Nazi state, women had received the opportunity to create the largest women's organization in history, with the
blessings of the blatantly male-chauvinist Nazi Party. Here was the nineteenth-century feminists' vision of the future in nightmare form. The
earliest crusaders for women's rights had believed passionately in their
distinct female nature and concluded that their political participation
and legal equality would elevate the level of public debate, redirect the
government toward more humane concerns, and calm male leaders' warlike predisposition. While fighting for equality, women defended their
difference, vowing never to become "masculinized." The dream lived on
even after war, revolution, and Depression had sapped the nation's idealism. As "man-made" institutions pitted worker against capitalist, socialist
against nationalist, rich against poor, a nostalgia for the natural grew.

The myth about a past that never was increased in beauty as it became
more remote from modern society. At the heart of this vision lay a dream
of a strong man and a gentle woman, cooperating under the stern guidance of an orderly state. The image did not die with the German surrender in 1945, but lives on in memory. Often it finds brilliant artistic
expression, as for example in Edgar Reitz's fifteen and a half hour film
Heimat, which recreates a Nazi past unfiltered by ethical questions and
unmarred by unpleasant references to victims or violence. National Socialism, as a movement before 1933, a state for twelve years thereafter,
and a memory since 1945, embodies the myth of an orderly world dominated by men and a gentle world of love preserved by women. Hundreds
of scholars had investigated the etiology of the regime that extended from
the SA and SS at the grassroots to the desk murders in Berlin. But what
about the women? That question brought me to Tübingen.

The woman who bore the major responsibility for creating a separate
female sphere in Nazi society was about to walk through the door. I had
followed her bureaucratic maneuvers, watching her establish a mam-
moth organization spanning virtually all aspects of German social life.
She had developed her own style of administration and cultivated an
intense loyalty among her followers. Often I had stared at photographs
of her modest figure surrounded by overdressed and overfed Nazi leaders. Because Scholtz-Klink's duty was to inspire other women to follow
her example, she always appeared as the peahen surrounded by plumed
ostentation. I recalled an American woman's account of a meeting with
the Führerin.

> One meets her surrounded by Nazi flags and uniforms. Her gentle feminin-
> ity is a startling contrast to the military atmosphere. She is a friendly
> woman in her middle thirties, blonde, blue-eyed, regular featured, slender.

> She sits in her wicker chair on her little balcony and chats with her visitor. Her complexion is so fresh and clear that she dares to do without powder or rouge. She talks, and one notices that her firm, capable hands have known hard work. . . . How does she feel about the possibility of Germany's going to war? She glances up at the swastikas and across at the black boots of the uniformed men beyond the doorway and she turns quickly away to hide the tears in her eyes. "I have sons," she says quietly. Her eyes are as sad as the eyes of so many other German mothers who know so well the German Labor Camp motto which says so plainly that sons must "fight stubbornly and die laughing."[4]

What would the Führerin say in 1981 about her massive organization that indoctrinated a generation of young women and girls to "be brave, be German, be pure"? After decades of silence, would she impart to a new generation words of guidance and contrition? From the archives I knew her as docile, self-serving, and rather noncommittal. For all her slavish devotion to the Führer, I had not encountered anti-Semitic prejudices in her orders or memos. Perhaps after so many years, she had decided to speak out to warn the world or simply to atone for her complicity.

Without really understanding why, I felt overcome with anxiety. I intended merely to listen and to record, occasionally to insert a probing question. Oral historians must remain faceless and value-free in order to capture the full truth. Still, I had never interviewed an ex-Nazi since those hitching conversations of my student days. Gazing out at the dismal garden, I wondered; my worries began to shift from the list of questions in my head to my image. Had I dressed appropriately for this encounter? What *was* the proper image for an ex-Nazi? Could I win her trust if I wore an A-line skirt (light gray), simple shirt (also light gray), hand-knit Irish cardigan (blue), sensible shoes (also blue)? Would my hair stay neat in its Germanic bun? Certainly, I thought guiltily, I had the right coloring for an "Aryan" image. These anxieties, I realized, masked my deeper forebodings. Why did I even want to win the trust of an ex-Nazi?

The door opened. A wiry, vigorous woman strode in and took my hand, smiling openly. "I'm very pleased to meet you," we both said. She, in an A-line skirt (dark green), a Black Forest hand-knit cardigan (also dark green), prim blouse (white) with a tiny brooch, and sensible shoes (brown), shook the rain from her umbrella. A hair net kept her white braids twisted neatly around her head. I had dressed so very correctly (and so instinctively), a shudder passed through me. Except for forty years of aging, Frau Scholtz-Klink looked just as she had in the photos —proud, athletic, and trim.

I had followed her trail through the fall of Berlin and knew that she and a small band of followers had been captured by the Russians at a bridgehead in Spandau. She had escaped from a prisoner-of-war camp and traveled secretly to the estate of an old friend, one Princess Pauline zu Wied, who offered her and her family a safe hiding place in her castle in the Black Forest. She and her husband worked as bakers in a small village nearby until 1948, when a local peasant reported their presence to the police.

During the intervening years, Scholtz-Klink was to tell me, she had lived in pleasant obscurity, wanting to forget the past and adapt to a new world. But then Albert Speer spoke out, openly confessing his role as the "Devil's architect." Frau Scholtz-Klink began to reconsider. As it turned out, she, too, wanted to speak out to a new generation, but not in the way I had anticipated. The newspapers, she said, had presented "such a biased view of the Nazi years." German youth of today should have the right to reclaim those aspects of Hitler's state of which they can be proud. Angered at the hypocrisy of the West German censorship of "unbiased" material, which depicted the Nazis in a favorable light, Scholtz-Klink rankled. She resolved to speak the truth about her past. I had anticipated a Speer-like contrition; she had been, after all, like Speer, very young and extremely ambitious. Instead I listened to pious excuses that reminded me of the rationalizations given during the war-crimes trials at Nuremberg. "How could I have known? We had our duty. You must remember the other side. . . ." Memories of these splendid autobahns filtered through my mind.

I had not been invited to hear a confession, and this was not an *ex*-Nazi. She remained as much a Nazi now as she had been in 1945 or 1933. This woman, who for twelve years imposed utter orthodoxy on her staff and dispatched Nazi propaganda to millions of German women, now castigated the current German government for limiting her freedom to extol the Nazi past. She did not care about preventing the rise of another murderous political system, but felt, on the contrary, deeply committed to vindicating the one she had supported.

As I evaluated the situation, I realized that I had come to get information and she intended to give me a sanitized version of Nazism that would normalize the Hitler state in the minds of contemporaries. She saw the chance to share her views with an American as a way of taking her message to not only a younger generation, but a new audience. I resolved to concentrate on the facts and resist the temptation to argue. Four decades and de-Nazification courses had not convinced her; it was unlikely that I would.

She talked on, dispensing advice for contemporary leaders, complain-

ing that no one listened to her anymore. I found it difficult to concentrate.

"You know, if our politicians learned from the past, they would not
have to complain about the unruly youth of today. Why don't they ask
us for advice on social problems? We senior citizens could tell them a
thing or two. In the Depression, we sponsored a national labor service
that took teenagers off the streets and taught them patriotism," she said
proudly.

"The organization that taught German boys to 'die laughing'?" I asked.

Dodging the question, she reminded me that our "great American
President" had initiated similar programs. Then she offered her proposals
for that other unruly segment of the population, women. "The new
French President, Mitterand, is on the right track, but he doesn't go far
enough. He created a ministry for women's rights. My own women's
division concerned itself with women's responsibilities. We formed almost a state within a state. In my ministry I directed departments of
economics, education, colonial issues, consumer affairs and health, education and welfare. No man ever interfered with us; we did as we
pleased." Her decision to create a separate bureaucracy for women had
"nothing to do with feminism," she insisted, but sprang from her own
intense pride in being a woman.

I remained mute, my reactions in disarray. Unconcerned, she pursued
her own stream of thought.

Within her own sphere, Scholtz-Klink smugly recalled, she had insisted on democratic principles. Did that mean elections and voting? I
asked. Not at all. If two staff members differed, for example, she did not
make a ruling, but told them to sit down and discuss their argument over
a cup of tea. "My women and I functioned as one big happy family. They
knew they could always count on my support. In all my years in office,
no one ever resigned, and I fired no one. Now that record shows how
harmoniously we cooperated. No man ever represented us in the outside
world. We spoke for ourselves." Without a trace of irony, she recalled,
"If you could have seen the women of Berlin defending their city with
their lives against the Russians, then you would believe how deeply German women loved our Führer." Even today she and her co-workers (like
SS veterans) meet regularly to reminisce, share news of their families
over *Kaffee und Kuchen*. Her whole bearing radiated satisfaction at a life
well lived.

"But, Frau Scholtz-Klink, you may have done exactly as you pleased
within your realm, but do you seriously believe you exerted the slightest
influence over the major policies you were supposed to carry out?"

"Of course I did. We enjoyed continual informal contacts with the highest officials. Göring, Rosenberg, Hitler, Himmler . . . I knew them all. Just before his death Goebbels admitted that he wished he had paid more attention to the women's division. Now, that's the mark of a real person, a *Mensch*. He admitted his oversight and, in the end, repented. You can't imagine what gentlemen they all were."

"But surely their manners didn't give your office power."

"You younger people always look for written records. You don't understand that Hitler did not make decisions on paper. I did just what all the other leaders did. When I wanted something, I spoke to Hitler. Or rather, I listened patiently as he rambled on and on. Eventually, he would get tired, usually after about an hour. Then, when his energy was spent, he would listen quietly. Then I had a receptive audience. You Americans have a saying about striking iron while it is hot. But I always knew to stay away from 'hot iron'—topics that made him angry. I waited until the iron had cooled off, until I knew I could count on persuading him, before making a formal suggestion. Sometimes that made my younger co-workers impatient."

"Then you were satisfied with Hitler's policies on women?"

"Absolutely. When we disagreed, I told him so. My voice was not loud but we accomplished much in silence. You historians always look for written words; but Hitler's style was to make it known that he wanted this or that and allow us to translate it into policy."

"Can you give me an example of a particular policy you changed?"

The answer came without hesitation. "Yes, it was in 1944, when my women were ordered to put on uniforms and volunteer for military service. I told them that I already had sons at the front and I was not about to send my daughters. My women did not put on military uniforms."

"But other women did."

"That was not my concern."

"And what do you feel your greatest contribution was?"

Again no hesitation. "Our job (and we did it well) was to infuse the daily life of all German women—even in the tiniest villages—with Nazi ideals. At least once or twice a month our local leaders would gather women together in small groups to inform them about our goals and to give them a chance to meet as women—without men. How often they told us with shining eyes, 'No one has ever talked to us like this, except, possibly, in religious services.' But the national purpose had never been brought home to them like this. We wanted to incorporate all women into the national community (*Volksgemeinschaft*). We didn't waste time trying to boss men around. You know, men today have not changed at all. And women have changed very little. When a man comes home for dinner, he wants to relax and maybe share the problems of his day at the office. He does not want to listen to her talk about *her* office. Men weren't interested in our offices."

For an instant I recalled Hitler had expressed similar views. "A highly intelligent man should take a primitive and stupid woman. Imagine if on top of everything else I had a woman who interfered with my work! In my leisure time I want to have peace."[5]

Scholtz-Klink mastered the art of the possible; a transformation of male nature lay beyond her control. Since men would not adapt, women did. After all, they always had. And she thought "we" should, too. "All your feminist efforts have placed a woman or two here and there in conspicuous places. But have you touched the lives of average women? We did. You have to start influencing women in their daily lives. And women still live for their families, now just like then. You young women just don't know what it means to create an entirely female world." She and her network relinquished claims over the sphere beyond their influence and directed their efforts at upgrading "their" own space. As Scholtz-Klink once put it at a Party rally, "Though our weapon be but a wooden spoon, it must become as powerful as other weapons."

"You young women think that you can tell average housewives they have wasted their lives. You presume to inform *them* their world is empty. And *then* you expect them to follow you gratefully. Take it from me, you have to reach them where their lives are—endorse their decisions, praise their accomplishments. Start with the cradle and the ladle. That's what we did."

Was that evil? Was it Nazi? The advice sounded very much like words I had heard so often from a community leader I admired on New York's Lower East Side. The conversation had drifted into platitude. Surely Scholtz-Klink could not think that I had sought her out only to hear her views on life in general and women in particular. I realized also that Scholtz-Klink could filibuster indefinitely on topics of motherly concern. Then, as now, she saw herself as a pragmatic bureaucrat, taking pride in a job well done. Like Albert Speer, she claimed that Nazi ideology had held few allures for her. She felt challenged by the task at hand. Speer years later admitted to his "blind ambition" and regretted that he had never concerned himself with Party doctrine. Looking back on his earliest association with the Nazi Party, he concluded,

> At this initial stage my guilt was as grave as at the end. . . . For being in a position to know and nevertheless shunning knowledge creates direct responsibility for the consequences—from the very beginning. . . . By entering Hitler's party I had already, in essence, assumed a responsibility that led directly to the brutalities of forced labor, to the destruction of war, and

to the deaths of those millions of so-called undesirable stock—to the crushing of justice and the elevation of every evil.[6]

Thinking of Speer, I asked, "Have you any regrets?"

"Only a few. I am sorry now that I was too busy in the early days of our movement to concern myself very much with ideology. I never mastered the intellectual underpinnings of the doctrine."

"But your job was to indoctrinate German women to be good mothers and loyal subjects." At least Speer, obsessed with buildings, did not need ideology to function. Scholtz-Klink must have.

"My day-to-day work unified all German women. I had so little time for reading theory."

"In subsequent years have you caught up?"

"Yes, afterward I did more reading. I understand much better the real core of the ideas that inspired us. Rosenberg, the kindest of men. But I did not often have time to read his books."

"And now that you have time, what do you think?"

"Of course, some notions seem extreme. But people today ignore the idealism that inspired us."

"What seems extreme?"

"Some of the aspirations were just unrealistic." She dodged again. Arrogant and bigoted and unreconstructed.

"To what do you attribute your success?"

"Rudolf Hess, Hitler's right-hand man, always said it was my charm and diplomacy. I never agreed with him on that. I feel I had influence because of my brain (*Geist*)." She glanced modestly at her hands folded quietly in her lap. Later I read of a very different career pattern than the one she described. Peter Englemann, exiled editor of a major German newspaper, recalled that he had interviewed Scholtz-Klink, who had told him about a meeting between Scholtz-Klink and Hitler that Nazi novelist Marie Diers had arranged in 1932. He credited Scholtz-Klink's behind-the-scenes maneuverings for her success.[7]

She chatted on, mouthing the phrases I had read dozens of times in archives. My own attempts at "charm and diplomacy" had not succeeded in breaking the surface. Scholtz-Klink talked on freely. But I did not like what I heard. Maybe this was not surface; maybe her innermost convictions had been frozen at the end of the war. As she relaxed, she began to speak more openly about the past, and proclaim her views more stridently. Normally, steadfastness is a virtue; in Scholtz-Klink's case it seemed more like arrested development. As my mind wandered, she worried about young Germans' need to be proud of their past, by which she meant Hitler. "You see, we genuinely believed in our ideals."

"Which ones?"

"National greatness, pride, our heritage."

"How did you become interested in National Socialism?"

"Oh, I never cared much for politics, although I supported my husband's views. During the 1920s I had all I could do to keep house, raise the children, and provide a good home. But one day my husband, who was an ardent SA man, did not return from a rally. They told me that in the excitement of the demonstration, he had suffered a heart attack and died. That's all anyone said." Angered and bent on vengeance, she reported at once to the local Nazi district leader and volunteered her services. Odd, I mused, that she blamed the enemies of Nazism, rather than the movement under whose banner he had marched to his death. "I wanted to replace him, to devote myself to the movement for which he had been martyred." When the district leader suggested that she organize the women in Baden, a tiny Catholic and liberal state in southwest Germany, she energetically set to work. The next years, during the depths of the Depression, saw her rallying women to provide the social services that played a crucial role in making every Nazi feel a sense of belonging to a subculture. They may have been scorned and ostracized by mainstream German society, but they created for themselves their own alternative to the materialistic and liberal culture from which they felt so alienated.

"Did you get on well with local Catholic leaders?"

"Oh, yes," she beamed. "We respected one another and soon became fast friends."

Odd, I thought, for I knew that in memos from 1932–33 those "friends" looked with deep suspicion at one "Frau Scholtz-Kling," whose name they did not even bother to spell correctly and whom they suspected of interference in their plans for a girls' volunteer labor corps.

With the Nazi takeover in January 1933, her position in Baden shifted rapidly. Instead of being repudiated by the community, she enjoyed the full backing of the new state. Efficiently, she established liaisons with non-Nazi women's organizations to provide jobs for unemployed women, food and clothing for the poor, and a volunteer labor corps for young women. Once, in late 1933, she had shared the speakers' podium with one of Hitler's adjuncts, who subsequently invited her to direct the national women's labor corps and establish headquarters in Berlin. From then on, she rose quickly to prominence. By February 1934, she had been named chief of women's affairs for the nation. I inquired about her bureau. She rummaged in her pocketbook, intent on discovering something. It turned out to be an organization chart of her realm.

Boredom hovered. *Bored?* I asked myself. How can you be bored? This may be the only Nazi leader you ever meet in your lifetime. All the same, this interview seemed interminable and oddly predictable, once it had become clear that the Reichsfrauenführerin had not changed at all in the years following Hitler's defeat. Boredom masks depression, and under depression, lowering rage.

Of course, Gertrud Scholtz-Klink presented the perfect image of a woman leader. Hitler, who consciously modeled his movement on Catholic organization and symbolism, discovered a mother of many children who had been the widow of a Nazi martyr and who swore total obedience to the *Vaterland*. Fertile and pure, she looked like a Holbein madonna. Annoyed at having lived the second half of her life in obscurity, in 1981 she wanted to take her place among Hitler's other ex-deputies who were beginning to grant interviews, publish their memoirs, and reenter the limelight to which they had once been so accustomed. I decided this madonna would lose her halo.

"Then you were not concerned about Hitler's policies on the Jews?"

The gentle smile did not fade. "Of course, we never intended that so many Jews would disappear. I had grown up in an anti-Semitic family, so the ideas did not seem unusual. We belonged to the upper civil service (*Beamtenbürgertum*), you know. Besides, until the war with Russia, all of our policies were strictly legal." I half expected her to blame the victims for their own demise by insinuating that because the Jews had overthrown the Czar in 1917, they provoked Hitler into invading Russia in 1941. She, however, shifted to new ground. "We always obeyed the law. Isn't that what you do in America? Even if you don't agree with a law personally, you still obey it. Otherwise life would be chaos."

"When a law passed by the government contradicts our personal moral code, and the Constitution, I would hope that we and all citizens of any state would refuse to obey."

"But, Frau Koonz, you don't seem to understand. We women stayed remote from the Jewish community. Our job was to direct welfare programs to help German people. As a leader I welcomed women from all political backgrounds, as long as they expressed a willingness to do the work at hand."

"Even Jewish volunteers?"

"None volunteered."

"What about those organizations you personally outlawed because they refused to expel their Jewish members?"

"When I arrived in power, I received letters from all major national women's organizations—all thirty-six of them—requesting to participate in our great work. If they had misgivings, why didn't they speak out? Do you know that the most important women's-movement periodical, *Die*

Frau, continued to publish right through 1944? Not even the paper shortage suspended publication." She had me there. I knew that Gertrud
Bäumer, the leader of the middle-class women's rights movement before
Hitler's takeover, had declared in a job application in the summer of 1933
that she had always subscribed to national socialist ideals. The officials
must have believed her, for during the next twelve years she continued
to lecture on the Woman Question, write articles, and lecture. After the
war, she implied she had resisted inwardly and had never printed a word
that contradicted her basic beliefs.

"Did you ever meet Gertrud Bäumer?"

"No. It was a disappointment. She must have known our door was
always open. She never visited us. We gave her no trouble and still she
never came." Scholtz-Klink gazed pensively out the window as a gust of
wind drove a torrent of rain across the garden. "What right do those
women have to complain now? Just because we lost the war, they become brave. We stick to our principles."

"After about 1937 you began to commemorate the birthdays of the
leaders in the pre-1933 women's rights movement. Yet in the early years
you had attacked them for being 'un-Germanic' and divisive."

"In the old days, when we were surrounded with enemies on all sides,
they seemed to present a threat. But after a few years in office I learned
a thing or two about the world. We began to rethink our position."

"When you took office, what seemed important?"

"At first, the men (when they thought about us at all) wanted us to
form merely an auxiliary—a sort of ladies' aid. . . . I was determined to
create a dignified and independent women's organization. To really accomplish something." Composed and smiling and looking intently into
my eyes, she offered me tea and cakes. What a pro, I thought. Strike
while the iron is hot, indeed! She just rambles on and on, keeping her
cool. High time, it seemed, for an interruption from me. Before I asked,
she moved of her own accord directly on to "hot iron."

"Of course, whenever I heard of injustices being done to Jewish
women, I helped out. But what could I do if I did not know?" Tea and
cakes first and the Jewish question next; like eating supper and watching
the TV news about starvation in Africa or atrocities in El Salvador.

Once she had sent money to a Jewish woman who went into exile.
Frau Scholtz-Klink became agitated at the memory. "What ingratitude!
After I helped her out as best I could, she publicly accused me after the
war of disloyalty." On another occasion, Scholtz-Klink said she had
heard too late that a Jewish acquaintance had been deported.

I recalled Adolf Eichmann on trial. He also claimed to have saved the
lives of two Jews in Vienna, but later regretted it. In fact, those two acts

were the only acts he regretted. They revealed a chink in his moral armor. If a law was right, then it had to be obeyed uniformly. If a moral precept held, then it, too, had to be kept—without sympathy. Eichmann had expressed himself very clearly on this point when he told his officers they must feel no pity when the orders came down to arrest and deport Jews–and ultimately to kill them. He himself had urged other Nazis to show no sympathy whatsoever to individual Jews. Eichmann had incorporated Himmler's warning to his men: "It's easy to say, 'Sure, that's in our program, we'll take care of it.' And there they come trudging in, eighty million Germans, and each one has a decent Jew. Sure, the others are swine, but this one is an A-1 Jew."[8] Behind the contorted thinking lay some consistency. Frau Scholtz-Klink, however, defended her actions by claiming to have broken the law while insisting that the treatment of the Jews was legal. The exception salved her conscience, but also proved the moral rule.

And I recalled Emmy Göring's autobiography, *At My Husband's Side*, in which she criticizes Germans who, after 1945, "pulled out their Jew to brag about (*Renommierjude*)" whenever it was politically correct.[9] I remembered, too, the cynical protagonist in Heinrich Mann's *Mephisto*, who went out of his way to protect one "enemy of the state" just in case the future did not turn out well for the Nazis. Studies of concentration camps report that guards and commandants typically declare they had saved at least one Jew.

"Then you must have had some doubts about the laws concerning Jews," I said. "Why did you not help more?"

"I did not know any." And, once again, a diversion.

"If you had, would you have helped them?"

"It's hard to say. I didn't. You know," she changed the subject, "in about 1938 we all knew something big was about to happen . . . perhaps a major shake-up in the Party leadership. We suspected a change. But not that." She took a lace handkerchief from her sleeve and dabbed her eyes. She had not changed the subject after all. As early as 1938, she knew. Maybe her eyes were moist. Maybe not. "Before the Russian war, everything was legal."

"Do you mean that whatever a government decrees must be obeyed because it is 'law,' even if that law violates a constitution or common notions of decency? After Germany began to lose, what changed?" This line of inquiry produced only obstinate detours. Time to change course. "What did you think when one day in 1941 you saw so many of your fellow Berliners appear with yellow stars sewed on their coats?" The sight of so many condemned and helpless human beings must surely have moved her. It did, but not as I had expected.

"I don't know how to say it. There were so many. I felt that my aesthetic sensibility was wounded."

"*Aesthetic*" concerns. No regret. Certainly no pity. Just the barely veiled variation on the "Jewish vermin" theme so vividly conveyed in Nazi propaganda. For her, Jews had ceased to count as human beings at all. When the yellow stars disappeared, Berlin must have seemed a cleaner place to live. Today *Heimat* reminds them of the pleasant side of a world without Jews. But Claude Lanzmann's *Shoah* preserves for us the memory of that day as seen by the people who had to wear the yellow stars. Inge Deutschkron told Lanzmann, "I remember the day when they made Berlin *Judenrein*. The people hastened in the streets; no one wanted to be in the streets; you could see the streets were absolutely empty. They didn't want to look, you know. . . . They had herded the Jews together, from factories, from houses, wherever they could find them. . . ."[10]

I poured more tea. Silence broken by rain pelting down on the roof. I repressed my only reaction: a fantasy . . . her face turning blue as hands closed tightly around her throat. She continued. I gulped the tea. "Some comrades after the war hesitated to admit they had been Party members." From a newspaper clipping, I knew that her husband, an SS general who supervised the schools designed to train the future elite, vigorously denied having belonged to the Nazi Party. Not his wife. "Of course I told the Americans I had belonged to the Nazi Party. I made a choice when I joined and I'm not ashamed." There was that steadfastness again. "The time has come for all of us decent Germans who served our people during the Third Reich to speak out. We must also salvage the memories of those comrades who did not live long enough to defend their honor." Again she went on about how they could not have imagined what happened in Poland.

Then she repeated the German maxim that I was to hear many times in subsequent interviews. "The soup is never eaten as hot as it is cooked." At the very gates of the gas chambers, guards calmed their victims by saying "What? How could you be suspicious? *This* is a civilized nation in the twentieth century! How could you think any harm will come to you here?" Who today can conceive of total nuclear destruction? I made another effort to break the dreary tone of our conversation.

Five decades of unfailing faith had insulated Scholtz-Klink in her Nazi world. Having sworn allegiance to the Nazi hierarchy, she simply went on about her business. "Do you mean that your Nazi women never knew about concentration camps? You thought they did not exist just because you never happened to see one?" My inquiries produced diversions. Stubborn, simpleminded, and self-righteous. But I had taken a long and expensive trip to hear this litany. Bury the rage and keep talking. Historians keep the record, they take notes. Maybe one day someone will decide how guilty the Germans were. Will unswerving loyalty to an immoral state count as guilt? If so, Scholtz-Klink stood guilty as accused (and proud of it). In 1984 George Orwell had described "crimethink." Scholtz-Klink's smug satisfaction suggested the possibility of "crimefeel." Where, I wondered, had pity gone? What kind of moral hardening had enabled this paragon of womanliness not only to participate in the Nazi state, but to defend it so mindlessly four decades later?

"But surely you knew about concentration camps."

"Yes." Her eyes strayed absently to the cup and saucer on the table. "Yes, once I visited a camp near Berlin. You know, just a normal inspection visit. Some of my women worked there as social workers. They had been sent to care for the asocial women inmates. As I toured the premises, everything appeared quite normal. In good order. After the inmates had been reeducated, they would be released to return to productive roles in society. Just as I was about to depart, a young woman pulled me aside and implored me to listen carefully to what she had to say. 'How can we rehabilitate them, Frau Scholtz-Klink, when we have not so much as a deck of cards or adequate soap? How can we do social work without handicraft materials? And the inmates seem so depressed. They don't seem to go home.' That young woman risked her job to warn me that something sinister was going on. I ordered that all my women be transferred from that assignment at once. And they were. We would not participate in something like that."

Once again, a chasm might have appeared in the defenses. Did she think it tolerable that other German women, not "hers," worked in concentration camps? Remember, she said, that the Catholic Church did not protest on behalf of non-Catholics or object when life-long Catholics with Jewish ancestors were banished. I thought of Dr. Edith Stein, a young theologian, admired by Heidegger, and a convert to Catholicism, who had become a nun. When the Gestapo investigated the nuns in her convent, she was reported as Jewish and deported.

"But surely women under your supervision participated in eugenics programs, turned unwilling people over to forced sterilization, and singled out 'undesirables' such as schizophrenics, alcoholics, and mentally retarded children for euthanasia."

"You know, I visited the mentally retarded child of my cousin the other day. And I wondered . . ."

But the racial laws? Again a pat response. Germans had been inspired by sterilization laws in many American states, American immigration quotas, Harvard quotas, eugenics research, hate propaganda against German-born Americans in World War I, and . . .

And the breeding programs? Germans applied biological discoveries to improving human life. Don't we Americans have genetic engineering? she asked. And isn't it humane to establish care for unwed mothers?

"Do you not think . . ." She peered intently at me, leaned forward in her chair and paused. ". . . that I committed a crime by believing in my ideals?" I knew she had indeed been brought to "justice" after being discovered. She told me proudly what I already knew: how she had outwitted her Russian captors and found refuge in the Black Forest.[11] She faced charges of assuming a false identity between 1945 and 1947. In 1949, Occupation officials pronounced her de-Nazified, and she continued her life, drawing a civil servant's pension after retirement age.

A well-known West German novelist, Ingeborg Drewitz, spoke to a group of Americans recently about her girlhood as a member of the Hitler Youth. She often wonders about "those concentration camp matrons: their brutal and tense faces. When they were arrested they pushed their chins forward, staring into nothingness. . . . Was the education of girls geared to producing such women?" Although Drewitz (unlike Scholtz-Klink) is horrified by her earlier faith in Nazism, like Scholtz-Klink she denies the connection between Nazi education and concentration-camp matrons. After all, she notes, Sophie Scholl and other girls in the Hitler Youth organizations rebelled against their training. Since a tiny minority did, anyone could have, Drewitz reasons. What could one say to Scholtz-Klink?

Pointless to argue. I sat face-to-face, over tea and cakes, with the everyday banality of evil, gazing at a woman who had embraced an ideology and surrendered responsibility to a closed system that left no doubts—or at least none that she would admit to. Never had she overstepped her bounds. Always she had followed the law. Never did she admit to pondering the ramifications of anything. She translated orders from above into obedience from below. And she had not broken the criminal code or the Geneva Convention. Thinking back on the archives I had visited, a new picture of the Third Reich began to take shape. Next to the dominant motif of male brutality, Gertrud Scholtz-Klink and millions of followers created the social side of tyranny. Busily administering welfare services, educational programs, leisure activities, ideological indoctrination, and consumer organizations, Nazi women mended while Nazi men marched.

Hitler's Eichmanns committed unspeakable acts in the name of an evil cause for an evil dictator. They acted. They dehumanized and killed. This woman, kindly and decent, sweet and hospitable, said she had committed no crime. Wherein lay her guilt? Adhering to the ideology subscribed to by millions of fellow Germans, she followed the paths trodden by women for centuries. No matter what, she did not doubt, but tried always to "make nice." Here at the tea table sat the Angel in the House—honored by John Ruskin, admired by Joyce Brothers, and praised by Germaine Greer. Virginia Woolf strangled her.

> The shadow of her wings fell on my page; I heard the rustling of her skirts in the room. Directly, that is to say, I took up my pen in my hand to review that novel by a famous man, she slipped behind me and whispered: 'my dear, you are a young woman. You are writing about a book that has been written by a man. Be sympathetic; be tender; flatter; deceive; use all the arts and wiles of our sex. Never let anybody guess that you have a mind of your own. Above all, be pure.' . . . I turned upon her and caught her by the throat. . . . Killing the Angel in the House was part of the occupation of a woman writer.[12]

Living by the Angel's maxims was essential in the life of Hitler's Reichsfrauenführerin.

Can we speak of "spectator guilt?" Such a category might be increasingly appropriate in a technological age or bureaucratized society where no one gives the orders and everyone performs only a tiny part of any given task. Scholtz-Klink and an army of bureaucrats helped to integrate racially "acceptable" women and girls within the Nazi network by 1939 —three million girls in the Hitler Youth; eight million women in Nazi associations under her rule. Over a million women subscribed to her journal directed at the most loyal Nazi women.

I knew as I looked at this composed and graceful grandmother that she had been guilty by choosing to serve a regime founded on war and racism. No one coerced her. Nazi officials tempted her. With what? She would not say. Perhaps by public accolades, the office, access to powerful elites, and influence over an entire administrative network. Philosopher Karl Jaspers reflected on *The Question of German Guilt* shortly after the German surrender. How, he asked, can we evaluate the moral guilt of "outward compliance, of *running with the pack* [italics in the original]?" While not actually committing a crime, had Germans been guilty of sin because of their "inner indifference toward the witnessed evil?" But Scholtz-Klink did not quite fit conventional categories. In addition, after 1945 she demonstrated no remorse. And before 1945, she directed a gigantic camouflage operation that flattered the famous men of the Nazi state and transformed the personal values of millions of women. In league with Goebbels' powerful propaganda machine, she dispatched speakers, community organizers, social workers, educators, mothers' helpers, and consumer experts. No less than Albert Speer, she directed Germans to harmonize their lives with state priorities: at first motherhood, and later, as Hitler rearmed the nation, working at farm and factory jobs as well as mothering while the men went to war.

Perhaps even worse, Scholtz-Klink was guilty of unrepentance. She introduced her book of essays with glowing praise for the glorious days when she enjoyed prestige and influence at the Nazi "court." Since she actually wrote only a small fraction of the book, she might well have blamed the articles on the women on her staff (most of whom were dead) who actually wrote them. But no. The layout gives the fraudulent impression that Scholtz-Klink herself wrote the essays. At the conclusion, fourteen photographs of racially pure "Aryan" women appear under the caption "German Fate in Woman's Face." In some German states the sale of Scholtz-Klink's book has been challenged in court because the Allied occupation authorities ordered in 1945 that freedom of the press shall not include the right to publish Nazi and neo-Nazi literature. But Scholtz-Klink's volume was "just" a women's book about the "positive" aspects of Nazi rule.

As I faced her that day—in a posh editorial office, with tea growing cold on the table—this book began to take shape. In it, I would bring to light the contribution to evil made by Scholtz-Klink and other women leaders, find out what they had done, what they *believed* they were doing, and why. I would ask how "normal" people (women, in this case) brought Nazi beliefs home in everyday thought and action. Above all, I would record the history of average people without normalizing life in Nazi society. This would mean examining the lives of Nazism's victims and opponents to recapture the picture of how Scholtz-Klink's women looked from outside their womanly sphere. How did "decent" people adapt to a state that inverted morality, perverted civilized traditions, and imposed distrust on all forms of social life? At what points did Hitler's charisma wear thin? When did Nazi policy contradict loyalty to religion and family? As I formulated these questions, I made a second decision. Although my book would depend upon archival research, I resolved to frame that material in a broad context and to write for an audience beyond academe, for people concerned about women's status in modern society, social history, and the impact of misogyny and anti-Semitism on public life.

Women's history during the Third Reich lacks the extravagant insanity of Hitler's megalomania; often it is ordinary. But there, at the grassroots of daily life, in a social world populated by women, we begin to discover how war and genocide happened by asking who made it happen.

1

INTRODUCTION: LOVE AND ORDER IN THE THIRD REICH

The state is based on the contradiction between public and private life, between general interest and private interest.

—Karl Marx

[T]he public and the private worlds are inseparably connected; . . . the tyrannies and servilities of the one are the tyrannies and servilities of the other.

—Virginia Woolf

After the publication of fifty thousand books and monographs about Hitler's Germany, it seems scarcely conceivable that any facet of those nightmare years remains unexplored, much less undiscovered. But in fact, half of the Germans who made dictatorship, war, and genocide possible have largely escaped observation. The women among Hitler's supporters have fallen through the historian's sieve, unclaimed by feminists and unnoticed by men. To be sure, Nazi leaders' lovers and wives receive their due (along with Nazi chiefs' sexual proclivities), and women as statistics appear in analyses of Nazi social policies and economic programs. A few historians note women only to blame them for Hitler's victory. A West German journalist comments, "Women discovered, elected, and idolized Hitler,"[1] and an East German historian draws the same conclusion: "Never in German history had so many women streamed into any political party, and never has a party so degraded women as the National Socialist Party."[2] But women do not appear as historical actors. If we think of women at all, we imagine masses of plain Eva Brauns with a Leni Riefenstahl here and there or perhaps an Irma Griese (the infamous "bitch of Auschwitz") in riding boots and SS uniform.

Historians have dismissed women as part of the timeless backdrop against which Nazi men made history, seeing men as active "subjects" and women as the passive "other," quoting Simone de Beauvoir's terms. However, this bifurcation encompasses only part of the complexity of Nazi society. Jean-Paul Sartre wrote *Anti-Semite and Jew* while de Beauvoir was working on *The Second Sex*. Although neither Nazi women nor Auschwitz figured in either book, together they analyze the fault lines that split the Nazi world. A double dyad rent asunder male from female, Jew from "Aryan." From the earliest beginnings of his Party, Hitler promised to eliminate Jews from "Aryan" society and expel women from public influence. Within the "master race," policy and ideology divided man and mother. These parallels, of course, did not merge Jews and women as victims, for there can be no comparison between the Nazis' drive to first ostracize and then eliminate Jewish citizens and Nazi social policy that relegated women to becoming bearers of children and poorly paid workers in the lowliest jobs. Women who decided to support Nazism accepted their inferior status in exchange for rewards, while cooperation for Jews was ultimately out of the question. Restrictive roles, no matter how severe, cannot compare with genocide. Yet in the model of Nazi society that inspired racial policy, ideology linked race and gender.

Because Nazi contempt for women was so blatant from the beginning, it would be easy to assume that women ought not share in the question

3

of German guilt. Perhaps women remained pure and powerless, repelled by the racism, violence, and masculine élan of the Nazi Party. But did women really remain immune to what Erich Fromm called "the craving for submission and lust for power" that had engulfed the nation? Voting statistics provide the evidence. Thanks to electoral officials' curiosity about how women would vote in the 1920s, German men were given gray ballots and women, white. We don't have to estimate—we know that women nearly as strongly as men supported the Nazis during the years of their spectacular rise to power between 1930 and 1932.[3]

Women do not appear to have played a role in the Nazi movement before 1933 or the Nazi state thereafter because historians have not defined women's support for Nazi Germany as a historical problem— i.e., a question that needs explaining. After all, the image of politically inert women reinforces cherished myths about motherhood. A fantasy of women untouched by their historical setting feeds our own nostalgia for mothers who remain beyond good and evil—preservers of love, charity, and peace, no matter what the social or moral environment. Against the encroachments of the modern state, we extol women who somehow keep the private beyond the reach of the political. When "feminine" ideals of love and charity flickered and were extinguished in the Third Reich, we assume this occurred because of a masculine assault against women as victims of either force or hypnosis, or of their own masochism. Sylvia Plath's "Daddy" reverberates still.

> Not God but a swastika
> So black no sky could squeak through.
> Every woman adores a fascist.
> The boot in the face, the brute
> Brute heart of a brute like you.[4]

The Third Reich, which left no serious ideological heritage or political admirers, has bequeathed a powerful reservoir of metaphors to the culture. When Plath hated her father, an image was available. From Riefenstahl to Wertmuller, filmmakers have exploited the erotic tension between the beauty and the brute, creating what some call a fascist aesthetic and others label fascist kitsch. The threat of violence barely contained by fastidious uniforms and martial discipline evokes hatred and love, terror and trust. But we must be wary. The symbolic language of Nazi propaganda, so alive in erotic culture today, misrepresents the real experiences of men and women who lived in Hitler's Germany.

Every woman Nazi in Germany did not "adore" a brute-hearted fascist. The women who followed Hitler, like the men, did so from conviction, opportunism, and active choice. Far from being helpless or even innocent, women made possible a murderous state in the name of concerns they defined as motherly. The fact that women bore no responsibility for issuing orders from Berlin does not obviate their complicity in carrying them out. Electoral statistics charted their enthusiasm, and Party propaganda depicts swooning women as well as marching men. But women did more than faint and vote for the only violently antifeminist party in Weimar politics. And they received more than a "boot in the face."

What did this overtly misogynist movement offer to women? Nazi men inadvertently gave women Nazis a unique opportunity because they cared so little about the women in their ranks. Men allowed women considerable latitude to interpret Hitler's ideas as they wished, recruit followers, write their own rules, and raise funds. In other parties male leaders welcomed women officially, but then curtailed women leaders' independence and chastised them at the slightest sign of separatism. In the service of womanly ideals, Nazi women sometimes behaved in most un-"ladylike" ways: managing the funds they raised, marching, facing down hecklers, making soapbox speeches, and organizing mass meetings, marches, and rallies. While espousing women's special nature and a reactionary view of the family, these women never thought they would retreat to the household. True, they crusaded to take women out of politics, but they did so in order to open up other areas of public life to women. Before 1933 Nazi women viewed the world around them in pessimistic terms, actively working in the public but not the political arena to preserve their nostalgic vision of a world that never was.

What, then, did women do for the men who ignored them? Before 1933, they provided men with an ambience they took for granted, complementing the stridently masculine élan of the Nazi movement and cultivating a homey domestic sphere for Hitler's motley and marginal band. They gave men Nazis the feeling of belonging not just to a party but to a total subculture that prefigured the ideals of the Nazi state for which they fought. Women kept folk traditions alive, gave charity to poor Nazi families, cared for SA men, sewed brown shirts, and prepared food at rallies. While Nazi men preached race hate and virulent nationalism that threatened to destroy the morality upon which civilization rested, women's participation in the movement created an ersatz gloss of idealism. The image did not, of course, deceive the victims, but it helped Nazis to preserve their self-esteem and to continue their work under the illusion that they remained decent.

To a degree unique in Western history, Nazi doctrine created a society structured around "natural" biological poles. In addition to serving specific needs of the state, this radical division vindicated a more general and thoroughgoing biological *Weltanschauung* based on race and sex as the immutable categories of human nature. The habit of taking psychological differences between men and women for granted reinforced assumptions about irrevocable divisions between Jew and "Aryan." In place of class, cultural, religious divisions, race and sex became the predominant social markers. To people disoriented by a stagnant economy, humiliated by military defeat, and confused by new social norms among the urban young, these social categories provided a sense of safety. The Jew and the New Woman, conservatives believed, had become too powerful in progressive Weimar society. The Nazi state drove both groups, as metaphors and as real individuals, out of the "Aryan" man's world.

For women, belonging to the "master race" opened the option of collaboration in the very Nazi state that exploited them, that denied them access to political status, deprived them of birth control, underpaid them as wage workers, indoctrinated their children, and finally took their sons and husbands to the front. The separation between masculine and feminine spheres, which followed logically and psychologically from Nazi leaders' misogyny, relegated women to their own space—both beneath and beyond the dominant world of men. The Nazi system rested on a female hierarchy as well as a male chain of command. Of course, women occupied a less exalted place in Nazi government than the men, and Reichsfrauenführerin Gertrud Scholtz-Klink, who stood at the pinnacle of the women's hierarchy, wielded less real power than, say, a male district chief or deputy minister. Standing at the apex of her own sphere, the woman leader minimized her lack of status vis-à-vis Nazi male leaders above her and instead directed her attention to the battalions of women under her command. As in wartime, women believed their sacrifices played a vital role in a greater cause. Scholtz-Klink saw herself as the chief of a lobby for women's concerns and as the leader of women missionaries who would bring Nazi doctrine "home" to every family in the Reich. Far from remaining untouched by Nazi evil, women operated at its very center.

As a politician and diplomat, Hitler remained within the limits of what we consider normal for a twentieth-century dictator. It is his racial schemes that evoke our horror and disbelief. When I spoke to Scholtz-Klink, I did not believe her disavowal of any role in the immoral facets of Nazi society. Hitler's plans for a racial revolution called for the extirpation of pity, empathy, and love toward those whom the Nazi leaders deemed unworthy. While Scholtz-Klink exalted gentle "feminine" virtues among "Aryan" women, Hitler's racial revolution depended on the elimination of pity for "subhumans." During 1933, the Nazi social planners who outlawed birth control and increased punishments for abortion among "Aryans" also decreed the laws that deprived Jews of their rights and forced the "racially unfit Aryans" to submit to sterilization. It fell to women to put all of these edicts into practice. Scholtz-Klink's social workers, teachers, and nurses turned over the names of the mentally retarded, schizophrenics, alcoholics, and misfits to Nazi sterilization agencies. Brides left the labor market in order to receive state loans and bear many children; housewives boycotted Jewish businesses and cut lifelong Jewish friends out of their social lives; women professionals founded eugenic motherhood schools and educated young women for housewifely careers; and women organizers carried on missionary work to convert the unconvinced. It fell to women to report "suspicious" strangers in the neighborhood, send their own children to the Hitler Youth, and finally to close the door firmly if anyone who looked "dangerous" begged for mercy.

How, I asked myself, could a political regime extinguish compassion and decency? Any ultimate meaning of Hitler's war and genocide must elude us. We cannot grasp "why," but thousands of studies have explained "how." They tell us that probably in any nation of sixty million people, several hundreds or even thousands can be recruited to carry out crimes on a horrifying scale. But the day-to-day callousness of ordinary people—how can we explain that? Millions of average women, no less than average men, contributed to the inversion of time-honored moral injunctions like "Thou shalt not kill," and "Love thy neighbor." Lotte Paepke, who survived in Nazi Germany as a Jew married to a non-Jewish husband, recalled how little life had changed in 1933 for the respectable people among whom she had always felt at home.

> Back then Germany was full of spotlessly clean sitting rooms, with pillow covers embroidered by the lady of the house. Germany was full of plush, overstuffed furniture and fringed window shades, with lonely Iphigenias on the wall and geraniums in the window boxes, a lot of righteousness, and unknowing innocence. . . . For the most part they were not inhuman, . . .[5]

The everyday brutality of the averted gaze, the firm insistence that "Jews are not welcomed here," or the ridicule of a frightened and hungry Jewish child fit comfortably into the life of the "lady of the house." Before the Gestapo summoned Jews to deportation centers, "Aryan" friends and neighbors had excised Jews from their society. Although the last stages of the "final solution" remained entirely within Himmler's authority, women as well as men delivered up the victims. Ordinary people, men and women in their separate ways, gutted compassion and made pity selective. Our understanding of the Third Reich will remain incomplete until these women have been restored to the historical record.

In 1978, I embarked on a research project to fill the lacuna. With generous aid from The College of the Holy Cross, The Rockefeller Foundation, and the German Marshall Fund, I spent the better part of the subsequent three years looking for the missing half of Nazi social history. Several concrete methodological problems made it difficult to obtain the sources from which to generalize about women in the Third Reich. During earlier trips, I had researched other topics in the West German Federal Archives in Koblenz, a modern building with massive holdings, meticulous indexes, and a cooperative staff. Monday through Friday, from 8:00 A.M. to 9:00 P.M., one can read memos and policy statements regarding men leaders' decisions *about* women; there, and at the equivalent centers in East Germany, "important" papers have been cataloged and preserved. But scarcely a woman's signature can be found among party leaders' biographies, cabinet protocols, military dispatches, personal papers (*Nachlässe*), police files, and economic reports. Public man had left an archival trail, but where might I find the voice of private woman?

The task appeared formidable, but the potential reward lured me on, for records of private life from Nazi Germany are rare. How often I recalled Goebbels' quip, "The only individual with a private life in Germany is the person who is sleeping." Women's records would, I hoped, reveal the contours of a forbidden world. Non-Nazi organizations had, of course, been outlawed in 1933, which typically meant the destruction of offices, libraries, and records. Printed sources, too, became rare after the infamous book burnings of 1933. During the last years of the Third Reich, Nazi offices themselves were partially destroyed by Allied bombing raids. In 1945, the Allied victory, in turn, created new lapses in the chronicle as individual Nazis expunged the evidence of their loyalty to Hitler. Documents that had been treasured before 1945, overnight became targets for the flames. Archivists everywhere in Germany received a ration of kerosene with orders to burn the records they had meticulously copied, cross-referenced, and preserved for twelve years. How they must have hesitated! Loath to destroy over a decade's meticulous labor, thinking about the price kerosene would fetch on the black market, how many archivists disobeyed the orders that could never be enforced? I asked Gertrud Scholtz-Klink how she used her kerosene. She hardly understood the question. Of course, she had obeyed, soaking the files and lighting the match herself.

All of these considerations helped to explain why few women Nazis' voices spoke from the past or, more precisely, from the sources in national archives. Acting on the assumption that perhaps less important archives would have the papers of less important people (such as women), I sent out dozens of letters to regional and local government archives in West Germany, asking if by chance they had papers relating to women in the 1920s and 1930s. Many responses seemed promising. I bought a map of Germany and plotted my trail. Before setting out, however, another idea occurred to me, so simple I had overlooked it. Women have never played a salient role in government institutions about which state archives provide so much information. Instead, for centuries the church has played the role for women in public life that politics has played for men. Men talked high theory and traded low gossip at the local *Stammtisch* (neighborhood pub); women gathered at the rectory to organize community projects and mind the parish's business. While men led political parties, served in cabinets, and ran for office, women organized nationwide religious, charitable, patriotic, civic, and social networks with their own leaders and goals. Naturally, these women's associations wielded less overt power than political institutions. Their lack of political clout proved to be a boon for historians, because when non-Nazi men's political and occupational organizations became illegal in 1933, women's associations were invited to participate in the Nazi state. This meant that their records ought to have remained intact; and perhaps because women's activities had been deemed unimportant, they had even been spared a post-1945 purge. Another round of letters to church archives brought more promising responses and more underlined cities on my map.

The idea of securing a place in history for their organization tempted some respondents. As one Catholic leader from the 1930s and 1940s confessed, "When we look around at the world today and see how young women fall from the faith, and how people rush around with scarcely a thought of God, we wonder if our life work was really important at all. Then a young historian comes along and tells us what we did mattered, and we feel proud once again." Ironic, I thought, as their work becomes meaningless to the modern world, we restore it by saving their reputation and consigning it to the past. I thought of myself fleetingly as a dealer in antique memories, enhancing value by upgrading "obsolete" and "old-fashioned" to "historical treasure."

A few of the people to whom I wrote resisted the temptation of being included in history, or perhaps they preferred to leave certain memories in the "obsolete" category. In my initial requests for information, I had avoided any hint that I specifically wanted to find sources about the Nazi period. "Have you material that relates to the impact of the Great

Depression on women's organizations?" One national Catholic welfare office told me curtly, "We regret to inform you that we cannot be of service. We, in *our* association, treat all people equally regardless of changing material circumstances." Others sent me an open invitation, and later reconsidered. A liberal Protestant women's organization, for example, invited me to their Hanover headquarters only to tell me, as soon as I arrived, that the papers seemed so disorganized the older members would have to arrange them after they retired. They wanted, they said, to spare me the aggravation of searching through unindexed files. Since historians Richard Evans and Amy Hackett had both used this excellent collection in research relating to the pre-1914 years, I knew that disorder had not precluded historical investigation that focused on material from a "safe" period. Judging from this organization's letters that I found later in other archives, I suspect that these valuable files will be purged before they are catalogued. Fortunately, the overwhelming majority of the associations and state archives I contacted cooperated with my every request. Ten months in Berlin, with its Inner Mission (social services) and Protestant Church archives, the Berlin Document Center, and the immense Prussian State Library, followed by itinerant searching in Freiburg, Cologne, Munich, Wiesbaden, Düsseldorf, Münster, and Hanover, produced pounds of Xeroxes and note cards.

When I began the project, I had assumed I would discover semi-public proclamations laced with heavy doses of propaganda, or private correspondence written on the assumption that a censor or zealous superior would read it. Of course, this sort of effusive praise was not lacking. But letter writers often communicated openly. "We returned from the rally this evening. As we ate stew on our balcony, we heard the Schmidt family (all red-blooded Nazis) playing a Schubert string quartet, and we knew our cause was just. *This* is what we're fighting for," wrote one woman Nazi during the Depression.

But in addition to enthusiasm (both fake and genuine), I discovered a very different sort of record. Hundreds of women leaders in religious and state-sponsored associations who perceived themselves as dedicated followers of Nazism knew that their own effectiveness depended upon accurate feedback and exchange of proposals. A complaint about morale, a lament about official corruption, or an admission of failure in one program did not, in their view, add up to disloyalty. This sort of commentary produced archival gems. "Dear Frau Polster," a letter might begin, "We are doing something here in our town that is not right." Or a neighborhood leader might tell her superior, "We have a problem here. On one hand we tell women to devote their time to their families; but on the other, husbands complain that their wives spend all their time on

Party activities. What can we tell the men?" A high-ranking administrator would complain to her male chief, "How can you expect us women to carry out our Nazification program among women teachers when you deprive us of adequate funds and treat us so arrogantly?" Nazi women saw themselves as strong-minded members of an elite. Emboldened by their genuine devotion to the cause, they spoke out clearly when they experienced conflicts.

Of course, women were not the only ones to evaluate programs frankly. Men Nazis, too, needed to assess morale, set goals, and confess errors; but they commanded more prestige, which, in turn, translated into railway passes and expense accounts for high-level conferences and secret discussions. Women labored under chronically inadequate budgets and had little money to travel or even to make long-distance telephone calls. But they did employ hundreds of clerk-typists, at very low salaries, who dispatched and filed memos together with carbon copies. On occasion, too, the contradictions inherent in any high-ranking woman bureaucrat's life produced extraordinary collections. For example, the highest woman official in the Nazi Teachers' Union, Frau Dr. Auguste Reber-Gruber, could not relocate to live near her job because her husband's desire for a wife at home took precedence over the state's needs. Thus, she conducted business by mail from her home and produced thousands of written "conversations" about daily routine that would normally have been lost to history. Such collections enliven the more typical fare of endless reports, bureaucratic debates about who would fund a particular activity, or what theme was to be featured on the national radio network's *Housewife's Week* program. Still, even the rather dull local and regional monthly activity reports tell us about both the types of work women accomplished and the sort of thing they knew their superiors wanted to hear. Interspersed among official letters one finds telling side comments about Marxists, specific Nazi programs, general mood, or personal experiences.

After working in public and private archives, I confronted a discontinuous narrative. Like an archaeologist who unearths the handle of a jug or the shard of a bowl, I had stumbled on fragmented records. I might discover hundreds of memos concerning a particular woman dissident or "Nazified" organization, enabling me to follow the minutest details of a feud, squabble, rivalry, or friendship. But then I would confront a complete blank. The paper trail would vanish. This could mean that the principal correspondents stopped communicating entirely—or, equally likely, they might have begun seeing one another on a daily basis and not written at all. Perhaps a circumstance described in the records was typical, or it might as easily have been unique.

As I began to organize my material, the last vestiges I might have had of a typical Nazi woman vanished, and I relinquished my initial expectation that chapter headings would spring naturally from my notes. German woman varied in both support and opposition, as victims and perpetrators. Even the blindest fanatics and crassest opportunists could on occasion protest a specific policy or take a great risk to protect a friend. The staunchest skeptics of Hitler's rule might comply with certain directives. Archives had (as they always do) broken up the monoliths with which I had begun my work. No one woman conformed to either the passive-docile or the heartless-brutish model. Few vapid Eva Brauns or cruel Irma Grieses. Instead, troops of Leni Riefenstahls—ambitious, determined, opportunistic—marched along, caught up in the Nazi tide. Far from fitting Plath's masochistic image, they imbibed an ideal of womanhood ubiquitous in the Western tradition and hoped to use it for their short-term advantage. The division between Nazi men and Nazi women had become very sharp in my thinking, but my archival explorations blurred the distinctions between non-Nazi and Nazi women. Women with a nostalgic vision of motherhood from either camp applied survival strategies that were as old as misogyny itself.

As I read, for example, Frau Dr. Auguste Reber-Gruber's description of women's special concerns and talents, I thought of nineteenth-century feminists who extolled women's uniquely humane influence. I remembered, too, the argument that women must preserve idealism and tenderness, because if they do not, who will guard socially necessary virtues like maternal love, religious faith, idealism, cooperation, and charity? Mothers, as mythical angels in the house, have preserved idealism, love, and faith while men made war, killed, and exploited. Even women's rights advocates' zeal for equality had dimmed after a decade of experience in the Weimar Republic. They reasoned that access to politics had not endowed women with political influence. Men would never relinquish their power, women could never wrest it from them; hence many concluded that the only effective women's strategy lay in cooperating with men and reaping protection as a reward. Experience had taught them that competition with men did not pay but compromise might. According to this logic, when the New Woman participated effectively in the man's world, she became like a man and relinquished her last bargaining chip in the sexual politics of everyday life.

Freedom, so essential to the confident, terrified the insecure. A decade of avant-garde experimentation during the Weimar period frightened conventional people. Long before Hitler came to power, many women called for "emancipation from emancipation." The new freedoms, which had exhilarated a few during the flapper era of the 1920s, unsettled the majority of women, for whom new opportunities meant loss of protection. "Emancipation," declared one woman, "threatens to emancipate our sons, daughters, and even husbands from our control." Women who conformed to traditional expectations demanded recognition in the motherly roles for which their childhood and education had prepared them. Viewing themselves as an endangered species in an abrasive modern world, they called for a virile patriarchy which, they believed, would protect them from emancipation. Democracy and choice had surrounded them with chaos, anomie, and competition. Women demanded their right to withdraw from that world, to devote themselves to familial concerns, and to be economically secure. Authoritarian rule would, they hoped, impose order and health on the nation and tie fathers to their families. Such an inchoate longing did not necessarily impel women to vote for the Nazi Party before 1933, but it did prepare them to welcome the Nazi state. Nostalgia about women and the family contributed to the Nazi appeal no less than other components of a proto-Nazi heritage, such as nationalism, fear of Marxism, hatred of the Versailles Treaty, and contempt for democracy.

The terms of women's discourse reflected the extent to which the notion of an exclusively female territory permeated their thinking. Catholic women called their periodical *Women's Country* (*Frauenland*), and a group of pro-Nazi Protestant women named their magazine *New Land* [*Neuland*]. Fearing that the individual mother in her home stood powerless against the forces that threatened her, middle-class women formed national associations to defend woman's interests as mother, consumer, homemaker, producer, and churchgoer. Traditionalist women dreamed of organizing a vast women's world within an essentially female space— under men's guardianship, to be sure, but beyond the surveillance of prelates or politicians. Beginning in the 1920s, they began to refer to their world as their own "living room." Hitler used the term as a fraudulent pretext for military conquest of the rich agricultural lands in eastern Europe. *Lebensraum* to women meant a peaceful social sphere within which women of all classes and ages would cooperate to revive the gospel of love and harmony. Such a "place" had, of course never existed. Women had never been so pure or men so protective. What alternative vision was there? Some socialists and stalwart feminists during the 1920s had fashioned a utopian landscape in which women and men would live equally together, sharing in families, in communities, and on the job. Facing two dreams, most women took refuge in the one rooted in a familiar past.

Nazi women adapted the dream of a separate space and forswore claims to "masculine" public power and in exchange expected greater influence over their own social realm. Health care, education, reproduction, folk traditions and handicrafts, social work, and religion all fell into the sphere women called their own social space. Scholtz-Klink told me smugly, "Men will always be self-centered, arrogant, and ambitious." Women will never wield power *as women*, although you will see a Margaret Thatcher or Indira Gandhi. "If you want to help women, then you need a women's bureau, not a woman president." But while Scholtz-Klink's "state within a state" reflected an important tradition, it also perverted two central principles. Whereas most conservative women viewed the family as an emotional "space" and bulwark *against* the invasion of public life, Nazi women saw it as an invasion route that could give them access to every German's most personal values and decisions.

Women's remoteness from public life, in the nineteenth-century view, endowed them with a certain moral leverage. They were supposed to remain aloof from corruption and injustice, admonishing their husbands, sons, and fathers to remain true to their principles. The ideal Nazi woman, by contrast, retained the remoteness from power, but forfeited her moral influence because she yielded to the state and enjoyed the rewards. Claiming that their work elevated women's status, Scholtz-Klink and her deputies intruded into previously personal choices related to issues as diverse as childbearing, education, consumer purchases, religious faith, menu planning, ethical values, and social life. Backed by state funds and lavish propaganda campaigns, Nazi women invaded family life with eugenics, ideological indoctrination, and anti-Semitism. Thus, they differed from the conservative tradition in their open retreat from politics and active entry into personal life. Whatever their doubts and disillusionments, women in other Weimar parties realized that they needed access to formal political power to defend their interests, even if, paradoxically, their major concerns revolved around preserving a private "space" in which a mother's influence predominated.

Motherly love in its separate sphere, far from immunizing women against evil, fired women's dedication to the Führer's vision of an "Aryan" future and expanded opportunities for women to reign in their own *Lebensraum*. Nazi women thought they ruled this "living room." But the state, which had supported its construction in 1933, began in the late 1930s to destroy it. The need for workers in strategic industries conflicted with official views of women's role. SS breeding programs violated customary views about marriage, as did a divorce reform that made it easy for husbands to abandon wives. Women Nazis felt betrayed when the state attacked both religion and the family. After German armies were defeated at Stalingrad, deception became threadbare and willful ignorance flaccid. Since Karl Jaspers in 1947 first spoke of Germans as "victims" of Hitler and his wars, the term has become common-place. But it is misleading. Most people touched by war lost control of their choices, whether as soldiers, prisoners, factory workers, or widows. They suffered. They became victims of Allied attack, but average citizens did not become the targets of their own government's murderous plans. Jews did.

During the early stages of my research, I had seldom come into contact with information about non-Nazis and victims. I had researched the women's world, which (to borrow a metaphor they often used) was contained by the walls around Catholic, Protestant, and Nazi organizations. These walls remained invisible as long as women did not venture too near the borders. But when a woman leader expected to participate with men in decision making (even in issues related to women), the alarms went off and she faced a storm of ridicule. Autonomy existed only in relationship to the women within her sphere and did not translate into bargaining power in male administrations. Women felt free only as long as their wishes were congruent with Nazi demands. Obviously, male Nazis faced constraints, but men's roles as wielders of power were not discordant with Nazi notions about gender-appropriate behavior.

Scholtz-Klink boasted, "My women and I did as we pleased," because she had so thoroughly internalized the Nazi leaders' definition of what pleased them. Self-esteem, for Scholtz-Klink and her underlings, depended upon never approaching the limits of their power. By blinding themselves to their own irrevocable second-rate status, they established their own satrapies on the margin of men's realm. Compiling the chronicle of this morass of self-deception and opportunism proved to be depressing work. What, I occasionally wondered, did these women look like from the other side of the social and legal wall that cordoned off "Aryan" from Jew and resister from Nazi?

One voice in particular jolted me out of the protective layer of indifference I had developed while perusing hundreds of documents depicting a grim topic. Erna Becker-Cohen spoke powerfully from the pages of her 1942 diary. Reading her words, written on yellowed paper, I began a new search that has not ended. A Catholic with Jewish ancestors and a Catholic husband, Erna Becker-Cohen needed desperately to communicate the pain she experienced under Nazi rule. Not trusting friends and reluctant to burden her already worried husband, she recorded her anguish in a diary remarkable for its restraint and honesty. Her straightforward, often telegraphic comments bear witness to the experiences of millions of women who risked (and usually lost) their lives because they did not fit into Hitler's schemes for a thousand-year Reich.

During the winter of 1942–43, Frau Becker-Cohen went to the store in Berlin at which she had shopped for years. The owner ordered her to get out. A sign said, JEWS ARE NOT WANTED. At first, the proscription took Becker-Cohen aback; then she adjusted quickly. Nothing, but nothing, could ever hurt as deeply as the day two years earlier when members of her parish had told her that "Aryan" Catholics found it unseemly to attend Christmas services in the presence of a Jew. How they had rejoiced at her conversion so many years before, and welcomed her and her husband into their community! Then, after 1933, these same Christian neighbors no longer greeted her on the street. Her disillusion with Catholics, however, did not diminish her faith in Catholicism, but she stopped attending the local church and traveled every day to a downtown cathedral where people would not identify her as Jewish. When the bombing raids began, her neighbors in the shelters behaved so crudely that she preferred to risk allied bombs rather than descend into the subterranean world of hatred and bigotry. She had learned to avoid ostracism and to pray alone. But how would she buy milk for her four-year-old son? She decided to send him to the store. Seeing the child with an empty milk container and ration book, the shop owner turned to her friends. "Just look at that Jew-woman, sending her son because we won't let *her* in!" They sent the boy home without milk. That night the mother confided in her diary, "How very hard people are! Not even mothers offer sympathy to me in my sorrow. Where," she asked, "can God be if his spirit does not live in the hearts of his faithful?"[6]

Where, I asked myself, did the spirit of resistance live if not among women? Somewhere within that society saturated with terror, someone must have preserved a humane tradition. German culture had, after all, produced Goethe, Schiller, and Heine; Mozart, Beethoven, and Schubert.

And the old question returned. Where had the women been? Germany, unlike Nazi-occupied countries during the Second World War, had not inspired any military resistance. Nor had terror played a significant role. That meant opposition depended upon skills that women have traditionally possessed in abundance, like the ability to "pass"—to shed any overt behavior that might attract the attention of Nazi officials, neighbors, teachers, policemen, or relatives, while holding on to an inner self-respect. Among Jewish Germans, too, I speculated, these womanly talents must have played a vital role. How did women, whom psychologists credit with sensitivity to others' needs and weaknesses, perceive sources of danger and safety?

Where Nazi power reigned, men and women remained separated by function, personality, and responsibilities. Beyond the limits of Hitler's authority, however, in small islands of opposition, women and men formed integrated communities, unified by trust and integrity. After the first wave of isolated and failed protests in 1933, resisters prepared for a long fight. Jews, devastated at their friends' betrayal, created new sources of support that likewise bound together men and women, young and old, rich and poor. To "resist" meant first of all to survive emotionally. It required the inner strength to cut oneself entirely loose from external systems of rewards and punishments and fashion a balance between conformity and opposition. Looking backward, evaluation of very limited information becomes extremely difficult. A wholehearted Nazi might be moved to perform one act of kindness toward a Jewish neighbor, or a diehard opponent would habitually give the "Heil Hitler" (called the "German greeting") salute to avoid suspicion. Next to fear of arrest, apathy was the worst threat. Immobilized rage turned inward produced political depression. Ruth Andreas-Friedrich and her husband, both members of the resistance, wrote: "The time of the lone wolf had passed. . . . Strength no longer depended upon those who appeared powerful. We had to build our own troops . . . what one person needs the other will supply. Everything depends upon our ability to divide up the roles intelligently."[7] We still do not know if hundreds, thousands, or tens of thousands preserved communities of integrity against Nazism, because courage among opponents and victims had to be hidden if it was to exist at all.

Looking back at Nazi Germany, it seems that decency vanished; but when we listen to feminine voices from the period, we realize instead that it was cordoned off. Loyal Nazis fashioned an image for themselves, a fake domestic realm where they felt virtuous. Nazi women facilitated that mirage by doing what women have done in other societies—they made the world a more pleasant place in which to live for the members of their community. And they simultaneously made life first unbearable and later impossible for "racially unworthy" citizens. As fanatical Nazis or lukewarm tag-alongs, they resolutely turned their heads away from assaults against socialists, Jews, religious dissenters, the handicapped, and "degenerates." They gazed instead at their own cradles, children, and "Aryan" families. Mothers and wives directed by Gertrud Scholtz-Klink made a vital contribution to Nazi power by preserving the illusion of love in an environment of hatred, just as men sustained the image of order in the utter disarray of conflicting bureaucratic and military priorities and commands.

Over time, Nazi women, no less than men, destroyed ethical vision, debased humane traditions, and rendered decent people helpless. And other women, as victims and resisters, risked their lives to ensure Nazi defeat and preserve their own ideals.

2

WEIMAR EMANCIPATION

War falls on the women most heavily, and more so now than ever before. This war should be a good argument for suffrage. It shows that men, as I have always believed, are as hysterical as women, only they show it in a different way. Women weep and men fight.
—Carrie Chapman Catt
The New York Times
August 6, 1914

An account of Hitler's Germany must begin with a survey of the Weimar Republic that preceded it, and here historians alternate between two perspectives, one myopic and the other omniscient. Opting for the first means portraying the 1920s as the people who lived then experienced them—depicting a relatively placid political landscape on which Adolf Hitler was a very small blot on the horizon. But the Third Reich casts a deep backward shadow that skews that perspective and places Hitler squarely in the center. We know what most Germans in the 1920s could not suspect: that a small band of fanatics who swore total allegiance to their Führer would after 1933 hold the fate of the nation in its control. Brutality, terror, and genocide from later decades intrude upon the picture of Weimar Germany as contemporaries saw it. This shadow calls for a retrospective double vision that encompasses both the prospect of emancipation and progress held out by Weimar democracy and the etiology of a disreputable and insignificant movement which spread, undetected, through the body politic and was diagnosed only after it could not be halted.

Because this is a book about women in a man's state, a second doubling in our perspective superimposes itself upon the first, for male and female worlds do not always harmonize, and frequently they do not even touch. Standard histories focus on the public sphere in which men determine foreign policy, negotiate economic deals, and declare social policy. Historians of Weimar Germany have often analyzed this world of their fathers, defining its turning points, diagnosing its structural faults, and singling out its heroes and villains. But behind and beneath the political chain of events that brought Hitler to power, the world of the mothers also underwent a transformation. Women's suffrage, the emergence of the economically and socially emancipated New Woman, the panic about falling birth rates, shifts in employment patterns—all sent tremors through society. The cataclysms of public life—war, defeat, revolution, and Depression—occurred against an emotional substructure torn by confusion, despair, and anxiety.

Formally, Weimar Germany began with the cataclysmic winter of 1918–1919, which irrevocably changed men's and women's lives. During the previous four years they had directed their efforts against foreign enemies. Then, in October 1918, when propaganda promised a quick military victory, German generals told their Kaiser to surrender or face invasion. He called for an armistice. Rebellion broke out, much as it had in Russia during 1917. The Kaiser abdicated and fled into exile. Just when Germans least expected it, the republic had been born. Just when women least anticipated it, universal suffrage became law. During the last weeks of 1918, an interim Socialist cabinet initiated a series of sweeping reforms. Because of Socialists' commitment to women's emancipation, German women became the first women to vote in any major nation. Neither democracy nor women's equality, however, found much support in war-torn Germany. President Wilson made it clear during the peace negotiations at Versailles that Germany could not end the war until its citizens had drafted a democratic constitution and elected their government. Refusal would have meant renewed war and an even more humiliating defeat. Germans elected a National Assembly that drafted the constitution. Because they feared revolution in Berlin, the lawmakers met in Weimar, gracing the new government with the name of Goethe's city.

No wonder observers watched German politics with intense interest. What would become of a liberation that owed its very existence to military surrender and Socialist victory? How would the beneficiaries use their new rights? In English, French, and United States history, political reform has often come as the result of victorious national revolution. But Germans had experienced their first taste of liberalism when Napoleon's armies invaded, and again in the wake of surrender in 1918. The high point of German history in the eyes of most citizens had come with the unification in 1871. That triumph had been achieved not by progressives, but by Otto von Bismarck and the reactionary Kaiser Wilhelm I. In some ways the Russian monarchy offers a comparison, for it, too, had provided a bastion against liberal reform. But after Nicholas I abdicated, moderates lost control in 1917. As in Germany, Russians suffered chaos after defeat, but Lenin's government relied upon military strength and not elections. Moderate Socialists in Germany defeated the Communists and pledged to uphold basic freedoms.

The sudden granting of women's suffrage likewise had no precise parallel. True, American and British women received the ballot during the 1920s, but their movements had been closer to success in 1914, and their nations emerged victorious in 1918. In France and Italy, women had contributed to the war effort, but received no rewards in the form of rights or suffrage until the end of World War II. In Germany, women's suffrage, like democracy, came as a by-product of chaos and defeat rather than as the immediate result of a long and hard-fought battle. What would emancipated women do with the promise of equal rights? A Socialist, Maria Juchacz, proclaimed, "The Woman Question in Germany no longer exists in the old sense of the term. It has been solved."[1] But other, more somber voices could be heard. Feminist Alice Rühle-Gerstel commented, "The war emancipated women; it is now up to women to emancipate themselves."[2]

The vote alone, she believed, meant little. Feminist-pacifist Lida Gustava Heymann predicted that women would encounter disillusionment: "Oppression that has lasted thousands of years leaves deep traces, which will not be erased overnight by women's suffrage. We have to bear those burdens for generations because it takes time to deprive the man of woman who has been cultivated to give him his comforts."[3]

In the 1920s Germans asked, Would the nationalists who dominated the Kaiser's regime concede victory to a coalition of liberals and moderate socialists? Would men allow women to take their place in public life as legal and economic equals?

The winter of 1918–1919 makes a convenient point of departure in any chronicle of Nazism. The trauma of surrender, economic hardship, and political revolution defined the real world in which most Germans lived. But emotionally they lived in the aftermath of wartime glory, on chauvinist slogans, images of brave soldiers and strong women, hymns to a national spirit, and appeals to sacrifice that persisted even as reality left them behind. As Germans experienced hunger, fear of invasion, revolution, and economic disaster, they clung to dreams created by wartime propaganda. Memories of the joyous upsurge of patriotism from 1914 alternated with the bitter shock of humiliation from 1918. The history of Nazism, thus, begins six years before Hitler took control of an insignificant party, with a war that galvanized Germans to action in the name of patriotic honor and imperialist greed.

On the last day of July 1914, Germans heard the news that their nation had been wantonly attacked by Russia, France, and England. The Kaiser called for a domestic truce between warring political parties, interest groups, and economic classes. Socialists, instead of launching an international workers' uprising as they had threatened, rushed to the recruiting tables. Women heard themselves summoned to save the Fatherland. As the troops marched to the front, Germans at home thrilled to the battle call and anticipated instant victory. The image of uniformed glory pulled citizens out of the daily humdrum into the vortex of flags, slogans, drives, and crusades. But "the boys" did not return victorious for Christmas in 1914, and the promise of instant glory became mired in the blood and mud of the trenches. Four years of mechanized slaughter at the front and desperate shortages at home, accompanied by fraudulent propaganda about German military triumph, sapped the fervor of civilians and veterans alike.

Fighting a common enemy, citizens experienced the thrill of national unity and a shared destiny. But men and women lived through very different wartime realities. After the defeat, soldiers returned—disillusioned, defeated, and bitter. Like Paul, the hero in *All Quiet on the Western Front*, they could not face "normalcy."

> All that meets me, all that floods over me are but feelings—greed of life, love of home, yearning of the blood, intoxication of deliverance. But no aims. Had we returned home in 1916, out of the suffering and the strength of our experience we might have unleashed a storm. Now, if we go back we will be weary, broken, burnt out, rootless and without hope. We will not be able to find our way any more.[4]

Soldiers' accounts of the war vividly chronicle their lives in the trenches and also depict their remoteness from civilian life. Their alienation from women (even the women they loved) haunts this literature. Paul, in *All Quiet*, discovers "a terrible feeling of foreignness" that severs his connection to the world back home. Even on leave, he cannot bridge the gulf, not even when his mother asks for his trust. "Mother, mother! You still think I am a child—why can I not put my head in your lap and weep? . . . I would like to weep and be comforted, too. Indeed I am little more than a child."[5] But Paul cannot weep, and mourns the loss of his ability to feel. Another author, far more popular in Germany, glorified this experience of being cut off from peaceful, "womanly" life. Ernst Jünger wrote best-sellers about his experiences at the front where he felt bound by profound ties of love and death to his fellow soldiers. "Though I am no misogynist, I was always irritated by the presence of women every time that the fate of battle threw me into the bed of a hospital ward. One sank, after the manly and purposeful activities of the war, into a vague atmosphere of warmth."[6] War, the "silent teacher," hardened a generation of soldiers against the seductive temptations of home, tenderness, and femininity. Remarque's soldiers experienced terror, madness, and grief that "feminize" them; Jünger's *Storm of Steel* preached vengeance, blood, and glory. The war had endowed Jünger's restless life with meaning and a higher purpose. Exhilarated, he marched with his battalion into Belgium, intoxicated by the "smell of blood and roses." The experience gave birth to the "new man," who was very different from the Weimar democrat or Remarque's burned-out veterans.

> War, the father of all things, is also our father. It has hammered us, chiseled us and hardened us into what we are. And always, as long as the swirling wheel of life revolves within us, this war will be the axis around which it will swirl. It has reared us for battle and we shall remain fighters as long as we live. . . . Under the skin of all cultural and technical progress we remain naked and raw like the man of the forest and of the steppe. . . .

That is the new man, the pioneer of the storm, the her
. . . This war is not the end but the new ascendar
forms will be filled with blood and might will b
fist.[7]

An insignificant trench soldier, Adolf Hitler, experien⌐
much the same way. After his first encounter with the enemy, he .
"Four days later we came back. Even our step had changed. Seventeen-
year-old boys now looked like men. The volunteers of the regiment may
not have learned to fight properly, but they knew how to die like old
soldiers. This was the beginning."[8] After 1919, a few pacifists called for
international disarmament, but most Germans remained in the thrall of
wartime propaganda and anticipated the day when a new army would
have a second chance to win the glorious victories promised by the
Kaiser's propaganda.

Because they experienced the war differently, women faced special
problems in the post-war world. War pulled women out of their families
and into public life, giving them a stake in the nation that most had not
previously felt. In 1914, women organized across political and religious
divisions to knit, nurse, collect scrap material, and donate to charity.
After 1916, as German generals realized the war would not end soon, the
government recruited women to take the soldiers' places at strategically
vital jobs. Overnight, it seemed, women were not only permitted but
begged to mine coal, deliver the mail, drive trucks and trams, keep account books, and work in heavy industry—as well as continuing to roll
bandages, nurse veterans, and perform charitable work. Suddenly a system that, until 1908, had made it illegal for women even to attend gatherings at which politics might be discussed and barred women from
earning university degrees, told women the nation's very survival depended upon their taking up jobs previously done by men. A woman
who joined the Nazi Party a decade later recalled, "It was a magnificent
and holy time for us, it made us feel tied to the front and our homeland
(*Heimat*). I don't think it would be an exaggeration to say that those first
war years pulled us all together in a true spiritual community."[9]

Ironically, the war, which slaughtered millions of young men, "emancipated" millions of young women by giving them the status and autonomy women's rights advocates had demanded for decades. The director
of German women's wartime efforts, Maria E. Lüders, admitted, "In a
certain sense, the war came at the right time for women."[10] Women
demonstrated their patriotism, energy, and skills, but they did so in a
topsy-turvy world that resembled antifeminists' worst nightmares: While
brave men marched to their deaths, women "stole" their jobs, took their

in the universities, and usurped their authority at home. Shibbo-
...s about "natural" feminine weakness dissolved in the face of clear
...idence that women could perform "men's jobs" with minimal train-
...ng.[11] Progress for women occurred in the context of trench warfare for
soldiers, and starvation, deprivation, social dislocation, and defeat for
society as a whole.

After the Armistice in November 1918, nearly two million German
soldiers did not return from the front; but six million did, some alienated
and others rebellious, but all of them needing jobs. A veritable social
revolution (soziale Umschichtung) broke out when men demanded the
jobs women had performed.[12] "A horrible war broke out between male
and female over bread and work," recalled a socialist woman.[13] Trade
unions, best-selling authors, politicians, government ministers, and industrialists (who could not agree on policy in any other area), cooperated
to expel the women they had lured into "men's work." Economically,
women could be demobilized, but psychologically what would become
of their aspirations? What would happen to the widows, to the wives
whose soldier husbands divorced them upon returning home, the unwed
mothers, and the nearly two million women who comprised what was
called the "woman surplus" created by the post-war scarcity of young
men? After experiencing independence and hearing themselves praised
as vital members of the nation, women found it difficult to return to their
former lives. "How could you keep 'em back in the kitchen, after they've
been to Berlin?"

> By now she (as a wartime worker) had been her own master for four years,
> and had earned her own money, a lot of money even . . . and was free to
> spend it as she liked, could come and go as she pleased, do what she liked
> or not do it. And suddenly, all this should come to an end.[14]

Overnight, it seemed, the propaganda campaign that had lured women
into the economy reversed direction. Instead of praise for her patriotic
service, the woman felt invidious comparison with the brave man of the
front. One young woman wrote,

> They go amidst the bullets for you.
> In the evenings you read about it by lamplight.
> They sleep stretched out in the wet grass.
> Your nice warm bed is in front of you.
> You can hug your loved ones close in your arms.
> Dying, they see a foreign face.
> And all your love and all your pain,
> Your warmest wishes cannot reach far enough

To make the last hour easier for those
Who die out there in murderous slaughter.[15]

Glory for the soldier meant guilt for the woman.

While Socialist women defended their equal right to work, middle-class women often put the needs of returning veterans first. For example, a women's periodical carried one man's complaint: "The man had to go into the field and, for a tiny wage, risk his life; the young women sat safely back home and enjoyed their complete personal freedom. And now they grumble because the man rightly demands that a place be made for him. The man at the desk! The woman at the stove!!!"[16] The cabaret singer Rosa Valetti sang Kurt Tucholsky's verses, mourning for a generation's lost hopes.

> I saw the world
> In fire enfurled—
> The women bent with sorrows,
> The reaper cut
> And they were struck
> With a hundred thousand horrors.
> And for what did they scream and die?
> Haho! For a filthy lie!
> The corpses—the corpses—
> They lie in the earth,
> We women—we women—
> Now what are we worth?[17]

Meanwhile, official Germany returned to normalcy. When we look at the public sphere, we see earnest democrats piloting their nation through the trauma of defeat after World War I, averting threats of revolution and right-wing putsches, trying to stave off disastrous hyperinflation, escaping a crushing foreign debt, and winning acceptance by their former enemies. Voter turnout also provided grounds for optimism as close to 90 percent of all eligible German women and men went to the polls in most elections. After a decade of democracy, liberals looked with satisfaction at the accomplishments of their experiment. This comes as a surprise, for often we hear that Germans overwhelmingly chose Hitler as their leader. A glance at election statistics shows that was not true. From the first Weimar elections in 1919 until the last free election of 1932, a majority of voters cast their ballots for parties that opposed fascist principles in general and the Nazi Party in particular.[18] Nazi candidates achieved a plurality that gave Hitler bargaining power, but he owed his appointment as chancellor to a reactionary President's prejudices and his own underhanded political manipulation.

Besides surviving politically, Weimar Germany provided the climate within which a brilliant culture flourished. The turbulent republic gave us the Weimar intellectuals who have shaped our own consciousness and informed our insights. Bertolt Brecht, Hermann Hesse, Robert Musil, Walter Benjamin, Thomas Mann, Rainer Maria Rilke, and Heinrich Mann set the parameters of dilemmas in which we still find ourselves. Freud's German-speaking followers—Karen Horney, Wilhelm Reich, Erich Fromm, Melanie Klein, and Carl Jung—illuminated new dimensions of our psychic world. Visual images crowd in: powerful messages from Käthe Kollwitz, Georg Grosz, Paul Klee, Walter Gropius, Emil Nolde, Ernst Ludwig Kirchner, Max Beckmann, Otto Dix, and Oskar Kokoschka. These stills are, in turn, overlaid by moving templates of a *Blue Angel*, a *Metropolis*, a mad *Dr. Caligari*, and many *Girls in Uniform*. In the background, we hear the discordant harmonies of Richard Strauss, Kurt Weil, Paul Hindemith, and Arnold Schönberg. Meanwhile, Karl Jaspers and Martin Heidegger, Karl Barth and Martin Buber searched for the meaning of it all. In that decade, German scientists captured seven Nobel Prizes; Albert Einstein taught at the University of Berlin and crusaded for world peace; and Max Planck directed his physics laboratory in Munich. The brilliance of their Weimar world overarches the Third Reich and speaks directly to us.

But the intellectual and cultural triumphs of Weimar Germany meant little to average Germans who experienced economic insecurity and political uncertainty that they blamed on the defeat. Those unrequited dreams from 1914 cast a dismal pall over the postwar generation, and the new civilian leaders could not speak to the inchoate longing for military triumph. The treaty they signed at Versailles demanded that the fleet be sunk and the army limited to a hundred thousand soldiers. Germans had no choice but to adhere to its terms. Judged in comparison to the treaties Germany had dictated to Soviet Russia in March 1918 and to France in 1871, the Versailles Treaty could not be considered overly harsh. But most Germans had anticipated a smashing military triumph right up to the end of 1918 and thirsted, with Ernst Jünger, for vengeance. The newly elected men and women, who had exerted no influence whatsoever upon the outbreak of the war or its conduct, ratified the treaty, while rabid nationalists looked back nostalgically upon an untarnished image of their own creation. The gallant German Army, ran the myth, had been stabbed in the back by defeatist collusion among Socialists and liberals, and, many reactionaries added, Jews and women. Against these insinuations women, like Jews, did their very best to demonstrate their patriotism. But they trod along a delicate border because whenever Jews or women defended their rights, their enemies derided them as pushy and selfish. Any move forward would be met with backlash. This tension between progressive aims and anxiety about conservative retaliation established the fundamental dynamic of the ill-fated republic.

Terrified by the example of Lenin, moderate Socialists sided with conservatives against threats of revolution. In their speeches, Socialists promised major reforms to win over the Communists; but in practice they refrained from keeping their word for fear of a backlash. Thus, Weimar leaders grafted a democratic state onto a traditionalist and conservative social structure and a thoroughly capitalist economy. All parties agreed that Weimar democracy represented the least of all evils. But grudging acceptance among reasonable people did not make for the enthusiasm necessary to launch any new political regime.

Nationalists attacked the Republic that left their *Vaterland "wehrlos, ehrlos, und heerlos"* (stripped of weapons, honor, and army), and fulminated against the Versailles Treaty that created a chasm between rich nations like France and poor countries like Germany. Communists, at the other extreme, despised the Republic for increasing the immense inequalities between rich and poor. Both extremes hated the compromisers in the middle, who apologized and cajoled in order to keep the combatants at the bargaining table. Women especially felt these contradictions, for the Weimar Constitution, which gave them the suffrage, also contained what Americans today would call an Equal Rights Amendment. But because the law code from the monarchy was not revised, women remained de facto bound to regressive laws and legal principles. To make matters worse, the liberal constitution was enforced by judges and civil servants who had pledged allegiance to the Kaiser before 1914 and hated democracy.

Any talk of further women's emancipation stirred the expectations of its advocates and the hatred of its enemies. On the surface it appeared that women's rights carried the day. Over 10 percent of the delegates to the 1919 National Assembly were women; and women took their places in local governments everywhere. Proportional representation worked to women candidates' advantage because this meant that each party sponsored lists of candidates, and contenders for seats did not campaign directly against each other. Thus, parties designed "packages" of candidates to attract a broad spectrum of voters. Although only Socialists had supported women's suffrage before the war, all political parties officially welcomed women's enfranchisement when they realized it was inevitable. Women's issues ranked high in politicians' promises; and every party included women on its list of candidates. For better or worse,

German women had, it seemed, entered politics. The reform could not be undone but it could be undercut. And women voters could do it. Paula Müller-Otfried, president of the national Protestant women's organization and longtime opponent of women's suffrage, ran for a seat in the 1919 National Assembly (and won). While advocates of women's equality rejoiced in having won the right to vote, Müller warned women that suffrage would not improve their lot, but she admonished her followers to vote anyway out of a sense of obligation. This sort of halfhearted support must have discouraged many from believing in their right to vote or in their claim to equality in general.

Except for the Versailles Treaty, the Woman Question was the most controversial topic in Weimar Germany. In 1919, as election time approached, people wondered if the new voters would form the much-dreaded "woman bloc" across party lines or merely vote like their husbands. Leaders of women's organizations that had vehemently opposed the vote worried that because Socialist and Liberal women had so much more experience, they would sweep the elections. Conservatives feared women would vote for Marxist candidates out of gratitude for emancipation. As it turned out, Paula Müller-Otfried need not have worried, but Socialists should have. Men and women distributed their votes in roughly the same patterns except that women voted less frequently for Socialists and more frequently for Catholics than men.[19] Socialists calculated that without the woman vote they would have captured the majority they needed to control the government. With women voters, they received only 47 percent and had to form a coalition cabinet. Women's preference for conservative candidates also meant that measures to implement the equality promised in the Constitution failed to pass the Reichstag. Throughout the next decade, Catholic and Socialist delegations to the Reichstag included the highest percentages of women, with the Nationalists including the fewest and the Nazis, none.

In regional politics, more dramatic changes occurred over the decade. While only 2 women served in provincial assemblies in 1919, by 1930 there were 52; and the 386 women on city councils increased to 506 in 1924. At any given time, between 400 and 500 women served in municipal elected political institutions at state and local levels. This was a dazzling record. A brief comparison with American history highlights this achievement. Between 1917 and 1976, 95 women served in the U.S. Congress, 37 of whom were widows who succeeded their husbands. From 1919 to 1932, 112 German women were elected to the Reichstag and comprised between 7 and 10 percent of the total. As with so many aspects of Weimar politics, the woman policy appeared to be the most progressive in the world. For over a decade the system worked.

As long as socialists, liberals, and conservatives all feare economic collapse, even bitter enemies settled on comp system functioned. Although long-term grievances feste the surface calm, everyone wanted to preserve the in well. If only life could be made to *appear* normal, if peopic carry on their old routines, then surely the reality would not linger far behind. Ilya Ehrenburg recalled the respectable quotidian existence of impoverished Berlin. "Nothing," he said, "prevented catastrophe from being presented as a well-ordered existence. The artificial limbs of war-cripples did not creak, empty sleeves were pinned up with safety pins. Men whose faces had been scorched by flamethrowers wore large black spectacles. The lost war took care to camouflage itself as it roamed the streets."[20] Official Germany marched forward away from the war; hidden Germany could not heal the scars.

Women experienced this double reality in a special way. On the one hand they were declared emancipated, which meant taking up their civic duties in public life. But they were also expected to guard private life and preserve the home against the ravages of economic and social turmoil. In practical terms this meant that while women heard themselves welcomed as equals, they had access only to a few areas of public policy: education, health, culture, religion, and welfare. Were women equal citizens or a special-interest lobby? Women's-rights activists had debated this issue for decades, but for the first time it had pragmatic ramifications. Conflicts and dilemmas that had been buried in the struggle for the vote now surfaced in the context of practical questions of the day. Because Socialist and middle-class women had organized rival organizations since the end of the nineteenth century, they faced their newly won emancipation with different expectations. Middle-class women had formed the Federation of German Women's Associations (BDF), which coordinated a broad-based struggle for women's rights without male participation. Socialist women, by contrast, worked closely with their male colleagues, who since the 1890s had incorporated women's equality into their party platforms.

Within both movements women straddled antithetical conceptions of emancipation. Writing in the 1930s, an American sociologist, Clifford Kirkpatrick, distinguished between two kinds of activist women in Germany. One (of whom he disapproved), the "protester type," wanted identical rights for men and women. These women rested their argument on the Enlightenment belief in universal and equal human nature. In the ranks of Socialists and the middle-class women's movements, this opinion was well represented prior to 1914. Socialists stressed the economic base of equality, while for liberals it was legal and political. Clara Zetkin,

.e dominant force among women Socialists before 1914, blamed capitalism for reducing women to mere breeders and housekeepers. After the Socialist revolution, she promised, women and men would experience liberation and equality. Her commitment to universal human equality led her to downplay women's special nature so resolutely that she had voted against introducing birth control as an issue in the 1890s. The progressives in the middle-class women's movement, too, insisted on women's fundamental equality. Hedwig Dohm, prominent in the late nineteenth century, declared, "Anyone who says women's nature is unlike men's is an antifeminist!" [21]

But another view became more popular with each passing year. Kirkpatrick labeled its proponents the "womanly type," who feared women's masculinization and worked instead to expand their influence over areas of public life they felt appropriate to their sex. The "womanly" movement incorporated romantic notions into its arguments for equality by emphasizing women's special idealism, loyalty, and selflessness. During the 1920s, the "womanly" women won. Among Socialists, a younger generation led by Maria Juchacz usurped Zetkin's leadership, and Zetkin resigned from the moderate Socialist Party and became a Communist. Younger women took up the ideology of middle-class women and proclaimed, "The woman is the born guardian of human life"—a statement that would have ranked as major heresy in Zetkin's time. [22] The middle-class Federation of German Women's Associations, led by Gertrud Bäumer and Helene Lange, which represented between 70 and 80 organizations, downplayed the struggle for legal equality while emphasizing women's special contribution.

Despite major disagreements, women had before 1918 felt unified by the very fact of their exclusion from public life. As soon as women delegates sat in the Reichstag, unity among them died. One debate in the Reichstag illustrates the fate of countless measures that addressed women's rights throughout the Weimar Republic. The Post Office, a major employer of women, ignored the constitutional guarantee of equal treatment to civil servants and routinely dismissed all unmarried women who became pregnant. But women state employees were entitled to maternity benefits. After 1919, left-wing Socialists demanded that these benefits be extended to unmarried mothers and, of course, that mothers not be fired. Men delegates generally tolerated the double standard and defended the postmaster. Women from all parties deplored the double standard and expected to use the constitutional guarantee of equality as a "weapon in our hands" to combat it. Agreement ended there. Middle-class women insisted that moral standards could be upheld only if all male postal employees who fathered children born out of wedlock were dismissed just like their female colleagues. Socialist women defended the rights of unmarried mothers to keep their positions, and Socialist men reluctantly followed their lead. Debate on the issue only deepened the divisions and the acrimony. The Reichstag sent the question to a committee—from which it never reemerged—and the postmaster continued as before.[23] Subsequent bills on divorce reform, protective legislation, education, abortion, and public morality met a similar fate. After a decade of access to politics, women had scored only two successes: protective legislation for women who did piecework in their homes and a program to combat venereal disease. Women from all backgrounds agreed in targeting the problems that affected their lives, but divisions among them appeared as soon as the discussion turned to practical solutions.

Disunity spread, too, among bourgeois women because their expectations had been unrealistic in the first place. Marianne Weber, active campaigner for women's rights and delegate to the National Assembly, believed that "it is our responsibility to infuse all life with our special mix of feminine and humane influence."[24] Katharina von Kardorff, moderate conservative Reichstag deputy, hoped that she and other women would "remove the poison" of masculine, materialistic interests and "purify political life."[25] Another woman leader from the moderate conservative People's Party wrote, "We offer reconciliation, steadiness and love."[26] Middle-class women cherished high-minded ideals for arousing "a new spirituality" and experiencing "an awakened power, a new feminine will, an elevated pride, and a sure, confident stride with the head held high."[27]

Women imagined they could rekindle the nationalist fervor of August 1914, but when they took their seats in the Reichstag these political Joans of Arc met severe disappointment. One liberal delegate confided to her friends,

> What passes for "high politics" is nothing but a heap of improper, disreputable, and mixed-up motions which would just make you ill. I have undergone a remarkable education. At first, the negotiations or the negotiators are almost totally unintelligible. But just as soon as I began to realize that concrete self-interest underlies every single issue, then it all becomes as clear as day. And the leaders are so passive! For the moment our feminine impact [*Einschlag*] can only consist of standing at the sidelines expressing continual astonishment at what we see happening—or at what fails to happen. . . . We can do nothing until we feel more secure. The routine is hopeless. Is there no place where we can get together with other women so we can purify our souls?[28]

Still, men expressed satisfaction at women's new political activities. "With surprise, I noted that among our parliamentary women delegates there was little evidence of the doubtlessly constitutional nervousness usually present in the female. Only once have I seen one of them burst into tears in a highly critical parliamentary situation," declared one politician.[29] Women leaders anticipated gaining leverage over political life by trading on their image of purity and virtue. Their first contact with politics drove them to despair.

Socialist women had never had much faith in spiritual power, whether men's or women's, but they confronted disillusionment on a different front. For half a century their male comrades had pledged support for women's equality. As they faced the test after 1919, Socialist women grasped the shallowness of their male comrades' support. As husbands, Socialist men preferred "their" women to devote themselves full-time to the family. As workers, they blamed women's low wages for undercutting men's earning potential. As politicians, they deemed other issues more vital than women's status. Women comprised about a third of the Social Democratic Party, served on party commissions related to the Woman Question, and worked diligently as organizers, public speakers, editors, and officials; nevertheless (as one woman put it in 1924), "Male comrades today still treat us with a sort of irrelevant benevolence."[30] Men welcomed women's participation, but ignored their requests. "The men are pleased if we don't make any demands on their time at all. At meetings they debate for hours on the most trivial matters. But if we want to discuss our concerns, then time suddenly runs out and the comrades have to go home."[31] Thus Socialist women concluded that women's constitutional victory had brought a new set of challenges. In addition to arguing the case for women's equality against reactionaries from rival parties, they faced their own comrades' apathy.

Women from all political parties argued with recalcitrant men by demonstrating their usefulness as women to the general goals of each party. These women often complained about men among themselves and occasionally chided them in public, but they relied on persuasion, not frontal attack, in their efforts to transform men's prejudices. Despite the frustrations of this approach, German women did not organize an all-women caucus in the Reichstag or attempt to form a national women's political lobby. Sensitive to accusations of separatism, women in politics deepened their bonds to the men of their parties. Conservatives and liberals pledged to support the *Volk*; Catholic women reaffirmed their commitment to their religion; and Socialists and Communists put class struggle first. Throughout the 1920s, Socialist and middle-class women closed ranks with the men who shared their political views and avoided appeals to cooperate as women across the political spectrum.

Two very different secular women's organizations worked for radical change outside the political sphere. Numerically, neither achieved a dominant position. One, a feminist association with liberal goals—legal equality for women, access to education and careers, equal pay for equal work, and pacifism—suffered major setbacks during the 1920s; the other, an organization lobbying for motherhood, remained numerically small but became extremely influential in left- and right-wing circles. The Nazi government declared both illegal and their founders went into exile for fear of being imprisoned. Women's reactions to these two very different movements tell us a great deal about mainstream concerns.

Before the war, Lida Gustava Heymann and Anita Augspurg had formed the radical wing of the middle-class movement, but as the BDF became conservative on women's issues and in 1914 supported the war, the rift between the two groups became a chasm that did not close after the war. During the next decade, Heymann and Augspurg made pacifism and women's absolute equality the cornerstones of their movement. During the 1920s, Heymann and Augspurg's feminist message proved too strong for Socialist women, and their commitment to social justice alienated middle-class women. As their support in Germany declined, they turned to the international Women's League for Peace and Freedom for collaboration.

The decline of a strong feminist organization fit in with younger women's general apathy about women's-rights issues. Even though the mainstream BDF became increasingly conservative, new members did not join the ranks. The younger generation, it seemed, believed that the Constitution solved the Woman Question and saw women's-rights leaders as shrill and doughty. The very word "feminist" remained anathema to many younger German women.[32] An American sociologist observed: "Almost all meetings of women's organizations, whether the League of University Women or the Association of Women Citizens, show the same picture. The generation between twenty and thirty is almost completely lacking. That between thirty and forty is sparsely represented.[33] A woman law student explained her generation's lack of interest in feminism: "We are neither bluestockings nor crusaders, nor rich or idle. The New Woman can be a genuine, one-hundred-percent woman now that women's rights have been won."[34] An older generation believed that women must choose between careers and marriage; a younger generation wanted both. Their optimism obviated the need to organize and the double commitment robbed them of the energy for collective endeavors. Prewar feminism never revived.

Under the leadership of Helene Stöcker, a radical association with very different concerns enjoyed great popularity among young and old, men

and women, left and right. Using the deceptively traditional name the
League for the Protection of Motherhood, Stöcker evolved a new idea of
woman centered on motherhood. Rather than escaping from childbearing, she advocated upgrading motherhood. Thus she proclaimed that
eugenic education, birth control, legal abortions, divorce reform, and
aid for mothers, whether or not they were married, were every woman's
birthright.[35] Throughout the 1920s, Stöcker worked closely with the sex
reform movement, which, through research and psychology, explored
ways to make sexuality freer and more fulfilling. A group of medical
researchers, calling themselves sexologists, inspired by Magnus Hirsch-
feld and Helene Stöcker, applied scientific methods to the study of sexual
behavior. Proclaiming sexual pleasure as every person's right, they
charted orgasmic curves for men and women, evaluated sexual prefer-
ences, analyzed arousal patterns, and dispensed contraceptives. In their
research, they discovered a new ailment that pervaded the culture: female frigidity. "Sex reformers and sensitive observers of daily life confirm
again and again that female frigidity in love and marriage is the most
fundamental major problem in today's erotic and family life."[36] Apparently their diagnosis struck a responsive chord, for over 150,000 Germans
subscribed to the sex reformers' journals and joined their organization.
Beneath the emancipatory glimmer reposed conventional themes: If
women found fulfillment with their lawful husbands, they would not
succumb to adultery, lesbianism, or masturbation. Women's emancipation meant the right to sexual pleasure, and motherhood became one of
the most popular causes of the decade.

Ultimately the Nazi state banned both organizations for their insistence on women's fundamental rights. Because these two were almost
the only women's associations outlawed after 1933, their activities during
the 1920s take on special significance. Stöcker's success and Heymann
and Augspurg's failure suggest that concern with sexuality and motherhood enjoyed greater support than pacifism and feminist reform. American and English women during this decade took up Margaret Sanger's
appeal for birth control to give women freedom to limit childbearing, but
German women demonstrated greater enthusiasm for the right to bear
healthy children.

Thus the fundamental dynamic of the Woman Question paralleled in
important ways the problems of Weimar Germany generally. Politicians,
artists, writers, and publicists balanced the promise of emancipation
against the fear of chaos, weighing the prospect of an uncertain future
against myths about the past. These opposites plague any society, but
two catastrophes made the balance especially unstable in Weimar Germany: the Inflation of 1923 and the Great Depression of the 1930s. The

second trauma encompassed all nations, but in Germany its effects came more quickly and more severely than anywhere else. The first shock, Inflation, had its origins entirely within German politics and had no parallel elsewhere.

In 1919, Weimar statesmen inherited financial problems of nightmarish proportions left to them by their negligent predecessors. The war had been financed by bonds and currency manipulation (instead of by taxation, as in England and France). The postwar leaders assumed the domestic war debt and with it the financial fate of millions of Germans whose savings vanished when General Ludendorff called for a surrender. The government resorted to deficit spending. Only one quarter of the annual budget was paid for by taxation. Loans covered the balance. Against the backdrop of a steadily devaluating German mark, financial crisis loomed: Allied leaders expected reparations to compensate them for wartime losses. They argued that because German soldiers fought on foreign territory and Germany caused the war in the first place, Germans must pay. The Treaty, however, did not stipulate the total amount of reparations due. After bitter recriminations on all sides, a final sum of 132 billion gold marks was established in 1921. Germans, already living at near-subsistence levels, swore they could not pay the debt; and the creditors insisted that they raise their taxes and balance the budget—in a scenario that reminds us today of the negotiations between the World Bank and Third World debtor nations. Germans asked how could they possibly pay such a sum with their industrial production all but ruined? But on the other hand, how could the nation return to the international economic fold without paying its debts? German payments soon fell behind. Ilya Ehrenburg, arriving in Berlin during 1921, noted that even as they faced economic disaster, Germans presented an obdurate front.

> Coming from Brussels, well-nourished and serene, I saw Berlin. The Germans were living as though they were at a railway station, no one knowing what would happen the next day. Newspaper men were shouting, "Latest edition! Preparations for a putsch in Munich and Communist demonstration in Saxony!" People read the paper silently and went on their way to work. . . . It seemed as though everything was about to collapse, but factory chimneys went on smoking, bank clerks neatly wrote out astronomical figures, prostitutes painstakingly made up their faces, journalists wrote about the famine in Russia or the noble heart of [General] Ludendorff. . . .[37]

Germans resumed their wartime habit of presenting a picture of order that masked their worst fears. But what would be done?

The British inclined toward leniency, but the French (at great cost to themselves) sent an occupation army into the industrialized Ruhr Valley until Germany resumed payment. German leaders ordered passive resistance, and then decided to destroy their own economy to thwart French intransigence. The resultant disaster, they hoped, would convince the creditors that European health without a sound German economy was impossible. Just a year before, Foreign Minister Walther Rathenau had warned while negotiating reparations debts, "Today Germany is dying economically. And the gangrened corpse that results will infect the entire world." [38] No one had listened to Rathenau, or to John Maynard Keynes, who wrote a powerful attack on the Treaty of Versailles. Rathenau fell to assassins' bullets in the summer of 1922 while he was still Foreign Minister, and Keynes was ignored for ten more years. By ordering vast increases in the money supply, Rathenau's successors proceeded to gut the German economy. In the process, they aided the economically powerful while impoverishing the average citizen who earned low wages or lived on a fixed income.

Average citizens may not have comprehended the causes, but they certainly grasped the consequences of the Inflation of 1923. The mark, which had been valued at about 4 to the dollar before 1914 and 75 to the dollar after the war, dropped in value as the government printed more currency. By July 1922, one dollar equaled 500 marks; and in late December the rate was 750 to one. During early January 1923, the rate of inflation reached 20 percent per day and the mark dropped to 22,400 to the dollar. Germans received their pay in the mornings and rushed out to buy groceries on their lunch breaks; Bruno Walter stopped rehearsals mid-symphony to enable his musicians to purchase food before the prices rose; banks returned savings accounts of several thousands of marks because the value was too low to make it worthwhile to service such tiny balances. An American might live handsomely on $5 per week at Berlin's most luxurious hotel while a German would spend his lifetime savings just to buy a trolley ticket for 40,000 marks. Life around Irene Delano Robbins, wife of an American Embassy official, became more unstable as her husband's American salary made them richer with each passing day.

> The mark was still going down . . . misery and disorder everywhere. . . .
> The dollar [by 1923] was at seven or eight billions. The theatres were full
> and we paid 20 billion or 3 dollars a seat. Yet lines formed in the streets in
> front of the open kitchens. . . . [When her husband went to the country],
> he had a private car attached tö the train to bring all our guests. When he
> paid for the luxury, he found it had cost him only 75 cents. [39]

Irene Robbins, like Ehrenburg, commented on orderly sufferir saw everywhere. Once, on a visit to a Quaker relief center, she obs̲_̲ ̲_̲_̲ "poor little girls and boys who looked younger than their ages—and got the shock of my life. They had the boys lined on one side and the girls on another and to my horror every boy from 10–15 got his bun and milk before any girl. I protested. 'Ach genädig [sic] Frau,' she answered, 'our future soldiers must be fed first.' " The wartime mentality did not vanish with the peace.

Berlin humorists kept abreast of the situation, telling about the man who walked down the street carrying his savings in cash in a wheelbarrow. A thief jumped from behind a building, beat the man on the head, and ran off with the wheelbarrow. The refrain of a hit song intoned, "We are drinking up our grandma's little hut and the first and second mortgage too."[40] Georg Grosz commented sardonically, "The only popular subject of the day was food. . . . Mornings, at a breakfast of turnip coffee, mildewed bread, and synthetic honey, one discussed lunch. At lunch of turnip cutlets, muscle pudding, and turnip coffee, one discussed a dinner of muscle wurst."[41]

Some men enjoyed the side effects of the poverty that drove thousands of women into prostitution. Klaus Mann recalled strolling past "fierce Amazons, strutting in high boots made of green, glossy leather. One of them brandished a supple cane and leered at me as I passed by. . . . She whispered in my ear: 'Want to be my slave? Costs only six billions and a cigarette. A bargain! Come along, Honey!' "[42] American film writer Anita Loos warned that "any Berlin lady of the evening might turn out to be a man; the prettiest girl on the street was Conrad Veidt, who later became an international film star."[43]

Not everyone remained lighthearted. People who lived through it called it a turning point in their lives. Looking back, they often called the Inflation "the time when money died." How does one measure worth without money? Impoverished and yet orderly, Germans continued their daily routines—hoping and fearing to hope. For women, especially, the Inflation accelerated irreversible trends that affected more than their economic status. Several years ago, a woman shared her memories of the period with historian Otto Friedrich:

The inflation wiped out the savings of the entire middle class, but those are just words. You have to realize what that *meant*. There was not a single girl in the entire German middle class who could be *married* without her father paying a dowry. Even the maids . . . saved and saved so they could get married. When the money became worthless, it destroyed the whole system . . . and it destroyed the whole idea of remaining chaste until marriage. The rich had never lived up to their own standards, of course, and the poor had different standards anyway, but the middle class, by and large, obeyed the rules. Not every girl was a virgin when she was married, but it was generally accepted that one *should* be. But what happened from the inflation was that the girls learned that virginity didn't matter any more. The women were liberated.[44]

The war gave them the vote; the Inflation brought social emancipation. A vignette in Ehrenburg's *Memoirs* illustrates the mood. A stranger approached him and invited him to a night spot. He agreed.

We travelled by underground, then walked a long way through sparingly lit streets and finally found ourselves in a respectable flat. On the walls hung portraits of members of the family in officer's uniform and a painting of a sunset. We were given champagne—lemonade with spirits. Then the host's two daughters appeared—naked—and began to dance. One of them talked to Lidin and it turned out that she admired Dostoyevsky's novels. The mother hopefully eyed the foreign guests: perhaps they would be tempted by her daughters and would pay; in dollars of course, marks were of no use, their value would fall during the night. "Is this life?" sighed the respectable mamma. "It's the end of the world."[45]

Putsches, protests, revolts, and the "death of money" cut away the rubble of Victorian standards, liberating people from old inhibitions. Once again, many German women felt themselves affected by an emancipation most had not desired in the first place.

Finally, as 1924 approached and the mark dropped to four trillion marks to the dollar, the government called a halt. Powerful industrialists reaped enormous profits; but millions of small businessmen declared bankruptcy, and unemployment figures rose to dangerous levels. Communist uprisings in North Germany and an abortive Beer Hall Putsch by an obscure rabble-rouser named Adolf Hitler in Munich deepened the general anxiety. Gustav Stresemann, first as Chancellor and later as Foreign Minister, stabilized the currency and directed foreign relations on the path of reconciliation with Western democracies. The French withdrew their troops. And Weimar democracy survived another challenge.

The strategy paid off handsomely. Just two years after the French evacuated the Ruhr Valley, Germany was invited to the Locarno Conference, which Austen Chamberlain called the great watershed between the two world wars. Germany joined France, Italy, and Great Britain as an equal and formally agreed to accept the western European borders as defined by Versailles. For the first time since 1914, Germans were integrated into Europe. Only a year later, the League of Nations invited Germany to join.

International financial arrangements proceeded just as auspiciously, for the American government arranged for loans to Germany to repay reparations and finance a major economic recovery. Over two billion dollars fueled the expanding German economy after 1924. The small businesses may have suffered from the inflation, but giant corporations had borrowed heavily to streamline their production methods, build new factories, and eliminate their smaller competitors. Powerful cartels undersold and outproduced their rivals at home and abroad. By 1928, 2 percent of all industrial operations employed 55 percent of all workers. Despite the demise of small business, the economy as a whole recovered. Wage earners took home 6 percent more than workers before the war. The British and French accused Germany of losing the war and winning the peace because their own industrial output (and wages) remained below the 1913 levels. German statistics showed that the gross national product had risen 12 percent above pre-war levels, and exports exceeded even those of the best pre-war years.

Gustav Stresemann converted this economic recovery into diplomatic triumphs. Ten years after a catastrophic military defeat, Weimar diplomats had restored Germany to a respected position among the great powers of Europe. The defeated nation stood poised ready for even greater successes in the decade ahead. Reparations were substantially reduced and the payments schedule extended until 1988, which was tantamount to admitting the debt would never be paid; the French promised that they would evacuate the last of their occupation troops five years ahead of schedule. While pledging international cooperation, the Germans secretly violated the Treaty by manufacturing and testing weapons in the Soviet Union. A German journalist who exposed these flagrantly illegal practices was arrested for treason and sent to prison.[46] Behind Weimar's liberal facade, Junker generals and powerful financial cartels still called the shots.

By the late 1920s, Germans enjoyed an international reputation for modernity as well as higher standards of living than other Europeans. They could ride the fastest train in the world (the *Flying Hamburger*) at 160 miles per hour. Automobile design leapt forward with the creation of a rocket-powered Opel that was clocked at 151 miles per hour. The first talking movie was screened in 1922, and in 1929 German engineers transmitted the first television program. Probably the most awesome technological innovation, however, was the zeppelin. Only the extremely wealthy could afford the passage to New York (which cost twice as much as a cheap automobile), but the idea of floating to the New World beneath an oversized balloon exerted immense appeal.[47]

Production rose; political stability replaced chaos; the bureaucracy administered a thriving economy; and diplomatically Germany escaped pariah status. Voters registered their satisfaction by electing moderate candidates. In the Reichstag elections of 1928, for example, only 2.6 percent of all voters chose National Socialist candidates, and a centerist coalition commanded a Reichstag majority. But an ominous trend began, which people overlooked at the time. Although very few Germans voted Nazi, 13 percent of all voters cast their ballots for single-issue protest parties that stood no chance of winning a significant number of seats. In addition, 10 percent of all citizens simply did not vote. These signs of disaffection occasioned little concern at the time, but only three years later Hitler galvanized this unhappy pool of voters into a unified movement.[48]

Another sign that the liberal coalition faced trouble came from the left in 1928. Just over a tenth of all voters supported Communist candidates —another form of protest vote. This means that, taken together, about one third of all eligible voters either did not vote or voted against the solid parties of the middle. When the unemployment rates grew after 1929, the Nazi vote would draw support from these ordinary men and women who felt alienated by the consensus politics and confused by the six major parties that campaigned for their votes. They awaited rescue from an alien world by a political or religious figure who would simplify, not confuse, the issues confronting Germany. But for most Germans, the wheelbarrow inflation diminished into the past like traces of a bad dream.

As material well-being returned, many Germans, especially the young, felt liberated from the legacy of monarchism and war. The quintessential symbol for the new freedom was the New Woman—youthful, educated, employed, socially free and autonomous. After the war had broken many stereotypes about feminine weakness, popular culture celebrated sexual liberation, and the Constitution granted equality between men and women in the 1920s, social life opened up vistas of freedom. Rebellious spirits turned to the apolitical frontiers of culture and society. Especially if one was young and lived in a major city, a new world began. Its center was in Berlin. This was Christopher Isherwood's Berlin—the city of Sally Bowles and Lotte Lenya. Madeline Kent, who married a German Socialist and later published her memoirs from the period, recalled the frenzied activities among the young.

> Some were vegetarians or ate only raw food; others went in for rational dress and regarded high heels and corsets as marks of spiritual decadence;

others made a fetish of personal hygiene, . . . and a great number practiced free love, not frivolously, but in the solemn conviction that they were thereby hastening the millennium and lifting mankind to a higher plane.[49]

Idealists and cynics rushed about in what Kent called the "faddism of the left." Visitors to Berlin unfailingly commented on the exhilarating atmosphere in this easternmost outpost of Western European culture. Some likened it to Chicago; others compared it to New York. "The air was always bright, you needed little sleep and never seemed tired. Nowhere else did you fail in such good form, nowhere else could you be knocked on the chin time and time again without being counted 'out.' "[50] Other European cities, of course, were as cosmopolitan; but only in Berlin did one enjoy such freedom from tradition. Novelist Vicki Baum recalled fondly, "Berlin was so marvelously alive, so enlivened with an unusual electricity." No one drank wine, but everyone ordered cocktails. "For our taste it was extraordinarily free and we turned up our noses at the doddering old men. That was just the freedom that we wanted and needed."[51] Social distinctions dissolved in these circles. Imperial Berlin had been replaced by a raw, unstratified society without established ranks or even manners. Young people in search of liberation flocked to the capital and created the life they expected to find.

Alex Swann, an Englishman, wholeheartedly approved of the relaxed social atmosphere. "When a girl wanted to pick you up, not a tart, just an ordinary girl in a shop, she used to bump you quite hard. . . . Bluntly, she simply was asking you to her rooms."[52] This emancipated world attracted an entire generation who refused to grow up and rejected their parents' values by striking out against adulthood. War had burned them out, seared their faith. Many sought to recapture meaning by turning to nature and away from politics. Stephen Spender recalled how this postwar generation searched for health in the wake of war's terrible destruction.

The sun—symbol of the great wealth of nature within the poverty of men—was the primary social force in this Germany. Thousands of people went to open-air swimming baths or lay down on the shores of the rivers and lakes, almost nude, and sometimes quite nude, . . . The sun healed their bodies of the years of war, and made them conscious of the quivering, fluttering life of blood and muscles covering their exhausted spirits like the pelt of an animal: and their minds were filled with an abstraction of the sun, a huge circle of fire, an intense whiteness blotting out the sharp outlines of all other forms of consciousness, burning out even the sense of time. During their leisure, all their powers of thought were sucked up, absorbed into the sun, as moisture evaporates from the soil. . . . I was fascinated by the worthless, the outcast, the depraved, the lazy, the lost.

. . . [And also by the young generation], which had been born into war, starved in the blockade, stripped in the inflation—and which now, with no money and no beliefs and an extraordinary anonymous beauty, sprang, like a breed of dragon's teeth waiting for its leader, into the centre of Europe.[53]

As Siegfried Kracauer, noted cultural historian, recalled, "Anyone who experienced those crucial years in Germany will remember the craving for a spiritual shelter which possessed the young, the intellectuals."[54] Inflated expectations once again fed longing for a stability that had never been. The Kaiser over the fatherland and the father over the family guarded this mythical hierarchy. Millions of Germans, displaced and frightened by defeat and democracy, felt a "hunger for wholeness" when they gazed at their inexperienced democracy maneuvering against former enemies in the west, menacing Communist revolutionaries in the east, and threatening civil war at home. Presidents, cabinets, chancellors, and Reichstags managed to cope with the material crises of Weimar Germany; but even Berliners had their doubts about emancipation. Count Harry Kessler, the sophisticated diarist-about-town, recalled one evening he spent, "*chez* Vollmöller on the Pariserplatz."

After midnight we . . . went to see Josephine Baker. He [Vollmöller] had assembled a strange collection of guests again. No one knew anybody—only his extremely charming lover, Fräulein Landshoff (dressed as a man again) stood out. Déclassé atmosphere. He is, or thinks he is, a déclassé poet and likes to surround himself with déclassé women in all stages of undress; one never knows who they are, whether they are "girl friends" or whores or ladies. You see young men who could be publishers or ballet masters, newly discovered "actresses" . . . I left at three. All in a sorrowful, almost tragic atmosphere.[55]

Christopher Isherwood looked back on those Berlin years when he wrote about a young German, Waldemar.

I'm sure that Waldemar instinctively feels a relation between the "cruel" ladies in boots who used to ply their trade outside the Kaufhaus des Westens [Berlin's largest department store] and the young thugs in Nazi uniforms who are out there nowadays pushing the Jews around. When one of the booted ladies recognized a promising customer, she used to grab him, haul him into a cab and whisk him off to be whipped. Don't the SA boys do exactly the same thing with *their* customers—except that their whipping is in fatal earnest? Wasn't one a kind of psychological dress rehearsal for the other?[56]

Pearl Buck reported a conversation with a German woman who commented, "The terrible thing is, we have to believe in something. When we do not know in what to believe, we believe every day in a new thing, and we have every day a new prophet. But better to have every day a new thing, than to believe in nothing."[57]

In 1928 signs of discontent occasioned little worry, for marginal movements exist in any political system, and dissent is a part of any healthy democracy. Experiments necessitate risks in the search of freedom. Berlin attracted the adventurous and avant-garde, but while its cultural life fascinates us today, it hardly touched the real life struggles of most women. Educated young women searched for their own better futures. As with so much in Weimar, the signs seemed auspicious. By 1929, the nation had over 2,500 women physicians, 300 women lawyers, and even a few dozen women judges and professors. University enrollments augured well for the future, since women comprised just under a fifth of the university student body. White-collar office jobs were being taken over, it seemed, by independent young women. American feminists gazed with admiration at their German sisters. Despite a long tradition of higher education, the percentages of American women among professionals had been dropping since the turn of the century. Another sign of German women's economic independence was the fact that about a third of all wage earners were women, as compared to about 15 percent in the United States. American women over the decades have displayed special enthusiasm for a job as the passport to progress and independence. Perhaps that results from the fact that until the late 1960s, American women had only limited access to paid work. In Germany, by contrast, women's share of the wage-earning population has remained at just over a third, with a variation of only a few percentage points. German women, with a longer tradition of wage earning, have fewer illusions about the relationship between a paycheck and freedom. They pointed out during Weimar that, as more women entered the job market, pay and conditions actually became worse. For example, although women startled contemporaries because they took jobs in offices and stores that had previously been filled by men, actually very little changed. More women than ever worked in factories, and by far the majority of women's jobs remained in heavy agricultural work, textiles, food processing, and assembly-line production, all exhausting, low-paid occupations.[58] In the United States, feminists place special emphasis on married women's right to a career, but in Germany (where over a third of all married women had worked outside their homes since the twenties), most married women felt chronically overworked and underpaid.

The increasing numbers of married and unmarried women who entered the work force during the Weimar Republic alarmed conservatives without really satisfying the women who worked for pay.[59] While American feminists were demanding entry into paid work, poorly paid German women dreamed of escaping from it.

An extraordinary collection of firsthand reports tells us about the constraints on working women's lives. In 1928 the Textile Workers' Union conducted a study of women employees' attitudes. One hundred fifty-eight women submitted entries to an essay contest on the topic, "My Work Day, My Weekend." This collection allows us to glimpse a slice of life that otherwise would have been lost to us. We see young women disillusioned by their jobs (which they found dreary and physically taxing) and yet unwilling to submit to the tribulations of marriage and childbearing. For a few years, perhaps, they might escape the "double burden" of paid labor and motherhood by living with their parents and working in an office or factory. At least then they had the chance to spend the money they earned as they wished—on entertainment, clothes, or vacations. However, they also realized that when they reached thirty, they faced almost certain dismissal as younger women replaced them. They understood, too, that if they did marry, they would one day return to the labor market when their children reached school age and the family needed more money. The women's essays portray the grim reality behind the statistics. "During the week I survive. On the weekend I live." Another woman wrote, "In the evening, it feels [as] if the cage door opens." Dominated by the clanging alarm clock and the piercing factory whistle, women workers mechanically lived out their lives in a frantic attempt to provide the most basic necessities for their families.

> It is 4:45. Still drunk with sleep the thought comes to me, "Time to get up, to earn your keep, like every day—sure, but how much? Not enough to live and too much to die." In a rush I wash, dress, slice the bread, then straighten up and ride three kilometers on the bike. I am exhausted even before I start work. I dread the thought of the next hours. It's 6:00 A.M. The siren sounds. Now begins the clamor. Chairs scrape; the belts screech; the foreman shouts; that is the daily concert and conversation of work.[60]

After several years at the assembly line, desk, or counter, most women abandoned underpaid jobs for unpaid motherhood. The former, they knew from experience, meant long hours of work at low pay; the latter, they dreamed, might bring them love. As we hear the poignant voices of "My Work Day," we see the limits of emancipation. The essay writers did not have careers; they had jobs. A paycheck did not buy emancipation.

The sight of women on the job gave the impression that Germans were among the most modern people in the world; but a closer look reveals that those women remained in the least-unionized, worst-paid, and most-exploited jobs. Similarly, the cultural liberation, which caught the imaginations of foreigners and pulled thousands of young people to the big cities, had its negative backlash, especially among people who longed for order more than security. Prostitution, rape, abortion, orgies, venereal disease, and pornography epitomized traditional women's worst terrors. Movies brought these fears home to them wherever they lived. One day Ilya Ehrenburg, whom we may assume to have been rather more sophisticated than the average German housewife, chanced to visit a film rehearsal at Germany's largest film studio. Even he registered mild shock at the plot.

> The heroine's father was trying to wall her up. Her lover lashed her with a whip. She threw herself out of a seven-story window, while the hero hanged himself. The director told me that the picture would have an alternative, happy ending, for export. I observed more than once with what rapture pale, skinny adolescents watched the screen when rats gnawed a man to death or a venomous snake bit a lovely girl.[61]

No wonder ordinary citizens worried about their future. Besides the runaway Inflation that destroyed their savings and eroded their wages, they sensed a pervasive disorder in their culture. The Kaiser—with his waxed mustaches, his helmet with its plumes and spike, his flamboyant uniforms, and bevy of obsequious ministers—had provided critics, no less than patriots, with a reference point. For his enemies he had served as a target against which they could practice their wit; for his devoted followers, he symbolized a sacred tradition. Both needed him. His departure left a vacuum. The framers of the Weimar Constitution recognized the nation's need for a strong leader figure when they provided for an elected President who presided over a democratic system. Except in emergencies, he remained a figurehead, but in a crisis, he could appoint a Chancellor, call up the army, and assume dictatorial powers. The first President, Socialist Friedrich Ebert, filled the role perfectly; but he died prematurely in 1925 and elections replaced him with former Field Marshal von Hindenburg, a man without political acumen or democratic principles. The young republic lost the leaders it needed to inspire unity. Left-wing critics, instead of praising the resultant freedom, attacked the very pragmatism that liberated them from ideological tyranny. They castigated Weimar democracy as a "soulless" system.

When critics attacked the "leaderless" democracy, they forgot that the very men who might have provided vision and inspiration were dead—victims of either French artillery fire before 1918 or assassins' grenades after that date. Just when the young republic desperately needed seasoned statesmen who believed in democracy, terrorists attacked the leaders they ridiculed as "November criminals." In the first four years of the Weimar Republic, assassins killed 354 liberal and Socialist leaders, while only 22 conservatives fell to assaults by the left. The sentencing patterns reflected the sentiments of the men who enforced the new democratic law: Of the 22 leftist terrorists, 17 received heavy sentences (the death penalty in ten cases); but of the 354 right-wing assassins, 326 were let off without punishment and the others received a few months in jail.[62] Judges, who had been appointed under the pre-war monarchy, simply could not bring themselves to hand down harsh sentences to criminals whose political beliefs they shared.

The day-to-day politics of Weimar Germany began to score solid successes in the late 1920s. Despite irreconcilable theoretical differences, legislators had learned to thrash out compromises on practical issues, while Stresemann orchestrated Germany's restoration to the international order. The Weimar experiment seemed so successful that a leading American political scientist praised the Weimar Constitution as the world's most democratic, and a respected Austrian economist confidently reported in 1928, "In no sense, in no area, in no direction, are eruptions, upheavals or disasters probable."[63] Germany had survived defeat, civil war, inflation, and international economic competition.

Within each success, however, lay the onset of future failure because the very reforms that made Weimar Germany look so healthy from a liberal perspective contained the sources of backlash. The republic had been founded in the first place amid defeat and despair, when expediency had driven bitter enemies to call a domestic truce and accept democracy as the least odious alternative to foreign invasion or civil war between Bolsheviks and reactionaries. Anxiety glued together an unstable alliance. After Weimar leaders succeeded in establishing a relatively stable national state, the threat of revolution and war subsided. Stability, therefore, robbed the republic of its pragmatic supporters. Immediate danger averted, its opponents could breathe more easily and ponder nondemocratic alternatives (monarchy, or dictatorship on the right and revolution on the left). The politicians who supported liberal reforms as an expedient were prepared to turn to a different solution just as soon as the system failed. Most Germans had accepted the democracy that had come to them as the result of military defeat, but they did so grudgingly and with reservations.

The same might be said about the fate of women's emancipation.

Women heard themselves welcomed as citizens, but experienced the erosion of their right to work, claim to equal pay, legal equality, and access to politics. Women's suffrage, far from opening up new avenues of change, may have actually retarded further inroads on male hegemony. Reactionaries rallied as never before to prevent further progress, while the women's-rights advocates found their ranks seriously divided on questions related to protective legislation, divorce, welfare policy, rights of children born out of wedlock, and education. This diversity, far from being a sign of weakness, was evidence that women had come of age politically and would have to come to terms with reality just like men in the political arena. The belief in a feminine unity had been born in the days when women were bound together only by their exclusion. Women legislators worked for women's equality as well as for the recognition of women's special needs and values. Both claims, however incompatible they may appear, emerged from real-life situations women faced and from their aspirations for a better future. Weimar legislators did not make great strides toward women's emancipation, but at least women, whether Socialists, liberals, Catholics, or conservatives, accepted their place in the political process.

3

NAZI WOMEN AND THEIR "FREEDOM MOVEMENT"

We want our women tried and true
Not as decorated toys.
The German wife and mother too
Bears riches no foreign woman enjoys.

The German woman is noble wine
She loves and enriches the earth.
The German woman is bright sunshine
To home and hearth.

Worthy of respect she must always be seen;
Not of strange races the passion and game
The Volk must remain pure and clean:
That is the Führer's highest aim.

—Curt Rosten
ABC des Nationalsozialismus

Were it not for the shadow of the Third Reich, the malcontents living in Weimar Germany would probably escape our attention altogether. As long as economic recovery held firm, they could not endanger the Weimar experiment. Middle-of-the-road politicians kept the major political parties on the democratic playing field and in doing so provided the freedom within which a lively cultural avant garde flourished. But the liberal government that produced a shimmer of emancipation also provided the setting for the National Socialist Party to grow. Hitler played by the political rules only long enough to destroy the playing field altogether and to "declare war on democracy in the name of the people." Nazi Party propaganda chief Joseph Goebbels stated flatly in 1928, "We are going into the Reichstag to arm ourselves with weapons from the arsenal of democracy. We are becoming Reichstag delegates so as to paralyze the Weimar spirit with its own sting. . . . We come as enemies! Like the wolf tearing into the flock of sheep, that is how we come!"[1] This sort of bravado leaves the impression that the masculine Nazi wolf attacked the Weimar sheep singlehandedly. In fact, while the wolves launched their frontal assault, Nazi women hastened the sheep's demise by gentler tactics. Women Nazis used the benefits of emancipation to destroy emancipation while men Nazis exploited democracy to demolish democracy.

What attracted women to the Nazi Party? Why did they not gravitate to another of the nationalist parties or the Catholic Center Party, all of which endorsed traditional women's roles and offered their women members a chance to hold office, organize, and wield influence over women's issues? The question is difficult to answer because in key respects Hitler's political values resembled those of conservative parties, especially when he fulminated against the Versailles Treaty and called for an end to the Bolshevik menace. But he added two more struggles to his agenda: the race war and the battle between the sexes. Hitler overtly demanded what other nationalist politicians only hinted at: "Aryan" victory over the Jew and male triumph over the emancipated woman. Hitler, who vacillated on nearly every other crucial political issue, never relented on two biological axioms: Separate the sexes and eliminate the Jews. Gottfried Feder, Nazi ideologue, linked the two aims. "The insane dogma of equality led as surely to the emancipation of the Jews as to the emancipation of women. The Jew stole the woman from us . . . We must kill the dragon to restore her to her holy position as servant and maid."[2] Alfred Rosenberg, in his *Myth of the Twentieth Century*, advocated polygamy and urged childless husbands to commit adultery.[3]

Why did some German women follow a leader who told them bluntly to leave politics to men? Politics, Hitler said, would only corrupt women, without improving men. "I am no friend of female suffrage. If however we must continue with this tomfoolery, then we should draw what advantage we can. . . . Women will always vote for law and order and a uniform, you can be sure of that."[4] One of Hitler's followers declared,

> The National Socialist movement is an emphatically male phenomenon as far as political power is concerned. Women in parliament are a depressing sign of liberalism. They insult feminine values by imitating men. We believe that every *genuine* woman will, in her deepest feelings, pay homage to the masculine principle of National Socialism. Only then will she become a total woman![5]

That men expressed such opinions comes as no surprise. But how are we to interpret the pledge of a leading woman Nazi who concurred? "National Socialism is a male concern and we women will gladly retreat just as soon as our Führer does not need us any longer."[6]

Throughout the 1920s, small groups of Hitler's brown-shirted SA men marched through the streets in military formation. Few observers paid much attention to these bands of ruffians, who swore to defend to the death a hysterical street orator and his crackpot schemes of "racial revolution." True, Nazi Party membership increased dramatically, but the numbers remained insignificant. Slightly over 100,000 had joined the Party by 1928, a tiny number when we think that the BDF (Federation of German Women's Associations) included over five times as many members, and the Socialist Party included well over a million members. In addition, the Nazi vote declined from just under 2 million in 1924 to about 800,000 in 1928. With over 30 million German voters choosing among six major parties, Hitler's marginal movement caused little alarm.

Sometimes men were joined by rows of women attired in blue skirts, brown blouses with white collars, neckerchiefs, and swastika armbands. Occasionally Nazi women disdained uniforms as too masculine. Singing folk songs or chanting Nazi slogans, they marched in earnest formations behind the men. One bystander watching such a parade exclaimed, "What! *Women* at this rally? To be a Nazi man, you have to be pretty mixed up (*meschugge*), but a woman who wears the swastika must be *really* nuts."[7] In 1932, an American journalist recalled that women had played a key role in Nazi popularity during the 1920s.

> Women have been among the strongest pillars of Hitlerism from its very inception. . . . At Nazi meetings the proportion of women in attendance is surprisingly large. Hitler has a fascination for Germany's weaker sex

which it will be the task of the psychologist to analyse. This interest is all the more unexpected because the Nazis want to deprive women of their voting right and want to send them back to their kitchen work.[8]

The reporter described several groups of people most commonly seen at Nazi rallies. "Ruined artists, over-burdened lower middle classes, discontented peasants, and youth of the universities inflamed against a world which offered them no future. The most fanatical adherents of National Socialism are to be found among the women."

New York Times reporter Miriam Beard, too, observed the thousands of women participating in Nazi rallies. Aghast, she wondered, "Why does the German woman vote for a group which intends to take the ballot from her?"[9] What made Nazi women different from the millions of women who voted for other parties? Nazi women shared many assumptions of other women activists in Weimar politics. Accepting conventional stereotypes about women's special nature, they worked to improve women's public status. However, at this point the difference emerged. Women in other political movements took their concerns into the male-dominated political sphere. But Nazi women, like members of nonpartisan Catholic and Protestant organizations, worked outside the political framework altogether. Rather than competing in the men's world, they expanded their own sphere beyond men's direct intervention, relying on men for protection against external enemies. Nazi women calculated realistically that women had not achieved sufficient force to make much of an impact on men. Their experience bred the cynical prediction that men would never change. Whereas feminists worked for an egalitarian future, conservatives spun out a vision of a past that never had been, in which strong men dominated public space and tender women guarded humane values. Nazi women accepted the promise of second-sex membership in Hitler's movement in exchange for the hope of preserving their own womanly realm against male interference.

During the 1920s, Hitler outlined his vision of women's role in a Nazi state. "The German girl [will] belong to the state and with her marriage become a citizen." As an afterthought, he added that women who did not marry might qualify for citizenship, but only if they performed important services for the nation. Goebbels in 1926 proposed multiple votes for mothers of many children and soldiers who demonstrated special courage.[10] Of course, these schemes to reward loyalty with citizenship or ballots would be rendered meaningless in a dictatorship, but they revealed an underlying axiom. Women were not born with rights; men conferred them. A man might serve the state in many ways; women's only genuine calling lay in marriage, defined in the narrowest biological terms: to guarantee "the increase and preservation of the species and the race. This alone is its meaning and its task."[11] Men in the Nazi state would direct politics, the economy, and the military; women would "breed absolutely healthy bodies."[12] The Party Program, which remained the only official list of aims as long as Hitler lived, mentioned women only once, in point 21, which pledged Nazi protection for mothers. With childbearing elevated to a major national goal, women would become the targets of a massive reeducation program to upgrade the traditional motherly traits that modern life had eroded. Hitler wrote,

> This work of care and education must begin with the young mother. Just as it became possible in the course of careful work over a period of decades to achieve antiseptic cleanliness in childbirth and reduce puerperal fever to a few cases, it must and will be possible, by a thorough training of nurses and mothers, to achieve a treatment of the child in his first years that will serve as an excellent basis for future development.[13]

Hitler's notions about both race and gender seem hopelessly unrealistic when we think about long-term trends in employment, demography, and social services. But as a marginal politician, Hitler had no reason to concern himself with the practical ramifications of his ideas. Instinctively telling his audience what they wanted most to hear, he held out a vision of the future that was as unrealistic as it was emotionally appealing. Germans who felt disoriented by hard times and national defeat could dream about building a new life on the mythical bedrock of a natural hierarchy based on biology. "The Jew" and "The New Woman" provided powerful metaphors against which people could direct their anger, and the anxieties generated by Hitler's warnings kept Nazis in a constant state of alert. In a certain way, the rhetoric about loving women offset their hate-filled images of Jews. Images of family life linked feminine roles to a healthy natural order. Goebbels, in a novel, described marital bliss among the birds. "The mission of the woman is to be beautiful and to bring children into the world. This is not at all as rude and un-modern as it sounds. The female bird pretties herself for her mate and hatches the eggs for him. In exchange the mate takes care of gathering food, stands guard, and wards off the enemy."[14] Hitler often repeated, "The Nazi Revolution will be an entirely male event."

As a boy, Hitler had dreamed of becoming an abbot, and since his young manhood he had lived in an entirely male society, first in the marginal world of the men's shelters in Vienna and then in the trenches of World War I. Not surprisingly, he cast his National Socialist Party in a stridently masculine mold. Scornfully dismissing electoral politics, Hitler at first plotted revolution and recruited a personal army of brown-shirted SA men to fight as propagandists and soldiers. Women had no place. In November 1923, he put his revolutionary strategy to the test in the Beer Hall Putsch in Munich. It failed miserably, and Hitler landed in jail instead of in the capitol. Years later he reminisced that during his brief prison sentence, women had been instrumental in keeping the Nazi faith alive while his men associates squandered time and energy in acrimony. "I left jail after thirteen months imprisonment to find they had sustained the movement. Instead of weighing the odds in a prudent and rational manner, they followed the dictates of their hearts and have stood by me, emotionally speaking, to this day." This did not imply Hitler considered women as part of his Party. When he saw girls marching behind the Hitler Youth at the Party Rally in 1932, he turned to the Hitler Youth leader, saying, "What have you done to me now?"[15] When he heard the girls came of their own will, he accepted them grudgingly, according to the Hitler Youth leader's wife. In the mid-1920s, a few socially prominent women in Munich introduced Hitler in influential circles and made sizable contributions to the chronically depleted Party treasury. Hitler, uncouth and unkempt, certainly profited from these contacts with Munich's elite, but women received scant thanks.

Reflecting upon the Beer Hall fiasco, Hitler realized the importance of working within the established democratic system, or, as Goebbels boasted, using democracy to destroy democracy. This meant striking alliances, attracting voters, and lobbying for specific legislation. In all of these activities, leaders of the other parties found women useful. Not Hitler. Nazi propaganda carefully designed campaigns to win specific occupational and regional followings (farmers, workers, and civil servants, for example); but Party literature ignored women until the early 1930s. The women who joined the Party did so in the absence of special efforts to recruit them.

Histories of the Nazi movement generally remained as silent about women in the movement as Hitler himself did. Party officials kept careful membership statistics, aggregated by age, occupation, region, education, and special interests. But they did not bother to separate male from female. For example, we know that 34,000 housewives joined the Party before Hitler took power, and we know that they constituted less than 5 percent of all members, but we have no idea how many women were included as "dependents," "workers," or "white-collar workers." If we had access to the original regional figures, we could recalculate women's participation. It seems clear that after about 1922, women's membership in the Party remained low. Firsthand reports reinforce this conclusion.[16] The initial Nazi meeting in Hanover, for example, attracted a typical mix of people: "two workers, three businessmen, two artisans, two officials, a writer and three housewives."[17] A popular writer described average Nazis as "young out-of-work shopgirls and disillusioned fighters."[18] Alfred Krebs, a district leader, noted, "though our opponents often claimed that Nazis wanted to keep women out of politics, the party never espoused this particular crudeness. In those early days of Nazism, when women were our most zealous agitators, such a position would have been utterly impossible."[19]

Given the paucity of information, a set of records from Hessia takes on added importance. Lists of applications to the Hessian branch of the Party over a three-year period have been preserved in the State Archives in Wiesbaden. Although we cannot know whether this information was typical of the nation, the collection provides a complete sample of data about men and women applicants. Of women who listed their occupations, none defined themselves (or their fathers) as factory workers, and virtually all had worked as sales personnel, office workers, dressmakers, or teachers before becoming housewives. One woman noted that her father had been a foreman in a lace-making factory, but most fathers had been civil servants, office workers, artisans, farmers, or small businessmen—and so were the husbands.[20] It may well be that some of the self-definitions mask working-class origins, but even if that is true, it shows that women applying for membership in the Nazi Party wanted to emphasize their claim to middle-class status.[21]

Membership statistics reveal one contrast between men and women: Women typically were a few years older than men.[22] This might appear odd at first, since Nazi women in the popular image passively followed their men, who, one assumes, were fathers, or husbands, and therefore older. But several factors explain this difference. The Nazi Party was well-known for its youthfulness—over two thirds of all members during the 1920s were under forty when they joined. Women under forty typically found their family responsibilities precluded any political activity. A few young women joined before marriage. Most, however, signed up only after forty, a pattern that, incidentally, holds up for women in all kinds of organizations in any industrialized nation. Young women's low membership rates resulted also from Nazi men's lack of interest in women. The women who did join and paid dues must have defined themselves as especially zealous, probably as leaders within the women's organization. When we compare women Party members' ages with men Party leaders, the age differential disappears. The conclusion seems clear: Women leaders joined the Party. Women rank and file did not.

Once in the Party, women did not integrate themselves within the dominant structure. Instead, they created their own hierarchy. Of course, the women at the very apex of their pyramid exercised far less authority and enjoyed less status than their male counterparts. But since the men ignored them, they could overlook their own relative inferiority and emphasize their status in a separate sphere. What did that sphere look like? Voting behavior and the histories of individual women's organizations provide a rough overview. Throughout the 1920s, women's vote for Nazi candidates lagged behind men's by as much as 50 percent.[23] As long as prosperity prevailed, most women supported moderate and conservative candidates. But with the onset of the Depression, the women's vote caught up rapidly, in some cases growing even more rapidly than men's.

Even the most ambitious women Nazis knew they could never aspire to high positions in a Nazi government after the revolution; nor could they identify with the powerful masculine Nazi élan. But that wasn't all. Some Nazi men routinely insulted women in the crudest terms. The pages of Julius Streicher's magazine for SA Men, *Der Stürmer*, featured illustrated stories of Jewish men raping blond women and derided women as stupid, lustful, and deceitful. Alfred Rosenberg's *Myth of the Twentieth Century* made Nazi misogyny clear to anyone who slogged through its turgid pages. Even in more public forums, Nazi men did not disguise their contempt for women. For example, after a Socialist Reichstag delegate spoke of having lost her son in World War I and of her desire for world peace, a Nazi delegate jeered, "That's all you nanny goats were made for anyway!"[24] Women Nazis managed to overlook the overt misogyny of Party leaders. Jews, after all, and Catholics, to a lesser extent, recognized Hitler's hostility toward them and avoided his movement. Why did women seem not to notice? Several factors played a role. Most Germans, including many of Hitler's supporters, found it hard to take Hitler seriously on the subject of either Jews or women. Because Nazi ideology was a haphazard conglomeration of many shopworn notions, people could (and typically did) agree with Hitler's general views while adding their own vociferous "except." Thus a voter might say, "I, too, believe in authoritarian state, hate Communists, and want to avenge the Versailles Treaty. Of course, the man's racism is crazy. Once he's in power, he will drop such crackpot schemes." Women Nazis told themselves that Hitler would never turn women into brood mares. Power would tame his extremism, they said.

They could also say, with some justice, that Hitler himself did not rage against women, although several of his deputies did. Julius Streicher and Alfred Rosenberg routinely insulted women, but Hitler avoided slurs in public except for diatribes against prostitutes who carried venereal disease. He made it clear that women would confine themselves to reproducing the next "Aryan" generation; but he expected women (unlike Jews) to welcome his program. Women, he insisted, would return to "natural" roles society had for centuries assigned to them. Compared with his rivals' hypocrisy, Hitler spoke forthrightly. Perhaps some women admired the Nazis' frankly conservative position on women. Liberal and Socialist women, by contrast, operated in an ambiguous ambience in which they were simultaneously welcomed and excluded.

Women Nazis operated in a familiar atmosphere, clearly demarcated into male and female domains. Having been raised on the Bible, they had learned to screen out misogyny from a doctrine they respected and still remain faithful to Christ. It was Saint Paul, a mere disciple, after all, not Christ, who made disparaging comments about women; just as Streicher, not Hitler, denigrated women. Although women voted in political elections, they did not enjoy similar rights in their churches, where they accepted their responsibilities within their own bailiwick and obeyed their superiors. Politically, we may find this choice cowardly and wonder why women seemed so happy to settle for second best, but emotionally the prospect of a separate women's world in public life held out the promise of fulfillment. The church, not the state, had for generations been the center of women's public life. And Hitler presented himself as a messiah. Women Nazis found themselves drawn to a vision of the future that was as emotionally appealing as it was practically unfeasible and morally indefensible.

Many observers noted that Hitler could be "all things to all men." His special charisma extended to women as well. American journalist Louis Lochner described Hitler's theatrical skills: "I have heard the Führer address a group of German women, speaking so tenderly of his mother, expressing such fond concern for the problems of the housewife, tracing so eloquently what the German women had done and could do for the Nazi cause, that the listeners were in tears."[25] A British visitor described German women's adulation for their Führer: "His words had power. He was emotional. He was sentimental, he was never intellectual. . . . The lonely bachelor, the non-smoker, the crusading teetotaller—the glorious fighter for Germany's honor who had gone to prison for his convictions. It was a richly emotional picture for [the women] to gaze on; in their day and night dreams."[26]

Statements by women Nazis are exceedingly rare. Most women found themselves too busy to take time for writing, a task that for many of them must have been hampered by limited education. One collection provides an especially rich set of testimonies, adding important psychological dimensions to our inquiry about Nazi women's motivations. Polish emigré sociologist Theodore Abel in 1936 sponsored an essay contest open only to "old-timers" who joined the Nazi Party before 1933. Writing on prestigious Columbia University letterhead, he circulated an announcement to all district offices in the Party, offering a prize for the best essay on the theme "Why I Became a Nazi." Among the over 500 entries, 36 were written by women, who ranged in age between seventeen and seventy-three at the time they "converted" to Hitler. These women represented a cadre of ambitious, articulate, and dedicated Party members whose stories emphasize life's tragedies—deaths of parents, poverty, insecurity, and deprivation. Virtually all respondents had been born to middle-class families, but only five ever enrolled in a university. Half were married and a quarter had at one point in their lives worked outside their homes or enrolled in trade schools. Three-quarters came from urban areas (which, incidentally, set them apart from Nazi voters in the 1920s, who tended to live in rural regions). Half had relocated (usually from country to city) at least once. This does not imply that objectively these respondents suffered more than most women of their generation, but it indicates that they saw suffering and sacrifice as the central experiences in their political lives. Women, like the men, came from circumstances that objectively seemed relatively secure, but anxieties dominated their memories of the past.

All except the youngest mentioned World War I as a major event in their youth, noting both extreme material deprivation and patriotic fervor. One woman wrote: "As the child of a soldier and peasant I always had the mission in my blood to serve and sacrifice for the *Vaterland*. I sacrificed my fiancé to the war, and after his heroic death, put myself in its service."[27] The author opened up a rest center for soldiers in Flanders, and followed the troops home to confront revolution and political unrest. In 1920 she became a fervent follower of Hitler, but joined the Party only in 1931. Another respondent recalled seeing the Russian army invade her East German homeland. "The war and my experiences in Poland caused me to take an interest in politics much earlier than women usually do."[28] Another (born in 1860), became a nurse during the war, after having served in the African colonies before. "I cannot forget the horror of the war which destroyed so many young lives in murderous fire of enemy artillery." But for others, the rapturous days of August 1914 stood out. "How bitterly I envied my male friends who had the good fortune to be able to fight against Germany's enemies!" recalled one respondent, and another remembered, "Oh, how I wished I were a boy so I could fight for my beloved homeland."[29]

Political scientist Peter Merkl, who analyzed both male and female essays, notes that about a quarter of the respondents had lost one parent (usually the father) while they were still children. He further suggests

that only about a fifth of the Nazi membership displayed violent feelings
of anti-Semitism. In this respect, women differed little from men. A few
statements give some idea of the kinds of anti-Semitism that appeared in
the writing of early Nazis. One woman initially rejected Nazi racism,
and only converted after her comrades' patient guidance.

> [I thought] racial thinking was un-Christian and unjust, especially concern-
> ing the Jewish question. I regarded Jewishness as entirely a religious issue.
> After many endless debates, I realized that this attitude confused religion
> and race—one of the world's greatest historical errors. . . . [Finally] I
> learned to reject the belief that appearance does not matter. Because I
> believe that a meaningful order pervades all creation, I understand that
> this order rests on unconditional differences among races.[30]

Gertrud Michael, by contrast, grew up in a North German Protestant
family (much like Gertrud Scholtz-Klink's), with a father "who was a
German nationalist and strict anti-Semite, as you would expect of a
German civil servant." Anti-Semitism became such an obsession that
she believed Jewish men paid special attention to her because, she said,
"of my delicate blondness." By the time she was a young woman, she
recalled, "I began to feel disgust and revulsion at everything Jewish."
Margarethe Schrimpff, probably more typical among the anti-Semites,
blamed World War I, the defeat, and all suffering on the Jews and the
Freemasons. "All nations must burn out this pestilential boil. Then we
would have peace and calm," she wrote in a metaphor that echoed Hitler's own ravings in *Mein Kampf*.[31] Violent anti-Semitism among a minority, backed by pervasive casual anti-Semitism, established an
ominous pattern. Supported by the state and propaganda, the fanatics
and followers would one day transform ideas to actions.

In describing their attraction to Hitler, these women borrowed unstintingly from a religious vocabulary they must have learned as children
studying the life of Christ. A teenager implored her Nazi uncle to tell
her bedtime stories about Hitler. "He had given me a little picture of him
which I kept like a shrine to which I could look up in adoration. I
enclosed him in my little heart and was determined not to rest until I
had finally grasped the meaning of his idea and battle."[32] "At last," wrote
another early convert, "I found a man willing to die for his faith; a feeling
rushed through me like fire."[33] "Whoever has looked deeply into our
Führer's eyes will never, not even years later, forget such a powerful
experience! I, who had never been able to recognize any authority over
me at all . . . I will follow a life of permanent obedience [*Knecht-
schaft*]."[34] Or again, "The joy inside me was impossible to describe. This

simple man with a true, righteous gaze streamed warm sunlight from his face into the 22,000 hearts in the audience. . . . Whoever has a pure heart and hears our Führer speak and looks into his eyes has no choice but to convert to him."[35] Upon hearing Hitler for the first time, one Nazi woman reported him as a Messiah figure. "From a thousand wounds rose his sweet face, enlivened by a childlike smile of holy self-confidence. Hitler strengthens the spiritual power of the entire *Volk*." She continued, "Heaven gave us more than we deserved when it sent us the fanatical crusader for honor and freedom, Adolf Hitler."[36] Maria von Belli described how she "waited patiently and confidently for Him who would make everything good without money" and Maria Bauer praised the "endless faith" of "the man who destiny and God have sent to (heal) a shattered Germany."[37]

These responses cannot be taken at face value as accurate descriptions of experiences that had occurred a decade earlier. Essay writers wrote the sort of statement that would win the competition and perhaps even, as a few suggested, open Americans' minds to the Nazi faith. "Every moment day or night, I am ready even to lay down my life in order to do whatever this Führer requires of me. May every moment of life be blessed [for] this Führer who has risen for us Germans!"[38] Whether consciously or instinctively, Hitler knew how to maximize his image as savior. Luise Jost's husband died penniless in 1928, and shortly thereafter her son joined the SA and was killed. When Hitler appeared at her doorstep, Frau Jost was overcome.

> In my pain and grief, Adolf Hitler came to me and looked deep into my eyes. He pressed my hand, and I knew that my boy did not die in vain. This man is worth a life sacrificed in his service. From the sixth of August, 1929, at ten o'clock, I became a National Socialist. My next son took my dead son's place. Whenever a Party comrade falls, hundreds, even thousands rise to take his place. . . . How wonderful those years of struggle were—I would not have missed them for anything, the wonderful success, the rallies and the demonstrations![39]

Another essayist in the Abel contest wrote, "He will help us. We believe that God sent him to rescue us from crisis and misery. Meet the challenge. German women! Carry on the battle with worshipful hearts [*mit betenden Herzen*]." "Because Adolf Hitler needed people who would willingly stand against Marxism and who were ready to bleed and die for the holy ideas of our beloved leader, I realized that I had at last found my goal and desire. I felt as if a fire flamed within me and I said to myself you do not learn about National Socialism, you have to experience it."

Maria von Belli declared, "The great awakener and warner . . . The liberator of all northern Peoples . . . must know he can rely absolutely on each one of us . . . in the union of blood and spirit."[40] Hildegard Passow, a Bavarian woman leader, endowed Hitler with similar qualities but within a secular framework. "Adolf Hitler, the Master Builder of the New Reich" had, she believed, researched and diagnosed the essence of the German People and constructed a political system which would strengthen the new structure.[41] Maria Engelhardt told Abel about her conversion in the 1920s: "And if you ask me today what brought me to the ranks of Adolf Hitler, I would not be able to dress it up in words and could only say that National Socialism is anchored in the deepest inner being of every German, and expresses the most primitive [ureigensten] sensitivities and emotions." Hitler offered "nothing new," she concluded, but evoked the "ancient Germanic nobility and altruism."[42] Such outpourings might tempt us to conclude that women formed an exceptionally hysterical cadre of fanatics, but men's memoirs contain similar oaths of utter surrender.

Male followers also outdid one another in fulsome praise. When we wonder how women could have joined such a misogynist party, we overlook an equally interesting question: How could the purportedly he-man types in Hitler's thrall have gushed such praise? How did men, brutal, brown-shirted, and radical, succumb so totally to a man who demanded utter surrender? What hidden needs yielded them up to this hysterical preacher and inspired them to write and speak about their Führer in the sentimental phrases stereotypically reserved for women? Goebbels borrowed love-at-first-sight imagery from popular fiction when he wrote to Hitler in 1923: "Like a rising star you appeared before our wondering eyes, you performed miracles to clear our minds, and in a world of scepticism and desperation, gave us faith. You towered above the masses. . . . We saw with shining eyes a man who tore off the mask from the faces distorted by greed, the faces of mediocre parliamentary busybodies. . . ."[43]

Like Christ among the money changers, Hitler came to cast out evil. Hermann Rauschning, one of Hitler's earliest disciples, confessed that in the early days of the movement he had been transfixed by Hitler's charisma—drawn by what he described as "a form of conversion, a new faith."[44] Hermann Göring spoke for thousands when he said,

In Hitler we have the rare combination of a keen logical thinker, a really profound philosopher, and an iron-willed man of action, tenacious to the highest degree. . . . For more than a decade I have stood at his side, and every day spent with him is a new and wonderful experience. From the

first moment I saw him I belonged to him body and soul, . . . I passionately
pledged myself to his service and have followed him unswervingly.[45]

Hitler released men from society's emotional straitjackets and rendered
them "feminine" in their obeisance and even obsequiousness.

Such surrender emanated from Hitler's personality, but it was also
aided by a special atmosphere that participants described as "electric."
Hitler's photographer recalled: "We were in a hall, thousands of thousands of people, and something monstrous happened. There was a mass
suggestion at work, a fluid in the air, and everybody, men as well as
women, abruptly began to tremble and weep and howl, and all the while
Hitler sat there without saying a word, without stirring, just staring at
them."[46]

Two women described early rallies. Louise Solmitz, a schoolteacher
in Hamburg and wife of a military man, wrote: "The April sun shone hot
like summer and turned everything into a picture of gay expectation.
There was immaculate order and discipline . . . the hours passed. . . .
Expectations rose." Then Hitler arrived. "There stood Hitler in a simple
black coat and looked over the crowd. Waiting. A forest of swastika
pennants swished up, the jubilation of this moment was given vent in a
roaring salute." The content of his speech was, Solmitz recalled, entirely
ordinary: "Out of all parties shall grow one nation." But still she recalled
looking out at the 120,000 people in the audience. "How many look up
to him with a touching faith! As their helper, their savior, their deliverer
from unbearable distress—to him who rescues the Prussian prince, the
scholar, the clergyman, the farmer, the worker, the unemployed, who
leads them from the parties back into the nation."[47] Interestingly, she
seemed not to notice the absence of women on the list.

Marlene Heder's essay for the Abel contest described another mass
rally. Early in the day, good-humored banter prevailed. As the afternoon
passed, the holiday atmosphere dissipated and "toward evening the tension began to mount. . . . The air grew denser as night fell; people
fainted; the mood became even better. A seventy-year-old woman with
tears in her eyes declared all she wanted to do before she died was to see
Hitler." Hitler arrived and spoke. After the tumultuous applause, flowers,
and cheers, people looked around. "But the man in the trim brown
uniform with the face marked by an unbending will and the small, expressive hands was no longer there," Heder wrote. When we read these
florid paeans to Hitler, we ask ourselves not simply why women found
themselves attracted to such a party but why all these people, male or
female, threw off the constraints of their upbringing and hurled themselves into the "feminized" throng.

The mood was not an accident. *Mein Kampf*, that collection of incoherent and hysterical ravings, contains Hitler's brilliant recipes for crowd manipulation. For example, he claims to have learned from Catholic masses that darkness or twilight allows audiences to "succumb more easily to the dominating force of a stronger will. . . ."[48] The style of Nazi discourse and theatrics had been shaped by religious metaphors. In addition, Hitler demanded the sort of *total* surrender that wives give to husbands or clergymen and nuns render to the Church. To become a National Socialist, one had to pledge obedience to Hitler and loyalty to the Party program. In addition, each Party member swore to "defend Nazi principles with his life."

Helene Radtke's essay for the Abel contest emphasizes the importance of this all-or-nothing faith. When she discovered she had received the right to vote, she "shopped around" and gathered information about all non-Socialist parties. Even though "women's suffrage was a terrible setback for Germany," she felt an obligation to become active. A Nazi rally convinced her. "Because Adolf Hitler needed people who willingly stood fast as fighters against Marxism and were prepared to fight and die for our beloved Führer, it became clear that my wish for certitude had been granted. I had found my political home." While hunting for a political party, she discovered a political religion and pledged loyalty for life.

Women *and* men converted to a movement that encompassed every aspect of their lives, feeling born again into a rich new life. "Feminine," more than "masculine," emotions provided the ideal model for Hitler's followers: blindly obedient, passionate, and weak. Hitler's comments to an old comrade, Ernst (Putzi) Hanfstängl, reveal his own understanding of the sexual chemistry at work when he spoke. "Someone who does not understand the intrinsically feminine character of the masses will never be an effective speaker. Ask yourself, what does a woman expect from a man? Clearness, decision, power, and action. . . . Like a woman, the masses fluctuate between extremes. . . . The Crowd is not only like a woman, but women constitute the most important element in an audience. The women usually lead, then follow the children and at last . . . follow the fathers."[49] Hermann Rauschning recalled that women were always seated in the front rows so Hitler could see "their expressions of rapturous self-surrender, their moist and glittering eyes . . ."[50]

According to the myth, Hitler as the master strode onto the historical stage and imposed his masculine will upon a disoriented and weakened *Volk*. But his magic as an orator originated in a more complex appeal, for alongside his bold and manly image, a certain softness could be seen. As Hitler sang the praises of brutal men and loving women, he himself transcended both stereotypes. Like the matinee idol (a similarity he him-self noted), he embodied a strong feminine component within his domi-nantly "masculine" image. While projecting an image of uniformed ruthlessness, he screamed threats in mixed metaphors, such as "He who has not himself been gripped in the clutches of this strangulating viper will never come to know its poisoned fangs."[51]

This did not mean Hitler was an androgynous figure, for he did not merge "masculine" and "feminine" traits—rather, the very dominance of his swaggering masculine self gave him a certain liberty to indulge in feminine gestures or styles. Before facing an audience he could thunder hate-filled tirades about excising the "Jewish vermin" and then clasp his hands imploring heaven for help like the innocent maiden. Leni Riefen-stahl's genius captured this juxtaposition of soft and hard. Think of Hitler in *Triumph of the Will* shrieking hysterically, striking the podium with his riding crop, and then quietly stepping back, timidly brushing his hair off his dripping forehead as he waited for the applause to subside. Hitler dictated "like a man" and absorbed his audiences' moods "like a woman." The very extremity of his male persona gave him latitude to indulge in emotional transvestism.

So important was Hitler's charisma that his early followers attributed Nazi successes entirely to their Führer's personality. Gregor Strasser, who more than anyone else provided organization within the Party, ana-lyzed the movement's success in 1927 entirely in terms of Hitler's person and doctrine. "For this is the great strength of our movement: an utter devotion to the idea of National Socialism, a glowing faith in victorious strength of this doctrine of liberation, and deliverance is combined with a deep love of the person of our Führer who is the shining hero of the new freedom-fighters."[52]

The picture of a hypnotic leader and masses of enchanted followers is compelling, and, indeed, Hitler was often linked to his predecessor of Hamlin. Accounts of Hitler the orator give the impression that his audi-ences heard the voice or looked into his eyes and began to vote and march for the Nazis. But after his release from prison until 1927, German authorities prevented Hitler (as an Austrian and a troublemaker) from public speaking altogether, and after that, several states banned both Hitler and Party demonstrations. Until Hitler became Chancellor, the Nazi Party had virtually no access to the media that Goebbels mastered so brilliantly after 1933. A few hundred thousand Nazis may have ac-tually heard Hitler speak, but by 1932, Party membership rose to over 800,000, and nearly 14 million Germans voted for Nazi candidates in July of that year. Enthusiasm depended on more than Hitler's speeches.

How, then, did the Nazi Party draw hundreds of thousands of followers into their ranks? Gregor Strasser, Hitler's chief administrator, asked himself the same question in 1932. He needed to know the Party's formula for success because whatever it was, he wanted to use it for greater victories. He told his colleagues that the Nazis projected the image of top-down authoritarianism, a "thoroughly anti-democratic political organization built solidly upon authority, discipline, and leadership. No other party has such striking power and self-contained unity." Beneath the allure of Hitler's dictatorial and charismatic image, however, Strasser knew that ideological ambiguity and organizational anarchy flourished.[53] Far from criticizing this disorder, Strasser rethought the question and revised his formula for success. Finally he decided that some degree of confusion gave tiny groups of Nazis all over Germany the sense they could determine their own doctrines and create their own institutions. "Our organizational forms are not laid out around a conference table at Party headquarters, but have grown organically from the bottom up, developed from the exigencies of daily struggle and from the ultimate aims of the movement." Each person in the movement gained in self-importance by seizing the initiative in response to local conditions. He boasted about the Nazis' "new and unprecedented manner of propaganda," as well as the creation of a "new type of political soldier, Adolf Hitler," flanked by the SA.[54] Strasser described a movement that was both decentralized *and* authoritarian. National Socialist popularity depended upon not only a powerful leader but upon thousands of little leaders in every corner of the nation. The tiniest organizational cell looked to a remote Führer for inspiration while developing its own program for local action. Had Strasser referred to *Mein Kampf*, he would have found that Hitler himself had emphasized the importance of "the indefatigable and truly enormous propaganda work of tens of thousands of untiring agitators."[55] In other words, the *image* of order and the *reality* of decentralization together constituted the winning dynamic behind Nazi victories.

Hitler's own bombastic revivalist style released charismatic potential in his audiences. On one occasion Hitler remarked, "A good speech is like a flaming javelin which sets the crowd afire."[56] The "flaming javelins" thrown by Hitler ignited his audiences to go out themselves and win new converts. This chain reaction was especially important to women, for many of them came to the movement without any background whatsoever and very few encountered opposition (or notice) from the male hierarchy. Nazi women recall both their newfound self-confidence and their joy at joining a cohesive community beyond the pale of stodgy neighborhood groups or boring ladies' clubs. Often they called their group a "fighting community." For them Nazism constituted far more than a party, and they themselves most frequently called it a movement, or "Our German Freedom Movement," or the "Hitler Movement," which encompassed every aspect of daily life. "Party" called up static images of interest politics, political trade-offs, and compromise. "Movement" meant constant activity. Its followers pledged their lives to a total crusade.[57] This sense of solidarity may have been inspired by leaders' speeches; but it was maintained by the tireless efforts of local and regional organizers who planned projects, rallies, meetings, marches, and campaigns. One leader wrote, "Womanhood gives us a community, a source of strength for the entire *Volk* [with which we] forge a powerful unified movement among all women and girls for moral renewal."[58] The promise of a strongly integrated community complemented a remote and charismatic Führer. Women Nazis invariably reported that after conversion their lives became both more active and simpler.

Overnight, the social world was divided sharply into "us" and "them." Often, too, women campaigners explicitly defined "them" as Jews or subhumans. In simplistic imagery, Maria von Belli contrasted the idealistic Nazis with "money types" (*Geldmenschen*), whom she described as people who followed "everything that sparkled without being genuine . . . without inner justification: the peace treaty, Marxism, the League of Nations, the government, demilitarization . . . as well as city people, cosmopolitans who loved Negro music and had no vision of the future." Often, she remembered, "you'd feel lonely, work hard, and wait. Just keep on waiting for the one without money to transform false into genuine values. In the true Germanic manner, we waited patiently." Theodore Abel reported that attending a meeting constituted the most typical conversion experience among the men and women who entered his essay contest. "The meetings became the spice of life for me," wrote one respondent.[59] Another remembered fondly the "wave of meetings which inundated our daily lives."[60] Belonging to the group, more than adulation for the leaders, brought the Nazi faithful back time after time. Fanatical belief in the Nazi cause provided the converted with a total cause and a program of action; while others floundered in despair, the tiny community of Nazis saw themselves as an elite. The Nazis were famous for constant activity—not only SA men's marches, but mass meetings, street-corner speakers, door-to-door canvassing, fund raisers, and lecture series. During one month prior to national elections in 1930, for example, the Nazi Party sponsored 34,000 meetings in Germany, which averaged out to be three meetings in every village, town, and urban neighborhood.[61] This constant agitation provided the Nazi faithful with limitless opportunities to experience the thrill of power at local levels, without worrying about surveillance from above. While sharing a crusade mentality that bound them together against a hostile world, Nazi women occupied a doubly marginal position: ignored or outcast by their male comrades and scorned by non-Nazi women.

Perforce, they created their own alternative women's community. With no status in the Party and no chain of command linking them to headquarters at the Brown House in Munich, a motley collection of women's associations evolved a variety of dogmas and activities. Nazi men's overt hostility toward women unintentionally encouraged women's autonomy. Depending on her personality and the local conditions, a woman leader might organize her bailiwick with more independence than a man. She could sew or wear a brown shirt and model herself on either a ladies'-aid or fighting-front ideal. Reports from the late 1920s and early 1930s tell of women's satisfaction at breaking free of established organizations and civic clubs.

Many Nazi women, in fact, performed quite ordinary women's work, as illustrated in the following examples. One small group of women collected money to purchase a sewing machine, which they used to make clothing for poor families in the movement and to sew banners and armbands for the men. "In the early days we had only a few women. But even our clumps of four or five would form an organization. . . . We plastered illegal posters on the walls, cared for homeless and unemployed SA men, threw parties at Christmas, and collected donations on street corners." [62]

Typically, women Nazis felt themselves to be poorer or from more humble social origins than the ladies in long-established associations. Nazi women spoke in clumsy, simple phrases and enunciated their dreams in platitudes. When asked how she happened to join the Party, for example, one woman replied, "Because so many men were unemployed, the women's work played a most important part in the movement. In order to reaffirm our close ties to the SA, the idea occurred to me to go home and sew myself a brown blouse." [63] Making a virtue of liability, many women recalled how the very smallness of their numbers enhanced their self-importance. "One hundred forty-six women may not count for very much in numbers, but if every single woman places herself totally and selflessly at the service of our great ideals, if she remains faithful in great and trivial things, and takes the swastika into her soul, then even a very few of us can rescue Germany!" [64]

Sewing circles gathered for women to read and discuss passages of *Mein Kampf* or Party pamphlets; often the members felt unable to comprehend the complexities of Nazi ideology, but always they eagerly sought more education. "Since I had no political background, I was quite inexperienced," wrote one young woman who joined in 1925. "To my astonishment, I soon was transformed into a fanatical fighter for the German Freedom Movement. I even put up posters and held meetings in my house because no one would rent public rooms to Nazis."[65]

"It was very difficult to attract a following here. Since everyone was Socialist or Catholic, they thought I was a fanatic. To this day, I don't know how I found the courage to join!" recalled Frau Dornberg in the North German town of Münster. "The membership dues were a real hardship for us, but our work was vital."[66] Often the poorest women felt proud that they could pay Party dues.

In their mundane actions, Nazi women displayed enormous faith in the importance of their trivial work (*Kleinarbeit*). They were not wrong. In a movement that perpetually fought off bankruptcy, women's door-to-door collections provided important revenue. Perhaps even more vital was the personal touch born of financial need. Hand-addressed and delivered invitations, individually painted posters, and free meals at rallies all conveyed the image of community that figured so large in the Nazi promise. "What all you couldn't do as a woman!" recalled Maria Engelhardt. "For weeks on end, I collected donations and spread the word. We had to depend on word of mouth because we were too poor to found a newspaper. We couldn't even borrow a typewriter. We lived, *really* lived according to the motto 'Collective need before selfish greed.' " Like members of an altar-care society for the Church, they would do anything, however banal it seemed, because they believed so deeply that it mattered. Women thought of themselves as the stable element in a quixotic male movement. Maria von Belli recalled how she helped carry the Party through lean times, such as the period when Hitler was in prison. After the Beer Hall failure, "we women had to pick up the thread of life from the floor and keep on spinning for the sake of our children. . . . The men wanted to hurl themselves at the fortress, to speed everything up."[67] But women counseled patience despite the deep mourning for a Führer in jail. This feeling of self-worth became a self-fulfilling prophecy, as Strasser realized when he acknowledged the value of a certain amount of anarchy among the faithful.

Without encouragement from Party leaders, several women Nazis independently organized in what one woman leader called "a sort of parallel movement," separate from the Nazi Party and yet supportive of it. Although Party headquarters did its best to contain men's enthusiasm into a centralized Party structure, no parallel hierarchy developed over the women's community. At the local and national level, women leaders emerged, each with her own style, objectives, and class of followers. National Socialism, as a new political organization, provided the ambitious with a unique chance to innovate and rise to leadership positions on the national level. So oblivious were Nazi men to the women in their ranks that they did not bother either to notice or control two major woman leaders during the 1920s. Elsbeth Zander appealed to little-educated poorer women, while Guida Diehl attracted more pretentious and "respectable" women to her cause.

Elsbeth Zander, the first woman leader to emerge, launched a double crusade for motherhood and Adolf Hitler. She went on nationwide speaking tours, set up rest homes for the SA, and published her own newspaper, *The German Woman's Service and Sacrifice* (*Opferdienst der deutschen Frau*). Until she was forty years old, Zander had ignored politics and devoted herself entirely to her career, home-economics education. Although she taught girls how to become good mothers, she herself never married. World War I roused her nationalism and the threat of Bolshevism drove her to activism. According to her account, she began to recruit women for Hitler's movement even before the Beer Hall Putsch. Other versions depict her sending picnic baskets to Hitler in prison. In 1923, she claims to have founded her Order of the Red Swastika. Because "swastika" (*Hakenkreuz*) means literally "twisted cross," the symbol embodied two traditions important to women: the Red Cross and the Christian cross, or emergency health care and faith. Zander twisted these traditions into a unique movement, dedicated to Nazi victory and to the removal of women from politics. Zander claims to have asked Hitler to include women in Party life during 1924. Casual remarks made by Hitler during the Second World War bear this out.

> In 1924 we had a sudden upsurge of women who were attracted by politics. . . . They wanted to join the Reichstag, in order to raise the moral level. I told them that ninety percent of the matters dealt with by Parliament were masculine affairs, on which they could have no opinions of any value. They rebelled against this point of view, but I shut their mouths by saying, "You will not claim that you know men as I know women."[68]

Party records indicate that in 1926 she requested (and received) official permission to consider herself the leader of all women Nazis.[69] As the price for her anointment, she pledged to obey Hitler's charge, given at the 1926 Party Rally in Weimar. "The Order swears to withdraw women from the turmoil of Party politics so it can employ their energies in the social domain; it must nonetheless acquaint itself with major political questions, and above all be familiar with laws that radically affect the family life."[70]

Zander shrewdly masked her own ambitions by cultivating an obsequious image and swearing absolute obedience to her Führer. From the beginning she carefully avoided calling herself the female Führer or Führerin and lavishly praised Adolf Hitler's every proclamation. Although she presented herself as his humble handmaiden, this self-styled woman leader, in fact, resembled her hero in several respects. Hitler, who referred to himself as "the little man" or "drummer" or the "corporal," never tired of boasting about his humble origins. Zander, too, made a limp and rather lackluster impression. Hitler, during those years, appeared in ill-tailored, frayed suits and made his middle-class followers uncomfortable by his lack of social grace. Zander, wearing shapeless housedresses, with her hair carelessly arranged in a bun, projected a most ordinary image. But facing an audience, her bearing changed, her voice rose, her speech became animated. Like her hero, she could move audiences to tears of sadness, rage, or joy. Uneducated and pretentious (like her hero), she spun long-winded declamations about racial purity and cultural decay. Instinctively she seemed to recognize the truth of Hitler's dictum that a great leader does not impose his will on an audience, but instead senses what the audience longs to hear, and tells them. Zander seemed to absorb her audiences' aspirations and give voice to their hidden angers and frustrations.

Emblazoned on the front page of her newspaper was a megaphone with the words ELSBETH ZANDER SPEAKS! When she arrived in towns and villages, her followers welcomed her with homely verses much as they greeted Hitler himself.

> *Willkommen hier in unserem Gau*
> *Du edle, tapfere, deutsche Frau.*

> Welcome to our district
> You noble, brave, German Frau.

Zander resembled her Führer in another respect as well. She founded her own organization and ruthlessly controlled every facet of its development. Swearing total devotion to Hitler, she expected in turn absolute allegiance from her followers. Zander's followers praised her in language laden with sentiments we normally call religious. One of Zander's young followers wrote, "The National Socialist movement is for us a religion. German youth will not cease to struggle until the ultimate goal is reached. . . . Of course, older people will read this and scoff. But despite the lies, treachery, insults, and prohibitions, the new youth stands upright."[71]

Zander lived in a polarized world, torn by forces of evil and virtue. At the head of her enemies' list were socialites and Socialists. The former had become mere decorative objects. Socialist women by contrast, she said, debunked motherhood and defeminized women by turning them into workers. However, she reserved her strongest invective for the "ladies" who played cards, read best-sellers, and met friends for coffee and cakes in the afternoon. "We are not a mere ladies' *Kaffeeklatsch* club!" she thundered. Zander, however, launched a moral-purity campaign. "We cannot, in this dire economic crisis, content ourselves with ladies' clubs, charity associations, or Socialist do-gooders." Emphatically, Zander rejected the women's movement, both Socialist and middle-class branches. Perhaps the Nazi who answered a British feminist's question about women's rights belonged to Zander's organization. "A humble greengrocer's wife in Berlin spoke for millions when she said, 'Your meetings are no place for women of my sort. You have to be educated to understand speeches like that.' "[72] Nazi women scorned the educated ladies who scorned them and formed what they called an authentic "working, living, and fighting community" that could unify young and old, rich and poor, Protestant and Catholic women from every part of the *Vaterland*. "We will make the nation worthy to receive liberation through Hitler."[73] Another woman said, "We must close ranks and form our own emergency community which is inspired entirely by a unique spirit and is determined to shun the bourgeois claptrap of welfare workers."[74] Nazi women under Zander created a dense network of "cell mothers" that would spread Nazi beliefs at the grassroots to the disenchanted and the alienated. Unconcerned with building a vertical hierarchy, Zander thought in terms of horizontal, neighborhood networks.

Zander's promise to leave politics to men did not at all mean that she envisioned women retreating into their homes. Instead, she encouraged them to take up tasks they judged *more* important. Let the men do the dirty work of cleaning up the streets; women, crusading behind the "holy flame of motherhood," would take on the more challenging task of purifying the national culture. By disengaging from the man's world, Zander believed she won new freedom for women to create their own sphere of activity. "No, we do not belong in the men's front. Let us affirm it openly! Despite all the modern teaching about women's legal equality, despite all her striving toward independence, toward personal and political influence, we women are overjoyed that Nazism is a purely male movement. . . ."[75]

From another standpoint, Nazism promised a kind of perverted equality by destroying everyone's rights. Zander put it simply: "We recognize no men's and no women's rights, but accept the duty of fighting, living, and working for the nation."[76] The devotion was universal, the tasks were gender-specific. Rather than protest failure, women decided not to want what they could not have. This meant yielding the external world to men and claiming for women the internal world.

Hitler called on men to fight for the future in the SA; Zander proclaimed a "motherhood crusade" to restore patriotism and increase the birthrate. Although (or perhaps because) her speeches lacked refinement, she attracted thousands by her impassioned call for a "mother's revival." For centuries, she exclaimed, women had sacrificed joyfully for their husbands and families; in the twentieth century they must learn to give themselves to their Führer and fatherland. Only then would their community triumph over the threat from the Jewish-Marxist-capitalist "poison" that threatened to destroy the race. Let the men destroy democracy, Zander concluded; women, under her leadership, would revive the German spirit.

From this she concluded that women must be liberated from the necessity of working for wages outside their homes. Because financial necessity, not personal ambition, drove most women to look for jobs, Zander and other Nazi women demanded the well-paid husbands every woman deserved. Women had become, one Nazi writer commented, mere "economic mechanisms," extensions of their drill presses, typewriters, sewing machines, or switchboards. The modern workplace, streamlined and rationalized, alienated male workers as well; but because of stereotypes about women's elevated (but fragile) spiritual nature, the impact on the nation seemed worse if women succumbed to materialism. Men had never been as spiritual as women in the first place. "Woman in the workplace is an oppressed and tormented being. Day in and day out, she sits for hours at the typewriter or holding her shorthand pad . . . day after day the same misery. . . . The woman has become a work machine. . . . National Socialism will restore her to her true profession—motherhood." How could a mere job compare to the calling of motherhood? Men had professions; women had families. "The women's movement of yesterday led thirty-six Parliamentarians into office and hundreds of thousands of German women out into the streets of the big city. It made one woman a ranking civil servant and produced thousands of wage slaves to the capitalist order," wrote Paula Siber, a leader in Düsseldorf.[77] A decade later, a British opponent of Nazism admitted that Hitler's promise of a husband for every woman "touched deeply the innermost feelings and desires of millions of women for whom 'equal rights' had til then meant merely the right to be exploited."[78] Emancipation, wrote Nazi psychologist Anna Zuhlke, robbed woman of her very selfhood by masculinizing her view of the world. When the social order appeared to have lost its moorings, a strong sexual identity provided men and women with the inner security with which to face a hostile world.[79] Such statements gave voice to longings for a world divided into (quoting a Nazi woman) "more masculine men" and "more feminine women." Rather than failing at masculine endeavors, women Nazis wanted to succeed in their own realm. In bombastic rhetoric Zander, too, picked up the popular theme in her attacks on "women without womanhood."

While Hitler's men brawled, marched, and paraded, Zander's women believed they could construct an alternative society based on women's traditional strengths: faith, love, and hope (*Glaube, Liebe, Hoffnung*). This trinity appeared on the red swastika insignia—its initials standing also for three heros in Zander's personal pantheon: Göring, Ludendorff, and Hitler. (Hostile rumors had it that Hindenburg had originally occupied the third place.) On occasion, Zander co-opted the Holy family for the graphics in her publications, but without religious emphasis. Always the politician, she carefully reminded "her" women that "above all we care for our Brownshirts!" Zander claimed that she had recruited a dedicated corps of 13,000 women by the late 1920s. A Munich police report on the "red swastika" estimated that Zander controlled 160 locals with 4,000 members.[80] We can not be sure, because Zander's style itself discouraged a structured organization, and she lacked any talent for the routine work of keeping records, distributing membership cards, or collecting dues. Like Hitler, she saw her task as inspirational not organizational. In fact, Zander's carelessness allowed her followers ample scope to tailor their own operations to local conditions. Zander's advice reinforced the message. "Ask, 'What can we do to help?' " Besides merely paying Party dues, she said, women could "give material aid. . . . But what is really important is that we do whatever needs to be done under the particular circumstances in which we find ourselves. We don't even need to join a group to be able to take in washing for SA men or offer once a week to cook an extra portion of stew for a less fortunate Nazi family."[81]

Blessings, she repeated, accompany the humblest acts of faith and charity. Zander herself, when not on speaking tours, supervised an SA rest home in Berlin. She recruited her own "brown nurses," designed their uniforms, and leased a suburban Berlin house as a rest and recreation center. Given to fits of enthusiasm and long periods of inactivity, she could not be relied upon. In good moods, she would sweep into her SA home and invite some of her favorite staff (usually that included her chauffeur) to an extravagant dinner; or she would indulge in a spending spree. Then she would withdraw completely into her room and leave the daily work to others.

This behavior exasperated her co-workers, but she proved her worth as a powerful speaker. Her emotional words converted her audience's anxieties into political action, and association with the Nazi Party provided them with a protective shield against the alien world. Zander dispatched her corps of mother-crusaders into battle. And as they discovered their own abilities, they moved beyond conventional stereotypes of ladylike behavior. Convinced they defended tradition, they felt few scruples about acting in outrageously out-role ways. Just as the most brutal SA man could shed tears during a Hitler speech, so the most loving woman could stand firm against her enemies. The emergency atmosphere created by Hitler's hysterical warnings recalled those days of World War I when women departed from normal roles. Zander empowered the weak to fight for their own self-interest while submerging themselves in a total movement.

Obdurate faith precluded reason, and the constant state of alert inspired by leaders' inflamed rhetoric kept Nazis mobilized. Emotionally, they revived the war experience, but this time they faced their enemies on the home front. If challenged, the Nazi woman retorted, "This is not a case for argument. It is a matter of creed!"[82] These women, many of whom had expressed a childhood desire to be boys, took risks, flaunted the law, and defied authority. Sissy Schneider, in her Abel essay, recalls the high point in her school years during the 1920s. Once when she had concluded a civics essay with "Heil Hitler!" the teacher took her to task for mentioning politics. "He singled me out. 'What's this? Hitler?' I stood up erect, like I had seen the SA men do. With my right arm out straight in a salute, I said, 'You bet it is! Heil Hitler!' " Later, she said, school chums, "especially three Jewish girls," jeered at her.

A woman from a small town near Münster reported, "In the evenings we would paste up illegal posters and on countless occasions we would stake out sentries to be sure our SA men were not intercepted by the police. When necessary, we carried weapons in our blouses for the SA."[83] Maria Engelhardt in her Abel essay described what happened one dark night when she answered her male comrades' cries for help. A "bandit" nearly stole their swastika banner, but Engelhardt ran to the scene with her house door key pointed like a pistol. "Stop or I'll shoot!" she screamed. They fled.

Wearing scarlet armbands, women marched in the streets of their home towns or neighborhoods to taunts of "Hitler whore!" "Brown goose!" or "Nazi pig!" They compared themselves to the Christians in the catacombs and described their joy at belonging to a genuine community. "What did it matter that we were nearly always ridiculed and stoned by Communists lurking in the shadows. . . . We were so despised in our neighborhoods that we hardly dared to walk alone in the streets."[84] In a most "unfeminine" voice, one early Nazi Party member declared,

"The world belongs to the courageous!" Maria Engelhardt was in her early thirties during the electoral campaigns of the Depression years.

> The party struggles began! We marched! SA and SS units and comrades! Before us, behind us, all around us, a howling, brawling throng. Bystanders threw flowers. Defiantly our battle song rang from our lips: "We are the army of the red swastika." How proud we were! Let them stone and curse us. Let the police work us over with rubber clubs! Let them attack us treacherously—what did we care? We had been there and would return again and again.

Insults only deepened their determination. The anonymous author of a booklet, "Mein Kampf als Nationalsozialistin" ("My Battle as a Woman National Socialist") recalled, "The more they scorned me, the more devoted I became." Non-Nazis, upon seeing women under the swastika banner, called out insults. Nazi women, who recalled having been self-effacing before, discovered they were braver than they thought. "Those years forged a fighting unity among us that no power on earth could rend asunder," recalled one early follower.[85] When the police chief confronted her, she told him, "You are sitting on a limb that's rotting out from under you!"

A housewife, speaking to apathetic passersby on a street corner, was confronted by an outraged businessman. As a good Nazi woman, he said, she ought to be home serving dinner to her family. Sneering at this "bourgeois heckler," she retorted, "The nation is in peril! I cannot remain happy and carefree at the supper table when Mother Germany weeps and her children die. Germany must live on, even if we sacrifice our lives!"[86] Germany, normally the "fatherland," became her mother as she transformed her feminine role into the heroic daughter who served her mother before her family. The Nazi movement, like a religious crusade, imparted a crisis mentality to its adherents and empowered them to behave in new ways. While claiming to care only for the community, they discovered their individuality and exercised broad influence within their own milieu. An account by a former SA man shows how women shared a sense of danger with the men: "I would like to say a word which will tell you something about the National Socialist spirit of our women. We were not allowed to carry weapons, and when the police showed up, they could not find any on our bodies. The weapons had all fallen under the skirts of the women present. My mother alone had six of those things dangling inside her clothes."[87]

Frau Huhn, explaining why she had joined the Nazi Party, described the satisfaction of flaunting the law. Women civil servants and teachers faced almost certain dismissal if they made their Nazi affiliation known. When swastikas were forbidden, Huhn ignored the order. "I wore my armband everywhere. I was thrilled to count myself among the little grey mice who dared to step forward to do the Führer's work."[88] Statements like this make it tempting to draw conclusions about Nazi women's feelings of inferiority; but men's memoirs contain the same sorts of self-deprecation. Fritz Thyssen, the Ruhr industrialist who supported Hitler at the very beginning of the Party, recalled, "People say to me so often, 'You are only the drummer of national Germany.' And supposing I were only the drummer?" Being only a drummer, he concluded, counted for more than standing aside and falling into the ranks of the passive bourgeoisie.[89] Hitler habitually called himself the "drummer" and played on his humble origins. His men and women followers picked up the rhetoric, emphasizing how once they had felt insignificant, but discovered their courage in the movement. Whenever a member of "the weaker sex" defied the police or heckled a liberal or Communist, her daring became especially noteworthy because it seemed so unexpected.

No doubt thousands of women Nazis conformed to rather conventional and passive models of appropriate feminine behavior, but thousands also flagrantly broke their own stereotypes about "more feminine women." As in wartime, they acted in new ways to defend old roles. Often they openly envied men. When Helene Radtke recounted her early activities in her Abel essay, she admitted how it had upset her to watch the men and boys from her town climb aboard the trucks and buses that took them to the 1928 Nuremberg Rally. They would see the Führer and she would not. Where we might expect a strong-minded woman to protest, she reacted by incorporating masculine traits into her character, identifying with the aggressor, in Freudian terms. Radtke in a later section of her essay mixed her metaphors in a telling way—turning herself into Prince Charming and the nation into the slumbering princess. "We are going to awaken our *Volk*, the sleeping beauty, from her slumber. That is an appropriate mission for women. I don't want my children to ask me one day, 'Mother, where were you when Germany faced utter ruin?' "[90]

These autobiographical sketches testify to women's discovery of self-worth and faith. The central tenet of Nazi faith was "You are nothing. Your *Volk* is everything!," surely a message that harmonizes more readily with women's upbringing than men's. In the service of this selfless crusade, Hitler's followers discovered their selfhood. Hundreds of thousands of "nobodies" began to feel like "somebodies."

But not all Nazi women saw themselves as the female equivalents of thugs and street fighters. While Zander rallied this sort of follower, a very different sort of leader attracted more solemn women to the Nazi cause. Whereas Zander's Order drew women with little education, Guida Diehl spoke to the conservative, well-educated, Protestant establishment. Diehl wrote books, addressed women's organizations, and founded a school for motherhood education.

From a nationalist and anti-Semitic family, Diehl boasted of her father's exploits as a German colonialist in southern Russia before 1914. When choosing her life's work, she sought out Kaiser Wilhelm's court chaplain, Adolf Stöcker, who hated Jews and supported the emancipation of unmarried women. Following his advice, she attended social-work school and later worked as a teacher of social work in Frankfurt. In 1917 the nation's very survival, she believed, depended upon women's efforts. Impatient with what she considered apathy on the part of Protestant women's organizations, she began her own New Land Movement. After the defeat, she found new enemies in Communism and cultural decadence and called for a new Fighting Women's League that spanned party differences.[91] Soon she claimed a devoted following of five hundred and opened a national headquarters, The New Land House, in Eisenach, Saxony.

She wrote in pretentious trinities. Truth, purity, and love, she believed, could survive only after women triumphed over the postwar "anarchy of values." Americanism, materialism, and mammonism threatened to overpower *Volk*, God, and fatherland. Germanic light, air, and sunshine had fallen under the cloud of humanism, individualism, and romanticism. As in World War I, Germans stood alone defending themselves against British, French, and American values. Men, as soldiers and statesmen, fought for territory, but only preserved life-giving values. Diehl called on women to "recognize the tremendous historical transformation of your sex and search for the rights, the paths appropriate to the female soul that will restructure women's lives. The new German woman's will must shape [together with the fighting masculine will] the future. Only then will a healthy, powerful German future emerge, and with it a holy German Reich."[92]

On occasion she rhymed her appeals:

> *Mit eisernem Besen*
> *Aus Herzen und Haus*
> *Das undeutsche Wesen*
> *Zum Lande hinaus!*

> With iron broom
> Drive un-Germanic creatures

Out of heart and house
Into the wilderness!

She published a newspaper that featured articles such as "The Dance as a Destroyer of Culture," "The Shameless Theater," and "The Devil-May-Care Attitude," which, she believed, undermined German values. The third annual convention in 1928 addressed "Our Battle Against Modern Sex Reformers!"

Such concerns spanned all political outlooks, she said, appealing to Protestants from all parties and occupations. A list of prominent members included novelist Marie Diers; Reichstag member Margarete Behm; nationally known politician Dr. Käthe Schirmacher; Dr. Elisabeth Spohr, delegate to the Prussian legislature; Martha Voss-Zietz, a leading educator, and Clara Mende, Nationalist member of the Reichstag. Men, Diehl declared, could apply for adjunct status.[93] Her views on the Woman Question harmonized perfectly with those of the conservative wing of the BDF, or Bund Deutscher Frauen (Federation of German Women's Associations). Like middle-class women's-rights advocates, she believed God had created healthy contrasts between men and women—physically, morally, and emotionally. "We women are in much closer touch than men with the hidden secrets of life." As a professional social worker, unmarried, deeply religious, and nationalist, she would have fit perfectly into a Protestant woman's organization except that, borrowing from Nietzsche, Diehl despised Christian meekness. An alarmist to the core, she told women to attack evil in the world and not just acquiesce to the trends they deplored. Diehl also exhibited a more obvious anti-Semitism than was considered tasteful in more conventional circles. "Woman is sacred to us in her predestined, natural role, and every man reveres her calling. She is the guardian of the German race and pure by nature" wrote Diehl in a book on women and National Socialism.[94]

In the early 1920s, she heard about Hitler and the Nazi Party. Soon she became a convert, but refused to join the Party, not even after 1925, when Hitler visited her New Land House at Eisenach. Organizing during the war had given her a taste for independence, and she was loath to relinquish her position of control to any men's organization. Besides, she pointed out, becoming a member of a male organization contradicted her separatist principles. In addition, she may have felt she could wield more influence outside of any large organization and that she could bargain on individual issues if she remained independent. Whatever her thinking, her devotion to Hitler was clear. "And so the Führer stands before us: upright, honest, thoroughgoing, God-fearing, and heroic—the sort of Germanic man we women long for and demand in this our

Vaterland's hour of direst need."[95] Her flamboyant verbiage prompted one observer to describe her mission as "scattering flowers" along the path of rough SA men.[96]

By the late 1920s, she boasted over 200,000 followers, surely an exaggeration, from more middle-class and respectable origins than the members of Zander's "twisted cross." Diehl spoke in overblown metaphors laden with religious references. In its florid rhetoric and glorification of women's culture, Diehl's style was a more pretentious version of Zander's prose. However, in important respects, Diehl departed from Zander. Diehl harmonized both Christianity and the women's-rights movement with Hitler's message, and recruited from the most conservative members of the BDF and the Protestant women's associations. Zander, by contrast, rarely mentioned God and despised Bäumer and the other leaders of the BDF.

The nineteenth-century advocates of women's rights, according to Diehl, had addressed genuine needs, but mistakenly concluded that these needs could be met by conforming to masculine values. According to Diehl, this capitulation produced two major sins. First, women's-rights advocates denigrated motherhood, housework, and women's culture because they had become so preoccupied with their careers. Women, she said, used to pity the spinster, but now intellectualized women felt sorry for the mother, who was trapped in her household and burdened by expectations she could no longer fulfill. Like so many of her contemporaries, Diehl alleged that excessive rationality and study atrophied women's motherly capacities. Secondly, Diehl launched a somewhat contradictory criticism: The erosion of women's roles had left middle-class women's homes and lives empty, which, in combination with ideas about emancipation, had produced in women an unhealthy preoccupation with sexuality and the search for personal pleasure. Self-indulgence thwarted the will to sacrifice. In short, she argued, the national spirit, as well as women themselves, suffered in a social milieu dominated by rationality and sexuality. And women themselves bore the blame.

Capitalism, Diehl conceded, changed women's outer lives, but women themselves brought on their own chaotic inner life. "If women sink, the entire nation sinks; and if the whole *Volk* declines, then women bear the largest guilt." Behind their guilt, however, lurked a more sinister culprit: the Jew, luring women into rational thinking and sexual pleasure. Diehl unambiguously attributed Germany's cultural and political collapse to an international Jewish plot. Claiming to bear no resentment toward Jews as a group, she nonetheless deplored Jewish leaders, by which she no doubt meant "the Jewish conspiracy." In thinly veiled anti-Semitic terms, she diagnosed the sickness of her times:

Behind it all stands Mammon, scornful and cold. He recognizes his success and ascertains quickly where money can be made. By the search for pleasure, the easy life, and overheated eroticism . . . he enriches himself most quickly wherever he discovers laziness. Wherever he sees an open wound in the body politic, he inserts his bacteria. . . . Therefore we must fight against the origins of the evil. That means against Mammon, which causes materialism and naturalism.[97]

This sort of coded anti-Semitism, incidentally, was standard in Hitler's speeches after he decided to work within the political system and therefore to moderate both his rhetoric and actions. This enabled his rabidly anti-Semitic followers to know that he still hated Jews; but his more respectable and probably more recent followers could tell themselves he had mellowed. After the Jews on Diehl's enemies' list came the New Woman and feminized men (both of whom she described as Americanized).

Unlike the pragmatic Zander, Diehl was not content with caring for SA men and dispensing charity to Nazi families. This ambitious organizer planned a Nazi women's paradise after Hitler achieved victory. Under no circumstances would women merely become handmaidens to the new leaders. In articles and books, Diehl worked out her vision of a separate women's sphere. Her proposals redirected women's desires away from "false" hopes for liberation to "true" needs for motherhood and reassured men that strong-minded women could make a vital contribution to male rule.

Diehl wanted to eliminate women from paid labor outside a home. This, she believed, would present no emotional hardship since, as many studies proved, most women took jobs for the wages and not for emotional satisfaction. Ambitious women who desired a career for egotistical motives should not be encouraged. But the few altruistic, intellectual women (perhaps she thought of herself) who sought a greater challenge in life than housework could always hire domestic servants. Although she was too shrewd to make the point explicitly, laws preventing women from working outside of a household situation, would depress servants' wages by increasing the supply, so middle-class women (like Diehl) would profit personally and financially. Up to that point, Diehl incorporated notions common among conservative women's groups, such as housewives' associations.

The second part of her program included the novel proposal of state subsidies to women whose husbands or fathers could not adequately support them. Although she would never have acknowledged her debt to a radical like Helene Stöcker, these proposals bore strong similarities to the demands of the League for the Protection of Motherhood. Ideally,

Diehl contended, a strong economy would be able to guarantee all husbands a sufficiently high income to provide for their families. In practice, she realized, many women might still face destitution. Rather than allowing such women to enter the labor force, Diehl proposed state subsidies to enable mothers to remain in their homes and devote their time to child rearing and housework. "Every woman deserves her home!" she declared. If the husband could not provide it, the state would. In a nation faced by declining birthrates, this solution promised a state-sponsored baby boom.

Diehl's political conclusions followed from her separatist instincts. The experience of Weimar politics demonstrated, in her view, that women could make no significant impact on their male colleagues. They did not vote as a bloc, nor did they impose their viewpoint upon the men in their parties. Why squander energy in a futile effort? Instead, Diehl called for a "women's chamber," a separate national legislature to which only women could be elected and for which only women could vote. Calling for a radical separation of spheres, Diehl envisioned a single-party state, with two political hierarchies. Women, in other words, would acquiesce to patriarchy, and as a reward receive influence over their own sphere. While men worried about diplomacy and economic policies, women would be liberated to devote themselves to the issues that most directly affected them: family law, health care, welfare programs, education, and public morality. Ultimately, she envisioned a corporate state in which women would be accorded their own housewives' chamber. In the meantime, however, a division into male and female legislatures would initiate a truce in the war between the sexes and give each German a forum in which to advocate his or her own best interests. If Diehl had her way, women would deprive themselves of access to traditionally masculine endeavors. Except for theology, girls ought to devote themselves entirely to home economics, psychology, arts and crafts, culture, and education.

Throughout the 1920s, Diehl pursued her own course, offering aid to overworked mothers, and, in a few cases, unwed mothers. Her newsletter and the pages of her somber books contained lavish praise of the national spirit, the *Volk*, and women's special crusade, aimed at middle-class women. Zander and Diehl represented the two extremes among Hitler's women followers. The charismatic unstable speaker and the self-styled intellectual never clashed in the early years of the Party. The records do not suggest that they ever met. The significance of their respective variations on the National Socialist theme lies in the fact that both flourished within the rubric of a dogmatic party. Women's ability to develop a specific set of ideals was enhanced by the tendency to view women as an occupational group with special concerns. The propaganda office encouraged recruitment drives aimed at particular occupations or interest groups and often published special tracts that stressed the grievances of a specific category of potential followers, provided, of course, that the ideology did not contradict the official program.[98] Women's independence within the Party structure occurred by accident. Variation among male leaders was carefully watched, while women created their own separate submovement de facto.

Of course, the informal nature of women's associations meant that virtually no records from those early years survive. On the basis of existing archives, it is impossible to sketch in a national picture. However, one rich local collection of memos, membership lists, and activity reports has been preserved from the northwest state of Westphalia. Women leaders in two urban areas, Münster and Bielefeld, provide us with a case study in the kinds of contrasts that separated the followers of Zander and Diehl at a national level.

The quiet middle-class atmosphere of modern Münster contrasts with its past. Four hundred years ago, this city was the scene of a dramatic confrontation between religious zealots and respectable burghers. In 1534, fanatic Anabaptists captured the city and held it for several months; when the townspeople, aided by imperial armies, reconquered their city, they tortured and executed the few survivors and then suspended their corpses in cages atop the church spires as a reminder to anyone who considered following a radical cause. In the twentieth century, these traces of religious warfare and class strife have been removed from the belfry. However, sharp class distinctions emerged along with divisions between Catholic and Protestant.

As unemployment doubled between 1931 and 1933, the Catholic Center Party maintained its popularity, but voters left the moderate liberal parties and Social Democrats. Communists and Nationalists increased their popularity slightly, and the Nazi vote grew from about 10 percent in 1930 to 24 percent in November 1933.[99] Economically, the region was somewhat anomalous as a relatively middle-class stronghold at the edge of the Ruhr River Basin, Germany's densely populated industrial area. In this setting, conflicts between Socialists and Conservatives, Protestants and Catholics surfaced frequently. The Nazi women's leader, Elisabeth Polster, emulating Guida Diehl, did her best to recruit the respectable ladies of the town to her meetings; without dazzling success.[100] Telling them to maintain their ties to traditional organizations and to participate in church activities, she blended Nazi doctrine with Christianity. To lend her words the ring of authority, she quoted Guida Diehl, not Elsbeth Zander. Rarely, and only during extreme crises, she admitted, might it become necessary for women to behave in an "almost military" fashion. But generally, they ought to remain in their own womanly spheres. After the Nazi revolution, she promised her audiences, women would once again center their lives on their families.

Polster attracted a small following using "ladylike" tactics. Striking a balance between vigor and respectability, she roused women from their passivity and told them they had a special mission. Polster worked closely with her chief, District Leader Adolf Meyer in Münster. While Zander's followers aroused fanaticism, Polster, like Diehl, demanded order. "We need a sisterhood whose goal is unquestioning obedience to our movement. The movement needs the total person." [101] By 1932, she employed a staff of nine women and counted 5,000 members in her organization. Polster recruited followers through a series of well-publicized community projects. In the summers, for example, she supervised a fresh-air fund that took urban children to the country for visits to farming families; during the winters, she sponsored charity drives to collect used clothing for needy families; and throughout the year, her organization operated a small soup kitchen. Her very favorite project, however, was a campaign to combat sexual license among the working class. Convinced that eugenically unsound sexual relationships produced offspring of a low moral caliber, she began a campaign to reform people's habits. Being of practical mind, she worked to improve the overcrowded living conditions that encouraged incest. She had no way of actually providing families with larger apartments, but she did mount a drive to collect bedding so children did not have to sleep with either their siblings or older relatives. It is not clear that sexual morality improved as the result of Polster's vigorous campaign, but her efforts lent her organization a solid bourgeois image that counteracted in part the brawling, masculine élan of the local Party organization.

In the nearby small industrial city of Bielefeld, a very different Nazi woman made dramatic headway in her campaign. Irene Seydel struck out on her own and recruited followers from among the less-educated working class and peasant women of the region. Bielefeld voters fell into the polarized model of the rest of the nation, with 40,000 voters choosing Communist or Socialist candidates, 20,000 voting Nazi, and 10,000 voting Nationalist in 1930. In this overwhelmingly Protestant stronghold with a large working class, the Catholic Center candidates made a poor showing. With the Depression, the vote for Nazi candidates shot up from 10 percent in 1930 to just under 50 percent by July 1932. Whereas Polster recruited middle-class and strongly Catholic followers, Seydel operated in a more secular milieu in which Marxist parties made a strong showing.

Daughter of a respected middle-class family and wife of an engineer, Seydel had joined the movement relatively late and without any prior political experience. Until the late 1920s, she had devoted herself entirely to her husband and children. In 1930 Seydel was thirty-eight and her teenage sons needed less attention. Like her neighbors, she became increasingly alarmed as businesses went bankrupt and dole lines grew. "Mother Germany," she believed, needed all of her children. Surveying the political options, she concluded that only the Nazis offered a dynamic alternative to more chaos because only they would be strong and decisive enough to prevent a Communist overthrow. Having read *Mein Kampf* carefully, she began her political life by addressing small groups of friends. To her astonishment, her first speeches proved successful. "Even my oaf of a brother, who sleeps through even the movies, stayed awake to hear me."[102] She traveled through the countryside speaking to whomever wanted to listen.

> From my own experience I can tell you about women who have responded to our appeal and begun to see things clearly because they discovered they could once again serve the nation. Women have something to offer their people—the purity of their hearts and the power of their spirits! Women long to hear that politics emanates from love and that love means sacrifice. The German woman's talents wither at the sound of commands barked by north-eastern [Prussian] trumpets. But she is eager to work for someone who sends a friendly ray of sunshine her way.[103]

Men, she said, contribute understanding and reason to politics; but no movement can flourish without women's emotions. Men create the form; women provide the content.[104] She told cheering audiences that the political battle began in the home. "Here, in the smallest possible framework, we will wage the battle against the internal enemy—the un-Germanic spirit."[105] While for many such a phrase might have connoted "Jewish," Seydel used the term in a different sense, and never referred to anti-Semitism. "Un-Germanic," to her, meant putting personal desires ahead of the public good. The "un-Germanic person," she said, might be a capitalist who valued his profits over his workers' welfare or a housewife who fed her own family well while her neighbor ate turnips. "Germanic" to her meant patriotic sacrifice of self-interest to the collective good.

Irene Seydel roused audiences into frenzied enthusiasm and appealed to their will to sacrifice. People, she intuitively realized, don't mind sacrificing as long as they are convinced that their cause is worthy, and that others in the community also undergo hardship. Seydel counted housewives, teachers, and unmarried daughters as her most dedicated followers. To them she promised a sisterhood that would transcend class.

> We know that for decades German women have longed to call one another "sister." Just let the ladies from the Liberal women's movement and their fancy clubs stand in *front* of us and lecture us! We stand in the *midst of the nation—beneath it as caretakers, guardians, and helpers. We will heal the wounds* inflicted by those dark and difficult years under the Weimar system.[106]

Women, according to Seydel, upheld the collectivist tradition of the nation, while men had always been trained for individualistic competition. The men in a National Socialist state would provide the hierarchy while the women could create its community. Traveling through the Westphalian countryside, usually by bicycle but sometimes by train, Seydel mastered the technique of the meeting. Taking her cue from Hitler, she listened to her audiences' responses and told them what they longed to hear. The advice offered in *Mein Kampf* seems especially tailored to women's putative capacity to be receptive (although Hitler certainly did not mean it that way).

> [The speaker] will always let himself be borne by the great masses in such a way that instinctively the very words come to his lips that he needs to speak to the hearts of his audiences. And if he errs, even in the slightest, he has the living correction before him. If . . . they do not understand him, . . . he will become so primitive and clear in his explanations that even the last member of his audience must understand him. . . .[107]

Independently of supervision by either national or regional leaders, Seydel and Polster recruited new followers using their own methods and beliefs and the audiences they sought to attract. As long as they produced growing numbers of women volunteers and voters for the party, no man bothered to question their activities. These two Westphalian leaders, despite their contrasting styles, shared two important characteristics: They swore unconditional allegiance to the Party hierarchy and they entered politics as middle-aged housewives with no previous interest in politics. They, or so it appeared to male leaders, could be trusted. Seydel and Polster, like Zander, Diehl, and the women who wrote the Abel essays, displayed a degree of anxiety about both national life and women's future that set them apart from the conventional women who organized within religious and civic associations. The depth of their alarm led them to search beyond established religious organizations for an outlet. As they entered vigorously into public life in order to restore motherhood, they stepped outside the limits of ladylike behavior and ultimately moral rectitude.

The Weimar scenario haunts liberals, for it is the story of a political house destroyed from within by a threat that was recognized only after it could no longer be halted. During the stable years of Weimar, the Nazi Party was only one of several minor movements. Beyond the mainstream, thousands, and then, after the Depression, millions, of Germans from many occupations, regions, and ages searched for security, and fashioned a nostalgic vision of the future based on a past that never existed. Nazi rhetoric exacerbated a crisis atmosphere that recalled those glorious days of 1914. We wonder how so many Germans who described themselves as decent and respectable could have been attracted to a Party whose public image was dominated by the SA.

Why, we ask, did these people not feel repelled at the flagrant brutality of men who tortured, murdered, and brawled, and then boasted of their exploits? Memoirs suggest a partial answer. Hedwig Eggert, writing for the Abel contest, recalled the 1929 Nuremburg Rally. "I can never forget the joy I felt as the 60,000 to 70,000 SA and SS men marched in absolutely perfect discipline."[108] Hilde Boehm-Stolz described the first time she saw the Brownshirts in March or May 1930. "In wonderful discipline they drove in cars through the inner city. . . . Tears of shame sprang into my eyes when I thought I had not seen the SA before. I felt so moved, that I shouted out, 'and they say you are such rowdies?? Such disgusting slander is not and never will be true!!!' "[109] When it is restrained by military formations and directed at one's enemies, violence turns repulsion to awe. Here is the core of the universal appeal of what Susan Sontag described as "fascinating fascism."[110] Crisis exaggerates both masculine and feminine stereotypes, and the strong polarities give the illusion of clarity where in fact chaos and danger reign. For men and women, the street demonstrations heightened the warlike atmosphere reminiscent of August 1914. Men marched and women pledged themselves to activities in the public sphere. In virtually all of their memoirs, women Nazis attest to their joy at feeling that even the most trivial work served a mighty cause.

Strasser indirectly acknowledged the importance of crisis when he noted that the Nazi movement had created "a political soldier, a totally new phenomenon in history . . . a preacher and a leader with a soldierly bearing and outlook. Honor and comradeship form the basis of this community."[111] Had he applied these insights to the female half of Hitler's followers, he might have described another equally vital political type whom he might have called a "mother preacher." This woman defended her separate responsibilities to preserve love and charity first within her family, and then within the Nazi movement and finally within the nation. Rather than using her newly acquired citizenship to enter into debates about foreign policy, the economy, or the military, she voiced her special anxieties about the spread of atheism, sexual chaos, poverty, and cultural decadence, to the center of national concern. She dared to be outspoken and even "unladylike" in her fierce determination to defend the mother against communism, atheism, sexual decadence, and materialism, all embodied in that powerful symbol, the New Woman. Erich Fromm wrote poignantly about the disoriented Germans who longed for *An Escape from Freedom*. But Zander and Diehl, Polster and Seydel called Weimar democracy "the system" and felt imprisoned by its materialism. They referred to the Nazi Party as "our German freedom movement" instead of using its formal name. Weimar limited their options and mocked their values. Hitler offered liberation from an alien and modern world.[112]

In an atmosphere of heightened danger and conflict, women as well as men experienced freedom in obedience to a rebellious movement. Although Nazi women shared many concerns of other politically organized middle-class women, they felt both more threatened in the world at large and more secure within their own subculture. True, open support for Hitler could unleash jeers, reprisals, or physical injury, but against that ever-present danger, the Nazi community closed ranks. Within this subculture, women played a vital role by offering material aid and emotional reassurance. The very existence of women's groups, however small their numbers, gave the impression to believers and potential converts that Nazism encompassed women's hearts as well as SA men's boots.

4

LIBERATION
AND
DEPRESSION

The surest, and often the only way by which a crowd can preserve itself lies in the existence of a second crowd to which it is related. . . . [G]iven that they are about equal in size and intensity, the two crowds keep each other alive. The superiority on the side of the enemy must not be too great, or, at least, must not be thought to be so. In order to understand the origin of this structure we have to start from three basic antitheses. The first and most striking is that between men and women; the second that between the living and the dead; and the third that between friend and foe. . . .
—Elias Canetti
Crowds and Power

The wonderful thing about nature and providence is that no conflict between the sexes can occur as long as each party performs the function prescribed for it by nature.
—Adolf Hitler

In *Freedom and Bread*, Frau Heese, a devoted servant in the household of a respectable widow, wonders, "What's this world come to?" Her employer's life, once so full of security and joy, was disintegrating with every passing day. Her income was declining, her daughter was dating a Jewish boy, and her son had fallen into debauchery. One day, the widow confesses she no longer has the money to pay her trusted Frau Heese. Disaster follows upon hardship. Frau Heese's children suffer hard times and her husband (once a rowdy Communist) joins the Nazi Party. After 356 pages, dozens of crises, and scores of coincidences, the widow and the servant together salvage the wreckage of their lives and begin anew. Two women, one working-class and one bourgeois, overcome class hatred, join Hitler's New Freedom Movement, and save the members of their families they believe are worthwhile.

In *Gilgi—One of Us*, one morning Gilgi stealthily leaves her foster parents' home and goes into the world to seek her fortune. Although the couple have provided her with life's basic necessities, they have never loved or understood her. Gilgi departs in search of autonomy and affection. Times are hard, but she keeps her office job and moves in with her lover, Martin. It is not clear whether she deeply loves Martin, but she does desire him physically and takes comfort in the stability of home life. Gilgi describes her attraction for Martin: "We enjoyed each other and our skin said yes to each other's touch. It was all natural and unpremeditated and without concern for consequences. I felt no prick of conscience and no inquietude whatever. I always felt clear and pure. I was sure of myself, followed my own free will, and set my own limit."[1] But Martin never does much, except sleep late and think about the world. One day Gilgi hears that one of Martin's former lovers has fallen into a desperate state. The woman and her husband are unemployed and their children are hungry. In a moment of mad frustration, the husband commits a robbery. He is caught. Unless the money he stole is replaced, he will go to jail. Gilgi searches frantically for money, even asking her mother (a prostitute whom she has never met before) for help. Too late. The parents have turned on the gas and the whole family dies. Then Gilgi discovers she is pregnant, and quietly slips out of Martin's life, making her way to Berlin, where she hopes to find a job and raise her child alone.

These plot outlines held thousands of readers in their thrall during the depths of the Depression. Both depict strong protagonists, women who believe in motherhood and learn they cannot rely on men for support. Frau Heese, a Nazi novelist's heroine, creates a network of women to salvage herself and her employer; Gilgi, a Socialist heroine, relies on no one and faces the unknown world of Berlin where she alone will raise her child. *Freedom and Bread,* by Marie Diers, and *Gilgi—One of Us,* by Irmgard Keun, dramatize the political and psychological impact of the Depression. Both addressed dominant themes in the war between the sexes that erupted with new force as politics and the economy crashed.

The world of the fathers had gone astray. Once again, as in wartime, the nation seemed to be on the brink of catastrophe and in need of cohesion. The "leaderless" republic was floundering. In 1928, at the height of Germany's economic recovery, Gustav Stresemann had warned, "During the past years we have been living on borrowed money. If a crisis were to arise and the Americans were to call in their short-term loans, we should be faced with bankruptcy."[2] Most Germans, however, believed economic recovery resulted from their own accomplishments and preferred not to think about the $20 billion that had fueled financial growth. Barely a year later, Stresemann was dead, and Black Thursday sent the American Stock Exchange into a frenzy.

American loans came due just as Stresemann had foretold, and the Depression hit Germany harder and faster than any other nation. Unemployment statistics charted the crisis. From a 1928 rate of 750,000 unemployed, the totals soared to 2.6 million in 1929 and 5 million in 1930. By early 1932, one of three Germans had no job. Six million people searched desperately for work that did not exist; and even the fortunate two-thirds with jobs earned only 65 percent of the real wages they had received before 1929. Germany's unemployment insurance program (the best in the world) could cope with a maximum unemployment of 1.5 million.[3] Forty-seven percent of all taxes collected went toward social services and welfare payments that barely deflected mounting malnutrition, sickness, evictions, and crime rates. When the Foreign Office defaulted on reparations payments, Germany was exonerated by the Hoover Moratorium in 1930. But still markets disappeared, factories remained idle, and new investment ceased. In the wake of the havoc wrought when the most powerful Austrian bank declared itself bankrupt in late 1930, the German Stock Exchange closed its doors for six months. Small banks failed, corporations went out of business, and the downward spiral continued.

Citizens from all political backgrounds looked to Berlin for leadership. But no successor to Stresemann emerged. By default, Germans fastened their gaze on the President of the Republic, Paul von Hindenburg. This staunch monarchist promised to defend the democracy as best he could. But how good was his "best"? True, he had pledged his allegiance to the Weimar Republic, but his character had been shaped by nineteenth-century values. He had already been retired for years when the Kaiser named him to the command of the German armies in World War I. Together with General Ludendorff, he restored German morale with victories on the Russian front. During the war, every Berliner who purchased a war bond received a nail that he or she could pound into an enormous wooden statue of Hindenburg in downtown Berlin. By the war's end, the steel-coated effigy testified to Germans' unflagging faith in their Field Marshal and *Vaterland.* In real life, too, Hindenburg made an impressive figure: well over six feet tall, with blue eyes and bristly white mustaches, he projected a stolid image. After the German surrender in 1918, millions forgot Hindenburg's role in the defeat and remembered only his victories against Russia. Their amnesia was no accident, for it had been Hindenburg who gave rise to the myth that his armies had been "stabbed in the back" by cowardly civilians. When President Friedrich Ebert died in 1925, the Field Marshal remained so loyal to the beliefs by which he had been raised that he awaited the exiled Kaiser's approval before accepting the invitation to stand as a candidate. Hindenburg won, and throughout the remainder of the decade, Hindenburg fulfilled his symbolic role as patriarch for the "fatherless generation." The very fact that such a staunch monarchist could broaden his political views and accept the democracy augured well for the future. But cynics worried about what would happen in a genuine emergency. Writer Theodor Lessing called the President "a zero" and commented presciently, "It may be said: Better a Zero than a Nero. Unfortunately, the course of history has shown that behind a Zero lurks always a future Nero."[4] Expecting this mythical figure to act wisely in the Great Depression, however, was like turning over political responsibility to George V. The British constitution, of course, precluded such interference. But the Weimar Constitution contained an emergency clause, Article 48, which empowered the President to assume temporary dictatorial powers if he believed the Republic to be threatened. For example, he could pass decrees when the Reichstag could not form a majority; if revolution threatened, he could call up the army; and in the case of a parliamentary deadlock, he could call new elections or appoint a cabinet. The drafters of the Weimar Constitution envisioned a President who, standing above parties, would stabilize politics by serving as a figurehead during calm times and a dictator during emergencies.[5]

When the economic crisis began in 1929, a coalition cabinet held power. Because two of the coalition parties, the Social Democrats and the conservative People's Party, could not compromise on the issue of unemployment insurance, the cabinet resigned in March 1930, and Heinrich Brüning, a moderate Catholic, became Chancellor. During the following summer, parliamentary deadlock persisted and democracy, for all practical purposes, ended. National elections in September 1930 produced the scenario that haunts all liberals: Crisis fragments political opinions, legislatures become paralyzed because no majority supports any proposal, and coalitions dissolve as quickly as they are formed.

In 1920, people had wondered if Germans would accept progressive reforms that came as the result of surrender to foreign armies. The answer became clear ten years later. Germans had, indeed, functioned under a liberal constitution as long as economic conditions remained favorable. But in crisis, voters spread their loyalty across the whole political spectrum. In the first Weimar elections of 1919, over 18 political parties had run candidates, and 10 attracted enough votes to win at least one seat; in the prosperous mid-twenties, voters shifted to the six major parties; but by 1930, 32 parties campaigned, and 15 secured seats. Record numbers of voters turned out, and astonished the world by their choices. The Nazi Party leapt from ninth to second place, increasing its Reichstag representation tenfold.[6] Voters who had earlier "wasted" their ballots on single-issue parties, or not voted at all during stable times, now coalesced into the amorphous but fanatical catch-all Nazi movement. Subsequent elections bore out the trend: The higher the turnout, the greater the Nazi and Communist gains. Polarization eroded the position of all moderate parties except the Catholic Center. Although the total vote for Marxist candidates remained relatively constant, voters within that bloc increasingly supported the Communist Party. Similarly, on the right the Nazi vote grew rapidly as support for Nationalists and the moderately conservative People's Party dwindled. The Democratic Party, which had played so crucial a role in the foundation of the Weimar Republic a decade before, diminished into obscurity.[7] No wonder a satirist quipped that political power looked like a dumbbell, with all its weight on the ends.

A state of emergency became an everyday affair. When the Reichstag could form no majority, decision making fell to the President. Hindenburg had no political acumen, and at age eighty-five it was improbable that he would acquire it. A small clique of unscrupulous advisers channeled his basically reactionary instincts and settled every new crisis in the most conservative way possible. Hindenburg, using emergency powers granted to him by Article 48, stabilized prices, reformed the tax structure, introduced a protective tariff, reduced salaries and social services, removed millions from the eligibility rolls for welfare and unemployment compensation, and supported failing businesses against bankruptcy. In addition, Hindenburg brought discredit onto the government when he approved a vast financial rescue scheme that netted handsome profits for himself and scores of other wealthy nobles. By 1932 the federal budget had been cut by a third; to prevent a worse deficit, massive layoffs and cutbacks in services were necessary.

Meanwhile the Reichstag remained in session, and national radio aired its acrimonious debates. Listeners recoiled as they heard the rowdy language, frequent uproar, and ubiquitous tinkling of the bell as the speaker demanded, "Order! Please let us have some order."[8] Citizens went about their daily routines, but a silent despair permeated every facet of life. Stephen Spender, as always an astute observer, recalled that

> There was a sensation of doom to be felt in the Berlin streets . . . the feeling of unrest went deeper than any crisis. It was a permanent unrest, the result of nothing fixed or settled. The regime was neither democracy nor dictatorship, socialism or conservatism, it represented no class or group. Only a common fear of the overwhelming disorder, which formed a kind of rallying place of frightened people. It was the *Weimardämmerung*. Tugged by forces within and without, by foreign powers and money lenders, industrialist plotters, embittered generals, impoverished landed gentry, potential dictators, refugees from Eastern Europe, it reeled from crisis to crisis within a permanent crisis.[9]

Thus began the "alienation of the representatives from the represented."[10] Hindenburg appointed a cabinet dominated by reactionaries, to serve a nation in which half of the population lived at subsistence levels and just over half of all voters cast their ballots for Marxist or liberal candidates. In this nation with only a brief democratic tradition, voters had seen twenty-one cabinets rise and fall in ten years; and during the worst crisis of its short history, the legislature yielded its power to President Hindenburg. Political paralysis and financial stalemate drove people to despair—but whatever their anxieties, they did their best to preserve their surface calm. The atmosphere of controlled chaos and quiet fatalism reminded Ehrenburg of the Inflation years.

> A middle-aged German with cropped hair and a high collar was in the railway compartment reading a thick newspaper. He told me he was a commercial traveler in patent notebooks. I asked him when we were due in Berlin. He removed a timetable from his wallet. "At thirty and a half minutes past eleven." He then picked up his paper again and said calmly, "It is the end of absolutely everything. . . ."
>
> The publisher of the radical newspaper *Neues Tageblatt* invited some authors to dinner. Everything was as usual: crystal glasses, good wine, flowers, conversation. Suddenly, the host said, just like the commercial traveler, "But you know all this will soon be finished."[11]

Helpless and resigned, Germans awaited their fate. Fear of collapse itself became a self-fulfilling prophecy.

Outside the political arena, another battlefield opened up. In wartime, a foreign menace solidifies citizens into a common front. But economic collapse opened up fronts that cut through the social fabric of the nation. Workers voted Communist and complained bitterly (although they did not dare risk their jobs by striking) against capitalists. Anti-Semitic publicists found growing audiences for their scurrilous attacks on the international plot to destroy finance. Youthful protesters scorned their parents' values. Clergymen combated the atheism they found everywhere. Everyone had a favorite theory; but no one produced a solution. Besides rekindling these traditional antagonisms, the crisis unleashed an unprecedented biologically based "war" that tore at the remnants of social solidarity. As the Depression deepened, the "sex war," which had broken out in the wake of women's demands for equality half a century before, flared up anew. Concern about the family formed the core of the Depression discourse about fundamental values. Whatever people *thought* about the Depression, they *experienced* it in their families and focused their anxieties on the changes they observed in moral codes and cultural trends.

Erich Fromm conducted a study of some of these private fears on the eve of the Great Depression that reveals how people cathected public disorder onto private anxieties. Fromm distributed a 500-question survey to a thousand working-class Germans. Most findings did not surprise him —except one. People (even those with progressive social ideas in other areas) replied with unexpected vehemence to questions about women's new role in society. Whether they discussed women's makeup, bobbed hair, or their place in the labor force, respondents displayed strong emotions. Fromm concluded, "The vigorous reactions point clearly to the amount of emotion which lurks behind apparently marginal problems like cosmetics. Here is an opportunity for political propaganda writers . . . to use for their purposes." The respondents viewed modernity for women as "immoral" or "un-German," or "not worthy of women." These staunch socialists may have voted with the left, but they experienced changing mores with the anxieties of the right. Parenthetically, Fromm noted the disappointing frequency with which working-class respondents expressed cultural attitudes remarkably similar to Nazi viewpoints.[12] People of all classes rallied to a bourgeois standard of respectability that combined patriotism with fixed ideas about appropriate manners, morals, and sexual attitudes.[13] When society broke apart, they looked for a cause and found it not too far from home in the New Woman who, in the popular mind, earned her own money and refused to settle into a wifely role.

Contemporaries feared that economic emergency unleashed a social war. "The times in which we live reach their low point in the relationship between the sexes . . . hostility plays the dominant role. An invisible revolution has taken place."[14] "The less noble characteristics surface . . . we revert to a lower stage in our social evolution. . . ."[15] This acrimony, which occurred beyond the limits of formal politics, pulled women into a nationwide and deeply emotional debate. "I can think of nothing more revolutionary than continued unemployment," warned one Reichstag delegate.[16] Misogynist laments had been increasing throughout the 1920s, but their tone became virulent after 1929. Social scientists pronounced German society sick and looked for the virus. Just as Hitler found it in the Jew, opponents of women's emancipation discovered the source in the New Woman. "The low point of German cultural life and morality has coincided with the high point of emancipation for women." Equality between the sexes, argued two academic opponents of women's emancipation (Hugo Sellheim and Max Hirsch), produced cultural decline.[17] Feminists, ran the ubiquitous complaint, wanted to become like men and steal men's personalities as well as their jobs and social status. Career women, they alleged, rejected marriage and belonged to the "third sex."[18] Respected professors wrote weighty books about *The Psychopathology of the Women's Movement* and *Sexual Character and National Strength; Basic Problems of Feminism* and *Feminism and Cultural Demise: The Erotic Roots of Women's Emancipation.* Sociologists warned about *The Nation in Danger: The Declining Birth Rate and Its Consequences for Germany's Future; Murder of the Future;* and *The Extreme Worship and Weakening of Women.* Political scientists worried about *The Rule of the Inferior.*[19] The tone of this assault marshaled "scientific" evidence and medicalized terminology to concentrate broad disorientation on one powerful symbol.

Germans were not unique in equating women's emancipation with cultural decline. In other nations, too, critics expressed horror at the license of the 1920s, and conservatives everywhere deplored women's equality as symptomatic of irreversible cultural decay. French legislators, alarmed at falling birthrates and cultural disorientation, initiated programs to keep women in their homes. British conservatives drew similar conclusions. George V declared, "The Foundations of National Glory are set in the homes of the people—they will only remain unshaken while the family life of our race . . . is strong, simple and pure."[20] Still, Germany was unique. In Britain industrial change had occurred earlier, and in France modern society evolved rather slowly over two centuries; German industrialization occurred rapidly and late (during the last decades of the nineteenth century). Since then Germans had experienced military defeat followed by revolution, women's legal emancipation, and the Inflation, accompanied by the moral thaw of the twenties.

Long-term trends and the Depression presented intractable dilemmas. But if the family could be stabilized, at least in the short term, tensions would be reduced. Politicians from all but the Communist Party concurred that "the family is the germ cell of the nation" and fought to protect it against emancipated women, who (depending on the stereotype) appeared as either "a girl type" who seduced men into debauchery or a masculinized "third sex" who competed against men for scarce jobs. Alarm about the family overlapped with fears about declining public morality. "Marriage and the family are the supporting pillars of every healthy people," wrote one anxious Protestant. "Industry and individualism have ruined us all!"[21] But not all families remained patiently, neatly unchanged.[22] For over a decade demographers had spread the alarm about the dropping birthrate, blaming it on women's "birth strike" and writing dire predictions about a "*Volk* without a future."[23] Behind the anxiety about the birthrate lurked the fear of unbridled sexuality. If the family failed to control its members, all of German society would, critics warned, fall into decline. "The family alone can contain the forces that economic disaster unleashed. Sexuality, that great gift from God, will destroy it. When human guilt is misused, that sexuality turns into a demonic power that pulls us down and unleashes endless disease into the world,"[24] declared a Protestant editorial.

Conservatives saw the restoration of family as the most effective method of preventing socialist revolution, while socialists worked for pragmatic reforms that would help parents cope with modern problems. "Marriage is the life and death of our People!" declared one conservative, and lamented dramatically falling birth- and marriage rates. What happened when husbands became idle and women shouldered financial responsibility? As during wartime, the social order became topsy-turvy, except that now men stayed at home instead of marching away. A serialized novel depicted the results. "We are now given too little to live and too much to die. In the narrow confines of these four walls, the man paces, his teeth clenched, looking on helplessly while his children quarrel. Bitter men and tired, despairing women cannot hold their families together."[25]

A team of psychologists who investigated the impact of massive unemployment in a small Austrian town noticed the increase in tensions between men and women. "Although I now have much less to do than before, I am actually busy the whole day, and have no time to relax. Before, we could buy clothes for the children. Now I have to spend the whole day patching and darning to keep them looking decent. My husband tells me off because I'm never finished. . . ."[26] All of the women interviewed reported that they preferred the old days in which they worked for eight hours a day in the factory. As one said, "It's not only for the money; stuck here alone betwen one's own four walls, one isn't really alive." The researchers themselves felt moved by the contrast between people's plans for a better future and the lack of opportunity to realize them. They described one man who had been known for his resourcefulness and ambition: "Now all hope is gone. He wishes so very much to live by his own earning. His wife, who had never been out to work, is now a complete wreck, . . . she is always ill and moody. . . . The will to resist is gone." Another resident commented, "What strangers we are to each other; we are getting visibly harder. Is it my fault that times are so bad? Do I have to take all the blame in silence???" Women with jobs suffered from overwork, while their husbands sat idle and sometimes began to drink heavily. Fearing they might hurt their husbands' pride, wives hesitated to ask for help with the housework and cooking. Neither mothers nor fathers seemed to be able to control the youth.[27] Crime, juvenile deliquency, suicide, out-of-wedlock births, and venereal disease increased. All these signs of social disintegration fed the anxiety that the family itself would lose its hold over its members.

In the popular novel *The Marriage of the Unemployed Martin Krug*, the protagonist grimly faces days of idleness while his wife bravely finds part-time jobs, does the housework, and cheerfully reassures him that soon all will improve. Her good humor and optimism gall him, and he envies her ability to earn money. Unable to find work, he looks instead for a mistress. After many melodramatic twists of plot, his wife takes the children and leaves him. In the end she returns for a joyous reunion.[28]

Real life offered few happy endings. Hundreds of thousands remained homeless after their welfare benefits expired. Living in tent colonies on the outskirts of major cities, people despaired of ever working again. They attempted to keep up the illusion of order even amid economic chaos. One Berlin citizen recalled the quiet desperation of the decent poor in tent colonies.

> Only the father went into town to collect his dole money. The more unemployed people there were, the bigger the camps grew. Visitors were amazed at their quietness. You saw men sitting in front of their tents just staring over the water. The rows of tents were neatly laid out, with street names and house numbers, and the space between the tents was decorated with patterns of slate.
>
> There was nothing romantic about camp life—it was clean, adult, and neat misery. Prussian in its straightness and its precision. The foresters and

the police were amazed at the discipline of the inhabitants. There was seldom any fighting or quarreling, acts of robbery or violence. Every tent town had its small parliament and its mayor. The children had their playground, and the fires on which the women cooked were laid out neatly with slate.[29]

As in wartime, the government called on women to make sacrifices for the good of the nation, and when conditions failed to improve, women were blamed for the disruption of family life.

At the heart of the hysteria about the disappearing family lay a deep fear that women would abandon their traditional roles. Politicians who disagreed about every other subject drew the same conclusion when they looked at studies on women in the work force: Because women employees' jobless rates remained at 10 percent as men's rose to 30 percent, and women's wages remained at about 60 percent of men's, even within the same job categories, legislators and social scientists declared that women "stole" men's jobs and emasculated the family father. To clinch the argument, they observed that women with jobs outside their homes bore fewer children than full-time housewives. From these assertions, lawmakers concluded that if women could be eliminated from the labor force, men would once again find jobs and stability would be restored. Opposition to women's emancipation, which had gained force during the 1920s, now intruded directly into working women's lives. In the wake of the Inflation, married women had lost their right to employment in government jobs, a clear breech of the Constitution.

The war between the sexes did not automatically pit women against men. Some women sided with men in the assault against working women. The BDF, the Protestant women's federation, and other civic associations opposed women's right to work. "The Federation of German Women's Associations [BDF] urges that working women ought to share fully the sacrifices and deprivations that are vested upon the entire population by the economic emergency. The Federation does not intend to be a lobby for women's interests.[30]

BDF leader Marie Baum suggested, "The best way to solve the problem of the employed mother is to make it possible for her to quit her job and devote all her energies to motherhood."[31] Women's-rights advocates sometimes reacted to men's hostility by forswearing women's rights. It ought to be noted, however, that middle-class women's organizations defended women teachers and social workers who were threatened with dismissal.

Two religious organizations kept their distance from the drive to return women to their homes. Jewish women appreciated the irrational component of popular hysteria about the Woman Question because they linked it with mounting anti-Semitism. Even though the pages of their periodical featured articles on traditional women's duties, Jewish women argued forcefully against anyone who questioned women's or Jews' fundamental human equality and loyalty to Germany. They formed self-defense committees and looked to longtime friends and allies in the BDF and other liberal associations for help. Except for Agnes von Zahn-Harnack (the president of the BDF) who gave public lectures against anti-Semitism, however, Jewish women's pleas fell on deaf ears. Neither the Protestant women's presss or *Die Frau* (the journal of the BDF) publicly protested either misogyny or anti-Semitism.

Because the Catholic network remained isolated from non-Catholic organizations, Jewish women did not consider looking in that direction for support. And, given the Pope's mandate for women to eschew any responsibilities beyond their families, it might seem that Catholic women's organizations would have joined the clamor for the restoration of motherhood by attacking women workers. They did not. Catholic women's organizations defended women's right to employment from a very different perspective. Because Catholic associations included a sizable constituency of working-class and peasant women, the leaders insisted that women—even mothers—absolutely depended upon their wages to support their families and relatives. Catholic periodicals based their defense of women's employment on the fact that women worked from unselfish and not careerist motivations.

The broadest support for women's right to employment came from the trade unions and the Communist and Social Democratic Parties, who pointed to the objective error of misogynists' claims. Because unemployment affected traditionally masculine industries (such as construction, iron and steel, and heavy industry) more adversely than feminine jobs (such as textiles, food production, and white-collar work) predominantly female sectors were less affected by the international financial crisis and fired fewer of their workers. Since over half of all married women who counted as employed worked in family businesses, they could not be replaced by waged labor. Women, in short, did not depress wages—capitalists did.[32] Finally, upholders of women's right to employment asked, what man would accept the poorly paid and menial jobs that typically attracted women (like domestic service, cleaning, the textile industry, office work, or agricultural labor)? Any "real man" would sooner face hardship and privation than accept dreary "women's work." Else Lüders, longtime advocate of women's rights within the conservative camp, estimated that a mere 200,000 women in the labor force might be replaced by men workers.[33] "Families cannot eat rhetoric," one woman commented. Defenders of women's equality compiled statistics, marshaled logical arguments, and appealed to sentiment.[34] Women reminded the legislators that marriage rates had actually increased since the nineteenth century; that 96 percent of all Germans lived in a family setting; and that the one million women who were widowed or divorced needed their wages, especially since half of them supported children. If indeed the family was really endangered, then it depended more than ever upon women's wages for its very survival.[35]

These efforts yielded little. In 1932, when a law renewed the prohibition against married women with employed husbands from working in state jobs, only the Communists voted no. Similarly, no political party protested the policy that mandated women demonstrate poverty before receiving unemployment benefits. For women, unemployment benefits were seen as welfare payments. For men they were an undisputed right. In family law and health, women's reform efforts met unyielding rejection.

As the Depression worsened, more and more women joined national associations to protect their status as wives and mothers. Germany's 230 national women's organizations pledged to remain nonpartisan while warning against cultural decline, sexual deviance, atheism, communism, foreign enemies, and occasionally Jews.[36] Since the turn of the century, eighty women's occupational, educational, and civic associations formed the Federation of German Women's Associations (BDF), which included 500,000 members. Once at the heart of the middle-class women's emancipation movement, after 1919 BDF had drifted steadily toward more conservative positions on women's issues as well as national politics. Nevertheless, many women found it too radical. Already during the First World War, the two-million-strong Protestant women's organization had withdrawn because the BDF supported women's suffrage. In 1932, 100,000 members of the Reich Association of Housewives resigned in protest against the BDF's purported liberalism. Thus, while the BDF claimed journalists' attention and appeared strong to the international women's movement, actually its influence and membership had begun to decline.

By contrast, during the 1920s a formidable force of anti-feminists had coalesced. In addition to the Protestant federation and the Housewives Union, over a million women belonged to organizations affiliated with the Catholic Church; 750,000 did volunteer work with the Red Cross; 130,000 participated in the elitist and nationalist Queen Louisa League; 90,000 belonged to the rural housewives' organization; and dozens of smaller women's auxiliaries to conservative men's organizations claimed the allegiance of thousands.[37] Youthful rebellion, factory-made clothes, store-bought food, sexual emancipation, flapper fashions, and the New Woman threatened to toss the old-fashioned mother on the scrap heap of history along with the skilled craftsman, sturdy peasant, and faithful servant. Because conservative women's organizations disavowed any political affiliation, their activities attracted little attention. But their mass membership, centralization, and publications made them an important force in shaping women's opinion. Wives wanted not emancipation from their families but leverage over their husbands. They supported family protection because they believed the family protected them. Helplessness, far from being a liability, comprised the wife's major weapon in controlling her husband. The "loving battle between the sexes," as one housewife put it, became so hostile that she found herself fighting on two fronts—politics and the economy. Organized housewives eschewed politics and instead extolled their own "invisible influence," first over their families and thence in society as a whole. Without major changes, they feared the demise of the family.

Besides lobbying for specific interests (like lowering servants' wages and increasing penalties for abortion), wives launched an emotionally charged crusade, complete with dire predictions about the decadent future and lofty paeans to feminine virture. "We housewives are a great power, but a silent one. We don't demonstrate, we don't speak in statistics or numbers. We don't tote up our scores. . . . But as a housewife, I administer the total property of this household and guide all of its members."[38] "We realize that we will win our rights only through large organizations!" wrote Clara Mende, longtime opponent of women's suffrage, and Nationalist Reichstag delegate. Antifeminist women seized upon the rhetoric of rights, but twisted its meaning to mean the "right" of women to remain protected in their domestic sphere. Many women, who had been apathetic about national issues before they could vote, used their newly won rights to mobilize against further change. Few grasped the paradox of their double mission of entering public life to defend women's private family sphere.

Without either education or upbringing that might have prepared them to take advantage of their new rights, these women wanted "Emancipation from Emancipation!"—a slogan later taken up by Nazi ideologue Alfred Rosenberg. Two-thirds of all married German women considered themselves primarily housewives. Swearing to reinforce, not threaten, male prerogatives, they set out to defend traditional morality against decadence, which they linked to large cities and poor people. Aiming to purify public morality by curbing male sexual license and saving endangered youth, housewives built their own subculture within religious and civic institutions and swelled the ranks of women's patriotic and civic associations. As liberals praised the unprecedented freedoms of Weimar culture, these traditionalists established their own protection against too much liberty.

In defending a mythic vision of the ideal family, they launched a crusade against modernity with political implications that became visible years later. During the Weimar Republic, women's organizations established rest centers for overworked mothers; directed orphanages; "saved" prostitutes; campaigned for stricter laws against smut literature, pornographic films, decadent theater, and loose morality; and founded associations for women's spiritual renewal. Needless to say, their main target was Berlin. The freedom that challenged and excited an artistic elite terrified women with traditional values. Organized women joined the political debate on the Woman Question and (like most men) did so not in the name of women's rights but the family. In the short term, this was a winning tactic; but by relinquishing women's inalienable claim to equality they mortgaged their futures.

Besides defending their feminine role and responsibilities as women, these middle-class women counterattacked by accusing men of failing in their responsibility to guarantee public order. While misogynists scapegoated women, public figures now blamed the Depression on a failure of the masculine will. "The man today is absolutely worthless!" wrote one stalwart woman academic from the old woman's movement. "He cannot protect his life, or his property, or his freedom!"[39] Turning the dominant rhetoric around, women replied in effect, "Yes, we will sacrifice, but only when everyone else does." When the major institutions of society collapse, citizens perceive their futures as threatened, and self-interest merges with sacrifice. The common good and individual advantage match. As in wartime, the national fate rested with the women who would revive morale by their contributions on the nonpolitical sphere. "We think back on the wartime when all economic freedoms ceased; when all able-bodied men not at the front worked for the nation; when a rationing system distributed vital goods fairly; when women had to meet their families' needs with these scarce provisions."[40] Masculine individualism, they argued, had produced financial and moral bankruptcy; only women could restore the collectivist spirit by treating the psychological depression that followed in the wake of economic disaster. Catholic women deplored the "crisis of confidence among men," while Leonore Kühn, a leader among conservative women's-rights advocates, attacked the "spiritual exhaustion of the modern man."[41] A woman sociologist gave this argument an air of objectivity by insisting that a society that had become sick now had to pay for so many years of domination by the "restless and rootless" masculine principle. Men, she insisted, were qualified only to be fighters and foresters, professions to which they ought to return.[42] The man, she continued, "constantly searches for a woman into whom he can place his life force. And then he tries to escape from his family."

What would keep the father at home after he lost his job? Not much. With over one-third of all people dependent upon welfare for survival, alarms spread that the father had lost his ability to care for his family, just as the politician had lost his power to control the nation. "The father who no longer supports his family ruins that family. [Without financial authority] he loses his kingly privilege and cannot any longer fulfill his monarchical duty to hold the family together," declared a Catholic author.[43] The patriarchy could not perform its most sacred function: protection of the social order. The time had come, many said, for women from all classes to assume extraordinary responsibilities. If family life was in trouble (and most middle-class women leaders believed it was), then the fault lay with male escapism, not with women's emancipation.[44] Women accused men of failing in their responsibility to guarantee public order and of simultaneously abandoning their patriarchal duties.

The women who flocked to conservative women's associations railed against men's default in their duties; and they stressed their own readiness to sacrifice. However, another theme emerged with full force: They expected a payoff. These women did not intend to return to their homes, but relinquished their claim to masculine turf with the understanding they would pioneer their own social "space," their *Lebensraum*. Before Hitler used *"Lebensraum"* to popularize conquest in the East, women had applied it in their own way, as "a space in which to live," or "living room" inside Germany—a social space where domestic tranquility and traditional values reigned. Thus women commonly used the term to describe a "space" beyond the materialist and abrasive masculine world of business, class struggle, and high politics. The leading spokeswoman for the middle-class women's rights movement, Gertrud Bäumer, wrote in 1926 that "our best forces do not lie in the conquest of new land, but in the quiet expansion of the area that we have already fenced in."[45] Five years later, she developed the theme in another book, *The Woman in the New Lebensraum*, in which she outlined women's responsibilities for bringing order and humanity to public life in times of hardship and chaos.[46]

To counteract economic dislocation, Germans from all backgrounds concurred that the family (like a precious national resource) ought to be protected. This put women at the nexus of the debate about ethical values, national health, and social cohesion. While cultural critics blamed women for failing to guard traditional morality, other authors looked back to prehistory for models to guide the future. In the midst of a cultural backlash against the New Woman came a revival of speculation about the glories of a long-lost matriarchy. The works of J. J. Bachoven, the nineteenth-century anthropologist who popularized this myth, were reprinted, and several writers took up the theme. Amid fractured modern society, writers dreamed about a mythical Magna Mater—a neoromantic deity who would purify and cleanse Germany. One of her admirers wrote, "The way of the *Volk* is the way of the woman, anonymous, without person, producing unconsciously, at work quietly like Nature." Helen Diner took up the theme in her book *Mothers and Amazons*, evoking a primeval maternal spirit deep in the "magic blood and earth spirit" and permeated by an "entrancing nest warmth of magic and feeling."[47] A female elite, she predicted, would overcome "intellectualism, the cult of technology, mediocrity, and male socialism." Behind such effusive praise of womanhood lurked an attack on the New Woman. Other authors demanded passive and loving women. What man would want to marry the "modern" women? critics asked. But if women once again became docile, experts promised that the male "urge to marry" (*Heiratslust*) would be rekindled. They did not consider the possibility that a New Woman might not desire an "old man."

In everyday life the cult of motherhood found expression in the increasing popularity of Mother's Day—a holiday introduced in 1927 by a florists' association and taken up enthusiastically by nationalist organizations. As the Depression forced most people to sacrifice, the praise of motherhood resonated among mothers who felt unappreciated.[48] While mother's-aid programs, rest homes for overworked mothers, special honors for mothers of many children, and public celebration of motherliness escalated, legislators took up eugenic and political questions. Throughout the many battlefields of the war between the sexes, one question remained unsolved. All sides of the discourse praised strong women. But what did the strong woman do? Did she tie her man more closely to her, or did she manage without him? Conservatives looked back to an idealized tradition and opted for the former. Liberals and Socialists gazed forward along an untrodden path and some dared to prefer the latter.

The debate about childbirth highlighted the contrast. Right and left polarized absolutely. Catholics remained staunchly reactionary, Protestants and Jews wavered in the middle, and Socialists and Communists called for more birth-control centers. All sides, it is important to remember, defended the family as an institution but disagreed about how best to support it. Whatever a few Berlin intellectuals said about family tyranny or bourgeois hypocrisy, for most people the family held out the

hope of material and emotional protection.[49] The left believed that families could be saved only by increasing husbands' and wives' control over
their lives. Throughout the Weimar Republic, Socialist and Communist
women had supported measures to ease the burdens of employed wives
and mothers. Acknowledging the reality that over 10 percent of all new
mothers did not have husbands, leftists wanted to legalize children born
to unmarried mothers, to end the harsh laws against abortion, and to
reform family law. They found it unjust that, for example, anyone con-
victed of assisting at an abortion was sentenced to seven years of hard
labor and that an adulterous husband whose wife won a divorce against
him still retained decisive rights over the couple's children. Working-
class women protested, too, that a husband could, and often did, legally
prevent his wife from using contraception. Socialist women advocated
abstinence and birth control and cautiously followed the lead of women
doctors in supporting legalized abortions to save mothers' lives.[50] Draco-
nian rules, they said, would never produce an ordered society. A Communist Reichstag delegate put the case simply: "Punishments have not
prevented the population decline; they have demonstrated only that
women will risk prison, illness, and sickness in order not to bring unwanted children into the world."[51]

A progressive filmmaker dramatized the plight of young people in a
movie that produced an explosive controversy. Two idealistic workers,
Hedwig and Paul, fall deeply in love. They decide to live together in
equality and independence. Eventually, when both have saved enough
money, they plan to marry; but in the depths of the Depression, they
barely earn enough to get by. Despite job insecurity, the two live bliss-
fully together and dream of the future. Then they both lose their jobs,
and Hedwig discovers she is pregnant. Paul, driven by destitution, steals
groceries so they can eat; his amateurish efforts lead directly to his arrest
and imprisonment. Hedwig, wild with desperation, decides to have an
abortion; she goes to a quack who bungles the operation, and dies.[52]
Censors in most German states banned *Cynakali* in response to women's
organizations' protests. Where it was shown, women picketed with signs
warning that the film was lewd and immoral. The slightest hint that
"good" people might land, through no fault of their own, in "bad" situations, met with implacable hostility; and the suggestion that a safe abortion might offer a humane solution to economic problems aroused
outrage from conservative women's groups. Women whose lives centered on home, husband, and housework, perceived any relaxation of
moral standards as an assault on their tiny kingdoms.

Erich Fromm's questionnaire, *Cynakali*, popular novels, and the
women's press attest to the depths of the controversy over men's and

women's proper roles. Hitler, as the most outspoken opponent of women in politics, emerged as the strongest spokesman for the strong-man ideal. Women might organize, argue, lobby, and volunteer, but many believed only a powerful man could bring other men back to order. Hitler embodied both the shabby respectability of the "little man" and the military swagger of the commanding personality. His political success revealed itself anew with each Depression election.

The dumbbell pattern held strong. Socialists lost while Communists gained; Nationalists lost as Nazis gained; youth and new voters increasingly voted for the Nazis, and clusters of adherents to single-issue parties also shifted their support to the dynamic Nazis. The impressive Nazi showing created a veritable bandwagon. Hitler fused the propaganda techniques from the revolutionary left with the nationalist, racist dogma from the right, producing what Sartre dubbed "elite of the ordinary."[53] Hitler himself ran for office on only one occasion, when he audaciously challenged Hindenburg in March 1932 and succeeded in rallying just over one third of the vote to come in second.[54]

From the early days of the Party, women's and men's support peaked at different points. Throughout the 1920s, when the Nazi vote remained low, many fewer women than men cast their ballots for Nazi candidates; and generally, despite their lack of political experience, women voters' party loyalty to Catholic and Nationalist parties remained slightly stronger than men's.[55] After 1928, women voters switched to the Nazi Party more slowly than men, but beginning with the 1932 July elections, they, like many new voters, converted quickly—even after many men, it appears, deserted Hitler's party, which seemed stalemated. It may also be that women who had not previously voted at all tended to cast their first ballots for Nazi candidates. This would indicate that their Nazi enthusiasm motivated them to vote.

Politics, however, meant more than voting during the last years of the Weimar Republic. Mass unemployment released millions of men from their 50-hour work weeks. After plodding dutifully to employment bureaus, many decided instead to march with paramilitary battalions. Four million men enlisted in private armies that served Socialism, Communism, Republicanism, Nationalism, and National Socialism. Members received not only food, shelter, and uniforms, but a sense of belonging, of being able to strike a blow against whomever or whatever they perceived as their enemy. Brecht characterized the thoughts of the one man who fell in behind the swastika.

> My belly rumbled with hunger,
> I fainted and went to bed,

> Then I heard in my ears a shouting—
> "Germany, Awake!" it said.
>
> And I saw so many marching
> To the Third Reich, they cried;
> I had nothing to lose and nowhere to go,
> so I joined them and marched beside.[56]

Paramilitary bravado recalled wartime heroics, providing the marching men with the thrill of battle, the élan of violence. Throughout Germany rallies turned into violent confrontations.

> Both Communists and Nazis were to be seen every weekend, parading in uniform, with a marching band at their head. They frequently came to blows. I wondered at first how they contrived to distinguish their enemies from their friends in those fracas, for their uniforms were remarkably similar. On closer investigation, I found the Nazis were mostly of middle-class origin, and the Communists were all working-class youths. But as regards outward appearance, there was little to choose between them.[57]

These weekend marchers may have been hungry, but this did not render them less dangerous. From the summer of 1931 until the summer of 1932, 182 men were killed in Berlin street fighting. One day in August 1932 saw over twenty acts of violence in the province of Silesia. On another occasion in the industrial town of Potempa, five Nazi storm troopers broke down the door of a worker's house and, in the presence of his mother, poked out his eyes with the thick end of a billiard cue, stamped on his throat, and killed him after inflicting twenty-nine wounds.[58] Political violence escalated. Leaders watched helplessly. Advisers warned Hindenburg not to use the army against the Nazis because the soldiers would refuse to fire on men who shared their values and backgrounds. They even convinced him to lift the ban against Nazi demonstrations. Violence erupted anew. Nazi brutality did not repel potential supporters; far from it. If victims were perceived as a lethal threat, then terror became heroic self-defense, a rescue mission and not a crime. "We will poison the poisoner!" Hitler screamed. Ruthlessness wielded by a manly yet restrained elite could be respectable. Because he swore to purify the nation of decadence, materialism, and military weakness, Hitler made his enemies seem evil. Many ordinary peace-loving people apparently tolerated Nazi violence. Terror does not terrify people as long as it is cloaked in respectability and aimed at movements or individuals they fear.

Beyond the dazzle of Berlin and the flicker of the movie screen, people longed for stability. The Nazi Party played to that longing. This motley collection of fanatics, which had attracted mainly derision during the economic recovery of the previous five years, doubled its following again and again. From 100,000 members in 1928, it had leapt to over 1.5 million by late 1932. In 1932 the League of German Girls (BDM) claimed 9,000 members. Before 1930, only 7,625 women (or 6 percent) actually belonged to the Nazi Party.[59] By 1931, the Party included just under one million members, less than 50,000 of whom were women. It is not clear how many women belonged to the various women's organizations. Diehl claimed 200,000; Zander boasted of 14,000. Nearly half of the over 4 million Germans who voted for Nazi candidates at election time were women. In other words, at least 2 million women supported the National Socialist Party without considering themselves part of the organization itself. District leaders reported that between 50 and 80 percent of their women followers did not officially belong to any Nazi association.[60]

The man whom foreign observers ridiculed as the Charlie Chaplin of politics, who called himself "the drummer," would lead his followers no less than his enemies to a *Götterdämmerung* without parallel. Chaplin looked at his audiences with a sad twinkle in his eye; Hitler sent his message out hypnotically, maniacally into his followers' souls, giving meaning to the millions who felt themselves alienated from the consensus politics of democracy and passed over by progress.

From his earliest writings, Hitler promised that not only would race replace class as the basis for understanding history, it would also supplant religion as the source for the myths that gave meaning to life. The second unchanging element in Hitler's biological goals was the absolute separation of "Aryan" women from "Aryan" men into separate functions, personalities, and civic obligations. Gender and race divisions, the bedrock of Nazi ideology, produced wildly inconsistent interpretations among Hitler's followers. As Nazis campaigned for electoral victory before 1933, this ambiguity provided minor leaders with the latitude to develop their own styles and values while remaining under the Nazi umbrella. Women particularly profited from this chaotic situation, and their activities before 1933 show how an utterly antifeminist movement can become attractive to masses of women who believe that society as they have known it hovers on the brink of extinction.

While SA men marched, the followers of Diehl and Zander collected funds and crusaded among the nonbelievers. Alarmed by the disarray of public life and impressed by Nazi successes, Diehl even reconsidered her earlier decision to shun male organizations and asked for a closer relationship with the Nazi Party. In 1931, she urged Gregor Strasser, the chief of Party organization, to tighten his command and simultaneously

strengthen his ties with non-Nazi groups, such as her own. While negotiating with Strasser, Diehl also opened discussions with the Protestant
Bishop in Berlin in the hope of establishing a close working relationship
with the Church.[61] When she wrote to Strasser, Diehl offered to cooperate with Zander's SA homes; but in writing to the Bishop she stressed
her efforts to combat pornography and to campaign against abortion.
Unlike Zander, Diehl was politically flexible and maneuvered to maximize her own importance with whatever group appeared powerful. The
Bishop, incidentally, investigated the request and wrote a polite rejection; Strasser accepted and promised to appoint Diehl to some type of
cultural office.

Diversity within the women's branches of the Party grew with the
rapidly expanding membership. Two young and vigorous women attracted considerable attention. Their views pushed Nazi dogma even
farther away from Hitler's narrow male-supremacist position, but no one
at Party headquarters seemed to care as long as their followings grew.
Pia Sophie Rogge-Börner, an anthropologist, examined race, which she
believed to be the fundamental determinant of character. This set her
apart from figures like Diehl and Zander, who insisted on gender as the
most important influence on human development. Rogge-Börner had
begun her career in the early 1920s with a treatise on matriarchy in which
she criticized men authors who saw women primarily in biological terms.
Superficially the matriarchists appeared to praise women and womanhood, but Rogge-Börner warned about the deeper implications of their
homage. In her book *Back to the Mother Right?* Rogge-Börner assailed
the "pervasive division of humanity into two species." The sudden outburst of praise for "motherliness, about which we have never heard or
read so much," aroused her suspicions. Glorification of a prehistorical
fantasy matriarch, she wrote, actually harmed real women by stereotyping them and generating expectations they could not possibly live up to.
She warned against any form of stereotyping, no matter how flattering,
because it reduced women to monolithic beings. The next step, she
predicted, would lead men to accept Nazi ideologue Alfred Rosenberg's
advocacy of polygamy. Rogge-Börner accurately perceived the danger of
an all-male elite turning women into breeding machines. Women, she
believed, had to participate in that elite in order to defend themselves.
Already she heard Nazi voices condemning monogamy because it
harmed the race by limiting men's procreative potential. Such determin-
istic, biological thinking, in her view, offered no hope for a better future.

Rogge-Börner exalted racial thinking as long as it did not diminish
women's participation in the master race. In lurid Nietzschean terms,
she depicted a glorious past that (not coincidentally) resembled the Na-

tional Socialist future of which she dreamed. At the dawn of recorded history she claimed men had "ripped us out of our lost harmony" and replaced the mother right with the father "Reich."[62] Advocating what she called "andromorphism," she demanded women's entry into public life because male-dominated institutions had brought humanity to the brink of destruction.

Rogge-Börner urged women to throw off layers of oppression and become psychologically independent and physically strong. "The woman must retain total control over her own body at all times," that is, she must have the right to say no to men's (even a husband's) physical advances. But Rogge-Börner believed a woman's autonomy ended with pregnancy. As soon as "another body exists within a woman's body," the mother has lost her right. Like the eugenicists, Rogge-Börner urged women from the "best" classes to reproduce more quickly so that Germany would not disintegrate into a "racial swamp."[63] To underscore her arguments, Rogge-Börner habitually noted that her opponents had fallen under Jewish-Freudian influence that reduced all human behavior to sex drives. Like Guida Diehl, she believed that women in the women's rights movement could be recruited to her cause and praised their commitment to women's pride. If Hitler became dictator, she believed the older generation would be easily integrated into the state. Besides writing for conservative periodicals, Rogge-Börner founded her own journal, *The German Woman Fighter*, in which she popularized her racial views and the Nazi cause.[64]

During the Depression another young woman leader with very different ideas attracted attention. Lydia Gottschewski, in her twenties during the 1920s, was a powerful speaker and tireless organizer who viciously attacked the leaders of the old women's movement.[65] During the war, she alleged, these middle-class women had hindered the war effort by demanding the right to vote. That generation's selfishness had cast shame on women ever after. Women, she said, needed a new collectivist movement because the old women's movement placed individual liberation ahead of a solution to the problems facing all women. Liberal women demanded (and to some extent achieved) access to expensive masculine education and entry into a man's professional world. Instead of closing ranks with women from all classes, however, these privileged women escaped from their womanly identity—and from the bonds of female solidarity.

> The fundamental experience of the old women's movement was the individual personality, woman's freedom and her pleasure. The fundamental experience of the new [i.e. Nazi] movement is the *Volk* and its community.

. . . Our banners proclaim our slogan, "The Volk must live on even if we must die. . . !" We want nothing for ourselves and everything for the community. We want only one right—the right to be able to serve. . . .[66]

Gottschewski criticized the old women's movement for its cooperation with women of other nations and its pacifism. Instead of discussing the goals and style of the conservative majority of the BDF (which resembled her own ideals), she blamed the BDF for opinions put forward by its ostracized feminist wing.

Gottschewski looked to Nazi men as the model for her organizing tactics because they formed a cross-class "male union" (Männerbund). The time had come for women to close ranks in their own interest in a Frauenbund. World War I had shaped men's consciousness; the Depression, and the desperate social conditions it produced, would create an equivalent rejuvenation among women. German men defended their nation against foreign foes; German women fought domestic, social decay. Gottschewski believed that women must form their own groups, modeled on male bonding and emulating Queen Louise of Prussia (a national heroine known for devotion to her husband and many children). Only unified women, she wrote, could offset a dangerous "exaggeration of masculine communal ideals. . . . What is the good of creating a new state if it fails to create new human beings? For over two thousand years, every revolution has failed because its leaders have failed to realize that the essential accomplishment of any revolution is not the seizure of power, but the rearing of a new generation."[67]

Gottschewski specifically criticized Nazi men for their close emotional ties to the "men's union." These intimate bonds (even if they were not sexual) by implication relegated women to a merely biological reproductive function. Far from being rebuked for arrogance, she was given the task of organizing girls and young women in the Hitler Youth movement. Under the banner of "spiritual motherhood," Gottschewski called on all women to devote themselves to motherly tasks, by which she meant not only biological motherhood, but all tasks requiring protection and nurture of the weak. Men, she implied, could never be relied upon to provide the community spirit that glued a Volk together.

As Diehl and Zander gathered supporters and Rogge-Börner published her journal and books, local leaders emerged in all Nazi strongholds to organize their own tiny groups. Without guidelines or standard rules, these women mobilized their neighbors and friends for National Socialism. In the name of motherhood and "Aryan" sisterhood, they struggled against democratic institutions. With no status in the Party and no chain of command linking them to the Brown House (Party headquarters) in

Munich, a motley collection of women's associations evolved a variety of dogmas and activities. Depending on her personality and the local conditions, a woman leader might organize her bailiwick with more independence than a man. The few reports from the late 1920s and early 1930s that have been preserved tell of women's satisfaction at breaking free of established charitable, religious, or educational organizations and being able to gather their own followers. Typically, women Nazis felt themselves to be poorer or less respected than the ladies in long-established associations. In the words of the 1931 guidelines for the Frauenschaft, Nazi women "avoided the false steps of the democratic-liberal-international women's movement which ignores the source of the woman's soul that comes from of God [italics in original] and nationality [*Volkstum*]. Instead they fight against men and ruin the deepest women's powers."[68] Nazi women, like men, organized themselves for battle and decried the passive and despairing people who refused to follow their call.

On the Woman Question, Nazis achieved no agreement whatsoever. Hitler showered sentimental praise on the "ideal mothers" of Germany, and Julius Streicher published soft-core pornography demeaning women. Nazi women themselves carved out their own sphere at the margins of Party activity, as well as on the fringes of bourgeois respectability. Among themselves they remained divided on several key issues, but they shared a pride in being women, found satisfaction in organizing for their cause, and believed deeply that biology determined character.

While they exalted women's special nature, they insisted that women dare not return meekly to their homes. Women belonged in their public "space." But what would it look like? Rogge-Börner and Gottschewski, perhaps because they were younger, openly criticized the stridently masculine élan of the Nazi Party, whereas Diehl and Zander said very little about the men's activities. Diehl saw Protestantism and Hitlerism as mutually reinforcing, whereas Zander, Rogge-Börner, and Gottschewski inclined more toward paganism. All saw themselves as nationalists, hated Communists, and made derogatory remarks about Jews. Equally important, they believed in radically separate spheres for men and women.

De facto autonomy allowed each leader the opportunity to develop her own talents and ideas. As long as the Party remained fairly small, their activities did not occasion much strife. As the ranks of the Nazi Party swelled, the structures that had served an organization of a few thousand dedicated members could no longer contain over a million recruits. The Brown House in Munich was flooded by complaints, questions, and demands. Letters from women Nazis bombarded the personnel office. Hitler delegated Gregor Strasser to place the organization on an entirely new footing. He hardly knew where to begin as he surveyed the scene, and, privately, leaders admitted that the Party was not at all as disciplined and unified as its image. The very fact that membership increased tenfold between 1930 and 1932 made chaos inevitable.

Divisions between women from Zander's and Diehl's organizations had turned into a sort of class warfare. "It is unbelievably difficult," wrote a Munich woman, "to try to defend this Nazi fortress . . . our enemies ridicule us . . . what's left is like the pulp of a squeezed lemon."[69] A Diehl supporter complained to Strasser of the "internal impoverishment" of the women's "freedom movement." Too much intellectualism, she warned, would undercut women's potential for action and spiritual inspiration.[70] Another disenchanted woman wrote, "I always thought that our Party work would be a sort of small example of what life would be like in the coming Reich. But I must tell you that if the Third Reich looks like our organization in Breslau, then every atom of energy and every spark of feeling has been wasted. . . ."[71] A woman leader from Lübeck complained, "It's simply unbearable not to have discipline. Just when you tighten the line of command from above, what happens? Splinter groups emerge!"[72] Success, it appeared, brought problems that the leaders had not foreseen. "We have dedicated all our energies to the cause and have doubled our membership," wrote women from southern Germany, "and now the rivalry is scandalous."[73] Frau Röpke from Chemnitz described the chaos that ruined their work. "Qualified women leaders have been fired. The treasury has even been snatched," by male leaders.[74]

Many women longed for the old days, when they closed ranks as an embattled minority, "when we worked with a select group dominated by energy and with an impeccable reputation." Mass success, this writer claimed, diluted the heart of the movement.[75] Addressing these problems, Strasser attempted to impose unity on the many branches of the women's movement.[76] Zander had already pledged her support to Strasser and reaffirmed her primary commitment to "removing women from the confusion of Party activities and turning their powers to meeting social needs."[77] Calling for the creation of "a nationalistic women's movement," Zander envisioned her German Women's Order as the official Nazi women's organization. Her followers praised her "discipline, courage, enthusiasm, and willingness to sacrifice." Zander, they agreed, had fought tirelessly for "motherhood and sisterhood."[78]

Strasser must have realized that Zander could not possibly unify Nazi women. Effusive praise for Zander was offset by bitter attacks. For example, Rogge-Börner told Zander,

All you care about is the glorification of your own image. You do not want to work collectively with anyone. All you want is creatures under you. You want mastery [*Herrschaft*]. Everyone who has the best interests of the Order at heart gets pushed aside. . . .You, Fräulein Zander, have to learn to recognize your own limitations. You cannot do *Everything!* Among other things you do not have the ability to edit a first-class, thorough, serious, and varied newspaper. Your remarkable and valuable talents lie in a totally different area.[79]

A long-time Nazi who stayed in Zander's SA home from February through June 1929 reported she wasted money, lied, and exploited her assistants. And then, the author added, she has the nerve to say, "I would starve myself for the SA."[80] Undaunted, Zander continued on her way.

The crescendo of attacks on Zander mounted, and the Party leaders dispatched an investigator to Berlin. Zander, it appeared, had allowed her organization to fall into debt, misappropriated membership dues, and kept a sloppy SA home. The party investigator, armed with a power of attorney, was shocked at the piles of unanswered mail, the low morale, and the haphazard record keeping. Zander, grasping the seriousness of these charges, blamed the Berlin SA, not her own conduct. In June 1931, a physician inspected her operation and reported to Joseph Goebbels, "The volunteers run around in their brown fantasy uniforms without the slightest connection with the National Socialist Sanitary Service and without sufficient training or skills. The irregular (*wilde*) activities of these pseudo-sisters must be regulated by our Sanitary Service."[81] He recommended dismissing the "psychopathological" Fräulein Zander and placing the rest home directly under his supervision. Extensive correspondence among Party leaders suggests that they fully understood Zander's limitations. Many found her newspaper, *Die Opferdienst*, embarrassing. Women members also complained about the image of Nazi women. For example, one woman demanded an end to "smoking and the mania for high fashion, dyed hair, extravagant clothes and hair styles, and flamboyant manner," and condemned the corruption of Zander's Frauenschaft, which, "with its gossip, pettiness, and bickering . . . and everything else lowly, obsequious, and misleading is destroying our womanhood. Every member of the women's movement must be educated to responsible behavior."[82] Surely the criticisms of the *Opferdienst* were justified, at least in our view. However, when compared to the slanderous *Der Stürmer* or even *Mein Kampf*, Zander's publication remained well within the limits of acceptable Nazi style. Zander, like other Nazi leaders, wrote to please her readers.

The Zander dispute placed Party leaders in an awkward situation. Her ability to recruit upward of five hundred new members a month and to raise funds placed Zander in a strong position. Even her enemies admitted they envied her "skills as an agitator, her flair for interpreting National Socialist doctrine." They admitted, too, that "the movement desperately needs a powerful woman leader." Thus, Zander remained at her post while a Party auditor inspected her operation and endeavored to bring order. When negative reports persisted, Goebbels dissolved Zander's organization entirely and considered bringing charges in the Party court. But despite a rather serious illness, Zander mounted a vigorous counterattack, charging men with jealousy. As soon as women succeeded at anything, she alleged, men suddenly became interested and then took over.[83] With Goebbels demanding her ouster and Zander creating dissent among women, Strasser compromised. Although he dissolved Zander's Women's Order, he named her the national leader of the newly created National Socialist Women's Organization, or Frauenschaft. By the winter of 1931–32, it appeared that Zander had maintained her own position against some of the most powerful men in the Party. Meanwhile, Strasser suffered a serious accident, and then in late 1932 resigned from the Party altogether.[84] From a broader perspective, it became clear that Zander would not mend her ways; and her appointment guaranteed not the end but the continuation of confusion among women.

One of the most difficult requests to understand is women's persistant requests for guidance in Nazi ideology, or, as they often phrased it, "in the thought of Adolf Hitler." Although it is difficult for us to take the content of Nazi doctrine seriously, women followers reported that they found the intellectual challenge exhilarating. Like religiously devout followers who desire guidance in reading the Scripture, women wanted access to Nazi doctrine. When they found *Mein Kampf* and Rosenberg's *Myth of the Twentieth Century* difficult to comprehend, they blamed their lack of intelligence and asked for help. Looking at the Nazi Party from the outside, women thought that ideological sophistication provided men with access to leadership; Nazi women foolishly believed that better training would advance their status as a separate branch of the masculine Party. From a more practical standpoint, women speakers and organizers routinely faced hecklers and quick-witted critics. They wanted greater familiarity with Nazi ideals to use as weapons in their own self-defense. "You just cannot believe how difficult it is to organize in a big city. To have to answer questions by bitter opponents and to face all sorts of encounters . . ." Without clear guidelines, one never knew when one risked being accused of heresy.[85] A woman speaker from a remote rural area who followed Guida Diehl requested ideological education so that she could translate *Mein Kampf*, or "My Struggle" into "Our Struggle." Implicitly she saw the individualist "my" as masculine and the collective "our" as feminine. She noted, "The activation of the male world has been achieved; but the woman's unique potential has not yet been tapped. The Party has not yet appreciated the faithfulness of its women and their emotional fanaticism." [86] Women had written their own books, tracts, pamphlets, and leaflets; but they wanted to come to grips with mainstream Nazi doctrine. They also faced for the first time the concerted opposition of non-Nazis who assailed their Party's misogyny.

On the eve of Hitler's electoral triumphs opponents issued blistering attacks on National Socialism and the Woman Question. Supported by funds from the Catholic Church, a psychologist published a scathing exposé of Nazi ideas about women; the moderate liberal People's Party issued warnings that women would be turned into breeding machines if the Nazis took over. Socialist women collected Nazi men's misogynistic statements and published them in a booklet that they then distributed to Socialist speakers. [87] These authors assumed that information and quotations would speak for themselves; any woman reading Nazi statements about women would, they assumed, recoil. This anti-Nazi propaganda makes sad reading. The authors naively assumed that women reading blatantly anti-feminist statements would waver in their attachment to Nazism. In reasonable, well-structured essays, non-Nazi authors criticized their enemy. Tragically, they neither comprehended nor countered the deep emotional basis of Hitler's appeal. Nazis depended upon speeches and rallies, holding their audiences with myth, bigotry, ritual, and violence. Election results showed that rationality did not prevail against passion and prejudice. Socialist leader Maria Juchacz despaired. "Powerful masses of unenlightened women threw themselves into the arms of political demagoguery," she wrote in January 1933. "The Depression has robbed us of more than bread and butter; an entire way of life has disappeared." [88] Overwhelmed by Nazi successes, anti-Nazi propaganda writers wondered how they could counter Hitler's dogma: Should they emulate it and promise better ways of restoring the family, stamping out decadence and revenging the Versailles Treaty? Or should they dare to defend a new vision of the family, looser definitions of morality, and peaceful coexistence with former enemy nations? Anti-Nazi propaganda presages a tragic future from another perspective as well. Although rival parties belatedly criticized the Nazis' hostility toward women, no similar attack on anti-Semitism emerged from the liberal or Marxist press. From the first, Hitler's opponents directly attacked his more traditional political opinions, but the core of his social revolution (sex and race) remained largely unnoticed.

While SA men marched, Nazi women sponsored meetings, rallies, charitable projects, and speeches. Men boasted about military conquest;

women launched a powerful mothers' offensive. Men played soldier; women compared themselves to Christians in the catacombs. Both fantasies seem rather silly to us. As it turned out, SA men's illusions about a military revolution proved to be as misplaced as women's dreams of "motherly" autonomy. Women's self-glorification as wielders of an unseen power strikes us as naive, but these women, so very powerless in objective ways, fabricated a view of the world peopled by hidden manipulators. Most of Hitler's followers believed in the myth of hidden Jewish networks working against them. Women inverted the myth and depicted themselves as clandestine, superidealistic, and potentially powerful. Such fantasies resembled the Reich Association of Housewives' proclamations about their silent influence and the middle-class women's visions of "spiritual motherliness." Christians looked forward to the day of judgment when the meek will inherit the earth. Nazi women blended such visions into an exaggerated sense of self-importance on earth. One representative of the Nazi Party told a London audience, "We firmly believe that the entire German womanhood is able really to 'make' the entire German manhood. This great power put into women's hands involves great responsibilities and sacred obligations which we are determined to shoulder."[89] Guida Diehl phrased it simply. "The truly Germanic woman is a fighter. She fights from mother love." How did she fight? For what did she fight? No one could be sure.

Since the "big world" of man and the "little world" of woman rarely overlapped before 1933, differences coexisted without causing much friction. Paradoxically, the two most emotionally laden themes in Nazi rhetoric, The Jewish Question and the Woman Question, were unattached to any concrete suggestions about implementation. This combination of emotional intensity and doctrinal fluidity provided an extraordinary opportunity for individual interpretation in a supposedly monolithic party. Within the Nazi world, opinions could coexist in a hodgepodge of prejudices and opinions, as long as everyone swore total obedience to the *person* of Adolf Hitler. The disarray that contemporaries sometimes found confusing gave ambitious leaders scope for their energy and inventiveness. Women, as the most overlooked category of the subculture, enjoyed the greatest latitude in action and ideas. Unconcerned about programmatic applications of Hitler's ideas, Nazi women enjoyed unparalleled freedom from male scrutiny while at the same time feeling they participated in a great religious-political revival. Women mistakenly attributed their autonomy to their own tactical prowess. Nazi victory would put their arrogance to the test.

After Hitler became dictator, promises had to be translated into policy; but in the frantic campaigns of 1930–33, all opinions that drew votes were accepted. Some debated the definition of "feminine" and "female," but generally few quibbled about such terms.[90] Estimates of the size of women's *Lebensraum* varied widely, but to everyone the term connoted a world of women that lay beyond the power, violence, and materialism of men's "space." How far would it be from men's power? Could women claim rights to education and employment? Could mothers? What was a "motherly" fighter? Would women command a separate bureaucratic domain? There were no answers.

Whatever form the women's world would take after the Nazi revolution, women Nazis expected to lead it. They hated the New Woman, but did not under any circumstances dream of returning women to narrow housewifely tasks. In the United States, we see the opposition between the New Woman and the return to the happy homemaker as a generational conflict between the women of the pre–World War II generation and their daughters' return to domesticity in the 1950s. In *The Feminine Mystique*, Betty Friedan described the New Women, who created "with a gay determined spirit a new identity for women—a life of their own," and asked why that determination dissolved. Why, she wondered, did the housewife image propagated by Nazi Germany come to prevail in the victorious United States? "Not long ago, women dreamed and fought for equality, their own place in the world. What happened to their dreams; when did women decide to give up the world and go back home?"[91] By looking more closely at those German women, we see that Friedan asked the wrong questions. In Germany during the 1920s, the housewife and the New Woman coexisted and contended for influence. But the housewife—even the Nazi housewife—did not see herself as "just" a suburban homemaker, or as her husband's docile servant. She did not glorify a life spent portaging children to the swimming pool, cooking tasty dinners for tired husbands, and keeping dust-free homes. The privatized motherhood analyzed by Friedan depended upon several post-1945 developments, such as single-family houses, with an automobile in every garage and a television in every living room. Nazi women conceived an intensely communal vision of motherhood that aimed at incorporating women into civic activities, welfare work, patriotic and folk organizations, and housewives' associations. They despised the New Woman because her image epitomized selfishness and autonomy. But they admired her vigor and ambition.

Feeling endangered and disoriented in the Depression, women Nazis looked to a powerful state to defend their sphere, not thinking that such a state would ultimately invade their *Lebensraum* and subvert their goals. Four decades after the demise of her administration, Scholtz-Klink told me that women belong in the public sphere only as wives and mothers.

She perceived feminine space not in the narrow confines of the family, but in a vast network of welfare, cultural, educational, and health-care institutions.

The confrontation between conservatives and the New Woman during the 1920s bears a similarity to the contemporary disagreement between fundamentalists and proponents of women's right to control their reproduction. Marianne Weber, feminist and politician, looked back on the 1920s. How sad it had been, she recalled, when after more than a decade of battling against men to win women's equality she looked backward and saw masses of women who opposed their own emancipation. "As we stride forward, we also have to look watchfully over our shoulder."[92] When Weber looked over her shoulder, she saw masses of women in brown.

Nazi women leaders fled from freedom and rushed to the security of group solidarity. One young woman summarized the collectivist mentality that to her seemed revolutionary in the context of Weimar emancipation.

> We will fight to uphold forever the living values of the Family, the Race and the Earth [*Scholle*]. In other words, we do not stand on the political front with the man like Marxist women do. Nor do we engage in politics like the fanatics in the women's rights movement. We do not demonstrate or call congresses, we do not care to meddle in day-to-day politics. But we will not let anyone play with us or degrade what goes on around us. We want to be open to a politics of the inner life. We have an unconscious, sure voice inside us . . . the feeling of responsibility. . . . We want to build the new *Volksgemeinschaft* [racial community]. . . . We want revolution, transformation, and constructive work.[93]

Women in the National Socialist movement expressed disillusionment with an emancipation they had not desired in the first place. They saw their democracy as expedient at best and dangerous at worst. When the economy cut away the material underpinnings of their homes, traditionalist women denounced the cruel and materialistic "system" that had set them free. These women created an alternative vision of an authoritarian state and strong families that would shelter them against alienation, poverty, and chaos.

5

"OLD-TIMERS" IN THE NEW STATE

The new things I wanted to happen were really a longing for old things to come back.

> —Pearl Buck, quoting a young German woman in the 1920s in *The Way It Happens*

The Weimar period, so scathingly denounced by women Nazis for its cultural decadence, sexual license, materialism, and disorder, ironically turned out to have been a halcyon era for those women Nazis. Weimar liberalism not only provided them with a target for their outrage, it gave them freedom to organize and protest. The Nazi Party, too, inadvertently allowed women Nazis wide latitude for their activities. Just as Hitler and his small band of fanatics operated at the very edge of politics, women leaders and their tiny groups worked at the periphery of the National Socialist Party. Excluded and ignored by male leaders, women formed their own movement with virtually no acknowledgment or interference from men. Turning their backs on the men who ignored them, women used the dominant male rhetoric to fashion their own message. Since Nazi dogma said so little about women's issues, Nazi women created on an empty canvas, developing several versions of Hitler's ideology and gaining experience as organizers, public speakers, and fund raisers.

Success for the Nazi Party, however, spelled doom for its women members. When their numbers had been small and their cause hopeless, desperation had welded them together. In 1932, with nearly 14 million voters, 850,000 Party members, and 400,000 SA men, chief party organizer Strasser undertook a thorough reorganization of the Party structure. This meant that women fell under men's scrutiny.

In the summer of 1932, women Nazis found themselves in much the same situation as Liberal and Socialist women's-rights leaders in 1919. Victory brought divisiveness and competition to organizations that had previously coexisted with little friction. In the "old days," their male colleagues accepted whatever contributions women made and did not bother to monitor their interpretations of Nazi doctrine. Women Nazis, under the protective brown coloring of fervent oaths to Hitler, had forged a subtext that spoke to women's special needs. Zander's crude bombast, Diehl's pretentious theories, Gottschewski's dreams of a fighting female community, and Rogge-Börner's arrogant racial notions coexisted and drew varied constituencies to the cause.

The Weimar Constitution guaranteed women Nazis freedom of speech, and Nazi men's disregard provided them with considerable liberty that they foolishly took for granted. While every early leader insisted on biologically based contrasts between masculine and feminine, none envisioned women's returning to their *Kinder, Küche,* and *Kirche* (children, kitchen, and church) after victory. Instead, they imagined they could create a female *Lebensraum* in public (not political) life, with "No Trespassing" signs posted at the borders. The success of Zander, Diehl, Gottschewski, Rogge-Börner, and scores of regional leaders gave women

Nazis the false hope that a strong woman could prevail against the Party machine. Having grown accustomed to operating beyond the margins of the male Party, Nazi women looked forward to Hitler's victory and the day when they could translate their informal influence into formal power. The Nazi Revolution, far from returning women Nazis to their hearths, would, they hoped, release them into national power as administrators, racial scientists, educators, propagandists, and social workers. By blending matriarchal strength with feminine zeal, one publicist declared, the Nazi revolution, would produce "a female race that is hard on itself, disciplined, and brave; but which has not lost womanly goodness and the redeeming majesty of earlier priestesses." Shaping Nazi propaganda to their own needs, women rationalized their expectations. After all, did not Hitler himself praise women's constancy and chastise men (who he said were more intelligent) for being less stable? "Masculine will," women concluded, had to achieve political victory; but "feminine faith" alone could restore domestic harmony in the wake of revolutionary violence. Men would coerce, women would convince.

Organizationally, Nazi women found themselves in an anomalous situation in the summer of 1932. On the one hand, Strasser had elevated Zander to national prominence and deputized Diehl as cultural chief; but on the other hand, each regional organization operated directly under the supervision of its male leader, or Gauleiter. Twice in 1932 women regional leaders met at national conferences to work out differences and compare strategies. Strasser praised women, and even called for a "movement of women's renewal" that would draw followers from all classes. Strasser assured women they would retain their right to jobs "except as soldiers and politicians [because] the Third Reich will not rest on half the *Volk*."[1] In the summer of 1932, the first national newsletter for women, the NS *Frauenwarte*, was established.

At election time, Nazi publicity for women voters denounced rival parties' accusations that Nazi men were misogynists. Liberal and Nationalist anti-Nazis, one broadside alleged, claimed Hitler intended to deprive women of rights and starve out women who worked outside their homes. Far from it, the author declared. "We want to win back for the German women the meaning which Nature gave to her. We want the man to earn the just wage he deserves so he can found a family. . . . Hundreds and thousands of women and girls, who today are forced to work, will be granted their real voice. Isn't that a healthy point of view?"[2] Zander took the effort a step further and in 1932 proposed that the Party run women candidates to offset its negative image. Strasser reacted at once. "The purely political battle remains the man's duty."[3] Despite this rebuff, the very fact that men paid attention to the Woman Question at all had important consequences. Starting in the fall of 1932, Strasser invited women from Zander's office to attend meetings with Party officials in charge of health and education, rural affairs, worker organization, and civil service. Accordingly, the Frauenschaft was elevated to Main Office status in the Party structure; within Zander's office new divisions were created that reflected the leaders' decision to keep women in public life and out of politics. Welfare and youth, hygiene and employment, consumer affairs and national economy, and public relations/indoctrination constituted the major subdepartments.[4]

Strasser's attention did not, however, end the rivalries among various women leaders. In addition to the endemic tensions between Gaulieters and national leaders, and between Zander and Diehl; Gottschewski and her League of German Girls (BDM) fought constantly with Baldur von Schirach, the boys' Hitler Youth leader for administrative control. The Frauenschaft declared that the principle of sex segregation mandated that "Girls belong to women."[5] Käte Auerbach, the newly appointed co-editor of the NS *Frauenwarte*, engaged in steady recriminations against Diehl and Zander. Thus, growing membership lists and official Party recognition exacerbated tensions and dampened morale within leadership of the Nazi women's world. The decentralized organization which had fostered autonomy among grassroots women produced disillusionment as women's organizations entered into the ranks of the official Party structure.

Women's discouraging reports from the fall of 1932 also reflected a more general malaise among Party members. For the first time since the beginning of the Depression, economic indexes edged up slightly and the Nazi vote fell by 2 million votes between July and November. That meant 34 fewer seats in the Reichstag and demoralization among Nazi leaders.[6] As the seemingly unstoppable Nazi crusade slowed and came to a standstill, Party members feared (and opponents hoped) that Hitler's opportunity had come and gone. *The New York Times* reported, "(T)here is not the slightest doubt that Hitler's chances to be Mussolini are gone. Whatever the future may hold for Hitler, he will not be the dictator of Germany. That, it has been made clear to him, is *verboten*."[7] Many Nazi voters abandoned the party that promised so much and delivered so little. They had never been stable as a voting bloc anyway, and observers believed that the economic upswing restored Germans' faith in the democratic process, or at least inspired them to support moderate Parties.[8]

At Nazi Party headquarters in Munich, no one could see a way out. The tidal wave of Nazi popularity had broken; the treasury was empty; and Hitler fell into depressions so deep that he threatened to shoot himself. With too many followers to stage a coup and too few to win a majority, Party leaders were hamstrung. December elections in Thuringia showed a 40 percent decline in Nazi popularity, and Goebbels noted, "The situation is . . . catastrophic!" Party disagreements eroded morale. In December, too, Hitler lost his brilliant organizer, Gregor Strasser, who had little use for the brawling, unruly SA. Accusing Hitler of moving "toward acts of violence and a German rubble heap," Strasser left the Party.[9] Goebbels confessed, "The most terrible loneliness is descending on me like dark hopelessness." Looking back on the previous few months, he voiced the despair shared by all Nazis. "The year 1932 has been one interminable streak of bad luck. . . . All prospects and hopes have completely vanished. We are all greatly depressed, mostly because of the danger of the whole party falling apart and all our work having been in vain."[10]

The rank and file shared these doubts. A Nazi woman in Berlin voiced the feeling of thousands when she decided politics offered no solution to anything. It had become too chaotic. "One cabinet followed another; one election came after the next; in a dozen years we had fifteen governments. . . . Our beloved Hitler had to suffer through hard times. How much we wanted to shake his hand to encourage him not to give up."[11] As the Nazi Party headed for apparent disaster, the government faced a new political crisis.

President Hindenburg's recently appointed Chancellor, General Kurt von Schleicher, could not create a cabinet that commanded Reichstag support. This meant that Hindenburg used the power of Article 48 and became a virtual dictator. But the elderly President had taken an oath to democracy and realized he needed a cabinet with a broader political base. Would Hindenburg look to the democratic left or radical right when he appointed his next cabinet and Chancellor? Following advice from Nationalist advisers, Hindenburg in late January invited Hitler (whom he had once denigrated as that "Bohemian lance coporal") to become Chancellor of the Reich and form a cabinet with Reichstag support. The aristocrats close to Hindenburg sneered at Hitler for being ill-bred, uncouth, and a crackpot, far less threatening, they said, than a Communist or a Socialist. "No danger at all," smirked former Chancellor Franz von Papen. "We have hired him for our act. In two months' time we'll have pushed Hitler so far into the corner, he'll be squeaking."[12] During the autumn of 1931, a high-ranking general deemed Hitler "an interesting man and an outstanding speaker with plans so fantastic that he needs bringing down to earth."[13] One of the few voices on the right that criticized the new Führer was a man who knew him well from the early days of the Beer Hall Putsch, General Erich von Ludendorff, who called Hitler "one of the greatest demagogues of all time" and told a Nazi friend this "damnable man will plunge our Reich into the abyss and bring inconceivable misery down upon our nation. Coming generations will curse you in your grave because of this action."[14] The popular and politically liberal German novelist Vicki Baum recalled how she and her friends had laughed at "this nut, this idiot, this *Hanswurst*." Later she understood that she had mistaken Hitler's greatest strength for his weakness when she wrote, "He was a child of the *Volk* and he knew just what the *Volk* wanted."[15] A harmless—even crackpot—image, combined with shrewd political sense, made Hitler a dangerous enemy.

For months Hitler had boasted that he would accept the chancellorship only if a majority of cabinet posts went to his supporters. But by January 1933 he had become so nervous that he accepted the post with only three of nine cabinet posts. No wonder conservatives cracked jokes about "Hindenburg's prisoner." Meanwhile, Hitler did not behave as if he had become anyone's prisoner, and displayed an uncanny ability to succeed just when people believed his luck had run out. Officially, Hitler had only been named Chancellor, but the Party behaved as if he had won an unqualified victory. Storm troopers celebrated his appointment with a seven-hour torchlight parade through the Brandenburg Gate in Berlin. Everywhere in Germany Nazis demonstrated, marched, and chanted.[16] Even non-Nazis thrilled to the spectacle. One bystander vividly recalls the impression the parades made on her at the age of fifteen.

> On the evening of January 30 my parents took us children . . . into the centre of the city. There we witnessed the torchlight procession. . . . Some of the uncanny feel of that night remains with me even today. The crashing tread of the feet, the sombre pomp of the red-and-black flags, the flickering light from the torches on the faces and the songs with melodies that were at once aggressive and sentimental. For hours the columns marched by. . . . At one point somebody suddenly leaped from the ranks of the marchers and struck a man who had been standing only a few paces away from us. Perhaps he had made a hostile remark. I saw him fall to the ground with blood streaming down his face and I heard him cry out. . . . The image haunted me for days. The horror it inspired in me was almost imperceptibly spiced with an intoxicating joy. "For the flag we are ready to die," the torch-bearers had sung. . . . It was a matter of life and death . . . I know I was overcome with a burning desire to belong to these people for whom it was a matter of life and death.
>
> I longed to hurl myself into this current, to be submerged and borne along by it.[17]

Renate Finckh, who was twelve in 1933, recalled forty years later the impact of Hitler's success on her family. Her parents had joined the Nazi

Party in the 1920s. "They both agreed. And their unanimity gave their marriage a new meaning." The parents' shared faith in the future after 1933 affected the daughter. "This Führer must be a wonderful man, if he could make my parents so happy. After the seizure of power the feeling at home was transformed into hope and triumph. They had been right all along. Now everything would get better."[18]

Nazi women who had campaigned for the Party before 1933 recalled their ecstasy at Hitler's seizure of power in language very much like Hitler's own rambling and emotional speeches. Longtime Nazi Party member Margarethe Schrimpff, in her essay for the Abel contest, rejoiced after the "long, difficult, and bloody battle." She and millions of Nazis believed they deserved their victory because the fight had been so hard.

> We wept with happiness and joy and could scarcely believe that our beloved Führer stood at the helm of the Reich. . . . A wedding [*Hochzeit*] of profound enthusiasm gripped the entire nation. A magnetic power radiated everywhere and eliminated the last traces of internal resistance. The Führer's electoral success showed that a new will to life would determine German history in the future. We were gripped by an inexpressible joy [*Hochgefühl*] when we saw our banners, once scorned and belittled, flying high on all public buildings. Enraptured, we watched enlightened workers burning their red flags in the marketplace.[19]

Louise Solmitz, a conservative who gradually came to see Hitler as Germany's only hope, recalls the victory in Hamburg. At 10 P.M. SA men marched together with the gray-shirted veteran's organization The Steel Helmets.

> 20,000 brown shirts followed each other like waves in the sea, their faces shone with enthusiasm in the torch light. . . . they sang battle songs, like "The Republic Is Shit." . . . We were drunk with enthusiasm, blinded by the light of the torches right in our faces, and always enveloped in their vapor as in a cloud of sweet incense. And in front of us men, men, men, brightly colored . . . a torrent![20]

As we read these accounts, we cannot help but wonder why non-Nazis did not become more alarmed at this show of utter dedication to a violent movement. Surely they had the power to oppose the Nazis. With over 5 million members, the predominantly Marxist trade union network outnumbered Nazi Party membership five to one. Over 600,000 workers belonged to Christian (mainly Catholic) trade unions that vehemently criticized Hitler's cabinet in February. They did not take up arms to defend the Republic. Nor did liberals. Many admired the Nazis' élan and shared their antisocialism. Besides, they told themselves, because the new Chancellor controlled only three positions in the Cabinet, they had little to fear. Superficially, their reasoning seemed impeccable. Hindenburg, the national hero, commanded the army and had pledged to defend the republic. These rational considerations overlooked Hitler's own analysis of the situation. "I have an advantage over my great opponent. The President is eighty-five years old, whereas I am forty-three. . . . I also have the conviction and the sense of certainty that nothing whatever can harm me, because I know that I have been appointed by Providence to fulfill my task. My will is tenacious, untamed and unshakeable."²¹ In addition, like the Great Powers that appeased German aggression in the late 1930s, Hitler's domestic enemies could not form a solid front against a common threat because they failed to perceive Hitler's longterm motives. Most importantly, the habit of democracy died slowly, and they still believed that elections counted for something and anticipated that if a majority of voters expressed their opposition, Hitler would fade from power. Hitler's decision to cloak his revolution in sham "legality" played into Germans' faith in law and orderliness.

Germans experiencing the turmoil of Depression and political collapse did not see the situation clearly. But surely, we think, foreign observers displayed more sense. They did not. Typically, journalists saw this charlatan as more foolish than dangerous. American writer Dorothy Thompson reported, "A little man has arisen in Germany. He has no weapons to speak of. A few pistols, some charged with water or caps; a few rifles; some brass knuckles."²² She scoffed at the idea he might be appointed Chancellor. "Oh Dolf! Adolf! You will be out of luck." Hitler's statements, so outrageously extreme, simply could not be taken seriously. A *New York Times* reporter assured his readers that Hitler would fulfill his nationalist promises "by emulating Mahatma Gandhi," leading "60 million Germans girding their loins with hand-woven cloth" to achieve 'total autarky.' "²³

One explanation of Germans' and foreigners' myopia lies in Hitler's brilliant decision to play up his role as the only force capable of stopping the Communist threat. In February 1933 (as at the Munich conference in 1938), Hitler warned that emasculated democracy could not hold back the tide of world Marxism. If he were not Chancellor, he told Germans just forty-eight hours after becoming Chancellor, revolution would sweep the continent. "Fourteen years of Marxism have ruined Germany; one year of Bolshevism would destroy her. The richest and fairest territories of the world would be turned into a smoking heap of ruins. Even the sufferings of the last decade and a half could not be compared to the misery of a Europe in the heart of which the red flag of destruction has been hoisted."[24] Behind the barrage of violent anti-Communist rhetoric, Hitler did not personally issue edicts against his enemies during the first weeks of power. Goebbels explained the purpose of this temporary truce in a diary entry dated January 30, 1933. "For the present we intend to refrain from direct countermeasures against the Communists. First, a Bolshevist attempt at revolution must flare up. Then we will strike at the proper moment."[25]

The wolf that plotted to destroy the sheep remained cautious. Then, during the night of February 27, the threat of revolution appeared when fire destroyed the Reichstag Building. Hitler, the master hypnotist, used the event to divert Germans' attention from Nazi terror by accusing the Communists of revolution. "Now I have them!" he exulted. One of his colleagues recalls Hitler's reaction.

> Hitler turned to the assemblage. Now I saw that his face was flaming red from excitement and the heat which had accumulated in the dome. As if he were going to burst, he screamed in an utterly uncontrolled manner such as I had never before witnessed in him. "Now there can be no mercy; whoever gets in our way will be cut down. The German *Volk* will not put up with leniency. Every Communist functionary will be shot wherever we find him. The Communist deputies must be hanged this very night. Every one in alliance with the Communists is to be arrested. We are not going to spare the Social Democrats . . . either!"[26]

Here we see Hitler blending a level of hysteria that our culture stereotypes as feminine with masculine violence. His deputies converted the mood into action. As Prussian Minister of Interior, Hermann Göring appointed 4,000 SA men as Berlin policemen and deputized 22,000 former SA men as assistants. He unleashed a massive attack on all suspects, declaring, "Every bullet that is now fired from the barrel of a police pistol is my bullet. If that is called murder, then I have committed murder. I take responsibility for it. . . . My business is to annihilate and exterminate."[27]

On the morning after the fire, Hitler rushed into Hindenburg's office with an emergency edict that cancelled constitutional safeguards for everyone. Hindenburg signed. This degree, euphemistically named "For the Defense against Communist Acts of Violence Endangering the State," remained in effect until June 1945.[28] Next Hitler used government funds in a massive Nazi electoral campaign designed to produce a landslide victory for the Party in the upcoming March Reichstag elections. Propaganda told the Germans "in hard hammer blows" to vote against Marxism. Hitler told Germans on the national radio: "Be proud once again. Now you are no longer unfree and enslaved; now you are free again. . . . Give thanks to God." Germans were asked to sacrifice their individual freedoms in the name of national liberation from bondage to the victors of World War I.

The National Socialist election campaign continued, aided by police intimidation and financed by government funds. Party publicity made Nazi aims clear. Women could have no doubts about their future in Nazi society. Rhetoric about men's and women's "equality in sacrifice" made it clear that this was the *only* kind of equality women might expect. "The thousands of women in our ranks, who actively participated with full equality from the beginning, decisively reject the dubious honor of joining the 'filth line' in parliamentary fights. As for the rest (i.e. nonparliamentary issues), we unconditionally recognize . . . the woman as companion of the man with perfectly equal rights in political life."[29] Behind the double-talk, the Nazis told women that they could participate equally in obligations without sharing the spoils. But Nazi women could ignore the threat because after Hitler eliminated *all* democratic institutions, elected office would lose its meaning for everyone anyway.

The election returns stunned Nazi leaders. Even though the SA and Göring's police force attacked their opponents, smashed their presses, outlawed their rallies, and confiscated their treasuries, the National Socialist Party did not win half of the vote. In fact, the Nazi vote increased only 7 percent above its previous high of 37 percent in July 1932.[30] A majority of German voters repudiated Hitler, even after Hindenburg had named him Chancellor. The chance to stop Hitler passed to the Reichstag.

Committed to maintaining the image of legality, Hitler needed a two-thirds Reichstag majority to suspend the Constitution. Even with the support of the 52 Nationalist deputies, Hitler needed to recruit more followers. The Catholic Center Party controlled the essential 73 seats. After much deliberating and negotiating, Monsignor Ludwig Kass, the head of the Party, led his delegation into the Nazi camp. Other, smaller, conservative parties and the remains of the Democratic Party followed suit. Only Otto Wels, chief of the Socialist delegation, dared to speak out against Hitler at the Reichstag session that was to vote Hitler four-year dictatorial powers. Wels swore to defend German honor by opposing Nazi dictatorship. Hitler mounted the podium and screamed,

> You seem to have forgotten that for years our shirts were ripped off our backs because you did not like the color. . . . For years your friends kept saying that I was only a housepainter. . . . You even threatened to drive

me out of Germany with a dog whip. . . . Gentlemen, the star of Germany will rise and yours will sink. . . . In the life of nations, what is rotten and old and feeble passes and does not come again. . . . Germany shall be free but not through you.[31]

The state broadcasting system carried the Wels-Hitler altercations into millions of German homes. Listeners heard the cheers of the Reichstag, the Nationalists' expressions of deepest gratitude for "so brilliantly putting Marxist leader Wels in his place." When the vote was called, the Reichstag delegates did what their constituencies had refused to do: Over two-thirds of all delegates (441) voted to give Hitler dictatorial powers for four years. Because the 81 Communist delegates had been arrested or detained, and 26 Socialist leaders jailed, the 94 Socialists who managed to arrive at the Reichstag session stood alone in opposition to the law granting Hitler dictatorial power for four years, officially named the Law for the Removal of the Distress of *Volk* and Reich.

Distress had just begun for millions who opposed Nazism. On March 31, every organization in Germany was required to submit to Nazification, which, in practice, meant the purge of all Jewish members and submission to Nazi control. Within months, non-Nazi organizations had been outlawed and dissident leaders jailed or exiled; "dangerous" books had been fed to the bonfires; and the press entirely censored. Hitler did not bother to abolish the Weimar Constitution. It was not worth his trouble. Once again, we might expect the foreign press to have recorded alarm at the state of affairs. Two days after Hitler's appointment, the *Le Temps* correspondent described Hitler as "merely an agitator" and doubted that he would ever become "a great politician like Mussolini."[32] The London *Times* cautiously suggested, "He deserves a chance of showing that he is something more than an agitator and an orator."[33] During the following weeks, *The Times* of London and *Le Temps* reported arrests, illegal searches and torture, as well as the mounting toll of political murder in their back pages. But in the front-page headlines, a new theme appeared. As the scale of repression mounted, reporters reclassified it from "unacceptable," within a democratic constitutional context, to "disciplined" and "controlled" within a revolutionary dictatorial setting. As its image underwent reclassification from hooligans to revolutionaries, the SA became more, not less, acceptable. Before March 1933, Hitler (as a "rabble rouser") had drawn harsh criticism from the foreign press. After March, however, reporters and statesmen judged him by new standards. *The Times* of London announced "the Nazi steam roller" had destroyed all opposition, leaving behind "only a brown uniformity." But rather than condemn the violence that accompanied so popular a "steam roller," reporters admired the order it created. "No one expects revolutions to be made with rose water."[34] *Le Temps*, which had deplored every storm-trooper excess until January 1933, changed its tone. Hitler became a moderate, with an extraordinary commitment to democracy simply because he allowed the March elections to take place at all. "No dictatorship in history has seen such a spectacle as this."[35]

As a ruffian upstart, Hitler's brutality had been denounced by the foreign press; as a revolutionary dictator, he won praise for his moderation. The London *Times* reported in March,

> All things considered, what may be regarded as tantamount to a revolution . . . has passed with remarkably little unpleasant incident. It is admitted that absolutely iron control over every unit of so vast a movement is impossible especially in view of the persecution to which the Nazis were exposed in their own opposition days [and] the party propaganda which . . . has set unstable minds aglow with hatred. . . . This movement is to be congratulated on the maintenance of a discipline which has enabled the election and other tense occasions to pass without any outbreak of violence on a large scale.[36]

Gradually, news of repression disappeared. "The everyday life of the average citizens," reported *The Times* of London, "is quite normal. . . . Residents and visitors see little or nothing of the violent outbursts and suffer no harm or inconvenience. . . ."[37]

Tourists in Germany during the spring of 1933 invariably commented on the astonishing impact of Nazi rule. Berlin, which during the 1920s had played host to Europe's avant-garde, after March 1933 epitomized order and tradition. A Swedish businessman who had traveled often to Germany recalled that in the old days, the capital had been "so flooded with pornography, verbal and pictorial," that it seemed "the German people concentrated all their attention upon the sexual life and especially its abnormalities." In the "new" Berlin of 1933, another impression superimposed itself upon tawdry images from the past. "The iron broom has made a clean sweep. . . . One has now the positive feeling that decency and good taste have won a victory." As if by a miracle, the "unwholesome, nasty and perverse" departed from public view.[38] May Day, once the occasion for labor demonstrations in "red Berlin," had been transformed into a spring festival. In past years, unless this socialist holiday fell on a Sunday, participants risked reprisals and lost a day's wages. Rather than banishing this Marxist rite, Hitler claimed it as his own by declaring it an official paid holiday. While the Gestapo arrested labor leaders, Hitler orchestrated a working-class celebration. Foreign reporters believed the farce. The London *Times* correspondent, for example, reported, "Instead of a rather meagre demonstration" as in the past, a "prodigious gathering" of one million workers massed on the runways of Berlin's Tempelhof Airport, "secure in the knowledge that they would receive a paid holiday. . . . Great columns of workers marched; the drabbest streets [became] gay and colored valleys," festooned with pine boughs, "spring foliage and a forest of flags." A zeppelin hovered in the cloudless sky while planes flew low overhead, "with the throb of their engines" echoing through the city. Berliners, the correspondent noted, "like the flags, the hum and the bustle, the noise in the air, the uniforms, bands and crowds." Everywhere in Germany, citizens heard their Führer promise "unity of spirit, mind and fist; of workman, peasant and bourgeois." [39] Once again, as in the days when Ilya Ehrenburg visited Berlin, desperation remained behind the scenes.

Even Hitler seemed surprised at how effortless victory had been. In early July, he told a Westphalian audience, "One would never have thought so miserable a collapse possible." For years his team had pulled hard in the political tug of war. Suddenly, the other side dropped the rope. Victory caught the Nazi leadership off guard. True, Strasser had organized the Party like a state within a state, with ministers, offices, and specialized responsibilities. But how would the Party actually take over the administration of an entire nation? The Depression continued, unemployment remained at about 30 percent, and people wanted action. Hitler had tailored his slogans and promises to win elections and had given no thought to implementation. Radios blared propaganda about the two key components in Hitler's racial revolution, the woman and the Jew, but no clear policy emerged. While casting about for domestic policies, Hitler diverted public attention to foreign successes. To the astonishment of enemies and supporters alike, he projected a new image of conciliation. In the "old days" before 1933, the Nazis had blustered about rearming Germany and "ripping up the Treaty of Versailles." But as Chancellor, Hitler shifted his rhetorical pace. In a speech that William Shirer called "one of the greatest of his career," Hitler called for international disarmament, swearing that "Germany is entirely ready to renounce all offensive weapons if the armed nations on their side will destroy their offensive weapons." War, he said, was "unthinkable . . . because it would cause the collapse of the present order" in Europe.[40] "The world was enchanted," Shirer reported. In London, Washington, and even Paris conservative and liberal newspapers demanded that Hitler be "given a chance" and "taken at his word." What a relief to hear Hitler tell the world, "Germany is not in need of rehabilitation on the battlefield."

Before Hitler's advisers settled on economic policy, they cultivated women's support by presenting themselves as the very soul of respectability on the Woman Question. No leader hinted that women would be deprived of the rights granted in the Weimar Constitution. Instead, Hitler defended traditional family values, which enhanced his claims to respectability and his image as the strong man of peace. Nazi propagandists paid homage to "the woman" and "the mother," and longtime women Nazis anticipated that their time had come to play a decisive and official role in the Nazi state. In an essay for Abel's study, one woman recalled, "The external battle has ended and we have been thrown into a new battle for a victory over the total German *Volk*. We want more than anything else to restore the outlook of the youth to . . . see their lives as sacrifice and duty so they can stride securely into the future."[41] Moving the "battle" out of the streets and into the hearts and minds, Nazi women prepared to launch a psychological revolution that would penetrate the private lives of all Germans. Despite the wide range of opinion among Nazi women leaders, they shared two expectations: that they would expand their power by creating a separate women's sphere in Nazi society and that they would face strong opposition from women's rights and religious organizations. Both proved false. Unlike Socialist, Communist, pacifist, and radical feminist associations, middle-class organizations were not outlawed but, on the contrary, given a chance to cooperate with the new government. After the victory in January, Nazi women leaders expected strong backing from a powerful state in their endeavors. Of course, they did not expect to participate in formal politics, but that did not mean they wanted to return to their homes. As one woman put it, "I would never have campaigned for Hitler at all if I had thought that we women would not be needed in the new state."[42]

Before becoming Chancellor, Hitler had carefully groomed his deputies for the day when they would carry ministers' portfolios. Observers noted that the Party itself was organized more like a "shadow state" than a political organization. Paradoxically, but not surprisingly, Hitler had given no thought whatsoever to the female half of his sex-segregated society, even though his racial schemes called for women's devoted participation, and his ambition to indoctrinate all children depended upon mothers' cooperation. Women leaders from the pre-1933 days, however, had given a great deal of thought to structuring their world. While differing widely on key issues, all agreed that women Nazis would lead a public assault on private life in the Third Reich. The female vanguard of Hitler's movement awaited orders from on high; but none came. So chaotic was the administration in 1933 that for a brief period the wife of the Propaganda Minister became the spokeswoman for Nazi leaders. Magda Goebbels, who had never evidenced the slightest interest in women's concerns, predicted that in the new state, women would enjoy access to all occupations except the military, law, and politics, which "required a cold, clear objectivity alien to women's warm and sensitive nature."[43] Women who feared they would be driven from public life must have felt relieved. But they ought to have sensed trouble when a minister's wife, rather than a woman leader, became the government mouthpiece. In fact, the Nazi chiefs probably selected Magda Goebbels because (with Strasser out of the Party) they had no notion about how to organize the exalted feminine sphere.

Several women would have been pleased to create a ministry of women's affairs. Guida Diehl, Elsbeth Zander, Lydia Gottschewski, and Sophie Rogge-Börner, each a dynamic leader and devoted National Socialist, made bids to become national director of women's affairs. But male leaders, who defined women as biologically and psychologically separate and subordinate, surely did not consider appointing an independent and charismatic woman to direct half of the population. The women leaders from the old days unwittingly disqualified themselves from posts in the Nazi state by demonstrating their ability and independence.

Within weeks of the March elections, Guida Diehl was quietly eased out of national prominence. However, she continued to operate her New Land association and unsuccessfully sought cooperation with the Protestant Church. In 1936 Scholtz-Klink apparently considered readmitting her to leadership circles, but Party headquarters in Munich rejected the possibility because Diehl was "headstrong and self-advertising," and more seriously, "she has no concept of discipline."[44] As long as she did not challenge Nazi policy, however, Diehl operated her New Land organization without interference. Elsbeth Zander received a transfer to a district office far from the center of national power.[45] The female half of Nazi society remained leaderless. Disorder at high levels of the Party and state meant that local women leaders' relative independence continued for several months after Nazi power had closed in on other areas of German life. They set out to convert the "inner spirits" of all Germans, now that the men had won political victory.

The press featured slogans like GRAB POTS AND PANS AND BROOM, SO YOU'LL QUICKLY FIND A GROOM! or NOT FOR YOU THE WORKING LIFE, BETTER LEARN TO BE A WIFE![46] Posters proclaimed, THE GERMAN WOMAN IS KNITTING ONCE AGAIN, but no one had decided what else she ought to be doing or who ought to be directing her. Hitler himself said nothing about policy, but did begin to praise women in public statements. For example, in July 1933, in an interview with American journalist Anne O'Hare

McCormick, he boasted he had always counted women among his strongest supporters. "They feel that my victory is their victory. They know that I serve their cause in working to redeem German youth, to create a social order, to restore hope and health."[47] Fine words after a long silence, but propaganda could not replace policy for long. On one issue, however, there could be no doubt: Socialist and Communist women's organizations became illegal overnight, their offices plundered, presses destroyed and leaders exiled. The Women's League for Peace and Freedom led by Lida Gustava Heymann and Anita Augspurg and the League for the Protection of Motherhood under Helene Stöcker disappeared. It was clear what the Nazi state did not tolerate. But no positive guidelines appeared.

The lack of a firm directive in part resulted from Nazi leaders' general confusion about all administrative issues. At a cabinet meeting in March, Hitler told his deputies to "divert attention to purely political affairs, because economic decisions will have to be postponed for a while."[48] Many people vaguely anticipated that the Nazi state would turn back the technological clock. One minor official summarized general expectations for Hitler's economic recovery program: "Rational distribution of available jobs, replacement of machines by hand labor . . . end of people working at two jobs. . . ."[49] Others hoped for a corporatist state on the lines of Mussolini's plans for a legislature that represented the various occupational interests. Either of these predictions might have led to relegation of women to wife and motherhood. The indecisiveness about women's roles that followed Nazi takeover is astonishing, given what we know about the firmness of Hitler's long-range goals for women. During the next few months, a deluge of proposals from women testifies to widespread aspirations for a revolutionary new future that would be constructed on myths of strong women in the past.

While Hitler and his ministers debated diplomacy, social policy, and economic recovery, a group of Nazi women academics drafted their own set of plans and published them under the title *German Women to Adolf Hitler*. They took Hitler's racist statements seriously and applied them to male-female relationships. If society was to be restructured along racial lines, they argued, and if women were to operate within their own distinctively female world, they would need education, status, and professional recognition. Leonore Kühn, long a leader in the middle-class women's movement, decided to support Hitler. Arguing logically from separatist premises, she declared that since women and men inhabited different worlds, it followed that women needed vastly improved educational opportunities so that they could staff and direct their own activities. "We applaud the traditional *Kinder, Küche, Kirche*, but we demand two more—*Krankenhaus* and *Kultur* [Hospital and Culture]." Another associate suggested more K's—*Kleider*, "clothes" (including the textile and garment industries) and *Kammer*, "chamber" (by which she meant a woman's legislature, but others meant bedroom).[50]

Another contributor to the volume proposed a sort of National Socialist equal-rights guarantee by insisting that male and female natures were so irrevocably different that laws to exclude women from masculine occupations could only be counterproductive. "Let us not," she wrote, use artificial means to "separate male and female into different professions, since biology keeps them so far apart." Under a National Socialist regime, the author continued, women would have the opportunity to prove their true capabilities. Because "decadent culture" had rendered women inferior, no one even knew how to measure women's potential. Men have written all the history books, she noted, and robbed women of their heritage. The author of a third article reinforced these views by claiming to have discovered that Nordic skeletons excavated in Scandinavia demonstrated that prehistoric males and females had been equal in size and strength. Because men had won the battle of the sexes, they continually underfed their women, who ultimately diminished physically. Like Chinese women's bound feet, she concluded, women had atrophied under male oppression. Nazi culture would equalize women and men by keeping women far from competition with men.[51] These authors, nearly all of them established in universities or professions, probably expected recognition from Nazi leaders. Of course, they received no attention at all, even though the book sold well.

Lydia Gottschewski emerged as the likely candidate to carry out the double mission of organizing women who already belonged to the Nazi movement and extending control over all non-Nazi associations that had not been outlawed. Her job prospects, however, remained hopeful only as long as Nazi Party bosses considered outlawing non-Nazi middle-class religious, civic, and women's-rights organizations. If, in other words, Zander's vision prevailed over Diehl's, Gottschewski had a chance. Her long-standing contempt for the "old" women's movement qualified her to stamp out the last vestiges of independence from Europe's largest women's-rights movement. "We do not begin with the liberal calculation that man is human and woman is human and therefore they can do the same things. Oh, no! We ask, What political contributions are appropriate for women's nature? How can we awaken women's special spiritual powers and make them fruitful?"[52] Women, she said, would happily surrender what little power they had won in Weimar Germany, and in exchange they would return to their "proper" sphere with a vengeance, which meant controlling what she called education, spiritual development, or inspiration. We would call it indoctrination. The strong-minded young organizer, however, verged on heresy when she called for a female fighting front or casually referred to Hitler's takeover as merely a political revolution, while intimating that the genuine and more important "spiritual" revolution lay in women's hands. "The band of men saved us Germans from the foreign Bolshevik threat. But now, whether or not the old-time feminists approve, we will create a spiritual Reich which will not break asunder."[53]

On May 10, 1933, Robert Ley, the Nazi head of the Labor Front, announced the formation of the Women's Front (*Frauenfront*) and deputized Gottschewski to integrate Germany's 230 civic and religious women's organizations. This meant pledging loyalty to National Socialist aims, including the expulsion of all women with Jewish ancestors from leadership positions, submitting financial records and agendas for state approval, and electing only Nazi women to office.[54] Each organization was given the choice of dissolving itself or submitting to Nazification. In the abrupt, almost rude memos, Gottschewski ordered German women's organizations to "fall in" quickly or face extinction.

All over Germany, women's organizations debated the merits of accepting the invitation to sign up. Gottschewski's arrogant style seemed designed to repulse middle-class leaders from respectable and "ladylike" circles. Moreover, her long-standing contempt for the BDF would not have inspired confidence in her aims. But, one after another, the acceptances came in. The bastion of patriotic women, the Queen Louisa League, capitulated at once with its 130,000 members, as did the Reich Association of Housewives with its 100,000 followers, the Rural Housewives with 90,000, the German Red Cross, which claimed 150,000 members, and several other conservative groups.[55] Their ready cooperation did not surprise anyone, for these groups had always espoused a virulent antidemocratic nationalism. But one association had, since the nineteenth century, formed the heart of the formidable middle-class women's movement. What, contemporaries wondered, would become of the powerful BDF, a national federation with over 60 member organizations and 500,000 members?[56] Gertrud Bäumer, writing in the BDF periodical *Die Frau,* had already declared that the struggle for women's rights remained oblivious to political institutions—"whether parliamentary, democratic or fascist."[57] President Agnes von Zahn-Harnack wrote to Leonore Kühn, by then a Nazi Party member, "We can only applaud the National Socialist regime."[58] In early May 1933, the leadership of the BDF discussed their options and voted (against Bäumer's advice) to dissolve rather than actively acquiesce.

In the same month, 40,000 members of the General Association of

German Women Teachers debated the same options. This association, long regarded as the very heart of women's emancipation, officially disbanded, but urged its non-Jewish members to join Nazi organizations and continue fighting for women's rights. The Association of Catholic German Women Teachers and Association of German Protestant Women Teachers refused to disband.[59] Women university students reached a consensus in October 1933: Dissolve their association, retain only Aryan members, and use the treasury to fund more politically acceptable projects. Women students in Berlin noted that the "Aryan paragraph" had lost its relevance, "because our Jewish members have already withdrawn or have for several years refrained from active participation."[60] About 2,500 women physicians (5.4 percent of the profession) faced the question of "Aryan" members squarely and decided to accommodate themselves to new circumstances. These erstwhile defenders of reproductive rights adjusted to Nazi demands. In Bavaria, women physicians explained their position. "We have always been more rooted and closer to nature, and therefore more instinctively race-conscious than elsewhere in Germany." One Jewish member of the Women Doctors' League in Berlin recalls the day when she arrived at a meeting, and her longtime friends and colleagues informed her curtly, "And now we request Jewish doctors to leave the local chapter. We have been Nazified."[61] After the organization reconstituted itself, its newsletters contained advertisements for women doctors to fill posts vacated by Jewish women physicians who had "resigned."

Women's organizations that had disdained the Nazis as "mere rabble" and "lower class," adapted skillfully to new conditions. The Nazi Women's Organization (NSF) membership increased by 800 percent between January and December of 1933. The ease with which independent organizations adjusted caught the Party unprepared. Instead of fighting a recalcitrant women's movement, Nazi leaders found themselves wondering how to organize middle-class women leaders' enthusiasm. The mass organizations that feminists in other nations expected would defend women's interests *against* the Nazi state actually hastened women's incorporation into Nazi government. Their capitulation resulted from more than cynicism. The middle-class women's-rights organizations subscribed to an ideal of motherhood shared by Hitler and his followers, and their nationalism made women susceptible to a dictatorship that promised a restoration of order and a revival of patriotism. Despite misgivings about Hitler's style, they welcomed his nationalistic, antidemocratic, and anticommunist stance. In contrast with the rather lackluster array of conservative and liberal politicians who led the parties to which these women belonged, the Führer offered an entirely new *élan*. BDF leaders protested vigorously when their own jobs were threatened, but believed their status as educated women with social standing would protect them from police terror. And they were correct. Bäumer was reinstated, her periodical Die Frau remained in print, the drive against women professionals halted, and the leaders of pre-1933 women's organizations were not harassed by house searches, arrest, or interrogations. Thus, far from building a barrier against Nazi encroachment, non-Socialist women leaders provided an avenue along which battalions of women marched into the Nazi world.

While economic plans remained nebulous and leadership in the women's sphere nonexistent, Hitler lost no time in shaping negative policy. Not surprisingly, women were excluded automatically from the government, but this decision affected primarily women officials with liberal or Socialist affiliations. Of 74 women in appointed political positions before 1933, none kept her job after 1933; all of the nearly 19,000 women officeholders at regional and local levels lost their posts; and the number of women teachers at all levels dropped by 15 percent.[62] By early 1934, Prussian bureaucracy had fired all married women. Although women constituted only 3 percent of the legal profession, they faced steady harassment. After 1936, women (even if they belonged to the Nazi Party) could not serve as judges or public prosecutors; and because they could not "think logically or reason objectively," women were also dismissed from jury duty. Lawyers appealed to the Prussian Ministry of Justice to bar women from the profession. The lawyers and magistrates rejoiced at the death of Weimar, because democracy "was a conscious rejection of the masculine way of thinking and coincided spiritually and chronologically with the end of conscription."[63] Married women physicians lost their right to practice; and by 1935, women physicians (like Jewish physicians) could no longer receive payments from the state-sponsored health-insurance system.

When criticized, Nazi leaders asserted that women professionals could always find outlets for their talents in volunteer activities or within specifically "feminine" occupations, provided they demonstrated their faith in Nazi ideology.[64] The "politically reliable" among these dismissed women knew they would be welcomed into the Nazi women's administration. However, in the fall of 1933, such a bureaucracy did not even exist, and in any case the option must have seemed unappealing indeed to women accustomed to participating in Reichstag debates, campaigning, and serving in municipal councils and ministries.

Women leaders, who during the Depression had not defended women factory and office workers' right to work, protested vehemently when legislation endangered the careers of women like themselves. But they did not base their defense on women's inherent claim to employment. Instead, they insisted that while women ought never seek "masculine" jobs, the nation needed middle-class women to perform "feminine" tasks, adding that "feminine" self-sacrifice, not "masculine" self-interest, motivated them to seek jobs.[65]

Agnes von Zahn-Harnack, who had presided over the dissolution of the BDF, complained publicly. "We anxiously await further developments. Numerous women administrators . . . have been removed. . . . Only two of them have been replaced by women. Fields of endeavor that indisputably belong directly in women's social and cultural working realms have fallen into men's hands."[66] Despite her antipathy for the "old" women's movement, Gottschewski paradoxically spoke out on the side of the former leaders of the BDF. Ambitious and talented women, she insisted, ought to serve the state.

> Women should be excluded neither from public nor from private life. . . . while the wife and mother ought to be removed from mechanized occupational drudgery and mothers need protection. Unmarried women should make their motherly traits useful for the entire nation. . . . [But] women should not disappear from politics. Where she has the expertise to give political advice and information, she can and must be heard. She should be listened to just as the early Germans listened to their priestesses before making decisions vital to the *Volk*.[67]

Women, Gottschewski insisted, must abide by the Nazi ethic and form their own women's union, a tightly integrated sisterhood that would carry the Nazi message beyond the circles of those who had already converted to the cause.[68] Sophie Rogge-Börner, a fanatical racist from the old days, openly challenged the exclusion of women from professional work. Her periodical, *The German Woman Fighter*, defended women teachers' right to work and cited a major Catholic survey from the late 1920s that demonstrated that three-quarters of all teachers needed their wages to support family members. Thus, because they saw their work as a necessity, they deserved to keep their jobs.[69]

Wilhelm Frick, Minister of Interior, capitulated. "I hear from the most diverse sources that a great alarm has spread among women teachers and state employees because they think we plan to dismiss them." Claiming he intended nothing of the kind, he insisted he wanted merely to make sure that women who did not need the extra income relinquish their jobs.[70] Women's success in reversing policy on this crucial issue gave them a misplaced belief that the totalitarian state could indeed be bent to serve their needs. Furthermore, their apparent success vindicated their strategy of the previous summer: to cooperate voluntarily with Nazi policy in the expectation of rewards such as concessions and organizational autonomy.

Middle-class women leaders' vigorous defense of their own jobs and organizations testifies to their tough-mindedness. Had they felt deep concern about dismissing members with Jewish ancestors from their organizations, we can assume that they would have registered their opposition. Yet no storm (or even drizzle) of protest was heard when middle-class women received orders to purge first their leadership and then their rank and file of women with Jewish backgrounds. Middle-class women leaders did not go down to defeat under the Nazis; they declared themselves ready to collaborate.

A few examples illustrate the pattern of compliance and self-interest. Gertrud Bäumer, the highest nonelected official in Weimar government, lost her position in the Ministry of Culture within weeks of Hitler's nomination as Chancellor. Angry telegrams and letters deluged Nazi government and Party headquarters, protesting her dismissal as an insult to women and a bad omen for the future.[71] Bäumer did not defend herself, but instead revised her curriculum vitae and submitted it together with her "pure Aryan" family tree to Nazi authorities. Adapting to new circumstances, she embellished on her collaboration with Friedrich Naumann, longtime liberal and founder of the German Democratic Party in 1919. Before World War I, Naumann had coined the term "National Socialist" to describe his political aims. Although neither Naumann nor Bäumer had any ties with the Nazi Party before 1933, Bäumer noted in her curriculum vitae: "I was active in the National Socialist wing of the Democratic Party."[72] Within months she received the offer of a new position, but rejected it. In her public utterances throughout the next twelve years, Bäumer spoke out quietly for expanded career opportunities for women while avoiding any criticism of Nazi policies. In her academic work, she returned to medieval themes. Although her name disappeared from the masthead of *Die Frau* for a few months, she contributed regularly. Already in 1933 her stance was obvious when she urged her readers to look at the bright side of the "national revolution" and persist in the fight for women's rights no matter what the context. "In a development whose essence requires a longer period of time than the life of any one generation, all is not finally destroyed. There is rather a guarantee that new viewpoints and forms will be developed."[73]

Bäumer followed her own advice. In August 1933 she supported quotas against women university students because she said that standards among women students had dropped in recent years.[74] In 1934, she defined the women's movement in terms that must have pleased her new masters. Organized women, she said, formed an apolitical force, with no desire to interfere in power politics, motivated only by the "longing for outlets for its spiritual powers."[75] *Die Frau* continued publication. After the war, Bäumer noted that throughout the Nazi regime she never published a word that contradicted her principles.

Another longtime leader of the Democratic Party, high civil servant, and member of the women's movement, Dorothee von Velsen, lost her administrative post and in 1933 withdrew from public life, but in private correspondence criticized Nazi rule.[76] Most of the longtime crusaders for women's rights used whatever access they had to the media to pursue their struggle, even though this meant lending respectability to the Nazi regime. Evaluating that choice presents formidable problems. The very fact that widely respected leaders with international reputations published in Nazi-approved journals gave credence to the Nazi claim that it respected women. Bäumer and her colleagues believed that keeping women's issues alive even in adverse circumstances justified their cooperation. The radical wing of the women's movement, like Marxist women's groups, disappeared.

Bäumer's conciliatory response to the Nazi state demonstrated her readiness to default on her predecessors' broad vision of human emancipation. The middle-class women's movement perceived itself as a single-issue women's lobby, determined to fight for women's rights within any political context at all, provided it was not socialist. Even before 1933, during both the postwar demobilization and the Depression, the BDF had not defended women's right to work across the board but rather had supported professional women's right to a career. Where average women were concerned, BDF leaders swore to put the national interest ahead of a "narrow" conception of women's rights, which meant they placed motherhood ahead of women's right to employment.

Before the Nazi leaders had evolved a stance on the Woman Question, middle-class leaders like Bäumer had solved the Nazi Question. One by one, professional and civic women's organizations made their peace with the new state and lobbied for favors within its institutions. While Nazi leaders floundered amid conflicting plans for the "women's world," the leadership of the middle-class women's movement adjusted quickly to the new reality. The organizations that might have resisted, or at least provided refuge for women who refused to collaborate, accepted the Third Reich. Rather than opposing dictatorship, these powerful associations, with branches in the tiniest towns, used their clout with the new masters. Organizations surrendered. Opposition, when it occurred, came from individuals. After 1945 several women who had either cooperated or withdrawn from public life in Nazi Germany wrote their memoirs, describing their compliance as inconsequential and inflating their reservations about Hitler into resistance.[77] From 1933 to 1945 they had sworn loyalty to Nazi policies in order, they claimed, to avoid arrest or harassment; and after 1945 they told the "hidden story" of their secret opposition. Recently, young German women have praised their fore-mothers for maintaining the "maternal spirit" against a hostile state.[78] While one can sympathize with a post-Nazi generation's need for inspiration, such claims serve only to denigrate the bravery of those feminists, socialists, and apolitical individuals who did resist. Few of these women lived to write their memoirs.

While the women's movement steered its course toward collaboration, and the Nazi women's bureaucracy remained chaotic, Hitler lost no time in implementing the central tenets of his solution to the Woman Question. Welfare and health administrations authorized policies that encouraged the "racially fit" to bear children and forbade the "unfit" to do so. Rewards for marriage and motherhood did not originate with Hitler's Germany. Already in 1920 the French government had instituted medals for mothers (bronze for five, silver for eight, and gold for ten children). During the 1930s, the French increased the penalties for abortion and provided allowances to large families, premiums to mothers who nursed, and subsidies for mothers who did not work outside the home. Stalinist Russia, too, rewarded mothers and made birth control next to impossible.[79]

Pro-natalist policies in Nazi Germany quickly surpassed similar programs in other nations in terms of funding, the number of people affected, and policy makers' ingenuity. In underlying goals, too, Nazi planners departed from precedent. Whereas policy makers in the United States and Europe justified their programs in terms of individual happiness as well as social health, Nazi pamphlets explicitly told Germans, "Your body does not belong to you, but to your blood brethren [*Sippe*] and your . . . *Volk*."[80] Within months of the Nazi takeover, a vast marriage incentive program offered government grants to newlyweds for up to RM 1,000 (or about a fifth of an average worker's annual salary). Couples had to meet two significant requirements to qualify: the wife could not work outside her home and the families of both partners had to be certified "Jew free" for two generations. To guarantee that couples did not waste this windfall, they received the grants in the form of coupons that could be used only for the purchase of household goods. To fund the entire enterprise, unmarried people paid a bachelor tax that amounted to between 2 and 5 percent of an average salary.[81]

The short-term impact impressed contemporaries. Five hundred thousand marriages created jobs for men by forcing wives' exit from the labor market. The coupons stimulated consumer spending and created more jobs.[82] But Nazi policy aimed at higher fertility, not happy couples. Marriages increased at once, but the effectiveness of pro-natalist measures would not become evident for two or three years.

In the meantime, however, propaganda advocated sterilization to eliminate the "unfit" from the mainstream "Aryan" population. Eugenics experts noticed, however, that the "most racially undesirable" people displayed the least ability to grasp the "fundamental truth" that their bodies belonged to the Volk.[83] To reinforce the propaganda, in July 1933 Hitler's cabinet passed a law that required social workers and nurses to report all "genetically defective" individuals to the health authorities, who would decide whether they ought to be sterilized. The government described its racial policies in technical-sounding terms to offset the moral reservations that inevitably arose. "Racial scientists" compared Hitler to Copernicus and Galileo, who revolutionized our understanding of the physical universe. Genetic laws, said racial scientists, would determine the future of the human race; policymakers' only option was whether to use genetic knowledge to advance humankind or to refuse to apply science and allow racial degeneration to destroy the Volk.[84] Nazi leaders may have been unique in their fanaticism, but belief in eugenics and, more generally, biological thinking about sociological problems flourished in both capitalist and communist nations during the entire inter-war period. In 1927, to take just one of many examples, the U.S. Supreme Court upheld the constitutionality of Virginia's involuntary sterilization law.[85] But in other nations sterilization programs for the most part remained voluntary; only in Germany did the full power of an authoritarian state direct its energy at a thorough "weeding out" of "unworthy" life. The phrase in German is even stronger: *lebensunwürdiges Leben*, or "life unworthy of life," which included (depending on the official in charge) people with supposedly hereditary diseases such as epilepsy, schizophrenia (as evidenced by moodiness or temper tantrums, indifferent housekeeping in women or irregular employment patterns in men), deafness, dumbness, prostitution, mental retardation, and certain forms of venereal disease.

The program provoked widespread fears, often expressed in humor. As soon as the eugenics law of 1933 became public, unenthusiastic Germans began to refer to sterilization as the *Hitlerschnitt* a word play on the term *Kaiserschnitt* (Caesarean "cut," or section). In Berlin, a story circulated about schoolchildren who were asked to memorize the categories for "sterilizable" people. One child answered "club foot." Everyone, of course, had seen photos of Joseph Goebbels, Director of Propaganda, that revealed his crippled foot.[86]

The very term totalitarian conjures up images of an absolutist state that reduces its subjects to automatons. Yet the policies on sterilization and marriage illustrate the constraints under which Nazi leaders operated. Hitler as a campaigner derived his power from his ability to mobilize people to do what they had wanted to do in the first place, releasing their energy rather than changing their will. As long as his rhetoric conformed to their desires, people did indeed seem to follow his will. But when Hitler imposed his own views on loyal supporters, conflict developed. The sterilization program provides an excellent case study in the result. The very idea of "life unworthy of living" introduced an alien concept into most people's thinking. The term, in eugenicists' usage, did not mean that the life for the disabled person would be so painful or so deprived that death would be humane. On the contrary, it meant that the individual labeled substandard ought not burden the community by living. Thus, parents of potentially "unworthy" children were encouraged to do their patriotic duty and forego parenthood to improve the quality of life for future "Aryan" generations. The government that exalted childbearing as each citizen's most solemn duty and source of happiness decreed that the "unworthy" must undergo sterilization (in German, literally "to be made unfruitful)."

Not only did this doctrine arouse general opposition, its administration fell largely to women, the least organized branch of the emerging Nazi bureaucracy. Because eugenic schemes constituted the heart of Hitler's plans for the future, women's cooperation would be crucial, and morale became a vital consideration. Morale, in turn, depended upon selecting the most appropriate woman leader. Hitler's deputies faced a choice between establishing a narrowly based association led by dedicated and seasoned old-timers or a mass women's association under newly appointed and moderate women. The former model might have offered the opportunity of indoctrinating a new generation of fanatically loyal women; while the latter held out the prospect of extending a pragmatically oriented and undogmatic form of Nazism to millions of women. In either case, it might have seemed logical to place the women's world under a single woman leader. But a woman with authority over half the population would have threatened the male elite, who swore to keep women out of politics. Instead, leaders squabbled over administrative control, treating women as bureaucratic territory to be captured. The Director of Welfare claimed women social workers; the Labor Front demanded workers; the Education Ministry insisted on teachers; the Ministry of Agriculture wanted farmers' wives. Even after the various contenders had staked out their claims, the need for a woman leader remained. A state that insisted on radical separation of male and female had to create an institutional framework to incorporate each half of the population. The ideal candidate would have the strength of character to organize women and yet yield to male superiors like Rudolf Hess, Wilhelm Frick, Baldur von Schirach, Hans Schemm, and Robert Ley, all of whom at one point or another laid claim to the task of organizing German women.

At first it seemed as if Gottschewski and Ley might win the bureaucratic war for women, but Wilhelm Frick promoted his own candidate, the popular district leader from Düsseldorf, Paula Siber. As consultant on women's affairs under Frick in the Ministry of the Interior, Siber was ordered to coordinate all women's activities that did not involve welfare, employment, or education. While Gottschewski organized her Women's Front from the Party headquarters in Munich, Siber established her Coordinating Committee for Women's Affairs in Berlin. Siber and Gottschewski ideologically and personally had embarked on a collision course.

Siber was more inclined than her rivals to support the religious organizations and recruit their leaders into her organization. She also vehemently opposed women's entry into any masculine type of work or political activity. Married and twenty years older than her rival in Munich, Siber presented a motherly and religious image. She had joined the Party relatively late (in 1931), but commanded respect as a speaker. As district leader in Düsseldorf, she proved to be a model of efficiency. While Gottschewski rallied young women, Siber attracted housewives, mothers, and teachers. She sharply criticized the bourgeois women's-rights movement, but sought to redirect its concerns and to point out that it had been "misguided." Whereas Gottschewski rebelled against the older generation, Siber intended to harness that generation into her own working committee for women's organizations. Women needed, she said, great ideas to keep them from becoming bogged down in pettiness.[87] Siber admired Guida Diehl and spoke often of God and religion; Gottschewski praised only Hitler and his racist doctrines. Her newsletter for leaders in 1933 exhorted her readers to banish pity from their hearts when it came to Jews.

> Often, much too often, one hears it still, "I find the fight against the Jews too severe. It does not seem right that the good Jews must suffer on account of their race" . . . and so it goes. Sentimental gush to say that the other person is also a human being and feels and senses like ourselves . . . [der Führer] has an inconceivably deep knowledge of final things. . . . This man knows what is necessary for us.
>
> We National Socialist women . . . should thank God that the movement exists and exert ourselves for it with word and deed. . . . Did not our entire people do penance for years for the sins of individuals? And who were these sinners? For the most part, Jews! The Jew with his quite different nature,

his essential being unlike ours is a subtle poison, since he destroys what is necessary to our life. The Jew has always felt bound to conquer the best places in the sun, ruthlessly destroying what was in his way. If we are to be healed as a people . . . and conquer a place in the world that is our due, then we must free ourselves ruthlessly from that parasite just as the body must get rid of poison if it is to be healed. . . . Christ himself drove the money changers out of the Temple.[88]

This sort of propaganda prepared its readers to dehumanize the Jew and exalt themselves. The metaphors in this passage echo the most virulent passages of *Mein Kampf,* which promise that the sick *Volk* can be healed by excising the parasite or poison. But where Hitler used pseudo-scientific jargon, the author of this pamphlet portrays Christ as a surgeon. If racial purification was to constitute women's chief responsibility, the youthful and fanatic Gottschewski would have been a perfect choice as national leader. However, her rival offered another alternative.

Paula Siber evolved a very different strategy, attracting women to practical tasks, such as charity drives. When women were fired in order to provide jobs for unemployed men, Siber (unlike Gottschewski) consoled the victims.

When today in these occupations preference is given to the man, this action means difficulties for the employed woman. Still it must be recognized that these sufferings are always slight in contrast to the agony which many mothers previously had to endure when year in and year out they could not nourish or clothe their children according to their needs.[89]

Unlike Gottschewski, Siber became more moderate in her opinions and less bombastic in style after Hitler became dictator. She stopped talking about the "Jews" and "godless Marxist-Bolsheviks," who had dominated her earlier speeches. Sensitive to the demands of the new state, she became more pragmatic. Although women had played a vital political role in Nazi triumph, she wrote, they must be "de-politicized." Eschewing rhetoric and ideology, she organized cooking and nutrition, sewing, day care, fund-raising, and "family culture." While these activities were all in theory family-oriented, Siber used them to redirect women's concerns away from the individual family and toward state-sponsored programs. Her vast network would be divided into economics, social welfare, and culture.[90] Siber, in teaching mothers how to improve their skills, ostensibly protected women's traditional roles; but at the same time, because she operated with the backing of a powerful state, she undercut the very privacy that women so valued in their familial lives.

It might seem that such projects were beyond reproach from a Nazi standpoint. One item in her plans, however, touched the sensitive issue, a concept she called "feminine culture." What, her suspicious superiors asked, did she mean? According to them the concept signaled female separatism, which they now condemned as heresy. Siber assured her critics, in carefully chosen phrases, that "culture" did not refer to any uniquely feminine traits, traditions, or aims; but merely delimited women's special areas of responsibility. She repudiated the existence of any sort of female culture, and emphasized women's potential contributions to the Nazi cause.[91]

Tension between Berlin and Munich created confusion and undercut morale. The Nazis, who had promised order, in fact brought chaos to the heart of the woman's sphere. Instead of creating a unified women's front, Nazi women rivaled one another for control of the women's world while defending themselves against ambitious ministers who extended their power over women. In the absence of national leadership, local chapters looked to their regional chiefs rather than to Berlin or Munich for guidance and protection. Many women expected the revival of Guida Diehl's plans for a "women's chamber" that would occupy the apex of women's separate sphere. Proponents of this plan followed the long-standing National Socialist vision of a corporate state, constructed according to occupational, rather than regional, divisions. Thus women, like other "occupations," would elect their delegates to sit in the same chamber as representatives of heavy industry, office workers, and peasants.[92] Instead, internecine rivalry persisted.

By allowing Siber and Gottschewski to compete for leadership, Hitler's deputies kept the solution to the Woman Question open and delayed a final showdown. Having legislated sterilization and marriage loan programs, they needed a dynamic leader with dedication and charisma, who combined the ambition of the New Woman and the values of her grandmother. Instead, two offices precluded a unified effort. The duplication of function and endemic jealousy undercut the effectiveness of both organizations. This very inefficiency was to become a hallmark of the much-vaunted Nazi organization. By allowing an authoritarian anarchy to flourish, decisions were deferred until the Führer himself could intervene and establish his domination. No one in the bureaucracy was ever quite sure of his or her situation, and everyone knew that he or she could be replaced by a rival at a moment's notice. Mutual and pervasive suspicion kept Nazis' eyes turned upward in the hierarchy and destroyed horizontal cooperation.[93]

By the fall of 1933 the chaos had mounted to unmanageable proportions. Non-Nazi women's organizations that wanted to collaborate in

Nazi projects and reap the rewards scarcely knew to whom they should turn. Longtime Nazis, meanwhile, became disillusioned. It was all well and good for Hitler to declare that every organization must be Nazified. But no guidelines told women leaders whether they ought to associate with Gottschewski's Frauenfront or Siber's Committee. Did "Nazification" mean joining the Party or the state, and what was the difference? Could one be a stalwart member of the Association of Women Academics, for example, and also a loyal Nazi? Even more basically, were Nazi women supposed actually to join the Party or one of the Nazi women's associations? From the statistical evidence the answer is clear. Women, even if they aspired to leadership positions, did not have to become Party members in order to retain the confidence of the new government. Men did. The Nazi Party, which had included under a million members in 1932, suddenly tripled its membership; and women's percentage in the Party membership dropped to under 5 percent.[94]

Between 1933 and 1934, women Nazis suffered because of the very disorganization that they had been able to use to their advantage before 1933. Decentralization had allowed prominent women to create their own autonomous enclaves; but bureaucratic chaos spread demoralization and confusion. During Weimar democracy, everyone had been free to dream about her own personal Nazi future; but in the Nazi state these visions dissolved as women from the old days found themselves replaced by the very ladies they had for so long scorned (and who had snubbed them). The new state, far from rewarding the independent and dynamic women who had for years followed Hitler, recruited from the more respectable and established middle class. Party stalwarts found themselves displaced by non-ideological community-minded women leaders who would win adherents to practical tasks.[95] At the local and national levels, conflicts surfaced. The old-timers saw Hitler's revolution as the starting point for a thorough Nazification of the entire society. But moderates, while welcoming Nazi power, hoped that Hitler would create a responsible dictatorship and leave traditional institutions alone.

The careers of old-timer Irene Seydel in Westphalia and her superior, Elisabeth Polster, illustrate the impact of this confusion at the regional level. Not surprisingly, Seydel joined the throngs in her native Bielefeld as they celebrated Hitler's victory. And of course she attended the next mass meeting in the town. While others cheered, Seydel felt let down. "All Bielefeld turned out! Just think what could have been accomplished! Everyone was packed together, forming a single, breathing, unified mass of humanity!" Expectations mounted. Nerves tensed. A perfect ambience for the Nazi meeting. Nothing happened. "No spark lit their imagination." Speakers intoned prepared remarks and the audience yawned. After the meeting, the women in the audience rushed to sign up with the non-Nazi Association of Housewives rather than going to the Nazi women's recruiting table. How would a colorless group of Party hacks ever inspire the spiritual revolution that Seydel believed all German women wanted?

The men did not bother to call women's meetings, and the local woman leader began her tenure in office by suggesting Nazi women march to Easter church services. "This is a grotesque parody of German women's traditions. . . . We appear ludicrous in the eyes of our fellow Bielefelders. We give the impression of military obedience. . . . Every time women march, it is awful. . . ." After years on the propaganda barricades, Seydel helplessly watched "petty and lackluster" men take over. Trumped-up stories of scandal damaged independent women's reputations—here stories of a Nazi woman leader who shopped at a Jewish store and there rumors that the district woman leader abandoned her family to spend too much time at Party headquarters in Düsseldorf. That was not the harmonious society Seydel had envisioned. When her protests met with rebuke from local Nazi men, her followers encouraged her to remain true to her beliefs even if that meant breaking with the Party. For the moment, Seydel stood firm against "the greedy and arrogant women whose personal pettiness makes it clear they have never read a page of *Mein Kampf.*"[96] For years, Seydel complained, Nazi women had asked for more guidance from Nazi men. Now they received it, and they hated it.

Throughout the summer of 1933, Seydel and her friends anticipated that the Nuremberg Rally would revive their flagging morale. When she arrived at the rally, however, Seydel and the few other women who attended were aghast. No activities for women appeared on the agenda. In seven days of speeches, spectacles, demonstrations, and meetings, not one hour for women had been organized. When she shared her disillusionment with a friend, she was told that Nazi men saw their women colleagues as "merely hysterical females in brown potato sacks." Seydel protested. "We women are neither ambitious nor proud. . . . We must give Hitler the impression that within the Nazi freedom movement there are not only hysterical women."[97] How could women change Hitler's impressions? Seydel reflected. She was a humble woman, and Hitler a busy man. In the tradition of Christians who turn to Mary rather than Christ, Seydel sent a letter to Hitler's sister, in which she unburdened her worries "about the fate of our woman's organization, which burns in my soul." After summarizing her own understanding of Nazi doctrine, she listed concrete issues.

Everything our feminine hands have achieved with endless effort and love now stands in danger of being destroyed. . . . No one asks women for their reactions or advice. . . . I am dedicated to planting in all hearts the ideal of a new female type—not the marching woman, but the woman who, uncomplaining as the earth itself, joyfully sacrifices and fulfills her fate. This type is not like either Lydia [Gottschewski] or Eva [Braun]. Whether it resembles Frau Siber, you know better than I. . . . I have reliable sources tell me that the Führer himself expects little leadership from that quarter. . . . We have entered a new phase of the battle and will need a staff and organization just like the men have. We pay our dues just like the men![98]

Nothing came of these proposals. Seydel returned from the Nuremberg Rally determined to carry on her work but without the satisfaction of having received an answer. On the other hand, her effrontery went unrebuked.

Confusion among Zander, Gottschewski, and Siber at the national level reached down to the grassroots. Simple women like Seydel found life more chaotic than under the Weimar democracy they despised. Then, the enemy had seemed clear. Now, the work of independent women faced a threat from the very leaders whose victory had recently made them so proud. At the same time Seydel protested this state of affairs, leaders in Berlin and Munich arrived at a unified approach to the organization of the Woman Question. Rudolf Hess had arranged for the creation of a Women's Bureau (Frauenwerk) under the Ministry of the Interior. For the moment this meant a triumph for Siber and Frick and the demise of their rival in the south, Gottschewski. Shortly after this announcement, the rebellious Gottschewski lost her job, although the decision did not make news in the Nazi press. Perhaps Nazi officials did not want to publicize the move, for they kept her name on the masthead of the magazine she had founded. Gottschewski immediately took legal action to defend her post. She failed. When the judge at the Party Court justified his decision, he explained that putting Gottschewski in charge of German women would be like putting daughters in charge of their mothers. Gottschewski, who before 1933 had received praise for her youthful vigor, had outlived her usefulness. After a few months she lost her editorial job and faded from view. She married in 1935 and attempted to pursue a career as a writer. However, the Nazi Writers' Guild denied her membership application, which in effect banned her from journalism.[99]

Siber's fate seemed more hopeful—at least for a few months. Besides advocating women's return to familial roles, she (unlike the blunt and youthful Gottschewski, the pompous Diehl, and the bombastic Zander) appeared as feminine and wifely. The appearance of order lasted for only weeks, for Frick's rivals challenged his control of women. Siber remained on Frick's staff as "consultant on women," and outlined her goals in flawless doublespeak.

> The German Women's Bureau will, as an umbrella association, not interfere with the independence [Eigenständigkeit] of its members, either regarding their organizations or their goals. But everyone ought also to understand that, as a creation of the National Socialist Party, member organizations must stand under pure National Socialist leaders, and that means absolute obedience and unconditional recognition of National Socialist authority.[100]

Peace did not last for long.

In October an entirely new face (and a masculine one at that) appeared at the leadership of Nazi women: one Gottfried Krummacher, a loyal Party member with no experience at all in women's associations. As a municipal official in Gummersbach, a small Rhineland town, and a leader in pro-Nazi Protestant circles, he had acquired the reputation of being spineless.[101] A security report said he displayed more loyalty to The Steel Helmets, a reactionary veterans' organization, than to the Party chief.[102] However, he had publicly defended the Nazis' expulsion of "non-Aryans" from all secular and religious institutions and fervently advocated a new religion that admonished Christians to revive pagan rites and place the Führer's command above the Bible. Followers of this German Christian movement saw Hitler as a messiah and wanted to expunge all Jewish influence from Christianity. Krummacher's utter lack of experience with women's organizations gave him the appearance of impartiality. His reputation as a good public speaker also enhanced his standing. Perhaps Party leaders believed a man would bring reason and order to the independent branches of pro-Nazi organizations. Krummacher quoted Hitler in describing his ambitions for women. "It is wonderful, indeed, to exercise power, but it is even more wonderful to win the love and trust of an entire Volk." Krummacher promised to launch a women's Blitzkrieg to "convert" the woman's soul and win her body to Hitler's dreams of a purified race.[103] Women, Krummacher realized, stood guard to the threshold of the family and held the key to Hitler's racial aims. Krummacher made his goals explicit:

1. Produce babies and educate them according to Nazi doctrine
2. Raise money for social services that make society more humane
3. Understand and apply racial principles in the selection of sexual partners

4. Support men's activities in whatever roles the leadership deems necessary
5. Maintain family-oriented values.[104]

Avoiding any mention of "feminine" nature, Krummacher stressed sacrifice and obedience as women's major duties. In his first public act, he dissolved all rival women's associations and declared himself leader of the newly reconstituted "Women's Front" and "Women's Organization." Whereas Siber and Gottschewski spoke of women's dignity and equality, Krummacher dispelled hopes for improving women's status. "The crusaders for women's rights demanded equality with men! And as soon as we gave it to them, they became even more dissatisfied because when they entered political life they saw for themselves how meaningless it really was." In the future, he said, only women without husbands or children at home would be able to serve the Nazi state in any public capacity. His women deputies, in other words, would form a sort of third sex, between men and mothers—a corps of nunlike workers devoted to carrying out his orders. At last, it seemed, the Nazi Party discovered a women's leader it could trust.

> The Führer has given me perhaps the most difficult job in the Nazi Party —that is, to bring order to the Women's Association and to pacify all of organized German womanhood. An extraordinary and unfortunate state of war dominates between the national [Party] leadership and [Interior Minister] Frick. Naturally, rivalous envy [Kampfwut] has falsified National Socialist doctrine and squandered money. Many use unfeminine and un-National Socialist methods to achieve their ends. My job is to bring them into line or quash them [kalt zu stellen] [with] iron ruthlessness.[105]

Krummacher made it clear that "in the new state it does not matter if a person is correct or not. What really counts is who, out of profound love for his Fatherland, is willing to submit to the unity of the community." When he spoke of excising the troublemakers, he used the bacteria metaphor so common in Hitler's tirades against the Jews: "The leadership is concerned that the carrier of the infection is closed out of the community and made harmless."[106] Nazi women did not welcome Krummacher as their leader. How, asked a contributor to *The German Woman Fighter*, could German women rally for women's work without women leaders?[107] Seydel reported from Westphalia that women resented having a male leader. Moreover, she accused Krummacher of "insulting" and "mocking" the Christian faith. The Hitler Youth organizations, she said, had already damaged family solidarity by splitting parents from children, and boys from girls. Krummacher would pit women against men.[108]

Other reports objected to their leader's religion. "Herr Krummacher can't talk three minutes without quoting the Bible four times." Besides, one Gauleiter reported, people found him arrogant, "school masterish," and authoritarian. The Party headquarters tactfully suggested that Krummacher share power with some women leaders, but he stood firm.[109]

During the late fall of 1933, confusion reigned as Siber in Berlin sparred with Krummacher, who refused to move away from the tiny Rhineland town of Gummersbach. Siber's husband, by contrast, reluctantly agreed to follow his wife to the capital. Nazi women had anticipated that dictatorship would replace democratic disorder with a strong, unified will. Precisely the opposite occurred. Ironically, when longtime Nazi women began to complain (and lose their jobs), many middle-class non-Nazis clamored to join the bandwagon.

The response of the Reich Association of Housewives provides an excellent case study of integration into Hitler's society. Led by Maria Jecker, the Housewives boasted a tradition of independence reaching back into the nineteenth century. Scholtz-Klink remembers Jecker as a "magnificent human being," and well she might, for Jecker proclaimed her support for Hitler before anyone had heard the name of the future Reichsfrauenführerin, praising Hitler's role that heralded "springtime in nature, springtime in the life of our *Volk*."[110] The Housewives proudly insisted on their independence from male-dominated organizations, such as church or political institutions. For decades they had bitterly opposed women's suffrage and grudgingly accepted the idea only after it had become a fait accompli in 1918. Although they associated with the BDF during the 1920s, they seceded in anger in 1932 because the BDF had become too radical.[111] The Housewives saw themselves as a lobby for the family, which they believed to be endangered by sexual license and cultural decadence. Behind lofty-sounding aims, they worked for more self-interested changes. For example, they cooperated with the reactionary Nationalist Party in educating servants to resist Bolshevik and Socialist propaganda. When Hitler became Chancellor, their president in Hanover, Bertha Hindenberg-Delbrück, waxed ecstatic. "I personally have supported Nazi aims on the Woman Question for years . . . cooperation will be a joy for me." She looked forward to a new era of peace and reconciliation. From smaller chapters came similar statements. "With deepest gratitude we welcome the determined national uprising. We will rebuild the nation and the state on the foundation of the family." They reported to Gottschewski and awaited further orders.[112]

Because they took seriously Hitler's promises to elevate their status, they felt entitled to make claims on the new government. Believing they alone embodied the ideal Nazi woman, they anticipated they would receive special privileges in the Third Reich. Even before the official Nazi women's periodicals discussed sterilization programs, for example, the *Deutsche Hausfrau* (German Housewife) popularized eugenics, quoting *Mein Kampf*, urging their readers to march along with the "population political campaign" to sterilize all "unworthies" and advertising the Nazi booklet *Mothers, Fight for Your Children!* [113]

During the fall of 1933, after Krummacher took over as chief of the women's sphere, the Housewives submitted all agendas and officers to local Nazi authorities for approval. [114] "We must put aside the fighting spirit that brought National Socialism to victory and saved us all from Bolshevism. Now we must recognize that the old methods of struggle brought difficulties. With peace and patience, they will be overcome." [115]

A major precondition for participation in Nazi programs remained expulsion of Jewish members. Even though hundreds of Jewish women had been members and leaders for years, the Housewives did not register a protest. But they did try to cloak their actions in euphemism, saying, "All members must be Christian and nationally oriented." The Nazi Party objected to such vague phrases because so many Christian women had Jewish grandparents. The Housewives then agreed to expel all "non-Aryan" women. They did, and confusion mounted. In the supposedly clear-cut "Aryan" society, based on "natural" distinctions, where did one draw the line? What about Frau Dieselhorst, who insisted that her executive committee needed the participation of a "half-Jew" who had played a key role in the local organization for years? Hindenberg-Delbrück could not understand how that had happened. "Where was she before? We don't have elections anymore, so it could not be an accident. How did this woman manage to get herself on the executive committee?" [116] The "half-Jew" resigned. But Hindenberg-Delbrück's problems persisted. She eased out several women, but confronted real problems with Frau Skutsch, "who unfortunately is a Jew and actually one of the most energetic of the directors of our experimental workshop. . . ." But the executive committee reasoned that Frau Skutsch was, after all, a member of a "visiting *Volk*" and ought never have expected equal rights in the first place. Another member of the executive committee, whom people suspected of being Jewish, presented a legal declaration that she was "pure German" and her husband "third-generation German." The leadership could not decide whether to trust the woman's declaration or local gossip. [117] Another member turned to Hindenberg-Delbrück to help her decide if she herself belonged or not. Her record of service to the association was impeccable, but her husband came from a Dutch-Indonesian background. What to do? Some said play it safe and banish everyone about whom any doubt existed. Others argued, "Some of our most faithful workers have a Jew in their family tree, and we would not want to lose their support."

At issue was the survival of the Reich Association of Housewives. Leaders balanced individual members' rights against state requirements. Counting on their Jewish members' "understanding," the Housewives tactfully proposed that their Jewish members display some sympathy for current "difficulties" and resign. No records suggest that leaders considered the moral dimensions of the problem, or reflected that the organization had made no distinctions between Jews and non-Jews in the past. The distinctions had always existed, latent and unspoken. Hitler's victory made unspoken prejudice not only respectable, but politically advantageous. Converting an ethical dilemma into a bureaucratic problem, the Housewives dispatched dozens of memos concerning administrative problems of definition.

In return for their cooperation, the Housewives assumed they would be granted advantages in the Third Reich. Soon they discovered they had made a serious miscalculation. Initially, they had supported the Nazi cause because they anticipated that a nationalist dictatorship would impose order on the nation and end the threat of liberal reform and Communist revolution. To this end, they assumed that Hitler would declare mothers (or at least housewives) an occupational category. Since the nineteenth century this had figured among the association's demands.[118] Chief among the goals of these "professionalized" Housewives was the destruction of servants' unions. In high-flown phrases about the "dignity of housework" or the "sacred responsibilities of the homemaker," the organized Housewives worked against improvement in servants' working conditions, hours, and pay, while keeping watch over their servants' private lives. For years before Hitler's takeover, Maria Jecker had opposed social security, unemployment insurance, health benefits, minimum-pay laws, and paid vacations for domestic servants. It had not occurred to her or her colleagues that the Nazis might organize servants against the Housewives.

But many servants had supported Hitler and anticipated the Third Reich would usher in a new era for them. The appeal to a classless society and "Aryan" solidarity had formed the core of Hitler's promises. Servants anticipated a very different sort of society from their mistresses. Melita Maschmann recalled the reaction of her family's dressmaker when she heard the news.

> For as long as I had known her she had worn an embossed metal swastika under the lapel of her coat. That day she wore it openly for the first time

and her dark eyes shone as she talked of Hitler's victory. . . . She announced that a time was now at hand when servants would no longer have
to eat off the kitchen table. My mother was displeased. She thought it
presumptuous for uneducated people to concern themselves with politics.[119]

The family servant believed the "Socialist" component of National Socialism would dignify her humble status.

Jecker and the Housewives heard disquieting news during the fall of
1933. Robert Ley ordered that all domestic servants must join the National Socialist Labor Front. "What?" exclaimed Hindenberg-Delbrück.
"Domestic servants belong in the Labor Front about as much as we do!"
In her view the Labor Front sounded suspiciously like a trade union,
which might demand higher pay and better working conditions.[120] "Our
servants come from all classes and we don't want them labeled as workers," she complained, adding that Marxist influence must have led the
Labor Front to encourage servants to form their own organization. "We
are convinced this is an oversight."[121] It was not. Letters from local
chapters quickly confirmed the truth.

> Dear Frau Hindenberg,
>
> Here in Uelzen, outrage has erupted! For the last four weeks, all of our
> girls have started to attend meetings of the National Socialist Labor Front
> Servants' Union . . . where [they are told] that the average middle-class
> woman knows only how to drive around in a Mercedes Benz, smoke ciga-
> rettes, and play tennis. Therefore, they must have servants . . . and not a
> word [do they hear] about servants' obligations to their employers. . . . Our
> girls have it really good here. . . .[122]

Hindenberg-Delbrück protested to the national headquarters and the
Labor Front. She dispatched spies to Labor Front rallies who reported
that "swarms" of poorly paid women who did piecework in their homes
flocked to hear Nazi speakers, whom Maria Jecker called "worse than
Communists."[123] Since the Labor Front had the backing of the state, the
short-term outcome was clear. The servants remained under the control
of the government-sponsored union and outside the jurisdiction of their
housewife-employers.[124] The honeymoon between the Housewives and
the Nazi state ended.

Jecker worked to create a world in which a housewife would rule her
domain much as an artisan presided over his shop, and like medieval
guild members the professional housewives would lobby for their inter-

ests. But Nazi policy, instead of empowering the housewife in her domain, pulled the servants out of her influence and organized them in the Labor Front. Jecker had been deceived. She and her associates had relinquished their own autonomy, dismissed long-standing Jewish members, and encouraged their "Aryan" members to join Nazi organizations. They traded off their own organizational integrity in anticipation of a long-term gain that did not materialize. When they discovered their miscalculation, they continued for a time to assert their independence. They realized belatedly that they faced only two options: total acquiescence or complete dissolution. They chose the former and pledged cooperation with all state programs. And, as it turned out, the government yielded, and within the next few years cut back servants' social security programs and appointed members of the Housewives' association to positions in Scholtz-Klink's administration. Ultimately, the servants lost their benefits, and the Labor Front, which they had mistaken for an ally, increased hours and told servants to be grateful for their jobs. Housewives in the long run won out and congratulated themselves on a victory.

As 1933 drew to a close, longtime women Nazis expressed their disillusionment and new followers grew restive. The idea of a man directing Nazi women did not improve morale. Nazi leaders renewed their search for a woman leader. The new government needed a very special type of leader: a woman who possessed sufficient administrative experience to take command of programs for millions of women, but also a woman who claimed no independent rights either for herself or women in general. Male leaders needed only an image: a woman to lead women and follow men.

Someone had to enforce and popularize women's removal from well-paid jobs, to lead a campaign to increase fertility among "racially desirable" Germans, and to mobilize women for unpaid volunteer work at the community level. The task presented serious intrinsic problems that only a social magician could overcome. The status of motherhood had to be upgraded even as its functions were taken over by the state. From an administrative point of view, the sheer scope of the office presented problems. The women's division was growing rapidly. Within months of the Nazi takeover, Paula Siber boasted that she had recruited over 8 million followers and enjoyed a good reputation with women regional leaders. After one year of power, Nazi leaders found fault with every woman leader who demonstrated leadership potential. In addition, Nazi chiefs Hess, Goebbels, Frick, and Ley competed for control of the women's administrative bonanza.

While male leaders made the transition from street fighting to desk jobs, female leaders fell by the wayside. They seemed, the men said, too rebellious, too angry and undisciplined. Women faced several obstacles in addition to men's hostility. To exercise influence in the Third Reich, any official needed access to Hitler. This, in turn, meant joining Hitler's entourage of cronies at after-dinner gatherings or at the opera. Because Zander, Gottschewski, Siber, and Diehl never enjoyed any contact with Hitler's inner circles, they had no opportunity to hear, much less adapt to, the Führer's latest proclamations. Moreover, men who made the transition from rebellious party to corrupt government received rewards in the form of regional leadership posts, ministries, and commissions. No woman leader was entrusted with control even over her own bureaucratic realm. Instead, women themselves became the spoils of victory in the male leaders' internecine competition. Far from becoming adept at leadership, successful women in the post-1933 bureaucracy learned how to surrender to male superiors.

Women, as welfare, office, and factory workers, were encouraged to work with (and pay dues to) the massive Women's Bureau (Frauenwerk), but they were also required to belong to Robert Ley's Labor Front, which controlled all German workers. Farmers' wives belonged to the Frauenwerk, but the Department of Agriculture, headed by Walter Darré, regulated the practical conditions of their lives. Social workers, while belonging to the Frauenwerk, received their orders from Erich Hilgenfeldt's Department of Welfare. Only women teachers, under Auguste Reber-Gruber, enjoyed a margin of independence as women in the overwhelmingly male Nazi Teachers' Union. Administrative flair and obedience, not charisma or even enthusiasm, became the qualifying virtues for women leaders.

Early fanatics did not measure up. The experience of autonomy had imbued them with the fighting spirit to defend their terrain against both "bourgeois bigots" and Communist "hecklers," in the words of one of the Abel essay authors. Their rebelliousness did not serve them well after 1933, when their principle opposition came from the men within the Party. Of the old-timers, Paula Siber and Lydia Gottschewski demonstrated the sharpest political acumen. Diehl had resigned from her Party post in late 1932, and Zander's close association with Strasser guaranteed her demise. Gottschewski and Siber had understood the importance of male protectors to represent their interests in high-level discussions from which they were excluded. But Gottschewski's youthful flamboyance assured her demise. Siber, backed by Wilhelm Frick, Minister of Interior, worked out moderate tactics for bringing German women under Nazi control. In one sense, Siber's choice was not a bad one, for Frick was the only incorruptible and hardworking of Hitler's deputies. However, as time passed, others overshadowed him. A rival quipped, "Göring and Heydrich weigh more than a hundred Fricks."[125] In regard to women, Frick's opinions differed not at all from non-Nazi conservatives. "The mother shall devote herself exclusively to children and family; the wife to the husband; and the unmarried only to feminine occupations."[126] By returning women to their homes, Frick expected to combat Marxism, which "destroys family life."

This narrow vision of women's place offered Siber and other ambitious women little scope for action. However, Siber swore allegiance to Frick's directives. On occasion, however, she took the initiative when it came to implementing Nazi guidelines.[127] This independence brought suspicions in the autumn of 1933, when Party chiefs accused her of having operated independently during electoral campaigns. Siber defended herself against having offered women too much authority. "We had to attract women not by empty words, but with authentic material that clarified women's position and rights in the National Socialist state." Because Nazi leaders themselves had remained silent about concrete programs for women, she campaigned on her own. The core of her promises seemed harmless enough. "The woman must create the family and the soul of the state," Siber told 30,000 cheering women at a district leadership conference in March 1934.[128] By defending mothers' rights, Siber believed she adhered to Nazi doctrine. For a time it appeared she was correct. Zander, Gottschewski, Krummacher, and Diehl lost their posts; Siber remained in office. Siber had elaborated her own ideological position in a book, several articles, and hundreds of speeches throughout Germany. She dreamed of a vast educational program that would incorporate millions of her followers into a tightly organized hierarchy. Under Hitler, she predicted, the German race would be divided into manly men and feminine women, each with its distinct sphere of influence and inspired by its "burning idealism" under God.[129] Siber wrote poetry, spoke eloquently, and inspired her audiences; she managed her finances efficiently; and was married to an old-time Nazi army officer. She presented the ideal image of the female Nazi leader and had every reason to expect she would be considered as national director of whatever women's organization finally emerged. Nothing of the kind happened. Precisely the traits that ensured Siber's success in the early days guaranteed her demise after 1933.

When her rival arrived in Berlin, Siber did not even notice. In fact, no one seemed to pay much attention to Gertrud Scholtz-Klink, who in December 1933 became the director of the Women's Service Year program. Without a national reputation or any special accomplishments, who would have guessed that within months she would become the

National Women's Leader of the Third Reich? For several years she had worked quietly in her own province of Baden, a small German state on the Swiss-French border. During the fall of 1933 she shared the speakers' podium with the chief of the Labor Corps, who invited her to join the government. At age thirty-three, she was ten years younger than Siber and considerably less experienced. Among Hitler's close colleagues, only Speer was as young and as recent a convert. Like Speer, she displayed little interest in doctrine. When she spoke in public, she avoided troublesome topics such as women's role or nature; instead she outlined dull administrative details and told women vaguely to sacrifice. Unlike Siber and many early women leaders, Scholtz-Klink displayed no enthusiasm for Christianity. Her formal exit from the Protestant Church was unusually bold. Although they did not attend church, other Nazi leaders, including Hitler himself, remained nominal Catholics or Protestants. Devoid of "doctrinal stubbornness," as she called it, she willingly took up whatever theme Nazi leaders suggested.

Before the summer of 1933, she founded local support groups and recruited charity workers to aid poor Nazi families in predominantly Catholic Baden. Unlike the rebellious early Nazis, Zander and Seydel, Scholtz-Klink cultivated contacts with Catholic women's organizations. In 1930 she unified 14 local Nazi chapters in Baden and invited herself to cooperate with non-Nazi charity drives. Like Polster, she worked closely with the male Nazi leadership in the area and adapted religious women's activities for the Nazi cause. Her district chief, Gauleiter Robert Wagner, paid tribute to her success. "The women's organization here is completely unified and has spread its network throughout the district." [130]

Her opportunism, combined with an easy grace and flexibility, brought Scholtz-Klink to the attention of the male Nazi leadership. Her physical appearance did not harm her prospects. Already Germans were beginning to whisper jokes about raising racially pure children, "as blond as Hitler, as slim as Göring, and as athletic as Goebbels." Scholtz-Klink, young, trim, and blond, appeared as the most "Aryan" of the clique of leaders surrounding Hitler. Because Scholtz-Klink did not attend meetings of high-ranking Nazis, she, like Siber, instinctively sought a male protector and found him in Erich Hilgenfeldt, the director of national welfare. Although of far lower rank than Frick, Hilgenfeldt possessed shrewdness and administrative finesse. Co-workers report that he could display a viciousness rare even among Hitler's deputies. The two made a perfect team. A former colleague alleges that Hilgenfeldt and Scholtz-Klink for several years were involved in a romantic liaison, a suspicion deepened by the fact that Hilgenfeldt married only a day after Scholtz-

Klink married SS General Heissmeyer in 1939. Scholtz-Klink, of course, denounces such rumors as slanderous.[131]

Against this formidable team, Interior Minister Frick and Siber stood no chance. Besides being a wily bureaucrat, Hilgenfeldt shared fully Hitler's plans for a eugenic purification. For this he needed women to cooperate with "positive" measures to breed the super race, but to excise pity from their hearts when they watched fellow citizens suffering the assaults of "negative" eugenics. He told his social workers,

> We no longer appeal to humane values and to sentimental instincts—that is totally false! No more alms and pity! Softness and sentimentality must go. . . . The infection affecting the *Volk* must be countered by a tough position. We seize the initiative! *[Wir greifen an!]* We will succeed against *any* resistance. While we welcome anyone to our task, we will accept only those who have been transformed [by our doctrine]. The totality of our claim encompasses all areas of social work.[132]

Following *Mein Kampf*, Hilgenfeldt believed that "racial poisoning" could be corrected only by careful breeding. Of course, he conceded, this conclusion might appear cruel to the faint-of-heart; but because the health of the nation depended on it, eugenic selection must be applied. Women, in other words, would cooperate and men would lead.

While Scholtz-Klink maintained a low profile, Hilgenfeldt boldly announced his priorities. Women's job in the Third Reich, he proclaimed, was to leave all policy-making to the men. At Scholtz-Klink's first meeting with her district leaders, she said virtually nothing, except to make vague promises that women stood ready to join in culturally oriented activities, political indoctrination, and spiritually *(geistig)* related missions. Hilgenfeldt dominated the discussion. "The woman's duty is to augment the man's rule. . . . Women who want to be like men always are deeply unhappy . . . because they contradict nature." He defined the feminine role in terms of subservience to men rather than in terms of any particular activity. "Ultimately our goal is to create the type of woman who is needed in our era . . . as the complement of the heroic and fighting man." Of course, he reflected, women's work might well be considered the more difficult because the rewards were so small.[133] One of Scholtz-Klink's staff members had the solution for that problem too. "Woman is the tool *[Werkzeug]* of the state. . . . We will not itemize what obligations the state owes to us women; we know only that the state has given us obligations that we must recognize and cheerfully fulfill."[134] The rhetoric of sacrifice masked (however thinly) the brutal dictates of racial revolution.

Scholtz-Klink evaluated the position of a woman leader more shrewdly than her rivals. Today she proudly explains her success. "The time from July 1, 1931, until the end of 1933, was hardly praiseworthy as far as the Nazi Women's Association is concerned. Because men disagreed among themselves and women leaders were so weak, each regional leader was left to improvise according to local conditions."[135] In true Nazi style, she equated "weak" with "independent." In a way she is right because if she wanted to be a "strong" force over the women's division, she needed to yield absolutely to her male superiors. In retrospect, she praises the earliest women Nazis using adjectives that she would no doubt apply to herself.

> Never will I forget the first women who found their way to us—the ones with nothing to lose except their lives. They assumed burdens and made sacrifices without asking what was in it for them. Perhaps they did not have so much intelligence or intellectual grasp of the great ideas of the Party. But they stood by their men because they believed that the life and death of their *Volk* would be determined there.[136]

In a brief description of her work for Hitler, three words recur: "harmony," "*Volk*," and "duty." Indeed, these remained the watchwords of her eleven-year career as the director of women's affairs. Since those halcyon days her views have remained intact.[137] During the 1930s, she told women they had been betrayed by the sterile and overly intellectual women's movement, which fought genuine Germanic spirit with "alien" weapons such as intelligence and reason; she, by contrast, proved to be the mistress of "feminine" tactics. Over four decades later, she believed that, if women aspire to masculine positions, they become nervous and anxious. And well they might, for they sense keenly the hostility from their male colleagues. Instead of fighting a hopeless battle for equality— an ephemeral ideal in any case—Scholtz-Klink advised women to renounce material aspirations. Her self-righteousness was exceeded only by her hypocrisy.

The Nazi Party, which purged unruly SA men and demoted a few male leaders with heretical ideas, had little trouble dispensing with Scholtz-Klink's major rivals. Simple directives had pensioned off Elsbeth Zander (who in any case had passed the normal retirement age). Diehl (in her early sixties) complained bitterly about the shabby way in which she had been treated, but had no choice but to leave national politics and return to her own New Land organization. Her instincts had served her well during those many years when she did not join the Party officially. By remaining independent, she retained her own organization, which sustained her after she fell from grace. Gottschewski's enthusiasm collapsed in the face of powerful opposition, and she retreated into private life as a wife and a part-time journalist. Krummacher happily resumed his municipal responsibilities. However, Paula Siber refused to be eased out of her position. Ambitious and fanatically loyal to Nazi goals as she saw them, Siber fought to retain her position. Hilgenfeldt initiated a smear campaign against her, alleging she had embezzled funds from the Mothers' Aid fund drive to support her publications, undercut Krummacher's authority, engaged in friendly talks with Gertrud Bäumer, the leader of bourgeois women's-rights groups, kept careless records, and formulated her own views on the Nazi position about the Woman Question. In all, Hilgenfeldt drafted fifteen accusations against Siber. His campaign proved so successful, Siber's husband later complained that rumor alleged his wife had been killed in the "night of the long knives," the SA purge of June 30, 1934.[138]

Throughout these maneuvers, Frick duly defended his deputy and ordered a complete investigation of all charges, but he naively suspended Siber during the investigation, which meant she could not speak in public or in any way organize her own defense.[139] The scandal generated dozens of memos, letters of reference and calumny, affidavits and hearings. Gossip was so scandalous and contradictory it is difficult to know which allegation was the most damaging or accurate. Scholtz-Klink was accused of carrying on an affair with someone high up. But interestingly, this suggestion was topped by another rumor; that she had had a miscarriage. For a Nazi to have an affair was probably not so terrible (despite Hitler's own prudishness), but a "miscarriage" hinted at abortion, a worse sin in the racial state. Paula Siber got off lightly with only accusations of mental instability, while her defenders attacked Hilgenfeldt's putative homosexual predilections.[140] During the winter of 1934, Hilgenfeldt admitted his defeat, formally withdrew all allegations, and confessed he had committed slander.[141]

By then, Hilgenfeldt's guilt and Siber's innocence no longer mattered. Scholtz-Klink herself had remained aloof from the proceedings and used the time to anchor her position as women's leader. Frick's loyal intervention formally saved Siber; but Scholtz-Klink exerted her informal pressure on Hess. After Hilgenfeldt relented and it appeared that Siber might be restored after all, Scholtz-Klink, in what must rank as her only independent display of power, insisted on having her way. "As far as I am concerned, I want my wishes accorded the same respect that would be given to a man [of my status] in ideological and financial affairs. I insist on this attitude [Gesinnung] from my co-workers and I am determined to make it an iron law right down to the smallest local group."[142] Her male superiors granted her wish. Since Siber refused to fit smoothly into her chain of command, she must go. Without presenting a shred of evidence against Siber, Scholtz-Klink insisted on control over her own territory. In the prototypical Nazi trade-off, she would obey the male leadership and women would submit to her.

Siber refused to leave and the totalitarian state could not easily dislodge her. By early 1935, Frick had abandoned her, but her husband had not. The couple had moved to Berlin in order to advance her career; when she was dismissed, they began legal proceedings. Although trials and hearings might delay Siber's dismissal, the couple ought to have known they stood no chance of restoring her office or her reputation. As a last resort, Major Siber addressed Hitler directly. Like a host of early fanatics, he felt deeply hurt by the high status being accorded to the newcomers who had opportunistically joined the Party after it took power.

> My Führer, I protest against the impact and results [Austragung] of this dirty and most un-National Socialist battle. . . . Hilgenfeldt has launched a slander campaign and brought the blemish [Makel] of dishonor upon her reputation. . . . No rehabilitation has followed his confession of guilt. . . . Mein Führer, I believe that these events contradict the fundamental honor, sense of justice, and loyalty owed to loyal followers. This is certainly no reward for years of the most dedicated and faithful work. . . . One does not hunt down such followers . . . like the most faithless and unreliable dog . . . This sort of behavior, mein Führer, is treason against the loyalty which you have always demanded and displayed.[143]

In rambling, overstated prose, reminiscent of Hitler's own style, Major Siber lamented the opportunism of a once-idealistic movement. "This has been the biggest and bitterest disappointment of our lives." The letter remained unanswered.

The Sibers probably never realized that, in addition to Paula's independence, she suffered from another handicap. Ironically, in this state that extolled the virtues of the traditional family, a husband was a liability for a woman leader. No matter how high her status, she would remain a wife, which, in turn, meant that obedience to her spouse took precedence over the requirements of her job. At any time, for example, the husband of a Nazi bureaucrat might insist she resign, relocate, or have a baby. Clifford Kirkpatrick tersely summed up the dilemma created by these policies. "They criticized women leaders when they did not marry and fired them when they did."[144] When speaking at rallies, Siber asked to be introduced as "Frau Major Siber," making it obvious to all she was the wife of an officer. Moreover, her husband's behavior had been exemplary in every way, and he had even lost his job during the Weimar Republic because of her. Because military personnel in the Weimar Republic swore to renounce any public political activity, Major Siber was dismissed. By endangering her husband's career—even for the Nazi cause—Paula Siber contradicted patriarchal expectations. Krummacher, incidentally, during his short tenure in office had recognized this conflict of interest and devised his solution to the dilemma when he suggested hiring only unmarried women. But his superiors did not approve of that either. Recent comments by Scholtz-Klink suggest why. Such women did not project a motherly image. "Frau Zander, and the early women," Scholtz-Klink told me, "may have been passed over because they behaved too independently—you know, always with other women and not with family." Scholtz-Klink alone among the contenders for high office in the Women's Bureau possessed just the right combination: the widow of a Nazi martyr and mother of many children. In Nazi Germany, as in so many patriarchal societies, widowhood enabled some women to transcend the limitations of their sex.

After Hitler became dictator, he directed the energies he had once used to destroy orderly society under Weimar democracy to the establishment of discipline in his dictatorship. This meant that his male followers left the streets and moved into offices, and their erstwhile enemies were either murdered, driven into exile, or imprisoned. Many old-timers missed the demonstrations, brawls, and camaraderie of the old days, and perhaps they felt a certain nostalgia as they devoted their lives to filling out forms and answering memos. But high salaries, dress balls, opera tickets, chauffeur-driven Mercedes, lavish homes, and public accolades compensated for the loss. Women Nazis confronted a very different situation. They had anticipated that Hitler's victory would empower them to do battle against non-Nazi women rivals within the female sphere (who for the most part had not been arrested). Nazi women, dedicated to motherhood, resolved to convert the unconvinced in the "old" women's movement, religious groups, and civic clubs to join their cause. They need not have bothered because middle-class women decided to collaborate of their own accord. Even more astonishing, the old-time Nazi women themselves were excluded from the newly formed women's bureaucracy. Male leaders distrusted them for precisely the energy, autonomy, and commitment prized in men Nazis.

Women old-timers watched from the sidelines as the newcomers received accolades and appointments to office. The more "respectable" women from the member organizations of the disbanded BDF, together with civic women's groups from whom Nazi leaders had anticipated resistance, quickly declared their allegiance and asked for posts. These women shared Hitler's overall program for a "new Germany" and admired authoritarian government. Like other non-Nazis on the right, they overlooked Hitler's fanatical and racist notions and anticipated that the office of Chancellor would force moderation on him. Accordingly, they volunteered for tasks in the expectation of rewards. A new wave of women functionaries transferred women Nazis' crusades from the street corner and living room into a bureaucratized women's public world backed by all-powerful state. They saw the less respectable and more fanatic early leaders being dismissed, and anticipated inheriting the movement their predecessors had begun. Retrospectively, their arrogance facing Nazi power is staggering. Like so many conservative and nationalist men, women believed they could carve out an independent set of institutions, protected but unmolested by a powerful state. The old-timers before 1933 had, in fact, operated fairly autonomously, thanks to men's obliviousness; but the army of bureaucrats commanded by Scholtz-Klink, with no illusions of independence, were more cynical. They expected to wield power over women beneath them in exchange for rendering total obedience to the all-male chain of command above them. Within months Nazi women were joined by new recruits from older organizations.

The easy capitulation of those German women troubles us still, for one would expect that membership in a women's-rights organization would have immunized German women against Nazi promises—if for no other reason than because the level of violence (verbal and physical) reached such horrifying proportions. But the member associations of the BDF yielded quickly. Nazi leaders who anticipated a long fight found themselves confronted with a surfeit of new volunteers for their cause. Before 1933, the BDF had already defaulted on its commitment to married women's right to work. Rather than insisting on their inalienable human equality, bourgeois women had bargained for benefits in exchange for contributions to the national good. In other words, they used their special "feminine" qualities to gain privileges. A decade-long encounter with democracy left them disillusioned, divided, and hopelessly alienated from the liberal wing of their own women's-rights movement. The possibility of a women's coalition against the rising tide of Hitlerism never was even a remote possibility. Because women had not, even after decades of organizing, achieved sufficient power to stand their ground in a male-dominated political forum, their tactics made sense in some ways. Women dedicated themselves to improving their women's world rather than competing in a political contest they could not win. Recognizing their weakness, they cultivated their separate culture and institutions beyond concerns they defined as "masculine." But, by making these pragmatic choices, they shed the claim they once had to special virtue. An English woman who lived in Berlin during 1933 watched the collapse of women's organizations and asked, "Was it not very like the attitude of the old lady who, when asked why she curtsied to the devil, replied, 'Ah, well, one never can tell.' "[145]

The feminist "fortress" collapsed. But Kirkpatrick's metaphor had been inappropriate in the first place. Women's organizations, although massive in membership, resembled networks with grids reaching into the most remote villages and towns. They had no walls around their separate sphere. Thus, women leaders who might have objected to the Nazi regime actually led their followers into the new state in the expectation that their cooperation would give them leverage.

6

THE SECOND SEX
IN THE
THIRD REICH

The old trust him, the young idolize him. It is not the
admiration accorded to a popular Leader. It is the worship of a national hero who has saved his country from
utter despondency and degradation. . . . He is as immune from criticism as a king in a monarchial country.
He is something more. He is the George Washington of
Germany—the man who won for his country independence from all her oppressors. To those who have not
actually seen and sensed the way Hitler reigns over the
heart and mind of Germany, this description may appear extravagant. All the same it is the bare truth.
—David Lloyd George
Daily Express (London),
November 17, 1936

Looking back on her career, Gertrud Scholtz-Klink smugly commented that she had offered her followers an alternative to two role models she considered inimical to women's interests, the lady and the feminist. Although Nazi leaders had at first asked her to form "a sort of ladies' auxiliary" for their Party, she objected. To her and many of her generation, the word "lady" had foreign connotations that suggested a beautiful but useless socialite. Frauenwerk [Women's Bureau] women, by contrast, performed vital tasks for the entire nation. Rather than obeying men's whims, they carried out their own mission with considerable autonomy and concern for women's special interests, according to the ex-Frauenwerk leader. Looking on the world of the 1970s and 1980s, Scholtz-Klink perceived another danger that reminded her of the Weimar era. Feminists, she said, betrayed women by demanding motherhood, and they threatened men by demanding entry into male-dominated fields. Worst of all, she claimed, feminists, like ladies, were selfish. In her memory, Frauenwerk women achieved the perfect solution to the Woman Question by mobilizing women as mothers into active public service within areas that kept them far from men's political and economic concerns.

This had not been an original solution to problems spawned by the demand for women's emancipation. In the 1930s many Europeans shared a panic about declining birthrates, the decaying family, and economic crisis. The French awarded medals to prolific mothers. British legislators debated family subsidies and provided income tax relief for families with many children. Mussolini declared a "battle of the birthrate." Stalin sharply curtailed the rights granted to women during the 1920s. Everywhere politicians decreed harsher sanctions against birth control and abortion, and in many nations eugenics enjoyed considerable popularity. The Nazi revival of motherhood, like other aspects of Nazi social policy, carried to grotesque extremes plans that other nations advanced only timidly. The thoroughness of Nazi policy followed from Nazi leaders' frankly misogynistic view of women. In democratic nations, pro-natalist policies contradicted a commitment to women's legal equality, and even in the Soviet Union the state never rescinded its official support for women's emancipation. But Nazi policy, from its explicit ban on women in political life to its massive programs to revive motherhood, propagated a cogent set of imperatives for women. The sturdy peasant family that graced the covers of women's magazines and inspired Nazi painters provided an emotional appeal enhanced by material incentives.

Of course, the hope of restoring the lost family was based on a misunderstanding of historical fact and in any case stood no chance of being realized in an industrialized society. But because the industrial revolution occurred much later in Germany than in other Western European nations, the memory of a peasant past seemed fresher and thus more real. The mothers of Scholtz-Klink's generation could remember the day when most families lived in rural settings and Grandmother spun, gardened, baked bread, carried water, and perhaps kept a few hens or a pig. In the 1930s, the appeal of her mythic life lay not in the tasks she had performed as much as in the belief that the loving grandmother had protected her family from a corrosive modern world.

While propagating the myth of a bygone peasant family, however, Nazi policy flagrantly contradicted its central feature: the dream that the family could provide a bulwark against the tides of alienation. True, publicity exalted the family as the "germ cell" of the nation, but social policy emptied the household of its members. Eugenic laws interfered with private choices related to marriage and children. The demand for total loyalty to the Führer undercut fathers' authority. As indoctrination supplanted education, youth leaders and teachers rivaled mothers for children's devotion. When Goebbels had described the male and female birds in his novel *Michael*, he neglected to say what became of the mother bird after her babies had flown away. Scholtz-Klink devised the answer when she organized motherhood. State subsidies, leisure activities, official ceremonies, radio programs, degrees in home economics and other "feminine" subjects, sports, and bonuses in the form of household products all seduced mothers into a vast state-run network and simultaneously offered career opportunities for educators, social workers, and administrators. By rewarding assertiveness, ambition, and physical fitness, these programs offered the New Mother as an alternative to both the careerist New Woman and the cultured lady. Frauenwerk women, unlike these selfish caricatures, learned self-effacement. Scholtz-Klink exhorted them, "Say to yourselves, 'I *am* the *Volk*.' The tiny individual self [*ich*] must submit to the great you [*Du*]."[1]

Scholtz-Klink's notions about the restoration of womanhood accorded perfectly with a Nazi historian's statement that "The soil provides the food, the woman supplies the population, and the men make the action." On this model, women had no history at all, although they had a rich heritage. Because they exerted no force in politics and economic change, women would provide a constant backdrop to men's history. This ideal had a special meaning within the context of Nazi social beliefs, according to which all individualism in men and in women was to be destroyed. Goebbels, always an articulate observer about the consequences of his task as Propaganda Minister, noted, "The revolution that we have made is a total revolution. It encompasses every aspect of public life from the bottom up. . . . We have replaced individuality with collective racial consciousness and the individual with the community."[2] The psychological revolution that was to follow the seizure of political power required a vast institutional framework. "We must develop the organizations in which every individual's entire life can take place. Then every activity and every need of every individual will be regulated by the *Volk* community, as represented by the Party. There is no longer arbitrary will. There are no longer any free realms in which the individual belongs to himself. . . . The time of personal happiness is over."[3] At its most revolutionary, Nazi policy aimed to socialize people, not property. Hitler once commented, "Our socialism is much deeper than Marxism. . . . It does not change the external order of things, but it orders solely the relationship of man to the state. . . . What do we care about income? Why should we need to socialize the banks and factories? We are socializing the people."[4] Collective joy would make private happiness obsolete.

Given prevailing notions about gender, it might seem that women were perfectly suited to spread this ideal throughout the nation. Certainly self-surrender accorded well with values that have been traditionally praised as feminine. Indeed, early leaders like Krummacher and Gottschewski perceived the potential power in such a mission. Instinctively, Scholtz-Klink turned her energies in different directions. To have placed women in charge of ideological conversion would have centered too much power in a women's division of the government; and, equally important, the kind of fanaticism implied in such a drive would have alienated the average middle-class housewives whom Scholtz-Klink intended to recruit. Her superiors expected her to integrate as many middle-class women into a Nazi framework as possible. Hence Frauenwerk projects emphasized the kinds of charitable, community-oriented activities that had always attracted wives and mothers. Built into Scholtz-Klink's success at organizing masses of followers was failure at specifically Nazi indoctrination. As long as women harmonized their values with the state sponsored programs, they happily cooperated. After 1936–1937 this became more difficult.

Eugenic policies, the assault against Christianity, and the shift to a wartime economy exposed the hypocrisy about a Nazi commitment to "strong" families and motherhood revival. Despite propaganda about "more feminine women," the new priorities made it clear that docility was the only trait that counted in women. Concern for keeping mothers in their homes lasted only as long as economic necessity made it advantageous. Ultimately, it became obvious that the ideal Nazi woman cultivated flexibility rather than any specific skills so that she could leave the workplace and return to homemaking as the state demanded. Throughout history women have shifted their economic activities over the course of their life cycles to suit the changing demands of family life. But Hitler replaced family considerations with national needs. Accordingly, Scholtz-Klink introduced a new slogan into her speeches, "Tradition does not mean stagnation, but duty."

Despite the rhetoric about restoration of family life, Nazi policy was deeply revolutionary because it aimed at the creation of a family unit that was not a defense against public invasion as much as the gateway to intervention. The contradiction between promise and reality is nowhere more apparent than in the publicity for the weekly "stew day," when mothers all over Germany prepared economical stews and contributed the money saved to the national charity, the Winter Relief (*Winterhilfe*). In the posters advertising the drive, the happy family enjoys a tasty stew around a table, but above them appears the stew pot (*Eintopf*) to remind them that their supper serves a higher cause. Family happiness was not an end in itself but a means to a national purpose. Government-sponsored family protection programs hastened the destruction of individualism and privacy. Hitler on many occasions made the revolutionary implications of this sytem clear. "Anyone who interprets National Socialism as merely a political movement knows almost nothing about it. It is more than a religion. It is the determination to create the new man."[5] What would motivate women to conform? What sort of women would desire the New Man?

Hitler answered the question at the 1935 Party Rally.

> The reward which National Socialism bestows on women in return for her labour is that it once more rears men, real men, decent men who stand erect, who are courageous, who love honor. I believe that, having watched the marching columns of the last few days, these stalwart and splendid youth from the Labor Service, our healthy and unspoiled womanhood must say to themselves, "What a robust and glorious generation is growing up here!"[6]

This type of woman, Scholtz-Klink tacitly recognized, would probably not respond favorably to fanatical Nazi indoctrination. So she organized thousands of courses, programs, outings, lectures, and radio programs oriented toward practical activities. Over a million and a half women benefited from maternity school during the first five years of Nazi rule, and nearly half a million studied home economics.[7] All of these courses indoctrinated women in race, National Socialism, and national aims. This suggests that Scholtz-Klink recruited women who had already accepted conventional notions about women's roles and who probably enjoyed the public acclaim and government funding to foster their agenda for a women's *Lebensraum.*

Adept at manipulating social situations, Scholtz-Klink obeyed her superiors' orders without participating in any of the high-level discussions at which those orders were debated. However, she did attend leaders' weddings and parties. She depended upon Hilgenfeldt to represent her interests because any display of energy from her might bring charges of insubordination from worried male superiors. Thus, her opportunism itself was limited by very limited opportunity. To be sure, this tension was endemic in all branches of the government, but women faced an unusual degree of distrust from the stridently masculine elite. If they appeared too docile, their male superiors called them "sneaking hypocrites," and if they attacked a problem energetically, they provoked male ridicule as "amazons."[8]

The position of ambitious women was fraught with contradictions. Albert Speer recalls that even Leni Riefenstahl confronted obstacles when she was contracted to film the 1934 Party Rally.

> As the only woman officially involved in the proceedings she had frequent conflicts with the Party organization, which was soon up in arms against her. The Nazis were by tradition anti-feminist and could hardly brook this self-assured woman, the more so since she knew how to bend this men's world to her purposes. Intrigues were launched and slanderous stories carried to Hess. . . . But after the first Party Rally film, which convinced even the doubters of her skill as a director, these attacks ceased.[9]

Had he been more honest, Speer would have noted that the film director demonstrated more than professionalism by cultivating intimate relationships with key Party bosses. Shortly after the Party Rally of 1934, for example, Julius Streicher (the notorious anti-Semite and District Leader of Nuremberg) sent her a warm telegram, using the familiar *Du* form of address, in which he recalled their last visit together.[10] Riefenstahl made it clear that she would conform not only to Party aims, but to her leaders' expectations. Obedience, or, more accurately, obsequiousness, counted as much as doctrinal purity or skill.

Scholtz-Klink organized her workers on pragmatic lines, focusing on the particular task at hand and underplaying ideology. Like the old-timers from the 1920s whom she replaced, she found herself staying as far as possible from the male Party. So low was her profile that the men around Hitler hardly knew who she was. Her male counterparts never acknowledged her as an equal, although her name appeared high in the organizational charts of Nazi Party and state bureaucracy. In memoirs and letters we find her name chronically misspelled. In 1937, Bormann admitted he still did not understand precisely what Scholtz-Klink's position was. The German *Who's Who* overlooked her until 1936, and the British did not think to include her in their list of top Nazis. In an extraordinarily complete collection of documents on women in the two World Wars, historian Ursula von Gersdorff implicitly acknowledged how little input Scholtz-Klink had into policy decisions by mentioning Scholtz-Klink's name only twice in 560 pages. Although she shared the podium with Hitler on dozens of occasions, at no time did he consult with her regarding substantive issues. So unimportant was Scholtz-Klink in the broader scheme of Nazi power that she did not even receive the official portrait of Hitler which de rigueur hung above every state and Party official's desk. But Scholtz-Klink pointed to this and other slights as evidence of her lack of concern for ideological issues.

In the late 1930s, Scholtz-Klink must have noted an irony that reflected poorly on her status. Although she was considered fit to be chief of all German women without a special racial investigation, when she became engaged to marry SS General Heissmeyer, Party officials thoroughly investigated her family tree for over four generations to verify that she had no Jewish ancestors. In the perverse scale of Nazi values, this indicated that a general's wife ranked higher than chief of all German women.[11] Scholtz-Klink will not admit it, but it must have galled her, too, that her orders needed Hilgenfeldt's signature. On occasion, *he* was even called the Director of the Frauenschaft. With this man as the power in front of her throne, Scholtz-Klink told women to "guard, preserve, and protect [*behüten, erhalten, und bewahren*]" their realm.

The only situation in which she could count on her superiors' support was when she needed their backing in a dispute with her women subordinates (like Paula Siber). Nonetheless, she boasted to me about her informal, "invisible" power. "You know how it was—the most important orders were never written down; Hitler merely expressed his wishes, and we translated them into action." She alluded to two examples to illustrate her ability to make an impact on Nazi planning. The archives corroborate the first. In 1938, she asked Martin Bormann to promote a woman astronomer with outstanding credentials.[12] Bormann granted the request, but not merely because Scholtz-Klink urged him to. Leading male astronomers endorsed it, and Scholtz-Klink swore that the astronomer (although unmarried) had not chosen her career for "any sort of professional ambitions," but was driven by "passionate interest." Because this was so unusual in a woman, she argued that it would not establish a dangerous precedent.

On a second occasion (not established in the archives) at the beginning of the war, she recalled that she and her office had authorized the construction of a Frauenschaft (Women's League) center in the fashionable Wannsee district in suburban Berlin. Goebbels, who lived nearby, canceled the project because he did not want his children to see too many women lingering about. Overlooking the insult to her Frauenschaft, Scholtz-Klink claims the plans went ahead anyway.[13] Scholtz-Klink did not acknowledge, even when I brought it to her attention, Goebbels' contempt for "her" women—even the putative elite for whom the center in Berlin was intended.

After five years of Nazi power, only one-third of all functionaries in the Frauenwerk (and less than 70 percent on Scholtz-Klink's own staff) belonged to the Nazi Party.[14] Using membership statistics as a standard, the Frauenwerk ranked lower than any other branch of government. When I asked Scholtz-Klink about that, she proudly unfolded a stack of charts and pointed to elaborate lines of command, names and boxes to show the distribution of power. Then as now, it was the outward show of status that impressed her. The lack of authority vis-à-vis men enabled her, she said, to operate effectively in a female *Lebensraum* where pragmatic tasks, not Nazi indoctrination, brought masses of ordinary women together in a joyous spirit.

To the general public, Scholtz-Klink projected a self-effacing image. Her supporters found her "a simple National Socialist woman selected for her womanly qualities to bring women into line, using gentle womanly guile to restore the rights of women threatened in the turmoil of revolution." Under her "gentle hand" over 4 million women participated in the vast network of Frauenwerk organizations; 5 million women belonged to the women's division of the Nazi Labor Front (nominally under Scholtz-Klink), 2 million leaders worked under the rubric of the elite National Socialist women's organization, the Frauenschaft; and just over 100,000 women teachers officially fell under her supervision.[15] While stressing nonideological, pragmatic goals in the massive Frauenwerk, Scholtz-Klink prepared the leadership of the Frauenschaft through hundreds of courses in public speaking, racial doctrine, community organizing, and administration.

From 1934 until 1939, 950 specially selected women attended two- and three-week summer sessions at a castle in the town of Coburg. Each participant submitted a brief autobiography, a photograph, and application form; and before she left, her teacher turned in an evaluation of her comradely nature, ideological reliability, physical fitness, discipline, skill at public speaking, and (most importantly) her overall leadership potential. These records, preserved in the Federal Archives in Koblenz, provide a valuable source of information about the types of women

Scholtz-Klink saw as the leaders of future generations. Several general characteristics emerge. Virtually all of the students lived in rural areas or in small towns at the time they attended the leadership school. In an industrialized nation with over half the population centered in big cities, this imbalance suggests that Scholtz-Klink recruited from women who maintained contact with rural values. It may also indicate (although she denied it) that women from urban areas displayed too deep a loyalty to rival church and civic organizations. Scholtz-Klink relied on women like herself—ambitious provincial housewives.

The backgrounds show a remarkable similarity to those of the respondents in Theodore Abel's essay contest on "Why I Became a Nazi." All but a handful of the women had grown up in middle-class Protestant families. None noted a father with a working-class occupation, and only a few had grown up in peasant families. "Postal official," "railway man," "businessman," "government employee," "artisan," or "small factory owner" appeared frequently in the blanks after fathers' or husbands' occupation. Predictably, most had never attended a university or university-preparatory school. About half had graduated from the school known in Germany as the "Upper School for Daughters" (*Höhere Töchterschule*), which offered some academic training as well as courses in housewifely skills and deportment. A few had attended more prestigious private schools (*Lyceum*). One woman who did complete a university education became a dentist, but left her practice when she married. Interestingly, however, most women noted that they had received advanced training in technical, office, or homemaking skills. Except for one young woman (the daughter of a noble family and graduate of a Geneva finishing school), all had found jobs after completing school and before marriage. Just under half of the women born during the 1890s included descriptions of their wartime service in their autobiographies. A few women proudly mentioned having received medals from the military or Red Cross. These records sketch a general picture of a Nazi woman who was proud of her middle-class status, oriented toward activities outside her home, and, above all, respectable.

In a regime that touted the traditional mother of many children, it may seem surprising that only about half of these 950 role models were married at the time they attended leadership training sessions. Many had never had children, and those with children had only one or two on the average. During the first years of the program, most women at the training school had been born during the late 1880s or early 1890s; but starting in 1935–1936, a younger generation, born twenty years later, predominated. These young women, recruited directly from the BDM, were not married. Scholtz-Klink, in selecting her elite, must have been motivated by the same considerations as the men who had chosen her. A married woman, especially if she had small children at home, may have provided an excellent role model, but she did not have the time to devote to Party activities. Moreover, a husband could claim priority at any time over his wife's Party duties. From this perspective, the large number of unmarried and widowed women made sense, even in a state that praised mother-hood as women's only career.[16] The leadership school records reveal a striking lack of emphasis on "racial science." A handful of women leaders noted "racial education" as their specialty, but virtually all others listed "local leader" as their job. This substantiates Scholtz-Klink's claim to have cared mainly about pragmatic concerns, such as home economics and child psychology, nutrition and physical fitness.

During her early years in office, Scholtz-Klink administered programs to refurbish conventional notions about women's roles, "professionaliz-ing" traditional duties and bringing women together to share their expe-riences. In other words, she used up-to-date public-relations techniques to accomplish conservative goals. She did not speak to women about Hitler's racial theories, about his threats to destroy Christianity or his plans to conquer new territory. Ultimately, of course, Nazi leaders cared only about improving fertility, but they gave Scholtz-Klink a mandate to encourage childbearing with comprehensive programs that supported mothers in material and psychological ways. For a time it appeared that Scholtz-Klink facilitated the world's most ambitious fertility drive. Marriage rates skyrocketed after the unusually low levels of the De-pression.

On closer examination, however, the increasing marriage rates may not have resulted from Nazi policy but from demographic trends. The fatalities of World War I had reduced the number of marriages in the postwar decade; but as younger men who had not fought in the war entered their late twenties and early thirties, these low rates would have risen even without material incentives. Marriage loans thus encouraged many couples who had deferred the decision to marry due to lack of money during the Depression. Loans enabled them to cross the thresh-old, a step that contributed to unusually high marriage rates just after the plan was announced followed by a decline after 1935.

Scholtz-Klink propagated shibboleths about "strong" families, but Nazi leaders cared far more about babies than happy homes. Nowhere else in Europe or the United States has so comprehensive a drive been launched to increase the birthrate. In addition to the innovative marriage loan program, more legislation followed to encourage childbearing. For each child born to a couple in the Marriage Loan Program, the govern-ment reduced the principal by 25 percent. Income-tax deductions were increased so that the parents could deduct 15 percent per child of their gross income from taxable income, and parents of six children paid no personal income tax at all. The term "dependent" was redefined to include children of up to twenty-five years of age. Large families found it easier to hire domestic servants since servants were excluded from the unemployment-insurance program. Women who bore their fifth child could choose to make a nationally prominent man the godfather of that baby; Hindenburg, however, outran Hitler, and the plan was suspended before the President's death. Mother's Day was changed to Hitler's mother's birthday (August 12) and made a national holiday.[17] Finally, motherhood medals were introduced (bronze for five children, silver for six, and gold for seven). Whenever a member of the Hitler Youth met a decorated mother (with her award worn neatly on a blue ribbon at her neck), he had to snap to attention with a brisk *"Heil Hitler!"*

Material and psychological incentives were reinforced by coercive policies. Birth control was outlawed, and marriage-counseling centers were closed or replaced by "eugenic counseling" facilities. Arrests and convictions of people performing or aiding an abortion doubled, and punishments became more severe. Women physicians felt the force of Nazi law acutely. Although less than 5 percent of all physicians were women, the majority of physicians arrested on charges of abortion were women. This imbalance resulted from a combination of factors. A disproportionate percentage of women were gynecologists in the first place. Since legislation prevented them from practicing except in their husbands' practices and then excluded them (along with Jews) from receiving public health insurance payments, many must have chosen to continue their profession clandestinely.

For all the public pressure, the birthrate in the Third Reich did not ever equal the rates from the last years of the "decadent" 1920s. Although recipients of marriage loans bore 360,000 babies between 1933 and 1939, it is not clear that these births resulted directly from government rewards.[18] Throughout the 1930s, abortion as a percentage of the total crime increased steadily, a trend that the authors of a governmental report considered "stunning!" given the strength of Nazi pro-family legislation and propaganda.[19] Evaluating fertility statistics in a short period inevitably presents problems. In the case of Germany during the 1930s, we can tentatively conclude that the birthrate failed to increase as dramatically as social planners predicted, although, on the other hand, German fertility remained relatively high compared with other western European nations.[20]

The most carefully thought-out pro-natalist program in any industrialized state did not significantly alter parents' desire for children. Parents considered their aspirations for a higher standard of living, the atmosphere of Nazi Germany, the expense of raising children, and housing shortages, and they limited the numbers of children they bore.[21] The trend toward small families proved intractable. Not even strict enforcement of antiabortion laws seems to have made a major impact. A staff officer in the SS estimated that in 1936 as many as 500,000 abortions had been performed. "The fact that many abortions are committed in the racially most valuable circles," he reported, defied social planners. "If these abortions could be prevented, in twenty years we would have an additional two hundred regiments." Little had changed by the late 1930s, when statisticians' estimates of abortions ranged from 500,000 to 1 million annually. Even the lower figure would suggest that abortions outnumbered children born to Marriage Loan couples.[22] One Nazi official lamented,

> The state stands helpless before many things. The scornful smile, expressing the sentiments of the children in regard to the "stupid" people with large families, cannot be forbidden or restricted. The state cannot completely eliminate the manifold dangers of the large city and it cannot deprive mothers of their employment. At first it can only honour the mothers of children and remove from the fathers of large families part of their extra burden by reducing their taxes.[23]

The official assumed that Nazi policy unambiguously encouraged childbirth and that public opinion proved intractable. Actually, the situation was more complex. In unintentional and paradoxical ways, Nazi social policy merged new and old trends. By linking women to family life, it hearkened back to the nineteenth-century ideal of domesticity; by offering state incentives, it epitomized twentieth-century welfare policies.

No doubt both trends attracted support. Some Germans who decided to marry after the Marriage Loan Program began may have responded positively to state incentives, while others may have seen marriage and a family as a defense *against* an intrusive modern state. Statistical evidence cannot tell us why Germans married. Nor can it tell why the newlyweds did not produce more children than couples during the "decadent" Weimar era. Perhaps people remained immune to appeals that counteracted material self-interest, and non-Nazi parents probably did not wish to bring children into a Nazi society.

Records from the welfare office and Frauenwerk explain a large part of the failure. The Nazi administration, in fact, demonstrated very little concern about attracting working-class loyalty to its programs. In contradiction to the rhetoric about one unified, classless society, Scholtz-

Klink's "target" population was limited to full-time housewives, and implicitly to the middle class. Vacations for overworked mothers attracted only women who could afford to pay someone to take care of their children and husbands back home. The requirement that the wife of a couple who received a marriage loan had to leave her paid job meant that husbands needed a substantial income to qualify. Working-class women fell under Labor Front jurisdiction. The Frauenwerk directed its attention at "respectable" women, and excluded not only the "racially unfit" and Jewish women, but working-class participation as well. Although protective legislation covering mothers with factory and office jobs was the most stringent in the world, its provisions were not enforced. Women worked for up to sixty hours a week under poor conditions; accident rates skyrocketed; and miscarriage rates increased among factory workers.[24] For all the fanfare about increased birthrates, only 20,000 mothers received welfare subsidies from the state, and other supports, such as school-lunch programs and direct aid to children, hardly existed.[25] The Nazi "brown nurses" helped only the "worthy poor," whom they defined in terms of "biological" criteria and enthusiasm for Nazism.[26] Scholtz-Klink no doubt sensed the futility of recruiting from urban working-class neighborhoods, in which Socialism had been so strong for decades. Thus it is not surprising that participants in an oral-history project in a working-class neighborhood in Berlin cannot remember ever being approached by a Nazi organizer or social worker.

Often, however, Nazi women cooperated with the Gestapo to harass and intimidate people with anti-Nazi reputations. The memoirs of Ilse Koehn, daughter of a Jewish father and non-Jewish mother with socialist backgrounds, illustrates how Nazi social workers operated against racial and political enemies. One day after school, Ilse encountered two representatives from the Women's Bureau at her Jewish grandmother's door. "I faced what seemed to be a gray wall moving toward me. I had the nightmare feeling that it would come close, closer, and crush me. It consisted of two huge women dressed in long, identical gray coats with big black handbags and laced boots. Ugly, flat, black boots. They had pallid faces, and their hair was tied back so tightly they seemed bald."[27] They inspected the household on the pretext of judging her grandmother's child-rearing ability. In reality, they initiated proceedings to make Ilse a ward of the state and return her to her non-Jewish grandparents, who presumably would raise her to be a good Nazi child. This event occurred before the Nuremberg Laws, when children with one Jewish parent sometimes counted as "Aryan."

Behind the facade of "One Volk one Führer" Nazi rule established a highly segmented society, with the members of the respectable middle

class as its beneficiaries. Scholtz-Klink looked for women just like herself
—provincial, traditional, and ambitious—to participate in the Nazi state.
From this it followed that when Hitler declared incentives for marriage
and childbearing, they were offered principally to the middle class, in
other words, to people who had already demonstrated the lowest birthrates before 1933. While offering incentives to bear children and
propagating motherhood as every woman's career, however, Scholtz-
Klink's Frauenschaft attacked key aspects of the traditional family.

Gone were the days when love and marriage joined the happy couple.
In "racial science" courses, young women memorized the "Ten Commandments for Choosing a Partner."

1. Remember you are a German!
2. Remain pure in mind and spirit!
3. Keep your body pure!
4. If hereditarily fit, do not remain single!
5. Marry only for love!
6. Being a German, choose only a spouse of similar or related blood!
7. When choosing your spouse, inquire into his or her forebears!
8. Health is essential to outward beauty as well!
9. Seek a companion in marriage, not a playmate!
10. Hope for as many children as possible!

Compliance with "racial standards" was elevated to a moral obligation to
the *Volk*, as enshrined in the Ten Commandments. A corps of medical
professionals, under Hilgenfeldt's Welfare Bureau, was dispatched to
inspect the health and genetic fitness of participants in state activities
such as motherhood courses, vacation plans, and community organizations. More ominous programs threatened familial privacy.

Widespread objections did not slow down the effort to sterilize all
"unworthy" Germans. In early 1934, 205 special eugenics courts were
established throughout Germany to decide who was "worthy" to procreate. One year later, nearly 100,000 applications (most by social workers "on behalf" of their clients) for sterilization had been forwarded to
the courts, almost 56,200 operations had been carried out (28,000 on
men and 27,900 on women), and the waiting list continued to grow.[28]
The national chief of eugenics told German women in 1934, "What you
are and what I am and what I can become in my whole life, that has
been determined in part by my genetic inheritance."[29]

Social workers, physicians, and a special court system removed decision making about childbearing from individuals. This mission did not
easily fit with stereotypes of love, gentleness, or charity. But policy ap-

pealed to a "higher" duty, the collective good of the entire *Volk*, and played on that cornerstone of respectability, purity, or, as the euphemism put it, "racial hygiene." As candidates for sterilization were removed from the category "human" and consigned to "abnormal," their difference was medicalized. Here, too, a modern trend was at work. Traditionally, charity ministered to the needs of society's misfits, the helpless and weak, who were threatened by society as a whole. Nazi dogma described the mentally ill, sexually deviant, retarded, crippled, alcoholic, and other "defectives" as germs attacking a "healthy" society. The separation of the "genetically unfit" from the "desirables" marked an important step toward the exclusion of "racially" inadequate people from "Aryan" society. The similarity of the rhetoric regarding genetic and racial "dangers" was no accident.

Emotional and pseudo-scientific appeals elevated racial quackery to the level of ethical duty and in the process redirected the woman's "mission" from love to hatred. Nazi women, as Scholtz-Klink boasted, would not be superficial and superfluous ladies, but would take seriously a challenge that required the callousness of a storm trooper. In 1933 a Nazi woman wrote, "Women are the heart of a *Volk*. Their love is its love. Their hatred, its hatred."[30] In preparation for the April 1, 1933, boycott of Jewish-owned business Gottschewski's Women's Order newsletter told its readers,

> For fourteen years you, Party comrades, have marched and fought shoulder to shoulder with the brown front against the Jews, the deadly enemy of the German people.
> Now you will be called on to lead the indoctrination campaign. You must be sure no German woman buys from Jews. Because the battle is hard and ruthless you must close out personal reservations. Tell German women that Jewish hate propaganda is guilty for the deaths of two million dead, guilty for the starving old people, children, and mothers, guilty of Versailles, Dawes, and Young. . . . Awaken in every German woman the will to self-defense . . . Not just for now, but forever the Jew must be excluded (*ausgeschaltet*) from *Volk* and state.[31]

Käte Auerbach, one of the authors in the Nazi women's press, urged women to resist being trapped by slick advertising that lured them into the department stores and deplored the "good Catholic or Protestant who buys her bridal gown at a Jewish store."[32] American sociologist Clifford Kirkpatrick observed a few years later that the Nazi mission lay as much in spreading hatred through its women as in diffusing love. "People," he wrote, "were shaped . . . by an impulse to tribal-group intimacy based on love of the in-group and hatred of real or fancied outside enemies" (like Jew, Bolshevik, or foreigners).[33] While Scholtz-Klink made speeches about women's power to love, she admonished her Frauenschaft leaders to harden themselves for tasks ahead—to wield an "iron broom."

The words of one of her staff writers illustrate how Nazis blended masculine and feminine traits to suit their purposes. Nature, she believed, placed a hard will and a tough exterior in men and then tempered it with women's loving and gentle personality. Often feminine virtues (as well as masculine strength) have saved entire nations from decay. However, she concluded, as the bearers of national life in Nazi Germany, women received a new calling: "To overcome suffering on God's earth," she wrote, Hitler requires more: "a relentless dedication to improvement [of the race] with every means known to man, a drive to produce better, unburdened forms of existence, to achieve what our *Volk* has been destined to achieve." With "religious seriousness," she concluded, women must excise sympathy from their nature and replace it with devotion to their mission to purify the race.[34] The moral universe of Nazism required its subjects to place abstract and long-term ideals, such as a purified "master race," ahead of ordinary moral injunctions. While we deplore the principles for which they acted, Nazi women as well as men behaved according to what some psychologists consider the highest stage of moral thinking, in which the individual looks beyond the immediate effect of a particular action to ultimate benefits and the common good.

The mandate to "be hard" and to hate the outsider placed women in a contradictory position. Nazi women had to behave ruthlessly toward outcasts and entirely divest themselves of tough-mindedness when dealing with their male superiors. When a woman's own priorities matched Nazi policies no friction occurred. Scholtz-Klink so thoroughly accepted Hitler's notions about women's roles that she did not see herself as surrendering to him. She, like conservative women elsewhere, defended patriarchal institutions as the best method of tying men to their families, arguing that if family life offered support and services to the man of the house he would want to remain at home. No law, they believed, could change man's nomadic nature or tie him to his wife and children. He had to be attracted, not coerced. Many of men's prerogatives were psychological. In earlier times the father had been called the "king" or "lord" of his home; after 1933, the fashion transformed him into Führer. The Wilhelmine legal code, which remained in force throughout the Nazi era, guaranteed each husband's inalienable rights. For example, in family discussions, wives could contribute their opinions, but only husbands made decisions. This meant that men could prevent their wives from seeking employment, or could force them to work in the family business without wages. A wife could not freely dispose of either her earnings or the property she brought into the marriage. In the event of a divorce, even if she won the settlement on the basis of her husband's adultery and gained custody of the children, the husband still made decisions about the children's schooling and religion. Proponents of these laws believed that they served family stability. By underwriting male privilege, they hoped to make monogamy and lifelong marriage attractive to men.

Nazi judges, however, broke the link between privilege and protection by increasing the husband's power at home *and* making it easier for him to divorce his wife. The trend began almost unnoticed by most Germans because it pertained to "Aryan" spouses who were given the right to divorce their "racially undesirable" partners without proving "guilt." Within months of that ruling in 1933, judges began to grant divorces to spouses (usually husbands) of Jewish, "genetically inferior," or sterilized "Aryans." One contemporary commented that "to be married to a person of non-Aryan ancestry in modern Germany is like being chained to a corpse" and spiraling divorce rates indicate that many (usually men) agreed.[35] Judicial decisions gradually expanded to non-Jewish Germans. In 1938 a major divorce reform incorporated de facto trends and officially defined new grounds for divorce: adultery, refusal to procreate, immorality, VD, a three-year separation, mental illness, racial incompatibility, and eugenic weakness. The response was instant. In 30,000 divorces under the new law, husbands left wives in 80 percent of the cases.[36]

While claiming to stand on tradition, Nazi policy actually accelerated a distinctively mid-twentieth-century trend: Divorce rates increased more rapidly than marriage rates. Thus, in marriage as in childbearing, Nazi policy did not deflect long-range trends common in all industrial nations. Individuals shaped their lives according to their needs and did not generally yield to the dictates of an authoritarian state. More young people married, couples bore fewer children, and husbands won more divorces despite the rhetoric about tradition, marriage, and the family, Germany had entered the twentieth century. Whereas in pre-industrial societies, marriage choices had been dictated by parents' desire to conserve family property, in modern societies fulfillment and free choice play the predominant role. Greater percentages of all people marry and expectations of marriage shift from material to emotional concerns. Young people seek intimacy, warmth, and security, perhaps as an escape from an alienated public world. Because people bring new expectations to the altar, they more frequently consider divorce as an option when disappointed. Thus, in some ways the increase in divorce reflected trends in other nations that underwent higher divorce and marriage rates.

The ordinary housewives in Scholtz-Klink's programs remained personally unaffected by Nazi innovations such as involuntary sterilization programs, divorce reform, and a campaign against abortion. Probably, too, they had never known someone with even one Jewish parent, since Jewish Germans constituted less than 1 percent of the population and lived mainly in cities. But many of them had daughters, and over half a million of these teenage daughters belonged to the League of German Girls (BDM). Their mothers had a chance to witness firsthand the long-range implications of the totalitarian state they condoned. Although few Germans who grew up during that time admit it, the Nazi youth organizations exercised a strong allure. Christa Wolf, one of East Germany's most celebrated authors, shares her memories with remarkable candor. Wolf describes the gulf between Nelly and her Socialist mother when she was a teenager during the 1930s. After experiencing acute feelings of awkwardness, Nelly

> got over her discomfort by laughing out loud—maybe too loud—when the leader broke into gay laughter. It was a satisfying relief to laugh for the leader's sake, and to disregard her own . . . embarrassment. What a pleasure it was to enjoy the joviality of the leader, a merry young woman by the name of Marianne, called Micky. Just call me Micky, I look like Mickey Mouse anyway. Another kind of pleasure was to crowd around the leader, together with all the others, at the end of the evening, forgetting one's own shyness, to grasp her hand, to enjoy the extraordinary familiarity. And on the ride home, to become familiar with a new word by repeating it to herself: "comradeship."
>
> It meant the promise of a loftier life, far removed from the small area of the store, filled with cans of fish, bags of sugar, loaves of bread, sausages hanging from the ceiling . . . far removed also from the white figure in the store smock who was standing outside waiting for Nelly: her mother had probably been waiting for a long time. Why had she been this late? . . . Not a word about "comradeship." She wiped her feet. [Not a word to her mother. Nor could she admit to her mother that] Micky sang and played and marched with them . . . there was something her mother couldn't give her, something she didn't want to miss . . .[37]

When it came to a choice between participating in a cross-country hike with Micky and staying at home to welcome her mother after her discharge from the hospital, Nelly opted for the hike.

Christa Wolf recalls the impact of songs on her childhood. First they learned "To Freedom Only Have We Pledged our Lives," and then "From the Me to the We," by Heinrich Annacker.

The me once seemed to be the central pole,
and all revolved around its woe and weal.
But growing humbleness helped to reveal
that you must aim your eyes upon the whole.

And now the me is part of the great We,
becomes the great machine's subservient wheel.
Not if it lives—but if it *serves* with zeal,
decides the worth of its own destiny.

Here was the youthful version of Scholtz-Klink's admonition to forget the "little I" and think of the *Volk*. Well-known novelist Ingeborg Drewitz also joined the BDM without daring to tell her parents. "Why? Well, because of the things that one thinks at age thirteen: I wanted to rebel against my parents at all cost because they disliked everything that everyone else liked."[38]

Looking back at her teenage years in the Hitler Youth, Melita Maschmann described similar joy at the collective life in the German Girls' League, which she also joined without her parents' knowledge or consent. But while Wolf and Drewitz acknowledged afterward that their parents had been right, Maschmann's recollections convey the same self-justification of Scholtz-Klink's reminiscences. Before 1933, Maschmann's clandestine activities in the Hitler Youth brought her into close contact with an entirely new class comprised of "shop girls, office workers, dressmakers, and servant girls." She disparaged her erstwhile friends, the "well-born . . . superficial and boring" girls at her high school, who wasted time with snobbish social events and cliquish clubs. Two decades after the war, she expressed little remorse at the BDM pranks, such as marching boisterously through the Jewish quarter in Berlin, chanting, "This is where the rich Jews live. They need a bit of waking up from their afternoon naps."[39] Maschmann's memoirs depict the pride of a narrow-minded and arrogant girl's exhilaration at rebelling against her "ladylike" upbringing.

Two women who have written perceptively about their years in the Hitler Youth both discuss the impact of their parents' reactions after 1933 on their need for friendship. Gerda Zorn, daughter of Communist parents, recalls how gloomy her home life became after 1933, when they felt helpless to act against the Nazis they hated and were terrified of arrest for the slightest protest. Without informing her parents, Zorn joined the BDM and enjoyed the friendship, outings, and excitement "at working for a great cause." Renate Finckh, who had exulted at her parents' newfound happiness when Hitler became Chancellor, soon felt abandoned in the "empty nest" created by her parents' constant round of activities. "At home no one really had time for me." At age ten, she joined the BDM and "finally found an emotional home, a safe refuge, and shortly thereafter also a space in which I was valued."[40] The summons, " 'Girls! The Führer needs you!' moved me deeply. I was filled with pride and joy that someone needed me for a higher purpose." She also recalls her devotion to her leader, a teenager only three years older than herself. "She replaced my sister, who had already left home." Camaraderie was heightened by extreme competitiveness. "Always it was 'Who sings, plays, writes the best? Who picked the most herbs?' . . . I became very arrogant." Renate discovered self-respect in the "thoroughly aggressive" atmosphere of the youth movement. Older BDM members who joined the teenage division, Faith and Beauty, ought to have realized they confronted new and less exciting responsibilities when they prepared to meet the entry requirements: Memorize all verses of popular Nazi songs, pass an exam on Party history and ideology, run 60 meters in twelve seconds, and swim 100 meters. Girls who were accepted felt triumphant. "But beyond all else lay that comforting feeling we all longed for, the 'We consciousness.' We Hitler girls belonged together, we formed an elite within the German *Volk* community," Renate Finckh remembers. Girls experienced the end of isolation, glorying in being not alone but first among peers.

In 1933 many women anticipated that pro-family programs would restore their influence over their children. This did not occur. From Westphalia, for example, came the report of a girls' school in which the BDM regularly scheduled their meetings and rallies during school hours. When parents and principal protested, the girl leader (die Führerin) reported them to the Gestapo.[41] Renate Finckh looked back almost bewildered as she recalled how obnoxious she had been when trying to convert a beloved aunt and a respected teacher who made no secret of their hatred for Nazism. Finckh wanted desperately to make the people she loved feel and think as she did about her ideals. She recalled, too, her own absolute intransigence against non-Nazi friends' and relatives' attempts to tell her the truth about her faith. Her total devotion held fast even through the bombing raids. Retrospectively, Renate Finckh said that Nazi society provided her with a consciousness that was ersatz but nonetheless gave her entire life meaning. Since then she, unlike Scholtz-Klink or Maschmann, often asked herself how so evil a doctrine could have inspired her so deeply.

She also wondered that the girls accepted with little rebellion the misogyny endemic in the Party. The statistics made the reality so clear. In 1932, 55,365 boys belonged to the Hitler Youth, as compared to 19,244 girls in the BDM.[42] Only in 1939 did the gap narrow to 1,723,886 and 1,502,571 respectively. When 100,000 boys attended the Nuremberg Rally in 1936, only 900 girls were invited. The 1935 National Labor Service Law obliged all young people to devote six months to a work program. One year later, the program created over 300,000 places for young men and less than 20,000 for young women.[43] The organization that inspired them with self-worth by telling them they belonged to the elite also told them, when they reached maturity, that they must settle into the dull life of a mother. How could the thought of selecting "racially fit" husbands, cooking wholesome food, keeping house, and bearing many children excite them after the years of sports, hiking, camping, and adventure that had attracted them to the movement? How could mothers share the communal spirt, the élan of the swaggering Hitler Youth? When Gerda Zorn confided to a boy in the Hitler Youth how much she wished she could be a boy, he reassured her, "We need girls like you so we won't die out." That was not enough for her. She still longed to share the masculine élan of the Führer elite. When the boys told her that "girls have to remain morally pure, clean, serious, nondrinkers and -smokers, and Germanic in appearance," she retorted, "I'm not a simp from the country. I am a Berliner. I drink, smoke, love to dance—and I want to go along with the boys." Finally, the boys accepted her after they decided she was a "mother of the race" (*Stamm-Mutter*).[44]

The BDM prepared girls for a lifetime membership in the second sex, as exemplified by the Hitler Youth motto for girls: "Be Faithful, Be Pure, Be German!" Boys, on the other hand, were told: "Live Faithfully, Fight Bravely, and Die Laughing!"[45] Boys heard the command to act; girls to be. Youth leaders encouraged rebellion against parents among boys and girls; but as adults, girls were to put adventure behind, while boys accepted the challenges of more active careers in the Party or military. Girls lived between the arrogance of the "master race" and the humility of the inferior sex. Biology, which predestined them to second-rate status vis-à-vis "Aryan" men, elevated them above their "racial inferiors."

As long as motherhood remained the official credo for women, traditionally minded women could enjoy the benefits of state support for programs in which they believed. But when in 1935–1936 new policies prepared women (even in the middle class) to accept the double burden of motherhood and job, confusion began. Economic reorientation shook the women's world to its foundations. Plans for conquest called for a higher birthrate; rearmament demanded more factory workers. Both needs rendered conventional notions of motherhood obsolete. Women would still be rewarded for bearing children; but these children would be educated by the state; their mothers recruited into war-related work and their fathers to the front. Reality became starkly clear: Motherhood would henceforth be viewed entirely in biological terms, just as Hitler's enemies had warned.

In 1933 the first signs of a new Nazi attitude toward motherhood had appeared, but the change, like so many policies, had passed unnoticed because it seemed to be an extension of older traditions. New views of motherhood blended demands made by both religious women's organizations and socialists in Weimar Germany. For four decades, pioneers in the middle-class women's movement and in church organizations had operated homes for unmarried mothers to rescue them from prostitution and protect them from social hostility. At first the sponsors welcomed Nazi support for their financially precarious programs. But a second development aroused their suspicions because it took up a long-standing Socialist demand for the end of all legal disabilities for children born out of wedlock. Although the law did not change until after World War II, judicial policy began in the mid-1930s to recognize the rights of mothers without husbands and children without legal fathers. Both homes for unmarried mothers and the end of prejudice against their children grew logically from Nazi ideology. If women's obligation to the *Volk* centered on childbearing, then public agencies ought to assume the obligation to care for those women and their children. In some ways, this reform harkened back to Helene Stöcker's defense of every woman's right to bear children, with or without a husband—except for one crucial difference: Nazi policy rested on the right of the nation to force women to bear children, whereas Stöcker placed women's needs and desires at the heart of her argument. After the mid-1930s, unmarried pregnancy no longer constituted grounds for dismissing state employees (which included teachers). Shortly thereafter, propaganda began praising the heroic "racially pure" unmarried mother's loyalty to the Führer.

In the mid-thirties, as Hitler's obsession with "Aryan" breeding revolutionized conventional views of marriage, his dreams of conquest and war compelled women to leave their womanly *Lebensraum* and return to the factories. Officially, Scholtz-Klink took charge of this transformation, too, but in practice her subordinate Alice Rilke in the Labor Front assumed responsibility for the morale and well-being of the over 5 million women who worked in offices, factories, stores, and agriculture. Unless the archives from the Labor Front appear, Rilke's activities will remain largely unknown. In many ways she appears to have been, like Scholtz-Klink, a bureaucrat who took her charge seriously. But her task was far more challenging because she supervised women who had never seen themselves as the housewifely types that official policy encouraged. In addition, women workers had probably come from socialist and trade union backgrounds. While Scholtz-Klink worked to remove women from the labor force, Rilke tried to keep them at work. From 1933 to 1936, state priorities coincided with those of the Reichsfrauenführerin, but thereafter both Scholtz-Klink and Rilke received orders to recruit women into factories and offices as part of Hitler's rearmament policies.

The task turned out to be less difficult than one might expect, partly because women workers had not been driven out of their jobs as completely as propaganda suggested. Although women comprised a third of all workers in 1933 and only a quarter of the labor force in 1936, the shift resulted from the restoration of men's jobs, not women's departure. The Depression had affected male employment more severely, and recovery expanded heavy industry and construction, which traditionally employed men. Thus, when full employment returned in 1935–1936, the balance between men and women resembled that of the Weimar era so bitterly criticized by Hitler.[46] Looked at from another way, the lack of change is even more evident. When we compare the number of employed women to the total number of women in the population, we find that slightly more women had paid jobs in Nazi Germany than in the Weimar period.[47] Old Guard Nazi women expressed dismay at such figures. One woman social scientist complained that after three years of Nazi power, the labor market contained 600,000 *more* women than in 1932,[48] and other women observed that the government did not even dismiss women from its offices. For all the official misogyny, the Nazi years did not affect long-term trends very strongly. Women's entry into the job market and a decline in family size continued apace without a major break. Even though Nazi policy did not significantly reduce the participation of women in the work force, it had two important effects: restriction of women to poorly paid jobs and acceleration of women's segregation into feminine jobs.

As more women entered the labor market, the quality of their jobs declined. These trends had begun before 1933 and characterize women's employment patterns in all industrial nations. After three years of Nazi rule, 40 percent of all women wage earners worked at physically exhausting agricultural jobs for 50 percent of male wages. In other fields, women earned as much as 70 percent of men's wages for the same work—not worse than in other countries.[49] Only a war economy gave women the chance, in one worker's words, "to actually apply for the office jobs of which we had scarcely dared to dream before."[50] Wartime shortages eventually produced increases in women's wages, but even then the improvement remained minimal.[51] Women who cooperated with government-sponsored leisure-time programs, such as "Strength through Joy" (*Kraft durch Freude*), received benefits in the form of tours to Italy, week-long vacations at German resorts, concert and theater tickets, and weekend outings. These advantages, however, came as rewards for faithful service to Nazi programs, and not as rights in themselves. Throughout the twelve-year Reich, real wages for women and men dropped. But social planners understood the importance of nonmonetary rewards and exploited fully people's desires for leisure activities and state recognition as substitutes for wage increases.[52]

In 1936, Alice Rilke herself wondered how successful her programs had been. Of course, it was not easy to find out since censorship quelled any honest feedback. So she distributed a questionnaire similar to the "My Work Day, My Weekend" survey conducted by the Textile Union at the end of the Weimar Republic. The unsigned answers depressed her. Despite publicity about official outings and the efforts of female on-the-job social workers, women preferred unorganized and spontaneous outings to the Labor Front leisure activities. Most women, when asked about their reading habits, said they had no free time in which to read anything—and certainly not Party material. Finally, among unmarried women with some spare time, Rilke found that respondents evidenced what she called a *Lesehunger*, or hunger for "real books," as opposed to government-printed tracts or trite Nazi novellas. Married women who answered Rilke's questions hardly understood the concept of leisure, since they had none. Rilke herself must have empathized, since she herself felt often constrained by orders from her Labor Front chief Robert Ley and from Scholtz-Klink.[53] On occasion she complained about the general lack of understanding for women workers. Rilke knew morale played a crucial role in mobilizing "her" women, but institutional blocks precluded a solution. In 1938 Rilke protested, "One cannot expect people to perform at top capacity if they are simultaneously being made to feel that their activity, even their very presence, is undesirable."[54] Rilke, committed to improving women workers' lives, met with continual frustration even after the Nazi economy increased the need for women in the work force.

Scholtz-Klink epitomized the perfect Nazi leader, who really did not lead at all, but followed every directive that came from above and modified it according to her own style. The much-vaunted leadership principle of Nazi Germany in reality masked a confused feudal organization of bureaucratic lords and vassals, with satrapies for all. This quagmire, which historians have labeled "organized improvisation," "planlessness," and "polycracy," preserved confusion and rendered any independent initiative void. In a certain sense this chaotic organization operated effectively because it prevented the formation of interest groups that might have placed their own advantages ahead of the Führer's orders. The duplication of functions, while inefficient, created an endemic paranoia that kept each official on guard lest a rival spy on him or her. The woman leader, even more than the man, felt the pressure of suspicion. Because Scholtz-Klink had no goals of her own, she could change course and adapt; but at the same time she lacked the doctrinaire commitment to thoroughly Nazify her women. Scholtz-Klink perpetrated bureaucratic confusion but always under the image of order, virtue, and purity.

From the outset, impossible obstacles prevented success. How could the Reischsfrauenführerin elevate women's self-esteem as mothers while at the same time lessening their influence over their own families and depriving them of responsibility in political life? In itself, this would have constituted a nearly impossible task; but when rearmament mandated women's mass entry into the job market the fraudulence of her appeal was unmasked. Without a protest, the Women's Bureau prepared women to expand their notion of feminine roles to include employment in offices, factories, and, when war demanded it, even in the military. Scholtz-Klink's success in remaining in office depended on her lack of commitment to any ideological position at all. But Hitler's megalomania and breeding schemes demanded women's mass conversion to the Nazi faith. Without total devotion they would not reorient their values about childbearing and child rearing. Ambiguity was inevitable because women had only one status in the Third Reich: subordination. With "joyful self-sacrifice," they were supposed to follow whatever national priorities decreed: from farm to factory, or from office to home.

National programs to upgrade motherhood may have heartened women who in any case would have seen themselves primarily as housewives. But when it came to winning new and radical believers in "racial revolution," the obstacles proved insurmountable. The fates of Auguste Reber-Gruber in the Education Ministry and Irene Seydel in Münster provide dramatic examples of the dilemmas faced by ideologues.

Frau Dr. Auguste Reber-Gruber, consultant on girls' education, oversaw the activities of all women teachers in Germany. Her 100,000 teachers educated millions of girls and occupied respected positions in their communities. Unlike Rilke or Scholtz-Klink, Reber-Gruber was a self-proclaimed ideologue with a misson. "The task of our schooling . . . is simple: the molding of German girls as carriers of the National Socialist point of view."[55] Teachers formed the core of a crusade to win women's "hearts and the minds" for Hitler's goals. In 1933 it was not clear how this mission would be accomplished. The Ministry of Education, the Hitler Youth, the Women's Bureau, the Ministry of Agriculture, and the Department of Welfare competed for the direction of female education. The Minister of Education won out against his rivals and immediately repealed the gains made by women in the Weimar Republic.[56]

Within months of the Nazi takeover, all women school administrators were dismissed, and the number of women teachers dropped by 15 percent in the nation. Women professors, principals, educational consultants, and supervisors (even in girls' schools) were dismissed. No woman could receive the equivalent of tenure until after her thirty-fifth birthday on the grounds that she might bear children and therefore owe her primary loyalty to her family. Gradually, however, starting in 1934, "trustworthy" women returned to universities and teaching jobs. The archives do not reveal the considerations that prompted this reversal, but two considerations must have played a role. The logic of "separate spheres" created the need for thousands of well-educated women to staff the rapidly expanding bureaucracies and services for women. In addition, because so many of the organizations of the "old" women's movement had expressed their willingness to cooperate in Nazi ventures, trained women seemed less threatening. Although the number of women at universities dropped by 40 percent between 1933 and 1935, women's share of the student body stabilized at 10 percent by the late 1930s, and rose steadily after that. Under Nazi government the universities lost prestige.[57] The numbers of women students at the universities dropped from just under 20,000 in 1933, to 5,500 in 1939.[58]

Educators asked themselves how to inspire "Aryan" pride in girls while propagating notions about women's fundamental inferiority in all activities except homemaking. The woman's body belonged to the *Volk*, but who would indoctrinate the mind of its owner? No guidelines stipulated what subjects boys or girls ought to study. The Education Ministry sent out a questionnaire to teachers in early 1934. Not surprisingly, suggestions for boys' education outnumbered proposals for girls by ten to one. Predictably, too, virtually all proposals advocated total separation of the sexes. One woman teacher summed up the general consensus. "If I mix black and white, then a colorless gray results. Coeducation, too, produces just such a neutral result. That may have been fine for liberals, but [National Socialism] . . . demands the production of more masculine boys and more feminine girls."[59] Ministry officials also abhorred dull gray. Ultimately, they wanted brown. That could only be accomplished by de-schooling the younger generation.

Every proposal emphasized that the major goal of Nazi education must be to redirect students' values away from "decadent" Weimar individualism and toward Nazi self-sacrifice. "Race science" and physical fitness would replace "effete" subjects like Latin, art history, and French literature; and character, not intellect, would be the new focus for girls and boys. Male writers emphasized the importance of providing boys with strong masculine role models. Women advocated "the education of girls by women as an indispensable necessity. A state that so deeply commits

itself to the separate responsibilities of each sex cannot escape this conclusion. Only under a strong womanly influence can girls be raised to
womanhood."[60] A woman teacher predicted that "woman as the guardian of the race and working companion of the man" would require a
massive network of educational institutions to train girls to fill the roles
their grandmothers found natural. Nazi men writing about girls' education took the opposite view. "Only a firm masculine hand can guarantee
stability," and besides, "an entirely female school system for girls would
not prepare the students for real-life situations."[61] Paradoxically, educators endorsed a radically modern method of restoring what they considered to be "tradition." Mothers and relatives would be supplanted in
the pedagogical process by male-supervised state schools that aimed at
transforming women from the guardians of family and private life into
the vanguard of Nazi ideology.[62] Behind the call for tradition, a radical
agenda emerged. Nazified schools would inculcate racism, eugenics,
love of the Führer, and a pagan worship of the Volk. Women teachers
(in sharp contrast to men teachers) had been among the few professional
groups that strongly opposed Nazism before 1933. Decades of opposition
from male teachers had made them battle-wise in the fight for their own
interests. Thus, while male teachers acclaimed the Nazi regime, women
teachers had been more skeptical about the regime that threatened their
jobs and dignity.

As policy guidelines appeared in 1933, a dispute erupted between
extremists and moderates within the Ministry of Education. Its outlines,
however, did not replicate the rivalry between Scholtz-Klink and her
predecessors. In the Education Ministry, Frederika Matthias, the "old-
timer," represented the more temperate and traditional position, while
Auguste Reber-Gruber, the newcomer, was the zealot. The apparent
leader of the women's division of the National Socialist Teachers' Union
(NSLB), Frederika Matthias, drafted her proposals in 1933. She opened
with a pro-forma attack on the 1920s women's-rights movement, saying
that after the pioneers had won access to educational and political equality, women in the 1920s had squandered their privileges by caring only
about pleasure. The idle and unmarried woman, in her view, must be
put to work. Just as boys would study military subjects, girls would learn
Christian piety. Science, Latin, and math bore no relationship to motherhood, so these subjects would disappear from girls' curricula in favor
of home economics. Nothing in her proposals indicated a specifically
National Socialist orientation. She merely elaborated on conservative
criticisms of liberal education in the Weimar Republic.[63] "The prerequi-
site for future mothers of the Volk must be sound physical training
during their girlhood. The undue accumulation of academic knowledge

must be curtailed in favor of a girl's healthy development. This can only be achieved through biological instruction, gymnastics, athletics, and walking tours—all coordinated closely by the BDM and the school."[64] Like many of Hitler's women followers, Matthias blended Christian faith and *Mein Kampf.* And like the old-timer women in the Nazi movement, she faced a new rival in her quest for power after 1933. In the ensuing power play, however, Matthias was the staid and respectable Nazi, facing a challenge from a younger woman who combined fanatical belief in Nazism, administrative skills, and a charismatic personality.

Frau Dr. Auguste Reber-Gruber, consultant on female education in the Ministry of Education, a careerist with little interest in National Socialism prior to 1933, had converted late to what she called the "Nazi faith." Rejecting Christian religion, she imposed pagan and racial beliefs on her teachers. With a Ph.D. in gymnastic pedagogy, Reber-Gruber intended to upgrade the status of women's homemaking skills within the higher education system.[65] In 1934, when women Nazi teachers met at a resort in the Harz mountains to coordinate plans for girls' education, Reber-Gruber explained her position.

> The female mind differs from the male mind, which excludes inward involvement and takes a cool, businesslike pride in its "objective" attitude. Owing to her natural disposition, her greater reverence for life, woman has the capacity for that inner devotion which more deeply fathoms the nature of things and perceives their true value and substance by means of loving absorption.[66]

Behind the scenes, Reber-Gruber displayed none of these "womanly" traits and revealed herself as a competent bureaucrat with the instincts of a street fighter. In a smear campaign, she attacked Matthias' integrity. Like Paula Siber in the Ministry of Interior, Matthias complacently believed that her record of service to the Party, combined with her ideological orthodoxy, entitled her to an important post in the new state. She, too, misjudged the situation. Women like Matthias, with their own solution to the Women Question, especially if they advanced Christian beliefs, had no future in a Nazi ministry. Reber-Gruber, as a newcomer to the Party, had a shrewder perception of reality and adapted quickly to the prevailing hostility toward both organized religion and women in "masculine" jobs. Equally vital, she gained the protection of a powerful man, the popular Hans Schemm, Gauleiter and Minister of Culture in Franconia. Although her status as "Frau Dr." might have aroused men's anxieties, the fact that she received her Ph.D. in physical education enhanced the anti-intellectual stance that became so vital in Nazi educational politics.

Reber-Gruber endorsed Schemm's pretentious glorification of women. Schemm, having made it clear women were created inferior, asked rhetorically, "What are all the modern rights compared with the holiest right of the mother to sorrow, work, and sacrifice for her beloved children? Only there can she find heaven prefigured on earth. . . ."[67] Schemm and Reber-Gruber saw women as nature's antidote to class war because, while men belonged to classes according to their economic status, women were divided into mothers and nonmothers, regardless of economic status. And even if employed, Schemm added, women identify primarily in relationship to their families, not their jobs. Because "Marxism expels the working-class mother from her home and drives her into the proletariat," he expected working-class women would welcome Nazi men's chivalrous offer to liberate them from paid work. Women, he said, don't work for wages; they sacrifice for their families. An endorsement from such an antifeminist certainly did not harm Reber-Gruber's chances.

While she engaged in bureaucratic feuding, Reber-Gruber piously declared, "Women are not greedy for posts and titles. They have withdrawn from the fight for financial or organizational sovereignty and want merely to work for the Party." She drafted position papers, accusing her rival of being a pawn of the Protestant Church. Matthias looked to Scholtz-Klink for protection, but Reber-Gruber (adopting Scholtz-Klink's own maxim) relied on her male defender.[68] In early 1934, Reber-Gruber was appointed to the position of Consultant on Female Education with the Ministry of Education, and also director of the women's division of the National Socialist Teachers' Union (NSLB) in Bayreuth. Matthias had lost out.[69] Reber-Gruber offered an ideal blend of traditionalism regarding women's roles and radicalism regarding Nazi goals.

During the early months on her new job, Reber-Gruber devoted herself entirely to consolidating victory over her rivals. As Reber-Gruber secured her position, however, her old obsequiousness dropped away. Viewing her job as both overwhelming and essential, she commented, "It is not easy to take an entire army of [ideologically] indifferent teachers and transform them into a vanguard of National Socialism." Of 120,000 women teachers, 83,000 women belonged to the Nazi union. Her task was to convert the remaining 40,000 and impose discipline on the members. With a tightly organized cadre of devoted women backing her, Reber-Gruber intended to reform education so that biological differences between male and female would become as irrevocable as the contrast between "Aryan" and Jew. "Germanic life of the future will be dominated by two absolute axioms: the laws concerning race and the laws regulating the polarity between the sexes."[70]

After taking office, Reber-Gruber's first task was to prevent her teachers from being absorbed into the Labor Front and Scholtz-Klink's Women's Bureau. "If something is not done, we will disappear altogether," she said of her women teachers' union. Having declared her absolute support for the principle of women's separate sphere, she did not intend to have her own union absorbed into Scholtz-Klink's massive Frauenwerk or the Labor Front. Individual teachers might join the Frauenwerk, she said, but women teachers owed their primary loyalty to the male-directed Nazi Teachers' Union.[71] Realizing she personally lacked power in this situation, Reber-Gruber asked Schemm to dispatch one of his deputies to argue her case with Scholtz-Klink in Berlin.[72] So touchy was Reber-Gruber that, when she heard that Scholtz-Klink planned to send a delegation of women to an international conference, Reber-Gruber demanded to select some delegates, and again called on Schemm for backing.[73] The slightest oversight roused her to action. However, when it came to educating the elite of Nazi womanhood, Reber-Gruber lost. Heinrich Himmler signed an agreement with Scholtz-Klink that excluded the Education Ministry from training SS men's brides.[74]

Reading the hundreds of Reber-Gruber memos preserved in the state archives in Munich, it is not difficult to imagine why leaders passed over Reber-Gruber. Precisely because she believed so fanatically in Nazi doctrine as she understood it, she could not bend to comply with every changing priority. Unafraid of censure, she defended women's roles as staunchly as she criticized Nazi policies that undermined them. Already in June 1934, she drafted a protest. "For years we Nazis complained that the Weimar Republic divided people. . . . Now we want to centralize everyone and end schisms. Our women deserve more than the inferior education given by untrained professionals in the Women's Organization [Frauenschaft]. I stand absolutely behind the Führer in this."[75] Reber-Gruber kept women teachers primarily within the educational framework. Scholtz-Klink had met her match.

Men teachers provided Reber-Gruber with ample grounds for disagreement. One of the many reports about arrogant male teachers described a union meeting. "At a district meeting, Minister Schemm spoke to a gathering of union members. The women were separated from the men and placed in the gallery. Most women had to stand because it was so crowded. Meanwhile they could see numerous empty chairs among the men." No one invited them to join their male colleagues. "They saw themselves treated in a not exactly polite way," the author added. "We must convince women they are equal not only in the amount of dues they pay but in status too."[76] Since she owed her position to Schemm, Reber-Gruber said nothing.

In March 1935, Schemm died in a plane crash. Reber-Gruber proved more than equal to the challenge. Spicing her speeches with accolades for her friend, the dead hero, she perhaps found him more useful dead than alive. Schemm, personally charismatic and violently Nazi, had entered into the Nazi pantheon, and Reber-Gruber used his memory to defend herself against his replacement, Hans Stricker. For the next decade, Reber-Gruber demonstrated that she had mastered Nazi bureaucratic style. She cited *Mein Kampf*, frequently referred to the Führer's will, and claimed always to act according to highest Nazi principles, as elucidated by her dear comrade, the late Hans Schemm.

To Stricker's dismay, the vigor that inspired her activities on behalf of Nazi indoctrination carried over into her defense of women's rights. In order for her teachers to work effectively, she insisted, they had to believe they constituted an elite. But her daily mail brought her hundreds of complaints attesting to mass disaffection. The most common centered on male teachers' behavior toward their women colleagues. A Teachers' Union (NSLB) official, for example, belittled Nazi women's organizations as, "that teatime gossip circle." Meetings of women teachers were called without Reber-Gruber's knowledge, and male teachers habitually offended their female colleagues. Men not only took over the direction of girls' schools, but routinely excluded women teachers from faculty meetings.[77] "If you don't dampen men's aggression, I cannot assume responsibility for what happens among women teachers," Reber-Gruber threatened. When women are treated with respect, she added, they will comply with any orders, but when they feel insulted, they won't even follow directives they agree with. "I wouldn't be surprised if women teachers drift back to religious teachers' organizations," she warned in 1935.[78]

Reber-Gruber sensed the tide was running against her. In 1937, she, like all other women with advanced degrees, lost the privilege of being addressed with the honorable "Frau Dr." or "Frau Professor"—only the wives of physicians or professors retained that right. "Sometimes I lose the courage to continue," she confided to a friend, "because I see so much evidence of routine and deep contempt for our women's work." In private she confessed what she denied in public. "After four years [of Nazi rule] I have become used to haggling over every little thing." Rather than finding fault with Hitler personally, Reber-Gruber blamed the "harmless and innocuous" women close to the Führer who concealed from him the truth about how men treated women. Instead of acknowledging her male colleagues' hostility, she blamed their lack of respect on jealousy for her position. As the complaints built up, Reber-Gruber's tone became sharper, and by the late 1930s, her tact gave way completely when she heard the news that the Führer personally banned all women from high offices of any kind, even in "feminine" jobs.

> I do not see how we will ever accomplish the transformation of girls' education. Women school administrators have become a dying species. The high schools for girls are purely male-run. The few assistant professors for needlework don't alter the trend. Everything remains just as it was under liberalism. I am now the only woman with a contract in teacher education. It is really ironic that we women National Socialists constantly spoke about the failures of the women's movement—we complained that they wanted to raise girls to be masculine. But actually what has changed? Really, very little.[79]

Reber-Gruber's dual pride as a Nazi and as a woman provoked her superiors' anger.

Despite Reber-Gruber's barrage, Nazi officials did not authorize adequate budgets to accomplish a restructuring of girls' education. While boys' textbooks were rewritten, women teachers depended upon books from the Weimar Republic. A recent study of representative feminine stereotypes from the inter-war years concludes that the image of the ideal mother (or woman) had changed very little in any case.[80] Reber-Gruber in 1934 had warned of a "war between the sexes" in education. "Not only have women teachers a right to exist, but raising children requires the best possible training of mothers."[81] What was the point, she asked, of publishing a journal for women teachers or commissioning special textbooks for girls' schools, if misogyny persisted? Nazi men, she implied, were as bad as Jewish psychologists, who demeaned women with their sexual theories.

Reber-Gruber's zeal made her a rare bureaucrat in Nazi Germany, for she combined administrative skill, incorruptibility, and an authoritative style. For eleven years she repeated her message. "The ideological battle —the most difficult any *Volk* ever waged—cannot be won if the men pay no attention to the women. Sometimes I think that our men think of nothing except their jobs. I could slug them when I see the petty intrigues, greedy jealousies, and jockeying for new positions that absorb them."[82] Reber-Gruber fought a double bureaucratic battle: On one front she propagated Nazism to doubtful women teachers, and on the other she defended women's rights against the hostile men in the Ministry of Education.

She relentlessly attacked two tendencies among women teachers: "black" (slang for "Catholic") and feminist influences. She was furious that Catholic teachers in 1937 still published their own journal and met regularly. Because all teachers had to join the Nazi Teachers' Union or lose their jobs, membership statistics looked hopeful; but that only increased Reber-Gruber's anxieties about new members' hypocrisy. Many women teachers had long sympathized with the women's-rights movement. Bourgeois women's-movement leaders, whom she saw as remnants from decadent liberalism, still published their essays in *Die Frau*. When Scholtz-Klink commemorated Gertrud Bäumer's birthday, Reber-Gruber and other "old-timer" women were outraged. How could their erstwhile rival win public acclaim when long-time Party members disappeared from public view?[83] I asked Scholtz-Klink why she had softened in her attitude toward the women's-rights movement. She replied that early in her career the demands of Bäumer and her friends had seemed excessive, but that a few years in office had taught her "something about the world." I thought, but did not say, that Bäumer's adaptation to Nazism had also demonstrated that Scholtz-Klink had nothing to fear and a great deal to gain from cooperating with the erstwhile leaders of the women's-rights movement. Besides feeling men's hostility, Reber-Gruber felt betrayed by Scholtz-Klink.

During the late 1930s Scholtz-Klink abruptly reversed another position and began to acclaim women who shouldered the double burden of employment and housework. Without ever acknowledging that such statements contradicted her earlier views, she took up the new themes without an audible murmur. She told young women to prepare for careers in industry, office work, and other "masculine" areas, and she spoke out against the "narrow maternal education" taught in the public schools.[84] This meant less funding for Reber-Gruber's "maternal" programs and also growing cynicism about a state that for three years had told women to become mothers and then launched a campaign to send them into factories and offices.

Reber-Gruber sincerely believed that home economics, psychology, folk art, eugenics, and physical education constituted the ideal training for girls; when suddenly her less doctrinaire superiors reversed priorities, she protested. And they tried to silence her. "You are sabotaging our Führer's work," they said, or "You are defending female separatism," or simply, "You must halt your activities at once!" Reber-Gruber had entrenched herself firmly in the education network, and in the face of dozens of official reprimands, followed by her threats to resign, she remained in office until the Allied invasion.

Unlike the pragmatic Scholtz-Klink, who adapted to every new priority from Berlin, fanatic Reber-Gruber held fast to her own vision of a sex-segregated educational system. Both women were careerists first of all, but in very different styles. Reber-Gruber, like Scholtz-Klink, had not come into prominence until after 1933, but she shared with earlier women leaders an absolute devotion to her own version of Hitler's program. Like them, she expected encouragement but met with opposition. In contrast to Reber-Gruber the militant, who rebuked her superiors, Scholtz-Klink the opportunist maximized her position by compliance. Both women faced growing chaos in their ranks after national priorities destroyed the sanctity of the home with the double demand that women bear children and work in factories. The disarray during the late 1930s resulted in part from both Scholtz-Klink's and Reber-Gruber's prior success at reestablishing traditional womanly concerns within their own domains. German wives and mothers who had rallied to a revival of domesticity felt cheated when Nazi policy threatened them with "modernization" worse than the threat of New Womanhood in the Weimar Republic.

The disorder in Berlin caused strife at local levels as well. While propaganda and official reports announced triumphs, private memos discussed the disintegration of Nazi power. The conflict between Elisabeth Polster, the pragmatist in Münster, and Irene Seydel, the enthusiast in Bielefeld, provides a case study for the fundamental problem confronting Nazi organizers everywhere. Correspondence among loyal Nazi women who felt dismay at the new state attests to the chaos wrought by the contradictory ideals advanced by conflicting policies. Polster herself succumbed to disillusionment. Activities that had been voluntary had become compulsory; ideology, once subject for lively debates, now created factions; and obligation subverted free will. A sampling of letters from Westphalian women gives us a rare chance to glimpse the underside of the "devotion" so exalted in propaganda. One of Polster's deputies, who took charge of 29 chapters, reported dismally: "They [our men leaders] accuse me of being ineffective, but my women are poor and desperately needed at harvest time." From the town of Detmold, a leader wrote, "We women leaders are proud that we can hold office in Adolf Hitler's movement. It does not increase our joy, however, if our efforts receive no praise from the leading men of the district."[85] Men, she concluded, could not understand a woman's triple burden: of home, politics, and jobs. From a nearby town, leader Paula Werth wrote:

Dear Frau Polster—this is an SOS!

It is hardly surprising that fewer and fewer women ever bother to attend the evening meetings. . . . We have burdened our women far too much with financial obligations. We required too much time from them as well.

The women are always selling something or other for the Party. The Welfare Bureau has transformed us into salesgirls.[86]

Resentment of obligations supplanted joy in sacrifice.

Discussing this problem with Polster, Seydel recalled that in the old days, women voluntarily worked night and day for their cause. But after 1933, women resented their new obligations. During the old days, money had been scarce, but the comrades shared it gladly; now, with more funding, pettiness had set in. Werth described the impact on husbands of women's constant activity.

> One sales drive follows close on the heels of the last. The women who work in the drives hardly know their husbands and children anymore. Recently one man comrade asked me, "Say, how's my wife these days?" Under his joking manner, he took the subject seriously. Our educational activities retreat into the background. And how desperately we need them! There is far too much gossip and grumbling . . . much of which has nothing to do with National Socialism. The motherhood courses are wonderful, but what's the point of sponsoring them if the mothers are always away from their homes on Party business?[87]

"Our entire family life has been torn apart," they said when lamenting the empty nest created by Party programs. How ironic it seemed for women to spend their time selling subscriptions to the Nazi magazine *Mother and Child* when they were neglecting their own housecleaning.

Even apparent successes could mask deeper failure. The leader from one minuscule farming village reported that her Frauenschaft team had succeeded in reaching their quota for a charity drive. Contributors received a badge (made by poorly paid nonunionized household workers). Many people in this village still attempted to avoid giving money by saying that they had left their purses at home. "We succeeded anyway," explained the woman leader, because "the town is so small it couldn't take more than a few minutes to go home for money and there are only two streets, so no one can avoid us." The Frauenschaft sold 344 out of the 400 badges they had been allotted and reported success. A cover memo asked, "But is that success? We collected money but did not win converts. Even our own loyal followers felt guilty about coercing mothers to steal money from their families' budgets to purchase worthless badges." With 46 percent of the town residents on poor relief, the drives lowered the morale of the very women the Party wished to attract. "You asked for the truth," the author concluded, "and here it is."[88]

Another report highlighted the same conflict between family and state:

We dutifully attend meetings. . . . But we do something that is not right. We have tried, and still continue to try, to awaken in our women a feeling of responsibility for their families. But then we erode it by the constant drives to sell something. . . . I love my work and my women, and I am ready to fight for them. But what is the point if it all looks great on the outside and does not nurture a true National Socialist human being? [89]

Poor women were not the only ones to object. Polster's middle-class "target population" remained apathetic. "I begin to understand why the solid middle class refuses to have anything to do with us. The low morale and also the dishonesty cause so many difficulties. . . . As deeply as we love our Führer and want to carry on his work, we strongly reject the Party and its administrative organs. To many women leaders, it seemed as if idealism had disappeared beneath a morass of corruption. The Party's early goals, they believed, had been betrayed by humdrum bureaucrats interested only in appearing respectable. As Irene Seydel put it, disillusioned women leaders from before 1933 complained that the Nazis "offer[ed] us the same old song with new notes." [90]

Elisabeth Polster followed Scholtz-Klink's advice. Ignoring the disaffection among longtime Nazi faithful, she reached out instead to the women who had previously looked down their noses at the uncouth Nazis. Rabble-rousing speakers, like Irene Seydel, only alienated the ladies of Westphalia who remained loyal to their church. Throughout 1933, Polster attempted to compromise with the old guard women. With the national leadership in flux, she hesitated between orthodoxy and moderation. Scholtz-Klink's emergence emboldened Polster to reprimand Seydel for her "lack of discipline" and to request that her public-speaking permit be revoked. Seydel, in her view, had committed an unpardonable breach by writing directly to Hitler's sister a year before. Seydel resigned as regional cultural consultant. By return mail, the leadership in Berlin begged Polster to recall the dissident Seydel, who, they noted, was the only woman speaker with the "ability to speak with deep faith in her convictions." Others spoke in "dull and abstract" terms, but Seydel roused her audiences to faith and action. In the spring of 1934, news of the trouble reached Scholtz-Klink's assistant. "Keep Seydel!" the office ordered. [91] By this time Seydel herself had gained the upper hand and defended herself:

Throughout many hard electoral campaigns and battles I was always counted among those who did not let personal feelings interfere. I placed my entire private life at the service of the Party's needs, and I don't think I overstate my case if I venture to say that my whole life has been bound up with our *Weltanschauung*. Like all of us, I unconditionally serve the idea and not the person. The National Socialist movement always stands apart from personal squabbles. I feel a deep commitment to pitch in and help out. *Heil Hitler!*"[92]

Polster sent Seydel to the national women's leadership training camp at Coburg Castle for reeducation. Her supervisors there described that Seydel was "enthusiastic in her studies, very self-confident, and an excellent speaker. Despite some difficulties she cooperated with the community."[93]

Meanwhile, Polster did her best to improve morale among her followers. She organized a retreat at a nearby health spa, but, as one widely respected participant reported, "the women here are forever complaining." Catholics and Protestants could hardly speak to one another in civil tones. The author of the report, a Protestant, added, "They display such a Catholic stubbornness!" Anti-Catholic (or anti-Protestant) jokes seemed more popular than topics such as Hitler's childhood, women's mission, eugenics, the Jewish Question, and Nazi charity.[94] When this educational approach failed, one of Polster's co-workers proposed the introduction of a "morale medal," to be awarded to women who maintained the most cheerful attitude. The suggestion, however, floundered because no one could agree on how to define "morale."[95]

Meanwhile, Seydel's followers mounted a campaign to support her against Polster. One of dozens of letters in her personnel files typifies the simple devotion Seydel inspired.

> Oh, how consistent and clear you made our views! And with what stirring emotions you talk to us! We knew Germany and the *Vaterland* were God's creations . . . how tragic it is that we . . . who have defended our great Führer's ideas with all our might, are so often attacked and insulted and excluded. Sometimes one despairs, drained of courage and strength. But over and over the idea of our Führer and his inspiring example puts us back on the right course. Despite attacks, we will not allow ourselves to be pushed back. Dear Frau Seydel, we *must* remain brave and faithful. The truth will emerge victorious in the end.[96]

Other issues intruded into the affair. Seydel had recruited a personal following more loyal to her than to their local Nazi officials. In addition, Seydel reconciled her brand of National Socialism with Christianity. By invoking both God and the Führer, she spared women the distress of deciding between their earthly leader and their heavenly deity. Polster emphasized practical work in the community and ignored religion altogether, while Seydel's charismatic style drew a huge following from peasants and working people. The feud continued, with Polster praising "friendly understanding" and Seydel defending her total dedication to Hitler. Polster ordered Seydel to tone down her rhetoric and avoid mentioning religion. "Your speeches are so fiery that they polarize the audiences." Seydel retorted that most religious women could only be recruited if they reconciled their twin faiths to God and the Führer.[97] As summer approached in 1935, Polster remained hostile. Scholtz-Klink warned Polster that hasty dismissals of trusted Nazis lowered morale. "Please be careful," she wrote, "always say someone has been given leave."[98] Rudolf Hess, too, worried about women Nazis' flagging enthusiasm. He, however, blamed it on the generation conflict, suggesting that the old-timers be protected from humiliation at the hands of a younger generation of women Nazis.[99]

As the Nazi movement transformed itself into the Nazi state, Seydel's prospects dwindled. During the Depression, when women voters counted, she had performed a vital service by mobilizing thousands of women; but after 1933, Polster's moderation was designed to draw mainstream "ladies" into her apolitical community organizations. Seydel spoke to women who were searching for a new faith in both God and Führer—women who disdained the snobbish ladies of Polster's ilk.

During the summer of 1935 Seydel realized that her cause had been lost; not only Polster and her ladies opposed her, but Nazi men made their contempt for women more obvious with each year. When she heard the news that, for example, the Nazi Women's Organization banner could not be flown at the same height as other Nazi flags, or that a special order demanded the exit of all women from responsible positions, she (like Reber-Gruber) protested. The feisty behavior that won her converts drove her to turn against her superiors whenever she perceived injustice.[100]

Seydel, speaking in homely metaphors and bombastic phrases, intuitively felt her audiences' desires and transmitted their responses upward to her superiors. As the Party was superceded by the state, obedience replaced fanaticism as the order of the day. Seydel understood her usefulness had ended. Before 1933, in a rebellious movement, effective organizing depended upon people like Seydel who could sense the mood of their supporters; after Hitler seized power, the state relied upon obedient bureaucrats like Polster who could be relied upon to follow whatever orders local leaders issued. Seydel relented. Realizing that no reformation of civic life and faith would occur, she drafted her last letter of resignation. As the Christmas bells tolled for the birth of the Christ Child, she wrote melodramatically,

Dear Frau Polster,

You will always find petty people to follow you. New times demand new people. The snow is falling gently and it buries much unpleasantness and hatred. . . . Perhaps it will also make us more peaceful in the silence. . . .

Maybe it will bring to us loving, good-hearted ideals. . . . I know that we have become distant of late. Powers beyond our control are guilty for that. I want to avoid ill will as we part. . . . Your powers in the district are on the rise and mine are on the wane. . . .[101]

Seydel retired from public life, adding with a flourish that she would begin work on her memoirs. At this point, her Party file stops. No records indicate whether she continued to support the Party or that she openly rebelled. Probably, she did just what she had predicted disillusioned women would do—simply withdraw from public life and revert to a more traditional Christian nationalist faith. Polster won out formally, but the local organization was deprived of a charismatic and popular force.

Under Polster's guidance, Nazi women in Westphalia cooperated in practical activities. Teachers from the younger generation seemed particularly eager to participate in Nazi work.[102] Polster did not mention the obvious fact that tests of political "reliability" were a requirement for employment in public schools. Nearly 200,000 women participated in ten-week home economics, motherhood, and civics classes organized by Polster.[103] Between 300 and 500 women leaders from the region were considered sufficiently important to be invited to the Nuremberg Party Rally each year; by 1936, 66,500 women had joined the local National Socialist Women's Organization. Polster's monthly reports exulted in such progress.

Beneath statistical success, however, two types of complaints persisted. First, general confusion about the organizational chain of command did not die out. After three years of Nazi rule, people still could not distinguish between a "cell," a "block," and a "local" leader.[104] One of Polster's supporters in Münster tactfully suggested she follow Goebbels' advice to organizers: "One of the major questions in the creation of a unified organization is the delimitation of competences. Unless each area is clearly demarcated, a harmonious and varied program is not possible, even among people with the best intentions."[105]

Established local organizations refused to obey Nazi directives; they insisted that their loyalty to Hitler placed them above reproach and therefore beyond the requirements for Nazification. The Red Cross, the monarchist Queen Louisa League, church groups, and veterans' ladies auxiliaries all promised to cooperate with Nazi programs but refused to obey Polster. Having met external requirements by dismissing Jewish women and electing women who belonged to Nazi associations, they expected autonomy in exchange. What Polster had interpreted as programmatic cooperation turned out to have been grudging obedience, inspired not by devotion but by material incentives. As long as she made no demands to control these organizations, Polster felt successful; when, after four years in office, she interfered in women's organizations' internal affairs, the results proved dismal. "In the interests of achieving total unity, we are arousing implacable hostility," she confided to her regional deputies.[106]

Her leader in Detmold asked, "Is there no way we can siphon off some of these petty individuals—so we can wean them away from their devotion to the Red Cross? They make our lives so difficult! Whatever can we do with such petty people? All we want is to conclude an agreement with them so we can get on with our work!"[107] Polster decided simply to dissolve recalcitrant organizations; but again Scholtz-Klink's office cautioned her to preserve goodwill and keep trying. Far better, they urged, to dispatch infiltrators and undercut women's organizations from within.[108] But Scholtz-Klink's insistence on subservience reflected the new mood in Berlin. As Hitler prepared for his "racial revolution," only unqualified obedience counted as loyalty.

One of Scholtz-Klink's closest co-workers was Maria Jecker, director of the Reich Association of Housewives. Throughout Germany, Jecker's organization had cooperated enthusiastically with the government. And yet, by late 1935, strife became visible. In Münster, Polster declared an all-out drive to thoroughly Nazify the Housewives. For a generation, the popular Frau Kruckmann had served as chapter president. In 1935, Polster asked her to join the Nazi Party or resign. Kruckmann refused.

Polster praised Kruckmann's "steadfast loyalty to the *Volk* and Führer," but began a gossip campaign. To her superiors she reported, "Frau Kruckmann exerts an unhappy influence which makes meetings difficult." Interestingly, Polster did not dare to dismiss Kruckmann. Instead, she began to whisper allegations so preposterous that none of Polster's co-workers had the nerve to confront Kruckmann.[109] Kruckmann's neighbors called for an open meeting. "It is an unhealthy situation indeed when we must dismiss anyone who has unstintingly supported our Nazi cause." Polster closed the case. Then she brought charges that were more flimsy than the first but strategically better calculated. Kruckmann, Polster claimed, had "poked fun at Reichs Leader Scholtz-Klink during an outing." No one would serve as a witness. Scholtz-Klink (noted for her conciliatory approach to strife) could not tolerate even an unfounded insult, and one of her staff told Polster to "make an example of the Housewives' Union" even if it meant destroying their organization.

As it turned out, the Kruckmann case did indeed set an example, though not the one Scholtz-Klink intended. True, Polster dissolved the group, but not before Kruckmann herself heard the news. The House-wives rented a moving truck and emptied the equipment from their cooking-education center before the police could confiscate it. Polster's assistant arrived on the scene as the shiny new cookstove disappeared into the truck and the treasury was disbursed among the members. "All women stand behind Frau Kruckmann," the assistant reported. She tried to reason with them.

> Although I spoke with joy and enthusiasm, I encountered a stony si-lence. When I asked one woman if she did not want to work with the National Socialist Women's Organization, she shrugged her shoulders. Be-cause they realized I was a full-blooded Nazi, they did not dare say an outright "no" to me, but they conveyed their feelings wordlessly. I said to myself, "Something is not right here," and went directly to local headquar-ters . . . and found a depressing mood. . . . What I saw and heard dis-tressed me deeply . . . [especially] the sad condition of the Party.[110]

The Münster strife miniatured the conflicts that had been played out among old-timers Zander, Diehl, Gottschewski, and Siber, and then between Scholtz-Klink and Reber-Gruber. Local leaders were expected to create a new Nazi spirit, but Polster imposed such a narrow authori-tarian structure on the women she attempted to mobilize that she cur-tailed their initiative and damaged morale. Polster, adept at translating orders from on high into local programs, lacked the essential quality for any popular leader—a quality, incidentally, that marked Hitler's own brilliance: the ability to tell an audience what it wanted to hear.

Polster had imposed unity but only by alienating her enemies, not by convincing them to follow her. Seydel and Kruckmann, who refused to accept Nazi "guidance," vanished. Top-down authoritarianism killed the revolutionary élan of the pre-1933 days, at the same time as Hitler accel-erated the assault against Jews and the "eugenically unworthy." The process of either Nazifying or destroying rival middle-class women's or-ganizations had taken over three years and left a train of bitterness. Women who undoubtedly wanted to cooperate with motherhood edu-cation, Jewish boycotts, or indoctrination programs refused to do so because they valued their own autonomy more than they feared the state.

At the national level, however, Scholtz-Klink's progress reports presented an optimistic picture. She directly employed 25,000 women who, in turn, supervised the activities of 8 million volunteers. Four subdivisions reflected the government concerns: (1) economic status of employed women, (2) social work for employed mothers, (3) cooperation with the Labor Front to regulate employed women's status, and (4) home economics courses. "Indoctrination" no longer retained the salient position it had enjoyed earlier. In general, highly paid posts were held by Party members, while nonmembers were pressured and intimidated into becoming volunteers. As supervisor of a vast bureaucracy, Scholtz-Klink collected public honors, titles, awards, and wealth, even as she lost real administrative control over her women and alienated opponents. Unlike the male heads of divisions, who accumulated increasing numbers of employees and offices in their purview, Scholtz-Klink ensured her longevity by cutting loose key chunks of her subordinate organizations and turning them over to male leaders.

Against the background of disillusionment and anger within the ranks of loyal Nazi women, Gertrud Scholtz-Klink projected an image of docile efficiency. American sociologist Clifford Kirkpatrick reported in the mid-1930s:

> Addressing an audience, the Führerin looks like a Nordic priestess preaching the cult of womanhood. Thousands of simple women identify themselves with this symbol of womanhood enthroned and feel convinced that a wife and mother like themselves is speaking from the depths of her heart to the hearts of her enraptured audience. [However, he also noted that her enemies saw her as a] shrewd, selfish, ambitious politician who enjoys the limelight, takes pride in her huge automobile and finds satisfaction in her own sentimental speeches. This assumes the fairies blessed her with intelligence. Another interpretation of her political status is that she is merely a simple National Socialist woman selected for her womanly qualities to bring women into line to serve the ends of masculine Nazi leadership.[111]

Admirers said she was using "gentle womanly guile to restore the rights of women threatened in the turmoil of the revolution."

Scholtz-Klink's feminine intuition told her what she must do to enhance her own status: Yield to her male superiors and impose absolute obedience on her female followers. By avoiding ideology and striking a moderate image, she attracted a broad following; but in the process she alienated the vigorous and independent "true believers" required by Hitler's secular religion. Six years in office had hardened Scholtz-Klink. In 1933 she had idealistically declared, "No Nazi woman will ever be motivated to work for money." Once in national office, she recruited as many unpaid volunteers as possible. Needless to say, she herself enjoyed a full staff and exceedingly comfortable material existence. But, equally obvious, her style of living never approached that of her male colleagues.[112] Relative to male leaders, she enjoyed modest rewards; but compared to most women, Scholtz-Klink lived lavishly.

Scholtz-Klink provided the perfect complement for Hitler. Their speeches at the Nuremberg Rally in September 1934 foreshadowed subsequent developments. Men, Hitler said, often are led astray by their own intellectual prowess and "Jewish" intellectualism. Women, by contrast, provide the ballast with their steady hearts and sound instincts.

> The power of instinct so clearly demonstrated its superior strength and accuracy. It turned out that the over-subtle mind can only too easily be misled, that men of uncertain intellectual discernment can be swayed by seemingly intellectual arguments, and that it is just at such periods that there awakes in woman her inherent instinct for self- and national preservation. Woman proved to us in those days that her aim is sure![113]

Scholtz-Klink put it this way to the same audience. "The conscience of the German *Volk* rests in its women's hearts, just as the *Volk* rests in their *Schoss* [which means both 'womb' and 'lap']."[114] Nazi women were not supposed merely to follow their hearts (which might be fickle); they were to follow their Führer.

Scholtz-Klink's followers worked to restore the strong family, as defined by lifelong monogamy, many children, and mothers' dignity. These women anticipated the creation of a biologically demarcated society with protection against both male intruders and the "racially unworthy." Within its sphere, Scholtz-Klink's office won support from a broad network of supposedly nonpartisan women's organizations, but chiefly for the activities they already engaged in before 1933. Although individuals here and there withdrew rather than cooperate, their associations contributed to home economics, psychology, medicine and health care, arts and crafts programs, and home industries to restore a strong, household-centered society. Epitomizing the dreams of many nineteenth-century women's-rights advocates for a separate sphere in the modern world, these women retreated from "manly" politics in order to participate more fully in "womanly" areas of public life. Redrawing gender lines promised them careers in public health, family law, administration, education, and culture, as well as state support for mothers. About 40,000 women worked at the district level, and another 280,000 at local levels of the Frauenschaft. Besides the 950 leaders trained at Coburg, nearly 4,000 women took courses in Nazism.[115] No doubt these women saw themselves as a convinced elite. But as doctrine became more central and the

Party more intrusive, Scholtz-Klink's strategy for attracting masses of women to pragmatic "motherly" tasks was undermined. While pledging to place the communal good above personal advantage, these "self-sacrificing" women carried that spirit to their own positions. They delivered services and expected a handsome payoff, as well they should have in the feudal world of Nazi bureaucracy. Reality proved to be very different. Women, even the most loyal and obedient, never gained access to powerful positions in which they might have decided policy. Party leaders trusted neither the doctrinaire nor the opportunistic woman administrator because the former could become strong-minded, and the latter might foster cynicism and apathy.

Independent administrators like Reber-Gruber and charismatic "true believers" like Seydel faced jealous superiors. Docile leaders like Scholtz-Klink and Polster, on the other hand, directed moderate programs modeled on traditional charitable activities. But Hitler's plans for racial revolution demanded dynamic leaders to recruit fanatics who would endorse unconventional notions about unmarried mothers, forced sterilization, and violent anti-Semitism. To succeed in Nazi terms, women leaders needed status, which as women they could never have. One loyal Nazi, in a telling vignette, experienced this contradiction when she received a motherhood medal. She returned it because, "since the medals don't even rate a swastika on them, they are not worth much."[116]

Two ideals of marriage and the family coexisted in the late 1930s. Max Horkheimer, writing in the mid-1930s from exile, saw the Nazi family as the basis of the "authoritarian character" because it repressed the urge to independence and rendered children anxious and docile. But at the same time he held up an ideal of the family with a very different sort of power. The family could also, he believed, serve as "a reservoir of resistance to the complete dehumanization of the world." The mother, as guardian of that reservoir, had the potential to create a space apart from a public arena.[117] Increasing German marriage rates may have resulted from forces quite different from Nazi policy. The drive for a new Nazi family may have actually deepened most people's nostalgia for tradition. As their leaders prepared Germans for war in a society permeated by suspicion and force, perhaps average people did long for a home life. In an alien world, deluged by propaganda and filled with terror, the idea of a family as a peaceful respite held considerable attraction. Women's support for the Nazi crusade during the early years testifies to their desire for a society based upon what sociologist William Goode called the "family of western nostalgia." Such a society never existed; but the wish for its "return" springs from a longing for meaning in a mechanized and bureaucratized world, a longing that is with us still.

Signs outside public bath in La Blaubeuren, 1937. A Jewish woman is standing in front of signs reading "Dogs not permitted" and "Jews forbidden." *Courtesy of the Leo Baeck Institute*

As part of a clean-up campaign against vice, SA men arrested suspected prostitutes and publicly ridiculed them. The sign around this woman's neck reads: "I am the biggest pig in the neighborhood and only associate with Jews!" *Ullstein Archives*

"Mother" Guida Diehl, leader of the pro-Nazi New Land Movement in the 1930s. *Ullstein Archives*

Gertrud Bäumer (1873–1954), delegate to the Reichstag, leader of the middle-class women's movement in the thirties. *Bildarchiv Preussischer Kulturbesitz, Berlin*

MUTTER UND VOLK

Herausgegeben für den Reichsmütterdienst im Deutschen Frauenwerk

7. Jahrgang / Nr. 9 / Berlin, September 1937
Verkaufspreis 10 Pfennig

Die Reichsfrauenführerin, Frau Scholtz-Klink

Gertrud Scholtz-Klink's portrait on the leaders. cover of the magazine for Nazi women

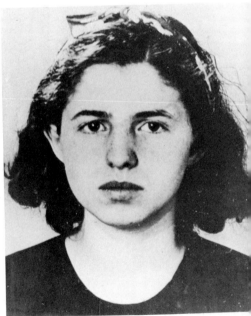

Hella Helene Hirsch, born 1921, executed 1943. A member of the Communist Jewish Baum resistance group. *Bildarchiv Preussischer Kulturbesitz, Berlin*

Seamstresses and superiors, Berlin, 1933. *Landesbildstelle Berlin*

Members of the Nazi League of German Girls at a harvest festival, 1933.
Landesbildstelle Berlin

League of German Girls
at summer camp.
Berlin. *Ullstein Archives*

Aryan girls practicing
gymnastics in stadium.
Landesbildstelle Berlin

Irma Griese, the "Bitch of Auschwitz," and Josef Kramer, sponsor of the Women's Orchestra at Auschwitz, after their capture in 1945. *Bildarchiv Preussischer Kulturbesitz, Berlin*

Guards from the concentration camp Bergen-Belsen, after the liberation in 1945. *Bildarchiv Preussischer Kulturbesitz, Berlin*

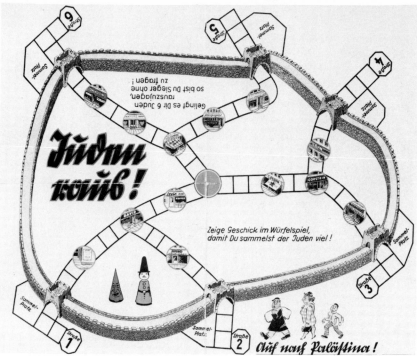

Children's board game called "Get the Jews Out!" The winner of the game is the child who manages to chase six Jews from their businesses and homes (represented by the circles in the center). At every exit ("collection center"), only one road of five goes to Palestine. The rhyming instructions are as follows: "Be skillful when the dice you throw/and you'll collect Jews by the droves/If you succeed in throwing six Jews out/You're the winner without a doubt." *Ullstein Archives*

Illustration from a children's book showing the separation between "Aryans" and Jews. Interestingly, it is the Jewish teacher who takes the initiative by leading his students out of Aryan society, in which they are not wanted. The "Aryan" teacher, by contrast, stands passively in the background. *Courtesy of the Leo Baeck Institute*

A boy in SA uniform at the
National Youth Rally in
Potsdam on October 1, 1934.
*Bildarchiv Preussischer
Kulturbesitz, Berlin*

Wartime cover of the
Nazi women's magazine,
Frauen Warte.

Women at Birkenau-Auschwitz being chosen for the gas chamber. Irma Griese is supervising the selection process. The watercolor, entitled *Frauen-Selektion in Birkenau*, was painted by a former prisoner, W. Siwek, after 1945 and now hangs in the Auschwitz Museum. *Bildarchiv Preussischer Kulturbesitz, Berlin*

Part of a collection of wallet-sized inspirational Nazi photographs. The original caption on the back of the photo reads: "November 9, 1935. The Fuhrer talks to a party member who is the wife of a man killed in the 1923 Beer Hall Putsch." The building in the background is the Party headquarters in Munich. *Peter Hammer Verlag*

7

PROTESTANT WOMEN FOR FATHERLAND AND FÜHRER

We have all of us . . . been thrown into the tempter's sieve, and he is shaking and the wind is blowing and it must become manifest whether we are wheat or chaff.
—Martin Niemöller
Fourth Sunday before
Easter, 1934

Often it seems to me as if we are all being tested by the Devil and Satan. And we must pass through Hell together until we finally obtain ultimate victory.
—Adolf Hitler

In his memoir of Nazi Germany, *The Nightmare Years*, William Shirer recalled,

> Adolf Hitler had become such a public figure and so reveled in it and spent so much time exposing himself to the multitude, that I wondered if he had any private life. . . . No German newspaperman or broadcaster would dare to raise the subject, in print or on the air. "You can say," one member of Hitler's entourage told me, "that he leads a Spartan personal life. He is a vegetarian, a teetotaller, a non-smoker, and a celibate."
>
> No one around the dictator dared, or at least ventured, to speak about the women, if any, in this celibate's life. One party member did confide that he was sure Hitler would never marry.
>
> "Why not?" I asked.
>
> "He considers he is married to Germany. Germany is his bride."[1]

Other sources report Hitler saying, "My only bride is my motherland."[2] Hitler once compared himself to the matinee idol who loses his allure once married, and remarked on another occasion, "For me, marriage would have been a disaster."[3] Indeed, Hitler consented to marry Eva Braun only hours before their mutual suicide in the Berlin bunker, when it became clear to him that he was, after all, only a mortal and not a messiah. Until that realization, however, Hitler depicted himself as his nation's divinely appointed suitor-savior, who swept his bride off her feet. After the "marriage" Hitler reminisced about the courtship in rambling, hypnotic tirades.

> Long ago you heard the voice of a man and it struck your hearts, it awakened you, and you followed that voice. You followed it for years, without so much as having seen him whose voice it was; you heard only a voice and you followed. I feel you, and you feel me! It is faith in our nation that has made us, a small *Volk*, great; that has made us, a poor *Volk*, rich; that has made us, a vacillating, dispirited and anxious *Volk*, once again brave and courageous. A voice that has made us who had gone astray, able to see— able to join together.[4]

To enable all citizens to hear their Führer's magic voice, the government subsidized the production of radios (called *Volksempfänger*—literally, "people's receivers"), and the tradition lives on today in West Germany, where reproductions of the Hitler radio grace the homes of people whose parents "heard the voice" and took the vow. Millions tuned into the national station and "married" their Führer by chanting together, "Adolf Hitler is Germany and Germany is Adolf Hitler. He who pledges himself to Hitler pledges himself to Germany." The bridegroom demanded absolute fidelity. A jealous, if psychopathic, god tolerated no rivals.

Like most suitors, Hitler had rivals. In 1933, they had literally vanished from sight in the wake of mass arrests, torture, and sometimes murder. After Hitler outlawed all non-Nazi associations, his victory seemed total. But the Führer wanted a love match, not grudging acquiesence. For this he needed not only the coercive mechanisms of the state, but the seductive wiles of his Propaganda Minister and the plethora of social and cultural programs offered by his Party organizers.

In the conquest of German "hearts and minds," he faced one last rival that could not be arrested, tortured, and browbeaten—organized religion. Rounding up his political opponents—"cleaning up the streets," as he called it—occasioned little protest from most Germans, who probably believed that the Communists were plotting revolution when the Reichstag burned. But not even Hitler believed he could arrest thousands of clergymen without massive protest. Seeing himself as a secular messiah, he intended to convert, not coerce, those who had still not "heard the voice" in 1933. Men had figured largely in formal Party politics during the early years of the movement and also during the first stage of Hitler's consolidation of power in early 1933. But the next stage in Hitler's courtship depended on women, for they formed the core of organized religion. As mothers they raised their children with religious values and as churchgoers they outnumbered the men. On a more practical level, they staffed the vast organizational networks of both Catholic and Protestant churches and operated hospitals, charities, welfare programs, and schools. If Hitler's vision of racial revolution was to succeed, he would have to convert women as well as men. Did that mean a loyal Nazi had to renounce her religious faith? Or could she combine her faith in God and her Führer? In the early days of the Party, Zander had preached a pagan Nazi dogma that implied giving Nazi loyalty absolute priority, while Diehl insisted on the compatibility of Christianity and Hitlerism. By the spring of 1933, both women had been dismissed, and Gertrud Scholtz-Klink avoided the question.

People who remember the atmosphere in Germany in 1933 recall Nazism as an all-or-nothing faith. They describe the revival-like atmosphere of Nazi meetings, which, more than any aspect of the Nazi state, horrified and fascinated them. French diplomat André François-Poncet (no admirer of Nazi principles) attended the annual Nuremberg Rally. Awed and repelled, he felt swept away by "an almost mystical ecstasy, a kind of holy madness."[5] William Shirer remembered: "I had seen vast throngs in India moved by the sight of Gandhi and in Rome by Mussolini. But this

German horde was different in a way I could not yet comprehend." At the Nuremberg Rally, the young reporter found himself literally caught up in a frenzied crowd that reminded him of Holy Rollers and participating in ceremonies that "had something of the mysticism and religious fervor of an Easter or a Christmas Mass in a great gothic cathedral."

> Hitler rode into this medieval town at sundown today past solid phalanxes of wildly cheering Nazis who packed the narrow streets . . . thousands of Swastika flags blot out the gothic beauty of the place . . . about ten o'clock I got caught in a mob of ten thousand hysterics, who jammed the moat in front of Hitler's hotel shouting: "We want our Führer!" I was a little shocked at the faces, especially those of the women. . . . They looked up at him as if he were a Messiah, their faces transformed. . . .[6]

The charismatic image that had attracted Hitler's earliest followers was after January 1933 packaged for mass consumption and transmitted to the entire nation. Having triumphed so easily over his political enemies, Hitler upstaged his religious rivals. Germans who tuned in to the national radio network a few days after Hitler became Chancellor heard their new leader shout, "I promise you a new Reich [kingdom] on earth!" And they heard him rave in his high-pitched, hysterical voice about "the inseparable trinity of state, movement, and *Volk*." With mighty cheers in the background, he offered a prayer for "power and glory. Amen."[7] At the Nuremberg Rally in September 1933, he spoke more like a prophet than a politician: "The German form of life is definitely determined for the next thousand years! For us, the nervous nineteenth century has finally ended. There will be no revolution in Germany for the next one thousand years!"[8]

This self-anointed savior of the *Vaterland* proclaimed himself the father of a Germanic heaven on earth. "This Reich has just begun to live through the first days of its youth. It will continue to grow throughout the centuries," he promised.[9] Having maneuvered his way into power backed only by a third of all Germans and a doddering former Field Marshal, Hitler looked heavenward for authority. "Ultimately, the individual man is weak in all his nature and actions when he acts contrary to almighty Providence and its will. But he becomes immeasurably strong the moment he acts in harmony with Providence! Then there pours down upon him that force which has distinguished all the great men in the world."[10]

As a revolutionary dictator Hitler had few predecessors—perhaps Napoleon I, or Mussolini. They did not impress him. He wanted more. "I am not a dictator and never will be a dictator. Any clown can be a dictator!" What did he desire? He had already suggested the answer in *Mein Kampf.* "I consider those who establish or destroy a religion much greater than those who establish a state, to say nothing of founding a Party."[11] After the "revolution" that had given him political power, Hitler in his more emotional moments yearned to inspire a "reformation" that would place a new secular religion at the core of his domain. Luther, Calvin, and Cromwell had set the pattern here; but they crusaded in a religious age, before mass literacy or mass communication. And they believed in an Almighty. In the intervening centuries, only Robespierre, preaching a union of virtue and terror, presaged Hitler's design.

After centuries of religious diversity, Hitler intended to expel Jews and subvert Christianity. Ultimately, in Hitler's plans, Catholics and Protestants would dissolve into a single state church. Jews would be expelled and Christians united under one National Bishop. Newsreels of Nazi rallies portrayed fervent masses of Germans chanting, "One *Volk*, one Reich, one Führer!" Would they add, "One God!" to this trinity?[12] Hitler said yes. The nation that had been given one Führer would now, Hitler announced, have one faith. As Hitler said so often, "We are not a movement; rather, we are a religion."[13]

Ultimately, Hitler aimed at subverting Catholicism and Protestantism into a single pagan religion. However, in the first stage of his campaign, Hitler deepened the chasm between both major religions. History aided him in this task, for Germans (divided along religious lines since the 1500s), insisted on their identity as Catholics or Protestants, which meant living, working, and above all, marrying within one faith or the other. Members of the two faiths had learned to coexist, but did not merge. Realizing the difficulty of unifying and paganizing both religions, Hitler approached the task piecemeal. In the short term, he developed contrasting strategies to destroy each church. In July 1933, he signed a pact (the Concordat) with the Vatican, which guaranteed on paper that the Church could continue to function independently much as it did in Italy. The Catholic Center Party and political Catholic movements, of course, were outlawed, but the structure of the Church itself would remain intact. Stage one for Catholics appeared to be a pact of friendship and mutual respect.

By contrast, Hitler proceeded against the Protestant Church with uncharacteristic recklessness. Perhaps he had begun to think himself infallible; or maybe his contempt for Protestantism led him to miscalculate. Raised in the Catholic faith, Hitler respected its teachings and admired its ceremonies and organizations. And he saw the Catholic Church as a more dangerous foe than the disorganized Protestants. In attacking the Protestant Church, Hitler forgot the most important secret of his success, as he described it to an assembly of district leaders gathered at the Vogelsang Castle, an SS training center supervised by Scholtz-Klink's future husband, in 1937. In this revealing speech, Hitler boasted of the patience and "iron calm" that assured his victory in any struggle. "I always know that I must never make a single step that I may have to take back. Never a single step that might damage us. You know, I tread always on the outer limit of a risk, but never beyond. You have to have a nose to sniff out the situation, to ask, 'Now what can I get away with and what can't I get away with?' "[14]

From his failure at the Beer Hall Putsch through January 1933, Hitler had proceeded cautiously, building electoral support, striking alliances with other parties, and participating in Reichstag politics. Even when some of his deputies clamored for a violent coup d'état, Hitler silenced them and waited, as he said, for history to catch up to him. As Chancellor, he restrained the blood-thirsty radicals in his party until the Reichstag burned. Even then, he insisted on a legal transfer of dictatorial power through a Reichstag vote. The Republic, with only a fourteen-year heritage, had been moribund since the onset of the Depression, when Hindenburg began to rule by decree. The Christian tradition, however, had a thousand-year heritage. Despite the slightly declining church attendance, which alarmed some church leaders, 95 percent of all Germans declared themselves as Catholics or Protestants in 1933. This figure, incidentally, is not an estimate, but a precise indication of religious affiliation, because the government provided financial support for all organized religions and distributed funds proportionately, according to taxpayers' declarations of faith.[15] Politicians had allowed themselves to be deceived, intimidated, or bought off; but could the Christian religion be as easily destroyed? In one fatal respect, the religious situation resembled the configuration of Weimar politics, which Hitler had used to seize power, and the diplomatic configuration that he would exploit on the eve of World War II. The Christian religion was divided, and each church feared its religious opposite more than it feared Hitler.

After the Protestant Reformation, only Germany emerged without a single national religion. Since the sixteenth century, German-speaking people had lived in a conglomeration of small states, each with its own dominant religion. In most of these states (mainly in the north and east), Protestants outnumbered Catholics; while in the minority (chiefly in the south and west), Catholics predominated. Thus, when Germany unified in 1871, it contained a Protestant majority of about 60 percent and a sizable Catholic minority. In 1933, 45 million Protestants belonged to 28 separate churches, the largest of which, the Prussian Lutheran Church, had 18 million members.

Although Protestants constituted a majority, they lacked both the unified leadership and the international networks that sustained Catholics. In addition, Protestants had always been more receptive to Hitler's appeal—as voters and Party members they were overrepresented in the movement.[16] The Protestant clergy had not only refrained from criticizing National Socialism before 1933, but actually endorsed many of its election refrains, such as "The Common Need above Selfish Greed." Rhetoric about Germany's "mission" in the world and talk of "purity," "Providence," anti-Communism, and "spiritual" rebirth formed the heart of Protestant clergymen's social and political beliefs. Most Protestants felt more nationalistic than Catholics, who, they said, owed their allegiance to Rome. And they often implied that Jews—and Marxists, too—constituted an international plot. [17]

Hitler played on all these themes as he began his religious battle with offers of friendship. He reminded Protestants that the Party program guaranteed the protection of all religious rights that did not damage the state, and he pledged to defend Christianity along with all of its church-sponsored institutions. During the spring of 1933, he spoke of God and Providence more than at any other time in his career, spicing his proclamations with appeals to God, and even an occasional prayer. "Lord, let us never be weak and cowardly. Let us never forget the duty that we have taken upon ourselves! . . . We are proud that God's grace has enabled us once again to become genuine Germans."[18] Such words sound fanatic, but this sort of merging between national destiny and Protestant faith had a familiar ring to Protestant clergy.

Meanwhile, Hitler developed concrete strategies, beginning with the fulfillment of century-old aspirations for a single, unified national Protestant Church.[19] Hitler appointed a National Bishop to lead all Protestants. Ludwig Müller, a former army pastor and devoted Nazi, had no particular theological credentials, but the reason for his selection became obvious when he declared that Hitler had been sent by God to save the nation in time of peril. Removing Christ from his Jewish forebears, Müller claimed that Germanic heroes from Christ to Charlemagne led the way to Bismarck and finally to Hitler. Müller promised to do God's will by purging Christianity of all Jewish influence and surrendering Protestant organizations to state control. Clad in a brown shirt and riding boots, this rough-hewn pastor with close-cropped hair told the faithful, "A powerful nationalist movement has gripped and elevated our *Volk*. We shout our thankful 'Yes!' to this historical turning point. God has sent it to us. Praise the Lord!"[20] To thousands of cheering Protestants in the Berlin sports stadium, he swore to extirpate the Jewish heritage, expel all Jews from the Protestant Church, and continue the "revolutionary"

National Socialist Program. He promised, "We will create one mighty, new, all-encompassing German *Volk* Church." To aid him in his mission, Müller summoned 200 pastors to Berlin. They marched to Nazi songs, sporting brown uniforms, riding boots, body and shoulder straps, swastikas, and medals of honor as well as Christian crosses. As their voices swelled in a chorus of the "Horst Wessel Song," Müller told them, "The entire Germanic movement, with its Führer, is a present from God, given to us in a time of decision. . . . The old has passed away and the new has begun. . . . Now begins the struggle for the soul of the *Volk!*"[21] The bishop ordered his corps of preachers to fall in, "with the swastika on our breasts and the cross on our hearts."[22] While Hitler appealed to Providence and cultivated a Christian image, his bishop imposed pagan racism on Christian doctrine.

A few obedient pastors took up the challenge. Calling themselves German Christians, they synthesized Christian teachings with Nazi doctrine and guaranteed the preeminence of the latter.

> Just as Jesus liberated mankind from sin and hell, so Hitler saves the German *Volk* from decay. Jesus and Hitler were persecuted, but whereas Jesus was killed on the cross, Hitler was elevated to the Chancellorship. While . . . young Jesus renounced his teachers and was abandoned by his Apostles, sixteen of Hitler's disciples died for their Führer. The Apostles completed their crucified master's work. We hope that Hitler will be allowed to bring his own work to fruition. Jesus built for heaven; Hitler for the German earth.[23]

No sooner had Hitler accomplished his political takeover than he opened up a war against the Protestant Church. Meanwhile, within his own Party, Hitler posed as a staid and mature dictator, an image reinforced when he expelled the anticapitalist Gottfried Feder from the Party and ordered the murder of Ernst Röhm and his disreputable crew of storm troopers in July 1934. Thus Hitler crafted a moderate political image at the same time as he opened up a radical and reckless attack on the Protestant faith.

Aside from some German Christians, most ministers and their congregations expected to cooperate with the Nazi state and also to maintain their autonomy. When Hitler appointed Reichs Bishop Müller, only a few hundred pastors welcomed the choice, while 2,000 protested and 14,000 remained neutral. Between 1933 and 1945, only 250 Protestant ministers joined the Nazi Party. National Bishop Müller and the German Christians said that any devout Christian could be a loyal Nazi, provided he or she unconditionally supported the state, which meant putting Nazi above Christian dictates in the event of conflict. "When the state of Adolf Hitler summons us, we must obey!"[24] as the bishop put it. What would happen when Adolf Hitler decided what constituted Christian theology or intervened in religious faith? What could the good Christian do then? No one knew.

In 1934, two hundred pastors took a stand and broke away from the Nazified Protestant Church, forming the Confessing Church. Throughout the Third Reich, these protesters enthusiastically endorsed Hitler's foreign and domestic policies, but insisted on their right to decide religious questions. Pastor Martin Neimöller, one of the most well-known dissidents, had effusively praised Hitler in his 1932 autobiography. But when Hitler appointed a bishop who depicted Hitler as a savior, and who denigrated the "Jewish" Old Testament, Niemöller drew the theological line and organized the opposition against pagan influences over the Church.[25]

Insisting that "church must remain church," independent of the state, the small but influential Confessing Church went into opposition. This did not mean, however, that they always behaved bravely. When early in 1934 some Protestant bishops personally registered their objections to what they saw as paganism in Nazi dogma, Hitler lost his temper and screamed, "Christianity will disappear from Germany just as it has done in Russia. . . . The German race has existed without Christianity for thousands of years . . . and will continue after Christianity has disappeared. . . . We must get used to the teachings of blood and race. Just as the Catholic Church could not prevent the earth from going around the sun, so churches today cannot get rid of the indisputable facts connected with blood and race." The bishops insisted that they remained a loyal opposition and emphasized how deeply they admired secular Nazi doctrine and the Führer's greatness. Yet Hitler fulminated, "You are traitors to the *Volk*. Enemies of the *Vaterland* and destroyers of Germany!" Except for Pastor Niemöller, who had the temerity to object, the bishops were, in the words of historian John Conway, "so shaken with terror that they literally collapsed to the point of becoming dumb. . . . They gave Hitler their unconditional loyalty."[26] Hertha von Klewitz, Niemöller's daughter, recalled recently that this exchange marked the turning point, at which Protestant leaders ought to have realized the futility of confronting Hitler and begun a total resistance. Instead, they attempted for eleven years to balance loyalty to the Nazis' political programs while objecting to the pollution of religion by Hitler's creed. During the next few months, nearly 7,000 of 16,500 clergymen openly supported the Confessing Church. Throughout the remainder of the Third Reich they maintained their own networks and opposed the encroachment of National Socialism in areas they defined as religious. While remaining silent about the persecution of Jewish Germans, they defended Protestant theology against Nazi influence. Von Klewitz remarks sadly, "It was a church resistance and not political."[27]

At the opposite extreme on the religious question, Nazi radicals believed that true Nazis must totally reject Christianity in favor of faith in their Führer. Alfred Rosenberg insisted that devotion to Hitler and his Thousand Year Reich on earth must replace "primitive" Christian notions. Martin Bormann made it plain that "for us National Socialism and Christianity are incompatible." Gertrud Scholtz-Klink had years before cut all ties with her Protestant background and opted for her own vaguely pantheistic faith in Nature and the Germanic race.

This option remained far too radical for most Protestant women, who faced a three-way choice: Either they could belong to the neo-pagan German Christian movement, the dissident Confessing Church, or the mainstream Nazified Protestant Church led by Bishop Müller. Faced with these options, most Protestants wanted to compromise and to remain spiritual Christians and secular Nazis. Ultimately, Hitler insisted on the primacy of his doctrine over the Bible and assigned National Bishop Müller to bring his new flock into the fold.

At the threshold of Protestant faith stood women—two and a half million women—organized into hundreds of clubs, societies, and associations, meeting in private homes, parsonages, schools, and retreats and following their own hierarchy of elected leaders. Since the 1890s, Protestant women had been organized into two national associations: the Women's League (*Frauenbund*) which attracted the wealthier and better-educated women, and the Ladies' Aid (*Frauenhilfe*), to which working-class and lower-middle-class women belonged—the "ladies with the hats" and the "women with the kerchiefs," in the language of the time. The churchmen who authorized both associations explicitly did so in order to offer Protestant women an outlet for their desire to be part of the crescendo of women's voices that demanded access to public life. They saw the new associations as a way of keeping women out of the women's-rights movement. Motherliness, they believed, offered an emotionally satisfying and socially useful alternative to the atheistic demand for equality.

Both organizations, inspired by the Queen, pledged themselves to hold back the tide of industrialization, modernism, women's emancipation, sexual liberation, and atheism. And they followed their mandate right up to the end of World War I. Until the very end, their publications predicted glorious military triumph and urged women to keep the home front strong. Then came the defeat. Paula Müller-Otfried, president of the Women's League, wrote bitterly of the million and a half men who had died in vain—"for a total surrender to the most humiliating demands." As evil as the foreign enemy had been, she wrote, the Germans who expelled their beloved royal family and ushered in socialism deserved even worse condemnation. Starting with the winter of 1918–1919, Müller-Otfried pledged to remain nonpartisan.[28] "One thing we know: If the Lord God does not grant us a miracle, then we have been destroyed —morally, politically, and economically—for decades to come!"[29]

The Ladies' Aid, too, viewed 1918–1919 as its demise. Seeing no political solution to Germany's problem, its leaders awaited salvation from a merciful God. "This dreadful year which has just ended smashed everything of value in this world, leaving only rubble and refuse."[30] True to their word, Protestant women remained aloof from the Weimar democracy, which offered them unparalleled access to formal politics and even gave their leader, Paula Müller-Otfried, the chance to sit in the Reichstag until she resigned in 1932. Calling themselves apolitical, they denounced Marxism, Bolshevism, decadent atheism, and liberal political beliefs while endorsing reactionary causes.[31] When the Depression threw economic life into turmoil, Müller-Otfried looked heavenward, as she had after Germany surrendered in 1918. This time she prayed not for a miracle, but a "steel-hardened man" to save the *Vaterland* from Bolshevism, atheism, and moral degeneration. In her annual New Year's message in 1934, Müller-Otfried thanked God for granting her wish.

> When I wrote a year ago and saw only a glimmer of hope, I could not possibly have believed . . . my plea would be so richly fulfilled. . . . The vast majority of the *Volk* joyfully summoned the national regime, with its drive to purify public life, to combat unemployment, hunger, and need. . . . We prayed and the answer arrived. May God grant our rulers wisdom. May the "steel-hardened man" for whom we cried out a year ago . . . retain his power.[32]

Protestant women leaders dropped their apolitical stance and supported a state that denied them equality in economic or political spheres. Their reactionary prejudices blinded them to the futility of supporting the regime that promised to deny them any political influence at all. Their Christian faith, which ought to have made them sensitive to the brutality and injustice of Hitler's cause, served instead to accelerate their rush into the Nazi state.

Protestant women by and large expected Hitler's dictatorship to establish spheres of influence and bring a conservative order to German society. The lines of demarcation would be drawn on "natural" boundaries such as sex, age, and race, rather than on "man-made" divisions between capitalist and worker on the Marxists' model. As women, they anticipated carrying on their own feminine activities within the Church, and as Protestants they expected to be welcomed as independent participants in Hitler's state. Cooperation would replace wasteful and demoralizing competition among major groups that shared the same conservative ends. In their model, women and men, Protestants and Nazis, would occupy separate and autonomous spheres. This degree of self-deception can only be explained by Protestant women leaders' exaggerated sense of their own importance. By and large, they came from aristocratic and well-to-do families that had wielded considerable informal influence for decades; in addition, they were well educated and widely respected by their membership. All of these factors blinded them to the threat presented by Nazi leaders, whom they viewed as socially inferior, confused, and inexperienced.

The Protestant women's press instantly reflected the transformation. Eulogies to motherhood and women's spirituality predominated. "Our times have grown weary of thinking," wrote one author. "We demand reality . . . which we can actively control." Others admired Nazi family support programs. One writer said of the marriage loans, "The law had the effect of releasing a healthy stream that had become blocked by powerful forces damming up the healthy desires of the *Volk*. . . . Now the stream crashes through its limits."[33] Throughout the Weimar Republic articles in the Protestant press had opposed women's emancipation and supported pro-family legislation, so these views were not new. However, the women's periodicals had included commentary on legislation, columns on "women and politics," and moderate support for women who desired university training. The last vestiges of these themes disappeared in the spring of 1933. Contributors to women's periodicals saw 1933 as a crisis year, and they urged their readers to make sacrifices just as they had in August 1914. They did not ask at first what the new state could do for them. Swept along by the Nazi tide, they asked only what they could do for the state.

After the first few months of Nazi power, however, their normal concern for their own interests returned. When the "steel-hardened man" of Müller-Otfried's dreams insisted that leaders of Protestant organizations become Nazi Party members, she refused.[34] Already seventy years old, she resigned from the presidency of the Protestant Women's League. Although she hated democracy, she found it difficult to adapt to the authoritarian state. As a sincere admirer of Hitler, she believed her loyalty put her above suspicion and continued to speak her mind in articles that appeared in the Protestant women's magazine.

From the standpoint of women, we cannot find much good to say about the year 1933. One responsibility after another has been robbed from the German woman, however gloriously this process is embellished with rhetoric. We, however, have never asked to be "relieved" of our duties; nor have we welcomed it when we find ourselves suddenly pushed out of all places in which we once expected to make important contributions to church and state. We can only conclude that this stems from a lack of respect for our sex. We are simply washed away like unwanted specks of dust. Today one speaks so much about the German *Volk* . . . but one really means German *men*. Men's speeches are redolent with friendly words for the German mother. . . . The goal of Protestant women is to keep women's contributions to the nation alive. . . . We have by now lost virtually everything that we had hoped to achieve for *Volk* and church, but as Christians we must continue, saying, "Nevertheless."[35]

Müller-Otfried as a woman and a Protestant objected publicly to Nazi policy, while praising Hitler's more general aims. Like dissenting pastors, she reconciled herself to the Nazi state. But within months of this article she withdrew from the editorial board of the association's magazine, which she had directed for thirty years. Thereafter, we see nothing of her—not even a letter to the editor in a women's magazine. She died in 1946 without having written memoirs or reentered public life.

Müller-Otfried's response to Hitler informs us about two facets of Protestant women's *Weltanschauung*. First, they naively believed they could offer conditional loyalty to the total state and probably felt themselves above reproach because of their socially respectable position and their reactionary political record. Secondly, however, Müller-Otfried's willingness to speak out on women's issues suggests that, had she objected to anti-Semitism, she could also have found words to express herself. Because the Women's League archives remain closed, if she did find those words, we cannot find the record. As the record stands, however, Müller-Otfried must be counted among those who would have marched eagerly into the new state if only they themselves had been exempted from Hitler's hatred for Protestantism and women.

While they welcomed Hitler to power, the leaders of the Ladies' Aid, a generally conservative group, also viewed themselves as the loyal opposition within the Nazi camp. Blending self-interest and enthusiasm, they wrote,

The Protestant Ladies' Aid recognizes joyfully and consciously the authority of church and state sent by God. It will participate obediently in the reconstruction of the new Reich ordered by Adolf Hitler, the Chancellor of the *Volk*. It, however, expresses its deep pain and shame at the divisions created by the appointment of Reichs Bishop Müller. Unity is everything. We reject political battles in the church.[36]

At a meeting in May 1933, women from the Ladies' Aid asked for support for more women's theological training so that they could better react to the changes they saw around them. These women welcomed Hitler, but they refused to march behind the brown-shirted National Bishop Müller.

Müller-Otfried's departure did not make a major impact on her organization, for replacements were already waiting in the wings. Magdelene von Tiling reacted with more understanding to the new conditions. Besides having served as the director of the Ladies' Aid for thirty years, she had sat in the Prussian legislature and written a book and several essays on women and Christian education. During the Weimar Republic she expressed terror of atheism and godlessness and urged Christian (by which she meant Protestant) mothers to band together in the interest of their children. This woman who feared atheism received her Nazi Party membership card in the fall of 1933 and cooperated with Lydia Gottschewski in "integrating" her organization. For years, she said, Protestant women had been politically progressive and for that reason would be pleased to join such a modern, forward-looking movement and to "work without interference or reservations directly in the service of Volk and state." She, however, maintained a tight hold over her women and board of directors.[37]

Von Tiling and her generation of Protestant women welcomed Hitler's promise of racial renewal, economic recovery, and military glory. But they did not surrender unconditionally. Shrewdly, von Tiling insisted that her tightly organized and pro-Nazi following would not tolerate any "blurring of edges" vis-à-vis other, non-Protestant women's organizations. She promised to (as she said) "purge" or "renew" the boards of directors to please the Nazis. In exchange, she made it clear that she could never yield either her authority or the Protestant identity of her organization to a Nazi umbrella association. Protestants, after all, had withdrawn from the BDF; they were not about to merge into a Nazi federation.[38] Like so many nationalist politicians, it took months for von Tiling and her board to realize that they exercised no leverage whatsoever over policy within the state they had decided to support. Von Tiling and Müller-Otfried belonged to an older generation of women leaders who had created vast organizations of which they were deeply proud. Because Hitler spoke to them in reactionary language they could understand, they would eagerly have served his cause. But Müller-Otfried and, to a lesser extent, von Tiling, opposed the wholesale sellout of their Protestant women's network to the Nazi rulers. By the end of the summer, von Tiling had left her office. Müller-Otfried and her co-workers did not prevail against a new generation of women who calculated that they could best represent Protestant women by collaborating totally with the Nazi state.

New cleavages appeared along generational lines; the young reacted more flexibly to Nazi demands, while the old valued long-established ties. "Our enemies tell us, 'You are too young!' " wrote one young German Christian woman. "But I say thank heaven we *are* too young! Too young to be weighted down by old-fashioned liberal notions."[39] Younger women prided themselves on a more realistic assessment of the situation. Absolute loyalty to Hitler, they calculated, would purchase a privileged position for them in the new state. Theologian Meta Eyl rationalized women's loss of responsibility. "We must be like the vessel which, even though it has been emptied, is filled again with duties from bottom to brim. New challenges will always arise."[40]

Between adaptable careerists and the aloof old guard, another ambitious woman had emerged, whose success resembled Scholtz-Klink's rapid rise to national prominence. Like Scholtz-Klink, Agnes von Grone had no previous reputation that might inconvenience her, and approached her task fresh. Forty-four years old in 1933, von Grone had been born into the noble von Hammerstein family, which traced its lineage back to the twelfth century. Agnes (or Anni, as she was called) lived in a somber household because both parents suffered frequent ill health and emotional breakdowns. When her father died suddenly in 1907, her mother assumed full control of the family estate. Shortly thereafter, Agnes attended a wedding in what she described as a "Renaissance castle." At the dinner, the host of her table expressed his annoyance that he should have an eighteen-year old "young thing" near him. "When he discovered that I was the daughter of Bernhard von Hammerstein . . . Siegfried von Grone began to pay attention." His attentions were rewarded in 1909, when the two married.[41] In September 1914, her husband was shot in the head at the front and remained a semi-invalid all his life. The young wife assumed control of his family estate and raised their four children. When her eldest son came of age, she turned the family finances over to him and participated in charity work with the Ladies' Aid of Bielefeld. Within weeks of Hitler's appointment as Chancellor, she became associated with the Nazi Women's Organization and applied for Party membership. She received her card in May, and her reward followed quickly. Reichs Bishop Müller appointed her to bring all Protestant women's organizations "in line" under the National Socialist state. In the next few months, she eased von Tiling out of her presidency[42] and, with the help of Dagmar von Bismarck, created a federation for all Protestant women called the Frauenwerk, or Women's Bureau, and joined Paula Siber's national women's committee.[43] Von Grone agreed that Nazi women would wield the preponderant influence in her Frauenwerk, even if this necessitated replacing longtime members who refused to join the Party or who had Jewish ancestors.[44] Several women leaders would, in addition, serve in both Protestant and Nazi organizations. In response to von Grone's concern that Protestant women might feel invaded, Siber swore to defend Protestant women's independence "relentlessly" and guaranteed that Protestant women would enjoy as much autonomy as Catholic women did.[45]

Von Grone signed her correspondence with *Heil Hitler!* and called herself the Reichsfrauenführerin of all Protestant women. In 1935, she boasted of her "participation in the great constructive work of our *Volks* Chancellor and Führer." Our women, she said, "dedicate themselves in faithful and enthusiastic obedience to Führer and Party." Proudly she noted that her husband and sons belonged to National Socialist organizations and her daughters worked in local Nazi charity organizations. In 1933 she told Protestant women that under the authoritarian state, which they "could trust absolutely," civic work "took on a new meaning."[46] Von Grone took further steps to protect her new organization against state encroachment by imposing the "leadership principle" on her own followers. Von Grone, as the young director of a giant federation of all Protestant women's associations, quietly purged her domain of those who refused to join Nazi organizations. In tacit exchange for turning against these women, she expected to be rewarded with total control over her organization. As she once boasted, she had Nazified her own organization so thoroughly that outside help from the state would not be necessary.[47] In the future, she told her co-workers in December, members would express their opinions freely. But when decisions had to be made, she warned, opinions would be "weighed, not counted" because "reliable" voters carried more weight. By early January 1934, the work was complete. Newspapers announced: TWO AND A HALF MILLION GERMAN PROTESTANT WOMEN DECLARE THEIR READINESS TO PARTICIPATE IN MOTHERLY SERVICE.[48] The Frauenwerk dispatched a telegram to Frick praising him as the "protective Lord of all German women's work." Reichs Bishop Müller officially inaugurated von Grone's Frauenwerk within weeks of Frick's approval. In July 1934, Bishop Müller boasted that he had single-handedly created the Women's Bureau, a clear warning that trouble lay just ahead.[49] Flanked by her own authoritarian organization, von Grone prepared to defend Protestant women's rights within, not against, both state and church.[50]

Von Grone, it might seem, had every reason to congratulate herself on a series of successful moves. She had aligned herself with Siber and Frick and outmaneuvered her rival von Tiling, who had worked with Gottschewski's ill-fated attempt at a Frauenfront (Women's Front). While longtime Protestant women leaders offered qualified approval of Hitler's state, von Grone saw no reason to antagonize the movement that would clearly dominate the state for the near future. Her allegiance to Hitler together with Bishop Müller's personal endorsement gave her control over a nationwide organization that had been created by the women she had forced out of office. In her vision, Protestant and Nazi women together would raise funds, found new organizations, recruit new members, and collaborate in activities as they felt appropriate "to fulfill the will of our Führer, Adolf Hitler. . . ." By retaining the right to decide when and under what conditions they wanted to participate, Protestant women believed they would exercise some leverage in their negotiations with secular power. Protestant women leaders responded very much like Gertrud Bäumer and the BDF to the first year of Nazi power: pledging both a continuing struggle for middle-class women's concerns and absolute loyalty to the Nazi state. Within this general framework, however, individual women leaders disagreed about where to draw the line.

In one sense, von Grone and other younger women displayed a shrewder perception of the new reality than Müller-Otfried or von Tiling. In the short term, they were realistic in seeing that protest could not be effective. But the older women prized the status they had achieved and anchored themselves more firmly in their own accomplishments. In addition, they perceived how duplicitous Nazi words could be and pinned their hopes for survival on separatism from the new state. Von Grone optimistically believed she could enter the Nazi fray and hold her own. She could look back, for example, on Frick's surrender in the face of organized women's protest (which Protestant women supported) against the expulsion of women from their jobs.[51] She also watched the internecine wars between Hess and Frick, Gottschewski and Siber, Krummacher and Ley, which diverted their energies from the Nazification of non-Nazi associations. Ironically, this confusion at the top resulted in part from Nazi women leaders' refusal to yield their own authority to male bosses—precisely the issue that led von Tiling and Müller-Otfried to drop out of their positions. Longtime Nazi and Protestant women leaders had a strong commitment to the organizations they helped create and responded warily to Nazi declarations of friendship. Confusion in the upper echelons of the government and Party provided leaders like von Grone with an unrealistic sense of their own influence. After a year of Nazi dictatorship, von Grone accurately concluded that her own women remained better organized than Krummacher's and Siber's women Nazis. Learning from her predecessors' failures, she understood, too, that she could hope for influence only by cooperating with the political force that would dominate the nation for the foreseeable future. She differed from Müller-Otfried and von Tiling only in the degree of subservience she offered. But in Nazi Germany, degree made all the difference.

When Scholtz-Klink and Hilgenfeldt took control of the Nazi women's networks, "reorganization" produced disorganization on a mass scale. Jurisdictional questions created an uproar during 1933 and early 1934. Everyone wanted order. But no one agreed on the conditions. In this murky atmosphere, rumors replaced normal news channels, exacerbating confusion and helplessness. Scholtz-Klink did something that ought to have alarmed von Grone. She imitated the hallmarks of von Grone's successful organization, naming her bureau the Frauenwerk, calling herself Reichsfrauenführerin, and finally copying precisely the logo and format of *Mutter und Volk*, the Protestant magazine for mothers. As the Nazi Women's Bureau expanded, it imitated or absorbed successful Protestant programs (such as marriage counseling, mother-care centers, and mother education). For a time, Protestant women accepted imitation as a compliment and enjoyed advising the new government, which welcomed their contributions. A well-funded national welfare bureau would, they hoped, provide a setting within which they could adapt their social programs to state needs. Three general areas of concern appeared to offer the chance for cooperation between church and state: youth projects, eugenics, and support for motherhood.[52] In each of these areas, however, Gertrud Scholtz-Klink and her staff used Protestant programs as models, perfected the Nazi versions, and ultimately outlawed the Protestant originals.

A Protestant volunteer labor corps for young women had been planned during 1932, but only with the arrival of Nazi government did it take form. Besides providing employment, the program was designed to break down hostility between the rich and the poor, the countryside and the cities, and Catholics and Protestants. Personal encounters would create a true national solidarity. One Protestant medical student recalled her first experiences with the program in terms that any Nazi might have used. "What is the point of talking all the time? Why keep on reading about class differences? . . . For us [students], work is a good experience. Heavy household chores and work in the fields won't hurt any of us. We learn to adapt, to be modest, and to feel a healthy amount of self-confidence."[53]

The youth, instead of protesting or falling into "decadent" habits, would restore harmony. So effectively did Protestants run their Women's

Service Corps that the Nazi state did not even take it over until 1936. Behind the idealistic claims of fostering understanding between urban and rural Germans, the program really supplied cheap agricultural labor, either in work camps or in individual peasant families. Only 3 percent of the participants came from the countryside and worked in cities. As war approached, the service included over 200,000 young women; and after 1941, when all women under twenty-five not employed in war work were drafted into the program, it doubled.[54] During the early years of the Third Reich, Protestant women leaders looked on the Service Corps as an example of church-state cooperation, never sensing how fragile their hold on the program was.

Clara Schlossman-Lönnies, founder and president of the popular Protestant Mothers' Association, cooperated with the new state by voluntarily disassociating her organization from Protestantism and giving it to Scholtz-Klink's supervision. Her periodical *Mother and Child*, which she had founded in 1931, had from its inception supported eugenics and motherhood. In many respects, the periodical took up the same causes as Helene Stöcker's League for the Protection of Motherhood, but with an important difference. Schlossmann-Lönnies denied women's right to decide when and if they desired to bear children, which had been the very cornerstone of the outlawed League. After 1933, Schlossmann-Lönnies took one more step to demonstrate her total devotion to Hitler by divorcing her Jewish husband and demonstrating her own "Aryan" ancestry. Her husband, incidentally, was "deported" during the war and never heard from thereafter.[55] Nothing seemed to stand in the way of a brilliant future in motherhood services for this thirty-five-year-old careerist.

Protestant women welcomed a state that promised support for their talents as mothers and organizers. Protestant social workers had for years lobbied for state subsidies to encourage marriage and support large families; in addition, they had developed a network of rest centers for overworked mothers and organized homemaker helpers for large families.[56] Protestant women had joined the national alarm about the falling birthrate, calling it "family suicide," or "*Volk* murder." Protestant social workers (unlike their Catholic counterparts) emphasized quality as well as quantity and urged that "racially" substandard people not be allowed to bear children. One specialist called for "a new morality, a new will for purity, healthy marriages and healthy families—together with physically, spiritually, and psychologically healthy children."[57] During the Depression, the Inner Mission, the progressive Protestant national welfare institution, spurred on by a sense of economic emergency, appointed commissions, formed study groups, and published studies related to eugenic schemes to improve the race.

The Nazi Party, by contrast, formulated no specific plans to implement the racial notions that Hitler had advocated for over a decade. Although Hitler fulminated against Jews and "racial poisoning," Nazi doctrine contained no specific eugenic proposals. But after making himself dictator, Hitler adopted as his own the programs that Protestants had long advocated. During the summer of 1933, the government announced both the marriage loan and the forced sterilization programs. Meta Eyl, the newly appointed director of the Women's League (Frauenbund), hailed the reforms, especially the latter.[58] "Only when the entire *Volk* recognizes the need for this [sterilization] law and its benefits can Adolf Hitler's will be fulfilled."[59] The organization backed other edicts that increased punishments for abortion, homosexuality, pornography, and prostitution. Since the 1920s, the Protestant Standing Committee for Racial Hygiene and Racial Protection had produced pamphlets urging individuals to place the public good above their own individualistic happiness by participating in the scientific program to remove genetic defects from the German race. Eugenic scientists complained about the burden of Germany's 180,000 feebleminded, 80,000 schizophrenics, 20,000–25,000 manic depressives, 60,000 epileptics, and about 30,000 blind or deaf-and-dumb citizens. Armed with the latest "scientific" discoveries, Protestant eugenicists expected to cooperate with the government to prevent "damaged" citizens from transferring their genetic defects to the next generation.

Women leaders welcomed this opportunity to expand and modernize their concern about motherhood.[60] Childbearing and rearing had entered into the forefront of national interest, and Protestant women saw themselves in the vanguard of this movement.[61] Women, instead of feeling like failures because they could not emulate masculine traits, could return to their proper "space" and reign unchallenged as the purifiers of national life. The "motherly type" praised by sociologist Kirkpatrick had triumphed over those bothersome "protester types" who cared only about entering masculine careers.

According to the official record, the cooperation proceeded splendidly. Nazis and Protestants, each with a different creed, cooperated together around a shared concern for motherhood. But the private record, hundreds of activity reports and memos carefully preserved at the Protestant Central Archives in Berlin, reveals a complex picture. The monthly communications sent to von Grone's office ranged, according to one woman's summary, "from enthusiastic agreement to absolute rejection."[62] Protestant women expressed universal gratitude for the strong male leadership that promised to protect their endangered feminine sphere within which they could reconstruct their own institutions. Beneath the surface calm of von Grone's official statements, Protestant women reported bickering, feuding, power plays, and scandal at every level. The authoritarian state, which imposed public silence, unleashed conflicts among groups of citizens by forcing individuals to confront their own religious, moral, and political values. The state that swore to uphold family values tore at family ties, pulling children into the Hitler Youth, mothers into volunteer service, and fathers into Party activities and rallies.

The demands of the state became so heavy that, in practical as well as ideological ways, Protestant Nazis faced difficult choices: Which, for example, counted for more, the Protestant Frauenwerk Bible society, or the Nazi Frauenwerk sewing circle? Women's letters from the period describe the crisis atmosphere that pervaded and, some added, poisoned every aspect of daily life. A woman leader wrote, "We stand amid a great time of struggle. Major values are at stake; it is time to gather, cooperate, and work together!" But to what end? Special meetings called to produce a unified front vis-à-vis National Socialism ended in discord. Not only did some Protestants support and others reject Hitler, more typically one individual would endorse certain Nazi programs while condemning others with equal vigor. [63] "Terrible battles infect social harmony in even the tiniest hamlets," reported one village. [64] "If *Volks* Chancellor Hitler knew about the confusion here, he would certainly feel distressed. We need mutual respect so badly." [65] "A burning battle has broken out! Unbearable situation! Denunciations and oaths . . . no hope for a solution here." In one village, where there had been barely enough volunteers to keep religious organizations alive before 1933, two factions among pro-Nazi Protestants formed because the German Christians placed Hitler above the Bible, while others placed the state below the church. "Now we have two choirs, two altar-care societies, two motherhood groups, and two executive committees. . . . We spend more time fighting with each other than in doing common work." [66] The authoritarian state that had promised order brought chaos on a scale unequaled even in the Inflation or Depression.

Agnes von Grone, no less than her Nazi counterpart Scholtz-Klink, wanted an end to this demoralizing chaos. Imposing her own "leadership principle," she ordered all local groups to integrate into her Protestant Women's Bureau. Several chapters refused to obey either set of mandates; they cut all ties to national networks and maintained their traditional organizations. Hundreds of letters flooded von Grone's office. In some areas, Nazi district leaders (Gauleiter) ordered Protestants to join the Nazi Women's Organization, while in other places they were expelled from Nazi-sponsored organizations altogether. Some Nazi women believed they ought to infiltrate Protestant organizations; others remained aloof. Whatever the specific problem, most women shared the opinion of one district leader from Kassel, who turned to Berlin for an answer. "If we don't receive some firm instructions soon, our Protestant organizations will continue to flounder. We will lose ground to the National Socialists. Peace in our community has been destroyed. This is a fundamentally National Socialist region, but people want to remain religious, too."[67] The police broke up Protestant women's meetings; the government press slandered individual members; Nazi men rebuked Protestant women's organizations (calling them, in one case, "bunny-breeding associations"). Complaints poured in. Often Protestant women took their Nazi assailants to court, and sometimes they won; but whether they won or lost, the experience of going to court made them more cautious in the future. In some towns, Protestant women received orders to cease all forms of activity that could not be defined as strictly religious.

> The increasing humiliations and hatred and insults have ruined our religious work. There is no alternative. . . . There is still work to be done. The times are economically hard. The poor still come to my door asking for charity—but I am forbidden by law to give handouts. With heavy hearts, we have to say no because it is forbidden. *Forbidden!* Under penalty of arrest.[68]

The author did not have permission to give charity because she had not received proper clearance from the local Nazi women. Other women protested that Church organizations lost members because the Nazi women offered substantial material advantages that Protestants could not match. For example, in some areas women had to attend Nazi- (not religious-) sponsored motherhood courses in order to qualify for the Marriage Loan Program. Funds raised in joint charity drives typically remained in Nazi coffers. Women's groups that protested were dissolved by the Gestapo; membership lists and financial records were confiscated; and Protestant women's charitable actions were subsumed under the Welfare Bureau. Many women even began to appreciate the Weimar Republic they had lost, as fissures appeared where none had existed. In the old days, Protestants had denounced Socialists, atheists, Catholics, and legislators. Now they attacked each other over priorities, loyalty, doctrine, and faith. German Christians, members of the Confessing Church, and loyal adherents of the neutral majority rivaled one another; and the Nazi Party undercut them all.[69]

Protestant women faced a conundrum. While they welcomed a strong centralized government that esteemed motherhood, they fought against the encroachments that such a state would naturally make onto Protes-

tant territory. Hitler's rule, far from streamlining social programs, cre-
ated conflicting bureaus, bitter feuds, and duplication far worse than the
"confusion" so commonly attacked by conservatives during the Weimar
Republic. In addition to jurisdictional strife between church and state,
Protestant concerns coalesced around the impact of social programs and
Nazi paganism.

Protestant women leaders lost influence, but during 1934 recovered
their voices and deluged their religious superiors with protests, suggestions, demands, and complaints. This phalanx of respectable German
society could not be ignored or repressed. Nazi officials dismissed un-
cooperative women from their own ranks, but hesitated to oppose openly
autonomous women like von Grone. Ideally, National Bishop Müller
ought to have been able to bring them into line and thus deflect the
brunt of women's resentment away from the government. But he lacked
the tact and base of support within the Church. Between 1933 and 1936,
a three-way competition persisted, marked by altercations between Nazi
bureaucrats, ecclesiastical leaders, and Protestant women. The Protestant Church, too, was torn by a three-way battle among the pro-Nazi
German Christians, the oppositional Confessing Church, and the majority in the middle, who wanted to avoid taking sides. The tempest in the
Church provides a dramatic case study of a totalitarian state faced by
opposition from a group of citizens who generally supported its long-
term goals but objected to specific policies.

Nazi policy divided Protestant women; von Grone, however, refused
to let them conquer and reinstated her organization's apolitical stance.
She and her followers would eschew the masculine world of Nazi politics, but she realized that a woman leader needed a male defender in the
Third Reich. Von Grone turned to the proverbial fox in the henhouse
and asked for protection from her National Bishop, the man with "the
swastika on his breast and the cross on his heart." Bishop Müller had no
intention whatsoever of defending the Church (much less its women
members) against state intervention. Short of turning to the Confessing
Church (which would have ruined von Grone's hopes for receiving state
funds and support), the National Bishop was the only hope. But von
Grone ought to have perceived what was obvious to virtually everyone
—that the Protestant clergy under its bishop welcomed Nazism and cooperated, even, at times, against their own organizations. As one dissenting pastor wrote to Berlin, "If this does not stop soon, we will be
forced to conclude that those gentlemen [the clergy] actually welcome
the Nazification of all activities!"[70] Müller, not surprisingly, responded
to appeals for protection with orders to integrate all church associations
into Nazi-sponsored institutions. By early 1934 he had dispatched

700,000 members of the Protestant Youth League to the Hitler Youth; women's occupational associations (social workers, teachers, and health workers) had been integrated with his approval into the Nazi Labor Front; and Protestant motherhood organizations under Schlössmann-Lönnies had been absorbed into the Nazi Department of Welfare.[71]

In January 1934, Müller set the stage for the wholesale integration of von Grone's Women's Bureau into the Nazi Women's Bureau.[72] When thousands of women leaders objected to Müller's sellout, Müller's male supporters responded indignantly. "What has become of our women?" demanded the Archbishop of the Rhineland. "What chaos will be introduced in our communities if even the women jump into the fray? . . . The chaos of the times has driven them out of their proper place!"[73] Women, however, did enter the political strife when they saw their programs taken over and their theological beliefs perverted. Von Grone on several occasions reaffirmed her unswerving loyalty to *Vaterland, Volk,* and Church, and punctuated her official correspondence with references to "our wonderful Chancellor" and closed with *"Heil Hitler."*[74] But when Hitler encroached on Protestants' religious faith and doctrine, von Grone objected. She and her followers refused to march to what they called their bishop's "heathen commands."

Despite a censored press, women criticized Nazified Christian theology in their periodicals. Their discussions remained abstract and theological, which readers would normally have found somewhat dull. However, discussing sensitive topics within a strictly religious context allowed women Protestants the chance to raise troublesome issues while bypassing the censors. The debate about women in the Old Testament, for example, which may have appeared arcane, revealed the nature of Protestant women's objections to Nazi rule. Nazi women journalists had blamed Christian misogyny on Jewish, Old Testament influences, singling out Saint Paul, who, they decided, had been unduly influenced by his Jewish heritage. Meta Eyl, President of the progressive German Protestant Women's League, vigorously defended the Judeo-Christian tradition, which had, from the times of Ruth and other Old Testament heroines, honored womanhood. But she qualified her defense of the Old Testament by reminding her readers that "the woman of Germanic blood had . . . an entirely different feeling for life, a different heritage and disposition. It is no coincidence that the women's movement began among northern women."[75] Protestant women, in defending the Jewish component of their heritage, preserved Christianity against Nazi defamation. They guarded their own version of Christianity against degradation by racial thinking. That did not necessarily inspire them to help Protestant women with Jewish ancestors.

As the heirs of Luther, they grounded their theology on salvation by faith, not by works or by any other material criterion, such as race. One woman theologian, Fräulein Damaschke, put it this way: Nordic-Germanic ideas about God presented as serious a threat to Christian faith as Marxist atheism. Furthermore, she found it heretical to speak of a "thousand-year Reich" on earth and ignore the kingdom of heaven. Protestant women could accept the belief that Nordic races might be destined to rule the world, but they objected to Nazi doctrine that predicted who went to heaven.[76]

Most Protestant women leaders said they accepted Nazi ideas about race, *Volk*, and state as long as these concepts affected only civil life. But they did expel members of their organizations who had Jewish ancestors. Mainstream Protestant leaders blamed the fanatic German Christians for polluting the sanctity of the Church by mixing religious doctrine and politics. With no sense of their own complicity in Hitler's regime, they piously criticized women who, to quote one German Christian, explained, "Ours is a total ideology which admits no other allegiances."[77] Only about 10 percent of all Protestant women joined the German Christians. So small a minority had no chance of controlling or even influencing mainstream Protestant women's work, but as they demonstrated on countless occasions, they had the power to disrupt and confuse. German Christians within the Protestant Church played a destructive role reminiscent of the Nazis' strategy when they had existed beyond the fringe in the 1920s.

In this fragmented situation, von Grone attempted to steer a safe course between Nazi fanatics in the Church and Nazi bureaucrats in the state. Her first disillusionment occurred during the summer of 1934, only months after Scholtz-Klink and Hilgenfeldt took control of the women's bureaucracy. On different occasions Krummacher, Siber, and Scholtz-Klink had all promised not to interfere with the normal functioning of "Nazified" religious organizations. Then, in July 1934, Protestant women's groups were forbidden to recruit new members or found new chapters, which to von Grone counted as major interference.[78] A week later she attacked Scholtz-Klink's ban as a sign of bad faith and, aided by her organization's new theological adviser, asked Bishop Müller, "What purpose would it serve if the church retained only its external structure but lost its content—its living members and their faith?"[79]

Protestant women leaders had offered their loyalty on the condition that they remain autonomous. They endeavored, as one woman recalled in the early 1980s, to "admire the positive" in National Socialism, and "criticize the negative." Willingly, and even enthusiastically, they volunteered to carry out Hitler's social programs; but in exchange for their energetic support they demanded sufficient autonomy to do their jobs effectively. When von Grone believed cooperation with Scholtz-Klink would enhance the power of her Frauenwerk, she curried favor with the state authorities; but when Scholtz-Klink undercut her independence, von Grone (again acting in defense of her organization's best interests) told her membership, "In no circumstances will we comply with the radical demands of Scholtz-Klink."[80] In the fall of 1934, some of von Grone's most influential supporters informed their bishop, "We refuse merely to dissolve into the Nazi Women's Bureau."[81] Protestant women reaffirmed their "love for the freedom offered by the new state," but warned that they would not disband until the government had solved the Woman Question.[82] Women leaders from southwest Germany drafted their own appeal to Müller. "Your dictatorial behavior and the resulting religious struggle seriously impairs all hope of unity. . . . For the sake of our nation and our church, we implore you to stop issuing edicts. . . . If you do not, then our nation so recently unified by our Führer will be confronted by a divided Protestant Church. *Heil Hitler.*"[83] The records do not indicate that Müller responded at all.

Von Grone escalated her protests, and in November drafted a fresh and more strongly worded demand.

The current bishop's leadership fails to protect our Protestant Frauenwerk —and, in fact, threatens its very existence. For four months the National Socialist Frauenwerk has seriously eroded the internal operations of our organization and violated every agreement we have concluded with it. They thereby destroy the solidarity among our *Volk.* . . . The reputation of the church suffers, and dissent poisons even the tiniest villages. . . . In September, I warned the bishop that he must cease his dictatorial ways and restore his spiritual leadership. . . . Our church is grounded in eternal faith. . . . May God grant us strength to carry joyfully and bravely the responsibilities of these trying times. . . .*Heil Hitler!*[84]

Perhaps remembering Nazi leaders' experiment with Krummacher in 1933, Bishop Müller in 1934 promoted the career of a male leader, German Christian pastor Hans Hermenau. Scholtz-Klink made a more conciliatory choice and asked if she and von Grone could talk over their differences.[85] Bypassing male hierarchies, she negotiated directly with von Grone during December 1934, and the Protestants emerged as the temporary victors. Scholtz-Klink promised autonomy for Protestant women and guaranteed their right to expand their organizations. Von Grone then asked her followers to make peace with Nazi rule and continued her feud with Reichs Bishop Müller. At this juncture she believed she had secured from Scholtz-Klink the right to retain complete control over her Protestant Frauenwerk. This, in effect, would allow her to decide when her organization would cooperate and when it would withhold participation. But she played a double game because by insisting that she remain directly responsible to her religious superiors, von Grone attempted to preserve her organization from direct Nazi intervention. Müller ruined this tactic by ordering her to merge her Frauenwerk directly into Scholtz-Klink's Frauenwerk and to forget about church protection.

Müller's own position had become tenuous by late 1934. His high-handed manner and fanatical German Christian speeches alienated the mainstream Protestants whom he was charged to recruit. Compromise was alien to this former army chaplain. A more intelligent leader might have called a strategic retreat, or (like Scholtz-Klink) suggested negotiations. Instead, he dismissed von Grone. In her place he appointed his protégé Pastor Hans Hermenau, who, at age forty, already enjoyed a considerable reputation as a fiery preacher and devoted German Christian. After completing his theological studies, Hermenau had specialized in the study of biblical texts as they related to women and wrote extensively about the holy state of motherhood. By the early 1930s he had founded a sort of cult of motherhood and served as the spiritual adviser to the Federation of Protestant Women.[86] This ambitious and radical preacher made German women the center of an unorthodox woman-centered theology that in its details resembled strongly the Catholic Marian movement. Hermenau flirted with heresy as he rhapsodized, "Who in these dark times remains as close to God as she has always been? Who is so close to creation? Women." Women, whom God had brought into "the innermost circles of holiness," had been entrusted with "motherly creation."[87] With little apparent concern for theological orthodoxy he waxed eloquent about "woman's soul, the streaming light that emanates from God's eye" and "enlightens the entire German Volk."[88] Other theologians saw woman as Eve; Hermenau saw a German madonna.

> Mutter, Du Wächterin still in der Nacht
> Mutter, wer hat Dich so stark gemacht?
> Mutter, Du Kelch voll Leid,
> Mutter, Du Ewigkeit!

> Mother, Oh Mother, silent guardian in the night,
> Mother, Oh Mother, who has given you such might?
> Mother, Oh Mother, chalice of pain,
> O Mother, through you heaven we will gain.[89]

Hermenau's sentimental praise for mothers outdid even Schlossmann-Lönnies' essays in her magazine *Mother and Child*. Woman, said Hermenau, had been liberated from Eve's sin in the Garden, and now possessed special powers to do God's work on earth. "Where German women's hands are busy, where German women's souls are steadfast, there it cannot remain dark."[90] In Protestant theology, such powers of intercession do not exist, but Müller did not seem to care. He wanted Hermenau to deliver Protestant women to the state and to outbid von Grone. German Christians could not understand von Grone's reluctance to share their joy. One pastor's wife described her faith. "Every genuine National Socialist rejoices at the thought that at last the odious gulf between state and church . . . is at an end. Our first duty is to retreat from all special groups and enter joyfully into the religious-minded *Volk* community. . . ."[91] Von Grone, the strong-minded organizer, had no sympathy for such sentimental surrender to any secular power.

In the ensuing power struggle, von Grone was outflanked by the German Christians, beaten at at her own game by Scholtz-Klink, and ambushed by Hermenau. Scholtz-Klink commanded her women deputies to form a tightly integrated corps of missionaries to spread the Nazi gospel. In her public appearances, Scholtz-Klink spoke glowingly about a pantheistic universe, faithful hearts, and sacred missions.

> In the final analysis, the success of National Socialism rests on the question of leadership. It is our duty to produce this new Führer personality . . . to create and mold people who are ready to devote themselves totally to Germany. . . . No longer will we entrust our fate to God! No. We Germans will take destiny into our own hands. Just walk in the deep forest, and there you will find God. Our Eternity is the *Volk*!

Then, in her final sentence, she paraphrased Luther's famous "Here I Stand" Speech to the Catholic hierarchy at the Council of Worms. Replacing Luther's "I" with "we," she told her cheering audience, "Here we stand. We cannot and we will not retreat."[92] The reality of Nazi paganism could not have been more obvious.

With Hermenau and Scholtz-Klink as rivals, von Grone counted on her followers' devotion to provide her with political ballast in the growing controversy. A few months later, Nazi secret service reports vindicated von Grone's arrogance. In September 1935, a classified secret service memo concluded, "In the rivalry between the Women's Bureau (Confessing Church) and the Women's Aid (National Church), most women's organizations have backed the Women's Bureau (under von Grone)."[93] Flanked by women who refused to acquiesce to Nazi intervention in their activities, von Grone declared her opposition not only to the Nazi bureaucracy but to her own Reichs Bishop as well. She called a national meeting of 800 delegates for late January 1935 to plan a campaign to strengthen women's defenses against Nazification.[94] When the Bishop threw his support behind the rival Women's Service,[95] von Grone severed her connections with the official Protestant Church. Defying her bishop and Scholtz-Klink, she took virtually all members of Protestant women's organizations with her.

Before striking out on her own, she tried one last gamble and requested an audience with Hitler so she could explain her position.[96] When her proposal was ignored, she persisted despite a nagging sense of her own powerlessness. Müller dismissed her a second time and simultaneously von Grone resigned in protest and turned to her own organization for protection. She played out her political struggle against the background of a badly divided Protestant Church. Her archenemy, Bishop Müller, had managed to attract fewer than 2,000 pastors to his cause, despite financial and police support from the Nazi state.[97] Müller had failed on two fronts. He had not protected Protestant institutions from Nazi incursions, as von Grone expected; and he had not managed to Nazify Protestantism, as Hitler demanded. Müller unflinchingly supported Hermenau, while the newly appointed national unification committee refused to recognize his existence.[98] Meanwhile, the Nazi leadership in Berlin realized that their effort to Nazify Protestants had failed. Although they did not openly admit their defeat, they deprived Müller of his power and turned the religious question over to a newly created Ministry of Religious Affairs.

At first, Müller's defeat must have seemed like von Grone's victory. But after breaking with the Bishop, von Grone declared in the spring of 1935, "We are leaving the men who have left us in the lurch."[99] Her supporters faced a difficult choice. They could cut themselves off from any other religious or secular hierarchy or they could ally themselves with the Protestant dissenters. They opted for the latter course. "Independently organized and free-standing, we support the Confessing Church. . . . The church must speak out about the burning questions of the times. To remain silent in the present situation would be to disobey the Lord of the Church. . . ." The working committee listed specific grievances, notably the neo-paganism of Rosenberg and other fanatics, the indoctrination of German youth, and the mass rallies that substituted for religious services. "We are forced to watch as the state sponsors paganism while taking away the rights of the church to defend itself. The state has launched a spiritual crusade and only succeeds in creating martyrs."[100]

At no point did von Grone raise moral objections to any facet of Nazi policy, only to her exclusion from power. The sincerity of her commitment to Nazi principles strengthened the self-righteousness she needed to persist in her hopeless effort. She reiterated that she needed autonomy for pragmatic reasons; without it she could not effectively work for Hitler. In May, she felt confident enough to report to the membership that she had "navigated through dangerous reefs" with Scholtz-Klink.[101] Throughout her struggle against Müller and Scholtz-Klink, von Grone counted several influential supporters, such as Freifrau Dagmar von Bismarck, who in August 1935 interceded directly with Scholtz-Klink. "Even if you cannot work with Frau von Grone," von Bismarck told Scholtz-Klink, "you must allow her to operate independently. Only by preserving some degree of autonomy can the Protestant women's organizations serve the Führer."[102] Scholtz-Klink, stunned at such a suggestion, told von Grone, "Your behavior is unacceptable for a Party member. We can tolerate no division whatsoever between church and state!"[103] Von Bismarck openly joined the Confessing Church shortly after this exchange. Scholtz-Klink reiterated the Party orthodoxy: "For National Socialists, there is no division between religious and *völkish* [ethnic] interests. We must bring the church into line."[104]

In 1935 the newly appointed Minister of Religious Affairs upheld Müller's support for Hermenau who, with a generous budget, his own publications, and a network of German Christian pastors, set to his new task with great energy. Like the well-organized and dedicated old-fighter Nazis in the Weimar Republic, he and his followers saw themselves as an utterly loyal minority with a mission. "Call out to the women! Spread the truth by word of mouth! Fight for the coming Protestant German Reich!"[105] Hermenau accused von Grone of breaking the sacred Lutheran pledge to obey secular powers that supported religious faith. She already, he said, "stands on pillars which are crumbling beneath her," whereas his women stood "at the beginning of a new age as the vanguard of the coming imperial church." Piously Hermenau preached, "We ignore pettiness and stand on the words of Luther! 'Faithful to the Führer and loyal to Christ.' "[106] Despite (or perhaps because of) this bombast, it was Hermenau, not von Grone, who stood on a crumbling pillar. By the autumn, even by his own calculations, he had managed to attract only 120,000 followers compared with a total of 2.5 million who remained under von Grone's leadership.[107] Of 704 regional associations, Hermenau attracted only 32.[108] Hermenau had failed, but von Grone had not yet won. She had defended her terrain. No wonder she cherished the illusion of power. In Germany, with the world's most finely tuned police network, she had led over 2 million women away from the official church and remained free of Nazi Party control.[109]

Three months later, Scholtz-Klink's objections took on legal form: Von Grone received a summons to appear before the Party court on charges of treason.[110] Von Grone, emboldened by her own clear conscience, continued on her way. After all, she noted, Protestants listened to Nazis disparage their religion, so why could Nazis not bear to hear mild criticisms of their faith? If Scholtz-Klink could tell women not to "search for your Lord God in dusty old Bibles," why should Protestants not have the right to defend those Bibles? Von Grone, after nearly three years in Hitler's Germany, still refused to comprehend the facts of life in a totalitarian system. What were the facts? In retrospect, we assume that the Gestapo could simply have sent her to prison. But von Grone, having escaped the Bishop's control, was not arrested even though she faced charges of "tendentious misinterpretation and illegal interference in religious affairs," as well as general "resistance." Von Grone continued to send newsletters, make speeches, and complain to her superiors.

In September 1935, her district leader expelled her from the Nazi Party, and von Grone appealed immediately. In March 1936, the court upheld the exclusion. At this point, von Grone told her followers she probably ought to resign for the good of the organization. They responded with a vehement "No!" In June, a higher Party court upheld her excommunication once again because, it concluded, von Grone displayed a stronger allegiance to her religious commitment than to her Nazi faith.[111] In July 1936, the official Protestant Church ordered her to sever all ties with women's organizations, and the Confessing Church did not take up her cause.

The state, which outlawed all political parties within three months of Hitler's takeover, took four years to banish von Grone and her Protestant Women's Bureau. Gertrud Scholtz-Klink appealed to von Grone's followers, without criticizing von Grone, to join her Nazi network in leadership positions.[112] Nazi leaders with the power to destroy the Protestant women's organizations negotiated and bargained before finally deciding what to do. While the judges deliberated and delayed, Scholtz-Klink made proposals of reconciliation, and Hilgenfeldt even held out the prospect of a nationwide legislative body for women only (a *Frauenkammer*).[113] Women received orders to chose between their Protestant affiliations and Nazi Women's Bureau memberships. By the end of 1936, the Protestant Women's Bureau was dissolved, and leading supporters banned from speaking in public or organizing new associations. Hermenau left the German Christian movement altogether and returned to the official Protestant Church. Meanwhile, the German Christians themselves fell into steady decline. National Bishop Müller retained his post in name only and suffered severe depressions in the wake of his failure. After the Second World War began, he committed suicide. Hermenau made use of his formidable political skills. Although his independent Women's Service steadily lost followers, he stayed at his post. In

1945 he lost his ministerial position and worked in an office in Wiesbaden. Eventually, he was given a parish in Versailles for the NATO forces.[114] The records do not indicate that he ever underwent de-Nazification or recanted.

In 1938, a Nazified skeleton Protestant federation of women's organizations remained, bearing the traditional name Ladies' Aid (*Frauenhilfe*), just as it had before 1933. Over the next two years, virtually every important member organization was dissolved by the Gestapo or harassed out of existence by the courts. Officially, the expulsion of von Grone was a Nazi success. The state had silenced one of its most "undisciplined" members and outlawed a powerful rival to Scholtz-Klink's Nazi Women's Bureau. But from another perspective, the case against von Grone signaled Nazi weakness. Three years of propaganda, material incentives, and official government status had attracted hundreds of thousands of Protestant women to Nazi organizations; but it had *not* motivated them to resign from their religious associations.

The Nazi Party had expelled and humiliated a dedicated leader who owed her position to the Nazi leadership in the first place. Von Grone, dynamic and ambitious, had rigorously applied the "leadership principle" on her followers, complied with Nazi guidelines, and endorsed Party doctrine. When, however, in late 1934, she realized that Nazification would force her to accept officers proposed by the Party and to prohibit new members, she had refused to preside over the destruction of her own organization. Although she had willingly followed the New Testament advice to "render . . . unto Caesar the things which are Caesar's," she refused to render unto the Führer what was God's. Like the majority of the Protestant clergy, she approved of Hitler's worldly goals but opposed "de-Christianization."[115]

Having suffered defeat, another person might have allowed the matter to rest and washed her hands of the entire corrupt affair. Knowing she had no chance whatever of reclaiming her office, von Grone decided to go to court in defense of her reputation. She demanded that her case be reopened in June 1937. At this point, Scholtz-Klink expelled her even from local volunteer work.[116] But von Grone appealed her case. In November 1938, the highest Party Court in Munich reopened the case and decided that the lower courts had indeed erred. Nonetheless, the court found von Grone guilty of damaging Scholtz-Klink's reputation and undermining National Socialist doctrine. In an effort at reconciliation, the court rephrased the terms of von Grone's original punishment. She was not "expelled" (the equivalent of a dishonorable discharge), she was "released" from Party membership.[117] In its final judgment, the court accused von Grone of loyalty to the Bible, which was incompatible with

Nazi discipline. As we read of the von Grone affair, we are not surprised that she was found guilty. What is astonishing, however, is that the Nazi Party spent nearly four years in its attempts to slander and undercut the efforts of a powerful woman leader who had declared herself absolutely willing to do the bidding of the state.

As an eighty-year-old grandmother in the 1970s, von Grone still worried about her reputation; and in 1981 a Protestant historian rehabilitated her. In a recent interview, her son insisted that his mother had always been a monarchist and "never really believed in National Socialism,"[118] but had hoped Hitler would be a strong leader like Franco or Mussolini. Fifty years after her trial, von Grone told of her heroic "resistance" to Nazi rule, saying that the Nazi judges had been right after all. To the credit of Protestant archivists, however, the files detailing von Grone's altercations with the Nazi state remain carefully preserved in Berlin. Her words—for example, from 1935—speak plainly. "In my public speeches you could never hear anything other than the most thankful and joyous subservience [*Gefolgschaftstreue*] to the Führer and the Party. . . . Witnesses can testify that I never became involved in one-sided church politics [against the state]." Looking back, she remembers only conflicts with Gertrud Scholtz-Klink; but at the time, she swore, she wanted only "sisterly cooperation with the Nazi Women's Organization [Frauenschaft]."[119] Looking back, she passed lightly over her work in the Third Reich; but then she boasted that 2 million German women trusted her loyalty to Hitler—"mothers of SA and SS men who guarded the precious *Volks* heritage and religious faith through the terrible Marxist years; these women trust my National Socialist leadership. . . ."[120] After 1945, von Grone, like Scholtz-Klink, defended her work for Hitler because women had remained far from the horrors of war, terror, and genocide. Ignorantly and innocently, they did only what women always do—make the best of the situation and try to preserve love and human warmth in whatever environment they find themselves. Von Grone looked fondly backward, exalting the charges against her that she had spent four years disputing. Among Protestants, her private war for power counts as resistance, although she did not display a shred of doubt about any National Socialist program or doctrine until after 1945. Americans would find a more apt word, perhaps *disillusionment* or *opportunism*. The records that would illuminate the nature of von Grone's collaboration or her putative resistance exist in the Protestant Women's League offices in Hanover. But despite the efforts of the National Protestant Archives in Berlin and private requests (including mine), its officers bluntly refuse to allow access until they have screened the holdings. It seems unlikely that we will ever know the full history.

Von Grone's conviction for treason signaled the beginning of a new era in which Protestants would have to choose between their faith and their Führer. To be considered trustworthy, the National Socialist had to do more than join the Party and subscribe to Nazi ideology—she had to render total obedience to the state and relinquish her last claims to autonomy.[121]

The impact of von Grone's trial on her followers in the Frauenwerk was predictable. Women who welcomed Hitler's economic, political, and racial programs deplored the Nazis' insistence on total power, which in practice meant total interference in every aspect of their operations. Letters of support for von Grone declared Protestant women's determination to carry on God's work as they saw fit and to remain organized within their own local communities. Friendship networks and social gatherings would preserve the tradition of Protestant women's organizations. By making excessive demands for total loyalty, the Nazi Party repelled broad segments of middle-class Christians who welcomed Hitler's foreign and domestic policies. A secret report on morale from 1939 attests to the effectiveness of the Evangelical Church agitation. Unlike the Catholic Church, the Protestants could not form a solid front, and so they, "especially the women's associations," decentralized into massive small-scale operations (*Kleinarbeit*), which, the report implied, proved even more difficult to monitor than their centralized networks had been.[122]

German Christians made the situation worse by holding out the promise of radical Nazification, thus generating expectations they could not fulfill. Anxieties grew. Morale declined. As it became clear by 1935 that their movement had failed, German Christians felt betrayed. A small incident from Westphalia illustrates a more general trend. To repair the "damage" caused by von Grone's stubborn opposition to Nazification, Scholtz-Klink sent out a call to trusted deputies in areas where strife was particularly damaging. One of these, Eleanor Liebe-Harcourt, sent distressing reports from Westphalia to her chief even before the final condemnation of von Grone. Dislike for the Nazi state in Westphalia, she said, had grown so extreme that people who had hated each other for decades now made peace "with former Communists and other dissatisfied people."[123] The report blamed "the fanaticism of the Confessing Church" for the disruption. Of 783 Westphalian women's Protestant organizations, 740 remained loyal to von Grone; and most of them had begun to work more closely with the Catholic organizations they used to deplore. Liebe-Harcourt, however, did not despair. "The Westphalian may be more difficult to convince and convert; but I think (and I am no Westphalian) that once he has been really converted he is more reliable." She kept on working to attract women to the "faith based on the firm foundations of the Bible and of confession to [*Bekenntnis zu*] Adolf

Hitler and his Third Reich."[124] Still, at times she and her co-workers succumbed to discouragement when they realized that three years after Nazi triumph, hostility to the Hitler State seemed worse than ever. Loyal Party members often felt outcast and inferior because of the "hateful defamation of our cause and the humiliating insults against our leaders." She continued, "Protestant women hold their Nazi sisters in contempt. This really hurts when our National Socialist women, early fighters for our cause, receive no gratitude for their service during the hard times when they had encountered ridicule and rebuff."[125] At first Liebe-Harcourt and local Nazi leaders attempted to infiltrate the ranks of Protestant women; but after a few months, they felt so unwelcome that they withdrew. Even wives of Nazi leaders in small towns resigned from Protestant organizations because they faced such hostility.[126]

Frau Liebe-Harcourt and her husband, a convinced Nazi pastor, wondered why so many Germans remained hostile to the Führer, who had "struck a terrible blow with his strong fist against the Communists and saved Germany from economic collapse." The answer, Pastor Liebe-Harcourt concluded sadly, lay in the conduct of the Nazi leadership itself. Instead of attracting followers to a new faith, the Nazi leaders applied pressure. For the Liebe-Harcourts, Nazism was like a religion, and they knew that conversion could be forced. The Nazi police destroyed their rivals but proved unable to attract new followers. "I wonder if this is the way to build faith?" the pastor asked. Surely, he noted, the old Prussian adage had been discredited: "If you will not be my brother, then I will bash your skull in." As he tried to make sense of the dissension in the society he expected would produce social harmony, he summed up his concerns:

> Expressed in the briefest way possible . . . the German Christians are absolutely loyal National Socialists; unless you are a National Socialist you cannot be a German Christian! But the Confessing Church says a *real* Nazi cannot be a good Christian. This contrast arises dramatically in regard to the Jewish Question. The National Socialist cannot imagine how a Jew can be allowed to remain in a position that would influence Germans; the Confessing Protestant recognizes baptized Jews as full equals.[127]

While von Grone and the moderates despaired at the Nazis' totalitarian claims, extremists like the Liebe-Harcourts knew that coercion applied to "lukewarm" supporters only created fear and resentment.

Because dissent within the Protestant Church did not spring from ethical considerations, Nazi persecution of it appeared gratuitous. Indeed, by attacking von Grone and the moderates, the Nazi state lost the cooperation of women who expressed no objection whatsoever to Hitler's general aims. Long before Hitler had given much thought to specific measures to wage his racial revolution, Protestant committees had drafted legislation, supported eugenics research, and established support networks for mothers. But just at the time von Grone entered into the last stages of her rivalry with Scholtz-Klink and Müller, Protestant women objected to certain programs on pragmatic grounds. Often the results of particular policies Protestants had supported did not measure up to expectations.

In 1936, the Protestant welfare office dispatched a questionnaire to evaluate the impact of sterilization on its clients. Women social workers who, three years earlier, had welcomed the introduction of eugenics measures, reported the dire impact of sterilization on both victims and society.[128] In hundreds of cases, they saw a negative impact on morale and social relations, although generally the victims suffered minimal physiological after-effects. Social workers watched their clients' reactions and themselves expressed shock. Protestants had endorsed the apparently progressive application of genetic science to human life, without envisioning the psychological cost. In practice the "Aryan" community turned against its genetically "unworthy" members as if they belonged to inferior races. By 1939, 370,000 Germans had been sterilized. Despite official statements that "genetic damage is no one's fault, and sterilization does not change a person's character," and that "genetically ill people have suffered a hard fate and should not be mocked," public opinion persisted in treating sterilized people as second-class citizens. Women, after being sterilized, often without their advance knowledge and almost always without their consent, felt the double stigma in a society dominated by biological thinking. Raised to believe motherhood would be their only calling in life and that they belonged to a superior race, sterilization came as a shock.

After several months, a second source of conflict appeared. The eugenics courts that ordered sterilization swore total secrecy, but that promise contradicted a second provision: Sterilized persons could not marry because the primary goal of marriage could never be achieved. To enforce this prohibition, every sterilized person's records followed him or her throughout life. Soon, too, rumors of scandal spread. Nazi Party members received dispensations for relatives, behavior that certainly did not inspire confidence in the ethical merits of the law. Prostitutes often applied to be sterilized and if successful, it was rumored, they became more debauched since they did not fear pregnancy.[129] Protestant women who still approved of eugenics in principle despaired as they observed the results of the practice. Originally, they had dreamed of a purified race and given no thought to the immediate consequences of their campaign. Now, however, they stood by aghast as controversy and personal tragedy pervaded their communities.

Initially, Protestant social workers had assumed they would be called on by the state to direct these programs; but by 1936 a very different trend became obvious. The Nazi welfare organization under Erich Hilgenfeldt removed all "racially valuable" clients from religious institutions, leaving only the "discards" for religious programs. One Protestant social worker from a small town in Westphalia in 1984 discussed her reactions to the "reduced work load." On the one hand, she said, these pathetic people needed love more than ever; but on the other hand, Protestant social workers had almost no opportunity to care for individuals who might strengthen their own community. The final consequences of this separation of "healthy" and "unworthy" became obvious in 1941, she recalled, when Protestant social workers realized their clients were being shipped en masse to concentration camps, where ultimately they were killed as part of the euthanasia program.[130] When they believed they would control eugenics programs, Protestant women approved; but when Nazi programs excluded them from influence and left them to repair the social and psychological damage, they objected.

Protestants' distress over sterilization, the von Grone affair, pagan theology, and jurisdictional disputes did not constitute resistance to the Nazi state. In most cases such disagreements did not lead to arrest, prison, or torture. The worst fate was loss of position or expulsion from the Nazi Party. The degree to which the Gestapo tolerated such protests reveals how much latitude certain individuals retained in the Third Reich to criticize particular policies without much retaliation. In fact, von Grone held her ground longer than early Nazi women leaders like Zander, Diehl, and Gottschewski. Even Siber managed to retain her post for only a month or two after she was harassed.

The Party that arrested and murdered its own dissident men did not proceed quickly and ruthlessly against Protestant women critics. These women leaders' determination to bend Nazi policy to suit their beliefs implies something about Protestants as well as Nazis. Leaders who spoke out against Nazi policy that hampered their organizational and charitable work remained silent about the possible ill effects of anti-Semitic laws. Today, Protestants say little on the subject of their "non-Aryan" co-religionists. But the few Protestants with Jewish family trees who survived fill in the silence. Even Protestants who miraculously survived the Nazi era because of underground resistance networks make it clear that acts of courage occurred as exceptions. Principles were guarded by a few brave individuals; Nazi policy destroyed national networks, and average Germans preferred not to know about injustice.

Still, despite feelings of betrayal, many women who had been born into Jewish families and converted to Protestantism remained in Germany. One of the most remarkable of those women wrote her memoirs after finally assenting to pressure for her to emigrate. Alice Salomon, the Jane Addams of German social work, had converted to Protestantism in 1914 and founded the first school of social work in Berlin. While associated with the BDF, Salomon had occasionally experienced affronts even from friends because of her "Jewishness." But she learned to overlook the slights. Perhaps the experience of having successfully confronted such hostility (combined with her international reputation) gave her confidence that she could rely on trusted friends to help her face Nazi opposition after 1933. She discovered her error.

> The attitudes of my most intimate group of fellow workers . . . most of whom were Protestant in predominantly Protestant Berlin, were typical of educated women. There were instances of human strength and human weakness. Some came out of the battle finer and stronger personalities, others lost whatever moral poise they had ever possessed. There were some women on our staff who would have been considered irreproachable by Nazi standards but for having worked closely with me. They tried to atone for this with redoubled fervor, saying *"Heil Hitler!"* twice when others said it once. Long before Aryans were forbidden to talk to the "wrong" people, it was painful for me to see them because with every word they felt a nervous urge to declare their new faith.[131]

Except for her longtime housekeeper, Salomon's Protestant friends found it more convenient to sever ties with her. Still, she felt more fortunate than others in her situation because her international prestige and preeminence in the social work profession protected her from the earliest waves of official persecution. Far worse off, she recalled, were women who before 1933 did not even know they had Jewish ancestors.

> We had a teacher who was born a Lutheran, but of Jewish descent. She had lived exclusively among Christians, and it was only when she was nearly grown up that she heard of her so-called Jewish "race and blood." A Nazi administrator imposed on the College dismissed her at once. She felt that she had lost not only her profession and her income, but her church and her country as well.[132]

Perhaps children felt the impact of anti-Semitism most strongly and earlier than their parents. Children of Protestant parents considered themselves Protestants even if they had Jewish grandparents. Suddenly, their Jewish heritage mattered. Alice Salomon wrote about a friend who worried about what would happen when her daughter's school friends discovered she had a Jewish background. The child, Ada, insisted nothing unusual happened. "The teacher is nice and the children are nice," she repeated every day to her mother.

> But one day she came home humiliated. "It was not so nice today." What had happened? The teacher had sent the Aryan children to one side of the classroom, and the non-Aryans to the other. Then the teacher told the Aryans to study the appearance of the others and to point out the marks of their Jewish race. They stood separated as if by a gulf, children who had played together as friends the day before. The Gentiles scrutinized their former playmates. Poor things. What else could they do? Finally a child said about little Ada, "She has curly hair. . . ." In Nazi Germany this child was marked, isolated from that day on.[133]

Thousands of Protestants with Jewish ancestors or relatives lost their longtime friends who severed all "dangerous" connections. "In the places that had been the shrines of truth, of the humanities and of intellectual integrity—the universities—the adjustment was the most complete," Salomon recalled.[134] "In the higher ranks of the professions, among teachers and artists, physicians and lawyers, the adjustment was made with few exceptions. They became interpreters of Nazi doctrine of blood and soil, changing their ideas, their theories, and their vocabularies. Many . . . were eager to replace their colleagues, often former friends, when these were ousted from their jobs or forbidden to practice, perform, to publish, or to exhibit." The atmosphere of freedom, which Salomon had taken for granted, disappeared overnight, without protest. "In a country dominated by a tyrant virtually everyone is spied upon from morning till night and from night till morning. What is worse, almost everyone is liable to become a spy."[135]

Protestant women who summoned the strength to defy their Nazi leaders and their Protestant bishops seldom found words to defend their own Protestant co-workers' with "non-Aryan blood." Von Grone had briefly won suspension of the "non-Aryan" paragraph in early 1934, but memoirs from the period suggest that it was applied socially even where it was not legally enforced.[136] On rare occasions, some women questioned the exclusion of "non-Aryans" from the Christian community.[137]

Evaluating fragmentary and scattered evidence about millions of Protestant women presents formidable obstacles. Especially on the subject of anti-Semitism, generalization is risky because the paucity of archives makes it next to impossible to judge whether silence indicated that women leaders deplored anti-Semitism but knew protest was futile or that they generally complied with "legal" restrictions against Jews. Women leaders under von Grone, like the pastors in the Confessing

Church, knew their options were severely constrained. One step too far (in a situation where one never knew where boundaries lay), might mean major reprisals against institutions, family, and friends. Archival sources and memoirs make it clear that Christians rarely aided Jews, and when they did they extended sympathy to fellow Christians with Jewish ancestors rather than to Jews. When they did offer aid, it was pathetically little and came tragically late. Because Protestant opponents of Nazism believed their own religious institutions stood at extreme risk, they did not lightly decide to endanger their situation by defending racial outcasts. While some individuals were brave, institutions were not. On occasion, even the Confessing Church ignored appeals for aid.

One of those occasions occurred when two Protestant women appealed to the leaders of the Confessing Church for help on behalf of "non-Aryan" Protestants. Marga Meusel and Charlotte Friedenthal, social workers in Berlin, began to worry about "non-Aryan" Protestants in late 1934. They asked leaders in the Confessing Church to set up a counseling center to advise and offer spiritual guidance to Protestants with Jewish ancestors. Although Friedenthal assured the church leaders that the venture would cost virtually nothing and provide immensely important support to bewildered and depressed members of the congregation, no answer came. One leader assured her that he knew from his own experience the agony of the "non-Aryans." Friedenthal told him, "We are constantly horrified by the fates and life stories of those we meet . . . and by the gratitude with which they accept every bit of our advice. Even when we cannot provide material aid, just knowing that someone who cares exists at all makes such a difference." In Stuttgart Bishop Wurm established a counseling center, and individuals sheltered "non-Aryans," but the Confessing Church as a whole did little until after the November pogrom in 1938.[138] At that point Heinrich and Margarete Grüber set up an aid station that helped Protestants with Jewish ancestors escape. Margarete Grüber recalled forty years after the Nazi era how their efforts had deeply involved every member of their family. "There were so few people who cared. We all shared the risk." After 1938, when she was in her late twenties, Helge Weckerling worked with the office, and recalled how difficult it had been to overcome the anti-Semitic feelings with which she had been raised. But becoming acquainted with another young Protestant whose parents had been Jewish helped her to a new understanding. Still, her memories of those years are painful. "They [Protestants with Jewish parents] came to us in dire need! But I don't know if you will understand what seems so absurd to me. These people's very lives were in the gravest danger. And what did we do? We read the Bible together and celebrated the Last Supper!" When her friend Inge Jacobson and other "non-Aryan" Protestants were summoned to the deportation stations, Weckerling carried her suitcases. "I helped her. Just the thought of that still makes me crazy today. . . . We were so sure that somehow they would be rescued."[139] Grüber's arrest in 1940 and imprisonment in Sachsenhausen and Dachau terminated their work.

The few memoirs or letters that remain usually leave a mixed impression, as the recollections of an extraordinary woman, Katarina Staritz, demonstrate. After Jews were ordered to wear yellow stars in public places or face instant deportation, Staritz organized a small group of Protestants in the border town of Breslau to protect Jews. "Legal" anti-Semitic policies that hampered social contact between Jews and non-Jews or economic regulations that put Jews at a disadvantage were perhaps tolerable. But forcing people to display a humiliating symbol that targeted them for ridicule and arrest violated Staritz's principles. They began to smuggle Jews out of the country and provide aid for those who remained. Most members of the group were arrested in 1943.[140] Staritz, courageous enough to have risked her life in opposition to the Nazis, after the war was brave enough to admit that under Nazism she had experienced the vestiges of anti-Semitic feelings that prevented her from empathizing as much with Jewish prisoners in Ravensbruck as she could with non-Jewish Communists and other dissidents.

Assessing the depth of anti-Semitism either before or after 1933 is extremely difficult. In their publications, Protestant women avoided outright slurs against Jews and, during the early years of Hitler's power, even occasionally defended the Old Testament from a theological standpoint. Eva Reichmann, a political scientist who lived in Germany during the 1930s, wrote recently that although after 1945 Germans claimed they knew nothing about genocide, "no outcry was ever heard" as Germans began to hear of plans for deportation.[141] Interpreting a silence, like interpreting an event that failed to occur, is counterfactual and risky, especially when the silence occurred under rigorous press censorship. But religious faith, if it has any meaning in the practical world, endows believers with the courage to speak and act. And the record reveals that few Protestant women did either on behalf of any cause except their own.

Von Grone and her organization demonstrated extraordinary alacrity in their maneuvers against the Bishop, Scholtz-Klink, and Hermenau. She may have been arrogant, but she was hardly naive. Moreover, her protest against what she considered shabby treatment by the Bishop and the Nazi state attests to her courage and independence as surely as it illustrates her fundamental faith in Nazism. Most Protestants' religion, far from immunizing them against Nazism, in many respects prepared them for it, for they had seen the world in polarized terms of Christian nationalism *versus* atheist socialism. When Hitler's state, which promised strength, brought disorder worse than their deepest anxieties in Weimar Germany, they were stunned; but they did not launch a broad protest against the tenets of National Socialism. They genuinely upheld Hitler's basic aims, except possibly for murderous anti-Semitism and abuses of the sterilization law. And von Grone's deep loyalty to Nazi doctrine in secular matters provided her with the fortitude to continue her battle for respect within the Nazi system long after any possibility for reinstatement had disappeared. Instead of working to alleviate abuses in the Nazi system, she dedicated herself to restoring her own damaged reputation. Her fall and subsequent efforts at self-justification after 1945 reflect the reactions of the Church as a whole, which never quite surrendered and never really resisted.

Hitler attacked and destroyed his Protestant rivals using the technique he outlined in the Vogelsang Castle speech while discussing his "nose" for the possible. Boasting that he lacked a sense of fair play and did not like sports, he said that he did not particularly enjoy fighting for its own sake. Caring only about total victory, he allowed his opponent to decay from within before striking, and then he would declare total war, telling his foe, " 'I want to destroy you! And now, so help me, I am going to get you into such a corner, you won't even be able to fight back, and then you will get a stab directly in the heart.' That's how I do it."[142] Hitler had switched metaphors from bridegroom to killer during the course of his fight against the Protestant Church. Steady harassment whittled away Protestant solidarity, and by 1937 the Church had lost its ability to defend itself against the state. Von Grone's protracted fights contributed to the inner decay of Protestantism, which rendered it helpless when Hitler planned the "final stab." A secret Security Police report described the situation. "The Protestants broke apart into an internal institutional and religious battle of opinion in which each divergent group insisted on its deep loyalty to the National Socialist state."[143] One reporter for an underground newsletter summarized Protestant opposition. "This was no struggle against the system, but a struggle *within the system* for a share in the domination, power, and booty in the new authoritarian state."[144]

The encounters between Hitler and the Protestant Church point to a fundamental duality between the messiah and the moderate in Hitler's own personality. If he intended to "convert" Germans absolutely and extinguish their Christian faith, then he had to keep up the momentum of the old days, when his movement had battled on the fringe of society.

But wild fanaticism before and after 1933 repelled mainstream respectable citizens, who (unless they had "dangerous" Marxist reputations) displayed an extraordinary eagerness to sign up for service in the Nazi state. Reichs Bishop Müller unleashed a drive for total Nazification that confused the vast majority of Protestants, who believed they could obey their faith in matters of religion and their state in political issues, to say, "Our politics is Germany! Our Religion is Christ!"[145] Taking the division between church and state for granted, they expected to cooperate in the new Reich. A Secret Service report on morale among Christians exposed the fundamental impasse into which Müller's radical Nazification plans forced state policy. After coercion had ended visible dissent, police worried that they had merely forced opposition beneath the surface, thereby making it even more difficult to ferret out. They did their best to work out a set of guidelines by which they could separate loyalty from opposition among Protestants and Catholics who swore allegiance to the state but maintained reservations about specific issues of Nazi policy. The problem was, as the author of the security report saw it, that people believed they could merely add Nazi allegiance to other earlier beliefs. These "and also Nazis" did not grasp that only total devotion counted. But he did not acknowledge Hitler's responsibility for having created the dilemma in the first place. During the 1930s, Nazi electoral victories came as the partial result of an extraordinarily fluid and eclectic mix of campaign promises.

Before 1933 the healthy diversity had to be pruned into a set of doctrines that could be used to determine loyalty. "Leadership, obedient loyalty, race, community, Nationalism, socialism, and Germanness," counted as the pillars of Nazi dogma. Still, these issues seemed so universal that Nazi leaders feared alien religious forces could subvert them to serve an enemy cause. Behind every affirmation of faith could lurk an unspoken "but" or a heretical misinterpretation that might "undermine" the state by spreading "degeneration [*Untergang*] and chaos." Of course, "degeneration and chaos" had been unleashed by the Nazis' own bureaucratic ineptitude and ideological confusion. Hitler claimed to have founded his state on solid doctrine and a new order. Nazi leaders' inability to establish either a clear administrative apparatus or a set of beliefs meant that they relied on only one test of loyalty, "for or against Hitler."[146] Protestant women's organizations that would have cooperated with virtually all secular programs launched during the 1930s discovered that their contributions did not win them a privileged position in the Nazi state. Von Grone gladly supported the Nazi state, but she drew the line when politics encroached on her organization's autonomy and a pagan doctrine threatened her faith.

8

CATHOLIC WOMEN BETWEEN POPE AND FÜHRER

"When I use a word," Humpty Dumpty said, in a rather scornful tone, "it means just what I choose it to mean —neither more nor less."

"The question is," said Alice, "whether you can make words mean so many different things."

"The question is," said Humpty Dumpty, "which is to be master—that's all."

—Lewis Carroll,
Alice's Adventures in
Wonderland and Through
the Looking-Glass

Catholic women leaders reacted to Hitler's appointment as Chancellor with silence. Unlike Müller-Otfried, von Tiling, and von Grone, they did not cheer during the spring of 1933 as Hitler constructed his dictatorship on the ruins of the republic. They avoided comment of any kind. This silence did not originate from a commitment to democracy, but from a tradition of waiting for an official policy statement from the bishops or Vatican before commenting on any issue. As women and as Catholics, they evaluated Hitler's state from a different standpoint than either Protestant women or Catholic men because Hitler's plans for eugenic engineering affected them directly. While Protestants had cautiously considered the dilemmas of birth control and sometimes abortion and divorce, Catholic dogma precluded doubts or questioning. Of course, Catholic men believed in the same precepts as women, but children and family rarely played as central a role in their lives. Nazi policy rested on the axiom, "Your body does not belong to you," but where Catholics placed procreation within God's province, Nazi doctrine placed it with "your blood brethren [*Sippe*] and . . . your *Volk*."[1] State and Church made total and irreconcilable claims that lay at the very center of women's concerns as mothers and as Catholics.

The temptations to endorse the state were great. After feeling like second-class citizens in predominantly Protestant Germany, for the first time their Pope and the head of their state had declared mutual respect. While Catholics felt vulnerable to accusations that they obeyed Rome, not Berlin, they also prided themselves on their self-contained Catholic world. As part of a well-organized minority, Catholics operated their own charity programs, schools, hospitals, and community groups under the direction of a highly centralized administration. They followed a total faith that addressed their daily problems, told them to vote for Catholic Center Party candidates, ministered to their material needs, and dictated absolute obedience. Their faith provided Catholic women with the psychological and ethical prerequisites for resistance. Decades of defending their minority rights had equipped them, too, with a political wariness toward any centralized government. The convent tradition and cults of the Virgin and female saints gave them a strong sense of their own identity and mission. Over a dozen major nationwide organizations unified a million women, as mothers, teachers, servants, housewives, unmarried women, and charity volunteers. Two hundred thousand women belonged to the liberal Catholic German Women's League (KDF, or Katholischer deutscher Frauenbund) and lobbied for women's rights within church and community.

During the first months of 1933, no one knew whether Catholic women, protected in their own total creed and church, would welcome Hitler or withdraw into a critical distance. While Hitler appeared as a secular messiah in the eyes of fanatic Protestant Nazis, he emulated the priesthood for the benefit of his Catholic followers. Aside from appealing to the Almighty in speeches, Hitler said virtually nothing about religion, but he was working out long-range plans behind the scenes. He set about his task carefully, following the advice he had laid down in *Mein Kampf*: "Never destroy religious faith without offering something better to the faithful." While fashioning "something better," Hitler did not directly assault Catholic institutions, but stalled until he could establish his rival Nazi "church." Meanwhile, the Nazi state took on several distinctive characteristics of its Roman rival. Joseph Goebbels' Ministry of Propaganda (a term borrowed from the Vatican) would communicate "holy conviction and unconditional faith."[2] Albert Speer, Hitler's architect and confidant, tells of designing a massive temple, a "secular cathedral," which was "basically a hall of worship. . . . Without such cult significance, the motivation for Hitler's main structure would have been senseless and unintelligible. . . ."[3] In elaborate ceremonies, Hitler honored the movement's martyrs. The centerpiece of Leni Riefenstahl's brilliant film of the 1934 Nuremberg Rally was the tribute to the soldiers of World War I, in which Hitler, like a priest, marched up the aisle, with thousands of his faithful standing at silent attention on both sides. Wordlessly, he laid a wreath on the tomb. The sound track falls silent. In the next scene, we see him preaching from a pulpit on high, flanked by swastika flags against a cloudless sky.

The state replaced hymns with Nazi marching songs, religious holidays with festivals commemorating the great events in Nazi history, and catechism with Nazi primers, such as "The ABC's of National Socialism." Ritual, obedience, ceremony, and immutable doctrine formed the core of Hitler's secular church. Authority emanated from Hitler alone, but a host of Nazi saints and martyrs, priests and crusaders enhanced his power. The similarity was not a coincidence. As a boy, Hitler had dreamed of becoming an abbot; as a man, he modeled himself on the Pope. Shortly before becoming Chancellor he covertly revealed his plans in grandiloquent phrases. "I hereby set forth for myself and my successors in the leadership of the party the claim of political infallibility. I hope the world will grow as accustomed to that claim as it has to the claim of the Holy Father."[4] Hitler, who rarely credited any source of inspiration outside his own genius, once admitted, "Above all, I have learned from the Jesuit Order."[5] As the Jesuits swore unconditional loyalty to the Pope, the black-shirted SS pledged obedience to Hitler. Besides reading Hitler's *Mein Kampf*, SS men (one quarter of whom were

Catholics) were urged to study the *Spiritual Exercises* of Saint Ignatius of Loyola to learn discipline and devotion.[6] To women, Nazis offered the chance to become "brown nurses"—clearly an adaptation of the Catholic nursing orders.

The question facing Catholics during Nazi rule was whether the affinity between Nazism and Catholicism meant Catholics ought to cooperate with the state, or whether the parallels signaled a grave danger to Catholic institutions and teachings. Catholics generally and women especially faced the dictatorship behind the walls built of a powerful and international institution. The difference from Protestantism could hardly have been more striking. Twenty-five dioceses in Germany, each with its own bishop, guided the faithful. To promote unity, representatives from each diocese met regularly at the Fulda Bishops' Conference, where they established theological, pragmatic, organizational, and social policy. In the Weimar Republic, the ecclesiastical hierarchy had not made its peace with democracy but remained nonpartisan, a euphemism that really meant *hostile*. Cardinal Faulhaber, later to become an opponent of Nazism, hated democracy because, he said, it "gives equal rights to truth and error."[7] The combination of reactionary politics and religious unity immunized Catholic voters from the Nazi appeal. With their own total church, why would they wish to gamble on a fanatic whose claim to absolute priority could only threaten their own? Perhaps it was this skepticism that prompted a few priests (unlike Protestant ministers) to warn their followers against joining the Nazis before 1933. In February 1931, Bavarian bishops warned Catholics: "What the National Socialists describe as Christianity is not the Christianity of Christ."[8] One bishop, after Nazi popularity rose dramatically in his district, admonished Catholics not to join the Nazi Party because it placed the "Nordic race" above Catholic teachings.[9] By 1931–1932, several bishops had warned their faithful to boycott all Nazi activities.[10] The pages of the women's press supported the Catholic Center Party, but remained nonpartisan regarding the other parties.

At the Fulda Conferences in 1931 and 1932, the bishops attempted to formulate a common policy. With Hitler's meteoric rise to prominence, the temptation to endorse this virile political force increased. Nazi violence shocked them, but the fear of Communism also held them captive. Why should the Church not support a political movement that would play a powerful role in the future? Would they risk losing followers if they took a strong stand against so popular a party? Ought they stand on principle and condemn a party that (in addition to preaching pagan theology and racial revolution) attacked Catholic beliefs? The bishops, like other conservatives, achieved a consensus by deciding not to decide, a solution that left Catholics free to support Hitler without suffering pangs of conscience, unless it happened that an individual parish priest they respected told them otherwise. The bishops' vacillation reflected the mood in Rome. The Vatican, which had not hesitated to condemn godless Marxists in Russia, Spain, and Mexico, remained silent. Rather than directly attacking Hitler, many priests wanted to "find the healthy core" of his doctrine and encourage Nazism as a "true reform movement," thereby joining a popular cause. Of course they objected to Hitler's pagan rituals, but aside from that, they generally approved of Nazi aims. "Why should it be impossible," asked one bishop, "to achieve in Germany what in Italy has proved so beneficial for the country, the people, and the Church?"[11] A minority of priests went one step farther and embraced Nazism because, they said, the Party program guaranteed religious freedom as long as the Church did not "militate against the moral sense of the Germanic state." The failure of the ecclesiastical hierarchy to speak out boldly against Hitler in the early 1930s was not surprising because the priesthood generally despised the Weimar government and hoped for an authoritarian solution.

But Catholicism meant more than priests and clergy; it included the influential Catholic Center Party. During Wilhelmine and Weimar Germany, Catholic representatives in the Reichstag formed a powerful "swing vote" by giving their votes on specific issues to whichever party offered the most support for Catholicism.[12] The Center Party emphasized educational and cultural concerns and demonstrated a strong commitment to programs to protect the family. Thus, although the Center had vehemently opposed women's suffrage prior to 1919, it incorporated more women into its leadership than any party except the Socialists after that date. Catholic women delegates voted with the ultraconservatives when it came to family policy, but they understood that many mothers' wages provided a crucial source of financial well-being and on occasion found themselves voting with the Socialists to defend protective legislation for women and to support women's right to employment.

Had it not been for women's enfranchisement, the Catholic Center would have slipped into inconsequence because Catholic men deserted the Party. But as male voters dropped out, women voters compensated for the loss, which meant that the Center regularly attracted about 15 percent of the vote in national elections. More significantly, when Hitler drew voters from nationalist and liberal parties to his cause, Catholic Center voters remained more loyal than the members of any other party. These broad trends have led political scientists to conclude that Catholicism "immunized" its faithful against the appeal of Nazism more effectively than any other non-Marxist party.

The rank and file stood firm even in the March 1933 elections. But as Chancellor, Hitler accelerated his assault, alternating carrot with stick. In his first speech as Chancellor he promised, "to defend and preserve the basic principles on which our nation has been built up. . . . Christianity is the foundation of our national morality and the family is the basis of our national life."[13] But then he showed his other face. During the electoral campaign of March 1933 Göring ordered Catholic presses seized, funds confiscated, political centers closed, and speakers harassed. Then the police arrested 3,000 Catholics. Despite nationwide objections from Catholic citizens, Catholic Center leader Franz von Papen (ex-Chancellor and Hitler's Vice-Chancellor at the time) did not protest. Quite to the contrary, he praised the tough authoritarian leader. "Considering the state of affairs in Europe and in view of the social disintegration proceeding in Germany, the rescue effort of National Socialism was inevitably the last chance of saving Germany from the abyss of social annihilation."[14]

In the March elections, over 5 million (or just under 15 percent) of all voters remained faithful to the Catholic Center Party. But at the first Reichstag session, the delegates did what the voters had not done. They voted for the Enabling Act, which ceded dictatorial power to Hitler. Historian Ian Kershaw, author of an outstanding study of popular responses to Nazism in Bavaria, summed up the collapse: Catholics were the last to hold out and the first to capitulate.

Their support did not buy them privileges, for the Civil Service Law of April 1933 purged all Catholics (and Jews) from the government. Although the Church hierarchy did take a stand, many Catholic leaders and organizations voluntarily cast their support with the new government. Joseph Lortz, the internationally respected historian of the Catholic Reformation, wrote a small book praising the parallels between Nazis and Catholics, both of which were founded on "an heroic and grand faith."[15] Bishop Conrad Gröber of Freiburg rejoiced at the new dictatorship, citing it as "proof that two powers, both totalitarian in nature, can find agreement if their domains are separate."[16]

During these tense months of temptation and fear, women remained far from the crucial decision-making processes. Looking back on a tradition of autonomy within their cloistered sphere, they awaited their superiors' decision. During the spring of 1933, as one woman Catholic recalled, "We knew things had changed. Just as soon as the Nazis took over, the telephone of our Berlin headquarters started ringing all the time with offers of this, invitations to that. But we held our peace."[17] Paula Siber, then director of women's activities with the Department of Interior, courted Catholic cooperation by paying tribute to Christian faith. At a rally of 10,000 women in Düsseldorf in July, she praised Christian religious values and included several popular hymns in the ceremony. The celebration closed with the "Horst Wessel Song" and the traditional "We Walk to Prayer" *(Wir treten zum Beten)*. [18] While Nazi men brought swastika banners into the cathedrals and churches, Nazi women brought Christian prayers, hymns, and rituals into their rallies.

Catholic women, however, held their peace. Their periodicals said nothing about Nazi policy or even about Hitler—in marked contrast with the Protestant women's press. Catholic women's silence in itself did not indicate opposition as much as caution. Tradition had prepared them to await a Vatican pronouncement before acting. Besides, given heavy press censorship, they had to word their public pronouncements carefully. Gerta Krabbel, the president of the Catholic German Women's League, KDF, commented cryptically: "In times of transformation, it has fallen to women to carry the torch of spirituality [*Fackel des Geistes*] and dedicate themselves entirely to guaranteeing that love and goodness enlighten the world." [19]

This reticence contrasted with Müller's, von Tiling's, and Müller-Otfried's initial and unreserved enthusiasm for Hitler. It also contrasted with Catholic men's reactions. For example, while the Union of Catholic Men Teachers enthusiastically endorsed Hitler, the Association of Catholic German Women Teachers withheld comment. The men declared that only Hitler could lead the nation in "overcoming the un-Germanic spirit"—a shabby euphemism for expunging "Jewish influence." But the women teachers broke with the men, saying, "We women Catholic teachers constitute an influential minority within the great mass of our male Catholic colleagues." The women teachers warned the Fulda Conference. "It will become very difficult to educate students as girls and Catholics. The new leaders openly admit that all children will be pressured into joining the Hitler Youth." [20] As women, they objected to the Party's antifeminism as well as its hostility to Catholicism. Male Catholic teachers probably shared the the endemic misogyny of their profession. Certainly they registered no protest when women faced dismissal. Catholic women defended their right to careers. When the Women Social Workers' Association expressed misgivings about the Nazis, their spiritual counselor urged them to cooperate with Hitler. "Yielding," he suggested, "is better than saying 'Heil.'" [21]

Behind his facade of support for Christianity, Hitler gave Catholic bishops ample opportunity to know his long-term goals. They responded no more bravely than their Protestant counterparts. In April, Hitler met with two bishops to clarify his plans for the future. Christianity, he told them, had proved itself too weak to accomplish the monumental moral tasks ahead. "He spoke with warmth and equanimity," the bishops reported. As he concluded the meeting, Hitler swore that he would follow the Catholic doctrine, which had for fifteen hundred years defined Jews as parasites and persecuted them accordingly.[22] Faced by a clear future danger, priests wondered how to react: to comply early and hope for rewards, or to oppose danger before it had a chance to develop? In early July, an astonished world heard the news. The Nazi regime had concluded its first treaty. Hitler and Pius XI agreed on a Concordat in which Hitler swore to defend Catholic rights and the Vatican promised to support the Nazi dictatorship. The agreement seemed to remove Catholics from pariah status and welcome them as equals in the new dictatorship.

Amid mutual congratulations, few Catholics noticed that one serious question remained open: Hitler pledged to respect all Catholic institutions that were not related to politics, but who would decide which organizations belonged in the political category? Officially, priests could publish pastoral letters; Catholic hospitals and schools would remain unharmed; charities, lay organizations, and other nonpolitical Catholic associations would continue as before. Of course, the Center Party had been outlawed, but so had all other parties. Two institutions with total claims faced one another: a church with a powerful political arm and a state with strong religious overtones. Naturally, the Church defined "political" as narrowly as possible, and the state narrowed "religious" to only matters of faith and ritual. Both sides claimed jurisdiction over a vast array of Catholic hospitals, schools, social service agencies, and community organizations. Catholics *felt* safe but ultimately *were* not because the outcome of this crucial debate depended not on logic or principle, but upon power. Ironically, in 1933, Catholics felt more protected as subjects of Nazi dictatorship than they had as citizens of Weimar democracy.

While the prelates congratulated themselves on victory, Hitler boasted to his inner circle, "Now we have brought the priests out of the party-political conflict and pushed them back into the church. . . . They will never return to that area for which they were not intended."[23] As with subsequent international agreements, Hitler made this pact in order to violate it.

The Concordat stayed in force until 1945. Along with the Nazi-Soviet Pact of 1939, it remains the most controversial treaty of the Nazi years. Ascertaining the proportions of opportunism, arrogance, and despair that motivated both sides is difficult. We know, however, which party benefited most: Hitler. The Church, having admonished all Catholics to obey the Nazi state, never revoked its support for the regime. Hitler, of course, never bothered to declare the Concordat itself void; he simply ignored it from the beginning. With the iron calm of which he had boasted at the Vogelsang Castle, he waited for the Catholic position to erode from within. In many respects, Hitler's strategy paid off. Negotiations continued for years about a violation here, a misunderstanding there. Expecting the Concordat to offer genuine protection was like believing Hitler could be swayed by other "scraps of paper," such as the Weimar Constitution or the Treaty of Versailles.

In the long run, the Concordat preserved the illusion that the Church had something to defend and thus blinded its leaders to their own complicity with the Hitler state. Rather than reexamining basic principles, leaders squandered the Church's moral credit in debates over details. Carefully inspecting each tree that fell, they never noticed the forest was on fire. Moreover, participating in the negotiation process itself, the churchmen came to see their Nazi opposite numbers as colleagues, amiable men with whom they lunched, smoked cigars, and traded jokes. The web of connections unified the negotiators, blurring black and white moral distinctions in a mass of bureaucratic gray.

When communications sped between the Vatican and Berlin in 1933, no one bothered to contact women. Awaiting the results, Catholic women took no stance. Unlike Agnes von Grone, they did not make their own contacts with the women leaders or venture to form their own evaluation of political events. They waited. What they saw may have astonished them. Even before the Concordat had been concluded, they watched a remarkable drama unfold. While Hitler, flanked by his black-shirted SS, boasted about his own infallibility, priests took up popular Nazi themes. Fearing they would make themselves unpopular with their followers by attacking so popular a national leader, prelates joined the chorus. In a handwritten letter, Cardinal Faulhaber told Hitler,

> Your statesmanlike farsightedness has achieved in six months what the old parliamentary parties failed to achieve in sixty years. . . . This agreement can bring for the inner life of the German *Volk* . . . an increase of faith and with it an increase of the ethical power of the *Volk*. . . . This handshake with the papacy, the greatest moral power in the history of the world, is a feat of immeasurable blessing.

The Cardinal closed with "Blessings from the bottom of my heart. May God preserve the Reichs Chancellor for our *Volk*."[24] In Berlin a special high mass commemorated the Concordat. National Socialist flags and banners adorned the cathedral and the Nazi marching song, the "Horst Wessel Lied," accompanied the recessional. The Church leadership, which only months before had opposed racial thinking, had reversed its position. Bishops like Conrad Gröber concluded, "Race and Christianity are not contradictions, but orders of a different kind that supplement one another." Expressions like *"Heil Bischof"* and "Jesus is our Führer!" became the clergy's stock-in-trade. In some churches, priests held memorial services in honor of two Catholics who had been "martyred" for the Nazi cause before 1933. One priest, exiled for his left-wing views, commented cynically that the Catholic leaders advertised their nationalist wares with a sign outside their shop window that read, "We carry all items that are sold by the competition, but our quality is better."[25]

On the Woman Question, Catholic men rivaled Hitler in proclaiming the restoration of motherhood in a warrior nation. Vice-Chancellor von Papen boasted about "the Germanic aversion to death on a mattress," and urged Germans to revive warrior virtues.

> What the battle-field was for the man, motherhood was for the woman.
> . . . The maintenance of eternal life demanded the sacrifice of the individual. Mothers must exhaust themselves in order to give life to children. Fathers must fight on the battle-field in order to secure a future for their sons. . . . A man who is not a father is not a man. . . . Even more true is the saying that she who is not a mother is not a woman. . . .[26]

With Catholic men espousing such beliefs, Hitler's sentiments hardly seemed radical at all.

Hitler, far from being pleased by such emulation, began to worry. Taken by surprise at the collapse of his rivals, he wondered why his former enemies took up Nazi themes. Perhaps, he feared, rapid surrender masked a more devious plan to subvert the Nazi state from within. A top-secret report on morale deepened his suspicions. Why, it asked, did so many priests suddenly praise "nationality, authoritarianism, leadership, blood, and soil?" Alarmed, Hitler called a halt to full-scale borrowing of Nazi rituals. He, by implication, could emulate Catholic rites; but Catholics could not copy Nazis.

News of the Concordat transformed women leaders' silence into acceptance. This does not mean that all women active in Catholic organizations agreed, but it did mean that the women with doubts did not express themselves in public. As soon as the Pope himself pronounced the Nazi state trustworthy, Catholic women leaders transmitted the message to their followers. No doubt some calculated (like von Grone) that they might derive some benefits from a pledge of cooperation. In a rush of enthusiasm, they overlooked Hitler's plans for "racial revolution," and instead gazed upon those aspects of Nazi policy that accorded with their own values. The Marriage Loan Program, for example, conformed precisely to Catholic women's vision of womanhood. "A touch of genius!" declared Antonie Hopmann, social worker and a leader in the relatively liberal Catholic German Women's League in August 1933.[27] Besides, since it appeared that Hitler would dominate German life for the foreseeable future, Catholic women did not want to be left out. As a minority religion, they were sensitive to slurs against their patriotism and wanted to be accepted by the majority Protestant Nazi alliance. "We stand with our strongest will ready to participate in the new state . . . not at the side, but at the very core of the activity."[28] The mood of August 1914 resounded through the Nazified land.

Catholic women leaders noticed, during the fall of 1933, a remarkable change among their fellow citizens. The events of 1933 had, in Krabbel's words, "transformed the entire face of Germany overnight. . . . These are exciting times to be alive!" She called 1933 "a period of great world-historical importance!" and "a holy year!" This normally sober woman allowed her emotions to guide her pen as she wrote, "In our hearts we feel that the future of Germany and the fate of Europe are at stake. . . . The breath quickens and the heart trembles." At last the republic (which had funded the Church so handsomely) was dead. No one mourned the demise of Weimar democracy in the Catholic women's press or even looked back nostalgically. Instead, authors told about that decade when "we all watched helplessly as that terrible and monstrous power (materialism) with demoniacal intensity tried to wrench the thought of God out of the human heart!" Germans now had "masculine men" to restore order. With "the hero" in control, "feminine" women could joyfully return to the "garden of helping love," to ideals of virginity and motherhood, "great, strong, and deep."[29] In a similar mood, Antonie Hopmann, longtime advocate of women's responsibilities in public life, summarized the "year of our Lord 1933."

As the Christmas bells pealed out over a peaceful land, "the Führer strives to accomplish superhuman tasks in the midst of world economic collapse . . . to lead the various classes and Germanic tribes [*Stämme*] toward unity . . . [and] to create a worthy place for Germany in the world." This longtime leader in the Catholic women's peace movement praised Hitler's sincere desire for disarmament and enjoined her readers to pray for his success.[30] Gerta Krabbel told her readers in the Christmas issue of the national women's magazine, "The current epoch demands from us women Catholics the dedication [*Einsatz*] of all our power and energy—more than ever before." Catholic social workers rejoiced in the unification and coordination of all welfare bureaus promised by the Nazis. At last, they believed, efficiency and planning would streamline the network of charitable and social work agencies in Germany.[31] A powerful state and a strong church, they hoped, would bring order to the nation. The women's press reflected the new priorities.

Although their praise was slightly less effusive than Protestant women's, Catholic women leaders' public statements about the Woman Question reflected the Vatican's stance. Ignoring papal pronouncements, Catholic women leaders had endeavored to reconcile motherhood with employment as options for women. In 1933, motherhood eclipsed its rivals. The traditionalists won out, and even liberals dramatically changed their tone on the Woman Question. Writers who had once defended women's place in the paid labor force now advised girls to take up home economics. Praise for motherhood, which, to be sure, had always constituted an important theme in Catholic women's literature, now prevailed unchallenged by countervailing considerations. Catholic writers, once the defenders of celibacy and women's claims to jobs and careers, now joined the new consensus urging women to retreat from the "masculine" sphere.

A series of essays on "We Women and Men's Professions" warned of the problems women would cause if they strayed from feminine callings. Where women authors had spoken of women leaders and used the word *Leiterin*, which has connotations of "director," they now called for a Führerin to step forth, using the female form of "Führer." Catholic women at their annual convention in 1933 decided on "Catholic Womanhood and the German *Volk* Heritage" as the theme. Earlier conventions, by contrast, had discussed such topics as women's place in the modern world, the economic depression, and women and peace. In the Catholic women's press, poems euologized the Germanic *Volk*, and a diagram of "the Mother of God's Family Tree" graced the cover of one issue of the national magazine *Frauenland*. A leading social worker welcomed the new regime once the Concordat had been signed, praising extraordinary change in German life. "The private sphere is totally transformed, women's entry into the highest levels of public life is amazing. We see the creation and work of women—of Catholic women, too." [32] She welcomed the "professionalization of women's nature" and hoped that women could recover from the "deep shock of the women's movement" in the Weimar Republic. Catholic women's periodicals, which had long endorsed their own peace movement, dropped the appeal for world understanding but stopped short of joining the clamor for war. Following the Pope's reasoning, women believed that the Concordat gave them the responsibility of supporting Nazi policy, but also the right to defend their organizational autonomy against any encroachments from the state.

Most Catholic women, like Protestant women, welcomed the arrival of an authoritarian regime in Berlin that promised to combat atheistic socialism while restoring a bygone harmony between feminine and masculine spheres. As one Catholic woman who had greeted Hitler's "revolution" recalled, "The Concordat gave us hope that after Hitler achieved power, he would lose his revolutionary character. He would become responsible and gradually normalize." Realizing this statement might appear flimsy in the clear light of hindsight, Elisabeth Denis reminded her readers that similar justifications characterized Pius XII's explanation of the Vatican's "prudent silence," which he did not break until Allied troops liberated Italy.[33] As soon as Hitler's armies had been defeated, however, the Pope lost no time in condemning the "satanic spectre," and "arrogant apostasy from Jesus Christ, the denial of His doctrine, and of His work of redemption, the cult of violence and idolatry of race and blood, the overthrow of human liberty and dignity." The Fulda bishops, by contrast, appear to have learned humility after Hitler's armies collapsed. "We accuse ourselves of not having professed more courageously, believed more gladly, and loved more intensely," they declared after the war.[34] Generally, women's recollections resemble those of the Fulda bishops more than the Pope's arrogant self-righteousness.

Whatever their retrospective explanations, the Concordat opened up the way for women to rejoice at Hitler's state. Although their endorsement came about six months after the Protestant women's declaration of friendship, Catholic women belatedly declared themselves open to the idea of cooperating with the new dictator. Of course, Hitler welcomed the support of one million organized Catholic women, many of whom had administrative and educational skills. But the courtship between a powerful man and frightened women was bound to end in a mismatch, for the partners were too unequal, and negotiations for the marriage contract broke down.

For a time, Catholics and Nazis co-existed amicably, because of the absence of unified leadership in Berlin and Nazi women's own uncertainty about the future. A woman Party leader in a small district explained her caution to her followers. "We do not want to destroy an organization just because it is not entirely constructed according to our liking. We can only do that when we have something to replace it with."[35] But having formally allied itself with the state, it was not clear precisely how the vast Catholic network of educational, health, and welfare institutions would function. Catholic women did not greet the new partnership unconditionally; indeed their private correspondence shows that from the beginning they insisted on their own terms and resisted a wholesale takeover by either the Nazi Welfare Department or the Women's Bureau. But qualified acceptance was not enough for Hitler, who wanted devoted cooperation, not grudging participation.

Catholic women leaders, like Protestants, said a cheerful Yes to cooperation and a determined No to merger. Unlike Protestants, Catholics were not pressured into joining the Nazi Party. In practice, this meant that Catholic women could, for example, volunteer to collect money in Nazi fund-raising drives, but they would do so as Catholics, not as Nazis.[36] Women used their position in the hierarchy as a pretext for bypassing offers to cooperate too closely with Nazi women, saying in effect, "Thank you for your invitation. We must ask our superiors."[37] When Paula Siber invited Catholic women to participate in a national conference, for example, Gerta Krabbel did not refuse immediately. Instead, she insisted she had to await the Bishop's permission. Catholic women stood directly under the Church, she argued, and owed their first allegiance to their male superiors, not their female, non-Catholic colleagues. Like von Grone, Krabbel expected her superiors to protect her against Nazi women's attempts to swallow up Catholic organizations directly into the state bureaucracy. But unlike the Protestant leaders, Catholic women avoided direct negotiations with state officials.

The district of Baden, predominantly Catholic and also traditionally liberal, was the headquarters of national Catholic Charities. During early October 1933, Scholtz-Klink, then the local Nazi leader in Baden, called a conference of prominent women leaders of the district, assuming that all women had agreed to merge their organizations totally into the new state. But Catholic women quickly disabused her of the notion. After much equivocation, they reported that they would willingly work in any motherhood-training programs, but only under the following conditions: that they retain their special Catholic identity and the courses include no mention of "racial hygiene." Scholtz-Klink, of course, found this unacceptable and closed the meeting with a curt farewell and a reminder that all leadership positions in the Nazi mothers' programs would be held by Nazi women.[38]

At the national level, when Paula Siber invited Catholic women leaders to participate in a national planning committee, the response was similar. Catholic women shrewdly agreed to cooperate only if Siber could promise them total freedom of religion, strict adherence to the Concordat, nonbinding discussions, and government subvention of expenses for participants in planning sessions—none of which was possible.[39] They did not join Siber's committee. Temporarily, at least, Catholic women seemed to be holding their own against pressure to participate in Nazi programs.

Meanwhile, Catholic women heard alarming reports about Nazi attacks against specific women's organizations. Already in July 1933, for example, the Nazis in Rottenburg broke into the meeting rooms of the Catholic Young Women (*Jungfrauverein*) and removed their organizational flag from the church. This left "a feeling there is no justice," and a "depressing impression." Speaking of the women's associations, the report continued, "Our organizations have been a bastion of support for church and state . . . despite the insults and jeers of Socialists and Communists. . . . We have remained faithful to order and willingly submit to the New Order and place our powers at its service. We . . . had never expected such attacks to come from the conservative powers of the Vaterland."[40] From a small Rhineland town came reports that Nazi children were not allowed to participate in Catholic youth programs and even jeered at Catholic children. "If we mothers have to stand by and merely watch, we may as well close up shop right now."[41]

While Protestant women plunged into close cooperation with the new regime, the Catholics followed a different strategy. Supported, they thought, by the Concordat, Catholic women endeavored to maximize their influence by remaining outside governmental spheres. They would participate on an ad hoc basis under carefully negotiated conditions. Officially, they insisted on the absolute primacy of their religious aims, the "deepening and inner direction of our members' faith" (*Vertiefung und Verinnerlichung*)." In reality, behind these pious official goals, they continued to work in areas the Nazis considered "political," such as professional organizations, women's education, health care, publicity (press, radio, theater, and cinema), marriage counseling, and campaigns against pornography. Women leaders whose lives had been dedicated to organization-building used every means at their disposal to preserve these networks, and they looked to the church hierarchy as their fortress against Nazi paganism. Shielded by the Church organizations, they expected to continue their work as always within the larger society. After all, they must have reasoned, if the bishops had provided them with a safe "space" during a republic they defined as atheistic and alien, would it not be able to shelter them under a dictator who had signed a treaty with the Pope?

That they underestimated the power of the Nazi regime in 1933 is surely understandable. During the bureaucratic chaos of 1933, Catholic women, like their Protestant counterparts, must have laughed at this "authoritarian" state that promised law and order yet delivered a succession of ludicrous women leaders. Who could worry too much about Zander's hysterical pleas, Gottschewski's "Frauenfront," or Siber's call for order, with Krummacher undercutting her every move? In retrospect, we may wonder why Catholic and Protestant women did not use their organizations to resist Nazi power more effectively. One part of the answer may be that, in 1933, the new rulers did not appear as a major threat to them. Catholic women believed they could compete and win, backed by a powerful church and the Concordat. They mistakenly saw the agreement as a defense against, not an offer to cooperate with, the Nazi state.

The euphoria that erupted during the summer of 1933 did not last long. After the Concordat, Catholics who opposed the agreement observed sadly, "The bishops cannot fight where Rome concludes peace." Then, women began to wonder how they might fight when the bishops concluded peace. The hierarchy behind which women sought refuge crumbled from the top down. Because the first signs of weakness appeared in relation to reproductive issues, which directly impinged on women's lives, women generally became alarmed before Catholic men. Beneath the polite, and often obsequious, tone of their official correspondence, a new note of anxiety appeared in discussions of their status under Nazi rule. They spoke of defending "genuine freedom of personal choice" for Catholics and the creation of an atmosphere in which women of all ages and marital status might communicate openly. Only four months after the Concordat had been signed, women from several organizations listed their objections to the Nazi regime that: defined motherhood in narrow biological terms, without mentioning love, education, or family virtues, promoted a martial style that threatened to masculinize women, and sponsored pro-natalist propaganda that insulted women who did not marry.[42] Facing the "Third Reich," Catholic women leaders looked upward for defense within their hierarchy. In so doing they made the same miscalculation that other non-Nazis did by failing to seek allies among other dissidents outside their organizations.

By late 1933, Catholic women realized that the protective "walls" upon which they counted offered little protection. One archbishop suggested that the Catholic German Women's League either moderate its stand or dissolve altogether. Maybe, he suggested, the new Reich had no use for any exclusively women's groups at all since the very term "woman's organization" was anathema. The women leaders assured their bishop that until the Woman Question was answered, Catholic women would remain organized.[43] They promised to continue to cooperate with Nazi women on an ad hoc basis only. In their own way, these women (like many priests) attempted to work with the "healthy core" of Nazism by rewarding those facets of the government they applauded and boycotting those programs that offended their morality. Thus, Catholic women believed, they could influence government policy while keeping their own consciences clear. Even though their superiors had disappointed them, Catholic women could at least take pride in the fact that their associations remained more intact than von Grone's Protestant Frauenwerk. The Catholic hierarchy, while encompassing a broad range of responses to the Nazi regime, did not openly split, as did the Protestant leadership; and Catholic women managed to protect their organization from Nazi takeover or dissolution.

Catholic women ought to have taken warning from the events of July 1934, when the Catholic hierarchy failed to defend even its own priests or to protest against Nazi crimes. During the notorious Blood Purge of June 30, Hitler ordered hundreds of his own SA men, as well as their leader and his friend, Ernst Röhm, murdered. For two days Hitler's police broke into homes and shot their victims; Hitler admitted to 77 killings; the Ministry of Justice claimed 207; and the total was probably much higher.[44] But murder extended beyond the SA. Catholic liberals also fell to Nazi terror—Dr. Erich Klausener, the director of Catholic Action, Father Adalbert Probst, director of the Catholic Youth, Fritz Gerlach, editor of the independent Catholic periodical *The Path*, and Father Stempfle (an old comrade of Hitler's) were found dead within hours of the SA purge. Each victim had openly criticized the Nazi regime. Except for Bishop Galen, who issued a mild protest, the Church failed to deplore the deaths of these independent and liberal churchmen.[45] Conservative church leaders, rather than protesting the murder of fellow Catholics, congratulated Hitler after the purge. The bishop of Hesse-Nassau sent his "warmest thanks for a firm rescue operation, along with best wishes and renewed promises of unalterable loyalty. We pray for God's blessing on our beloved Führer."[46] No pretenses of legality, no trials, no charges were made. Hitler ordered all documents related to the murders destroyed and returned his regime to normalcy as quickly as possible. On July 1, even as the firing squads were killing the last of their victims, Hitler chatted amiably with his guests at a garden party; on July 13, he addressed the Reichstag for three hours, introducing metaphors that presaged more violence. "In this hour I gave the order to shoot the ringleaders of this treason, and I further gave the order to cauterize down to the raw flesh the ulcers of this poisoning of the wells in our domestic life. . . . Let it be known for all time to come that if anyone raises his hand to strike the state, then certain death is his lot."[47]

Hitler personally would identify traitors and "cauterize" well poisoners. Judges, trials, juries ceased to have any meaning. Conservative Catholic leaders watched as Hitler's ruffians attacked the liberals in their own church. And they joined the chorus of obedient Germans who praised their Führer. Hitler, for his part, had indeed trodden along the "outer edge of risk" and succeeded. Evil stood unmasked. Opponents remained silent.

If the Catholic leadership said nothing in response to direct attacks against its own priests, would it speak out about life-and-death concerns that affected the lives of ordinary women of their faith? The answer came within the year. Danger signs had first appeared in July 1933 for anyone who cared to read them. The first eugenics law had been formulated in July 1933 at the same cabinet session that approved of the Concordat. The plan called for the elimination of "racially unworthy" offspring by sterilization of "inadequate" adults. Nazi leaders shrewdly decided not to make the law public until after the jubilation about the Concordat had passed. When they did, the Fulda bishops protested that the law would put Catholics in a conflict of conscience. But they spoke in conciliatory tones. Church teaching, the bishops decided, does not preclude eugenics generally, and even allows "morally permissible" means of achieving eugenic aims. Although they condemned forced sterilization, some bishops thought that voluntary sterilization might be acceptable.[48]

Equivocal Catholic statements allowed government agencies to misrepresent the Vatican's stance on eugenics by publishing articles designed to "relieve the consciences" of Catholic women health workers. Only one prelate, Cardinal Clemens August Galen of Münster, spoke out openly and directly against the sterilization law and eugenics.[49] His words had no impact on policy. A bland restatement of Catholic opposition to eugenics appeared in the *Osservatore Romano*, but it was not translated from the original Latin for the benefit of German readers.[50]

The Nazi government remained adamant and the Church kept its "prudent silence." Priests who advised against sterilization would, in certain districts, be dismissed by government orders.[51] Catholics in marriage-counseling centers received instructions not to give advice on family law or discuss eugenics. Since virtually all couples seeking advice asked questions related to one or both of these topics, this measure crippled the centers.[52] In January 1934, Catholic social workers received orders to submit the names of clients who ought to be sterilized, and Catholic nurses had to assist in the operations they believed to be immoral.[53] Nazi social planners allowed no exceptions for Catholics in health-care professions.

The Fulda bishops responded with a strategy that set a pattern for the next decade. Rather than attacking the broad principles behind the involuntary sterilization law, the bishops conceded the principle and negotiated for exceptions. The bishops bargained and won permission for Catholic physicians to refuse to perform operations related to sterilization. This strategy split apart the Catholics who were covered by exception clauses from those who were not—in this case mainly male doctors from female nurses and social workers. By conceding an immoral principle the Church damaged its moral authority. In exchange, government officials conceded that "racially unworthy" Catholics who committed themselves for life to residential institutions would avoid sterilization.

Women, as mothers and health-care professionals, registered their objections. Catholic nurses appealed to Father Kreutz, the national director of Catholic Charities, for support. When they refused to participate in sterilizations, nurses lost their jobs and were replaced by non-Catholic "brown sisters," who belonged to the Nazi Order of Nurses.[54] These women, with a crash course on Nazi doctrine and eugenics as well as basic nursing skills, took the jobs of registered nurses who had received a minimum of four years of formal education. The "brown sisters" received lower pay than nurses and, perhaps more importantly, they brought Nazi beliefs to their clients. Observers in Bavaria reported in 1937 that "patients complain because these sisters care more about Hitler-agitation than them. Their hatred for Catholic Charities goes so far that one woman who was scheduled for a recuperative stay in a mothers' home was refused because she had allowed herself to be cared for by a Charities nurse."[55] Elisabeth Zilliken, the director of women in the Catholic Social Workers' Association, appealed to Kreutz for support. He curtly ordered her to inform her membership that they had to report "genetically damaged" children to the eugenics courts. He discussed the matter with Hilgenfeldt (who was an old friend from Baden), and he scolded Zilliken for being overly scrupulous, saying her vivid imagination always conceived of the most extreme cases. Kreutz reasoned that since the Church could not hope to win all disputes, it was wise to discuss only issues on which Nazis might yield. In any case, he concluded, Catholic leaders had no certainty they would exert any influence over either government or population.[56] When Zilliken asked for a clear statement of Catholic doctrine, she received admonitions to keep quiet and hope for the best. That was not enough.

Catholics all over Germany asked for spiritual guidance on how to reconcile contradictory axioms from church and state. The files from Archbishop Gröber's office in Freiburg testify to average people's despair at the eugenics policies of the Third Reich. The overwhelming majority of these inquiries came from women with questions related to childbearing. A few representative examples illustrate the range of such concerns. A woman teacher inquired how she could ascertain whether a twelve-year-old boy who performed poorly on IQ tests suffered from brain damage, retardation, or cultural deprivation.[57] In times of moral decline, she wondered, how could anyone confidently prescribe sterilization for someone who displayed "an absence of ethical concepts"? A social worker asked if a "depraved" or even "endangered" young woman should be sterilized at her request. What if sterilization removed the fear of pregnancy and she fell even more deeply into sexual license?[58] Social workers reported that formerly responsible but slightly retarded citizens became "asocial" after sterilization because they felt society already re-garded them as hopeless. Since expectations of marriage often motivate people to behave morally, sterilization would undermine the character of unmarriagables. In Mainz, a Catholic social worker, Martha Herter, without guidance from her male Catholic superiors, advised the wives of alcoholics not to allow their husbands to be sterilized. "Is it so serious," she asked, "if your husband comes home drunk now and then or if he has a few outbursts of temper?" She doubted Nazi health officials' prom-ises that after sterilization husbands would spend their evenings at home and provide better financial security for their families. The police ar-rested Frau Herter and she was found guilty of trusting her own opinions over those of the government. "The state cannot and ought not tolerate subjective opinions that endanger the collective health of the German Volk."[59] A higher court ruled that while the state could not absolutely require citizens to support sterilization enthusiastically, it did insist that no one had the right to complain about the law.[60]

Although the combatants were unevenly matched in the sterilization controversy, they agreed on one issue: The individual ought not be en-trusted with the right to make decisions related to his or her reproductive potential. Catholic women disclaimed women's rights to limit pregnancy except by abstinence; Nazi women extolled motherhood as their highest goal in life, while denying to thousands of "undesirable" women the chance of ever marrying and bearing children. Neither group of women believed they had the right to control their bodies. According to Catholic dogma, no individual could interrupt a pregnancy for any reason without disobeying God's will because every human life was equal in the divine order. Nazi doctrine, founded on the distinction between "worthy" and "unworthy" life, enforced selective breeding by increasing penalties for abortions and prohibiting birth control. Both doctrines took decision-making away from the individual. According to eugenicists' logic, be-cause the "racially undesirable" usually displayed the least ability to grasp this fundamental truth, forced sterilization alone could prevent their reproduction.[61] When Scholtz-Klink's Frauenwerk spread propaganda to this effect, Catholic women leaders protested to the Reichsfrauenführ-erin, but to no avail.[62] These debates continued without resolution. Women stood at the nexus of two competing value systems, both of which denied them the responsibility for their own reproductive deci-sions.

· As time went on, sterilization proved to have negative practical con-sequences, as Protestant women also discovered. Social workers were instructed not to inform prospective candidates for sterilization that Nazi marriage law prohibited sterilized persons from marrying (even from marrying other sterilized people). Although the Catholic tradition has long glorified sexual abstinence as a virtue in nuns and priests, forced infertility was quite another matter. Sterilized people felt betrayed when they discovered they could not marry. Propaganda urged them to act patriotically and submit to sterilization in the interests of the community. And yet Nazi law prevented them from ever leading the only life that propaganda described as normal and healthy.

Despite social workers' objections, the Church complied with the ban on marriage for sterilized people. Archbishop Gröber, in Freiburg, defended the law so vigorously that a local Gestapo official requested him to tone down his statements. "Great confusion," the official noted, arose when Catholics heard that leaders support a doctrine "of imposed unmarriedness" that deprived worthy citizens of marital bliss. In addition, they wondered how the Archbishop could advocate divorce in cases of sterility. In order to minimize the "lively unrest" of the Catholic population, the Gestapo requested Gröber to declare that sterilized persons might be allowed to marry.[63] In late 1936, the bishops reversed their decision and allowed sterilized people to marry other infertile people. Perhaps this change of heart resulted from the fact that so many Catholics had by then been sterilized.[64] In fact, Baden (the district of Gröber and the national headquarters of Catholic Charities), reported by far the highest sterilization rate (2.7 per 1,000). Protestant Berlin and Braunschweig claimed the lowest rates (.94 and .88 per 1,000 respectively).[65] Even Gröber seemed embarrassed by the "success" of sterilization in his province; and he attributed it to the superior efficiency of the Baden administration. Soon, he predicted, other, less well-organized areas would catch up.[66] But Gröber ought not have been surprised, as the percentages of Catholics in the Nazi Party in Baden exceeded the averages in several other (predominantly Catholic) Rhineland states.[67] Organizational safety did not bring Catholics either peace or influence because the strife over sterilization drained their energies and disillusioned them about their male superiors.

Catholic women faced another special conflict. Unlike the Protestants, they operated their own school systems, protected by the Concordat. Catholic teachers and mothers asked how they could prevent their children from joining Nazi youth organizations. A Catholic mother recalled how her son looked enviously at the "uniform, badges, neckerchief, dagger, and flags" of the Hitler Youth and longed to join his friends in their "snappy marches and rousing songs."[68] How could Catholic mothers help their children with homework that required, for example, memorization of the following prayer?

Adolf Hitler, you are our great Führer. Thy name makes the enemy tremble. Thy Third Reich comes, thy will alone is law upon earth. Let us hear
daily thy voice and order us by thy leadership, for we will obey to the end
and even with our lives. We praise thee! *Heil Hitler!*

Younger children learned this bedtime prayer:

Führer, my Führer, sent to me from God, protect and maintain me
throughout my life. Thou who has saved Germany from deepest need, I
thank thee today for my daily bread. Remain at my side and never leave
me, Führer, my Führer. My faith. My light. *Heil, mein Führer!*[69]

One Catholic mother recalled that "The younger generation wanted to
be 'with it,' to advance in life, to be proud, to become 'something.' Who
cared about Mother's old-fashioned notions?"[70] Recollections from convinced Nazis validate Catholic mothers' anxiety. A member of the
League of German Girls described her contempt for women who refused
to take sides:

The Christian teachers pretended to themselves and to us that one could
be both at once without dishonor: a Christian and a National Socialist.
They had not yet taken the measure of what was afoot in Germany, or they
did not want to take its measure, because they would then have needed a
great deal of courage in order to go on living as Christians. So people
floated along in a confused jumble of Christian and National Socialist
attitudes.[71]

As long as neither church nor state forced an absolute declaration of
total loyalty, Catholics could "float along." We will never know how
many children attended youth meetings and preferred not to tell their
parents; nor can we ascertain how many children obeyed their leaders'
order to report on their parents' anti-Nazi sentiments.

In Bavaria, Catholics confronted an especially difficult situation in
1936, when the Nazis stepped up their drive to abolish all religion-affili-
ated schools. Everywhere in Germany parents were asked in rigged pleb-
iscites whether they wanted to end parochial education. State-controlled
elections produced pro-Nazi results. But in Bavaria virtually all schools
were Catholic and parents did not easily agree to send their children to
Nazified schools. Three-quarters of all nuns were dismissed without pen-
sions, state aid to Catholic schools was terminated, convents were dissolved, and schools attacked. Catholics protested. Priests broke Nazi
orders and read sermons condemning the action from their pulpits. Pro-

tests flooded state and church offices. As one former Nazi supporter put it in an unsigned letter:

> Which Catholic mother did not weep in the last few days when she was told about it [convent dissolution] by her children? I happened to be a witness as to how the children cried on the streets for their sisters, and all the grown-ups who came with them. Must the sisters go to make way again for bigwigs [*Bonzen*], or because they are Catholic? In fifty years' time the children will still have fond memories of their good sisters, while certainly no one will give a damn about these Nazi *Bonzen*, whether they disappear today or tomorrow. . . . *Heil Hitler!* The father of a family . . .
>
> P.S. Would the wicked Communists have attacked us Catholics in such a way?[72]

Although the pattern of harassment differed from place to place, Hitler's insistence on an all-or-nothing commitment to his ideology deprived the Nazi state of the morale that he considered absolutely vital to carrying out his plans for a Third Reich.

In communities where Catholic leadership remained strong, the population found ways of making its opinion known. Throughout Catholic Germany, graffiti artists defied street cleaners' best efforts with slogans such as "There is only one Führer and he was born more than 2,000 years ago."[73] In the small Franconian town of Leidersbach, residents voted No in a plebiscite on de-Christianizing the schools, hung yellow-and-white Catholic flags, and threw stones at Nazi leaders. In this closely knit Catholic town, Nazis remained outsiders. "The work of every teacher in Leidersbach has been made difficult . . . but recently positive work on behalf of the National Socialist state and Party has become completely impossible. This secret sabotage is becoming increasingly unbearable." Catholic mothers behaved more resolutely than ever. In a veritable mothers' revolt they threatened to withdraw their children from schools in which crucifixes had been replaced by swastikas. One nervous Nazi district leader reported that the mood at Catholic protest meetings reminded him of the revolutionary days of 1918–1919.[74] Opinion polls, morale monitors, and security police testified to widespread outrage against the Nazi policy. One reporter dispatched a description of the situation to anti-Nazis abroad, saying that the mood of the Catholic population was "without exaggeration, despairing," and claimed that the fighting spirit brought out by the school struggle had given way to general indifference that had its cause in the passive approach of the higher Church dignitaries.[75] The bishops registered their protests by reaffirming their commitment to Nazism and asking for Catholic rights within that context. Catholic women thus stood between the Nazi state that directly attacked their institutions and their bishops who equivocated.

Catholic parents and teachers inculcated into the youth a belief that they belonged primarily to the Christian community—that they must sacrifice for others and put the collective over the personal. Nazi youth leaders preached precisely the same collectivist values, but defined "community" in racial, not religious, terms. .

Barely a year after Hitler had seized power, Elisabeth Zilliken, director of the Catholic Social Workers' Association, reported that the younger generation no longer looked to Catholic leaders for guidance. Instead, they turned to the National Socialist Welfare or to the youth groups. Similarly, the most highly qualified graduates sought jobs within the state bureaucracy. Who could blame them? They were, after all, both ambitious and idealistic. She asked Kreutz how Catholics could compete with the Nazis in recruiting the youth. "We must now know, most respected Father, if we have to go along with this or if we can oppose it. . . . I think that I need not tell you how great the magnitude of this decision is. A spiritual issue of the first order is at stake: The religious education of our children . . . cannot in any way be guaranteed by the state . . . [all of our good work] will be choked."[76] Zilliken's fears were well grounded. Although Nazi officials promised that Nazi youth programs would provide religious instruction for children of all denominations, in fact children rarely heard about Christ in these classes. One child, for example, reported, "In our religious-studies periods we have to speak about our Führer and we have to learn poems about him. We do not have any poems or sayings about Paul and John."[77]

Reports flooded the headquarters of Catholic Charities in Freiburg— all with the same concern: "Where will this Nazification [*Gleichschaltung*] stop? People call it 'churchnapping' [*Kirchenraub*]! Will no one raise his voice against it?"[78] How, others asked, can the Concordat protect us against the "claim to total power of the new political powers [*Totalitätsanspruch der neuen Machthaber*]?" During the first four years of the Third Reich, anyone could belong to Nazi and Catholic organizations simultaneously, but Catholics feared that one day they would have to choose. Of course, certain policies contradicted Catholic doctrine; but what power could the bishops bring to bear against the popular dictator? Even Cardinal Galen, among the most courageous opponents of Nazism, advised against telling Catholics to boycott Nazi organizations. The majority, he believed, would side with the Nazis.[79] Without faith in their own flock, the bishops saw no alternative but to follow the Vatican's lead, negotiate with Hitler, and avoid a public test of faith.

However, conflict did not cease. One of Catholic women's gravest concerns was with the question of children born to unmarried mothers. Rumors and government policies suggested that soon children born out of wedlock would be granted equal rights, which in the minds of pious Catholics meant an endorsement of "free love." In July 1934 an article in a newspaper for textile workers suggested that the "children of love can be considered of much higher value than those who are conceived in conventional relationships." In his conclusion the author proclaimed, "The voice of the blood cannot be repressed!"[80] After thousands of concerned Catholics addressed their clergy, the Fulda bishops made a mild protest in defense of the family. But police harassment of women's organizations and the state takeover of homes for unwed mothers proceeded unabated.

Women turned to the Fulda Bishops Conference, asking for support. "We address you . . . with the enormous plea that you will defend us mothers. Please support our concern by asking the priests to pay much closer attention to the care of our children."[81] Elisabeth Denis, prominent director of a women's charity association, begged for help when Nazi officials forbade Catholic employment agencies from advertising because they defined such services as political. "We defend our [Catholic] tradition, and in so doing we are defending human values against the increasing power of the anonymous state."[82] From Regensburg came a similar request. Local priests, it seemed, had taken it upon themselves to transfer charitable and educational activities from Catholic women's organizations to the National Socialist Women's Organization—without consulting Catholic women. "What are we to do when priests behave like that?" women asked the Fulda bishops. "Church activities offer us our only chance in these times to build bridges toward better times in the future." How, she continued, can priests act without even consulting us? "The confusion is so great that some women are beginning to waver, which is hardly surprising." All over Germany, women complained about harassment that typically took the form of anti-Catholic posters, slurs against priests, and SA or Hitler Youth attacks. Propaganda urged Germans to boycott Catholic charity drives. "Don't send your money to Rome!" shouted uniformed Nazi hecklers. Women objected. In one town, fifty women demonstrated to win the release of a priest from jail, threatening to throw away their motherhood medals.[83]

Gradually Catholic women faced the truth: Nazi bureaucrats broke their commitments to Catholic leaders, and Catholic leaders, in turn, reneged on their promises to Catholic women. Few prelates defended Catholic women's right to bear and raise children according to their consciences. In 1934–1935, Catholic women, like Protestants, took matters into their own hands. But they did so at the local level. In small towns in Westphalia, for example, indignant Nazi women reported that Catholic women harassed their efforts. When Nazis and Protestants planned joint charity drives, Catholic women scheduled their own religious retreat.[84] Other women Catholics protested directly to the local Nazi women leaders.

Local Nazi welfare offices decided which Catholic services would remain loyal. As in the case of Protestants, this left Catholics with the obligation to care only for "hopeless" clients. Negotiations failed. One Catholic woman from Heidelberg reported in the summer of 1934: "Total Failure! Basic Nazi attitude: 'That's how things are. That's how they remain. . . . We insist on overseeing your work and activities so we can select those areas and cases with which we want to work.' " After the attempt to negotiate directly with local Nazi officials, Catholic women decided that it would be more effective to appeal to the national Catholic hierarchy.[85] The Fulda bishops did not negotiate a reversal, and Catholic social workers were given only the cases that Nazi agencies did not consider worth their while. Catholic women leaders, for lack of a better alternative, continued to appeal for help. How could they preserve faith if the Nazis indoctrinated their children and relegated trained teachers and social workers to the thankless tasks of maintaining "racial castoffs" allocated by Nazi agencies? Protestant women maneuvered within the same parameters, but the two groups did not form a common front.

Besides continuing the sterilization campaign and claiming absolute control over the education of all non-Jewish children, Nazi social planners in the mid-1930s unveiled a program to undercut the traditional family, which Hitler had praised so lavishly in his campaign speeches. Social policies prepared citizens for a society based on peer-group associations. Increasingly, the family came to be viewed as a pragmatic institution: to breed, feed, and house the youth. Motherhood became biologized and child-rearing was Nazified. The Fulda bishops drafted a routine protest, threatening vague "dire consequences." Their declaration brought no change, although months later Nazi officials did apologize for the "overzealousness" of certain statements.[86] On the issue of children born out of wedlock, just as on education and sterilization, Nazi programs continued as planned. Official protests produced official apologies, but no substantial change in Nazi policy.

During 1935, Nazi welfare officials banned all motherhood-training programs that were not directed by the Nazi Women's Bureau.[87] Mothers, the order declared, must be trained without regard for class or religion. According to the government, Catholic teachers had too often advised their pupils to boycott Nazi programs, and frequently Catholic teachers warned against obeying eugenics measures. Once again, women protested; but the bishops did not forward their objections to the Nazi hierarchy. Gerta Krabbel discovered the limits of her superiors' willingness to support women's organizational autonomy when Kreutz, the director of Catholic Charities, suggested that perhaps the time had come for her to make her peace with Scholtz-Klink, saying Catholic women ought to withdraw from all social programs and renew their primary (and exclusive) commitment to spiritual matters. Protestant women, Kreutz noted, had surrendered their control over practical activities; why not Catholics? "Perhaps you might speak openly with Frau Scholtz-Klink to get a feeling of how she personally sees things. . . ."[88] Although Scholtz-Klink boasted of her good relations with the Catholic women from Catholic Charities in Baden, she did not recall having spoken with Krabbel.

On another occasion, in 1937, the director of the St. Elisabeth Association asked Kreutz for support after the membership had voted against the nomination of a Nazi-appointed director. In private correspondence, Kreutz complained about these women as too "stubborn and tradition-bound" to be dealt with.[89] In the pages of their own periodicals, Catholic women authors refrained from mentioning the name Adolf Hitler or "Führer" even when they praised German greatness or discussed social policy. After the Concordat, they had sworn to avoid politics and, construing their pledge strictly, they did not mention the Nazi Party, which would have been "political." Nor did Catholic women leaders sign their letters with *Heil Hitler*, as von Grone and her associates did. Altogether, Catholic women did not walk as far along the path with Nazism as Protestants did. Instead, they used their religious activities to preserve their own communities against psychological and institutional intrusion from a state they belatedly perceived as menacing.

Catholic mothers' organizations deepened their commitment to religion and used their concern as a wedge into public life. "This winter our work must be strongly guided by the question: How can we help the mother in the battle against the alienation of the youth from the Church?"[90] Catholics saw little hope of claiming the right to care for the physical well-being of mothers; the Nazis had won that contest. But they insisted on their obligation to guide mothers' spiritual lives. While emphasizing their religious concerns, Catholic women knew that their drive to prevent Nazi indoctrination of their children had intensely political and anti-Nazi implications. Against the tide of paganism and indifference, Catholic women reaffirmed their commitment to religious life.

The stream of complaints from women Catholics testifies to the anxiety they experienced. Balanced between two total systems—a state with messianic goals and a religion with a political tradition—they did not know which to choose. One unidentified woman asked, "How can we educate Catholic German mothers? Church competes against the state for the total loyalty of the people. That presents the question: Is the education by each to proceed in tandem or is it to be merged? This drive for unity affects the woman in her deepest nature. She cannot tolerate a split at the heart of her life."[91] The unknown author of this letter complained that Concordat negotiations produced no satisfaction at all and concluded that, if Catholic schools were forced to tailor their teachings to suit Nazi doctrine, they might just as well be given up altogether. The *only* point in maintaining a separate institutional identity was to defend a separate viewpoint. Although they met resistance in relation to motherhood schools and projects for "wayward" girls, by and large Catholics survived direct attacks on their youth programs and bypassed the assault on their community organizations.

Secret morale monitoring surveys confirmed Catholics' sense of accomplishment. Nervous officials reported that opposition had not been destroyed, but merely driven underground. "Political Catholicism," they agreed, was being preserved within the family, in private life beyond the reach of spies or teachers. The youth, too, seemed less eager to join Nazi associations after about 1935–1936. Rudolf Hess, Hitler's closest adviser, warned against any obvious assault against tradition. "The less the parents' opposition is aroused on church matters, the less they will inculcate into their children opposition to their Hitler Youth leaders."[92] Hess' counsel prevailed for the first three years of Nazi rule. The harassment before 1936 seemed bad enough at the time but later measures made the earlier period seem calm.

During endless negotiations with church officials, which always yielded Nazi victory and religious compromise, Hitler was sustained by the knowledge that the recalcitrant Catholics would simply die off or retire; the youth belonged to him. As the Catholic Church rotted behind its mighty facade, he told himself, Nazism would inherit the next generation. But disquieting reports arrived daily. The young, in fact, had not yet been monopolized by the Nazi youth structure. After an initial surge in membership after 1933, only 60 percent of all German youth between ten and eighteen had joined Nazi youth organizations.[93] In addition, the average age of Party members increased steadily throughout the period, indicating that as Nazi ideology became bureaucratized, its ability to recruit young people declined.[94] Thus Hitler had been too optimistic in anticipating that Germans' allegiance to Catholicism or Protestantism would diminish and they would become Germans united under a pagan, Nazified God, or perhaps a vague "Providence." Few Germans left the Church, which suggests they integrated their Nazi and Christian beliefs.[95] Security reports reinforced Hitler's concern about widespread apathy, and also informed him of a still more alarming trend. In some places, Hitler Youth leaders subverted the Nazi cause by using their position as cover behind which they inspired their followers to criticize the corruption, materialism, and oppressive conformity of their society. A 1937 report from Münster noted that the leaders had not converted to Nazism and used the "appearance" of loyalty to spread the Catholic faith.[96] People were growing impatient with the bureaucratic invasion of daily life, bored with the steady drone of propaganda, and angry at state encroachment into their private lives.[97]

Often Catholic women leaders adopted the prelates' tactics, much as von Grone had done. Professing their deep admiration for all aspects of Hitler's social policy except those that directly contradicted Catholic dogma, they reiterated in 1935 their pledge: "As faithful Catholic women, we remain lovingly and obediently loyal to the Church and the Holy Father. As faithful German women, we remain obedient to the leadership in their efforts to support the Volk community. We ask for intercession to aid our nation, our Volk, and our Führer."[98] By contrast, Scholtz-Klink increasingly appealed to a pantheistic, pagan Germanic faith.[99] "God is love," she told her audience. "I do not say, 'German mothers, stay away from the Church'; I say, 'Be as in olden times the priestesses in your own homes.'" Women, she believed, had always been more religious than men, and they ought, therefore, to feel more grateful for the fact that Hitler saved them all from Bolshevik atheism. She closed her speech, however, with a clear warning: Every German woman owed to the state her "total power and total love."

Most Catholic women leaders swore their loyalty to the Nazi state but withheld the *total* devotion demanded by Scholtz-Klink. They did not accept a secular monopoly of education, eugenics programs, and interference in the affairs of women's organizations. Nazi women, for their part, declared their faith in a vaguely Christian doctrine, but did not disguise their determination to outmaneuver and finally to destroy an autonomous Catholic women's organization. Still, as 1935 drew to a close, Catholics retained their organizational network. Catholic women leaders wanted a stronger initiative from their own male superiors, but they also realized that they had been spared the intense harassment meted out to their Protestant counterparts. Despite persecution, Catholic women by and large retained control over their programs for teachers, mothers, welfare workers, and health care. Thus they experienced the split perception of reality that characterized life for all Germans who objected to Nazi methods. While saying how terrible conditions had become, people added, "Thank God things are not worse."

Catholic women naively attributed their successes to their own skill at negotiating. In reality, they had been spared harsher reprisals because Hitler had decided to play a waiting game and because the Catholic hierarchy had capitulated with less trouble than the Nazis had anticipated. Once again, Hitler's remarks at the Vogelsang Castle reveal his tactical thinking on the religious question. The "Catholic problem" fell into the category of worries that "take care of themselves." With more pressing issues on his mind, Hitler applied his strategy of attrition: "to belabor people as long as necessary until they succumb to us." Moderates near Hitler, notably Rudolf Hess, also feared that repression against Catholics would produce martyrs and ultimately strengthen the faith. Blending bigotry with political acumen, Hitler suggested, "We should trap the priests by their notorious greed and self-indulgence. . . . I shall give them a few years' reprieve. Why should we quarrel? They will swallow anything in order to keep their material advantages. Matters will never come to a head. They will recognize a firm will, and we need only to show them once or twice who's master."[100] As long as the Catholic Church placed no major obstacles in his path, vicious repression would not be wise. After terror had decimated enemies on the political left and the Nuremberg Laws cordoned off Jews from public life, Nazi leaders were not eager to coerce their potential supporters. Besides, it appeared in early 1936 that, except for a few scruples about eugenics, the Catholic Church as a whole could be counted among the friends of the Third Reich.

At the end of 1936, however, Hitler called the showdown Catholic leaders had dreaded. Just when it appeared that the Nazi state might stabilize and become more tolerant of some diversity within its ranks, Hitler lost patience. The time had come for a new test of loyalty, and Catholic women began to experience the same kind of harassment that had driven von Grone from her office a year before. The accelerated drive for total loyalty occurred against the background of increasing complacency on the part of average citizens who appreciated the full employment, international prestige, state-funded leisure-time activities, and the orderly appearance of daily life. Statistics tell us that actual wages did not rise, but by 1936 everyone had a job. When the United States faced the worst years of the Depression, Hitler's decision to rearm had pulled Germany back to normal. This stability, which would have gratified a "mere dictator," was not enough for Hitler.

Once again, his speech to the elite youth at the Vogelsang Castle reveals Hitler's motivations for accelerating his drive against conditionally loyal Catholics and Protestants. Success brought problems, he mused. In a state where everyone must obey and most people had settled into complacency, how does one test for bravery? How can the future elite be recruited? "In the old days, selection of leaders was very easy," Hitler mused, because the battle against Weimar democracy itself drew the "most talented, courageous, respectable, brave, and idealistic" to the ranks of Nazism. But with opposition destroyed, where was the testing ground? The commitment he sought in his future elite often turned up among the opponents of his regime. As he planned for the next stage of his rule, Hitler feared that his own ranks had grown too "soft." The very stability that made Germans feel secure resulted directly from Hitler's success in transforming the Nazi Party itself from a brawling, unruly troop of followers into a respectable and obedient cadre of administrators. This success sowed the seeds of Hitler's discontent. Put another way: When Nazism as a state stabilized, Nazism as a movement floundered.

Another anxiety fed Hitler's impatience. Painting glorious verbal vistas of a thousand-year Reich pleased his sense of destiny; but who, he wondered, could realize these dreams if he died or became seriously ill? He admitted to the men at Vogelsang that he worried about his "damaged" health, saying that "I must restore my nerves. . . . This is obvious. Worries. Worries. Insane worries; an absolutely astonishing burden of worries." [101] Haunted by fears of death, Hitler lost his ability to outwait his enemy or rival. As he "sniffed out" the limits of the possible in 1937, he decided to escalate a war he had begun on the Protestant front and carry it onto the Catholic battlefield.

As the time for a change had arrived in Hitler's impatient mind, dissident bishops convinced the Pope to speak out. Cardinal Faulhaber, in February 1937, publicly condemned the Nazi state for breaking the Concordat, and in March 1937, Pius XI's sermon "With Burning Sorrow" denounced Nazi racial policies. When priests circulated it illegally in their parishes, the battle was on. Shortly thereafter, Hitler removed the religious issues from the Ministry of Religious Affairs and assigned them to the SS under Heinrich Himmler. Coercion would take up the crusade where conversion had failed. A specially created section of the SS under Reinhard Heydrich attacked the enemy: "political churches, sects, and Jews." [102] Hitler closed the ranks of the Nazi Party to everyone except graduates of Hitler Youth; all Party members had to resign from non-Nazi organizations; and schools like the one at Vogelsang Castle indoctrinated the new elite.

A new time of choice was at hand. Hitler made it explicit. "The totalitarian claims of the church challenge those of the state. Between the National Socialist state and the Catholic Church there can be no compromise." [103] Alfred Rosenberg (as usual) put it more bluntly: "When we put on our brown shirts, we cease to be Catholics or Protestants and become simply Germans."[104] By and large, the clergy dreaded such a choice because, as Cardinal Galen feared, most Catholics might well prefer the state. However, some priests told their congregations that the time would come "when each Catholic would have to vote whether he wished to remain a Catholic and still have a priest."[105] Hitler told his elite that a new time of testing had arrived, and he ordered them to become utterly loyal, as in the "days of struggle" before 1933. Every German had to choose between allegiance to the Führer and loyalty to his or her religion. Hitler declared a new reformation and simulated the battle conditions of the old days. "Believe me. The entire secret of our success as a Party, that I can assure you, consists in my having delegated an extraordinary amount of authority. . . . Each one of you must become an educator [*Erzieher*] as well as a soldier. . . ."[106]

Although the numbers remained small (less than 100,000 per year), statistics show increases in the number of Catholics who cut their ties to the church.[107] The attack on religion was part of the drive for total control. During this time Hitler attacked the last vestiges of independence in the judiciary, the bureaucracy, and the churches, unleashing a second revolution against the last holdouts who failed to worship at the Nazi shrine.˙ The drive to separate fanatically loyal Nazis from moderates coincided also with the campaign to recruit women into economic life.˙

As the showdown approached, Catholic women felt the impact. Their motherhood associations, charitable institutions, and educational facilities were outlawed, or totally absorbed into Nazi organizations. For four years, Nazi women leaders had urged Catholic women to join their organizations, and now they ordered all Catholics to resign from religious associations.[108] And the term "religious" was defined in the narrowest way. This meant, for example, that even charitable organizations that had already been relegated to helping only the clients Nazi agencies did not want and youth groups became illegal.[109] That left altar-care societies, Bible-discussion groups, and religious retreats. All meetings had to take place on religious property, not in public places, large meeting halls, or even in parishioners' homes. Nazi spies regularly monitored religious activities. Initially, some exceptions were granted (for example, for railway-station rescue missions and homes for wayward girls); but by 1939, they, too, disappeared.[110] Catholic publications, when they were allowed at all, were put under strict censorship.[111] Zilliken's letters to Kreutz, the director of Catholic Charities, became more anxious. "The Inner Mission [Protestant national charity association] resists state encroachment, why will you not help us?"[112] Kreutz favored patience.

We will never be able to gauge the extent of the illegal activities that

continued under a strictly religious guise. Scattered reports in Gestapo
files as well as in the archives in Freiburg describe small enclaves of
women Catholics with few ties to larger networks. Women who look back
on this epoch recall that the decisive change brought a certain relief.
During the first few years of Nazi power, church leaders had counseled
moderation, cooperation, and compromise in an effort to demonstrate
that loyal Catholics could remain faithful to both Führer and *Vaterland*.
With a choice forced upon them, each woman had to examine her conscience. One recalled:

> During those early years [1933–1936], our hesitation was not in the least
> heroic. We [hoped for the best], avoiding senseless sacrifices, whether in
> the form of isolation, defamation, or ostracism from the *Volk* community.
> I must admit that for me it was often very hard to endure the condescend-
> ing smiles of our neighbors, who saw us as "unregenerate" women. . . .
> Whoever came to our homes fell under suspicion, and whoever paused to
> speak to us faced subsequent unpleasantness.[113]

One Catholic teacher from a large urban area reported, to a woman
she did not realize was a reporter for a clandestine resistance newsletter,
that she had initially supported the Hitler regime because the "photos of
nuns' coffins from Spain" terrifed her, but after 1937 she declared, "Now
I reject the Hitler government because it is against the Church, because
it allows no freedom of expression at all, and because it has forced some
of my friends into exile. I don't traffic with Nazis. We Catholic teachers
stand solidly together. Our director harasses us. But if it's illegal to meet,
we will meet privately." The informant despaired because she felt so
helpless but believed that, until Germany was rescued, the only recourse
lay in maintaining their Catholic networks and faith.[114] "How could we
know what was right? How could the majority of our friends and neighbors have been wrong?" many wondered. After 1945, one Catholic leader
commented, it became fashionable to look back almost nostalgically on
those days, saying smugly "Faith needs a dark night." But such complacency, she added, ignores the fact that, in the testing period, most Catholics said *"Heil!"* first and rationalized their religious commitment later.

During the early years of Nazi rule, organizations had opposed encroachments into their activities that they called "religious" and the state
termed "political." Women leaders turned to prelates, bishops negotiated
with state officials, and petty arguments wore away patience on both
sides. Still, Catholic organizations had managed to remain intact. Faced
by curtailed activities in the "political" spheres of education, social welfare, and health care, they redoubled their concern for religion. When

they did that, a new wave of repression hampered religious activities with more restrictions, and Catholics realized they confronted a state that claimed their total obedience. In this atmosphere, after 1937–1938, the smallest actions took on major significance. Hanging out yellow-and-white Catholic flags; saying *"Grüss Gott"* instead of *"Heil Hitler"*; attending mass instead of a Party rally on Sunday; and celebrating saints' days, paying tribute to mothers on Catholic, not Nazi Mothers' Day, or participating in church rituals instead of Nazi festivals: All expressed opposition to Nazi leadership. Under the new repressive situation, religious objectors adopted the tactics used by the Nazis themselves when their Party had been outlawed in certain states under the Weimar Republic. Not surprisingly, anti-Nazis drew the most idealistic and independent people to their cause—the same kinds of people who became Nazis before 1933 according to propaganda. Despite persecution, the KDF (Catholic German Women's League) circulated illegal pastoral letters, turned their homes into "small chapels," and continued their underground networks. Ironically, their letters and reports from this period reveal the sort of deep beliefs and stubbornness that characterized the memoirs by those old-timer Nazis who wrote essays for Theodore Abel's contest in 1934.

Hitler's internal security reports warned that repression only created deeper problems. In destroying the community base for welfare and for educational and social programs, the government had also killed the popular support upon which such organizations depended. An official of the Ministry of the Interior reported on the Nazification of social and cultural life to Rudolf Hess in 1939. "We are trampling on an important component of local administration, on which the Führer himself says the new state must rest."[115] From a practical standpoint, too, social services suffered from the depletion of skilled personnel caused by the withdrawal (or expulsion) of so many Catholic women.[116] But in private networks, women Catholics continued. The very decentralization on which their existence depended made it dangerous to keep records. Informal reports from Catholic Charities give the impression of extraordinary activity, especially by the women of the KDF. Lectures in living rooms, discussion groups in kitchens, and youth group meetings in the woods became a routine part of life. Women felt honored when their bishop gave them his blessing. "These days the ancient history of the Church repeats itself. We see that in the most dismal times, human beings enrich themselves so that the intentions of the enemy are reversed."[117]

In general, very little information has been gathered about daily life among Catholics who refused to "adapt to the times"—as Gestapo reports put it. But shortly after the war, the president of the Association of Catholic German Women Teachers asked the membership to describe their lives under Nazism. The essays have been preserved in manuscript form at the association's headquarters in Essen. None of the authors described defiant and courageous actions or participation in a well-organized resistance network. These were ordinary women who spent their energy preserving faith and finding a way of making a living. Most belonged to the first generation of women to gain admission to the universities and teaching colleges during World War I. They tell of their pride at receiving a diploma, and of their despair at receiving notification that no openings existed for women teachers after 1919. They put their names on waiting lists and took whatever jobs they could find—as social workers among "fallen women," teachers in factory settings, bookkeepers, assembly-line workers, or clerks in stores. They knew that marriage would take them off the waiting list forever. Twenty years after the experience they expressed no bitterness. Mathilde von Thiel, for example, recalled, "The work in that office did not agree with me. . . . But still it was a very important time for me. I had grown up very sheltered, but I realized that I would get nowhere that way. So I learned to trust myself, to speak out justly, and to persist in taking risks—and to evaluate the world of workers in a way that a dutiful teacher would never learn."[118] During a decade of undeserved waiting time (as they called it), these teachers informally conducted educational seminars to keep abreast of the latest teaching techniques so that they would be prepared when they were called to face a class. In the early 1930s, they began to receive their long-awaited appointments. Despite prejudices against women in state schools, they found employment in Catholic schools. By 1934, they had been incorporated into Reber-Gruber's Teachers' Union (NSLB), which meant paying dues, subscribing to Nazi periodicals, and attending workshops on ideology and eugenics. These were the women at whom Reber-Gruber fulminated, the "black" retrogrades who resisted her invitations and undercut the morale of "her" loyal women. Each Catholic teacher charted her own course, rendering enough superficial loyalty to keep her job while teaching enough about Catholicism to pacify her religious conscience. One woman teacher even became the local leader of the Nazi Frauenschaft and succeeded in keeping it oriented toward religion until a male leader attended one of her meetings in 1935 and asked who had not yet joined the Nazi Teachers' Union. When he discovered that the only nonmember was the Nazi women's leader, he dismissed her on the spot.

Teachers who were suspected of less than total devotion to Nazism found themselves subjected to forced transfers away from the Catholic communities in which they enjoyed respect to predominantly pro-Nazi (and usually anti-Catholic) towns. This meant painful separation from parents, friends, and religious groups. The trauma rendered Catholic teachers helpless and often depressed. Once a teacher had fallen under suspicion, she never escaped surveillance and regular interrogations. Wherever she moved, her police files followed her. Teachers had to choose. Many relented and joined the NSLB. An officer in the outlawed Catholic teachers' union wrote, "We fear about half of those who resign [from the Catholic Union] do so with their priests' approval. . . . This is the bitterest experience. When we feel our superiors tell us to retreat . . . After our union is destroyed, how can we create anew?"[119]

But dissent did not stop. Clandestine networks spread the word. Perhaps the most notorious of these chain-letter campaigns occurred after the nation's number-one ace pilot, Werner Mölders, had been shot down in 1941. Catholics circulated a letter supposedly written by this national hero—describing the deep Catholic faith that enabled him to face death fearlessly. Mölders had voiced his criticism of the Nazi regime after the Gestapo raided a convent in which his sister was a nun in 1941. In the letter, supposedly written to his confessor, the pilot wrote that non-Catholics' "scorn turned to respect and love" when they saw that Catholics, because of their faith in heaven, behaved more courageously than Nazis in the face of death.[120] The letter played on Catholics' patriotism. Gestapo agents declared this "resistance," because in their perverted frame of reference it seemed to imply that Catholics died more bravely than Nazis for their Führer. Another letter that occasioned Gestapo persecution criticized Nazi failure to stop the Allied bombing raids. "If the dead could talk today, they would scream flaming protests and say, 'We were Christians, we were neither Jews nor heathens, and we want to be buried under the Christian crosses and not under piles of rubble.'"[121] Implicitly, Jews and heathens deserved to die, but Catholics, as good "Aryans," merited a better fate. Both letters are interesting because of the extent to which they incorporate Nazi values and Catholic faith.

This sort of protest counts as resistance in some circles today. I interviewed a retired leader of the Catholic Women's League, Maria Prymm, at the organization's headquarters in Cologne. When I asked if she had criticized the Nazi regime in any way, she proudly recalled that during the war she sewed special mass cases for Catholic army chaplains. She also has her share of stories about Gestapo agents knocking at the front door while fugitives fled through the garden. Subsequently, while working in the Gestapo files in the Düsseldorf State Archives, I came across a report on the arrest of a regional leader of the Catholic Women's League, Emma Horion, which occurred as a result of incriminating evidence given by Frau Prymm.[122] Horion, it appears, had maintained close ties to members of the outlawed organization.

The Düsseldorf Gestapo files yield information about other forms of dissent. Take, for example, the following report. At one retreat to a country inn in the Black Forest, a speaker [one Herr Werkshage] told his audience [mostly nuns] "that Germany is threatened by a monster and a dragon, and that the monster lives as a man—gifted, smart, and refined —at home in all social settings. . . . And the worst of it is that he appeals to God and brings sacrifices to Him."[123] When it finally dawned on her that the speaker meant Hitler, the "informant" was horrified and rushed to the local police. It is difficult for us to take such single-issue opposition seriously as resistance because participants gave priority to deepening their own Catholicism against the paganism they felt engulfed the nation. These private activities saved no one. Participants, if caught, faced fines or short jail sentences. But they did preserve a tradition, "kept the light burning," as they said, during a time when church institutions surrendered their claim to integrity. On the balance, such invisible opposition did not compare with the resistance of Germans who risked their lives to shelter Nazism's victims or attack its defenders.

Catholics' responses to the euthanasia program of 1941, however, demonstrate their capacity for moral outrage—and their potential to deflect seriously (if not to halt) a program. News of the heavily laden buses with the blackened windows traveling to a "clinic" in the Black Forest and then leaving without any passengers aroused worries. Relatives of euthanasia victims would receive highly improbable explanations for death, together with the victims' ashes. Catholics, like Protestants, objected to the very idea of "mercy killings." But even the few who might have accepted mercy killing deplored the bungling and secrecy. One Catholic woman wrote to the local Nazi leader.

> I could only find peace if I had the certainty that, through a law of the Reich, it was possible to release people from their incurable sufferings. This is a good deed both for the patient himself and also for the relatives. . . . I myself and my relatives stand firm on the ground of the Third Reich and we would certainly not go against such an ordinance [if it were really official].[124]

Opposition could spring from many sources. Apart from these mundane and ambiguous efforts at resistance, a few Catholic women distinguished themselves by extraordinary courage. We have only a few histories and will never know whether they represent the tip of an iceberg or its entire mass. Often Catholics reached out beyond their own religious circles, to political organizations and to victims. Maria Grollmuss was one such woman. In the last years of World War I she began her university studies and continued through her Ph.D. in 1925 (with a dissertation on German resistance to Napoleon). At the university she broke out of her Catholic upbringing and made friends among student radicals. "Politics stands alongside religion and love," she would say as she integrated Catholic and Socialist principles. As her guide, she referred to Rosa Luxemburg's prison letters and to nature. "The loneliness of the summer fields, the colorful berries, animals' soft eyes, all these quiet things give the woman's soul the strength to keep on fighting."[125] During the first weeks of Nazi power, Grollmuss sensed the growing danger and knew she belonged in the opposition. Because her family had summered in their house near the Czech border for years, she believed that she could do the most good by moving there to act as a courier and to smuggle anti-Nazis to safety. Her fluent Czech and trustworthy neighbors aided her in her work and after a few months she began to feel safe. One day when she was engrossed in a conversation with a colleague, a black limousine parked outside and the Gestapo surrounded the house. She was arrested and never tried. After three years of hard labor, a judge offered her the chance to recant and return to freedom. She told him, "I stand behind what I did; and I would do the same thing again, even knowing I would be arrested." After six more years of hard labor, she was transferred to the women's concentration camp at Ravensbruck and killed in 1944 at the age of forty.

During the worst of the anti-Semitic persecutions, a network of Catholic women worked to establish an underground railway out of Germany. We have only the barest information about the group of women around Dr. Gertrud Luckner, who set up a War Aid Station to help "non-Aryans" escape via Freiburg, Switzerland, and Vienna. Luckner, with a degree in economics and a Ph.D. in social science, had been active in the Catholic peace movement before 1933. Upon hearing about the Nazis' racial persecution, she decided to work for Catholic Charities to help the victims. Using her position with Catholic Charities as a cover, she and her co-workers sent packages of food to deported people—"as long as we believed it mattered." Then, by 1939, they realized that it did not. She received what she called "huge sums," probably from Freiburg's notoriously pro-Nazi Archbishop Gröber, who experienced a change of heart after World War II began. In 1942, Luckner understood that "deportation" meant death for Jews, and began her rescue operation. Luckner went about her business with extraordinary courage, convinced, it seemed to some, of her own invulnerability. But on March 24, 1943, the SS arrested her en route to Berlin with RM 5,000 to be used to help Jews escape. After nine weeks of interrogation and months of detention, the Gestapo deported her to Ravensbruck where she remained until her liberation in May 1945. After 1945, she worked closely with an organization that fosters interfaith cooperation and advocates missionary work to convert Jews to Christianity.[126]

Alongside legends of courage appear examples of betrayal, opportunism, and fear. The frontal attack against the Church, which began in 1937, escalated with the outbreak of war. While some were brave, most Germans, whatever their faith, retreated from choice and conflict. Because the historical record will always remain fragmentary, generalization is impossible. Letters and memoirs by Catholic women with Jewish ancestry give a mixed account of bitter disappointment in individual Catholic neighbors and friends, combined with a deepening faith in the Catholic religion itself. Erna Becker-Cohen's diary epitomizes the emotional polarization of those years. With the birth of her child in 1937, Becker-Cohen's anxieties overtook her. What would become of her son, cursed with a Jewish mother and a father who was guilty of "racial crime" (i.e., marrying a Jewish woman). . . . And what of her husband? "Even though he loves me and stands by me, he will not be able to prevent others from rejecting his wife and child. How I hope God will grant the child a loving heart, because that will be his only hope for survival in this hate-filled world."[127]

With the war, the mother and son experienced such daily hostility from their neighbors that the husband found them a safe refuge in a convent on a lake in suburban Berlin. "The neighborhood was hateful," she recalled, "especially the [Nazi] woman leader." War enthusiasm endangered their very lives as Jews. After several months of peace behind convent walls, "one nun who felt particularly German told me that she could not bear to see me every day. They don't even take pity on the child." Still, as Christmas approached in 1940, Becker-Cohen remained, playing Christmas carols on the piano with a kind Dominican monk, Erwin Hus. As the isolation grew, she wrote, "I nearly collapse under the guilt with which Judaism has burdened me," and she wondered if she had been cowardly not to reconvert to Judaism. She returned to her husband at home, and life became worse. After her confessor warned her that she endangered anyone with whom she spoke, life became unbearable. By Christmas 1942, she could find consolation only in chamber music. "I sit quietly next to [my husband] and dream of another, peaceful world, in which I am a fully human being. . . . Beethoven, Bach, Brahms, and Mozart are our only friends. . . . I have no inner peace. Life is so relentlessly difficult. Torment . . . Where is God? If He cannot be found in Christians' love and goodness, where can one ever find

Him?" In March 1943, the Gestapo "removed" her to a "collection center," from which the deportations departed. Miraculously, she escaped and rushed to a nearby Catholic hospital that she knew. The sisters there could not be bothered. At that point she became a *U-Boot* (submarine) and lived underground, seeking protection in a new place every few days. As the war came to an end, she closed her diary. "How petty these people are! This super race which will not acknowledge anyone else's right to exist at all, who hated me, and shut me out. Now, they grovel for my friendship. That's harder to bear than their hatred." After the war life in exile brought only more difficulties, and in 1954 husband, wife, and son returned to Germany. "Thank God we are in Germany," she wrote, "we did not find happiness abroad [*in der Fremde*]." Germany, after all, was their home.

From Düsseldorf Gestapo files come reports of women like Else Müller Cohen, who had been raised a Catholic (without any idea she had Jewish ancestors) and joined the National Socialist Women's Organization in 1931. She discovered her Jewish family tree but, until the late 1930s, she did not worry. "I assumed that my Catholic childhood and marriage to an Aryan, and my personal dedication to the Party, counted for more. . . . After the revolution in 1933, I felt myself to be a thoroughly German woman." When the Gestapo questioned her in 1939, she sought counsel from two priests, who told her that religion can never offset race. She was sentenced to Ravensbruck, the women's concentration camp. After being released and rearrested, the Sisters of Charity secured her release in 1941 and found her work as a seamstress. As of July 1944, she disappeared from the records.[128]

The most well-known Catholic woman philosopher, Edith Stein, met a tragic end. Having been brought up in an assimilated Jewish family, she converted as a young woman and attended the university. She completed her Ph.D. under Martin Heidegger, and then pursued her academic career and also lived a devout religious life. In 1933, she joined the Carmelite Order. When the Gestapo became curious about why one sister in the convent did not register to vote (which required a certified "Aryan" family tree), the Mother Superior told the police about Stein's ancestry. Stein moved to a convent in Holland. When the Gestapo discovered her whereabouts, the nuns could not protect her. Within months she had been deported and killed.[129]

From the early spring of 1933, Catholic women, like Protestants, expected guidance from religious leaders who cooperated with the regime. This placed the women in a difficult situation because criticizing the state implicitly meant doubting the Church. Outright resistance required repudiation of the dominant religious and political powers. As Catholics,

women operated within their own subculture, far from the male ecclesiastical hierarchy and remote as well from other women's associations.
They, no less than other middle-class women, cherished their own
"woman's space." In their metaphoric spatial model, they saw themselves
as being in a lower position relative to the priests' theological and administrative authority. As women and as Catholics, they operated at the
margins of national organizations, but their central concern with cultural and social issues—childbearing, eugenics, education, and the family—placed them at the very center of Hitler's plans for breeding a
genetically superior and totally obedient future generation. As devout
Catholics they had been raised to believe they endangered their immortal
souls if they complied with Nazi eugenics laws, so when church superiors
uged them to comply, they faced a conundrum.

Like the Protestant women, Catholic women's organizations, which
despised the Weimar Republic, had grown accustomed to its benefits,
such as generous financial support, guarantees of free speech, and respect for religious institutions. But they feared the republic would prove
too weak in the face of atheistic Bolshevism, cultural emancipation, and
secularization. Catholic women's concerns placed them at the very heart
of the terrain over which the bishops and government officials fought:
the borders between church and state. More precisely, in keeping with
the metaphor, church and state both claimed total control over the areas
between: culture and society. These were women's spaces. Catholic
women, from childhood accustomed to operating within a religious milieu that structured their lives and dictated their values, believed that
evil existed in the world. While many Protestant women temporized and
filtered "good" from "bad" Nazi doctrines, Catholic women had been
raised with absolute principles regarding their sphere. Interference with
childbearing and the family counted as evil. Catholic women's organizations laid down a strict doctrinal position that enhanced their decision
to remain aloof from direct negotiations with Nazi women. When the
"walls" of the church eroded, many women rebuilt them around their
own *Frauenland*, within which they fought to keep their faith free of
paganism and their families far from Nazi indoctrination. Bound absolutely by a total faith and a doctrine that guided every aspect of their
lives, the Catholic women who opposed Nazi rule preserved private
spaces of freedom. Like Protestants, they did not so much work for the
demise of the Nazi state as attempt to keep their distance from its claims.

9

COURAGE AND CHOICE: WOMEN WHO SAID NO

Rebellious thought cannot dispense with memory.
—Albert Camus
The Rebel

We, as women, have learned and forgotten more than they have ever set down in books. . . . We are sustained in our weakness by something they have never even heard a whisper of.

—Kay Boyle
"Decision"

Hundreds of books and articles have been written about (and occasionally by) the Germans who said No to Nazism. As the Third Reich recedes into the past, these works do not slide neatly into what we normally call history. Historians reconstruct the past in order to explain the events they chronicle. They disentangle the web of causes that enabled Hitler to gain power, analyze the factors that drew Germans into the mesh of Hitler's state, and above all ask how the Nazi system functioned. They explain what went wrong; who went crazy; and who ought to have done what when. But resistance against the Nazis defies this sort of analysis for methodological, as well as emotional and ethical, reasons. Sociologists and psychologists generalized about the backgrounds of Germans who tended to support and oppose Nazism at particular times.[1] But no one has analyzed why a tiny minority of individuals within generally anti-Nazi communities risked their lives for a value system they knew was morally right in a world that had gone wrong—in which conventional maxims such as "Thou shalt not kill" and "Love thy neighbor" were inverted to "Hate thy neighbor if he/she is Jewish, Communist, an enemy of the state, or 'asocial' " or "Look the other way while your 'racially unworthy' neighbor is taken away.' "

Inspired by the courage and integrity of those Germans who said a resounding No! to Nazism, we keep the record, disinclined to analyze, but wanting to admire and to reconstruct a narrative, preserve a tradition that very nearly died out. Admiring what they cannot explain, scholars of the resistance write in the traditions of Plutarch, hagiography, and martyrology. Chroniclers of the resistance ponder individual choices in all their unpredictable complexity.

Methodological problems in evaluating the sources on resistance against Nazism are legion. The fragmentary evidence and random source material upon which this chapter is based contrasts with the documentation for the earlier chapters. Women who participated in pro-Nazi movements (unlike their enemies) operated in clearly defined, coherent settings. By contrast, resistance against Nazi rule emanated from tiny islands of people acting semiautonomously to aid victims escape, to protest, to undercut morale, and to transmit news about Nazi oppression. In the Nazified world, by contrast, members of one faith or association shared points of reference and ideals. And they kept records. While they are sometimes difficult to locate, masses of documentation on the workings of the Nazi state have been preserved. Catholic and Protestant archives too, measure their holdings in running meters. We can read foreign reporters' accounts from the period and peruse secret reports on microfilm. But women in the resistance dared to trust only a very few other people and typically did not know the names (coded or otherwise) of more than a handful of comrades.

In true *1984* style, the Nazi system blotted out the memory of its victims almost as efficiently as it killed them. When we do retrieve names, facts, biographical detail, and primary accounts, we cannot know if we have discovered a representative case that hints at thousands of unrecorded deeds, or if we have stumbled on a unique display of courage. At no time did Germans who opposed Nazism organize military or terrorist activities, as did the resistance in occupied nations during World War II. Hence, we have no newspaper accounts of a major action here or an assassination there and no police records tracking down a centralized command force. Further complicating the historian's task is the fact that records (when they exist at all) are most complete for individuals who resisted and failed; successful resisters, by definition, remained undetected. Because no one working in a clandestine network would have kept a diary or even an accurate date book, primary sources about anti-Nazis have been spoken or written retrospectively or by the Gestapo at the time. A study of women within the opposition to Hitler confronts all these problems plus the added difficulty that until very recently most people assumed resistance was a man's affair, often with the innuendo that women accepted Nazis more easily than men.

H. G. Wells found it astonishing that "There has been no perceptible woman's movement to resist the practical obliteration of their freedom by Fascists or Nazis."[2] As the previous chapters demonstrate, those organized women from whom Wells expected protest adapted rather easily to Nazi rule because they shared two fundamental tenets of Nazism: intense nationalism and a deep belief in women's separate *Lebensraum*. But it would be inaccurate to conclude from the complicity of most non-Socialist women's organizations that women in general played no role in the opposition to Hitler. Wells is correct in one respect. Women *as women* did not in general resist. Nazi power severed male from female worlds, but resistance networks depended upon women and men working closely together. Women who opposed Hitler did so in the context of a clandestine and integrated subculture, whose history has been recorded by men. Because resistance in Germany was nonviolent, it did not depend upon the military skills normally attributed to men. Rather, active opponents of Nazi rule survived by applying skills that the culture normally considers as feminine: deception, analyzing the enemy's personality, manipulating weaknesses of the more powerful, and cultivating an innocuous appearance.

In one sense, then, adjusting the historical record by focusing only on women in oppositional networks is artificial. The emphasis on women in the previous chapters accurately reflected the subjects' experiences. Women Nazis, Protestants, and Catholics lived their public lives separate from men. Opponents, by contrast, guarded their humanity in an integrated society of people from varied backgrounds and both sexes. To pull women out of that context skews their experiences. Nevertheless, I have chosen to write of the women because most historical accounts have all but omitted discussion of women's roles in the opposition to Hitler, and, more importantly, because women's experience of a shared reality differed from men's in crucial ways.

This chapter, in terms of subject matter and source material, differs from the earlier chapters in this book. It is also distinct organizationally, because it does not present a chronological account of one cohesive group of people. Instead, it begins by asking why Hitler's takeover occasioned so *little* active opposition among those who hated all he stood for, then compares degrees of opposition among women, and inquires about the motives that inspired individual choices. In every case, women risked their lives to aid the victims of Nazism, but also to preserve their ideals.

Ultimately, each individual in the Third Reich faced his or her own conscience and decided between "yes" and "no." Most answered "maybe" and did not ask too many questions. Guided by religious, intellectual, and political leaders they trusted, most Germans cooperated with the Nazi regime even if they disagreed with some of its policies. Opposition, when it finally did develop within mainstream circles, came only late, and was born of disillusionment with Hitler, not opposition to his goals. Even the few brave Catholic and Protestant leaders who spoke out against specific Nazi policies reaffirmed their fundamental loyalty to both the person of the Führer and his policies. When Hitler failed, they accused him of betrayal. After a few years of Nazi rule, untold numbers of youths in Germany rebelled against the uniformity of Nazi life. In the Ruhr, for example, gangs of young men and some young women calling themselves the Edelweiss Pirates routinely defied the Gestapo and harassed the police.[3] Some opponents, like the members of the White Rose group around the Scholl Family, were young; others, like Count von Stauffenberg, belonged to an older generation and operated at the very center of Nazi power. Many disillusioned Germans who decided to "give Hitler a chance" during the 1930s realized their error only after World War II began. I will exclude these opposition movements born of disenchantment from consideration in this chapter and investigate instead those Germans who from the very outset of the Third Reich opposed Hitler's fundamental aims.

How can we assess who despised the principles of Nazi rule? A rough estimate must include the 13 million Communists and Socialists (about one-third of the 1932 electorate). In addition, many voters from the ranks of the liberal and moderate parties must have felt betrayed when their leaders acquiesced to Hitler's demand for dictatorial power in March 1933. Still, the overwhelming majority of all Germans from non-Nazi backgrounds found ways of existing under a regime they despised. If they had "Aryan" family trees and no major Socialist activities to mar their records, they could, and almost everyone did, conclude a truce with the new regime. A few even cooperated with the Nazis, but in so doing they had to face up to the fact that they betrayed their respective heritages and disappointed longtime friends. It is difficult to know how common such betrayal was, but people who went over to the enemy earned contempt from both sides. Communists and Nazis ridiculed such turncoats as "beefsteak Nazis"—red on the inside and brown outside. Private misgivings notwithstanding, their decision to collaborate brought a measure of security to them and their families. At the other end of the statistical and ideological spectrum were the 20,000 Jehovah's Witnesses who, practically to a person, unequivocally refused to render any form of obedience to the Nazi state.[4] In addition, nearly 500,000 Jews existed in so vulnerable a situation; their reactions will be discussed separately.

Contemporaries wondered about the lack of opposition in 1933. As a journalist writing for *Le Temps* put it, "Hitler's enemies defend themselves with a timidity that contrasts starkly with the Nazis' hardness."[5] Although the possible answers to this question do not add up to a completely satisfying answer, several factors played a role.

People who took major risks to oppose the Nazi state had to believe that their actions would win approval, that other Germans besides themselves would welcome liberation. Many of Hitler's opponents lost that belief in 1933 as they saw non-Nazis acquiesce. Millions who had not voted Nazi in March 1933 felt utterly disoriented by the extraordinary success of Hitler's propaganda *Blitzkrieg* and succumbed to the drama of torchlight parades, a Reichstag in flames, and a powerful authoritarian leader. Klaus Mann spoke for his disillusioned countrymen when he said, "My mistake was not that I underrated Schickelgruber [Hitler's father's born name] but that I overrated the Germans. They were smitten with his grammatical howlers and brassy lies, his slimy humor, his illiteracy, his bullying, his whining, his nervous fits, his half-crazed megalomania. . . . What is wrong with the Germans?"[6] Mann despaired as he watched people who had voted against the Nazis in the March 1933 elections decide to yield rather than fight. Protestants, Catholics, moderate conservatives, nationalists, and liberals listened as their national leaders told them to cooperate with the regime that had saved the nation from Marxism. Most of these non-Nazis found some aspects of the dictatorship distasteful. Some disliked Hitler's style; others laughed at his "crackpot" economic schemes; others worried about his bellicose rhetoric; and most criticized his hostility toward religion. People (we will never know how many) who had not previously voted Nazi made their peace—or at least a provisional truce—with Nazism. Within a few weeks in the spring of 1933, Hitler had shifted the national consensus so sharply in his direction that moderate opponents realized that they had been outbid.

Before accepting foreigners' or exiles' comments about cowardly Germans, we ought to remember how arbitrary much of the Nazi repression was. Even the smallest acts had consequences, often graver than people realized. Individuals later recalled that their lives changed radically, if only in small but symbolic ways. The shopkeeper who said "hello" instead of "*Heil Hitler!*" to her customers lost business. The housewife who contributed to Catholic Charities and did not drop a few pennies into the Nazi Winter Relief box fell under state-employed social workers' suspicion. Students told police about the teacher who told her class, "Long live Germany!" and then added, "And all other peace-loving nations." Often, too, suspected "opponents" (usually Communists and Socialists) were arrested preemptively before they had actually committed any "crime." In Kiel, a woman grumbled to her grocer, "Hitler hasn't made anything better," and within twenty-four hours she had been sentenced to ten months of hard labor. The most common crime for which women were arrested during the early years of the Third Reich was making offensive comments. For example, in Munich (one of the very few cities for which records exist), the most common crime for which women were tried before the Special Court was based on the December 12, 1934, *Heimtückegesetz* (Law Against Malicious Gossip).[7] Thus, a Bavarian peasant woman might be sent to prison for repeating the following joke to a neighbor, who then reported her to authorities. "Why does Hitler press his cap against his abdomen when reviewing parades? Answer: He is protecting the last unemployed member of the *Volk*."

Olga Koerner, an ex–Reichstag delegate, and Emma Beier, a former city councillor, each spent two years in prison because Gestapo searches of their homes turned up expired Communist Party membership cards. Women were particularly affected by the practice of arresting members of the households of individuals who had escaped. Often male leaders departed quickly, leaving children and wives as potential hostages. The Gestapo also tortured servants (typically women) of "suspects," until their employers had been captured.[8] A worse fate than arrest awaited other hostages. When, for example, the Gestapo decided to retaliate against Erich Maria Remarque because he made an anti-Nazi broadcast from the United States, they arrested his sister, Elfriede Scholz, who later died in prison. Although no records describe her death, the Gestapo no doubt gave her a chance to publicly denounce her brother in exchange for her life.[9]

Fearing that criticism of the popular new leader would reflect badly on them, not Nazism, some of Hitler's rivals muted their criticism and watched from the sidelines. Annie Kienast, a young Socialist, recalled her response in 1933. "Too many people were enchanted by the Nazis. We were totally surprised, depressed, and despairing when neither the Socialist Party nor its paramilitary forces nor the labor unions called us to battle. We felt totally disoriented. We hid our weapons and pamphlets."[10] Hannah Tillich's memoirs convey a similar theme. "The *Machtergreifung* [seizure of power] . . . left us and our friends . . . with a feeling of uttermost helplessness. We had been glued to the radio, listening to the election returns, when we heard the summary announcement claiming for Hitler the number of votes he needed for victory. Overnight Germany had become a country of block wards. . . ."[11] Hannah and Paul Tillich gave up. A prestigious theologian with an international reputation had options ordinary people did not have in the depths of an international Depression.

Although with hindsight it seems scarcely credible, people who lived through the period say they simply could not realize the extent of the danger presented by Hitler's chancellorship. Communists confidently predicted that a Hitler dictatorship would deepen the crisis of capitalism, which in turn would generate massive support for their revolutionary politics. The Communist International told German Communists not to oppose Hitler because the Social Democrats presented a worse threat to Communist plans for revolution. Some opposition leaders who ought to have known better even expected the Nazi government to respect civil rights and the Constitution. After the Reichstag fire, for example, the head of the Communist Reichstag delegation received news that he would be arrested. Fearing that flight would make him appear guilty, he stayed home. When the Gestapo pulled him rudely from his bed, he complied willingly with the arrest orders because he knew he had not broken the law and expected to defend his honor in court. Within the week he was incarcerated in Dachau.

The Socialist Party, too, urged caution on its followers. Before January 1933, its leaders had boasted that Hitler could accomplish nothing as long as their voting bloc held strong. And they threatened an armed uprising by Marxist fighting units in the event of a Nazi coup. None came. Hitler did not stage the sort of coup they expected, but manipulated Weimar political leaders into ceding power to him. And paramilitary formations never marched. When votes ceased to count, the left had no alternative strategy. Socialist leaders urged their members to destroy their party cards and Marxist literature that might be used as evidence against them.

While Hitler's enemies on the left debated whether his government really presented a threat or not, the Gestapo and SA lost no time. During the first months after Hitler became Chancellor, the escalating level of violence claimed many completely innocent people as its victims. SA men, disappointed that Hitler had deprived them of the chance at fighting a violent revolution, often became trigger-happy during demonstrations. One afternoon in February 1933, a woman in a working-class residential district looked out of her window as an unruly SA demonstration passed by. A loudspeaker warned people to close their windows. She did not. Within seconds, she had been shot dead. By a marksman or a stray bullet? We do not know. The London *Times* called her a "humble working class creature to whom not even the press of the Right troubles to attach the label 'communist.' "[12] Terror—massive, swift, and random —silenced many Germans. A few statistics give a rough idea of the extent of Nazi repression. In January 1933, 300,000 Germans had belonged to the Communist Party; one year later, half of them were in jails and camps or dead. Most who were free went into exile. In the aftermath of the Reichstag fire, police imprisoned 18,000 suspected Communists. During the next few months they executed 200 "political enemies," most of whom were Socialists or Communists.[13] In March and April alone, 25,000 "detainees" had been sent to prisons and concentration camps in Prussia.[14] By October 1933, the death toll among all "enemies of the state" had risen to over 500 men and women. While the media spoke of a "cleanup" and a "battle against terrorism," 3 million suspects were arrested for questioning in 1933. At any given time between 1933 and 1939, at least 150,000 Germans were confined to workhouses and concentation camps for political crimes. Between 1933 and 1939, it is estimated that a million anti-Nazis served jail terms. Wartime drove those statistics still higher. Between 1933 and 1945, over 7 million Europeans would be cast into concentration camps and "deported" to extermination centers; only 500,000 survived.

At every stage of Nazi terror, most foreigners and Germans chose to believe the news only after it was too late.[15] Hitler launched a brilliant propaganda drive that portrayed his police state as orderly and disciplined while unleashing ruthless terror on an almost inconceivable scale. The Gestapo and SS, in the tradition of Robespierre, blended a fastidious concern for order with savage brutality and pretensions of virtue. Murder, threats, and prison haunted Socialists, Communists, labor union leaders, and Jehovah's Witnesses who refused to swear loyalty to the Nazi state. Without warning, the legal system, judges, and police, from which even the most cynical expected some sort of protection, became instruments of violence. Cautious people dared not display their sentiments overtly and realists knew better than to embark on futile escapades.

Hundreds of thousands of Germans, faced with ruthless state terror and fearful for themselves and their loved ones, assessed their situation realistically and escaped psychologically or geographically. A member of the Women's International League for Peace and Freedom bluntly explained this choice. "What's the point of resistance? It could lead only to defeat." Although she and a few friends met regularly and secretly throughout the Third Reich, they at no time contemplated active resistance or recruitment of new members.[16] Christabel Bielenberg, a young British woman who relinquished her nationality in 1934 to marry a Socialist lawyer, recalled how simple it was to maintain one's integrity without collaborating with Nazi rule or actively resisting it. "There was nothing to prevent us from showing our disapproval by lack of cooperation. . . . And we had learned to watch out for the subtle signs from others who were doing the same."[17] Many Germans, protected by birth, reputation, foreign connections, or simply good fortune, lived in the Third Reich they detested. Often they met under the guise of a social gathering or hiking expedition to share their discontent openly in their closed circles.

The main purpose of such secret communities lay in the preservation of the members' ideals and sanity. "We lived in a community bound by an oath," said one woman after the war, as she thought back on her group's efforts to spread disillusionment with Nazi rule among neighbors and friends. "It was trivial work for a great cause. . . . We were little people, workers, artists, and scholars, without an organization." In her opinion, genuine resistance lay not with the much-publicized plot against Hitler's life in 1944, but with "the ordinary Germans who in their daily life took risks to dampen morale."[18] Such communities, much like their counterparts among religious dissenters, worked to preserve a faith, not to overthrow a state.

Afterward, Germans who had participated in these discussion groups told of their opposition to Hitler. Their pride raises interpretive questions. Take, for example, the case of political scientist Margaret Boveri, who in private bitterly condemned Hitler. Many of her friends participated in the Red Orchestra plot during World War II, but she opposed revolt on the "patriotic" grounds that because Hitler remained the nation's legitimate ruler, citizens had no right to rebel.[19] She lived a comfortable enough life, and after the war justified her choice in a widely read book called *Treason in the Twentieth Century*. This convenient position enabled millions to swear their allegiance to Nazism before 1945 and to assure the Allied occupation forces that they had opposed Hitler all along. Immediately after the war, West Germans exalted the courage of such "spiritual resistance" among the elite that guided the post-1945 nation toward capitalism and NATO.[20] We cannot ascertain how many Germans fell into this category, since in 1945 virtually everyone described his or her life in Nazi Germany as "silent opposition." If "resistance" is to have any meaning at all, it does not apply to those Germans. But complexities arise.

As we attempt aided by hindsight to evaluate the impact or the morality of this choice, other examples come to mind. Did it serve the Nazi cause to fulfill one's minimal obligations to the state while preserving a private world (usually among family or trusted friends) where humane values prevailed? What about the parents who hated Nazism yet feared their own children? A second set of questions relates to the circumstances of each individual. Elderly people not only had deeper roots in German society, but many fewer options to emigrate. The lives of two well-known women, both in their late sixties, illustrate the difficulties of rendering a clear judgment of what Germans call "internal immigration."

Ricarda Huch, a popular poet and writer, lived in Germany under the Nazi regime she detested. Her books were not banned, and she received permission to lecture. Gertrud Bäumer honored her birthday in *Die Frau*. After the war Huch wrote a tribute to Germans in the resistance. Käthe Kollwitz, an artist with long-standing ties to Communism, also remained in Nazi Germany. Huch and Kollwitz submitted their family trees to demonstrate their "Jew-free" lineage and were admitted to the National Socialist Writers' and Artists' unions. Sensing the impossibility of active revolt from within Germany, both women chose to wait out the Nazi years without openly confronting their enemies.[21] Kollwitz filled out official questionnaires, but always irreverently: "citizenship? Prussian; religion? dissidentic [*sic*]; public monuments designed? only to the dead." She remained a member of the appropriate Nazi guilds that enabled her to continue her work, although she did not publish and exhibited only rarely. Amazingly, in 1942, she was allowed to exhibit her graphics in Bremen. The police reports expressed outrage—first *that* a Communist sympathizer could show her work at all, and secondly because the press notices were so favorable. They also criticized her "utter refusal" to "adapt" to Nazism. In 1942, a London resistance group praised her as "a great artist and—an almost rarer thing still—a fine human being."[22]

As long as they *did* nothing and protected no one, silent dissenters did not dislodge power in the Third Reich. Indeed, if they were well known, their very decision to live in Hitler's state enhanced the claim that Germany was not such a bad place after all, provided one was not Jewish—and over 99 percent of all Germans were not. Untold thousands who despised Nazism loved their families and refused to consider putting them in jeopardy. Non- and anti-Nazis who eschewed political activism withdrew into their private space and enjoyed a certain freedom. "Liberty to breathe provided you don't breathe too deeply; liberty to sleep if your conscience permits it; liberty to work if not too many questions are asked," as Kay Boyle described this fenced-in freedom.[23]

For thousands of Germans, however, that was not enough. Longing to breathe deeply in a liberated society, they lived a breathless, wary, and anxious existence. Even those who fled from Germany lived in constant dread of arrest. Dorothy Thompson remarked in the mid-1930s, "Practically everybody who in world opinion had stood for what was currently called German culture prior to 1933 is now a refugee."[24] Sometimes people became exiles almost by accident. For example, Lida Gustava Heymann and Anita Augspurg, leading feminists since the 1890s, happened to be vacationing in Italy during the winter of 1933. They decided not to return until the Nazis had been defeated. Neither lived to see the day.[25] Helene Stöcker, longtime crusader for reproductive rights, left at once for exile.[26]

Most who chose exile were younger and believed they could oppose Nazism more effectively and earn a living outside Germany; often, however, they returned to their homeland with severe consequences. The examples of Lotte Eisner, Johanna Kirchner, Maria Juchacz, Irene Wosikowski, and Käthe Niederkirchner illustrate women's different options and choices. They demonstrate, too, the risks faced by activists who chose not to compromise. Lotte Eisner, prominent film critic and collaborator with Henri Langois in the Cinémathèque Française in Paris, looked back on her departure from Berlin and recalls, "I didn't even decide to leave. Fortunately for me, the Gestapo made it absolutely clear I had no future in Germany." One day in March 1933, as she was about to leave home for her office at a left-wing journal of film criticism, the phone rang; a voice said, "Take the day off. The Gestapo ransacked the office and destroyed the presses." Eisner, a radical and a Jew, packed her belongings and took a sleeper to Paris, where her sister lived. "That was the last time I ever traveled first-class." After the fall of France, she was arrested and escaped, then went into hiding as a cook in a girls' school and joined the resistance under the name Louise Escoffier.[27] Eisner managed to survive the occupation and salvage the films that comprised Cinémathèque. The German government invited her to return to the Berlin Film Festival in the mid-1950s, which she did, but she traveled under her underground name Louise Escoffier and spoke only French.

Johanna Kirchner decided to leave her children in Frankfurt and to work with German Socialist exiles along the French border. Daughter of working-class parents, she had grown up in an atmosphere of political debates, campaigns, and long meetings. As a teenager in the early 1900s, she had joined the Socialist Youth League. Shortly thereafter she married a Socialist. Their children thrilled to stories about their ancestors' heritage and especially liked to hear tales about the time when Grandma had hidden red flags under her petticoats during the anti-Socialist raids in the 1880s.[28] During the Third Reich, Johanna Kirchner carried on the tradition. In a small Alsatian city she found work as a waitress and provided shelter for refugees as they crossed the border. When the residents of the region voted in a plebiscite to join Germany rather than France, the Gestapo noted that "Frau Kirchner was not gripped by the overwhelming wave of enthusiasm," and put her name on the "wanted" list. Meanwhile, she escaped to the nearby French town of Forbach and contined her work. The Gestapo watched her children cross the German border to visit their mother, but never arrested them. "You can see to what depravity the woman has sunk," the police noted, "when you see her exploiting her children for political purposes."[29] Kirchner aided veterans of the Spanish Civil War and edited a clandestine newspaper that reported on conditions in Nazi Gemany. When the Germans occupied France, Kirchner fled once again, but the French police arrested her and sent her to a French concentration camp. From there she was extradited, tried, and executed in May 1944. In her farewell letter, she told her daughters to "remain brave and utterly loyal. Don't let pain weigh you down. Think of Goethe's words, 'Stirb und Werde ['Die and become'] . . .' Please please do not cry. . . . Your love and your courage are my consolation and comfort in my last hours. . . . A better future is coming for you. My love stays with you always."

Former Socialist Reichstag delegate Maria Juchacz also went into exile in the Forbach area and, like Kirchner, provided shelter and food to refugees from Germany; despite Gestapo harassment and Vichy surveillance, however, she managed to escape and returned to an active public life after 1945.

Irene Wosikowski, a native of Hamburg, was twenty-four when the Nazis came to power. As a Communist, she participated in anti-Nazi activities until 1935, when she received news that the police had issued an arrest order for her. She managed to escape to Marseilles. After the fall of France she joined the resistance there. When the Nazi armed forces occupied the south of France in July 1942, she and thousands of German exiles were sent to the French concentration camp at Gurs. She escaped miraculously and took on the task of talking to Nazi soldiers in the occupation force to undermine their faith in Hitler until French police arrested and deported her. On September 27, 1944, she was executed. In her last letter, she assured her mother that she regretted none of her decisions, but apologized for not being a good daughter. "Except for this I bear my fate, certain that you would not have wanted me to act otherwise. . . ."[30] Other women, with the option of remaining abroad, evaluated their situation differently.

Besides suffering material hardship in foreign countries where they felt unwelcome, many anti-Nazis abroad felt deep homesickness and succumbed to their longing. Often, too, they felt guilty at not being able to participate more actively in the resistance. Käthe Niederkirchner grew up as a leader in Berlin's Young Socialist circles and also participated in sports. During the Weimar Republic she had been jailed for her participation in the Communist transportation strike, so when Hitler seized power she was twenty-four years old and in jail. When the Nazis released her she fled to France, where she remained for the next decade. In 1943 the longing to see her homeland drove her to return. She was arrested at once, sent to the workhouse, and then to a concentration camp. In September 1944 she wrote from her cell, "My dear, good Hilde . . . every day I say good-bye to life and think they will come for me tonight. But then it is dawn again and the torment begins anew. Will they come today?" A few days later she added, "This morning the director read out my sentence with such disgust and scorn. The Beasts! They have gotten so used to murder that they take a special pleasure as they graze on their victims' misery. Tonight they will surely come. Oh, how much I wanted to live to see the dawn of a new age."[31] These women who opted for exile and resistance paid heavily for their choice. Besides aiding refugees and surviving themselves, they preserved a tradition. But very few lived to witness the liberation.

Accounts of resistance nearly always end in martyrdom, as Ricarda Huch put it in 1946. "It was not granted to them to save Germany; it was only granted to them to die."[32] When they pitted their wits and principles against the Gestapo state, surely they experienced the truth of Camus' postwar comment, "Rebellion is not realistic." Realistic or not, what did Hitler's opponents expect to accomplish in 1933? Clara Zetkin, a dominant force within the Social Democratic Party before 1914 and during the 1920s in the Communist Party, enunciated the priorities. Like so many opponents of Nazism, she assumed that Hitler would soon discredit himself and fall from power. She did not urge violence, but called for, "solidarity with those who fight and material aid to preserve life for the victims of murderous fascism; that is the most pressing need of the hour for everyone who emotionally and intellectually abhors the crimes of fascist terror."[33] She did not translate this vague appeal into a plan for revolution or even suggest who the "fighters" were. Socialist flyers urged individuals to "build cells in your places of work. Form groups wherever you find people who agree. Take a firm stand!" What was a firm stand in Nazi Germany, and how could an individual who hated Nazi rule act without firm leadership? Ironically, the two forces in domestic politics with international institutional power, the Communist Party and the Catholic Church, both opposed radical protests against Nazism during 1933. Thus the first resisters acted out of their own consciences on an ad hoc basis. Without thinking through long-term aims or unified strategies, they voiced their opinions and opposed injustice much as they had during the Weimar Republic. Some Communists and Socialists worked individually to overthrow Nazi power before it became deeply entrenched. Too often, they overestimated their own strength and misjudged their fellow citizens. The lives of Lore Wolf, Franziska Kessel, a couple known only as Willi and Maria, Hedwig Laufer, and Grete Messing illustrate individual assessments of the situation and represent the courage and integrity of the few.

Lore Wolf had traveled widely in Europe, the United States, and Soviet Russia. As it happened, she resided abroad with an emigration permit during the early months of Nazi power. Wolf returned immediately to help her family in Germany, after making sure her exit visa and work permit would enable her to return to France. When no one welcomed her at the station, she felt something amiss. A stranger sought her out and whispered, "Don't collect your bags. Gestapo waiting." But she had brought presents and went to the baggage room. Within ten minutes, police officials had confiscated her passport, exit visa, work permit, and baggage. Looking back, she tried to explain her failure to comprehend Nazi reality. Years of faith in the Communist Party had imbued her with the certainty that Hitler's rule by its violence would touch off a world revolution against capitalism. She returned to Germany convinced that victory was only months away. During the next twelve years she worked underground with false identity papers and a strong network of comrades. She was arrested twenty times, but each time managed to escape or secure release to survive Nazi defeat.[34]

Because the first victims of planned arrests were frequently leading politicians and because relatively few women were politicians, women fared rather better than men at first. But they were not completely exempt. Of over one hundred women from all parties who had served in the Weimar Reichstag, more than a third were arrested within months of Hitler's takeover.[35] Committed to political action, they had refused to surrender passively. In early 1933, a Communist ex–Reichstag delegate, Franziska Kessel, took over the direction of the Communist women's group in Frankfurt and continued to speak and write against Nazi terror. Because she had been arrested several times during the Weimar Republic, she believed she could withstand Nazi repression as well. Within weeks, her name appeared on Gestapo "most wanted" lists and she went underground, but continued to gather facts about Nazi prisons and torture. Escaping to France under a false name, she presented the truth about Nazi terror to an international conference in Paris. In early 1934, she chose to rejoin the underground in Germany and asked an acquaintance in Frankfurt, Frau Senger, to provide her with shelter in her home. Frau Senger, herself vulnerable as a Jew, an immigrant without proper papers, and a Communist, sheltered Kessel. But she worried. Her son, Valentin Senger, recalled, "She made her point. Our guest left us the following night. Later she was arrested . . . the plain truth was that Mama's fears for her family were stronger than any ties of solidarity with a comrade in flight."[36] In the spring of 1934 Kessel was betrayed and arrested in a nearby town. Shortly afterward, at age twenty-eight, she was murdered in her cell.[37] Kessel, like so many radical politicians, had grown accustomed to taking risks, and a decade of experience in a democratic setting had not equipped her with the paranoia needed for a clandestine existence in Nazi Germany.

Annemarie Jacobs, like Kessel a seasoned political organizer, did not await orders but immediately participated in drafting a call for "Political Mass Strikes against the Hitler-Papen-Dictatorship." She and a few comrades distributed over 200,000 copies. Then they printed 100,000 copies of a pamphlet accusing Hitler of planning the Reichstag Fire. Convinced that demonstrations could halt Hitler's march to power, they used tactics they had always used in Weimar democracy. Tragically, they failed to be sufficiently wary of spies, and by 1934 the entire cell of activists was in jail.[38]

Other members of the political resistance behaved more cautiously. Fear of betrayal motivated Socialist and Communist youth to close ranks into tiny groups of trusted friends, united by not only ideals but years of shared political activism. In August 1933, Anna Nolan in Munich established secret contacts with young Communists in Augsburg so they could distribute copies of the The Young Guard. Within a few months, Nolan and twenty-two comrades were sentenced to prison.[39] At about the same time, Katharine Haag joined a group of five young people in another section of Munich. Every week or ten days, they met to exchange information and distribute illegal literature calling for an uprising against Hitler. By 1936, these and virtually all other small groups in Bavaria had been arrested. Few survived the Second World War.[40] Until the end of 1933, some Socialists and Communists placed a great faith on an uprising for which no plans whatsoever had been made.

Few people, politicians or otherwise, imagined the sadism of their new rulers. Beneath a carefully cultivated image of martial order with columns of impeccably uniformed, goose-stepping troops lurked a realm of violence so unbelievable that many people dismissed the truth as pure invention. The regime that glorified the family ruthlessly exploited familial bonds as instruments of psychological torture. A young couple, Willi and Maria, married in 1933. Fearing the worst, they lived separately and worked out secret codes and meeting places. One day, Maria asked Willi to meet her because she had discovered she was pregnant. A Gestapo officer awaited her at the agreed-upon place. "Aha! You thought your Willi would be here. Your Willi, a ridiculous bloke, is dead." Maria refused to believe him and would not cooperate with the interrogators. The Gestapo man took her to the graveyard and exhumed his corpse. "See what you get if you're stubborn," they told her. Maria revealed no secrets, but this encounter ended her active resistance.[41] Minna Cammens distributed Social Democratic pamphlets in Bremen one Sunday in March 1933, much as she had on other weekends. A few days after her arrest, her husband received her ashes in a cigarette case.[42] The chasm between crime and punishment was scarcely conceivable.

In a small town in eastern Germany, the Gestapo ordered an elderly social worker (and longtime Socialist) to appear at the police station for questioning. When she refused to give any information, she was "stripped to the skin in the Nazi barracks and so terribly beaten that she later died in the hospital after photographs of her wounds had been taken. One of her kidneys had been crushed." A Socialist woman who was also Jewish was arrested with eighteen colleagues while at work in an employment agency. She herself was not tortured, but SA men forced her to watch as they beat up her male comrades. Then they turned to her, dragged her by the hair, and shaved patches of her scalp. After being forced to pay for the "haircut," she was released. Believing she had rights, she reported the incident to local police. The officer in charge called her crazy and said she must have cut her own hair. "I suggest you not make trouble," he warned. She notified the clandestine press but asked that her name be withheld.[43]

Hedwig Laufer from Fürth, a small town near Nuremberg, lived to recount her activities between 1933 and 1945. Apart from the fact that she survived internment, her story was typical of hundreds of women in the resistance because it illustrates a lifelong predilection to question authority and "make trouble." From childhood on, Hedwig's parents and teachers had doubted that this rebellious "black sheep" would ever amount to anything. She refused to sing in the school chorus or attend religious services. As a young woman she met other nonconformists in an Esperanto course. A rally converted her to Marxism, and she discussed politics with other women at work. "I found mostly open-minded women who understood that the fascists threatened workers. I sold *The Woman Fighter*, which was the woman's paper of the Communist Party." During the Depression she was jailed for political activism. After her release, Laufer continued her organizing. "On March 10 [1933], the first warm springlike day, we met secretly in the woods. The police arrived and searched us. Later, they searched my mother's apartment and took me away. My mother screamed at the window, 'You may just as well take me, too!' Ten days later she was also in prison." The entire membership of the Communist Party in the town of Fürth was tried as a group and sent to prison. Throughout Germany, unknown hundreds and maybe thousands of people followed their instincts and ignored their left-wing leaders' advice to "lie low." They acted on lifelong principles and suffered heavy reprisals.

Grete Messing, arrested by the Gestapo for "pro-Communist activities," managed in 1933 to obtain release from prison. As she walked through the gates to freedom, the guard saluted her with *"Heil Hitler!"* Her political reflexes intact, Messing snapped back, "Red Fighting Front!" The guard killed her. Violence so ubiquitous and random defies our comprehension and baffled opponents, especially when they had become accustomed to a state that guarantees basic rights. Victims of police attacks did not understand how suddenly traditions they regarded as natural simply disappeared.

By 1934 or 1935, opponents of Nazism recovered, regrouped, and drew up new plans. Irma Keilhack, a Socialist, recalled, "In 1933 we told ourselves, 'Germany is not Italy,' and 'the Nazis have absolutely no notion about how to solve the economic problems,' and 'the Nazis cannot begin to get us out of the insane crisis we're stuck in.' . . . All vain hopes." Even though left-wing Germans had for years warned that fascism spelled disaster, war, and repression, when the time came they did not really believe it.[44] Because they had failed to understand the Nazis' mass appeal, many Germans on the left judged Hitler by their own standards and could not imagine that he would ever manage to rule for more than a few months. Often, too, Marxists exaggerated their own strength and looked to international Socialism as a weapon against the Nazi state. The unpredictability of Nazi terror during the early months of 1933 threw Hitler's enemies off guard—much as Hitler's *Blitzkrieg* stunned western European leaders into submission in 1940. In part, however, the news blackout hampered anti-Nazis' ability to assess the danger and plan a strategy. When they began to regroup and evaluate their situation in late 1933, the creation of underground news networks replaced isolated acts of defiance as the first priority. Surveying the situation, anti-Nazis confronted two dismal realities: First, they realized the extent of the terror they faced, and secondly, they began to grasp how little most people wanted to believe the truth about Nazi violence.

Ellen Wilkinson, director of a British association to aid refugees, despaired when she heard tourists praise the "decency" and "moderation" of the "new Germany." People chose not to see the prisons, concentration camps, and torture chambers. "Silence and order have descended upon Germany. . . . Everything here is very much quieter than anyone has ever known it. No one speaks of politics at all anymore. In the trams and buses, shops and public places, any mention of politics produces shocked silence."[45]

Even foreigners with access to a free press often chose not to believe. The legacy of the First World War cast an ominous shadow. People of all nations, unaccustomed to mendacious and "slick" propaganda, had naively accepted as true whatever their leaders told them. That included hate stories about the enemy as well as false proclamations of victory. The slanderous portrayals of "the Hun" and wild atrocity stories made dramatic copy for a gullible homefront. When passions cooled and peace returned, many French and English people (especially liberals who despised the war and opposed fascism) felt shame at ever having believed such outrageous anti-German lies and vowed never to be deceived again. By the 1930s they had developed a psychological resistance to hate propaganda as well as a commitment to pacifism. The discrepancy between official pictures of wildly enthusiastic Germans and the clandestine reports of terror caused many to assume an air of detached objectivity—to "wait and see." Delayed guilt feelings about the past blunted the alarm on the part of those people who ought to have been most outraged at Nazi dictatorship.

Unless they happened to experience it personally, most Germans themselves did not realize the extent of the terror. Madeline Kent, who lived in a left-wing neighborhood, reported:

> The Nazis are perfectly accurate when they claim that their revolution barely ruffled the surface of daily life. This deed was done by daylight, because they knew how much the ordinary populace would enjoy seeing the wicked Marxists brought low, yet without bloodshed. But their blackest deeds were done under the cover of darkness, so that none but the victims' friends should know about them. Night after night we were awakened by the powerful light of police cars that had come to fetch the suspects in the settlement to concentration camps.[46]

While millions succumbed to the "crime of silence," the Nazi police made as little noise as possible.

Eyewitness accounts bring to mind the contrast between surface calm and subterranean fears described so poignantly by Ehrenburg a decade earlier. The Gestapo made its arrests during the night, and by day propaganda smothered news of torture under euphemisms. Victims were kept in "protective detention"; prisoners frequently died "of unknown causes" or "suicide" in their cells, thus avoiding the publicity of a trial; the guilty were not sent to prison, but to ninety special "rehabilitation centers," also called concentration camps, where they underwent ideological "reeducation." Germans who talk about those days recall hearing SA men in streetcars or cafés complain boastfully about their tired and stiff right arms; but to understand precisely what that meant, one had to take the risk of finding out via underground contacts. Knowledge, in any case, brought the burden of facing difficult moral and political choices. Most preferred not to know.

Whatever else Hitler's opponents did, they had first of all to break through the silence that descended behind the curtain of Nazi propaganda. This meant pitting their clandestine mimeographed leaflets and chain letters against the world's most sophisticated communications network. While Leni Riefenstahl commanded a well-funded battalion of cameramen, technical assistants, and lavish settings for her film of the 1934 Nuremberg Party Rally, opponents of the regime risked their lives to smuggle fragments of information about the underside of Nazi reality. The messages in these early pamphlets are strikingly simple. Appeals called for overthrow, resistance, and justice; and the news concerned instances of Nazi terror or hopeful reports of support from abroad. Handbills predicted "a death blow to Nazi terror!" and denounced "Gestapo swine." Inserts in library books told readers: "Hitler is a butcher!" "Nero burned Rome to persecute the Christians and Göring burned the Reichstag to persecute Communists!" "Don't kill yourself working for Nazi war!" Or simply: "Long live freedom!" A poster bearing a woodblock print of a mother and her two children read: "Save the family!" and others said: "Thou shalt not kill."[47] Women played a crucial role in the rebuilding of oppositional networks because information exchange was so vital.

Because the Nazis' claims were total, resistance workers believed that even the smallest sign of opposition cracked the facade and opened a wedge in the supposedly impervious system. We cannot assess their long-term impact, but according to Gestapo reports, twelve major groups with 6,100 members still printed and distributed anti-Nazi literature in 1935. Two years later, arrests had thinned their number to several hundred.

The paper lifeline among resisters depended upon several specifically feminine capacities. First of all, women (many of whose husbands were

in jail or underground) could meet for *Kaffee und Kuchen* in the after-
noons without arousing suspicion. While appearing to gossip, they exchanged vital and secret information concealed in shopping bags, books,
or napkins. Without a typist, the news could not reach the page. That
required not only skill, but an illegal typewriter (and/or mimeograph).
Maria Deeg (a former Socialist who became a Communist in the Depression) recalls: "The typewriter was kept in our apartment. My mother was
still alive and we sublet a room to an SA man. Since he had few possessions, I asked him if I couldn't store the washing in one of his drawers.
And along with the dirty clothes came the typewriter."[48] From then on,
whenever the police searched the house, mother and daughter would
always ask whether they wanted to inspect the room of the "old fighter."
Of course, that never happened.

To disseminate information, they needed paper. Because Nazi law
proscribed the sale of paper in large quantities to unauthorized people,
women would take their babies for a stroll in the carriage. In large cities
they would purchase small quantities of paper from as many as fifty stores
in one day. At night the mimeograph would turn. Finally, the pamphlets
and handbills had to be distributed; the news had to be sent abroad; and
paper is heavy and difficult to hide. Carola Karg, disguised as a pregnant
peasant woman, made dozens of border crossings at different check-
points, each time chatting informally with the guards while carrying
pounds of illegal printed matter beneath her maternity dress.[49] Gertrud
Staewen, a Protestant, told about the circle of women from all backgrounds who used to collect motherhood medals in order to pin them on
Jewish women who then (accompanied by their own or borrowed children) would escape across the Swiss border.[50]

Everywhere in Germany, women with babies and buggies would take
strolls, chat amiably with Gestapo officers, and drop forged identity papers and illegal printed matter at pickup points. One woman member of
a resistance circle was carrying a suitcase filled with illegal pamphlets
across Berlin when suddenly she confronted a spot check. Approaching
the policeman, she cried for help. "I'm in my fourth month." They
smoked a cigarette as she told him of her husband's great interest in
collecting Grimms' fairy tales, the books on top of the hidden material.[51]

The covers of many resistance pamphlets suggested another way in
which women played an important part. Much illegal literature was disguised as harmless reading material—and logically addressed to the most
harmless readers. Who but the housewife became the putative reader for
booklets entitled, "Eleven Ways to Better Vegetarian Cooking," "Excen-
tric [sic] Shampoo," or "New Blood with Biomalt and Iron"?[52] Women
and men found other ways to spread the word. Workers might discover

scraps of paper on the conveyor belts with crudely lettered slogans; pedestrians occasionally noticed graffiti on the walls if they were out before the street cleaners arrived. The pages of thick volumes were cut out to smuggle illegal leaflets, and toilet paper was often used for printing slogans because it could be repackaged to appear harmless. As women workers entered the labor market in increasing numbers after 1937–1938, new slogans directed at women appeared. "Women! Will we continue to work twice as hard as men for half the wages?" or "Slow down on Tuesday." A few of these cheaply printed appeals have been preserved. They crumble with each turn of the page. How they contrast with the enamel paper and slick photographs of Nazi publications, which have scarcely yellowed over the years. Sometimes the corners of a resistance pamphlet have dozens of pinpricks in the margins. In order to maintain anonymity and yet provide one another with a feeling of solidarity, each reader made a tiny hole before passing it along.

In addition to issuing printed material for Germans, Hitler's opponents established a communications network using Social Democratic Party ties. Each month, the Paris office of this organization (SOPADE) compiled information about morale in every region of Germany and distributed it in mimeographed booklets (published on tissue paper). So accurate were these reports that the police did their best to obtain copies to evaluate the effectiveness of its own internal security reports.

Participating in this network involved terrible risks. Here, too, women played a vital role in deception. Maria von Maltzan, daughter of one of Prussia's oldest noble families and sister of a devoted Nazi officer, recalls how she regularly got the latest news reports onto the international night trains.

> First we had to register with the SS [at the gate]. "Mail for abroad, press mail." And I was a very friendly young woman back then, and had my method. Before the suitcase was searched, I drank one or two. I always carried a flask. I come from Silesia, so I can hold my liquor. Then it would become terribly late. I would cry, "Oh, God! In five minutes the train leaves! My mail!" The guard would quickly look at a couple of letters on top . . . and open a few envelopes. I would beg him to help me. He would carry the heavy suitcase to the baggage car.[53]

Around 1939 the paper in these slim publications became thinner, and the number of reports per issue diminished. With the war, the SOPADE reports virtually died out.

People in anti-Nazi circles confronted a dilemma: The existence of police spies mandated accepting no new members in any group, but as arrests diminished those groups and repression mounted, it became vital to reach out to other dissenters. This meant cooperating with former rivals and even enemies in a society permeated by spies and informers. The ever-present threat of betrayal led most resistance groups to close ranks and trust only longtime friends and comrades. But occasionally members of the underground formed ties with other opponents of Nazi rule. One of the most surprising forms of cooperation appeared between Communists and Catholics in northern Germany. Maria von Maltzan recalls that around 1936, friends ("some very devout" and others "very red") began to work together against "brown dictatorship." Feeling powerless against so ruthless a foe, both sides decided not to squander their resources in mutual hostility.[54]

Bertha Karg, a young Communist, in 1932 returned to her native Düsseldorf after attending a political school in Moscow. Hitler's victory came as an utter shock to her, and she immediately contacted a group of dissidents gathered around the Jesuit Joseph Rossiant. The Catholics aired their hatred of Hitler's state and Karg spoke in glowing terms about life in the Soviet utopia. Despite Rossiant's aversion to Communism and Karg's dislike of religion, both groups forged a unity based on shared "democratic ideals and common disgust at the increasing fascist power." Together, they called on workers of every religious and political persuasion to unify in a great uprising against Hitler. In addition, they cooperated in several protests. One day in 1935, for example, the Catholics laid wreaths on the graves of people whom the Nazis had murdered; meanwhile, Karg's group distracted the police by racing past the cemetery on bicycles. By 1936, every member of the group had been arrested, and nearly all were killed shortly thereafter.[55] Karg survived her prison term, the last five years of which were in solitary confinement.

By 1935–1936, Hitler's opponents realized that their enemy was becoming more, not less, popular, even as repression against the churches escalated. Massive rearmament and public-works projects had revived the economy. Even workers seemed quite contented. Although wages remained low, unemployment had ended; leisure programs provided vacations to cooperative workers; bold diplomatic decisions elevated German prestige abroad; more people married; and Germany was at peace. Socialists who gathered reports on morale concluded that it would be very difficult to turn popular opinion against Hitler. Aside from complaints over specific policies, most of their informants agreed generally with a young woman who was interviewed by a reporter for the clandestine SOPADE reports. She worked in a grocery store, was engaged to an SA man, lived at home, belonged to the National Socialist Clerks' Union, saw politics in personal terms, and respected Hitler, whom she called an

Übermensch (superhuman). Extremely anti-Semitic, she worried slightly about rumors of war, but feared Jewish conspiracy most of all. Other reports noted pervasive grumbling, disillusionment, and apathy, but these did not provide the raw material for recruitment into a resistance network which demanded that its members risk their lives.[56] Feelings of powerlessness undercut morale and sapped the energy for brave stands against the Nazi state.

Rather than working for overthrow or hoping to convert new supporters to their cause, opponents thought in terms of self-defense and survival. In a state that controlled every aspect of public life and private existence, preservation of a community beyond policy surveillance constituted in itself a major achievement. Opponents of Nazism eloquently described their helplessness and rage, emotions that psychologists describe as the ingredients of depression. In an environment saturated by propaganda and terror, dissenters frequently succumbed to political depression within their own social and familial circles. "Open conversations became increasingly rare . . . the possibility of meeting without consequences diminished. Hopelessness cast a pall over us like death. As if everyone pulled their heads in. As if everything had already been said. You already knew just what your friends thought and feared . . . so intense discussions diminished. They lost their meaning."[57]

Conversation, even among trusted friends who despised Nazism, gradually degenerated into platitudes because people tired of the daily repetition of the same shared beliefs in the absence of any way to act on them. Without a free press, wild rumors replaced the news with whispered stories of concentration camps, hideous tortures, and gruesome accounts of Nazi leaders' personal lives. Neighbors turned into informers. Because no information was reliable, people could easily decide nothing was true and withdraw from knowledge and activity. Anxiety blunted the determination to act. But those who did enter a resistance network found that the very decision to plot with others against a common enemy overcame alienation.

Children recall how they suffered when their parents kept them out of the Hitler Youth. And parents talk about how difficult it was to believe that virtually all of society beyond one's close circle believed so fervently in an incorrect or immoral doctrine. Historian Gudrun Schwarz interviewed a woman who had participated in the Socialist underground throughout the Third Reich. She dreamed of the day when Allied soldiers would liberate Berlin, and in her fantasy she pictured the Nazi leaders hanging from the Brandenburg Gate. When Berlin did fall, she passed the Gate every day and listened to the radio. She also naively anticipated being congratulated by her fellow Germans for having aided in the liberation. Not only did the Allies fail to purge the West German government of its former Nazis, but after the war she said she felt even more ostracized than before because her neighbors resented her for making them feel ashamed.[58]

Opponents needed strength. But they also required time—to plot, test, develop ploys, gather intelligence, make contacts, and above all to trust. The preservation of anti-Nazi islands amid the overwhelmingly apathetic or fanatically Nazi majority became the precondition for rescuing victims, exchanging vital information, and maintaining morale. Survival mandated preserving a superficial image of loyalty, of saying *"Heil Hitler"* or smiling when the grocer commented joyfully on the Invasion of the Rhineland, or sending one's children to Hitler Youth meetings to avoid the suspicion of disloyalty. Sporadic and spontaneous acts of protest diminished; and in their place appeared the coordinated, conscious group action.

The most cohesive group of resisters were sustained by religion. From the first, Jehovah's Witnesses did not cooperate with any facet of the Nazi state. Even after the Gestapo destroyed their national headquarters in 1933 and banned the sect in 1935, they refused to do so much as say *"Heil Hitler."* About half (mostly men) of all Jehovah's Witnesses were sent to concentration camps, a thousand of them were executed, and another thousand died between 1933 and 1945.[59] The reflections of one former Jehovah's Witness suggest the trials and dilemmas this group encountered. Elizabeth do Pazo, who was born into a Jehovah's Witness family and attended grade school in 1933, recalls that suddenly everything her family did became illegal. "No more bicycle trips to neighboring farms. No more visits to other Jehovah's Witnesses. No more talking to kids of other anti-Nazi families. Overnight, everything you did had consequences." But her parents and relatives seemed not to notice and continued as usual.

"This was our way of life. Papa was not going to give it up for anyone. 'We live for our principles. We have already pledged allegiance to God, we cannot pledge allegiance to a mortal man, and certainly not to someone like Hitler! . . . We don't pay homage to the flag of this or any other country. We are peace-loving Christians. The main thing is that Jehovah our God is pleased. It does not matter what people think. Maybe by your good example you can persuade others not to harm other human beings.' "[60] During 1933–1934, Jehovah's Witnesses faced business boycotts, unemployment, and even torture at the hands of local SA officers. In some cases, parents lost custody of their children because they refused to deny their faith. Elizabeth do Pazo's father was sent to a concentration camp.[61] Jehovah's Witnesses had since their foundation stood resolutely apart from any state, which meant not taking an oath, voting, or performing any civic duty. From these principles it followed that resistance consisted of remaining steadfastly outside the Nazi sphere. They did not work to overthrow or undercut Nazi power because they did not believe in violence.

Jehovah's Witnesses believed that absolute noncompliance with even the most trivial Nazi laws was justified in God's sight. By taking a public stand, they inspired all who knew them. Paradoxically, their complete trustworthiness made them the most trusted inmates in any prison. An SS man knew he could relax while a Jehovah's Witness shaved him, for example, because the morality that inspired opposition to Nazism also guaranteed that the razor would not slip. The political resistance, by contrast, depended upon duplicity because success at serious tasks (such as counterfeiting identity papers, sheltering Jews and political refugees, or smuggling illegal information) depended upon deceiving Nazi neighbors by overt conformity to Nazi mores.[62] Effectiveness required invisibility. Detection meant prison, deportation, or execution. Public enthusiasm could very well mask private opposition, which is what ultimately drove the internal spy system to its paranoid persecutions of "internal enemies" during the late war years.[63] Hitler's opponents lived by luck, whim, and instinct. In this setting, "resistance" denotes a commitment to dangerous acts as implied by the Latin *resistere*, to stand firm. Camus defined *The Rebel* as the man who says, "There is a limit beyond which you shall not go," or "up to this point yes, beyond it no."[64] "Standing firm" and overtly saying "No" conforms to our expectations of "manly" behavior.

Dictionaries include three key terms in definitions of "resistance": organized, clandestine, and military. The term itself is oriented toward "men's work" such as throwing a bomb, sabotaging an armaments factory, or ambushing a Nazi leader.[65] Almost by definition, such activities precluded women's participation. Very few studies of the German resistance mention women at all expect in passing. Yet inside Germany resisters eschewed assassinations, sabotage, terrorist attacks, and other forms of violence and concentrated upon underground communications, clandestine rescue networks, and secret publicity campaigns. These activities fell into what we think of as "women's work." Women, with a realistic sense of their vulnerability, know that they will prevail only if they manipulate the situation. Intelligence and the ability to assess the enemy's personality play a key role in this tactic. Camus did not pause even to consider a rebel as woman. But men and women shared the daily tasks of resistance.[66]

Since 1945 historians have measured resistance by counting the numbers of Germans who were arrested or tried. Police and court records do not, however, provide a reliable index of opposition. The status of the accused, the judge's personality, and ever-changing Gestapo guidelines could produce wildly different conclusions about the seriousness of any particular act of opposition. Sentencing and arrest patterns were inconsistent—and it was never clear whether people reported their neighbors for "malicious gossip" to settle old grudges, thwart their rivals' goals, or to bolster the Nazi state. Often, too, basically loyal citizens could find themselves in jail for acts they never imagined would be criminal. The definitions by which the accused were tried allowed the widest possible latitude to state and local officials. Judges in the special courts for political crimes (*Sondergerichte*) were charged "to warn or destroy unsettled spirits [*unruhige Geister*] by the swift and vigorous use of state power, so that the smoothly functioning state will not be interrupted in times of political tension."[67]

Living under a constitutional framework, we assume that some relationship exists between crime and punishment, between risk taken and result achieved. Nazi justice diabolically destroyed that link; beneath orderly fetishes, a sort of feudal anarchy dominated daily life. We cannot know if arrest records represented grossly exaggerated Nazi paranoia about enemies everywhere, or revealed the exposed edges of a vast clandestine network. To take only one example from thousands, did Else Breuer (a Protestant sales clerk who married her boss) commit an act of opposition when she asked a colleague in 1937, "How can you respect a man like [Rudolf] Hess, who is so racially doubtful he looks like an orangutang?" When I read that account in the archives, I smiled and nearly cast the file aside without taking a note. But I realized that although I grinned, the Gestapo had not. These charges occasioned extensive investigation and produced a thick file on Breuer. She paid a fine of RM20 and spent twenty days in jail.[68] Because she was also an official in the local Nazi Welfare Bureau and rumor said she was involved in abortions, she faced serious charges. It is hard to judge which considerations aroused the Gestapo. Court records abound in a maddening volume of detail with few hints of the values that made a particular action criminal. When major "criminals" were brought to trial, by contrast, evidence is often sparse because officials did not want the memory of those actions preserved. Finally, the police who monitored public opinion and reported on seditious acts exaggerated the threat in an effort to justify and expand their responsibilities. Resistance publications, for very different reasons, were also prone to exaggerate the extent of disaffection. These considerations make reliable generalization impossible.

However, in some objectively measurable ways, the Third Reich was indeed different for women and men who opposed Nazism. The police arrrested fewer women than men (not only for political crimes but for being Jewish). When women were arrested, officials avoided sending them to concentration camps, but instead jailed them in local facilities or workhouses. Of the ninety camps constructed in 1933, only one (Mohringen) was used for women inmates.[69] About half of the total female prison population had been accused of "ideological" crimes, and the rest were charged with prostitution, abortion, or undercutting morale.[70] In 1934, seventy-five women had been imprisoned in Mohringen and were guarded by women from the Frauenschaft, although Scholtz-Klink insisted that her women did only social work. In March 1938, the women prisoners were transferred from jails to a new women's camp, Lichtenburg. This marked a turning point in Nazi attitudes and in prison conditions, for the new facility fell entirely under SS control. After this point Scholtz-Klink's women did not guard women prisoners. No reliable statistics have been found; but one list indicates 1,415 women were in prisons in 1938. In the following May, 860 German women were transferred to the Ravensbruck concentration camp. Most were Jehovah's Witnesses, and 120 were political criminals.[71] By 1945, 92,000 women from Germany and occupied nations had died at Ravensbruck, the largest women's concentration camp. Forty thousand survived.[72]

Court records indicate that about one in five people accused and found guilty of political crime was a woman. Hannah Elling, author of an excellent survey on women in the resistance, estimates that one in five prisoners was female. Statistics based on arrests made in 1933 in one strongly Socialist city suggest about the same one-in-five proportion of women to men.[73] A recent study of court records from Düsseldorf produced similar ratios of men to women prisoners, and the historian who compiled them concluded that more men than women actively resisted Nazi rule. In addition, she concluded that non-Jewish men more frequently violated the race laws than non-Jewish women. "Men were much more likely than women to aid Jews and to have sexual relations with them. Males were not only more active as Socialist opponents . . . they were also more active as opponents of racial persecution." The same author also discovered that opposition correlated positively with age. Thus, the German who aided Jews tended to be over forty and male.[74] On the one hand, this seems plausible, since people who feel more secure (usually men) often find it easier to take risks than people who feel vulnerable (usually women). If these generalizations did reflect general trends, it would mean that opposition to Nazi rule came from the same socioeconomic groups that constituted the majority of government and Party adminstration.

Other sources, however, suggest a different reality. When historian H.

D. Leuner compiled information about individual Germans who saved the lives of Jews and fugitives from the Gestapo, he concluded that women outnumbered men in the files he studied.[75] In the 1960s, the Berlin Senate began a program to honor those Berliners who had risked their lives to save Jewish victims. Over the years hundreds of citizens have been recognized, and the balance between men and women is roughly equal.[76] Frances Henry, an anthropologist, who returned in 1980 to the small German town from which she and her Jewish parents had escaped, found that women had typically offered different kinds of aid than men. For example, women would leave food for Jewish neighbors after dark—not an act that spies were likely to see. Women, she suggests, may have performed more routine, but equally lifesaving work than men and escaped detection.

In evaluating arrest records, we cannot overlook the mentality of the police and judges, who were reluctant to damage morale by arresting women. In two nationwide dragnets, women were not targets for arrests. In 1933, very few women were arrested in the random attacks against suspects after the Reichstag fire. After the Crystal Night pogrom in 1938, the Gestapo arrested 30,000 Jewish men and no women (or teenage boys or very old men). In fact, before 1938, no Jewish woman was arrested at all unless the police found her guilty of another offense (for example, belonging to a Socialist cell, carrying false identity papers, or aiding the escape of a refugee).[77] In Hitler's view of the world, men were powerful and dangerous; women passive, protected, harmless, and not very intelligent.

In the Third Reich, the second sex was beneath suspicion. The regime that defined women as incapable of political participation did not readily perceive them as sufficiently intelligent or independent to commit treason. Heavy-featured "criminal" male faces with menacing expressions conformed to Nazi prejudices.[78] Stereotypical thinking (and behavior) dominated Nazi shibboleths and precluded efficient investigation. Hitler, to the end of his life, contrasted men (who, he said, barely pay attention to women) with women (who devote themselves completely to men). "The woman loves more deeply than the man. But in her, intellect plays no role. . . . In political questions, the woman, even if she is extremely intelligent, cannot separate reason from feeling." Behind his bragging, however, Hitler harbored a fear of the unknown sex. "Women's political hatred is extremely dangerous," he added. Perhaps, as Germany approached inevitable military disaster, Hitler became more paranoid about women, which may explain his personal insistence that some women resisters in 1944 be executed rather than sentenced to life in prison.[79]

Had the police rounded up masses of women, eventually people would have realized that women suffered at the hands of the Nazis. This would have undercut the official image of the Gestapo as "clean" and "noble" by unmasking male brutality toward the "weaker" sex. In addition, arrests of women would have demonstrated that women could act independently outside "feminine" roles. Annie Kienast looks back on her work in the resistance and smiles. "The image of women then helped us a lot. The Nazis regarded women as stupid—capable only of being good housewives and mothers."[80] She played her role to the hilt, so the Nazi neighbors never suspected. "The little dummy with plush earmuffs was my recipe for survival." Nazi proclamations about mindless women enhanced the opposition's chances for success by throwing up a protective screen around resisters who pushed baby carriages, gossiped around a tea table, and flirted with men in uniform. Propaganda portrayed the Nazi rulers as knightly guardians of womankind and women as their grateful wards. When women were arrested, this image crumbled; the arrest of men, by contrast, reinforced the dominant myth by enhancing the notion of a dangerous anti-Nazi conspiracy.

Nazi judges waited until 1937 to sentence a woman to death for treason (although countless women died while in prison). This woman, Liselotte Hermann, a twenty-two-year-old mother and a Communist, had during the 1920s attended school in Berlin, written a thesis on Marxism, and designed a book of antiwar fairy tales. In 1929 she moved to Stuttgart and became involved in a Socialist youth movement. After 1933 she signed a petition against war and fascism, which resulted in her dismissal from the university. Assuming a false name, she moved to Berlin. After the birth of her son Walter, she returned to her parents' home in Stuttgart and continued to organize against the Nazi regime. In December 1935, an informer turned her in. Her captors placed her son in the next cell so she could hear him ask, "Mommy, when are you coming?" They threatened to have him raised in a fanatical Nazi home if she did not inform on her friends. "It is very difficult," she wrote, "to leave and also to say good-bye to a child, knowing that Germany will be destroyed by war." After nearly three years of interrogation and torture, "Lilo" Hermann was executed on June 21, 1938.[81] A letter by a loyal Nazi woman protesting Hermann's execution may explain the relative infrequency of charges against women. "Was it really necessary," the Nazi woman asked, "to kill a German mother because of her opinions? With 99 percent of the Volk solidly on Hitler's side, why did someone choose to make her baby motherless?"[82] Execution of a twenty-two-year-old mother of the "Aryan" race defied the understanding of Germans who took Nazi propaganda about motherhood seriously. Internationally, too, the Nazi image suffered. Several aristocratic English women sent a joint

protest telegram to Hitler with copies to the English press just at the time
when German diplomacy hoped to form an Anglo-German entente.[83]
Gestapo tactics in reality were brutal enough; Hitler could ill afford publicity about executions and torture of women.

Domestically, too, the government displayed great concern about
women's public actions against the state, especially after women were
being recruited for work in war industries. Nazi officials, who scrutinized
weekly reports on morale from even the smallest towns, must have been
sensitive to scenes like the following, reported by Hannah Sost, whom
the Gestapo attempted to deport from Berlin.

> We were about 1500 women, who early in the morning, between 5:00 and
> 5:30 A.M., were brought to the Stettin Railway station. Just when the work-
> ers were on their way to the early shift, we stood there bound together. We
> could go no farther. The SS stood helpless. The workers saw us and let
> loose. "That is unheard of!" "How can you lead women around tied up like
> that?" "What is this? *Affenschande!*" "So it's come to this—that women are
> led around by ropes!" "Let the women *go!*"[84]

In this context, the courage of two hundred non-Jewish wives of Jewish
husbands stands out. Their husbands were rounded up at their work-
places one day in February 1943, and the Gestapo refused them the right
even to notify relatives. The wives, nevertheless, discovered the truth,
and day after day increasing numbers of them gathered at the assembly
centers from which deportations began. They loudly called for their
husbands' release and passed food and clothing to them. Suddenly, and
without explanation, the Gestapo released the men. Such a protest was
unprecedented; so was the result.[85] Goebbels noted the impact of non-
Jewish spouses in his diary. "The evacuation of Jews from Berlin has led
to a number of untoward happenings. Unfortunately a number of Jews
and Jewesses from privileged marriages [between Jews and non-Jews]
were also arrested, thereby causing fear and confusion. . . . Because
shortsighted industrialists . . . warned the Jews in time, we therefore
failed to lay our hands on about 4,000."[86] In armament factories, workers
circulated rumors of German defeat and staged slowdowns. Repression
and resistance grew apace, and pulled people into opposition who formerly had accepted Nazi rule. Despite Nazi preconceptions, however,
deceit, daring, steady nerves, and endurance were not gender-linked.
Irma Keilhack recently reflected on her life in the resistance before she
was imprisoned. "Hiding was our great strength. We hid the flags, we hid
our books, we hid our papers. Everything was hidden. . . . We did not
even go to the Socialist Party offices. [In all of this] women were more
protected than men."[87]

Just gathering information about the thousands of women who resisted is a monumental task—for the records often note only birth and death dates of those who mysteriously "disappeared." Hanna Elling's list of women—with biographical information when available—who died for their resistance activities makes depressing reading. In publishing their names, Elling hoped that people with more information would write to her so the stories of these extraordinary women might be preserved. A small excerpt testifies to the anonymous bravery of women about whom we can discover virtually nothing: [88]

	NAME	BIRTH		DIED	REASON
		DATE	PLACE		
195	Sennholz, Käthe	9/3/1902	Duisburg	2/2/33 shot by SA	Communist
196	Stein, Edith (nun)	10/12/1891	Cologne	8/9/42 Auschwitz	converted Catholic arrested as antifascist
197	Stimming, Gerda	11/19/1889	Miersdorf	8/11/44 executed	"unfascist" remarks
198	Stöbe, Ilse (foreign correspondent)	5/17/1911	Berlin	12/22/42 executed	collected information
199	Struth, Wilhelmine	?	Duisburg	2/3/33 shot	spread information
200	Szaidel, Emma (servant)	2/18/1917	Cologne	11/12/43 executed	*in restaura*
201	Taro, Gerda (correspondent)	1911	Leipzig	7/28/37 fatal wound	fought in Spain

A few of these women were sufficiently well known to have left records and inspired biographies.[89] But most, by far, remain names with a few sparse pieces of information. The majority were killed after 1941 on suspicion of holding anti-Nazi views.

Life in opposition communities took sudden and unexpected turns, frequently compelling people to assume new roles and identities. Necessity often required women to take up command positions or men to do the laundry. More often, however, emergency mandated that both women and men perform the traditional tasks to which they were accustomed. This meant that everyday tasks fell to women, who sheltered and fed refugees, did the typing, took notes at meetings, or cared for children. Many of the male leaders from the Weimar Republic who escaped arrest continued to organize foreign support, attend conferences, fight against fascism in Spain, and write for the underground press. They generated a written record and often wrote memoirs that historians find relatively accessible. Because women as well as men took women's everyday activities for granted, few bothered to comment on them. Luise Rinser, who describes herself as "an instinctive antifascist," recalled, "I was never at the front lines of the resistance; I worked behind the lines."[89] Hannah Elling concludes that women "directed underground classes to inform people about the political situation; traveled to secret meetings in other regions; smuggled illegal material that had been printed abroad."[90] Vera Laska, who has collected information about women in the resistance from all European nations, describes women "partisans, freedom fighters in the truest sense of that word; they were radio operators, code clerks, spies, double agents, messengers, smugglers of documents and people, yes, even secretaries, cooks and nurses for the resistance."[91] Recently a historian confronted a leader in the French resistance with the question, "Where were the women? What did they do?" "What did they *do?*" he responded, "Why, they did everything the men did, plus they cooked, provided shelter to refugees, kept house, and took care of the kids."[92] Women's participation made resistance possible, and courage knew no gender. Käthe Popall, arrested in 1937, looks back on life in the German resistance:

> There were no special women's groups. The women were . . . everywhere in the whole resistance. Many worked totally in silence, their contributions scarcely noticed. I think about when all the men were arrested right away in 1933. Without the women, their courage and bravery, the men's actions would not have been conceivable . . . And what about all those men and women underground? Where would they have been without the women who provided them with illegal quarters?[93]

Few people thought of women as a special category at all. Thousands of slogans and headlines in clandestine anti-Nazi literature denounce capitalist exploitation, police terror, and warmongering. Very few mention women (or Jews) as victims of Nazi brutality. The international press after 1936 made much of the Nazis' failure to honor mothers as they had promised, but largely ignored women as either victims or resisters.[94] Occasionally handbills urged: "Take care especially of the children, orphans, and wives of all political prisoners."[95] One leaflet accused Nazis of holding women as hostages in Hamburg prisons and deplored the Gestapo's habit of arresting wives and female relatives of the men they had labeled as ringleaders.[96] Only when the Nazis began to pay special attention to women's morale because they wanted women in war production did oppositional pamphlets address women as victims.

In the first few years of the Third Reich, left-wing opponents courageously took aggressive stands against Nazism. As they realized the magnitude of the threat they faced, their hope and their numbers diminished. Self-defense became the top priority. Wartime brought a new epoch. Despite some disillusionment, the state and police remained intact; Hitler's armies dominated Europe; opponents could hope for only two developments: invasion from abroad or the decay of Nazi society within. In fact, they did not overthrow or undercut the Nazi state. Whisper campaigns and illegal pamphlets focused and exacerbated general feelings of malaise; work slowdowns hindered production; and German women's reluctance to work in war industry after 1939 increased the labor shortage, which was only partially compensated by slave labor. The Gestapo reports blamed the resistance for what they called women workers' "blues," or low morale.[97]

Resisters could not escape the guilt they felt for jeopardizing family and friends. After the war, many children of parents who had died in the resistance wrote glowing testimonials. But Elizabeth do Pazo admitted how difficult her parents' religious intransigence made her childhood. She asked,[98] "Can you realize what it would be like to grow up without friends?" Her parents forbade her to play with other children of non-Nazi parents because association with other Jehovah's Witnesses would endanger their already fragile reputations. "So you could only be friends with children of Nazi parents whose reputations were above reproach." Then Hitler announced conscription. "You did not have an option. You were either for Hitler or against him." Her father was sent to a concentration camp in 1936. "I had an uncle in the SS, jovial, very funny guy, a stamp collector, and very interesting. . . . He put on his full-dress SS uniform to go to ask the commandant to release my father.

" 'That's my wife's brother. I want him freed,' he said. The commandant agreed.

" 'Of course. You can have him right now,' he said and brought him to the desk dressed in civilian clothing. . . . But my father refused to sign the papers renouncing his faith and admitting to the error of his thinking. . . . He just said '*Auf Wiedersehen*' for the last time and went back into the camp. We never saw him again."

Do Pazo continued, "You might think we were very proud of my father because he withstood all the pressures. But we were not. We said he should have signed because Papa should be with us and maybe he could keep a low profile and even a lot more. . . . Our teachers told us, 'Your father was a coward.'. . . And we were boiling over inside, but we couldn't say anything. . . .

"Grandmother told us, 'The main thing is Jehovah knows he was not a coward.' "

The family lost its house, the Gestapo arrested Elizabeth's mother, and the children moved to Lübeck with her parents. Elizabeth's grandmother realized that if she continued to attend services and associate with her religious community, she would endanger her relatives. "Grandmother just stayed home, studied her Bible, and talked to us." Then Elizabeth took a rebellious step. She joined the Nazi BDM (League of German Girls) because Party officials threatened "grave consequences" to families whose children did not join. "My grandmother cried and asked how I could do such a thing after my father and mother had been so brave. I said, 'Listen. I don't believe . . . I cannot believe in a God like that who lets these things happen. He's supposed to be the God of love. I don't want that religion. . . . I did not want to see the Bible. . . . I got a uniform and marched right in."

At age fifteen, Elizabeth experienced friendship for the first time, wandering and hiking in the countryside, doing charitable work, helping farmers, and singing in the BDM chorus. "We were just kids. We didn't care about the Nazi stuff." Within months she had been nominated for a leadership position. That was too much. "I flunked the test because I had no interest in where Hitler was born and Göring and all that. That let me off the hook." The BDM brought her friends, outings, singing, and community service. Only after the end of the war did she and her siblings appreciate her father's decision to remain in the concentration camp. "After we were teenagers it dawned on us that he had been more than courageous," she said quietly. As soon as the war ended, she left Germany forever and emigrated to Massachusetts. While Elizabeth do Pazo's faith in God never returned, she carries on the tradition of her father by working with community groups as part of a project to combat racism in American society.

Whether as political or religious dissenters, the opponents of Nazism preserved their own integrity and at immense risk created tiny spaces of freedom. Resisters failed to dislodge Himmler, Göring, or Hess, who operated the machinery of coercion; but they undercut Goebbels' drive to intrude into private life. Like numbers looking for meaning behind the "green wall" in Zamiatian's novel *We*, or Julia and Winston meeting in "prole" districts in Orwell's *1984*, these Germans maintained for themselves and for us a tradition of humanity. The police files of the Third Reich testify to the Nazis' obsessive concern with morale and leave the clear impression that resisters succeeded not by destroying the Nazi state, but by eroding Nazi society. The authors of Nazi reports on morale did not dare to suggest that perhaps Nazi policy in itself alienated more and more Germans; and ascertaining the precise balance between disenchantment and opposition is difficult. But we do know that resisters formed a tiny minority within an inert political mass of Germans who listened to their leaders. Catholics and Protestants heard their clergy urge them to cooperate with Hitler. If they resisted, they did so against orders from both church and state. Although some churchmen did protest specific Nazi policies, they insisted on their absolute loyalty to Hitler's overall aims. Charismatic leaders, by definition, inspire loyalty even among people who dispute their policies. Jehovah's Witnesses, by contrast, had absolutely refused to give their cooperation to any state. Marxists attacked the nationalism, militarism, racism, and exploitation that lay at the heart of Nazi policy.

Because the record is so sparse, it is difficult to know what motivated resisters. Women resisters from political and religious backgrounds explain their choices in nonideological personal terms. Take, for example, an employee in Berlin's notorious Plotsensee Prison, commonly known as the Berlin Deathhouse, who for twelve years risked her job and even her life by smuggling messages between prisoners and their friends and families outside. When asked later to explain her choice, she said simply, "How could I have done anything else? I had to do it. I was placed in that position. How could I have acted differently?"[99] In the words of one member of the Catholic-Communist group led by Karg and Rossiant: "We had to protest the terror and the persecution. We had no choice but to act as we did with the small amount of freedom left to us." Helene Jacobs recalled in a recent interview: "The first stage of activity was a completely personal support for people in trouble."[100] Then, once one had taken the first step, it became increasingly difficult to refuse further actions.

A woman who protected a Jewish family hardly understood the question when a historian asked her to explain why she had taken the risk. "Basically, that's just how it was. I say to myself simply, 'This is a fellow human being in trouble and I can stand by him. Well, that's just my damned duty [Schuldigkeit].' God, or maybe it was just life, gave the orders. I am no heroine."[101] In the memoirs of virtually every German who left for exile we find words of gratitude for the family servant who risked prison or a fine to help "her" family. Ilse Rothschild remembers vividly the neighbor woman who came to the back door at night after the Crystal Night pogrom with a key and a message. "God help you if you ever need this. But if you do, it is the key to the outside entrance to my attic. Come after dark; don't tell me you're there; but know you will be safe."[102] She did not need to explain.

Maria von Maltzan, protected by family, money, a Ph.D. in natural science, and an influential social circle, refused the invitation to emigrate to England. When she came under suspicion in 1934, she left for a five-month trip through Africa. "The English offered me a good position. . . . I could not relinquish my homeland. I returned, which was probably a mistake. But then life itself consists of a chain of more or less well-constructed mistakes. And too, I could accomplish more here than abroad. . . . You just helped whomever needed you. Jews, Socialists, or Communists. You cannot just let someone get killed because you don't agree with their opinion," recalled von Maltzan. [103]

Since the 1970s, historians have sought out "everyday" opponents of Nazi rule and asked them not why they opposed Hitler (which now seems obvious) but how they found the courage to act on their beliefs. The informants in retrospect say they did not see that they faced a choice. Virtually all answered like Doris Masse: "Not to oppose fascism would have been unthinkable. . . . Either you had your beliefs or you did not. If you did, well, you just had to pay the consequences." [104]

People who said No to Hitler did not begin to be brave in 1933; the habit of perceiving injustice and defending one's principles had developed in childhood. In interviews I have noticed that, whereas ex- (and not-so-ex-) Nazis routinely justify their participation in the Third Reich in terms of "higher" ideals, like patriotism and admiration for Hitler's authoritarianism, the resisters minimize the decision-making process altogether. They state simply that they saw no alternative; they do not recall suffering agonies of doubt. Looking back, they see their choices as personal and moral rather than ideological. Phrases like "my belief in Marxism" or "my Christian principles" occur only rarely in their memoirs. [105] Instead, people recall that events in daily life—friends and neighbors in trouble—led them to resist. Jehovah's Witnesses felt that they acted out of a direct personal responsibility to God, rather than from a commitment to abstract principles. [106] Thinking back on my hitchhiking conversations in 1960–1961, I recalled that references to abstract ideals had colored former Nazis' self-justification for participating in evil. "I didn't approve of Hitler's anti-Semitism, of course, but his other goals were so inspiring" ran their refrain.

Moral choice depended upon empathy and conscience that grew from direct personal contact with injustice. I listened to some of these people, wondering to myself about the millions who never considered saying No. These Germans explain their inaction in terms of their love of family and fear of endangering loved ones. They lived in a setting in which "every action or inaction had consequences," as one woman recalled. No one could escape choice. To act against the state endangered cherished friends and relatives; but to acquiesce meant betraying others whose very lives depended upon help. Germans who supported Hitler from the beginning did not face this dilemma—in fact they hardly noticed 1933 as a watershed date at all. People in their community did not fear repression because they did not fear Nazism. By contrast, opponents found themselves drawn incrementally into resistance networks, from one act to the next. Maria von Maltzan, although raised a Protestant, did not link her actions to religion. "One didn't jump to action in order to be somehow heroic and to save people. But one was somehow *hinein-geraten* [slipped into it] through one's values [*Haltung*]. And once you had entered, you could not easily disentangle yourself." [107]

Against the bleak record of millions of Germans who said in varying degrees *Heil* and *Ja* to Hitler, resisters risked almost certain death to preserve a tradition of honor. For them, the horror of Hitler's rule lay as much in Goebbels' perversion of truth and decency as in physical oppression. In their very worst fears, Goebbels would triumph in the end and their courage would be recorded in history as treason—or, worse, snuffed out altogether. They saw their deaths as a continuation of their commitment in life. "My dearest Mama! You understand, my poor Mama, my life was rich, and I will live on in many people's hearts. . . . I go into endlessness. And I am happy that I lived in the service of humanity," wrote Käte Tucholla, a thirty-three-year-old secretary, on September 28, 1943, just before she was executed. Elisabeth Schumacher, a graphic artist, was thirty-eight when she wrote her last words. "Dearest Mother, . . . I wish I could console you. The most difficult thing is for me to have caused you such pain. But please, one thing above all. Do not be ashamed of us. You know that we are not subhumans." [108] Liberatas Schulze-Boysen and Mildred Harnack, together with their husbands, were arrested in connection with the Red Orchestra plot in Berlin in 1942. The judge had initially sentenced the two women to life in prison, but Hitler personally ordered their execution. In calling out to a world beyond the prison, these women defied the "memory hole" and defended their integrity. Their last words tell us why they risked their lives and speak directly across the divide of 1945. As she died, Harnack said, "And I have loved Germany so deeply." Schulze-Boysen, who was sentenced to death in August 1942, managed to smuggle a last letter to her loved ones, telling them "I love the world, I bear no hatred. I have eternal spring." To her mother she wrote, "If I may ask one thing of you, tell everyone, everyone about me. Our death must be a beacon." [109]

10

JEWISH WOMEN BETWEEN SURVIVAL AND DEATH

A hierarchy of needs is built into the very structure of
reality and is revealed when a misfortune touches a
human collective, whether that be war, the rule of terror, or natural catastrophe. Then to satisfy hunger is
more important than finding food that suits one's tastes;
the simplest act of human kindness toward a fellow
being acquires more importance than any refinement
of the mind. . . . A great simplification of everything
occurs, and people ask themselves why they took to
heart matters that now seem to have no weight.
                        —Czeslaw Milosz
                        "Ruins and Poetry"
                        The Witness of Poetry

"The broth is never eaten as hot as it is cooked." I had first heard that expression from Gertrud Scholtz-Klink, but since then I had heard it often. For centuries this adage has guided Germans through adversity as surely as "His bark is worse than his bite" has reassured English-speaking people. After the war, non-Jews used the adage to explain that if they had really believed Hitler they would have behaved differently. Jewish Germans, too, remember that their liberal values and milieu had sheltered them from people who took racial hatred to heart. They simply could not take seriously the ravings of an uncouth and hysterical extremist. After 1933, Hitler cultivated his image of unpredictability, confusing his victims by alternating swift, massive attacks with periods of calm, and by aiming each stage of war against the Jews against only one section of the population at a time. Thus those not affected could tell themselves, "Thank God, they did not select me" or "You see, it wasn't as terrible as we feared." By alternating between threats of a blitzkrieg and the mirage of a "phony war," Hitler kept his victims on the defensive and gave them false hope. Perhaps more important, Hitler launched his earliest attacks against political and social opponents, not Jews. Therefore, Jews knew that, as painful as their isolation from their Christian friends and colleagues was, others fared worse. Socialists, religious objectors, prostitutes, homosexuals, and "genetically damaged" Germans were arrested and often tortured and killed. Until after 1938, Jews in general did not experience this kind of repression.

Still, given the verbal violence of Hitler's own words, we wonder why so few people became alarmed. Germans, whether or not they were Jewish, did not comprehend that Hitler really meant what he said in *Mein Kampf*. It seemed too insane. True, Nazi propaganda was laden with portentous metaphors, but few translated those images into concrete threats. Madeline Kent, a British woman who lived in Germany at the time, commented on the difficulty of ascertaining the Nazis' true aims in 1933. "Their vocabulary was oiled with euphemisms which served a treble purpose: They deceived the simple-minded both at home and abroad, added insult to the injuries of the persecuted, and pleased . . . the slave mind of the masses."[1] Deception, diversion, and euphemism shrouded Hitler's true intent.

Because government policy appeared so inconsistent, victims found it hard to chart a steady path of action to defend themselves. Shifting Nazi policies kept people busy debating the significance of each new law or anti-Semitic outburst instead of plotting their escape. Behind every ominous event, they could discover an indication of hope: an individual act of kindness, a legal loophole, or a stroke of good fortune. By grasping at

347

good news and minimizing bad omens, many Jews blinded themselves to their own powerlessness. While a common threat pulled Jewish communities and families tightly together, anxiety could also rend solidarity asunder when opinions clashed. Individual family members disagreed violently about practical survival strategies. In those dark times, as public society forced Jews out, the family took on a deeper significance as a guardian of sanity, humane values, and culture. Although some Jews turned to Jewish organizations, for most the family replaced lost ties, and also provided the setting for intense debates and deep emotion.

Martin Buber told Jews in the 1930s, "It does not matter if one leaves or if one remains. What counts is how one leaves or how one remains." We know how tragically wrong he was. Life itself depended on how Jews answered one question: whether to leave or remain. When beginning the research for this chapter, I assumed that because so much had been published about the German resistance, genocide, and daily life under Nazism, I would find the record of Jewish Germans available in bookstores. I was wrong. Not only is Germany today virtually "Jew-free" (to quote a Nazi term), but historians typically eliminate Jews from their scholarship on general history. A recently published two-volume collection of sources on German women contains no section on Jewish Germans; a social history of "Class and Status in Nazi Germany, 1933–1939," includes no chapter on Jews.[2] A left-wing editor of the journal *Aesthetics and Communication* blames his own appalling ignorance about Jewish Germans before 1939 on the absence of Jews who will explain their heritage to him.

In addition to the empty space in recent histories of Germany, the history of women within the Jewish community has all but disappeared. Gestapo searches destroyed family records; individuals burned their own papers to avoid suspicion; the press was censored; and fewer women than men wrote their memoirs.[3] My task in this chapter is to suggest some partial answers to questions related to women, family life, decision making, perceptions of danger, and experiences of anti-Semitism within the Jewish community.

Retrospectively, we see clearly that Jewish Germans who consoled themselves with peasant wisdom about the broth at serving time ought to have heeded a very different adage:

> *Dieses war der erste Streich,*
> *Doch der zweite folgt sogleich!*

> That was only the first blow,
> The second comes at once you know.[4]

Often it was young people and women in Jewish families who accurately read the danger signals before fathers and husbands, for they did not feel as deeply invested in their milieu as the men. We know, too, that women suffered far less from violent attacks than Jewish men. Until the deportations began in 1941 the Gestapo, SA, police, and angry mobs assaulted only men. Since men bore the brunt of overt brutality, it might seem that fathers and husbands would have urged their families to emigrate before mothers and wives. Many Jews, like other Germans, adopted a wait-and-see attitude, telling themselves that Hitler had changed his mind about so many questions, he might moderate his views about Jews as well. The chancellorship, many anticipated, would transform a rabble-rousing speaker into a more responsible leader. Hitler encouraged this hope during the first months of his rule. He toned down his wild threats of war and scurrilous anti-Semitism. This enabled many non-Nazi Germans to overlook particular policies that seemed "extreme" and opt to cooperate with those programs that promised hope. Such rationalizations seemed absurd at best, tragic at worst. But the pragmatic fluidity of Nazi doctrine, enhanced by leaders' indecisiveness and vacillation, appeared as a lack of seriousness. Most Jewish Germans failed to understand that although Hitler and his leaders disagreed about how to implement their anti-Semitic feelings, Hitler's determination to launch a "racial revolution" remained bedrock in his long-term goals.[5]

Although anti-Semitism had figured large in Nazi rhetoric during the 1920s, the word "Jew" did not appear in the official platform, which stated that "only a racial comrade can be a citizen" and that "noncitizens shall be able to live in Germany as guests only, and must be placed under alien legislation." True, the overwhelming majority of all Nazi Party members shared a dislike and perhaps even hatred of Jews, but this did not automatically mean they advocated terror against Jewish Germans. Hitler himself discussed specific anti-Semitic policy with his deputies on only one occasion before January 1933. At a meeting in 1932 they agreed on two contingency plans: If the Nazis seized power by force of arms, Jews would immediately lose their citizenship (which implied violent attacks against Jewish Germans); but if Hitler took power legally, Jewish rights would be eroded gradually and administratively.[6]

Without awaiting orders from Berlin, local SA units sporadically attacked Jewish businesses; dragged Jewish judges from their chambers and even courtrooms; and publicly humiliated community leaders. In these sporadic attacks SA men attacked Jewish men (along with homosexuals, prostitutes, and other "asocials"), but ignored women. In Berlin, all except thirty-five Jewish lawyers lost their licenses to practice; in the Palatinate, a region in southwestern Germany, Jewish bank accounts were confiscated unless their owners had resided in Germany prior to 1914; and in several cities suspected prostitutes were driven through their streets by uniformed SA men. In Nuremberg and other small cities, women were forced to carry signs: "I have committed racial treason" or "I fornicate with Jews." Julius Streicher unleashed an unprecedented attack on Jewish residents in Nuremberg. Fifty male leaders of the Jewish community were arrested and sent to Dachau, where "they were beaten, forced to eat their own feces, and to drink their urine. Nine were killed . . . and their bodies returned with bullet holes in the back."[7] In Kiel, a riotous mob broke into a jail, dragged out a Jewish man accused of a crime against a Christian, and murdered him.

Such random brutality sent shock waves through the Jewish community. Lucy Maas-Friedmann, then a teenager, recalled: "We sat speechless in front of our radios and listened to one of the Nazi bosses scream, 'Anyone who buys from Jews commits treason!' in his hysterical voice."[8] Nazi newspapers proclaimed: 800,000 JEWS MUST PAY FOR THEIR LEADERS' CRIMES. During March the violence became so widespread that Hitler worried about international and domestic repercussions. Anti-Semitic outbursts in Berlin produced a drastic fall on the stock market; the Woolworth chain threatened to withdraw its capital from Germany; and the international press registered outrage. In Germany, respectable middle-class people who did not complain about the mass arrests of Communists and Socialists deplored the harassment of middle-class Jewish citizens. While many and probably most Germans harbored anti-Semitic prejudices, they did not endorse lawlessness against the middle class. Shunning Jews socially was one thing; but unsanctioned attacks on Jewish individuals and their property was quite another. Erna Lugebiel, a seamstress who sheltered Jewish Germans during the war, recalled that her anger at the Nazis began in 1933. Nazi political actions did not upset her, but she commented, "What finally drove me into the resistance was the way they treated the Jews. That made me radical. . . ." Her own industrious nature had always led her to respect Jews. "You wanted a good dentist? A good physician? They were always the best. Virtuous, industrious . . . I began *only* to shop at Jewish stores." After describing some of her acts of kindness toward Jews, she added, "I never saw that as resistance. You simply reacted to your emotions."[9] Hitler's seizure of power did not transform Germany into a nation of Jew-hating fanatics overnight; it took six years of steady propaganda and anti-Semitic legislation to isolate Jewish from non-Jewish Germans.

Jewish Germans' trust in the *Vaterland* did not disappear overnight either. Jews had made their home in Germany for centuries, and nowhere in Europe had Jews felt more settled. To the East they lived in separate communities and constituted a higher percentage of the population than in the West, where they were more integrated into mainstream society. Partly this feeling of safety stemmed from Germany's religious diversity. In all major European nations the Protestant Reformation ultimately produced one dominant religion, which per force made Jews a minuscule religious minority within an otherwise monolithic nation. But the Lutheran Reformation fractured political authority and religious uniformity. Germany's religious diversity resembled, albeit on a small scale, the melting pot that we associate with the United States. While not quite ethnic pluralism, Germans did experience religious dualism. For three centuries, Catholics and Protestants had lived side by side in varying degrees of peace; and for over ten centuries a tiny Jewish minority of less than one percent had made its home within the Christian community, mainly in urban areas.[10]

Germans from Catholic, Protestant, or Jewish backgrounds grew accustomed to ethnic jokes, some social taboos, and occasional hostility. When Jews felt the brunt of ethnic prejudice, they consoled themselves that Catholics, Protestants, and immigrants experienced similar slurs. They observed, too, that in some ways, Catholic Germans lived more separatist lives than Jews because they looked to a foreign religious leader, sent their children to parochial schools, and constituted a large enough demographic force to form separate social communities. When recalling the 1920s, Jewish Germans recount occasional slurs and remember a few very exclusive social clubs from which they were excluded, but they add that in Protestant regions Catholics similarly felt excluded. Often they note in passing that since arriving in the United States they have encountered the same sorts of prejudice. "Remember, Ivy League colleges all had quota systems. What American country club would have accepted us? That you can live with. And an ethnic joke now and then won't kill you either." Germans, like Americans, had accustomed themselves to both religious diversity and ethnic rivalry. Jews confronted the limits of their integration, knowing that Catholics (and sometimes Protestants) experienced similar limits. Some blamed anti-Semitism on orthodox new immigrants from eastern Europe who refused to take on the ways of their new homeland.

German society, confined by rigid etiquette and clear ideas of "good form," allowed for a considerable amount of mutual acceptance in the neighborhood and at school. Women in their friendship circles and volunteer activities cooperated in civic programs. Children played together and their mothers visited back and forth for the afternoon Kaffeeklatsch; at Christmas, Jewish children and sometimes their parents joined Christian families at tree-trimming festivities; at Passover, Jewish families gave matzoth to their Christian friends; on Sundays, Christian families invited their children's Jewish friends for dinner; on Friday evenings, Jewish families reciprocated. Only in one's late teens did signs of social segregation appear. Frances Henry, now a professor of anthropology in Toronto, grew up in a small town on the Rhine until her family fled in 1939. Forty years later she returned to her childhood home to interview her former friends and neighbors. She looks back on an entirely integrated social world—until the question of marriage arose. Then it was understood that even if one dated a youth of another religion, one would not marry. Ilse Rothschild, whose family also immigrated, agrees that she had no concept of prejudice as a child, at least not until she entered her late teens. "Once my friend's family invited a bunch of us to an evening party when the older brother brought some friends home from the university. I thought it might be nice to invite them back and my parents said that since they invited me, it would be okay. But when I did, an awkward silence followed."

I spoke in 1986 with Charlotte Blaschke, who grew up before World War I in a liberal and assimilated Jewish family. Because her classmates came from well-to-do and enlightened families, she did not think much about having a Jewish background, until one day her very closest friend announced she could never see Lotte again. The brother, a young nobleman in the military, inquired about the girl's school and asked about her friend's last name. From that point, the friendship ended.[11] As they approached adulthood, young people realized that an unseen barrier divided Jew from Christian. But they also realized that strictures against Protestant-Catholic marriages remained just as strong. When parents warned their children against a mixed marriage (*Mischehe*), they hardly thought about the possibility of Jewish-Christian unions, but worried about the more likely event of a match between Catholic and Protestant. During the 1920s, 15,300 non-Jews married Jews, a tiny percentage of all marriages. This statistic, however, represented a very high percentage of Jewish marriages, and religious Jewish parents routinely warned their children against marrying non-Jews.[12] In 1931–1932, the annual total increased slightly to 3,400.[13]

Assimilation increased, the Jewish population decreased, and most Germans hardly thought about the Jewish Question. At the end of the nineteenth century, marginal politicians had mobilized people around anti-Semitic and anti-feminist issues, but their parties died out before World War I. Weimar Germany created a security that enhanced a long tradition of neighborliness and sociability. Shortly after being so abruptly rebuffed by her best school friend, Charlotte Blaschke studied at the University of Munich and struck up a deep friendship with a young woman who one day made a cutting comment about "those Jews." But when Blaschke responded by saying, "Why, don't you know I am a Jew?" the young woman stood "still as a stump" for several moments and then responded that this fact would only make their relationship more meaningful. Painful experiences intermingled with joy and discovery.

Government reports on morale registered widespread opposition to violent anti-Semitism during early spring of 1933. Hitler stood between the rabid anti-Semites at the core of his movement and millions of Germans who detested violence against law-abiding people. Persecution of Jews differed from political repression. Jews and Christians lived in the same middle-class neighborhoods, whereas political opponents lived in working-class districts. Attacks against Jews occurred in public. SA men bullied and humiliated Jewish businessmen by daylight. When reports on morale registered widespread disapproval, Hitler called a halt. To mollify the extremists and create the illusion of moderation for his foreign and domestic foes, Hitler declared a "legal" national boycott against all Jewish-owned businesses—to begin on April 1, a Saturday. Distancing himself from the action, Hitler left the planning to Julius Streicher and the Party leadership in Munich. He further diverted responsibility for the action by blaming the victims—in this case by linking foreign criticism of his politics to an international Jewish press conspiracy. In effect, Hitler held Jewish Germans hostage, swearing to continue the boycott until the international press ceased to protest against Nazi atrocities. On April 1, SA men stationed themselves at the doors of Jewish-owned businesses and offices, holding placards admonishing "Aryan" patrons not to shop there; photographers took photos of people who ignored the boycott and published them under captions like "Frau Schmidt is a Jew-lover." The boycott had its effect. The London *Times* correspondent declared, "The boycott revealed strikingly how preponderant Jewish influence is in business life."[14] Ann Froendt, a special observer sent by Protestant churches in the United States to report on the Jewish Question, exonerated Hitler for the boycott and criticized the "extremists" in the movement.

> Hitler himself has not said anything hostile to Jews in his speeches; but his followers have here and there dropped some anti-Semitic comments in their electioneering speeches. Hitler himself emphasizes the positive position, that the Germanic race must hold itself together, which may in fact come to the same thing, but does not sound as inflammatory.[15]

Froendt believed that newly emigrated Jews from eastern Europe bore the brunt of Germans' hatred, but concluded that assimilated Jews had little to fear. This, of course, communicated precisely the message Hitler intended foreigners to hear.

The domestic significance of the boycott, however, became clear when Hitler called it off after only twenty-four hours.[16] Secret-police reports agreed that the action had failed; most citizens remained apathetic, and a courageous minority actively flaunted the boycott. Many Jewish store owners had closed up shop for the day; some stayed open and reported brisk activity; and a few confronted the SA men who came to harass them. One store owner in the small town of Wesel put on his World War I uniform (with medals for bravery) and stood with his own sign: "To Our Reich Chancellor Hitler: Reich Ministers Frick and Göring have repeatedly declared, 'Whoever insults a combat veteran in the Third Reich will be punished with imprisonment,' " and appended his family's military record from the days of Napoleon through the 1918–1919 fighting against the Communists in Berlin. "We view this instigation as an insult to every decent citizen. We remain convinced that the same moral courage which Bismarck once called for still exists today in Wesel, and that German faithfulness is backing us now. . . ."[17] The SA departed.

Bonds forged over the centuries held strong, at least for a while. Jewish citizens took heart when their neighbors defied Nazi orders and even offered support. Marta Appel, a middle-aged resident of a small city on Germany's western border, recalled that after the boycott strangers and neighbors she scarcely knew made a special point of telling her how outraged they felt.[18] And Dr. and Mrs. Salomon told me, "We will never forget how a couple we knew very well donned their Sunday best that day. They strolled around the block three times, so people could see them, and then they called during my office hours." The personal courage of their friends compensated for the menacing actions of the SA ruffians. The SA men who actually enforced the boycott had been transported from nearby towns because Nazi officials feared they would not bring themselves to harass friends and neighbors in their hometowns. Toni Lessler, the director of a school in Berlin, recalls that she and her teachers feared the parents of non-Jewish students would keep their children home from school on boycott day. As it turned out, Jewish children stayed home to avoid attacks; but every non-Jewish child appeared. Still, when Frau Lessler ventured outside to survey the scene, she saw disgusting posters: "Every mark in a Jewish hand weakens the German Fatherland" and "Why buy Jewish? You'll do better with Christians." Placards appeared on the "pillory" in the square on which the names of people who did business with Jews were posted. But, as observers commented, these state-directed efforts demonstrated the lack of natural inclination to comply with economic anti-Semitism against friends and neighbors. The abrupt end of this experiment reassured reasonable people.

Gradually, life returned to its normal course. Non-Jewish students did not desert their school, anti-Semitic signs disappeared, and Lessler remembered that "friendly relations between Jews and Christians continued as the spring of 1933 spread its glorious blossoms over our beautiful school grounds." But she added, "Everything beautiful seemed to have lost its charm. We did not notice the splendid surroundings so many envied. We lived in constant worry about what would happen if any of the threatened edicts were ever imposed."[19]

Individual expressions of solidarity obscured a portentous reality. The institutions that ought to have led protests against Nazi outrages remained silent. No Catholic or Protestant prelate, no judge, no cultural or intellectual leader, and no educator publicly condemned the boycott, even though, as Rabbi Leo Baeck noted, "the little people in Germany remained good." Baeck, noted scholar and leader, remembered the impact of the boycott. "One speaks of the day when Jewish businesses were boycotted; in truth, justice was boycotted." Presciently he added, "Each retreat begins with a great cowardice. We have experienced it."[20] Although some "little people" displayed great integrity, most did not.

Jewish women felt institutional betrayal in very personal ways as their non-Jewish counterparts in Protestant, Catholic, and civic women's organizations faced the decision whether to expel all "non-Aryans." The Jewish Women's League (JFB, or Jüdischer Frauenbund) shared the assumptions of women in other religious organizations and civic associations. The pages of their monthly magazine before 1933 reflect their concern about "women's renewal" rather than "emancipation." Like other middle-class women, they had lamented the falling birthrate and decried divorce as moral decline. Calling for a "more feminine" education, they argued that since one generation of pioneers had demonstrated women could achieve excellence in "masculine" fields, the time had come for gymnastics, training for future mothers, and professionalized motherliness. They, no less than Christians, extolled women's unique closeness to nature and sensitivity. The Jewish Women's League leader, Rahel Straus, declared, "We [women] are nearer to nature; tied, in fact, to nature," (unlike men, who were divided by class, occupation, and ethnicity). This insight, she said, required a fundamental rethinking of women's priorities during the 1930s. "Thirty years of women's higher education proved beyond a doubt that girls and boys were equally endowed. But today we must ask different questions. Today women face the problem differently: Is it the right path for the woman if she studies the same subjects as the man?"[21] Straus concluded that just as girls develop their bodies in special feminine exercises, girls could best improve their minds within the context of a feminine curriculum in all-female schools. Along with Helene Lange, Gertrud Bäumer, Gerta Krabbel, and other women in the old guard, Jewish women worried about growing hostility to women generally and called for a physically strong, morally pure "fighting woman" who would defend maternal values against threats from an industrialized, masculinized world. However, Jewish activists differed in important respects from their Christian sisters. Unlike Catholics and Protestants, Jewish women unfailingly supported women's emancipation and the BDF.

The Jewish Women's League took an independent stance in relation to issues concerning race and reproduction. Jewish women tended to be more supportive than Catholics of birth control, and more skeptical than Protestants about abortion. Articles in the Jewish women's periodical press argued that while abortion was morally wrong, it did not constitute a crime. Like Catholic women pacifists, the Jewish Women's League called for peace among all nations. But unlike either Protestant or Catholics, they warned about racial conflict within Germany. As Jews, they linked growing misogyny and rising anti-Semitism, and they asked their non-Jewish colleagues in the women's movement to join them in defense of human equality and dignity in the face of both. Throughout the Depression, Jewish women had noted an alarming rise in anti-Semitism and acted to stem the tide within the social spheres to which they had access. One woman in the Jewish Women's League wrote:

> The Jewish people has always encountered anti-Semitism throughout its history. But today this hatred comes from powers that are completely out of control, and less than ever amenable to reasonable discourse about rights and justice, understanding and judgment. Looking into the darkness of the future and standing on uncertain terrain, we ask ourselves: What should we do?[22]

As the Nazi Party scored electoral triumphs during the Depression, Jewish women redoubled their efforts at what they called *Kleinarbeit* (little work), reaching out to non-Jewish women in their own social circles, pleading for understanding, tolerance, respect, and sisterhood. But signs in public parks and stores announcing that Jews were not wanted, billboards blaming the economic Depression on Jewish capital, and proscriptions against Jewish students all alarmed them. This was a level of bigotry that no other religious group faced, even in the Depression. What could be done?

Lilli Kretzmir, president of her local chapter of the Jewish Women's

League in a small Rhineland city, remembers having volunteered to pay social calls to non-Jewish individuals who expressed an interest in interfaith understanding. One such individual turned out to be a young woman she had met socially just a few weeks before. Upon being announced by the maid and chatting over tea with the lady of the house, her hostess finally inquired what had prompted her to make an unannounced social call. "Why, I thought you invited me," Mrs. Kretzmir replied. "I am the representative from the Jewish Women's League." After a few moments of utter disbelief, the lady of the house began her education about Judaism. Even after older non-Jewish friends began to avoid the Kretzmirs, these conversations continued and deepened their faith in assimilation. Believing in their own right to equality, most Jews decided to resist and not run. To remain proud in the face of the Nazi threat was, as Lucy Dawidowicz phrased it, "a legal right, a moral necessity and a religious imperative."[23] Jewish women leaders warned: "You render no service if you senselessly leave Germany! . . . Do your duty here! Do not blindly push away people you love and strike out on your own to face an unknown fate!"[24]

Even as they wrote these brave words in their publications, women experienced betrayal at first hand in their neighborhoods and organizations. The precise chain of abandonment varied from place to place, but the behavior of the nationwide BDF (Federation of German Women's Associations) set the pattern. For decades prior to 1933, women had looked to the BDF as a model of integration, within which they could express their special concerns as Jews. A longtime Jewish leader recalled that the high point of her life had been the day, in 1931, when a Christian woman had addressed the assembled Congress of the BDF and praised Jewish women's contributions to the women's emancipation movement.[25] After the Nazis seized power, Jewish women expected their women friends and associates to support them. Some did, privately. But in public, silence prevailed. Not a word in the women's press about the boycott; no files of protest letters or BDF memos about Jews. As Jewish women awaited a reaction, the Federation declared itself dissolved in May 1933. At first this seemed like support because the BDF rejected Nazi rules. But although individuals may have objected, the member organizations marched ("Jew-free") into Hitler's state. "From the standpoint of *Realpolitik*," wrote Dr. Margarete Edelheim in the Jewish women's magazine, "that meant expulsion of the Jewish woman out of the organized women's world in contemporary Germany."[26] Over 50,000 Jewish women in 450 regional chapters had been ejected from the women's movement within which they had always felt so accepted. "Perhaps the most hard-hit are Jewish academic women who have grown up with the older fighting generation of women's-rights advocates, either as long-time sisters or as grateful students." A generation of women who had taken "interconfessionalism" for granted found themselves locked out of a sisterhood that had seemed so safe. "We depart with deep pain," wrote the Jewish leaders.[27] Rejection taught the Jewish community a lesson. Archives and memoirs do not reveal that Christian women felt anything at all.

Jewish women, having just begun to feel accepted as women in public life, were excluded as Jews by the very "sisters" with whom they had worked for entry into the male world. In the face of non-Jewish apathy, Jewish women extolled the virtues of self-reliance. "We must depend entirely upon ourselves in this trial by fire. Until now we have achieved no success in our efforts to obtain the cooperation of the great Christian religions. With a few exceptions, intellectual leaders have also remained silent."[28] Following the lead of Martin Buber and other Jewish leaders, Jewish women called for independence and courage. Jewish pride replaced building bridges as a survival strategy. For women this meant a reaffirmation of both their Jewish and feminine identities. As they felt themselves excluded from a series of social networks, they regenerated their subculture. The revival of the Jewish community, however, often blinded its members to the menacing world beyond.

Many concluded that survival depended upon retreating from public places altogether. Jewish women expanded their own organizations and called for strength in adversity. "The seriousness of these times can provide us with a preparation for a healthy and joyous future," declared Jewish women leaders in public. But at the same time it became increasingly difficult to avoid internalizing the insults. Paradoxically, self-assertion could produce statements such as the following warning against appearing too "Jewish": "We must avoid doing anything that will attract attention to us and possibly arouse hostility. Adhere to the highest standards of taste and decorum in speaking manner and tone, dress and appearance."[29]

The Jewish women's magazine throughout 1933–1934 advised its readers to maintain a "non-Jewish" image. Simultaneously, however, contributors wrote of Jewish pride—inspiring them to preserve in private the stubborn courage that would have provoked anti-Semitism in public. The doublethink could not have been easy, and yet survival itself depended upon Jews' ability to internalize their self-esteem even as they inured themselves against public humiliation. Where women had once felt patriotic about their German nation, now they were to take pride in agricultural and cultural achievements in Palestine. Sadly, many redirected their nationalism away from the culture in which they had been raised and toward a land that to many seemed to be a strip of desert on a remote shore.

Invisibility became the order of the day. Lotte Paepke looks back on the years when she lost her entire social world, although she survived because her "Aryan" husband protected her. She recalled how she learned to suppress her personality, to don the negative image reflected by people around her. In a revealing and mixed metaphor, she recalled how she assumed a humble public persona.

> One tries on this dress, separateness, one tries it on over and over in various situations. Almost like when one has ordered an extraordinarily flashy evening robe that still feels totally alien. You go home and stand before the mirror; you move back and forth; and you try to feel at home in it, so that later in fancy society no one will notice that it is so new and only ordered for this very special occasion.
>
> In these years I learned better and better how to wear this robe, until it seemed to be fashioned on my very body; and gradually I noticed that I could no longer take it off.[30]

One Jewish woman survived during the entire Nazi period in Berlin because she was the favorite seamstress of Nazi leaders' wives. They cautioned her to remain invisible and never appear in public, but every now and then she simply had to go out. She would sew herself a high-fashion evening dress and attend the opera with the Nazi bigwigs. Defiantly she sat in the lavishly dressed crowd, knowing she could look every bit as beautiful as they. Women's memoirs and recollections reveal an extraordinary sensitivity to the dilemmas of loyalty, appearance, and stereotypes. No solution was simple.

Most Jewish Germans could not transfer their patriotism from Germany to Palestine. Even after the humiliation of the boycott and the betrayal of non-Jewish organizations, they decided for fight and against flight. Reinforcing their choice, Hitler changed course after the April boycott by issuing edicts. For the next few years, hatred of Jews took pseudo-legal forms, embodied in over 400 regulations and laws designed to sever the Jewish community from non-Jews. Compared, however, with the erratic and murderous outbursts of the early spring 1933, subsequent legislation seemed manageable. Where a law existed, exceptions might be discovered and modifications won. In addition, some edicts affected certain non-Jews, too. University quotas restricted both Jewish students and non-Jewish women.[31] Until 1935, officials could not even define "Jew" legally. Every discriminatory law contained escape clauses. For example, public school quotas adjusted the percentage of students allowed from the Jewish population (ranging from 1½ to 5 percent). Small towns ignored the laws because no Jewish schools existed as an alternative and national legislation outlawed truancy. Children of veterans were exempted out of deference to popular opinion and Hindenburg's concern for veterans. The April quotas against Jewish professionals and expulsion of Jewish doctors from the national health program *(Krankenkasse)* excluded World War I veterans. To the Nazis' astonishment, half of the nation's 717 "non-Aryan" judges and 30 percent of all lawyers remained exempt.[32] The Civil Service law of April dismissed all Jews and Catholics but exempted all government employees who had received their jobs before the Weimar Republic began and veterans of World War I. After a few weeks of chaos, the Civil Service law was modified to apply only at the very top ranks since qualified "Aryans" could not be found to replace thousands of trained civil servants. Moreover, anyone dismissed in 1933 received his or her full pension and fringe benefits, whereas the later victims received little or no compensation.

Individuals who managed somehow to slip through the maze of regulations did not realize that they enjoyed only a temporary respite. For example, in Berlin Charlotte Salomon, an extraordinarily gifted artist, had been allowed to study painting at the prestigious Akademie der Künste after the law excluding Jews had been proclaimed.[33] When, however, one of her paintings won a competition of unsigned works, her professor worried that the award would call the Gestapo's attention to her. She continued to study and paint until she fled to France in 1938. The Jews who found escape clauses to protect them in 1933 were more severely affected when the laws eventually were extended to include them. Ultimately, the harshness of the early measures saved the lives of those affected because they realized they must leave Germany. "We had no choice after that," recalls the widow of a physician; "thank heaven we *could* not hesitate. As difficult as it was, we packed the family and relatives off for New York."

In retrospect, it became clear that Jews had no choice; Nazi leaders never at any time had the slightest intention of working out a permanent modus vivendi. In one way, Alice Salomon, the pioneering social worker and convert to Protestantism, noted, this proved to be fortunate. "In spite of the misery and the ruin that has come to the Jews and those of mixed ancestry, I have always considered them lucky in one thing. They did not have to make the wretched choice of accepting the Nazi creed or not. The Gentile *had* to make that choice."[34]

Many middle-class Jews, like many middle-class Catholics, had welcomed an authoritarian state except for its anti-Semitism. Some Jews might actually have supported Nazi policies had it not been for anti-Semitism. In 1933, Klaus Mann observed:

There can be no doubt that the vast majority of German Jews would have remained in the Reich, if only the Nazis had allowed them to stay. There is nothing derogatory or malicious about this statement. I just do not believe that the reactions and insights of the shop keeper Moritz Cohn differ basically from those of his neighbor, the shop keeper Friedrich Müller. Why should the Jewish sector of German bourgeoisie have protested against a government that was hailed, or at least accepted, by millions of their non-Jewish counterparts?[35]

Harold Rogers, formerly Hans Rosenberg, looks back on the 1930s in Mannheim, where he worked as an enamel cookware salesman. "Of course some Jews supported Hitler. They marched, many in their World War I uniforms, with swastika flags—you know, like Jews for Jesus."[36] Such overt support, of course, stands out as an exception. Generally, Jews and Germans within similar social and economic situations wanted a state that could impose order, banish labor unions, and quell the threat of Socialist revolution; they hoped for a revival of Germany's status as a world power; and they worked to restore traditional values. Jews for centuries had lived in urban centers and were as a group less frequently found among the peasantry or working class than among professionals, white collar workers, and in the service sector.[37] Jewish Germans thought like their non-Jewish counterparts. When they referred to the Nazis they used phrases like "this Hitler business" or "that Nazi nonsense" or "crackpot bigotry," and thought it would pass. Jews, like other educated and liberal Germans, had lost touch with the passions that motivated 14 million of their fellow citizens to vote Nazi.

Alice Salomon herself shared a certain sympathy with the Nazi rhetoric about restoring class harmony and national pride. She and other Jews had no opportunity to choose, whereas non-Jews balanced "position, income, and family" against their political and/or ethical principles. A simple oath to Adolf Hitler smoothed the path to occupational security at a time when unemployment remained at 30 percent, whereas refusal to join brought "a daily rise in danger for them and their families. It was far from easy." One Jewish refugee after the war recalled bitterly something a neighbor told her: " 'We Aryans envy you Jews. You don't have a choice. I have to become a pig. You can remain as you are.' "[38]

Alice Salomon, however, glosses over the agonizing choices faced by most German Jews. She decided not to leave Germany until the Gestapo gave her thirty days to leave. After years of foreign lecture tours, she counted on dozens of friends who might help her find work. As it turned out, Salomon died alone and embittered because her erstwhile colleagues could not find work for a woman over sixty. Jews without international ties, however, agonized over the decision of whether to leave and make major sacrifices to buy their way out. The reflexes that had deepened their acceptance into the Christian community for generations provided them with precisely the wrong concepts for judging their situation realistically in the 1930s. Looking back, an elderly Jewish woman who lives in Berlin says that Jews who remained in Germany faced three and only three alternatives in 1933: suicide, a clandestine existence, or deportation.[39] When they ought to have been searching desperately for visas, they concentrated on the meaning of each new law, reacting piecemeal to every escalation in danger. Adaptation, they believed, would see them through even those difficult times. For every Jew who decided to emigrate before 1938, four calculated that they could continue to live in Germany, albeit at a reduced level of comfort and security.

In 1933, Jews obeyed the order to surrender their passports and identity papers so that a large "J" could be stamped on them. During these months, non-Jews searched baptismal records and birth certificates to produce their "Jew-free" family trees. Anxious Christians paid specialists to procure the documents. Many Jews worried that their passports and, with them, their civil rights, would vanish. But the return of the papers dispelled their worst fears and led them to sigh, "It was just another formality after all." The most portentous law went virtually unnoticed by Jews and non-Jews alike. In July 1933, all Jews born outside Germany lost their right to apply for German citizenship. The nearly 150,000 Jews who were affected by this ruling had remained marginal to the Jewish community because of their poverty, their Yiddish language, and orthodox religious faith. Assimilated Jews had often blamed these oddly dressed, uncouth newcomers for the hostility toward Jews in general, and did not become alarmed when their citizenship was voided. One author in a 1931 issue of *Blätter des Jüdischen Frauen Bundes*, the Jewish women's organization magazine, expressed such hostility. "The West Jewish woman is tired of hearing one scream for help after another from the East Jews. Not that there is no need, and not that no shiftless poor (*Luftmenschtum*) exists, but the monotonous emergency tone of these calls for help in the long run has a dampening effect."[40] But Jews from the East were not expelled, at least not in 1933, and German-born Jews did not feel the edict affected them.

As we look back on 1933, we wonder why all Jews did not pack up and leave at once. Thirty-seven thousand did join the panic exodus of 1933. Those Jews had read the signs correctly, either because they had experienced pogroms in eastern Europe and instinctively sensed danger or because they belonged to Marxist organizations, which directly experienced Nazi terror. Most Jews, however, felt integrated in the German community, with long-standing social and economic ties that they were loath to sever. Until 1939, the annual American immigration quota of 25,000 for Germany was never filled; and by 1935, over two thousand Jews who had left decided to return to their homeland. From 1933 to 1939, between 20,000 and 30,000 Jews emigrated to various foreign nations each year. But gradually, most Jewish Germans forgot Goebbels' warning: "The Jews in Germany are guests. If they believe they can misuse our hospitality, they are sadly mistaken." [41]

Frequently, family discussions about the future divided men from women because each sex encountered anti-Semitism in different ways. Jewish men by and large withstood the economic pressures of the 1933 edicts and consequently faced the future with confidence that their world of finance and business would offer them a niche as long as they could find a loophole here or an economic necessity there. The editors of one Jewish national newspaper looked back on nearly a year of Nazi rule in November 1933 and declared:

> If we look at the events of the past year, we must note that many German Jews have lost their economic base for existence. Yet it appears from the pronouncements of authoritative sources that in the future our economic existence will be guaranteed, though limited, by the new legal situation. . . . In this light we can understand Dr. Goebbels' remarks that what needs to be solved concerning the Jewish Question has been solved by the government. [42]

Not only did Hindenburg order Hitler to ease anti-Semitic violence, but Hjalamar Schacht, the banking genius who guided Hitler's economic recovery, accepted his new job on the condition that anti-Semitism not interfere with economic recovery. In the Bavarian countryside, where most Jewish businessmen were in the livestock trade, peasants did not curtail their dealings with Jewish bankers or cattle dealers. As hundreds of angry letter writers told the government, no "Aryan" businessmen offered such good rates or could claim so long a tradition of trust. [43] When the Tietz Department Store faced bankruptcy in 1933, the Nazi economic planners ignored their pledge to destroy Jewish department stores and granted Hermann Tietz a government loan to save the jobs of 14,000 employees. Thus, it appeared in late 1933 that Germany's economic institutions would protect men in their sphere.

Fathers, proud of their achievement, stood firm. "Do you see that granite building there, with my family name chiseled on it? That is my fortress and it will protect us," declared M. M. Warburg, president of Germany's most influential private banking house. Although Warburg spent much of his fortune helping other Jews leave Hamburg, he himself refused to depart because he had his family's name to defend and his "fortress" to protect him.[44] Frau Hilde Gerson Stahl, from Munich, recalled that her father resisted all her mother's entreaties with two statements: "Our family goes back twelve generations in Munich. When the museum began its internationally famous crèche collection, did they ask a Christian to donate a genuine crèche from Oberammergau? No. *We* Gersons donated that hand-carved Bavarian crèche to the Munich Museum collection." If that did not seem to convince his wife, he added the second argument: "When Hermann Göring was wounded at the Beer Hall Putsch, who took him in and called a doctor? He stood at our apartment door, and when the doctor came he swore to us that he would protect us no matter what. We are not in danger." As it turned out, the Field Marshal proved to be more reliable than the crèche, and Frau Stahl managed in 1941 to use Göring's pledge to arrange for the family's escape.[45]

Many women with strong ties to business judged the situation much as men did. Frau Gerson, Frau Stahl's sister-in-law, a dignified woman of ninety-three in 1983, gazed pensively out of her window onto the Court Garden in Munich. In 1939, she had escaped from the Gestapo via Shanghai to Seattle, Washington, where she made a living by scrubbing floors, and then returned to Germany after 1945. This seemed inconceivable to me. It had seemed that way to her, as well. But, she said, the thought of her family tradition and property gave her courage. When she approached the German border in 1947, her terror increased, but soon rage replaced her fear. The border police kept her out—she had no right to a visa, they said, because she had neglected to renew her German passport during the war. Aghast, Frau Gerson waited in France, her anger mounting together with her anxiety about returning. A lifetime of courage and pride had equipped her with a habit of resistance. "When I was a teenager, I rebelled," she told me. When I asked what she did she responded with a glint in her eye. "I got married without permission." Because her husband was at the front in 1918–1919, when rioting soldiers stormed Munich, Frau Gerson defended the family business with a revolver against a former employee who called himself a Communist and attempted to take over her mother's profitable commercial laundry and dry-cleaning business. A broad grin broke her somber expression. "And I was a crack shot, too." I could easily imagine her intimidating her assailant. Over sixty years after the event, she stood straight and composed, proud and tall. During the 1920s, it turned out that her husband cared more about sports than business, so Frau Gerson managed her mother's laundry business as well as her husband's family's fuel company. She remembered how stunned they had felt when their sports club put up a sign that said: "Jews not welcome here." Did the Gersons consider leaving? Certainly not. They had the foreign connections and the money to emigrate. The determined businesswoman who had defended herself against Communists and her athletic husband did not dream of fleeing their erstwhile friends. The Gersons retaliated by organizing a Jewish tennis club. They purchased a tract of land with a clubhouse and sponsored competitions against their former non-Jewish friends. "And we won our share of matches." She smiled proudly. "But then," Frau Gerson continued, "then one day they just destroyed it, took it away. We had a thousand members, and we won so many matches against Nazi sports clubs." Only after they had lost their home, commercial property, and savings did the Gersons decide to leave for Shanghai. After the war the same fighting spirit that had kept them in Munich long after they ought to have left drove Frau Gerson back to claim her family's honor. When the West German government offered to pay her for her misfortunes and the property stolen by Nazi officials, she disdainfully refused. "I could have gotten a financial payoff by staying in America. I came back here to get *our* factory, office, and home back. That property does not belong to the Nazis who 'Aryanized' it." Her honor was at stake. I wondered, too, whether she did not want to give the postwar Germans one more chance, an opportunity to show that only the Nazis, not all Germans, had behaved disgracefully. Generations in Munich tied her to both her heritage and the city. For over a decade she battled in the German courts and twice argued her case before the Supreme Court. To no avail. German justice left the factory, the family home, and the fuel business in the hands of the Nazis who had taken them over in 1939. The West German judges had not themselves confiscated the property, but they defended the rights of the Nazis who had.[46] The legal battle produced no victory, but the years in Germany restored her roots. "This is home. I have a very few very dear friends. My son and his wife live in Nuremberg. They speak my language." Her gaze traveled between the Court Garden outside and me. "You know how you will feel when you are my age? Old age is a disease. Your mind stays young but your body never gets over it." As we spoke, I thought of Alice Salomon's words. Like Frau Gerson, she felt deeply integrated into a tradition. Salomon recalled: "Yet, in spite of pogroms, danger, spying, many of my friends remained in Germany. We were convinced that our duty was there, that we had to take a stand and defend a tradition, that we must not give in."[47]

In these and countless other reminiscences, fathers (and sometimes mothers with strong economic and community ties) wanted to remain in Germany to defend their honor. Believing themselves protected by their education, their business ties, and their professions, they stood their ground. However, younger men without wives and children or professional ties joined the pre-1939 emigration in larger numbers than either young women or older men. By the late 1930s, 123,000 Jewish women and 91,000 men remained in Germany.[48] The changing age structure of the Jewish population contributed to the larger number of women in Germany than men. In 1933, 10 percent of the Jewish population was over sixty-five years old; by 1938, the percentage had doubled.[49] "Old trees can't be transplanted," said Lotte Eisner's mother, who returned to Berlin from her safe home in France in 1940, leaving a note for her daughters saying she wanted to buy baby clothes in Berlin for her first grandchild. Within months she disappeared.

Young men without family ties, like recently arrived Jewish immigrants from the East, interpreted the danger accurately and found it easier to conceive of a new life outside Germany. Many sons struck out on their own in order to prepare for their families' immigration. Young women had considerably less freedom to leave their parents. Within many families, however, it was the wives who felt the impending disaster and often overrode husbands' objections. In a society where fathers ruled their families this was an unusual role reversal.

Motherhood played a role in Jewish women's acute awareness of the dangers ahead. For mothers "the future" meant not only financial success for themselves and their husbands, but their children's happiness. Marta Appel's memoirs suggest some factors that made women's outlook special. She recalled a dinner party when the guests debated the merits of emigration. Men had deplored flight as cowardly while the women protested vehemently that forging a new future required even more daring. "Why stay and wait for our ruin? Better to leave while we still have strength and our children still have a future." Every woman, without exception, agreed. As they drove home afterward, her husband still seemed shocked at her lack of patriotism. "How," he asked, "can you possibly consider giving all this up?"[50] "All of this" meant profession and community standing for men, but it meant family and community for women.

Women, because they maintained close ties with their neighborhoods and organizations, more frequently felt the brutal affronts in daily life than did their husbands who typically spent their days in offices or stores. Frances Henry recalled her mother's experience.

> She was walking down a street in Sonderburg, wheeling me, then a very small child in a baby carriage. On turning a corner, she was accosted by a group of youths who shouted at her, "Here comes the dirty whore who

goes to bed with a Jew and has the nerve to wheel around her bastard!" This comment referred to the fact that my mother, born and raised Protestant, converted to Judaism upon marrying my father.[51]

When doing their marketing, Jewish women (or their servants) encountered signs telling them nothing would be sold to Jews. Even beggars who appeared at the back doors for their weekly handouts, as was the custom, began to greet their benefactors with a snappy *"Heil Hitler"* salute; and they soon stopped accepting money from Jews.[52] Ruth Nebel, who survived concentration camps at Jungfernhof and Kaiserwald, recalled,

> I was fourteen years old in 1935 when anti-Semitism slowly crept into our little town. If one chose, it could be ignored, made excuses for, or denied altogether. But insulting remarks were being spoken publicly. "Jew, we'll get rid of you"; "it's good we have a Hitler, he'll do the job right"; "Jewish swine." It became difficult for Jews to secure jobs, and eventually all the Jewish children were not permitted to continue their schooling.[53]

Anticipating life in an urban area would offer more protection, in 1937 the young woman moved to Würzburg, where life turned out to be even worse. "I was afraid to go out at night. Gangs would attack Jews, beat them and leave them bleeding in the streets. I missed my family terribly."

Mothers encountered anti-Semitism through their children's experiences. Often, too, mothers and children agreed not to burden "Papa" with additional worries. Lucy Maas-Friedmann one day in 1934 returned from grade school in tears and inquired whether her father had fought at the front. If he had, the girl reported, she could continue to study with her class like other children; but if not, she would be treated like the Jewish students and barred from extracurricular activities and field trips. Instinctively, Frau Friedmann rushed directly to the principal's office, who, she noted, coincidentally "had the comical name *Holzbein*, or 'wooden leg.' " Indignantly, she launched into a tirade, but the Fräulein Doktor did not seem to care much. Finally, Frau Friedmann resorted to the threat to remove her daughter from the school unless she was treated equally—regardless of her father's military record. When Fräulein Doktor shrugged her shoulders and handed her the students' registration book to sign her daughter out, Friedmann understood the gravity of the Jews' situation.

Jewish parents had to decide whether their children ought to fight to remain in public schools or to transfer them to overcrowded Jewish schools where they would be at least treated with respect. What, for example, ought the rabbi's wife have said when her daughter asked for help with homework that included the following educational information:

1. The Jewish race is much inferior to the Negro race.
2. All Jews have crooked legs, fat bellies, curly hair, and an untrustworthy look.
3. The Jews are responsible for the World War.
4. They are to blame for the armistice of 1918 and the Versailles Treaty.
5. They caused the Inflation.
6. They brought about the downfall of the Roman Empire.
7. Marx is a great criminal.
8. All Jews are Communists.
9. They are the rulers of Russia.[54]

What was the honorable response?

Worse dilemmas confronted those parents who had never told their children that the family had any Jewish heritage. Inge Deutschkron, for example, had been educated in secular primary schools and raised in an atheist milieu. She remembered returning from school one day: "I can still hear my mother's voice. 'You are Jewish and you must show the others that does not make you less important.' But what *was* a Jewish girl (*eine Jüdin*)? I decided not to inquire just then."[55] Soon, her "Aryan" teachers told her what it meant, and her parents transferred her to a religious Jewish school. Many parents recall that in some ways educational anti-Semitism in the schools took a greater toll on their daughters than on their sons; or at least it had a special impact on girls. Boys, they say, had always roughhoused, insulted, and joked with one another; but the girls had behaved politely. Suddenly, girls encountered harsh verbal abuse from children they did not even know; cliques formed on the basis of "Aryanism," and their friends apologized for not talking to them any more. "After several weeks, I was afraid to walk to school alone, so I found some other Jewish girls. The boys would throw stones and insult us," remembered Ilse Wischnia, who grew up in Rothenburg. Shortly thereafter, her parents sold the dry-goods business that had been in the family for generations and moved to Frankfurt, hoping there would be strength in numbers.

Margarete Buber-Neumann, who spent nearly a decade in Soviet and German prison camps, met Milena Jesenska, Franz Kafka's close friend, who talked to her about the pain of betrayal so common in every Jew's life. Jesenska recalled, "I discovered then what *Rufmord* means: death by gossip, by lies, hostile comments, *Nachrede* (slander), and false allegations. . . ." Even the poorest of the poor felt their lives draining away as neighbors made normal life impossible.

An Aryan woman she [Jesenska] had known for sixteen years had as a young woman been deceived by a Jewish good-for-nothing who married her, took her property, and left her pregnant. She moved in with her mother and raised the child by her own skill with the needle—every day sitting until she was utterly exhausted at the sewing machine. Stitch by stitch she earned a living for three people. Then the proud Nordic race with its heroic ideology of "attack the weak" found her out. News of her misdeed spread rapidly. After that she received no more orders, and her boy, who had been apprenticed, lost his job.

Milena Jesenska concluded, "*Rufmord* is an altogether new weapon, and it wounds more deeply than steel. You bring a murdered person to the cemetery. There he finds his peace. The victim of *Rufmord* has to keep on living and yet cannot really live."[56]

Gossip, schoolchildren's insults, neighbors' indifference, friends' aloofness, community excommunication—all made life wretched for Jewish women as their husbands' earnings began to diminish. Men and women approached crisis during the 1930s in different ways because their evaluation of the situation depended upon values instilled from childhood. Men, for example, had often served in the military and felt a kind of commitment to defending their patriotism; men in middle-class families had been steeped in German culture when they attended the Gymnasium. "You have to remember that for us Germany was not the land of authoritarianism, dictatorship, militarism, and police. Our *Deutschtum* (Germanness) was rooted in the Enlightenment, in Goethe, Schiller, Luther, Heine, Kant, and Mendelssohn. Our families arrived with Caesar before anyone at all lived in the Rhineland," recalled Dr. Robert Salomon. Luther's notorious anti-Semitism escaped his notice.

Men identified with a proud masculine tradition and saw no manly alternative to standing their ground and defending their rights. As businessmen, many had invested their lives in attaining a certain economic and professional security that emigration would certainly destroy. Professionals felt an obligation to clients and patients not to flee. Civil servants remained loyal to the charge of their office. Families were easier to export than businesses. The family meant emotional bonds more than public status. Often women possessed special skills that meant little in Germany but could support the family abroad. While many men read Greek and Latin fluently and could discourse comfortably about life in fourth-century B.C. Athens, their wives had typically learned English and French, along with more practical trades such as child care, office work, teaching, and nursing. Women's skills transplanted more easily than men's. Jewish women's organizations sponsored crash courses in skills useful in immigration—child care, foreign languages, cooking, and office work, while men learned new skills such as shoemaking or wood-working, or studied agriculture. Even before leaving Germany, the occupational structure of Jewish Germans was changing radically. The percentage of Jews employed in commerce and communication, for example, dropped from 61 percent in 1933 to 19 percent in 1939; while domestic service (mainly women) rose from 1 percent to 13 percent during the same period. Manual laborers increased by nearly 48 percent.[57] Humor kept up with changing realities as jokes circulated that laughed at ambitious parents boasting about "my son the electrician" or "my daughter the floor-scrubber" because semiskilled and unskilled trades offered the best job possibilities abroad.

On the surface, of course, women exercised little overt influence. Ilse Rothschild recalled that in the old days the father made all the decisions. "There was no conception of divided authority." Her own father was no exception. But more often than not, the mother made her wishes known covertly. As a teenager in the 1930s, Ilse Rothschild had never heard her parents disagree about anything at all. Her father never so much as considered emigration because his job at the banking house held firm—and in the family his word was law. Then one day in the late 1930s, his wife (for the only time in anyone's memory) stood up to her husband over an incident the daughter recalled as trivial. When Father wanted to remodel the bathroom, Mother said firmly, "We will *not* give the Nazis a new bathroom. And that's that." When the Nazi family moved in a few months later, they did not find a new bathroom, and the cost of the repairs had been applied to ship passages and exit visas. Officially, the father had the last word—but the mother said it first.

Other families did not remain unified, especially if one spouse was classed Jewish and the other "Aryan." In the late 1920s, a young couple (both physicians) settled in a small village and gradually established their practice, bought a tiny home, and together with their five children, enjoyed a quiet and comfortable life. "A joyful, lively atmosphere pervaded the tiny rooms," recalled an old friend. Lilli, the wife, had been born Jewish but had lost all connection with her faith; the husband restlessly alternated between Protestantism and Catholicism. But that did not matter much, as both partners enjoyed the friendship and intellectual companionship of the local pastor. Then, in the spring of 1933, local SA men ransacked their home; the husband became increasingly morose; Lilli was forced to stop practicing medicine; then her husband divorced her. Shortly thereafter, she was arrested and sentenced to prison in Lippenau. The old friend, who recorded her story in her own memoirs, remembers Lilli's utter despair. "Over and over, she asked, 'How has all this come to pass?' and 'Oh, how will it ever end?' and 'Why did this have to turn out this way?' "[58] Ultimately, Lilli was deported and killed.

No pattern emerges from memoirs of the 1930s that might enable one to understand why some people behaved decently and others overnight turned into rude bigots. Jewish Germans from the Rhineland suggest that Catholics behaved better because they understood what it meant to be regarded as inferior by Protestant North Germans. Jews who had lived in the north, however, defend the region in which they were born, saying that Protestants (as the majority religion) felt less threatened by people with a different faith—and besides, many add, Jews were more integrated than Catholics. Memoirs tell of a more depressing reality. Although every recollection about Nazi society includes one or two accounts of a brave friend, colleague, or neighbor, virtually all contacts between Christians and Jews ceased by 1935. Frances Henry noticed that women seemed to have parted from their "unacceptable" friends with considerably more emotion than men. "Aryan" men simply turned away from their lifelong friends. "When you would walk down the broadest street in Mannheim," recalled Harold Rogers, "your best friends would make a point of looking away and marching off to the other side or would push you into the gutter." Dr. Salomon recalled that his former colleagues at a major Frankfurt hospital from which he had been dismissed ignored him totally when they met him by chance at a health spa. But then, when he went into the men's room, they all followed him and behaved as if nothing in the world had occurred. " 'And how are you, old man? How are you doing, buddy?' they asked, clapping me on the shoulder. They seemed to think I would feel better if I knew they still had feelings in private that they did not dare display in public. But they didn't talk about it." Dr. Salomon never saw them again. An old family acquaintance told Frances Henry about her lifelong friendship with a Jewish woman who had moved to a nearby town just after she married. One day Frau von Himmel dropped in to see her Jewish friend in Sonderburg and spend the afternoon. " 'For God's sake, Frieda, leave, don't come, we are already being watched!' [her friend said.] They stood at the door, tears came to both their eyes, and Frau von Himmel slowly walked away. She said in recounting the incident, ' I was stunned, I didn't think there could be anything wrong in visiting an old friend.' She cried all the way home."[59] Henry observed that women openly expressed their sorrow, whereas men distanced themselves coldly from old friends.

After the random violence of early 1933, the April boycotts, and the occupational edicts, many Jews believed Hitler had accomplished his aims and life would normalize. Jews adjusted to the new constraints; the relatively few (like physicians, professors, and lawyers) who felt themselves economically unable to survive made plans to leave the country. The painful encounters and ruptures with friends that marked 1933 blended into the past and the Jewish community strengthened its own network. The Nazi government enhanced their belief that Jews could remain in Germany as long as they existed in a social ghetto.[60] Ominous signs, however, continued for those who cared to read them. When Hitler announced a universal draft, he excluded Jewish men. Jewish men, especially veterans, protested against this insult.

In September 1935, Hitler wanted a dramatic piece of legislation to crown the annual Nuremberg Party Rally. At the last minute he ordered his legal advisers to draft a law prohibiting marriage between "Aryans" and "non-Aryans." He still did not use "Jew" because no one had been able to define the term. A team of medical researchers had searched in vain for special Jewish blood; racial "experts" could not identify any special biological features. This presented a paradox to proponents of "scientific" racism. Finally, the Nuremberg Laws declared that anyone with four grandparents who had been born Jewish were Jews. "Jewish" then legally related not to biology but to one's forebears' religious choices. (By implication, one could have eight great-grandparents who had converted to Christianity and be considered "Aryan.") Statisticians faced a problem. Since "mixed race" had never been a census category, they did not even know how many people the racial categories covered. By 1939, the Nazi Office of Racial Affairs under eugenicist Dr. Walter Gross estimated that 64,000 half-Jews and 43,000 quarter-Jews or *Mischlinge* lived in Germany. People with two grandparents who had not been baptized counted as Jewish. However, the statistics do not reflect the people who lived in Germany in 1933, since many had left by the time the statisticians made their calculations. The law vacillated about people with one or two Jewish grandparents, but it made all Germans with three or four Jewish grandparents "state subjects," without inalienable rights.[61] It appears that just over a half-million Germans were considered Jewish under the new law.

Like the loopholes in the legislation against Jewish professionals and students of 1934, these categories divided the Jewish community by offering slim hope to the fortunate *Mischlinge*. Instead of feeling solidarity with other Jews, people with mixed ancestry tried to make themselves "exceptional." A front-soldier father, a spouse or child with a foreign passport, an American aunt who might send an affidavit, two "Aryan" grandparents, a baptismal certificate or forged identity papers might make all the difference. Escape offered survival. Solidarity meant suffering. Ilse Blumenthal-Weiss asked, "After all, was it really so sinful to long for a baptismal certificate?"[62]

Besides hoping for "exception" status, many Jews welcomed the Nuremberg Laws, which they anticipated could contain anti-Semitism within lawful bounds. Intermarriage had all but ended in any case; ties with Christians had eroded; civil rights meant little for "Aryan" or Jew in the Nazi state anyway; and Jewish children already had withdrawn from Christian circles. True, a new edict forbade non-Jewish servant women under forty to work for Jewish families; but in most cases where Jewish families had employed servants for years and years, the servants were over that age. Probably the origins of this absurd law stemmed from Hitler's own dread that his grandmother had been a servant in a Jewish family and had borne an illegitimate child in his own lineage. Meanwhile, Hitler began to plan for the 1936 Berlin Olympics and he had no intention of arousing foreign animosity because of his Jewish policy. Signs banishing Jews (especially in tourist areas) disappeared; economic assaults diminished; and the press toned down its propaganda. Once again, the public image of order prevailed. At the Olympics, leaders from every democratic nation returned Hitler's salute in the reviewing stand. In the lull before the Holocaust, most German Jews felt that the worst had passed; perhaps this "Hitler nonsense" would not quickly disappear, but both sides had worked out a modus vivendi.

In 1938, however, the pace of anti-Semitism accelerated and Jews recalculated the balance between hope and despair. On the one hand, Jewish firms that produced material that was essential for military rearmament were protected, and labor shortages promised employment, albeit at low wages and under terrible conditions. Although no new laws were declared during the first part of 1938, Goebbels announced a radical acceleration in his "Aryanization" campaign. *All* Jewish property had to be itemized and reported to Party authorities; and all real estate and businesses must be sold to Aryan buyers, usually at between 10 and 20 percent of its market value. During the summer of 1938, Jewish Germans received notices that their middle names would be changed to Sarah for women and Israel for men. At the end of the summer, an even more ominous event occurred. About 50,000 Polish Jews who had been deprived of the right to apply for citizenship in 1933 were arrested and on twenty-four hours' notice deposited at the Polish border. Deportations had begun, and no one seemed to notice. After all, these were the *Ostjuden* who, assimilated Jews told themselves, displayed virtually no loyalty to Germany and no understanding of its culture.

Instead of saying "We could be next," most Jewish Germans reassured themselves: "Thank God it wasn't us." Throughout the summer of 1938, random violence against synagogues (especially in Berlin and Munich) increased, perhaps as a test for what was to come. As after the April 1933 boycott, some non-Jews objected and many helped Jewish victims; but the institutions—notably the churches—remained silent.[63] Jewish organizations remained helpless in the face of this apathy. Amid the silence after the first storm, one person acted. A seventeen-year-old Jewish student in Paris, whose parents had been deported from Germany to Poland, shot a German diplomat in November 1938. Nazi fanatics used this act of resistance as pretext for a nationwide pogrom on November 9, 1938.[64] The night has gone down in history as Crystal Night because of the piles of shattered glass left on the streets in front of Jewish owned property. This, more than any other single event, made it clear that, as the leading rabbi of Berlin told his congregation, "for Jews there is no future in Germany."

The violence of early 1933 had touched relatively few people directly; and the April 1 boycott largely failed. Subsequent legislation made it difficult to earn an adequate living, but not impossible. Even the Nuremberg Laws became mired in technicalities. But Crystal Night brought SA men into every neighborhood and community. A Sonderberg resident told Frances Henry, at about 6:00 A.M., five young men broke into Minna's house, led by a fellow worker in the local department store. They destroyed everything with axes and left; later, schoolchildren came by and threw stones through the windows.

> My father had a heart attack in the kitchen, so they didn't come in there, but the living room was all a mess. The man who worked with me said nothing; I looked at him and he looked at me but he lowered his face. Among the four was the veterinarian and he came to my father's bedroom and said, "*Mein Herr*, following orders from above, we must destroy your house. You and your wife, go out." The vet had been father's superior in World War I, which may have explained his saying anything at all to my father.[65]

Frau Kramer, who was not Jewish, recalls her mother coming home that evening with tears in her eyes and saying to her father, "They're at the Mandels', the Loebs', and other houses, throwing everything out of the window. The street is full of feathers [from the comforters]. Why are they doing this? What did the Jews do to us?"

Other Jews were more fortunate. Mrs. Anne Bader and her physician husband happened to be in Munich on Crystal Night. Having heard no news of the pogrom, they arrived the next morning at a medical supply house to pick up equipment that had been ordered and paid for. At the door stood an SS man who saw the "J" on their identity papers. But when he attempted to arrest Dr. Bader, the quick-witted reserve officer snapped back: "Sir, how *dare* you speak that way to a former officer of the Bavarian army!" and showed his war papers. The SS man wilted and stammered, "Oh, but . . . sir." He saluted. "I am terribly sorry to have troubled you." Alarmed about their son back home, the Baders rushed to use an old family friend's telephone. But the elderly Catholic widow on a pension (who was not in any way beholden to the Nazis) suggested curtly that they find another telephone. The Baders drove rapidly back to the Rhineland, secured visas, and took the last ship from Hamburg to Shanghai.

Dr. Bader narrowly escaped the fate of approximately 30,000 Jewish men who were arrested. Wives and daughters frantically called influential friends, offered bribes, staved off SS searches, and wrote appeals to Nazi judges to secure their safe release. Veterans' wives bearing their husbands' military honors and discharge papers accosted commandants. Lilli Kretzmir remembers watching as the SS entered her house after her husband had been arrested. Shortly after the men had begun to take paintings, silverware, and whatever caught their fancy, the officer arrived. Suddenly he caught sight of a portrait on the grand piano. "What is *that* picture doing here?" he asked. Frau Kretzmir answered, "That is my late father." The officer went white and ordered his men to leave everything they had taken. "I cannot bring harm to your father's family. He was a wonderful, wonderful man." They departed. Luck, quick wits, and persistence resulted in most cases in the liberation of the men— exhausted, ill, humiliated, and terrified, but alive. Then the last shreds of hesitation vanished and Jewish Germans frantically searched for nations that might grant them visas.

Again, women's skills proved useful because often this meant writing letters to total strangers abroad begging for help and promising never to be a financial burden. "Do you know what the number-one best-seller among German Jews was then?" Helen Sachs asked me, her eyes twinkling. I, of course, did not. But I tried, "The Torah? Goethe? Heine? Mann?" All wrong. "It was the Manhattan telephone book. We spent hours, days looking for Jewish-sounding last names and writing letters. It was our only chance. And many, many answered back. But not enough." In wealthier families, if the husband still had a job, the wife sometimes took trips abroad to look for immigration possibilities; women aroused less suspicion than men because they could always say they were visiting relatives, taking a health cure, or just shopping. Magda Meyersohn, for example, left her children and husband in North Germany while she took a steamer to New York in 1938. Once in the United States, the Council of Jewish Women helped her to prepare for her family's immigration. But over 200,000 Jews (plus 100,000 *Mischlinge*) could not arrange their exodus. They knew disaster lay ahead.

Hitler spoke to the Reichstag in January 1939. "If the Jewish international financiers inside and outside Europe succeed in involving the nations in another war, the result will not be world bolshevism and therefore a victory for Judaism; it will be the end (*die Vernichtung*) of the Jews in Europe."[66] In Hitler's mind, this was "fair" warning. During his last few days of life, while the Russian troops approached the outskirts of Berlin, Hitler wrote, "I have always been absolutely fair in my dealings with the Jews. On the eve of the war, I gave them one final warning. I told them that if they precipitated another war, they would not be spared and that I would exterminate the vermin throughout Europe."[67]

Immigration figures chart Jewish despair. For the first time, U.S. immigration quotas for Germans were filled; and President Roosevelt refused to expand them or even to apply the unused spaces from earlier years to the thousands of applications on the waiting list. In 1938, 40,000 Jews left Germany, and in the following year, 78,000 departed. One refugee bitterly commented on the callousness of non-German Jews.

> I was stunned by the fact that . . . almost all American Jews did not have the slightest conception or understanding of the life we had led. . . . Even after the war, Americans would ask how many eggs a day Jewish prisoners received, or they would tell us about how hard it was for them because they had to walk twenty-five blocks to be able to save a nickel. That was the biggest stumbling block—to finding my balance in the United States . . . the total insensitivity and ignorance of our own Jewish people.[68]

Yet without the aid of non-Germans, emigration was not possible.

Jews in Germany had after 1933 turned for spiritual and material support to the Jewish community, which offered them a space within which they could find respect, dignity, and even humor. Tragically, their choice to identify with the Jewish community marked them as Jews and targeted them for subsequent destruction. Perhaps one of the saddest aspects of this increasing isolation between Jewish and Christian Germans occurred among left-wing political groups, which after 1933 faced a strange set of options. Although non-Nazi political organizations became illegal in the spring of 1933, Jewish organizations, which remained legal, seemed relatively safe. Cultural associations even received government support. Moreover, because of extremely severe punishments for Jews arrested for political agitation, many Jews often worried they would jeopardize their non-Jewish Marxist comrades if the group was arrested. These considerations separated Jews and non-Jews in outlawed political networks while long-standing ties based on family and friendship assumed ever greater importance as Jewish radicals severed their connections with underground political groups. We have no way of knowing for certain how many Jews continued to cooperate in Marxist groups, but Gestapo reports suggest that by 1935, only about one hundred Jews had been arrested for political crimes in all of Germany—a number so low that even Nazi chiefs expressed surprise.[69] These statistics suggest that Germans from Jewish and left-wing backgrounds decided to leave Germany or to carry on their work within the Jewish community, even though they were not religious.

The extremely scarce records provide us only with scattered names and ages of individuals with Jewish backgrounds who participated in various underground networks. Memoirs, combined with police records, suggest that hundreds of Jewish youths decided, after the Marxist parties became illegal in 1933, to continue their work in the context of Jewish youth organizations (Hachomer Hatzair and the Ring of Jewish Youth), which still remained legal. Marianne Awerbuch, a student in the 1930s, recalled in an interview how a tiny group of young Jews had worked day and night to train adolescents for a new life in Israel. By an agreement with Nazi officials they were allowed to obtain exit visas for some Jews bound for Palestine. But, after the 1938 pogrom, it dawned on them that by choosing the strongest and most talented young people they indirectly contributed to the selection process. At that point she left for Palestine.

Despite the paucity of records, we know some details about one group of youthful resisters who gathered around Herbert and Marianne Baum to work for Communism among Jewish youth. Perhaps, they hoped, the fact that young Jews had been forced into proletarian occupations might increase their receptiveness to Marxist ideas. Under the cover of hiking expeditions, musical evenings, and sports events, the Baums, together with Hildegard Jadamowitz, Hella Hirsch, and Richard Holzer, formed a network of about thirty Jewish-Marxist opponents of Nazism. After 1937, they distributed anti-Nazi literature, circulated illegal books, put up posters denouncing Hitler, and plotted clandestine protests. After 1941, when Jews could no longer walk in parks and forests, their meetings became more dangerous. Two young women, neither of whom was Jewish, provided the group with vital funds and contacts. In 1940, the group held a public memorial service in the Jewish cemetery in Berlin to honor a comrade who had been executed. In 1942, Herbert and Marianne Baum, plus two men and three women, planted explosives at a Nazi exposition; the Gestapo discovered the bombs, and within a few days, all known members were imprisoned. All participants, except three women, were executed; and the three women were soon deported to Auschwitz, where they died. Two participants, Richard Holzer and Charlotte Paech Holzer, miraculously survived and managed to find each other after the war. Their first goal after their reunification in Berlin was to hold a memorial service for their dead comrades. The East German government approved, but insisted that the ceremony be held in the cemetery for Communist heroes. The Holzers, lifelong Marxists, saw the Baum group as Jews first and political dissidents second. They conducted the service in the Jewish cemetery.

Starting in September 1941, all Jews had to wear a regulation-size yellow star on the left side of their coat when they left their homes. To be caught in a police check with papers showing a "J" and without the star meant immediate deportation. To be caught without identity also meant deportation. About 20,000 Jews decided to remove the yellow stars from their coats and become "submarines" (i.e., to live underground). Frau Iselotte Themal told me how she decided to take the risk, even though her husband rejected the idea as too dangerous. Shortly before she had given birth to a boy and he had been assigned the name Uri. In 1941 she said to her son, "Uri, that means 'light.' You are my light. And together we will go through the darkness." The Allies already had begun to bomb German cities. Rumors told people where, in the local slang, "it burned." She took Uri to the Gestapo headquarters in one recently bombed-out district, told them she had forgotten her papers during the raid, and now the house had burned. In extraordinary detail she fabricated a life history and false identity. With temporary ration card and passport, her journey began. After fleeing from informers and police, she once again went directly to the enemy and got a job working for the *Gauleiter's* wife as assistant postmistress in occupied Poland. After the war, Uri became a rabbi and moved to Australia, but Frau Themal, who described herself as a Berliner "down to the marrow of my bones," stayed in Germany.

Of the nearly 20,000 Jews who became "U-boats," about two thirds survived. But the decision to abandon loved ones and families as they faced deportation had not been easy. Inge Deutschkron told Claude Lanzmann in his film *Shoah*, "This was the day when I suddenly felt so utterly alone, left alone, because now I knew we would be one of the very few people left. . . . This was also the day when I felt very guilty that I didn't go myself and I tried to escape fate that the others could not escape. There was no more warmth around, no more soul akin to us, you understand. . . . And this feeling of being terribly alone and terribly guilty that we did not go with them. Why did we try? What made us do this? To escape fate—that was really our destiny or the destiny of our people."[70] The fact that some Jews survived underground tells us that some individual Germans behaved courageously. One of the few Jewish German women to live through deportation and write about it pauses midway in her narrative.

Dear Reader! Can you possibly imagine that you could be uprooted from your home completely by surprise? Out of your community, friendship networks, with whom you live and whom you love—brutally uprooted from all of your habits and needs? Suddenly someone else's will, a powerful hand, pulls you out of everything that had actually made up your whole life? . . . No, dear Reader, that you cannot possibly really imagine unless it has happened to you.[71]

The tiny number of Jewish Germans who did survive genocide did not resist in the normal sense of the word; far from it. Survival depended upon the extent to which they appeared legal. After 1939, they knew their chances were slim. Statistics testify that they were correct.[72]

JEWISH POPULATION FIGURES: 1933, 1939, 1944

	Religious Jews	Non-religious with 3–4 Jewish grandparents	Two Jewish grandparents	One Jewish grandparent	Total
1933	499,682	40,000	unknown	unknown	539,682
1939	213,930	19,716	52,005	32,669	318,320
1944				hidden	14,574
				survived camps	5,000

It is not clear from these estimates what percentage of the Jewish Germans who survived genocide in Germany were *Mischlinge* (persons with one or two Jewish grandparents), but it seems overwhelmingly likely that they comprised a majority.[73] As late as December 1942, it appears that a few Jewish women *Mischlinge* still belonged to the Nazi Women's Organization (Frauenschaft).[74] Probably it is also true that women's chances of being protected were better than men's because any man under forty-five and not in the military (or in strategically essential occupation) aroused instant suspicion. Moreover, in a male-dominated society, non- Jewish husbands with Jewish wives had more influence over Nazi officials than non-Jewish wives with Jewish husbands.

Those few Jewish Germans who managed to stay alive underground owed their success mostly to good fortune. Among non-Jewish Germans, a tiny minority—perhaps one in a hundred—protected Jews. Although isolated acts of kindness by non-Jews before 1939 often contributed to Jews' tragically (even fatally) misplaced sense of security, after 1939, those acts of kindness saved lives. The scale of courage and cowardice, risk and punishment escalated beyond our imagination. In the recollections of Jews who remained in Germany, stories of a neighbor who blocked police inquiries, of a grocery clerk who dropped off milk at 3:00 A.M., or of a pastor's wife who offered a bed in the attic play a crucial role. Ironically, the war itself had a double impact on survival possibilities. On the one hand, it made Hitler's mass genocide possible, but in a fraction of cases, the war—with its critical shortage of labor and massive dislocation after bombing raids began—also enabled some victims to live. Lucy Maas Friedmann and her husband fled to the south, where she found work as a mother's helper while her draft-age husband remained in hiding. By telling people that her house and all of her identification papers had been destroyed, she managed to remain undetected. Perhaps many Germans suspected new arrivals like Maas-Friedmann of being Jewish, but the apathy that led them to stand aside when Jews were being deported from their neighborhood may also have led them not to ask questions about a woman who seemed not only personally pleasant but possessed valuable domestic skills during a servant shortage.

Three hundred thousand Jewish Germans, however, did not evade the mass arrests and were deported. Only five thousand of them survived the concentration camps. In addition to extraordinary good fortune and a strong constitution, personal factors played a crucial role in enabling some individuals to adapt to the inhuman conditions. Upon arrival in the camps, the Nazi guards perverted chivalry by sending "women and children first" directly to the mass execution sites. Women seemed weaker and less able to work. In addition, guards obeyed priorities from Berlin, where leaders worried that the most "eugenically fit" women might survive to reproduce and threaten the "Aryan" future. For those given the chance to exist after the first selection, the decision not to become what Nazi guards derisively called "Moslems" (*Musselmänner*) and (for women) "Pretty Pieces" (*Schmuckstücke*) constituted the first step in resisting.[75] Helen Kopmann, a young woman who lived in the Warsaw ghetto and was deported during the rebellion in 1942, recalls the moment she decided to live no matter what. "I held my little brother in my arms all night in the freezing boxcar. All around people cried and moaned. I just held him and held him. He was sick and lay very quietly. Then I realized he had stopped breathing. For the first time, it became clear to me. I said to myself, 'Hitler *wants* us to die. He *intends* to kill us.' At that point, I said to myself, 'I will live.' "[76]

Hannah Levy-Haas, who spent months in Ravensbruck for her participation in the Yugoslavian resistance as well as for her Jewish ancestry, noticed the contrasts between women and men inmates. She speculated that women's upbringing had prepared them for hardship because they arrived in the camps with certain survival skills. Memoirs of male survivors suggest that they underwent a certain "feminization" similar to soldiers' experiences on the front in wartime. They learned to share, trust, and comfort one another, admit their fears, and to hope together. But most men had to learn behaviors women already knew. Levy-Haas found the disparity between men and women upsetting. On August 26, 1944, she wrote in her diary:

> One thing here upsets me terribly, and that is to see that the men are far weaker and far less able to stand up to hardship than the women—physically and often morally as well. Unable to control themselves, they display such a lack of moral fibre that one cannot but be sorry for them. . . . To be sure, however, their behavior here is merely a natural continuation of their past.

Levy-Haas also recognized how difficult it was for anyone to continue to act in civilized ways when surrounded by barbarism. "Our hut is like a madhouse. Only a few are capable of controlling themselves. The slightest incident leads to vicious arguments, threats, insults, and abuse. Everyone is irritable . . . full of distrust, suspicion and deceitfulness. It makes one shudder."[77]

Women and men both kept alive in their minds the vision of a world beyond the barbed wire and searchlights. Sometimes this meant clinging to the hope of seeing a loved one who one knew must have died; it meant, too, maintaining faith by keeping alive the vision of a world beyond. Inmates found the psychological energy to recall in vivid detail precious moments from the past; they would exchange favorite recipes and household tips, tell jokes, or sing folk songs. These and dozens of other acts of faith preserved a sense of normality by tightening connections with a distant world. Clinging to a common humanity, inmates pledged themselves to a shared future beyond the death camps. The smallest acts of kindness cost precious energy and rarely resulted in effective change. Still, even the most trivial choice in itself preserved a realm of freedom over which the SS had no control.

For some Jewish men and women, preserving dignity meant remaining in Berlin to give aid and comfort to desperate people. Hannah Karminski and Cora Berliner, the mainstays of the Jewish Women's League since before the First World War, remained, working themselves to exhaustion, using, in Karminski's words, "the morphine of work" against "this sense of infinite loneliness. . . ." But what they did "did not the least resemble social work" because the misery was too deep. On the day Cora Berliner was to be deported, Hannah Karminski paid a last visit. "C. and our other friends took books along. They agreed on the choice. To my knowledge C. took *Faust I* and an anthology. When I went to visit them on the last day, shortly before their departure, they were sitting in the sun in the garden reading Goethe."[78] Gertrud Staewen, one of the Protestants who worked with the Grüber Office to help Jews, recalled her visit to Hannah "Kaminski" in Berlin shortly thereafter. There, in her center for children, she knew that one day she would be picked up. Staewen felt something terrible would happen after one particularly serious German defeat. "I went to her during the night. In her room was only a seven-branch candlestick on a cushion with a Bible. That morning she had read to the children, '*Ziehe in ein Land, das ich euch gewiesen habe.*' She told the children that God, not Hitler, would send them there. We read from Abraham until about four o'clock."[79]

In 1943, Vera Friedländer, then a teenager, was arrested and forced to work in a slave-labor factory in Berlin with Polish forced laborers and a few French prisoners of war. Throughout the months of deadening work, the Nazi woman supervisor harangued the workers with threats of the concentration camp. She insisted on impossible quotas and allowed no breaks. Resistance seemed impossible. Still, the workers (who hardly shared a common language) silently agreed on a permanent slowdown. Vera agreed (since her post was near the door) to pass along the signal to speed up if she saw a supervisor or police official approach. What kind of a "factory" was it anyway, Vera wondered as she looked into the eyes of her fellow prisoners. The workers did not produce anything; they just repaired worn-out shoes. But what strange customers, she thought. They drop off their precious shoes before they are totally worn out—without tags, without instructions. How do they think they will ever get their shoes back in the midst of bombing raids? Vera asked herself, Where are the clients? Only half-worn-out shoes, from all sorts of factories. Without quite saying it, Vera knew, and she thought about the endless world of pain outside.[80] She and her close friend Hannah spoke little, but shared a determination to help one another live to recount the story of this Salamander shoe factory, West Germany's largest shoe-store chain today. How many Germans, I wondered as I read her memoirs, know the story about the "shoes without owners"? And if they know, where do they buy their shoes?

Jewish Germans who remained learned to live a double existence, to "disappear" beneath an obsequious public persona, and yet preserve their psychological health by not internalizing Nazi stereotypes about skulking Jews who sneaked through Aryan society. Most of all, Jewish women maintained ties with their families and a few friends they had loved since childhood. As they watched others depart for Chile, Cuba, New York, Shanghai, and Argentina, they maintained warmth in their diminishing social circles. Fighting off inevitable demoralization, they participated in family decision making even as their options swiftly narrowed. While men did their best to cope with the hostile world of business, profession, and bureaucracy, women struggled to preserve their families as a refuge from a menacing world outside.

11

CONSEQUENCES: WOMEN, NAZIS, AND MORAL CHOICE

What is so horrifying, so simply indescribable is the silence of the Third Reich, is its insane stillness accompanied by so much surface noise. The Reich makes the whole world its business, and only keeps quiet about what it has made of its people [*Menschen*]. That, despite all the news reports, remains the deepest secret. . . .

—Heinrich Mann
Foreword,
Deutsche Frauenschicksale

Human wickedness, if accepted by society, is changed from an act of will into an inherent psychological quality which man cannot choose or reject but which is imposed on him from without and which rules him compulsively.

—Hannah Arendt
Origins of Totalitarianism

Suspended over all accounts of Nazi Germany hovers the question of responsibility for genocide. Who bears the guilt? A mad dictator, his fanatical deputies, SS men, the "desk murderers" in Berlin, Party members? Who? Dozens or thousands? Raul Hilberg, distinguished historian of the genocide of European Jews, formulated the beginning of an answer.

> There is one conclusion we may draw from the past. A destruction process is not the work of a few mad minds. It cannot be accomplished by any handful of men. It is far too complex in its organizational build-up and far too pervasive in its administrative implementation to dispense with specialized bureaucrats in every segment of society. The perpetrators who were responsible for "The Final Solution" . . . came from all parts of Germany and all walks of life.[1]

The mechanization of death required the participation of people from all backgrounds. How often have we asked with Edmund Burke how so many good men did nothing? And inquired, with Peter Drucker, about the "Indifferent Man" who did so much?

> I have often wondered which of these did, in the end, do more harm, the "Monster" or the "Lamb" and which is worse . . . lust for power . . . or sin of pride. But maybe the greatest sin is neither of these two ancient ones; the greatest sin may be the new, the twentieth-century sin of indifference, the sin of the distinguished biochemist-physiologist who neither kills nor lies but refuses to bear witness, when in the words of the old gospel hymn, "they crucify my Lord."[2]

These speculations direct our eye away from the dictator who conceived genocidal schemes and toward those who carried out orders to arrest, deport, brutalize, and murder. Who was guilty? Who was complicit? If responsibility extends beyond a "handful of men," where does it end?

Hilberg speaks of "men." What about women? Who has pondered the role of the "inferior" gender in genocide against the "inferior races"? The chain of command from chancellery to crematorium remained entirely within men's domain; women took no part in planning the "final solution"; and, except for a few thousand prison matrons and camp guards, women did not participate in murder.

But, to a degree unprecedented in any other Western society, the Nazi state institutionalized a rigid social system based on polarized conceptions of "man" and "woman," "Aryan" and "Jew." The effects of this system transcended the activities of particular individuals in the final act

387

of the Third Reich. This concluding chapter thus moves beyond the women's *Lebensraum* and explores the implications of a social order founded on race and gender. The radical consequences of this biological restructuring were masked by the Nazis' endorsement of the family as a bastion of tradition. From the days when he wrote *Mein Kampf,* Hitler had praised the family as the "germ cell of the nation," and after 1933, rhetoric about the "strong" family resonated with people's deeply felt need for security amid the chaos of economic depression and political uncertainty. The very language of family evokes powerful and conservative images of a domestic order that protects its members' freedom, privacy, and dignity against a corrosive public sphere. In contrast to public institutions that reward social skills and a pleasing, conformist, and flexible personality, the home fosters character (moral, solid, and independent).[3] This dichotomous view of public and private obscures another vital family function. The family, which offers refuge to its members, simultaneously prepares them to face society outside.

While Nazi rhetoric evoked the nostalgic myth of a sheltering family, state policy promoted a submissive family that delivered up its members to the total state. This revolutionary family model pitted Nazi children against their unconvinced parents and also emptied the Nazi home by recruiting parents and children into state-sponsored leisure, professional, charitable, and educational activities. As peer bonds replaced ties to siblings and parents, the emotional function of the family yielded to the expanding psychological claims of the state. This concluding chapter investigates the consequences of a social system that promoted starkly polarized concepts of race and gender, while attacking the last vestiges of private family life among its supporters, victims, and opponents.

After I interviewed Frau Scholtz-Klink, I discovered that, indeed, the French had pronounced her guilty of carrying false identity papers, and sentenced her to eighteen months in jail.[4] A U.S. denazification tribunal called her a "major Nazi offender" but released her. By keeping "her" women safely beyond the reach of male politics, she believed that she had found a way of improving women's status despite a general climate that made her task difficult. She refused to see her role as complicit because she did then—and evidently still did in 1981—endorse Hitler's goals.

Scholtz-Klink restored motherhood. With the full backing of a totalitarian state, she used financial incentives, radio programs, vacation activities, advanced educational degrees in "womanly" subjects, career opportunities in the Frauenwerk, motherhood medals, and ceremonies to make women feel at home in their domestic *Lebensraum.* Eight million women stood directly under her command in 1940.[5] But strength depended on more than numbers. Because Scholtz-Klink depended heavily upon the state for backing, she undercut her own claims to autonomy, by which she had rationalized her work at the Women's Bureau in the first place. In a material sense, government-sponsored programs did revive traditional feminine roles; but at the same time they cultivated a dependence on state support that undermined the very privacy those roles normally protected.

The state lavished status, bonuses, and public attention on women as a reward for cooperation. Scholtz-Klink recalled that she removed women as a political force. But there was a blind spot in her hindsight. If Nazi leaders had had their way, nothing would have remained private; everything, including the illusion of loving families and apolitical women, had its political use. Like camouflage in jungle warfare or diversionary tactics before an invasion, Scholtz-Klink's image of the German woman made a vital contribution in a larger battle plan. Hitler needed women who would convey an illusion of clean-cut decency that masked a murderous state. Before the war, women in Scholtz-Klink's bureaucracy, often aided by organized Christian women, created their own women's world and marketed its feminine image. Because the ultimate meaning of their activities became clear only after 1939 and because I have focused on the pre-war period, these final comments will not be conclusions as such, but rather consequences. They examine the moral and social purposes to which women's "separate sphere" was put in war, repression, and genocide. As always when biological bigotry is juxtaposed with pragmatism, contradiction, paradox, and irony abound. Worse, however, this history of the "more masculine men" and "more feminine women" enshrined in Nazi propaganda unfolded against the background of unremitting tragedy in real life.

In early 1937, a clandestine survey of morale in Germany reported that people expected war and complied with preparatory measures "not totally without resistance, but still more willingly than one earlier might have predicted." The author, a Socialist, had been disillusioned at Hitler's success in winning over masses of previously hostile or apathetic Germans. Hitler, it seemed, understood his subjects' deepest longings and brilliantly used "mass psychology" to work his will. A contributor to the same report observed how complacent most Germans had become under the new order. "The German Volk is indeed such a fundamentally decent Volk. The people love above all else the so-called order. They do not want chaos."[6] As long as policy conformed to Germans' deepest emotional and economic needs, the state mobilized masses of followers.

Planning for war, however, injected different priorities into social life. Hitler's agenda for racial purification contradicted traditional moral beliefs. In planning for war, Hitler ought to have broadened his base of support, rallying everyone together for wartime unity. In a pluralistic political system, wartime leaders understand the importance of creating a solid front against the enemy. To improve morale and production on the home front, wartime leaders typically broaden the national concensus by welcoming men and women from all parties, classes, religions, and regions. Even bungling Kaiser Wilhelm II had forged a loyal home front at the outbreak of World War I. Hitler did the opposite. Starting in 1936, while rearming Germany for possible war, he escalated his attacks against the churches, "racially unfit Aryans," and Jews. Thus, for example, rather than trusting Catholic and Protestant pledges of loyalty, the Gestapo arrested religious leaders, defamed their reputations, dissolved organizations that objected, and outlawed any activities that might compete with Nazi programs. Instead of escalating the "legal" erosion of Jews' status, Nazi leaders unleashed a pogrom in November 1938 that horrified those average Germans who "loved their so-called order."

When the Nazi government ought to have become less ideological and more pragmatic, it veered toward dogmatism. The glorious days of August 1914 did not return in September 1939. William Shirer described the contrast. "In 1914, I believe, the excitement in Berlin on the first day of the world war was tremendous. Today, no excitement, no hurrahs, no cheering, no throwing of flowers, no war fever, no war hysteria. There is not even any hate for the French and British—despite Hitler's . . . proclamations . . . accusing the 'English warmongers and capitalist Jews' of starting this war.[7]

In the fall of 1939, instead of calling for solidarity against England and France, Hitler opened up a eugenic attack against German citizens by institutionalizing genocide, breeding schemes, and euthanasia. Rumors about "racial revolution" tore apart the morale so essential for success in battle and on the assembly line. Behind the acclaim for military triumph, the fabric of domestic life began to unravel. As long as German armies swept victoriously through Europe, shared triumph offset the havoc wrought by these measures.

While conquest glossed the psychological consequences of domestic programs, Hitler escalated his claims over life and death, making deep inroads into conventional morality. Nazi education, welfare programs, propaganda, culture, and material rewards urged Germans to think in terms of "us" and "them"—not only as Germans versus French or British, but as "Aryans" against Jews, as the "genetically fit" as opposed to the "unworthy," as men versus women, and often as children against parents. On the eve of the Polish invasion, nearly one-third of the total German population belonged to one or another of the Nazi organizations that guided each member from cradle to grave.[8] Not all Germans, and perhaps not even most, could be counted among the fanatically devoted, but virtually all gave their global assent to Nazi rule and happily obeyed Nazi directives. The Party leadership, instead of welcoming general acclaim, escalated the drive for totally loyal followers. Under the duress of war, conditional loyalty no longer sufficed. After 1939 Germans who considered themselves pro-Nazi in general often found themselves facing judges on charges of "anti-state" activities or "political treason" because they grumbled about a particular policy. Single-issue dissent counted as heresy.

With so many men at the front, charges of "political treason" fell heavily on women. Two cases illustrate the kinds of demands placed on citizens by a nation at war. Just after Hitler's invasion of Poland, Auguste Henke, a Protestant Nazi Frauenschaft leader in Cologne, wrote to a friend, "I cannot tell you how deep our outrage is against H. This will be the end of Germany. We do not believe in a glorious time. . . . We will have to pay. . . . It is not true that we needed this man. People are so bitter they don't keep their opinions to themselves. . . . We need no new land and have enough to eat." Frau Henke's letter was opened in a routine inspection and triggered a major investigation. She defended herself by arguing that she had not damaged morale, but had merely put into writing what everyone was saying. Her husband stood by her, although Party officials incited him to divorce her. After Henke had spent some time in prison on Heydrich's orders, she was released without trial. Although the records do not reveal the motivation for this decision, it is likely someone calculated that the trial of an articulate Frauenschaft leader would only provide more raw material for the whisper campaigns that worried officials in charge of propaganda and morale. A second example of an apparently loyal citizen falling under suspicion occurred in November 1939. Hilde Lehmann, whose physician husband served in Poland, did not make a contribution to the Winter Relief drive and allegedly blamed a Nazi "brown nurse" for the death of an infant in her care. Evidence against her filled twenty-eight pages in her Gestapo file. "The ideas of Adolf Hitler are totally alien to her," said one reference. "Her behavior outrageously wounds the *Volk*'s spirit," added another. "How long must we tolerate such insolence?" asked a neighbor.[9] After many reports, affidavits, and accusations, charges were dropped. These cases attest to the existence of demoralization within the generally pro-Nazi community. In addition, the time-consuming investigations and ultimate decisions to drop charges attest to confusion among the police.

Even during the heady successes of Hitler's invasion of Poland, Germans who basically approved of Nazi rule began to fragment in the face of the drive for total devotion. "Us" and "them" referred not only to Germans versus Poles or French, and not only to "Aryan" versus Jew, but to the fanatically obedient versus the halfhearted. To those within the circle, a Nazi offered comradeship, love, support, and sacrifice. But then one drew the line that placed the "others" beyond the edge of mercy.

In retrospect, it becomes clear that "racial revolution," not military triumph, stood as Hitler's primary war aim. World War II, to paraphrase Karl Marx's prophecy about revolution, was to be the midwife of Nazi society. In 1943, Goebbels recalled, "The Führer is right in saying that the war has made it possible for us to solve a whole series of problems which could never have been cleared up in normal times." When Hitler declared, "Everything from baby's first story book . . . must serve the state," women should have understood their real position.[10] The war accelerated Hitler's determination to establish an entirely new social order based on race and sex, with the ideal couple at its core: not a husband and wife, but a soldier and his mother, obedient to Hitler, the patriarch *über alles.*

Scholtz-Klink in 1934 had received orders to regiment the lives of the female half of this couple, but she had never received clear instructions to guide her. Nor did she command sufficient bureaucratic power to initiate any major change. With the approach of war, Nazi policy promoted an unstable combination, a passive-aggressive woman who actively facilitated the "race war" but surrendered to men in the "war between the sexes." The devoted mother was told to place her many children in day care and work for twelve hours a day in a factory. From 1933–1936, the Frauenwerk had issued invective against "double earners," wage-earning women whose husbands had good jobs, because childbearing constituted women's most important career. After 1936–1937, however, policy rewarded the "double earner" who patriotically shouldered the double burden of childbearing and employment. One official summed up the contradiction: patriotic Mother Cross recipients found themselves on the job in factories on Mothers' Day.[11] It became clear that from the beginning Scholtz-Klink had only one goal: to remove women from their homes and put them at the disposal of whatever national priorities Nazi leaders dictated. Powerless and self-sacrificing, women would enter public life as willing objects of state policy. As long as women believed they were going public in the name of motherhood, the policy worked, at least among the middle-class women who made up Scholtz-Klink's constituency. But by the time mobilization orders were drafted, the attacks against religious organizations had severely eroded loyalty to Nazi aims among the women Scholtz-Klink wanted to attract.

The switch to a war economy completed the process of disenchantment even for the middle-class women in the Frauenwerk. When the wartime economy required women's mass entry into "unsuitable" work in transport, mines, heavy industry, and communications as well as increased participation in agricultural and office work, moderates got off the bandwagon. By her bland rhetoric and pragmatic approach, Scholtz-Klink had recruited millions of these women. They stood ready to serve Nazi aims as long as they could reconcile these programs with their own beliefs about motherhood and the family. When the ideals enshrined in Women's Bureau programs fell before the needs of a war economy, the Reichsfrauenführerin had little political influence with which to defend her own programs. She and her staff paid the price of their opportunism as they saw their organizations gutted by the advance of a war economy.

Ever the realist, Scholtz-Klink adapted. She mouthed the new phrases called for by the wartime scenario, and urged women to study for technical careers and take up strategically essential factory work. But who would believe her? Nazi planners had not even consulted her as they drew up their plans for wartime mobilization. Only a few years before, Scholtz-Klink had sworn that "her" German women would never have to sully their hands with paid jobs. Because she had invested so heavily in the restoration of motherhood, she lost credibility when suddenly she urged women both to bear many children and work at factory jobs. As long as she propagated a popular and conventional message, women followed willingly. But when she broke with her followers' ideals about family and home roles, her credibility diminished. True, statistics showed that marriage continued to be popular. But figures do not reveal young couples' motivations. Perhaps marriage seemed attractive to people who resented the pollution of public life by continual propaganda drives, fabricated news, the third-rate fiction offered in government magazines, and indoctrination programs. Germans who drove the marriage rates upward may well have sought an escape from participation in the Nazified public sphere. Many couples married, too, on the eve of the new husband's departure for the battlefront. Birthrates did not rise, even though Nazi women social workers visited mothers to urge them to have a baby after eighteen months had elapsed since their last pregnancy.[12]

Although she had separated women's sphere from men's, in the process social policies and political indoctrination destroyed the privacy that had been the hallmark of the home. Far from honoring the family, Scholtz-Klink used it as an invasion route into ordinary people's ethical choices, emotional commitments, and social priorities. Women as a whole lost out; but she and her staff received material rewards and displayed very un-"maternal" ambition.

In the interests of separatism, Scholtz-Klink had relinquished the power she needed if her Women's Bureau was to serve both women and society as a whole. She claimed, in her interview, to have accepted the post of Reichsfrauenführerin in the first place only in order to establish a strong and autonomous women's sphere, a sort of Ministry of Women, she called it in retrospect. But within her first months as director of the Frauenwerk, she had traded in that hope of equality in exchange for short-term rewards. Gertrud Scholtz-Klink consistently retreated from confrontation with male superiors, foolishly thinking that socializing with the male elite would substitute for participation in policy-making discussions.

Once the war began, Scholtz-Klink remained in office, but her functions as Reichsfrauenführerin diminished. The virtual absence of Scholtz-Klink's name from the holdings of the Military Archives in Germany underscore women's total lack of influence on wartime social policy. The wartime chain of command usurped the influence of all Germans except a tiny elite around Hitler, rendering all women and most men helpless to change their situation. Although they lost what little control they may have had over the general conditions in which they lived, Germans in no sense became victims. Powerless to alter the fundamental nature of Nazi rule, German citizens did retain control over the degree and energy of their participation. The questions surrounding their moral choices and options remain unanswered. But by any standard, it is clear that Scholtz-Klink and her Frauenwerk yielded to temptation; they did not surrender to coercion. Despite an occasional objection to a particular policy that displeased them, they shared complicity in a system from which they reaped rewards.

Once the nation switched to a wartime economy, the Labor Front took over planning, and Alice Rilke, Scholtz-Klink's rival, formed the only link between the high administration and women workers. Publicity drives to lure women back to factory work also emanated from male planners. For the first time, the government reports on public opinion began to monitor women's morale as a special category. Women, as in World War I, heard themselves called into "masculine" jobs to demonstrate "feminine" virtues such as selflessness, idealism, and patriotism. A poster featured a picture of a happy wife-worker in an armaments factory. "Earlier I buttered bread for him, now I paint grenades and think, this is for him."[13] Wartime rhetoric told woman her nation and its soldiers depended on her. Propaganda abounded in appeals to fate, glory, emergency, triumph, and solidarity. Posters, speeches, and radio programs made the theme ubiquitous. "Total war equalizes everyone!" wrote the author of an important study of women in wartime economies.[14]

Auguste Reber-Gruber at the Education Ministry at first reacted bitterly to mobilization of women for war, complaining about the concomitant de-emphasis on womanly traditions and the shortages of materials for her needlework and cooking courses. However, this seasoned Nazi recalculated her position quickly. Soon she took up the equality theme and welcomed war as an opportunity to cultivate "readiness to fight, leadership, racial consciousness, hardened will, strong character, and love of life among women [because] a third of all women have entered into the competition for jobs just like the men in peacetime." How, she asked, can the state call us without offering anything? In 1940, she demanded access to the "latest psychological methods" that integrated the study of "race" and "soul" into a new science (Rasseseelenkunde). "That knowledge is vital for us women, even if the psychologists themselves create difficulties." Complaining about "organization egotism," which deprived her of influence over schools, she worked to gain control over women's education in the occupied countries and schemed to defend her Teachers' Union against rivals in the Labor Front and Frauenwerk.[15]

The war opened up opportunities for some women who in any case wanted or needed to seek employment. As in World War I, women students, professionals, and skilled workers received sudden and temporary encouragement. Studies proved the advantages of "tailoring the universities to meet women's needs" against creating "women who fit the universities." Engineers redesigned heavy equipment to suit women's size.[16] Industrial sociologists experimented with various on-the-job incentives to attract women (such as pastel-painted walls, half-time shifts, bouillon breaks, child care, and counseling services to ease working mothers' guilt feelings). And a few remarkable individuals came to the forefront. In Germany (as in the United States), women received assignments to fly the risky test models of new aircraft, presumably to save the lives of male fighter pilots. Hannah Reitsch's legendary skill and courage made her the only pilot Hitler and his deputies trusted in 1944–1945 to fly them into Berlin under enemy antiaircraft fire. Naturally, she was held up as a role model. But when she spoke to young women, she told them to follow her example of "feminine" dedication to the Führer, not to dream of becoming test pilots.[17]

Nazi planners agonized as they examined the success of the German World War I mobilization of women and the Allied women's labor market during World War II. Both of those drives had recruited more women workers and achieved higher productivity than the Third Reich.[18] In England, over 60 percent of all women worked outside their homes; in Germany, just over a third of all women had jobs—barely more than in peacetime. Already in 1939, the labor shortage had grown so acute that many manufacturers could not accept military contracts because they could find no workers. Only 13 percent of all women workers were employed in industry, which represented a substantial *decline* from the 1920s. A million and a half household servants might have heeded the call (or their well-to-do employers might have sent them into war work), but the number of servants did not decrease significantly. Three and a half million women without children under fourteen plus half a million new brides remained outside the labor force. These women, most of whom were between twenty and forty, would have made excellent industrial workers, but they ignored propaganda to work for victory.[19]

Leaders' ideas about women consistently impeded rational measures to attract women to war work. Compared with poorly paid, physically exhausting work in strategic industries, the private sphere offered a desirable respite, especially to women who had accepted their "motherly" roles. Planners faced an impasse. The middle-class women who had been the target of pro-natalist policies seemed reluctant to leave their homes and look for work. Labor-market experts, like their counterparts in other nations, advised either raising women's wages or reducing benefits paid to war widows and soldiers' wives. Increasing wages would, they feared, upset male workers and accelerate inflation, while maintaining low wages would dampen women workers' morale and give credence to accusations that capitalist profiteers exploited women workers' patriotism.[20] But Hitler's own ideology about women's nature hampered a solution. Because wages, Hitler believed, reflected the worker's status and not the value of the work performed, higher pay for women would have threatened men and upset social order. To encourage young women to look for jobs, marriage loan policy changed in 1937 to allow wives to work outside their homes. But other policies counteracted that incentive. Soldiers' wives and widows received extremely high subsidies—85 percent of the wage a husband would have earned at home.[21] If a wife went to work, her allowance was cut. In the summer of 1941, officials charged with paying these allowances began to investigate recipients' needs with an eye to reducing the payments. Child subsidies also alleviated mothers' need to earn wages. None of these incentives to remain at home was cut for fear of damaging morale at the battlefront. The hesitation to use coercion combined with the reluctance to raise women's wages left planners entirely dependent upon propaganda as the means of recruiting women.

The long debates about women workers reveal the irrational and self-destructive impact of rigid thinking about gender roles on the conduct of a war economy. However, conflict plagued war planners in every sector of the Nazi economy. Fear of dampening morale by labor drafts or cries of emergency led to what historian Burton Klein has called "a peacelike war economy," in which the declaration of total war coexisted with an effort to preserve the image of a placid society and a confident military.[22] Behind the facade of confidence, however, memo followed memo, one more tortured and convoluted than the next. To take just one example, in 1942 Robert Ley, the director of the Labor Front, explained why he denied Scholtz-Klink's sensible proposal to encourage both childbearing and factory work by extending maternity benefits for employed mothers. In high-level conferences with male leaders, Ley unsuccessfully argued for higher wages for women workers, but when confronted by Scholtz-Klink, he defended the official line, which argued against parity for women, symbolized for him by mechanical household aids (an issue entirely unrelated to Scholtz-Klink's suggestion). In Nazi society, *all* women ought to share one identity: motherhood, whether or not they were employed outside their homes. He told Scholtz-Klink that "national biological" (*volksbiologisch*) considerations took priority over material need because the "healthy" National Socialist state represented an improvement over the decadent Weimar Republic.[23] When Scholtz-Klink did offer her suggestions, this was the sort of response she received.

Even faced with dire labor shortages and acute production problems, Hitler, Goebbels, and Göring did not fashion a policy that tapped women as a reserve. Until 1943, Hitler repeatedly rejected desperate pleas from the men responsible for the work force, Albert Speer, Georg Thomas, Fritz Sauckel, and Franz Seldte, to conscript women into the labor market, and he refused to authorize increases in women's pay on the job. Even the moderates in Hitler's entourage worried about the impact of coercion. Ought employers, for example, punish soldiers' wives for absenteeism, or force Party members' wives to take full-time jobs, or devote major efforts to retraining women whose work records were poor?[24] Thus, Hitler's rigid ideas about race and gender combined with other considerations to thwart an all-out drive for women workers. Göring's barbaric forced-labor schemes only partly compensated the loss. Already by 1941, over three million foreign workers and prisoners of war had been imported to fill the demand for labor. After Stalingrad, nearly four million Russians augmented this total, but inhuman working and living conditions reduced their number to a million by 1945. Falling productivity resulted from Nazi leaders' obsessions.

In the final analysis, then, the carefully constructed system, which offered material and psychological benefits for motherhood, proved dysfunctional in Nazi leaders' plans for conquest. Although employed women's wages remained low and soldiers' wives' benefits remained high, funding for women's programs dropped off to almost nothing. Without material need, female leadership, or enthusiasm for the war, women did not enter strategic industries, and labor shortages crippled the military. Although propaganda recalled those glorious days of 1914, the mood did not return. In World War I, everyone had shared the "front experience" and felt threatened by the devastating loss of life at the Marne, Verdun, and the Somme. But until Stalingrad, Germans looked rather complacently at the war effort, in which only the German armies took the offensive and emerged victorious after every major battle. Easy military triumphs blunted people's willingness to sacrifice for what propaganda told them was certain victory. And after the tides of war turned against the German armies in late 1942, many began to suspect that the German cause had been lost no matter what they did.

After Stalingrad, Hitler's deputies overrode his opposition to drafting women into war work, and all citizens had to register for employment. But even after the declaration of "total war," women found it easy to evade employment because officials were reluctant to enforce the measure. Young women were conscripted into labor camps, a program that Gertrud Bäumer endorsed in the name of women's rights.[25] Nazi leaders' ambivalence was reflected in the strong proscription against calling women's quarters "barracks"; they were referred to, instead, as "wooden houses."[26] Eventually, women served as air-raid wardens and as privates in the military. In 1981 Scholtz-Klink boasted of having refused to allow "her" women to serve in the army ("I have sons in the war, I will protect my daughters"), but she herself learned to use a submachine gun as Allied soldiers invaded Berlin.[27] Having supported a powerful leader who vowed to restore strong families, women Nazis despaired as their worst fears about Weimar democracy and Bolshevism came true within the context of a dictatorship they had helped to power.[28] Reber-Gruber confided to a co-worker, "Oh, how our old rivals would rejoice if they could see how badly the Party treats its women."[29]

Hitler's idée fixe about women hampered his economic planners' ability to tap female resources; but his determination to wage racial revolution among the "Aryan chosen people" spread a more debilitating pall, even among convinced Nazis. Hitler had, since the days he wrote *Mein Kampf*, envisioned a nation led by an elite guard of black-uniformed troops who would obey him alone and live in their own world. Himmler applied Hitler's obsession with race in his exhortation to SS men to father as many children as possible without marrying. With the beginning of war, Himmler accelerated his *Lebensborn* program and praised the unwed mother who bore children for the Führer as well as the brave soldier who fathered them. In October 1939, Himmler told his SS men, "The greatest gift for the widow of a man killed in battle is always the child of the man she has loved." He continued, "SS men and mothers of

these children . . . show that you are ready, through your faith in the
Führer and for the sake of the life of our blood and people, to regenerate
life for Germany just as bravely as you know how to fight and die for
Germany." [30]

Considering that the SS included over three million men, this suggestion had potentially major ramifications. The order exposed the underlying axiom of all Nazi policy on the Woman Question: Women
performed only one function, breeding the children who would be raised
by the Reich as the soldiers and mothers of the next generation. The
policy had wider ramifications as well. Promiscuity within an elite movement, like chastity in a religious order, maintains men's loyalty to a
masculine corps and inhibits the formation of deep ties to women and
children. Women, by contrast, who bear children without husbands find
themselves wholly absorbed by activities related to motherhood with little
time or energy for influential political or civic tasks. Himmler planned
that in the future his SS men would sire as many offspring as possible
and the state would assume the financial costs. In the short run, however, Germans were not ready to accept such notions and the program
made virtually no dent in fertility statistics or out of wedlock births. [31] But
it did have a massive and negative impact on morale. Public outcry
forced Himmler to retract his statement and urge his men to avoid "unbridled behavior." [32]

Opponents of Nazism made much of these measures. Jokes ridiculed
women Nazis. Critics and cynics played on the initials of the League of
German Girls (Bund deutscher Mädel). The BDM became the League of
German Milk Cows (Bund deutscher Milchkühe); or "Baldur, drück
mich," (Baldur, take me—referring to the head of the Hitler Youth,
Baldur von Schirach); or Bedarfsartikel deutscher Männer (useful things
for German men). Melita Maschmann, a BDM leader, recalled that
every one of her comrades hated the orders to bear children without
husbands. They all agreed that "the family alone could be the place
where children grow up." When a woman leader became pregnant without getting married, the BDM dismissed her regardless of the official
policy, which said she merited special praise.

The careers of longtime women Nazi leaders illustrate the disarray
that followed in the wake of Hitler's much-publicized breeding schemes.
Ironically, Gertrud Bäumer, whom the Nazis had dismissed from her
Education Ministry post in 1933, declined to speak out on the issue of
Lebensborn, while several key longtime Nazi Party members objected
strongly. Reber-Gruber's office at the Education Ministry was deluged
with protests. How, teachers wanted to know, could they instill moral
principles in their children and at the same time praise the pregnant,

unmarried kindergarten teacher? [33] Reber-Gruber lashed out against glorification of unwed teachers, bitterly criticized her superiors' disregard for
women, and to the end complained that she personally was maligned.
Still, she did not resign. After the war, Allied soldiers sent her to a
denazification camp in the Alps and she died in 1947. The state's encouragement of unwed motherhood roused Guida Diehl from her qui-
escence as well. Having been forced from office eight years earlier, she
had remained silent, occasionally seeking cooperation with the pro-Nazi
branch of the German Christian Church. [34] The *Lebensborn* project angered her so deeply that she complained within the circle of her New
Land movement. In 1940, Gestapo officials began to monitor her mail
(producing, incidentally, an excellent archival collection). In the process, they discovered that she worked with Pastor Grüber's office to save
Jews. She was put on trial, but not by the state. The High Party Court found
her guilty of disloyal behavior and expelled her from the Party. [35] Diehl
did not speak out again. When she wrote her memoirs, she recalled only
the fondest memories. When, for example, she first met Hitler, she wrote
she had found him "serious, warm, and natural," adding, "he set out his
goals. He brought nothing new, just an embodiment of the very best of
our national tradition. He offered a dynamic organization where others
relied on uninspired party politics. We absolutely needed unification." [36]

While Diehl, Reber-Gruber, and other loyal Nazi women expressed
their outrage at the *Lebensborn* program, another conflict further eroded
confidence in the Nazi state. Already in 1935, Hitler had told the chief
of the national medical association of his plans to begin killing "unworthy" citizens. But he did not want to incite a major protest by churchmen
and felt that only wartime conditions would render them silent. Accordingly, the orders for T-4, the euthanasia program, were duly sent out
during the week of the Polish invasion. Shortly thereafter, letters from
parents, relatives, and neighbors arrived at Party and religious offices.
Although SS officers oversaw transportation to the killing centers and
male doctors actually administered the lethal injections, it was women
who, as nurses, social workers, hospital-staff members, teachers, and
counselors, bore a major responsibility for delivering up the victims. In
addition, women faced the grief-stricken and angry relatives as the news
filtered out. Ideally, the "politically reliable" brown nurses under the
Welfare Department ought to have staffed the entire operation; but the
corps remained too small to assume full responsibility. [37] After between
60,000 and 80,000 elderly and allegedly ill, retarded, and insane Germans
had been killed, a tiny number of Protestant and Catholic prelates spoke
out. By that time, thousands of victims' relatives, mostly mothers, had
written to their religious advisers objecting to the euthanasia program.
Although the program was conducted in total secrecy, parents' suspi-

cions were aroused by strange-sounding statements explaining the cause of death. Residents of towns near the killing sites sensed something ominous when they saw the buses with the blackened windows making deliveries and leaving without passengers. Both churches remained silent. But Cardinal Galen, in 1941, spoke out. "These are our brothers and sisters," he told his congregation in a sermon that was distributed clandestinely throughout the nation. Sending shock waves through Catholic Germany, he asked, "How many of us expect to live if we become ill and unproductive?" Galen declared his solidarity with the victims, begging Germans to empathize with the misfits, outcasts, and elderly. His words had their effect. Hitler ordered an end to euthanasia in Germany. No similar protest, however, erupted in the wake of orders confiscating Jewish property and compelling Jewish Germans to wear yellow stars, live in ghettos, and ultimately to die. No voice said, "These are our brothers and sisters." Before passing judgment on that silence, we ought to remember the consequences of speaking out. Catholic Bishop Bernard Lichtenberg of Berlin, one of the very few to publicly condemn the "final solution," was arrested, sent to Dachau, and died en route. Euthanasia was curtailed, but no order slowed genocide.[38]

War, with its attendant patriotism, anxiety, and material shortages, provided racial extremists with a cover for "biological engineering" projects. Nazi priorities held sway, and ordinary citizens did not register objections; but the fear of arbitrary and unexpected repression dampened morale even before the Allied bombing raids began.

Scholtz-Klink, of course, will not admit it now, but contemporaries reported that she suffered depression, failed to appear for speaking engagements, and felt increasingly unable to perform even her functions as a figurehead. After three years in war-torn Germany, Scholtz-Klink and her SS-general husband turned their backs on unpleasant reality, lavishing their attention and money on their country estate in occupied Poland. After a visit to Berlin, Goebbels jotted some notes about her report on women and war.

> Frau Scholtze-Klink [sic] reports on the problems of employing women. And there are all sorts. Who is to discipline the women? Female labour must become compulsory. Otherwise we shall never settle the issue. And camp life throws up so many problems for women. Frau Scholtze-Klink [sic] is quite despondent about everything. I chivvy her up a little. And then, of course, there are the sexual aspects of separating millions of men and women. War means regression to a primitive state for human beings. We must seize victory as soon as possible, and then restore order and discipline.[39]

A report from Schleswig-Holstein alleged that the "ladies" of the Frauenschaft offended the simple and hardworking women in war industries by their pretensions that their work as "bearers of culture" exempted them from work. Reber-Gruber accused Scholtz-Klink of devisiveness and resented her obsequiousness. From every region came reports that the "upper crust" of society women still preferred the Red Cross to the Frauenschaft.[40]

Scholtz-Klink hoped for the return to a more civilized postwar society, but her superiors planned to solidify the most gruesome aspects of wartime social policy as the cornerstones of the Third Reich. The short-term contempt for women encountered by women administrators stemmed from Nazi leaders' fundamental and explicit misogyny, which had been evident throughout Hitler's career. Had she bothered to read *Mein Kampf*, Scholtz-Klink would have known about Hitler's oath to eliminate the "ethical and moral poisoning," "the Jewish parasite," and the "department-store Jewess" who spread syphilis. Nor would the *Lebensborn* program have come as a surprise. "The struggle of the males for the female grants the right or opportunity to propagate only to the healthiest," Hitler had written.[41] These principles went into effect with the approach of war and prepared for a future world of absolute masculine superiority in which the largely middle-class membership of the Frauenwerk would breed racially pure stock, and poorer, working-class women would both work at low-level jobs and bear children.

During the last weeks of April 1945, Hitler lived deep under Berlin in a bunker encased by tons of cement. His last virulent tirades reflected the principles that had guided him from the first: He told his successors that they must "above all else, uphold the racial laws in all their severity, and mercilessly resist the universal poisoner of all nations, international Jewry."[42] And then he spelled out his plans to repopulate the devastated *Volk* by allowing war heroes to engage in polygamy with "racially superior" women. Of course, these were the ravings of a madman. But eugenics and anti-Semitism had been both insane and central to Nazi policy from the beginning. Had Germany won, the temporary wartime measures enticing women into the work force would have been dramatically reversed, but extermination and eugenics would have been accelerated. As Rudolf Hess wrote in a letter to an unmarried mother, "The new ideas born in the war must also hold sway after the war."[43] These ideas "born in the war" rested on the unworthiness of "the Jew" and "the racially unfit" and the subservience of the "Aryan woman," which had always constituted the foundation of Nazi social policy.

National Socialist policy produced chaos, while promising order. The organized female world of civic, religious, community, and ultimately Nazi organizations had been fragmented by 1939. Scholtz-Klink presided over the Frauenwerk and Frauenschaft that had been reduced to the auxiliary status she had sworn to prevent when taking office. Thus, because of the virtual disappearance of Nazi women's organizations, Scholtz-Klink's women did not directly participate in the "final solution" (a term she still uses). But this ought not blind us to the fact that individual women—as officials and as wives and as guards—not only understood that genocide existed as a policy, but themselves sustained it. Gertrud Scholtz-Klink had been one of those women. Three years after speaking with Scholtz-Klink, I discovered in the Leo Baeck Institute Archives the memoirs of a woman who had lived in Berlin on the eve of the war. Erna Segal recalled how "one Klink-Scholz—or maybe I have it backwards" sent a special "buyer" (a nurse) who removed the Segal family's valuables, then drew up a contract promising payment in full within four weeks. Since they were dealing with the Reichsfrauenführerin, they did not worry. Besides, the family desperately needed the money to pay a recently levied "tax" on all Jews. When no payment arrived, they hired a lawyer to collect the bill. Scholtz-Klink's representative agreed to pay a tiny fraction of the price written into the contract. "How can you reconcile yourself with this . . . blackmail?" Frau Segal asked the Reichsfrauenführerin. To no avail. The Segals accepted the sum of money and used it to escape from Germany.[44]

When employees of government programs wanted new furniture, meeting space, clothing, and equipment, they appropriated the property of Jews who had been deported. On one occasion, Reber-Gruber resisted the temptation to profit from this custom, but not for moral reasons. When she was offered the chance to acquire the castle owned by the Bleichröder family (whose ancestor had achieved prominence as banker to Bismarck), she declined. It would not set the correct mood for her teachers because "although Frau von Bleichröder was not Jewish, her husband was."[45] Four decades later, Scholtz-Klink expressed indignation about Jewish ingratitude. Willful ignorance dominated her hindsight as totally as it had determined her vision before 1945.

A few wives of government officials shared their husbands' interests. The wife of Hans Frank (the governor-general of occupied Poland) helped build the family fortune. While Frank reduced the ghetto populations to starvation levels, his wife profiteered by exchanging small quantities of food for large quantities of furs, jewelry, furniture, and art.[46] Emmy Göring insists that her husband never understood the full implications of the "final solution," but witnesses remember that she helped out in her husband's deceitful "business" dealings with Jews who "sold" him magnificent art collections for scandalously low prices.[47] One wife acted not only out of greed but also from genuine commitment to racial ideology. Gerda Bormann (whom Speer described as "browbeaten") wrote to her husband in 1944,

> My dearest Heart,
>
> Every single child must realize that the Jew is the Absolute Evil in this world, and that he must be fought by every means, wherever he appears [Bormann scribbled "quite true" in the margin]. . . . As long as there exists somewhere in the world Germanic *Volk* who want to work hard, cleanly and faithfully and to live according to their own laws, in a State befitting their breed, the Eternal Jew will try to prevent it and to annihilate all positive life.[48]

Frau Bormann, with her intense anti-Semitism and her commitment to her husband's career, stands out, however, as an exception to the behavior of most wives, who were not above greed, but generally remained uninterested in their husbands' jobs and Nazi doctrine generally.

At the opposite extreme of the Nazi hierarchy, a few women worked as matrons or guards in concentration camps. Although they were statistically insignificant, descriptions of them fairly leap from the pages of survivors' memoirs. Susan Cernyak-Spatz recalled: "In my experience the matrons were cruel, more vicious (sadistically vicious) than any SS man. These women who, as I read later, ranged from baronesses and countesses to prostitutes, were the most vicious. You rarely found SS men who played games with their dogs in which the point was for the dog to get the prisoners' derrieres, but the matrons did." Maria Kaufmann-Krasowski testified at a trial in Düsseldorf about Hildegard Lächert, who assigned her to wash floors and beat her mercilessly with a whip until she was only "scraps of a human being," and then barked the order, "Get this piece of filth out of here!"[49] Margarete Armbruster, who was deported to Ravensbruck, reports that besides the SS men, 2,000 women assistants made their lives wretched. "Only one NS sister treated me decently. And she was transferred as punishment."[50] Nearly every concentration camp had its women's section—guarded by its Ilse Kochs—and small brigades of booted, uniformed women guards. Irma Griese at Auschwitz brought horror to her victims with her sadomasochistic sexual exploits.[51] For a woman to become a guard required so major a departure from the normal values and experiences of women, perhaps the few who ended up on camp assignments were more apt to be depraved or deranged than the men. Or perhaps women guards *seemed* more cruel because their behavior deviated farther from our conceptions of "feminine" models than men guards' behavior departed from stereotypes about men.

Jolana Roth told me she had seen very few women SS guards at Auschwitz. "But the ones you did see—they were worse than the men. I will never forget the one who would stand at the peephole of the gas chamber just because she wanted to." Was the woman guard at the peephole "worse" than the SS men, described by Jolana Roth in a different context, who used live babies for target practice? Such comparisons lose their meaning. Greedy, bigoted wives and heartless matrons remained exceptional. However deeply their acts repel us, they did not affect the workings of the Nazi state.

Far more important than these exceptional cases was the system that prescribed polarized gender identities for males and females. After 1939, wherever Nazi power held sway, men and women, "Aryans" and Jews, occupied separate spaces—and that was as true among the dying as among the living.

"MEN TO THE LEFT! WOMEN TO THE RIGHT."

This phrase haunts concentration-camp memoirs. "An SS noncommissioned officer came to meet us, a truncheon in his hand. He gave the order: "Men to the left! Women to the right!" Those were the first words Elie Wiesel heard when he arrived at Auschwitz.[52] Victor Frankl remembered: "We were told to leave our luggage in the train and to fall into two lines—women on one side and men on the other—in order to file past a senior SS officer."[53] "There were loud announcements, but it was all fairly restrained: nobody did anything to us. . . . I followed the crowd: 'Men to the left, women and children to the right,' we had been told."[54] The phrase is ubiquitous. Miklos Nyiszli's account hints at a possible motivation for this practice. "To start, the SS quickly divided us according to sex, leaving all children under fourteen with their mothers. So our once united group was straightaway split in two."[55] Ilse Blumenthal-Weiss reported that at a camp for converted Jews in Holland (a privileged category), relatives could meet together during the day, but when they arrived in Theresienstadt, "families were torn apart."[56] Vladka Meed, one of the very few survivors of the Warsaw ghetto, recalled: "For me the final solution is the final isolation of women, men, and children, of both sexes, of young and old. . . ."[57]

Before the stripping, beatings, delousing, searching, and even the selection for work crew or crematorium came the separation of women and men. Camp life was planned to obliterate all signs of individuality: tatooed numbers replaced names; identical "uniforms" and shoes, shaved heads, and starvation reduced external differences to a minimum. From the prisoners' first minutes in a camp, however, gender remained as one of the few social markers. The other distinction (and this only for those "selected" to survive a few weeks or months longer in work camps) was a colored triangle: yellow for Jews, pink for homosexuals, blue for stateless, green for black marketeers (*Berufsverbrecher*), black for "asocials," red for politicals, and violet for Jehovah's Witnesses. Inmates with triangles of all colors shared common barracks and work assignments. Men and women were not allowed to mingle.

Nazi orders routinely linked genocide and gender. When Heydrich gave the first unequivocal and specific directive for mass murder on July 31, 1941, he included as a matter of course both separation according to sex and then extermination based on race.

> In pursuance of the final solution, special measures will apply to conscript Jews for the labor service in the east. In large labor groups, with the sexes separated . . . while constructing roads [they will be] directed to these areas, whereby undoubtedly a large number will drop out through natural elimination. . . . The possible remainders, and they undoubtedly will be the toughest among them, will be treated accordingly, for [history teaches us that] they, being a natural selection, would if released become the germ cell of a new Jewish reconstruction.[58]

In procedures that defy belief, even when the "deportees" at extermination camps were to be murdered within a few minutes, camp officials scrupulously followed the ritual: men to the left and women to the right.[59] This did not result in favored treatment for women, as the following remarks about women in Treblinka illustrate:

> [Menstruation] only afforded the Ukrainians and the SS one more opportunity for sadistic humor. There were, of course, no sanitary napkins, or even newspapers, and the girls used large leaves—burdock leaves if they could find them—to protect themselves. But any blood showing on a dress meant death; it was unaesthetic, and the SS were very keen on aesthetics.[60]

At Auschwitz, where able-bodied victims could at least hope to work and survive for a few weeks, or months or years, the same segregation prevailed—also without any special consideration for the "weaker" sex.

> The SS-men showed no consideration for women in the camp. From the initial humiliation, when they were ordered to strip in the presence of soldiers and were shaved on the head and body by men, they went through every form of ill-treatment. They were put to work at making roads, leveling the ground, cleaning out ponds [and] had to live in the crowded barracks with the three-tiered bunks. . . . They died of hunger and fell beneath the blows of the SS-men's sticks, just as did the men.[61]

The SS brutalized women and men separately and equally.

To some extent, the separation of men and women resulted merely from conventional ideas about sex-appropriate work. For example, where victims served as Kapos (prisoners assigned to help the guards and granted special privileges), a traditional division of labor prevailed. At Treblinka, the "upper" camp included gas chambers, the installations for the disposal of the corpses . . . and the barracks for the *Totenjuden*, the Jewish work groups. One of the barracks was for males, another, later, for females. The men carried and burned the bodies; the twelve girls cooked and washed."[62] But conventional notions about women's and men's work could have played only a small role in the basic decision to separate the sexes. More fundamentally, Nazi orders aimed at the destruction of family ties.

Separation of men and women meant more than preventing sexual activity, it meant eroding emotional bonds—leaving individuals bereft in a horrifying world. Survivors' memoirs testify eloquently to the truth of Nazi leaders' fears. Splitting women from men did stun the victims, but only temporarily. Nazi planners failed to realize that the separation from biological siblings or spouses did not prevent victims from restoring lost loved ones in new relationships. In a few cases, inmates found ways of clandestinely maintaining proscribed contact with family in other barracks. When this proved impossible (as it usually did), prisoners reconstructed lost bonds, for they carried with them the family as memory and model on which to build new ties. Eugene Weinstock recalled: "survival . . . could only be a social achievement, not an individual accident."[63] Kitty Hart made the same observation. "I soon realized that alone one could not possibly survive. It was necessary therefore to form little families of two or three."[64] These new "families" may not have looked like families. Usually they included only members of the same sex. But they felt like families. How many memoirs of concentration-camp life contain phrases like "She became my new sister" or "We were like brothers." These newly formed connections represented the first stage of resistance —the refusal to submit to the dehumanization of gender separation. And after the first stage, inmates formed emotional bonds by performing small acts of kindness that cost precious energy and food, thus preserving their own emotional world within the barbed wire and beyond the control of guards.

In society outside Nazi surveillance—among victims as among resisters—individuals unified behind a common goal. The family (sometimes in its biological sense, but more often as a myth or a model) formed the basis for secret preserves of decency, love, and trust. Victims and opponents of Nazism, searching for a vocabulary with which to describe the deep ties they formed to their fellows, adapted the familiar vocabulary that carried reassurances of steadfastness and shared devotion in the midst of a lethal environment. To them, as to us, the very word "family" brings reassuring visions of strength. But usually life underground or in the camps dissolved the patriarchal assumptions people brought with them. Memoirs written about that life suggest that often victims and opponents played out stereotypical roles for pragmatic reasons as well as because of unconscious assumptions. But memoirs also abound in stories about how men learned the skills that most women learn as children— nurturing, caring, cleansing, and sharing; and women discovered unknown strengths when they had to run dangerous missions in places where any man of draftable age would have been arrested on the spot.

In the camps as in the underground outside, women brought special skills to the errand, and the public-private split worked to their advantage. From childhood, they had learned to live in a bicultural world that severed the public persona from private feelings; as resisters, they "instinctively" knew how to appear harmless and even obsequious to their enemies while maintaining their inner integrity. Concentration-camp prisoners learned to avoid calling attention to themselves while preserving an internal set of values. Those who resisted Nazi rule knew that sporadic acts of defiance produced only martyrs. Resistance meant long-term, collaborative deviousness—pitting wit, not physical power, against the enemy. This quintessentially "feminine" strategy became universal in situations where resisters and prisoners commanded few of the superficial attributes of normal life and dignity.

Paradoxically but not accidentally, Nazi policy aimed at eroding family ties among victims and also among its own "Aryan" followers. In both cases, the goal was the same: to break down individual identity and to render people susceptible to whatever plans Hitler announced: eugenic breeding schemes for the chosen "Aryans" and genocide for the selected. Nazi guards sent "men to the left" and "women to the right" for the same reasons that they sent girls to the BDM and "Aryan" boys to the Hitler Youth. They divided up German society into peer-group associations, not only because each gender was to perform different tasks, but (contrary to rhetoric praising the "strong family") to weaken family bonding and enhance total loyalty to the Führer.

Given this strategic Nazi antipathy to family ties, however, it comes as a surprise to discover that the architects of death viewed the family in very different terms when it came to their own lives. While fostering a gender-separated social world for millions of ordinary people, the men around Hitler, who carried out his order for genocide, allowed for and even encouraged an older concept of womanhood. Eva Braun, dull, passive, and decorative, not zealous Gerda Bormann or opportunistic Scholtz-Klink, remained the prototypical wife. The reasons for this apparent paradox become clear only after reflecting upon the masculine roles and tasks assigned to this elite by Hitler's orders for genocide. This reflection begins at the end—with the trials in Nuremberg—and centers on men, not women.

When we wonder about those men who issued and carried out genocidal orders, we ask with the judges at Nuremberg, "How was it possible that all you honorable generals could continue to serve a murderer with such unquestioning loyalty?" How, they asked themselves, could the elite placed in charge of killing operations remain human with such acts on their consciences? Hitler's deputies, for all the unspeakable crimes they ordered, were not hardened sadists or pathological killers. When the defendants at the Nuremberg Trials watched films depicting the brutality of extermination and forced labor, William Shirer recorded their reactions.

GÖRING: Shielded his face with his right arm, and seemed especially upset as tortures were mentioned.

HESS: Showed sustained interest, glaring at the screen.

DÖNITZ . . . Was quite upset, clenching his fists, and covering his eyes with his hands.

SCHACHT: Refused to look at the picture at all, turning his back on the screen. Showed no evidence of emotion.

FUNK: Broke down and cried.

FRANK (the butcher of Poland . . .): Quite overcome. He bit his nails, clenched his hands, and showed evidence of great emotion.

The whole courtroom was as silent as a sepulcher. Justice Lawrence, hitherto equal to every occasion in his dry, matter-of-fact judicial way, even forgot to adjourn the court. The judges silently rose from their chairs and slowly strode out without saying a word.[65]

Just a few years earlier in Berlin, when Party leaders had translated the "final solution" from the Führer's wish into deadly reality, they had imagined the impact on the men who actually did the killing. Novels by Remarque, Jünger, and a generation of veterans vividly depicted the massive transformations wrought by four years of trench warfare. What would become of elite soldiers who slaughtered helpless men, women, and children? Nazi leaders devised several solutions, the most obvious of which was to employ non-German soldiers from conquered nations (like the Ukraine and Poland) to carry on most of the guard work; and to offer a few prisoners special treatment in exchange for performing the most horrifying jobs. Secrecy, too, helped. Members of the task forces (*Sonderkommando*) did not realize the exact nature of their job until the last minute.[66] Still, the camps required German administrators. The *Einsatz-*

kommando in the field were largely Germans, and eventually soldiers found out.

Raul Hilberg summarized the ways in which SS and Nazi leaders managed to remain sane while committing subhuman jobs. While Hilberg does not use the term, he describes traits that Western culture praises as especially masculine. First came patriotic duty. As Wilhelm Frick declared at Nuremberg, "I have a clear conscience . . . I am convinced that no patriotic American citizen . . . would have acted any differently in my place." . . . [67] This echoed Himmler's speech to the SS in 1940.

> In many cases it is considerably easier to lead a company into battle than to command a company responsible for some area where it has to hold down a hostile population, probably one with a long history, to carry out executions, to deport people, to remove shrieking, weeping women . . . to do this unseen duty—to maintain this silent activity . . . to be always consistent, always uncompromising—that is in many cases far, far harder.[68]

In the name of obedience to a higher law (the Führer, in this case), officers were admonished to abolish from their hearts "feminine" traits such as sentimentality or squeamishness. They were to think of the long-term gain for all "Aryans," which vindicated the evil they wrought in the short term.

Equally important, leaders encouraged their men to feel proud of their brotherhood—a tough, elite force. To perform well in a concentration camp or *Einsatzkommando* meant to be a "real man," to be ruthless, obedient, loyal, without moral scruples toward subhumans, and scrupulously honorable to equals. Himmler told his officers on October 4, 1943:

> The SS man is to be guided by one principle alone: honesty, decency, loyalty, and friendship toward those of our blood, and to no one else. . . . Whether other peoples live in plenty or starve to death interests me only insofar as we need them as slaves for our culture; for the rest it does not interest me. Whether 10,000 Russian women keel over from exhaustion in the construction of an antitank ditch interests me only insofar as the ditch for Germany gets finished. We will never be savage or heartless where we don't have to be; that is obvious. Germans are after all the only people in the world who treat animals decently, . . . but it is a crime against our own blood to worry about [human animals] and instill ideals into them, only to create problems for our sons and grandsons. If someone comes to me and tells me, "I cannot dig these antitank ditches with children or with women, it is inhuman, they will die on the job," I must say to him, "You are a murderer of your own blood, because if the antitank ditch is not dug,

German soldiers will die, and they are sons of German mothers. They are our blood."[69]

This extraordinary order commanded men to defend their own manhood, even though it involved killing women.

Although she was not speaking of this example specifically, American writer Susan Griffin describes the message conveyed by Nazi criminals at Nuremberg. "Implicitly, he tells his judges that he is not him*self*. He *is* only an empty shell of a man, a receptacle for the orders given him by the Nazi Party and by Hitler . . . he had acted only as a puppet."[70] SS men emptied themselves of their own autonomy and filled the void with a mythical vision of their own manliness to stiffen their resolve and still their consciences. Yet this picture of characterless automatons does not adequately convey the complexity of the men's personalities who ordered and carried out mass murder. On the one hand, Griffin describes a man who, contemporary sociologists would say, felt overidentified with his role. Like the careerist or workaholic, these men saw themselves as *totally* loyal, obedient, and rigorous. They saw themselves as paradigms of masculine virtue. In following orders, they cast aside the last vestiges of their humanity, but clung to a prefabricated and socially acceptable vision of masculinity.

But this portrait is too monolithic. To have totally internalized their tasks as the core of their identity would have completely brutalized them. This could (and occasionally did) produce men who identified with their jobs so enthusiastically that they began to find pleasure in them. Such a commandant or guard might then forget his overriding responsibilities to the SS and begin to enjoy his job. Nazi leaders wanted dedicated, cold administrators of death, not killers among their elite. Nor did they want madmen. Conventional ideas about "masculine" and "feminine" played a role in two very different aspects of genocide. First, male guards had been socialized to a code of behavior that prescribed gentleness toward defenseless people, especially women and children. Secondly, camp personnel brought with them deep emotional needs for contact with their own wives, children, and families, which enabled them to maintain their tenuous ties to the world beyond to a sphere of private happiness and sanity. Even as a guard identified with his role as murderer, he kept his sanity by cultivating what sociologists call "role distance" from his actions. Paradoxically, he overidentified with his career and simultaneously withdrew from it as a source of his identity. He was aided in this psychological feat by specific policies.

In addition to extolling the virtues of the SS, propaganda vilified and dehumanized the most helpless victims. Camp personnel continued the process. Journalist Gitta Sereny asked Franz Stangl, the commandant of Treblinka, why, if they were going to kill them anyway, what was the point of all the humiliation, why the cruelty? "To condition those who actually had to carry out the policies," he told her, "to make it possible for them to do what they did."[71] One inmate who survived asked the same question of a camp guard who had been "an absolute monster" when she had been in a camp. "You know," he said, "when you look at people . . . without any identity and that aren't human anymore, you feel so guilty you overcome the guilt with anger."[72] Saying "These are not humans," they could conclude, "I am not a murderer." By brutalizing their victims, they avoided brutalizing their own souls.

These shallow psychic tricks did not always work. Sometimes, like Adam Goeth (portrayed vividly in *Schindler's List* by Thomas Keneally) or Irma Griese (depicted by Olga Lengyel in *Five Chimneys*), guards began to enjoy their work—erratically and violently indulging their sadism. More commonly, the reverse reaction occurred. Despite psychological conditioning, horror at their actions seeped into administrators' and guards' consciousness. Stangl admitted that the undressing barracks were the most dreadful place in the camp. "I avoided it from my innermost being; I couldn't confront them; I couldn't lie to them; I avoided at any price talking to those who were about to die: I couldn't stand it."[73]

In Israel, Eichmann confessed he had been so sensitive that he could not bear the sight of blood and had become sick at the sight of Jews stripped in a large room. Mobile gas vans drove up to the door and sent carbon monoxide into the room. Eichmann had to watch. "I cannot tell . . . I hardly looked. I could not; I could not; I had had enough. The shrieking, and, I was too upset, much too upset. . . . I saw the most horrible sight I had thus far seen in my life. The doors of the truck were opened, near a ditch, and the corpses were thrown out, as though they were still alive, so smooth were their limbs. . . . I can still see the civilian extracting the gold teeth with the pliers. A physician in white overalls told me to look. I could not." Eichmann protested to an SS general in Lvov: "It is horrible what is being done around here. Young people are being made into sadists. Simply bang away at women and children. That is impossible. Our people will go mad, or become insane, our own people." The general shrugged. One of Himmler's officers reported after his men had witnessed the execution of "only" one hundred Jews: "Look at the eyes of the men in this *Kommando*, how deeply shaken they are! These men are finished [*fertig*] for the rest of their lives. What kind of followers are we training here? Either neurotics or savages!"[74]

More extreme measures had to be devised. This process began in Berlin and shrouded genocide at every level in euphemism, beginning with the benign-sounding code names devised by the "desk murderers" and ending with elaborate deception at the killing sites. Similarly, a series of schemes kept relatives outside the camps ignorant of the truth. The mother of a Dachau prisoner, who did not know of her son's death, received a packet with his clothes and a note: "Enclosed are the articles which the prisoner does not require on his discharge."[75] Stangl had a fake train station constructed (complete with painted clock with hands that never moved and signs TO BIALYSTOK), so that prisoners about to be murdered would not realize they were on their way to the "sorting house." And the anterooms to the gas chambers had carefully lettered signs telling prisoners to remember the numbers of the hooks on which they had hung their clothes. Each camp had its specialty—a greenhouse, a zoo, or park. Auschwitz had its orchestra, to keep *Kultur* alive. Fania Fénélon described the directors of the orchestra, Maria Mandel and Joseph Kramer, who both loved music passionately. "Kramer cried when we played *"Träumerei"* by Schumann. Kramer, who gassed 24,000 humans. When he was tired of his work he came to us and listened to music. That's what's so incomprehensible about the Nazis. They could shoot, murder, and gas—and afterward be so sensitive. We were not even humans in their eyes. We were lice. They wanted to exterminate us."[76] Fénélon's description itself suggests how such killers could love music. Kramer's and Mandel's ability to escape into music was not paradoxical but essential because it enabled them to identify with how they felt, not with what they did. As they divided the players from the music, so too did they split their own workaday reality from their deep attachment to culture.

Commandants and guards imposed on themselves a split reality, telling themselves that the fake world they had constructed matched their "real" inner selves. They relegated "obeying orders" to their public responsibilities, and created a private fantasy within which they deceived themselves into thinking they were not so bad after all. Speer, in his cell, wrote, "Today it seems to me that I was trying to compartmentalize my mind. On the one hand was the vulgar business of carrying out a policy proclaimed in the anti-Semitic slogans. . . . On the other hand there was my idealized picture of Hitler. I wanted to keep these two apart."[77]

Franz Stangl, awaiting his execution, made a similar remark. "That's what I am trying to explain to you; the only way I could live was compartmentalizing my thinking."[78] Later Stangl declared, "I had to do [my job] as well as I could. That is how I am." "My professional ethos was that if something wrong was going on [in the camp] then it had to be found out. That was my profession; I enjoyed it. It fulfilled me. And yes, I was ambitious about that; I won't deny that." Sereny asked Stangl, "Would it be true to say that you got used to the liquidations?"

He replied, "To tell the truth . . . one did become used to it."

"In days? Weeks? Months?"

"Months. It was months before I could look one of them in the eye. I repressed it all by trying to create a special place; gardens, new barracks, new kitchens, new everything; barbers, tailors, shoemakers, carpenters . . . and I drank."[79]

One central deception formed the core of all these pretexts: the ideal of womanhood. Paradoxically, the Nazi state, which sedulously undercut all forms of privacy and attempted to destroy parental influence over children, actually encouraged traditional notions of the family when selecting SS commanders who would oversee genocide. For all the emphasis on breeding programs and unwed motherhood, the Nazi leaders and SS chiefs remained as petty bourgeois as they accused their enemies of being. They relied on the sheltering family (or on its myth) to keep alive an ersatz sense of decency in the men who would work most closely with mass murder. Nazi policy for commandants and guards encouraged a vision of womanhood and the family that they had deeply opposed in social policy aimed at masses of ordinary Germans. They re-created the ideal of a family as refuge, as a place to renew contact with a private and more humane self. The SS man who excised "feminine" traits from his personality depended on a woman to salvage his sanity.

When Sartre and de Beauvoir analyzed anti-Semites and misogynists, they described the process by which the member of the dominant category objectifies the inferior social category. In Nazi Germany, the Nazi "subject" converted women and Jews into "objects" of both social policy and of their own fantasies. For Jews, there was no difference between the two processes. The propaganda that dehumanized the Jew prepared the way for the deportation and extermination. But for women the matter was more complex. Nazi men needed the women they subdued. On the simplest level, they viewed their wives as their property and did not want their possessions confiscated.[80] In addition, while designing vast programs to erode the family and the privacy it protected, Nazi leaders themselves realized they needed the haven they destroyed. Except for a few fanatics like Gerda Bormann, wives had little to do with husbands' careers; and records of Hitler's dinnertime conversations with women present testify to the apolitical mindlessness that predominated during those gatherings. Scholtz- Klink recalled when I spoke with her that Nazi husbands did not want fanatically loyal wives who might "talk shop" at the end of a hard day. Not even Nazi "shop." And leaders continually sent out memos warning their men against discussing their jobs with wives. When wives knew, the barrier between a "sane" and "decent" home life lowered. At a Party rally, Rudolf Hess reminded the elite, "In conversation with your wives, speak only of those matters which have been expressly marked for public distribution." Six months later, Nazi leaders in Prussia were told, "One does not chatter with women about politics; women must take care of their looks, politics is our business." Frau Hoess, wife of the Auschwitz commandant, eventually did begin to ask questions, and her husband told her reluctantly that he "bore the responsibility for hundreds of thousands of inmates."[81]

After choosing four hundred men to carry out euthanasia, one hundred were singled out as psychologically able to apply their skills to mass extermination. On the whole, good family men were chosen, and generous leave time was granted so husbands and fathers could rehumanize their psyches in the company of their families. When one of his physicians seemed to be on the verge of a nervous breakdown, Dr. Mengele sent for the man's wife to come to live in Auschwitz.[82]

After all the propaganda about totally loyal women who would select racially fit mates, carry out sterilization programs, direct a separate women's world, and indoctrinate their communities, most wives of the concentration-camp "elite" conformed to rather traditional expectations. Even Nazi memoirs keep the image of virtuous womanhood alive. Speer (who unstintingly criticized his male comrades), says of their wives:

> In general the wives of the regime's bigwigs resisted the temptation of power far more than their husbands. They did not lose themselves in the latter's fantasy world. They looked on at the often grotesque antics of their husbands with inner reservations and were not caught up in the political whirlwind in which their men were carried steeply upward. Frau Bormann remained a modest, somewhat browbeaten housewife, although blindly devoted both to her husband and the party ideology. I had the impression that Frau Göring was inclined to smile at her husband's mania for pomp. And in the final analysis Eva Braun, too, proved her inner superiority. At any rate she never used for personal ends the power which lay within her grasp.[83]

Scholtz-Klink, Reber-Gruber, and other women leaders directed their offices and shaped policy before 1939, but wives remained far from any public sphere, even a "womanly" one.

One of the central fantasies to which commandants and guards clung emerged from their love of their families. In the case of the Hoess family, the commandant and his wife lived together with their many children on the grounds of Auschwitz. In the memoirs he wrote while awaiting execution, Hoess reflected on his life.

> I had to go on with this process of extermination. I had to continue this mass murder and coldly to watch it, without regard for the doubts that

were seething deep within me. . . . In Auschwitz I had no reason to complain that I was bored. If I was deeply affected by some incident, I found it
impossible to go back to my home. . . . I would mount my horse and ride,
until I had chased the terrible picture away. Often, at night, I would walk
through the stables and seek relief among my beloved animals.

When I saw my children happily playing or observed my wife's delight
over our youngest, the thought would often come to me: how long will
our happiness last? My wife could never understand these gloomy
moods of mine, and ascribed them to some annoyance connected with
my work.

I was no longer happy in Auschwitz once the mass exterminations had
begun. I had become dissatisfied with myself. . . . My wife's greatest pleasure would have been to give a present to every prisoner who was in any
way connected with our household.[84]

Emotional stability, no less and probably more than false train stations,
euphemistic terms, and dehumanized victims, provided the murderers
with an ersatz sanity.

The reminiscences by men waiting to be hanged, however, ought not
lead us into believing that commandants' home lives really conformed to
such a loving and "humane" description. We know that often men with
unrealistically high and rigid expectations about family abuse their wives
and children. In Hoess's case, rumor reported that he had a lover-inmate
at Auschwitz who at one point attempted to murder him. Myths about a
happy home, like the fake train station and the symphony orchestra, did
not provide a permanent refuge from reality.

Among the thousands of normal people who participated in genocide
about whom Hilburg wrote, we have no evidence of any participant
taking a stand against mass murder—nor did any SS man go insane in
ways that hampered the efficient operation of the camps.[85] No man asked
for a transfer. After 1945, ex-commandants and guards seem to have
returned to domestic tranquillity and, although tormented by nightmares
and fear of arrest, carried on with their lives unless they were appre-
hended. Their postwar readjustment was, in all probability, smoother
than their victims' reentry into society.

The SS leadership, which in every other respect inculcated an entirely
masculine élan among its corps, placed men who cared about their
wives and children in charge of routine killing operations. This family
connection played a vital role in maintaining "culture" among the
murderers when they returned from "out there." Governor-General
Frank told a group of SS men at a Christmas celebration in Cracow
in 1940:

Some of you have mothers, others parents, and still others your wives, your brides, your brothers, and your children at home. They will all be thinking of you during these weeks. And they will worry, "My god, there he sits over there in Poland with so many Jews and lice . . ." It would be very nice of you if we would take photographs to send back to the loved ones at home.[86]

Jacob, whose full name we do not know, became a police chief in occupied Poland, and wrote to a friend, "I have a nice apartment in a former kindergarten, with everything. . . . Nothing is lacking, except naturally my wife and children. They would understand me best of all. My Dieter and the little Lene write very often in their way. It could sometimes drive you to tears. It is not good if one loves children as much as I used to."[87] He asked his friend back home to write. "One is so lonely and abandoned here that every piece of news from home does so much good."

Sereny asked Stangl, "In the midst of all the horror that surrounded you, . . . what was there for you to hold on to?"

"I don't know. Perhaps my wife. My love for my wife?" At first, in 1941, he had successfully concealed the nature of his work from her. "The little time we had together, we usually talked about the children and ordinary everyday things. But it is true [after she suspected], there . . . was tension." Among the concentration and killing camp personnel, caring was confined to the deepest emotional unit, the family, and excised from the routine activities of everyday duty. Sereny asked Frau Stangl what would have happened if she had forced her husband to choose between his profession and her.

"I have thought very hard . . . I believe that if I had ever confronted Paul with the alternatives: Treblinka or me; he would . . . yes, he would in the final analysis have chosen me."[88] Eventually, Frau Stangl realized the full extent of her husband's participation in mass murder. She told Sereny, "I began to see the terrible change in him. . . . I saw only glimpses." She urged him, " 'I am afraid for your soul, . . . you *must* leave.' " He refused. She "couldn't stand it any longer" and confessed to the Austrian priest. " 'I know you won't believe it but there is this terrible place in Poland and they are killing people—they are killing the Jews there. And my Paul . . . is working there. What shall I do? Please tell me. Please help us. Please advise us.' " Then she told Sereny, "He gave me such a terrible shock. . . . 'We are living through terrible times, my child. Before God and my conscience, if I had been in Paul's place, I would have done the same. I absolve him from all guilt.' I walked away like a zombie, in a dream, in a nightmare."[89] Stangl, aided by his vision of a family guarded by his virtuous and innocent wife, continued at his job, believing that one day he would return to the full-time role that matched his inner feelings. In the meantime, he removed his daily work from moral judgments altogether and reserved his ethical considerations for private life.[90]

What you do is public, how you feel is private. This is the essence of a system that severs masculine from feminine. Stangl, Hoess, and untold thousands of men felt their very sanity depended upon preserving an island of serenity where love, tenderness, and devotion reigned. A place to "touch base" and reaffirm one's humanity in the face of brutal criminality. A young SS man, writing to a comrade, ricocheted back and forth between descriptions of "the horrifying figures of the Jews . . . with big bulging veins, crippled, and stunned . . . not people, but ape-beings,"[91] to "sweet thoughts" of his "sweet girlfriend," the pharmacist's assistant, in Hamburg. Felix Landau (adopted son of a Jewish father in Vienna) worked with the Security Police and fell in love with a woman who deceived him. In suicidal grief, he volunteered to join the *Einsatzkommando*. On June 30, 1941, he was shipped to the front.

> Wonderful music, "Oh, Do You Hear My Secret Call?" How soft a heart can become. Strong are my thoughts about the person for whose sake I landed here voluntarily. What I wouldn't give if I could see her for only ten minutes. Hundreds of Jews with blood streaming down their faces, holes in their skulls, broken hands, and eyes hanging out, all running down the streets. A few Jews with blood streaming over them carried others who had totally collapsed. We traveled to a stronghold and there we saw things that certainly no one else has ever seen. At the entry stood soldiers with cudgels as thick as a fist and beat everyone in all directions.[92]

But the young soldier continued writing on July 12, 1941, "It is really so strange. You love battle, and yet you have to shoot unarmed humans *(Menschen)*. We got orders to shoot twenty-three, two of whom were women. They astonished us when they refused even to accept a glass of water from us. I was designated as a marksman and will have to shoot those who try to escape."[93] He confessed, "Evenings when I lie in bed, I get this desperate longing, this longing for peace, quiet and love."

As the Nazi state destroyed morality in the public sphere, wives and relatives were supposed to guard an emotional "space" for the men who oversaw the killing operations. "Each partner performed the function prescribed for it by nature," as Hitler put it. These wives did not directly participate in evil, but, on the contrary, fulfilled "nature's role" by normalizing a masculine world gone amok. While Nazi men expanded their German territorial *Lebensraum* and made the nation *judenrein* (literally "purified of Jews"), women chose between ignoring or recognizing their husbands' work. Meanwhile ordinary women decided whether to look away or offer an act of kindness when they knew a friend or neighbor was in danger.

Wives, when they remained in their "proper place," kept their family world apart from the masculine sphere of brutality, coercion, corruption, and power. As with so many other aspects of Nazi ideology, this vision of womanhood embodied a traditional ideal carried to extremes. Over a century before, Johann Wolfgang von Goethe, in *Wilhelm Meister*, described the ideal couple. "Man tortures himself with public affairs, . . . Meanwhile a sensible housewife truly governs her domain." By remaining outside politics, history, and change, women preserved an important part of what the Germans mean by *Kultur*, or the commitment to lofty ideals of humanity and creativity. At the turn of the century, sociologist Max Weber explained how *Kultur* functions in a highly developed nation such as Germany: "A people accustomed to refined *Kultur*, *and yet* capable of withstanding the horrors of war out there . . . and a *Volk* who then return *despite all that* as basically decent as the vast majority of our people, that is true humanity; this no one should ever forget. . . ."[94] When the man returned from "out there," woman would be waiting, like the "intended" in *Heart of Darkness*, ready to still his nightmares and restore his humanity. Kurtz decides that "we must help [women] to stay in that beautiful world of their own, lest ours gets worse," and Marlow agrees.[95]

In Hitler's Germany, women provided in a separate sphere of their own creation the image of humane values that lent the healthy gloss of motherhood to the "Aryan" world of the chosen. In addition, wives gave the individual men who confronted daily murder a safe place where they could be respected for who they were, not what they did. Stangl's daughter, after her father's arrest, said, "All I can say . . . is that I have read what has been written about my father. But nothing—nothing on earth —will make me believe that he has ever done anything wrong. I know it is illogical; I know about the trial and the witnesses. . . . I love him—I will always love him."[96] In a bureaucratized society in which men separate themselves from their public deeds, the home takes on special meaning. Although in many ways Nazi social policy invaded domestic life (with its racial fetishism, spies, and media control), the family continued to offer a haven from public horror for the men who arrested, deported, tortured, and killed those they defined as enemies of the *Volk*.

The private sphere, a "place" apart from the brutal world, offered respite to people at both extremes of the moral spectrum. Guards and commandants, victims and resisters—at the outer flanks of the Nazi world, all needed the psychological "space" offered by a home (or at least the myth of one) to gather strength with which to face the deformed world outside. In the Nazi world, man and woman operated in radically separated spheres. Leaders designed programs to drain the home of its emotional meaning for average people, but for the elite who actually oversaw the concentration camps and death camps, an older ideal prevailed. When the SS man returned home, he entered a doll's house of ersatz goodness in which he could escape from his own evil actions. He, in contemporary psychological terminology, "split" his identity as public man from his warm and loving feelings for his family. Nazi wives did not offer a beacon of strength for a moral cause, but rather created a buffer zone from their husbands' jobs. Far from wanting to share their husbands' concerns, they actively cultivated their own ignorance and facilitated his escape.

Victims and resisters, by contrast, did their best to integrate their private morality into their public acts—even as they learned to dissemble in public to avoid detection. Both men and women adapted, often learning new roles and attitudes from each other. Women as well as men operated in the public world they found repugnant and found solace in carefully guarded private spheres. Their personal lives remained clandestine, genuinely "private," and their underground communities genuinely moral. When they needed a vocabulary to express the concern, trust, and idealism they shared, words like "sister," "brother," and "family" came readily to mind.

Guards and commandants rationalized their participation in Nazi schemes for genocide and repression by divorcing what they did from who they were. Victims and resisters, in contrast knew that sanity and survival depended upon preserving private integrity against Nazi power.

EPILOGUE

"No, I don't mind the tape recorder at all. And if you could send me a copy, I would appreciate it. Just this afternoon my daughter called me from Italy and asked that I talk to you after she gets back home. She wanted to hear, too. My daughter has never asked before, I have never told her. Neither did my husband, and he had far more to tell than I. Five years in Theresienstadt. Of sixteen thousand in the group in the first deportation together, he and two others survived. We wanted our child to have a normal childhood, like we might have had ourselves if only . . . Maybe she ought to know. She'll be home tomorrow. I think I should talk."

Frau Dr. Jolana Roth reflected for a moment, framed by a vivid green lawn, fading pink roses, and red-checkered tablecloth. In her backyard, where the Munich suburban sprawl encounters the deep Bavarian forest, she had created her own island of peace, simple and spacious. The house, with white walls and marble floors, was devoid of frills. A stark, empty haven, with the smell of a paprika roast drifting from the kitchen.

"Wouldn't you like some wine or beer—or soda, tea, coffee? I normally have more to offer, but I just returned from Cannes this morning and started right in to work." I accepted mineral water.

"Where to start?" she asked, as the shadows lengthened over the lawn and her face softened in the twilight. "I had such a normal childhood. Perhaps even happier than most. It was my mother who made us all happy—my father, two sisters, one brother, and me. We had very little in the way of possessions, but we felt luckier than people today who have so very much. My parents' marriage was arranged; no one thought of selecting their own partners. There was no egotism. Mama always put in her opinions and was very strong-minded. She cooked, and sang, and sewed, and provided us with a wonderful home. You know, with all the social problems in the world today, it's a wonder someone doesn't realize that if only all married women left their jobs and just made their homes wonderful, people would be happier and unemployment would disappear. There was no egotism in our family. We came from four genera-

tions of rabbis, originally from Romania, but for generations in Czechoslovakia on the Hungarian border. In 1939, our region became part of
Hungary, after Hitler invaded Czechoslovakia. Papa was of the old
school. Very strict. No talking at mealtime, and all prayers in Hebrew.
We spoke Yiddish at home. My father had a modern side, too, so he
encouraged me to study to be a teacher. That's the only thing I ever
wanted to become. Papa suggested medicine; but I was too squeamish. I
felt faint at the sight of blood. After Auschwitz, though, I became a
physician because I wanted to help people. Papa would have been happy.

"Looking back on that time, it's like describing life on the moon. It
was so different. Our village was nestled in the mountains, so beautiful
and so remote. Everyone respected Papa, who was a firm Socialist and
the mayor of our village. It was a big village—three thousand or four
thousand people. My father was a farmer, too, and we all worked very
hard as children. So remote . . . as if we lived on the moon."

As if to underscore the observation, the roar of a jet burst into the
silence. The Munich airport lay just beyond the forest. I thought quickly
back to my first attempt at oral history: my day with Gertrud Scholtz-
Klink two summers before. In the 1930s, when she was riding through
Berlin in her limousine, Jolana Katz was studying for her high school
exams, singing Yiddish songs, and working on the family farm. Germany
had seemed so remote to her then that when an uncle from Berlin told
them about life in the big city, the Katz family could hardly believe his
description. "He came from a different planet."

I realized that a misunderstanding had brought me here. I had been
told Dr. Roth would be a source of information about Jews who had lived
in Nazi Germany. It had not been my initial intention to write about
concentration camps, a subject that has its historians. I did, however,
plan to write about Jews in Nazi Germany. As I spoke to Dr. Roth, I
doubted this conversation would be important. Memories from
a childhood that began in a peasant village in the Carpathian mountains
could not have been more remote from Scholtz-Klink's cheerful recollections.

"We played with the other children in the town. There were only a
couple of hundred Jews and we felt no stigma. Of course, we felt different from the others somehow. Why? Well, for one thing, we did not
drink. The others drank and the men did the most terrible things to their
children and wives. Now that I think of it, I don't think that even now I
have ever seen a drunk Jew. Jewish parents believed that their children
ought to be better off and worked hard for their children. Yes, we were
different, but our neighbors treated us very well. My father's very best
childhood friend fought in the war with him and was very close. He was

a Christian." Here Frau Dr. Roth paused. Her hands remained folded, and her gaze shifted to the tape recorder on the checkered tablecloth. "When they came to get us for the transport, when they came to get us, my father knew. He rushed to his friend and begged him to raise my ten-year-old brother, to save his life. On his knees, he begged him. The friend said No.

"All his life my father was proud of his farming equipment. 'That's my empire,' he would say. 'We will always be safe. Here I am master.' But the neighbors took it; and the government requisitioned our cow. We had nothing left. After the war I returned to the village and visited our neighbors. I saw my parents' bedroom set. 'Please, may I have it back?' I asked. 'You must be mistaken,' they said, 'that's ours. You are confused.' At another farm I saw our dining room table. 'Your father sold it, fair and square, and we don't intend to give it back.' And then, the dishes. The neighbor said, 'Listen. You have suffered very much, but you are alive. You should be grateful, and we won't give them back.' I didn't care about the money, but I wanted something to hold on to. I stopped asking. My brother-in-law did not stop. He took his case all the way to the high court in Prague, and the people in the courtroom nearly killed him, they were so furious. He got nothing. I stopped asking. People are not angels. Goodness is fragile. People are not good.

"I had a very happy youth. The best memories," she mused. "I was allowed to study at the *Gymnasium*, even though I was the only Jew. Our teacher was a terrible anti-Semite and used to tease me because of my name, which means 'cat.' Still, he was Hungarian and I was the only student who spoke Hungarian, so in a certain way I was his favorite. We could discuss literature and philosophy. Aside from that, I enjoyed my studies, and village life was calm. We had a beautiful family life. The whole community stayed very close—like the moon, no comparison with today. Some things are the same. Today they call it anti-Zionism, but we know it's just the same anti-Semitism some people believed in then. Anti-Jew is anti-Jew, no matter how you call it.

"In some ways it was not so bad that Hungary conquered our little village, because Admiral Horthy tried to protect 'his' Jews. You had to prove your family had lived there for generations (and that meant expensive legal fees), but if you could afford to prove it, you did not get shipped off to the Germans. But then the front moved closer to us.

"The Hungarians on their way to war did terrible things, chased Jews, I can't say. . . . We had to wear the Jew star, and my father was taken to a forced-labor camp nearby. But then they released him. Still we did not know. They took my little cousin to a small area in a field where they had to dig trenches. Then the soldiers shot the people, who fell into a mass grave. My cousin did not get hurt. So when night came, she crawled out and came home to warn us. Those were bad times. We left our farm and moved to a small city. My father said we must continue to pray. One Saturday, when my father was praying, the Hungarian soldiers came to the door and took him away."

A jet rose above the line of the dark forest; and silence returned.

"Then they brought him back weeks later. We had to wear yellow stripes. People treated us like animals. When people saw the yellow they did not see the human being who wore it. Maybe people are really all animals and only human on a very thin surface. In Holland, Germany, France, in all those nations if the local officials had not cooperated, it would not have happened. They all sleep peacefully today. The police shaved my father's head. He did not talk about his experiences in the camp. We all played happily together as children. Life was not easy.

"In March 1944, they made us walk to a tile factory several hours away. This was the collection place; we did not know it. On the first night the girls sang patriotic songs and hymns to keep up our spirits. On the second night, my little brother started to scream and scream. Somehow he knew. And somehow we knew that he knew. No words were exchanged. No one sang on the second night."

The telephone rang, its bell more piercing than the occasional jets that passed overhead. Frau Dr. Roth calmly excused herself. Soon I heard her voice, which no longer sounded like her voice, talking with a friend in animated tones punctuated by laughter. In rapid and expressive Czech, talking about the events of the day, Frau Dr. Roth produced a volley of sparkling phrases. Talking with me, staring at the tape recorder, she had spoken in a barely audible monotone—struggling beneath a surface tranquillity to form the words and recall long-buried images. Her telephone conversation ended.

Ours resumed. "When we entered Poland, we had never heard of Auschwitz. We knew nothing. How could we have known? The world's greatest historians and experts still cannot understand it with all the evidence in front of them; how could we have known? I was a high school student. Father knew and said that if he had understood sooner, his one wish would have been to get poison for us all. They let us sit in the May sun all day in the wagons. We smelled a horrible stench, but could not guess what it was. Along toward midnight, under searchlights, the SS unloaded us. My father took my brother's hand. If he had not, they would have remained alive. If you held a child close to you, you were automatically sent to the gas chamber. My cousin helped a neighbor child, too." Frau Roth paused. She must have wanted to stop here, switch off the recorder, and return to the present. But she did not. "How many times I have been sorry that I did not give my mother a shawl to keep her warm. If only I had found her a shawl. All my life I have accused myself because I did not give her a shawl.

"They sent my sisters and my mother to the right. I suddenly said, 'My sister is not as young as she looks,' She was barely sixteen. They said, 'How old is she then?' I answered, 'Eighteen.' To this day I do not know what gave me the courage to say that. Then he said, 'Good,' and she came with us. The SS looked so noble. They said that the old and the sick should come in the truck. Direct to the gas. But we had the feeling they were being taken for a bath or a change of clothes. We had not heard the word 'gas.' Later, when rumors spread, a handsome SS man, about forty, laughed. 'What? Don't be childish. This is the twentieth century. How could you think we would gas a human being? Here we have great factories. Once in a while the elderly die. We build the chambers for hygienic reasons.' Then he took a very lovely young woman, shaved her hair and put her in uniform, so we would know no harm could come to us either. We all were taken into the SS room, stripped and shaved and paraded in a fashion show. We felt degraded beyond belief. Elderly or pregnant women were sent directly to the gas. My sister and I asked about our father and they said he was already at work.

"Even the experts don't understand. The ovens worked overtime and often could not take care of the bodies. So the men would heave them in piles, you know, one took the feet and the other the arms—one, two, three, hoopla—they tossed them on the pile. When we passed by, I saw my sister's body. . . ." The telephone rang and once again Frau Dr. Roth pushed Jolana Katz into the past.

"That's what life was like. A very unhappy existence. They sent us to 'A' Camp in isolation from the others. They called it 'Canada'—no one knows why. Maybe they wanted us to think life there was as good as in Canada. We sorted clothing of the people who came from the gas. Often it was warm. We divided it into men's, women's, and children's sizes, and according to quality. We had to turn in anything valuable. We could not leave any trace of a yellow star, no yellow. I always did my best to leave a torn number or a fragment of a star, so the people outside would know where these clothes came from. One day I found my brother's shirt, the one I had sewn for him. It just happened to come to me. Had I stood a few paces to the right or the left, it would have come to someone else. Another day I found a scrap of my own high school portrait burned at the edge. My father always carried it with him. He was so proud. He would never have let it go. I tried to keep it, but we couldn't keep anything. It's gone now, with the rest.

"The very first day when I saw the piles of corpses I could not look;

and I could not *not* look. Their tongues, bitten through in anguish. And their open eyes, staring out at us. Telling us something. Sometimes the children on these piles moved. They were short, so the gas was not always effective enough to kill them outright. Sometimes we would open a suitcase in 'Canada' and find a baby inside, just barely alive. We never knew what do to. A mother had tried desperately to give her child a chance at life. We agonized but we could never conceal them. The Kapos came.

"Three of us girls who worked together are like sisters. We made sure that whenever anything happened to one of us, the other two would protect her and take care of her. We never left each other's sight. No matter how far apart we are, we visit and write and telephone. Last year we all got together in Canada—Calgary, Canada. We will never never lose track of one another. No matter what. We kept each other alive. In our barracks, we had a beautiful Greek actress who sang songs I had never heard, but will never forget. The song about the Jewish mama made us sob when we first arrived. The melody was very sad. But there were terrible scenes among the women, too. Mothers against daughters. And the women guards were the very worst. Worse than the men. One tall, blond SS woman would stand in her knee breeches, hands on her hips, with a whip and laugh as people went into the gas. Looking through a special window. A sadism no one can explain. The volunteers from the Ukraine were even worse. They chose to work here; they supported the Germans and became camp guards—hated the Russians and welcomed the German soldiers. They had grown up in a Socialist and moral state; yet they volunteered. They were not supposed to be like capitalists. They took our food from us, and ate it in front of us.

"Two things I will never understand: Why did they want so much music? If any of us could sing or dance, we had to play in the orchestra or amuse the SS guards. They always wanted people to seem happy. Then I don't understand why everything was so orderly. Always a system, forever a schedule. If enough new people did not arrive, they selected from camp inmates. But always the rules. Always German order. Once they came in and told us it was our turn. We marched to the ovens. Then they told us to turn around. It had only been a joke. And they laughed. They treated intellectuals and professionals especially badly. Once the women who worked in the arms factory nearby smuggled weapons to the men. I will never understand how they did it with the terrible searches. But they did. So the men inmates blew up the *Sonderkommando* sky-high. They blew up a crematorium. The very worst of the guards were blown up. But new ones came. The SS went crazy at the thought that the Jews had staged an uprising."

By now, dusk had turned to night. But the warm evening felt peaceful, and light would attract mosquitoes.

"Once Dr. Mengele made the selection personally in our barracks. We knew the situation was dangerous. When I would see him on the street of the camp I became terrified. His eyes. Like a wolf's eyes, but blood-red. An animal, not human. I saw the whole crematorium in his eyes. One day he visited our barracks, in a section where skin was unloaded and preserved. He strode in and looked up, very high near the rafters. He noticed a piece of skin clinging to a nail. 'If that doesn't come down in three minutes, you'll all go to the gas.' I looked in his eyes. To this day I do not know how I climbed up the beams, but I did. I brought it to him so the barracks would be neat and orderly. We were spared the selection that time.

"Sometimes people tell about decent SS guards. I never met one. They talk about one who actually loved a Jewish girl. When I first came to the camp, I saw him—his name was Wunsch, or Wünsch—from Vienna. He played at target practice by tossing Jewish infants up into the air and shooting them. Later he fell deeply in love with a Jewish girl. Real, genuine love. He adored her. In Israel afterward, they put her on trial. But she was found innocent, for she did nothing wrong. We never heard what happened to him.

"The other night I watched TV and saw David Irving. He said, 'Hitler did not know,' and 'Germans did not know.' I want to write him a letter and invite him to a nice home-cooked supper. Then I will sit him down and roll up my sleeve and say, "Look here, Herr Irving! How do you think I got this number on my arm? Whose idea was it to put it there? When I saw him on Austrian TV, famous and respected, without any German expert to contradict his 'scholarship,' I said to myself that we all had better talk about the truth.

"Several years ago, my husband and I heard about Emmy Göring driving around in a chauffeur-driven Mercedes; and we heard that a high government official received damage payments because the Nazi education system had not allowed him to pursue the career of his choice. We looked at one another, and said our claims deserve recognition. It was not for the money; we did it on principle. We said we ought to receive reparations for our "service" in the camps. For years afterward I lay in my room. I couldn't get up. Could not move. Finally the depression lifted and I went to medical school. Later we wanted the German government to recognize our suffering. For years we hired lawyers and took the case to the highest courts. The Germans did not want to deal with us because we had not been German citizens during the Second World War. Only citizens deserved reparations. Finally, they offered us a settlement after my husband had already died. Do you know how much I received for my time in 'Canada'?"

When I responded that I had no idea, I was making an honest statement. How could one calculate in money the impact of death-house labor on a teenager?

"The government awarded me DM 2400."

Even before the dollar rose and the mark fell, that was only about $1200.

"DM 2400. I would pay happily DM 10,000 or 50,000 or 100,000 just to have one single German spend a single day in Auschwitz doing that work. So they could report and tell the world what it was like; then people would believe. I stopped fighting. All I want is a quiet life and happiness for my daughter in med school. Germany will never come to terms with its past. There are almost no Jews here, and still my patients make cracks about Jews. It will never change."

I asked why she lived in this nation.

She had not really made a choice. After living in Prague, she and her husband had a chance to emigrate to Germany. Their dissatisfaction with life in Czechoslovakia overshadowed their dread of Germany—the land in which almost any citizen of the right age might have been one of their tormentors two decades before. In Munich they made a new life and raised a daughter.

The telephone rang. Again, Frau Roth spoke with joy in her voice. This time it was her daughter, who called from Austria on her way home. "She is coming with her boyfriend—an Italian. What can I say? He is a lovely young man. But somehow it seems so sad for her to marry into a mixed marriage. For all that we suffered through to end. For a tradition to disappear. Of course, with all I suffered, I cannot say anything to her. But it makes me sad. We wanted her to be normal, so we said nothing. And now she is normal and a family tradition comes to an end.

"I never doubted God or religion until I saw the bodies. Hundreds of thousands of corpses blur childhood faith. I asked myself if God had spoken there. One just cannot think about it . . . one dares not. I believe in God, and not so much in what my religion says I must do. It makes me sad."

Frau Roth suggested we go inside. She switched on the light, which brought me fast forward to the present. Again the Spartan furnishings impressed me. Although she had traveled widely in recent years, she had resisted the tourist's imperative to fill her home with exotic acquisitions. "Wouldn't you like to see my prized possessions?" she asked in a voice that began to assume its full range of modulation. Behind the glass doors of the bookcase, I saw an extraordinary glow. Dozens and dozens of glasses, plates, serving dishes of the finest Bohemian cut glass and rims of heavy gold. "This pattern was created for Queen Elizabeth's coronation, and the only other person to have a full set was Emperor Haile Selassie. I collected it gradually after the war. It's a lost art now. One does not use it, of course. It's too precious. Glass is so fragile. But when a rare artist touches it, it is good." Frau Roth's face broke into a smile, and she relaxed as we gazed admiringly at this splendid collection. Like people, her glass was so very fragile. But if protected, treasured, and cared for, it would last for generations, lending its luster to the lives in its sphere.

Her eyes seemed to reflect the warm light of the crystal as she turned and invited me to share the roast, which was just ready to come out of the oven. When I had met Jolana Roth only a few hours before, I wondered how had I arrived on her doorstep. As our conversation drew to an end, I understood that Jolana Roth's memories would conclude this book, which opened with Scholtz-Klink's self-serving recollections from, as Jolana Roth might have phrased it, the other side of the moon. The Reichsfrauenführerin, with ample opportunity to have informed herself before 1945 and four decades thereafter to repent, remained fixated on her ideal of Nazi glory. She spoke to me because she hopes people will remember the good side of Nazism. Jolana Roth, too, cares about history, and because so many Germans had taken up the search for a positive Hitler, she broke her silence.

NOTES

Preface

1. Mary R. Beard, *Woman as a Force in History. A Study in Traditions and Realities* (New York and London: Collier, 1971), 23. Cf. Ann J. Lane, ed., *Mary Ritter Beard: A Sourcebook* (New York: Schocken, 1977), 226–233.

2. William Shirer, *20th Century Journey. The Nightmare Years* (Boston: Little, Brown, 1984), 279.

3. Susan Sontag, "Fascinating Fascism," in her collected essays *Under the Sign of Saturn* (New York: Farrar, Straus, & Giroux, 1972), 99. Wherein lay the appeal, Sontag asks of a charismatic movement, "which transforms sexual energy into spiritual force, sexuality converted into the magnetism of leaders and the joy of followers."

4. Doris Kirkpatrick, "Role of Women," *The New York Times* (September 26, 1937).

5. Albert Speer, *Inside the Third Reich* (New York: Macmillan, 1970), 92. "Think of the problems if I had children!" Hitler had added.

6. Ibid., 19–20. In 1944 he drafted a memo to Hitler, " 'The task I have to fulfill is an unpolitical one. I have felt at ease in my work only as long as my person and my work were evaluated solely by the standard of practical accomplishments." Ibid, 112.

7. "When Hitler came to power, she shrewdly hung out three swastika flags and sent a letter to Diers by courier." Peter Engelmann, "Lady Führer über alles. Frau Klink is the Nazi Arbiter on 'Childbed and cookpot' matters," *Living Age* 359 (October 1940), 112–116. Engelmann had, incidently, been asked by Scholtz-Klink to serve as her press agent, but he chose exile.

8. Hannah Arendt, *Eichmann in Jerusalem. A Report on the Banality of Evil* (New York: Viking, 1964), 120–122. Arendt adds, "Whatever Kant's role in the formation of 'the little man's' mentality in Germany may have been, there is not the slightest doubt that in one respect Eichmann did indeed follow Kant's precepts: a law was a law, there could be no exceptions during the time when 'eighty million Germans' each had his 'decent Jew'. . ."

9. Emmy Göring, *An der Seite meines Mannes. Begebenheiten und Bekenntnisse* (Göttingen: Stütz, 1967), 64. This scorn, however, did not prevent her mentioning the Jew she tried to save.

10. Claude Lanzmann, *Shoah. An Oral History of the Holocaust*, preface by Simone de Beauvoir (New York: Pantheon, 1985), 50–51. Scholtz-Klink had reacted just as Nazi leaders hoped most non-Jews would. Report from

November 24, 1941, BA Koblenz, reprinted in Heinz Boberach, ed. *Berichte des SD und der Gestapo über Kirchen und Kirchenvolk in Deutschland, 1934–1944* (Mainz: Matthias-Gruenewald, 1971), 597–598. People felt shocked that so many were left. While church leaders cautioned their faithful not to make Jews feel uncomfortable, they also qualified their admonitions by suggestions that "non-Aryan" Christians attend early morning services.

11. "Schlossherinnen unter sich. Warum bot die Fürsten zu Wied der Reichsfrauenführerinnen eine Zuflucht?" *Neuer Tag*, March 5, 1948. The two were arrested in Altenheim, Kreis Kehl. Before then people had assumed Scholtz-Klink had committed suicide. *The New York Times*, (November 19, 1948), 12; (November 18, 1948), 12. Scholtz-Klink, *Frau*, 50–54.

12. "Professions for Women" (1943) based on "The Death of the Moth" (1931) in *Virgina Woolf, Women and Writing*, ed. Michele Barrett (New York: Harcourt, Brace and Jovanovich, 1979), 59.

1. Introduction: Love and Order in the Third Reich

1. Joachim C. Fest, *The Face of the Third Reich. Portraits of the Nazi Leadership*, trans. Michael Bullock (New York: Pantheon, 1970), 265. Originally published as *Das Gesicht des Dritten Reiches. Profile einer totalitären Herrschaft* (Munich: R. Piper, 1963). In a note, Fest adds that his statement is to be understood in the sense, "that men made the gods but women worshipped them," note 9, 377.

2. Jürgen Kuczynski, *Die Lage der Arbeiterinnen in Deutschland vom 1700 bis zur Gegenwart* (Berlin: Akademie, 1963), 255.

3. It should be noted that after the first national elections, constitutional challenges ended the separate ballots in many states. Gabrielle Bremme, *Die politische Rolle der Frau in Deutschland* (Göttingen: Van den Hoeck and Ruprecht, 1956), 76, and Richard Hamilton, *Who Voted for Hitler* (Princeton: Princeton University Press, 1983), 60–61, note 46 on 512–513, and 360–393; Thomas Childers, *The Nazi Voter* (Chapel Hill: University of North Carolina Press, 1983), 188–189 and 259–260. Michael Kater, *The Nazi Party. A Social Profile of Members and Leaders, 1919–1945* (Cambridge: Harvard University Press, 1983), 147–153.

4. Sylvia Plath, *The Collected Poems*, ed. Ted Hughes (New York: Harper & Row, 1981), 223.

5. Lotte Paepke, *Ich wurde vergessen. Bericht einer Jüdin, die das Dritte Reich überlebte* (Freiburg, i.B.: Herder, 1979), 30.

6. Erna Becker-Cohen, *Tagebuch*, 31. A 147-page manuscript, covering 1937–1954. The Leo Baeck Institute, New York. Hereafter, LBI.

7. Ruth Andreas-Friedrich, *Der Schattenmann. Tagebuch. Aufzeichnungen, 1938–1945* (Berlin: Suhrkamp, 1947) 188–189. English translation *The Berlin Underground 1938–1945*, trans. Barrows-Mussey (New York: Holt, 1947), 163.

2. Weimar Emancipation

1. Quoted in Jill Stephenson, *Women in Nazi Society* (New York: Barnes and Noble, 1975), 15–17.

2. Alice Rühle-Gerstel, *Das Frauenproblem der Gegenwart* (Leipzig: Hirzel, 1932), 124. Helene Dransfeld, a conservative Catholic, in a speech delivered on July 1919, asked, "What ought I represent, the interests of my sex or my party?" in Regine Deutsch, ed., *Politische Frauenarbeit*, 2nd. ed. (Gotha: Perthes, 1924), 6.

3. Quoted by Ulla Wischermann, "Die Presse der radikalen Frauenbewegung," *Feministische Studien*, III:1 (May 1984), 58.

4. Erich Maria Remarque, *All Quiet on the Western Front* (New York: Fawcett Crest, 1956), 160, 174. Remarque continues, "And men will not understand us—for the generation that grew up before us, though it has passed these years with us here, already had a home and a calling; now it will return to its old occupations, and the war will be forgotten—the generation that has grown up after us will be strange to us and push us aside. We will be superfluous even to ourselves, we will grow older, a few will adapt themselves, some others will merely submit, and most will be bewildered; the years will pass by and in the end we shall fall into ruin," 175.

5. Ibid., 113.

6. He admitted, however, that he appreciated the "clear objectivity of the Catholic nursing sisterhoods," Ernst Jünger, *Storm of Steel. From the Diary of a German Storm-Troop Officer on the Western Front*, intro. R. H. Mottram (New York: Fertig, 1975), 314. On occasion, alienation produced exaggerated worship. Klaus Theweleit, *Männerphantasien* (Frankfurt a.M.: Roter Stern, 1978), vol. I.

7. Ibid., 316. "I learned . . . that life has no depth of meaning except when it is pledged for an ideal, and that there are ideals in comparison with which the life of an individual and even of a people has no weight."

8. Adolf Hitler, *Mein Kampf* (Boston: Sentry, 1962), 165.

9. This autobiography has been preserved as part of a collection made by an émigré sociologist in 1936. Theodore Abel, *Why Hitler Came to Power: An Answer Based on the Original Life Stories of 600 of His Followers* (New York: Prentice Hall, 1938). His method is described in Chapter 3, note 7. Abel biography No. 145, by Maria Engelhardt from Frankfurt am Main. For the reactions of middle-class women, cf. Elly Heuss-Knapp, *Ein Leben in Briefen und Aufzeichnungen*, ed. M. Vater (Tübingen: Rainer Wunderlich, 1961), 149, especially her letter to F. Naumann, Sept. 25, 1914 that describes the end of euphoria; and Marie Baum, *Rückblick auf mein Leben* (Heidelberg: Kerle, 1950), 175–176 for a description of "masses of women."

10. Quoted in R. Hofstätter, *Die Arbeitende Frau. Ihre Wirtschaftliche Lage, Gesundheit und Mutterschaft.* (Vienna: M. Pereles, 1929), 22. Comments made by Susan Gubar and Sandra Gilbert at the Conference on Women and War, Center for European Studies, Harvard, January 6–8, 1984, informed these observations. Cf. Sandra Gilbert, "Soldier's Heart: Literary Men, Literary Women and the Great War," *Signs*, 8:3 (Spring 1983). Agnes von Zahn-Harnack, *Die Frauenbewegung: Geschichte, Probleme, Ziele*, 191, 308–314 and Idem. *Schriften und Reden* (Tübingen: Hopper, 1967), 9. Jürgen Kocka, *Facing Total War: German Society 1914–1918*, trans. B. Weinberger (Cambridge, Mass: Harvard University Press, 1984), 111–145.

11. During the war the percentage of women students at Heidelberg and

Freiburg (the first to open their admissions) rose from 6 to 35 percent. Ursula von Gersdorff, *Frauen im Kriegsdienst* (Stuttgart: Deutsche, 1969), 25, 198–199.

12. Charlotte Lorenz, *Die Gewerbliche Frauenarbeit während des Krieges,* vol. 6, James Shotwell, ed., *Wirtschafts- und Sozialgeschichte des Weltkrieges* (Stuttgart and Berlin: Deutsche, 1928), 311–417.

13. Matilde Wurm, delegate at Protokol der Reichs-Frauen-Konferenz der USPD Berlin: "Freiheit," n.d. (1920).

14. Quoted in Atina Grossmann, "The New Woman, The New Family, and the Rationalization of Sexuality," Rutgers dissertation, 1983.

15. Andrea Frahn, "Zu Hause," in Richard Klucsarits and Freidrich Kürbisch, eds., *Arbeiterinnen Kämpfen für ihre Rechte. Autobiographische Texte* (Wuppertal: Peter Hammer Verlag, 1983), 129. My thanks to Bonnie Anderson for calling my attention to this poem, which will appear in Bonnie S. Anderson and Judith Zinsser, *Women in European History* (New York: Harper and Row, forthcoming).

16. Rudolf Lust, "Die Frau im Berufe des Mannes," *Der Frauenbund* V: 5/6 (1919), 144. This complaint involves the feminization of a previously male field.

17. Lyrics by Kurt Tucholsky, quoted in Harold Poor, *Tucholsky* (New York: Scribner's, 1968), 53.

18. Arnold Brecht, *Prelude to Silence. The End of the German Republic* (New York: Oxford University Press, 1944), 47–49, 68–72, 126–132. The Socialist parties consistently received just over one-third of the electorate; the Catholic Party vote never fell below 15 percent; and the liberal parties (DDP and DVP) attracted between 12 and 20 percent of the vote. In the last election prior to Hitler's takeover, the Nazi Party candidates received just over 32 percent of the vote.

19. Gabrielle Bremme, *Die politische Rolle der Frau in Deutschland* (Göttingen: Van den Hoeck and Ruprecht, 1956), 69. For a perceptive contemporaneous view of women's participation in the government at all levels, cf. Hugh Wiley Puckett, *Germany's Women Go Forward* (New York: Columbia University, 1930); Gertrud Bäumer, *Die Frau im deutschen Staat* (Berlin: Junker und Dünnhaupt, 1932) and "Die Frau in der Gemeinde," *Die Frau* 55:1 (January 15, 1920). According to the tabulations in the latter article, over 1300 women served in elected offices at the local level in Germany. Hans Beyer, *Die Frau in der politischen Entscheidung* (Stuttgart: Enke, 1933) concluded that women remained constant voters with participation levels only slightly lower than men's, a conclusion born out by W. Phillips Shiveley, "Party Identification, Party Choice, and Voting Stability, The Weimar Case," *American Political Science Review* 66 (December 1972), 1203–1225. Cf. Heinz Herz, *Uber das Wesen und die Aufgaben der politischen Statistik* (Waldenburg, Saxony: E. Kaestner, 1932).

20. Ilya Ehrenburg, *Memoirs: 1921–1941,* trans. Tatania Shebunina with Yvonne Kapp (Cleveland and New York: World, 1963), 10, 12.

21. Hedwig Dohm, "Die Idealisten des Anti-Feministen," in Waly Zepler, ed., *Sozialismus und Frauenfrage* (Berlin: Cassirer, 1919), 28.

22. Clifford Kirkpatrick, *Nazi Germany: Its Women and Its Family Life* (New York and Indianapolis, Bobbs-Merrill, 1938) 280–281. On the failure of German feminism, cf. Richard Evans' excellent account in chapter 8, "The Bitter End," *The Feminist Movement in Germany 1848– 1933* (London Beverly Hills: Sage, 1976) 207–222, 253–265. Special issue on "Die Radikalen in der alten Frauenbewegung," *Feministische Studien* (Heft 1, 1984), 1–150; Renate Bridenthal and Claudia Koonz, "Women in Weimar Politics and Work," in Berenice A. Carroll, ed., *Liberating Women's History* (Urbana: University of Illinois, 1976); Rita Thalmann, *Etre Femme dans le Troisième Reich* (Paris: Robert Lafont, 1981), 46–57, and Barbara Greven-Aschoff, *Die bürgerliche Frauenbewegung in Deutschland 1894–1933* (Göttingen: Van den Hoeck and Ruprecht, 1981), 183 ff., and *Idem.* "Sozialer Wandel und Frauenbewegung" *Geschichte und Gesellschaft* VII:314 (1981) 328–346; and Ute Gerhard, " 'Bis an die Wurzeln des Übels,' Rechtsgeschichte und Rechtskämpfe der Rakikalin," *Feministische Studien* Heft 1 (1984), 77–98. Puckett, *Germany's Women,* 308–313.

23. *Stenographische Berichte der Verhandlungen des Reichstages* (hereafter referred to as SB), 348: 87 (March 17, 1921), 3161–3162.

24. While extoling women's superior spirituality and strong morale, she admitted that women had failed to prevent postwar chaos. "Die besonderen Kulturaufgabe der Frau," *Frauenfragen und Frauengedanken der Frau. Gesammelte Aufsätze* (Tübingen: J.C.B. Mohr, 1919), 279.

25. Katharina von Kardorff, "Der Konflikt der Frau in der neuen Zeit," lecture given either in 1927 or 1928, and "Gedanken zur Politik," n.d., BA Koblenz. Kardorff Nachlass, nos. 40 and 32. Women, said Kardorff, would bring to political life, "less theory, less red tape, fewer cliques, smaller egos, and especially less jealousy." Ibid 38/14.

26. Julie Velde, "Reden" DVP, Frankfurt am Main, BA Koblenz, ZSg 1/42/45 Speech to the National Assembly 1919.

27. Gertrud Bäumer, "Der neue Tag," *Die Frau* 35:12 (Sept. 1918), 388.

28. Gertrud Bäumer, letter to Marianne Weber dated April 11, 1919, *Des Lebens wie der liebe Band* (Tübingen: Wunderlich, 1956), 135.

29. Quoted in Rühle-Gerstel, *Das Frauenproblem,* 259.

30. Werner Thönessen, *The Emancipation of Women in Germany,* trans. Joris de Bres (London: Pluto, 1976), 239.

31. Ibid., 130.

32. On this turnabout, cf. Richard Evans' excellent *The German Feminist Movement* and Christine Wittrock's supurb survey of the intellectual continuity between the middle-class women's movement and Nazi women's thinking on "the women question." *Weiblichkeits Mythen* (Frankfurt, a.M.: Sendler, 1984), 14–34, 81–84.

33. Quoted by Kirkpatrick, *Nazi Germany,* 57.

34. Anna-Lise Schwelwitz-Ültzen, *Die Frau im neuen Deutschland* (Berlin: Staatspol., 1920), 15. On November 14, 1931, a Nazi woman, Elisabeth Rendschmidt, reported gleefully to Gregor Strasser on a middle-class women's organization meeting. "Bäumer spoke about the professional fate of a

younger generation, but the young were not there. . . . For the most part they will have nothing to do with liberal ideas." She warned that Jews ran marriage counseling centers and somehow were to blame for unemployment. BA Koblenz/NS22/348.

35. Amy Hackett, "Helene Stöcker, Left-Wing Intellectual and Sex Reformer," in Bridenthal, Grossmann, and Kaplan, *When Biology Became Destiny* (New York: Monthly Review, 1985), 109–130. Ann Taylor Allen, "Mothers of the New Generation: Adele Schreiber, Helene Stöcker, and the Evolution of a German Idea of Motherhood," *Signs* 20:3 (Spring 1985), 418–438 and Wittrock, *Weiblichkeitsmythen*, 55–72.

36. Margarete Kaiser, 1932, quoted by Atina Grossmann, "The New Woman and the Rationalization of Sexuality in the Weimar Republic," in Snitow, Stansell, and Thompson, eds., *Power of Desire. The Politics of Sexuality* (New York: Monthly Review, 1983), 154.

37. Ehrenburg, *Memoirs*, 9.

38. Rathenau quoted in U.S. Department of State, 862,00/1073.

39. Irene (Delano) Robbins, "German Diary," Box 18, 123. Family papers donated by children. FDR Library, Hyde Park. I am grateful to Blanche Wiesen Cook for sharing this material with me.

40. Pearl Buck, *How It Happens. A Talk about the German People 1914–1933* (New York: Doubleday, 1947), 81.

41. George Grosz, *A Little Yes and a Big NO*, trans. L. S. Dorin (New York: Dial, 1946), 61.

42. Quoted in Otto Friedrich, *Before the Deluge. A Portrait of Berlin in the 1920's* (New York: Harper & Row, 1972), 128.

43. Anita Loos, *A Girl Like I* (New York: Viking, 1966), 128.

44. Friedrich, *Before the Deluge*, 127.

45. Ilya Ehrenberg, *Memoirs*.

46. Istvan Deak, *Weimar Germany's Left-Wing Intellectuals: A Political History of the "Weltbühne" and Its Circle* (Berkeley: University of California, 1968), 187–199.

47. Alex de Jonge, *The Weimar Chronicle* (New York: NAL, 1978), 170.

48. Thomas Childers, *The Nazi Voter. The Social Foundations of Fascism in Germany 1919–1933.* (Chapel Hill: North Carolina University Press, 1983), 15–49, and Karl Braunias, *Das parlamentarische Wahlrecht*, Vol. I (Berlin & Leipzig: de Gruyter, 1932), 81–128 on "Parteizersplitterung." Eighteen parties produced ten representations in 1919; in 1930 32 parties produced 15 delegations. Voter participation was 83 percent in 1919 and 75.6 percent in 1928. In the Depression it increased to over 80 percent. In the U.S.A., by contrast, turnout averages between 50 percent and 55 percent in the twentieth century.

49. "These new games had to be played according to the rules, and anyone who took them lightly was snubbed . . . mercilessly." Madeline Kent, *I Married a German* (London: Allen and Unwin, n.d.), 112–113.

50. Carl Zuckmayer, *Als wär's ein Stück von mir. Horen der Freundschaft* (Hamburg: S. Fischer, 1977), 218.

51. Vicki Baum, *Es war alles ganz anders. Erinnerungen* (Berlin: Ullstein,

1962), 369. She called the secretaries *Neunuhrwesen,* "nine-hour beings" who came to life only at night.

52. Alec Swann, quoted in de Jonge, *Weimar Chronicle,* 127.

53. Stephen Spender, *World Within World: The Autobiography of Stephen Spender* (London: Hamish Hamilton, 1951), 107, 116.

54. Siegfried Kracauer, *From Caligari to Hitler. A Psychological History of the German Film* (Princeton: Princeton University Press, 1947), 107.

55. Harry Kessler, *The Diaries of a Cosmopolitan,* trans. Charles Kessler (London: Weidenfeld and Nicolson, 1971), 279.

56. From Christopher Isherwood, *Down There on a Visit* (New York: Simon and Schuster, 1962), quoted by Sheila Jeffreys, "Sado-Masochism: The Erotic Cult of Fascism." Unpublished manuscript.

57. Pearl S. Buck, *How It Happens,* based on conversations with Erna von Pustau.

58. Despite the demobilization of 1919, by 1925 the percentage of women working at industrial jobs had risen to 21 percent (as compared with 18 percent in 1907). Even before World War I, 22 percent of German married women had entered the work force. But one ought to remember that women who worked for a family business (small store or farm) were included as "working." In the U.S.A. only 10 percent of all married women worked outside their homes before 1914. Pinson, *Modern Germany,* 204–205; Quataert, *Reluctant Feminists,* 27, and "The Shaping of Women's Work," *American Historical Review* 90:5 (December 1985); Dörte Winkler, *Frauenarbeit im "Dritten Reich"* (Hamburg: Hoffmann und Campe, 1977) 18–28, Stefan Bajohr, *Die Hälfte der Fabrik* (Marburg: Verlag Arbeiterbewegung und Gesellschaftswissenschaften, 1979), 158–219. Angela Meister, *Die deutsche Industriearbeiterinnen* (Ph.D. dissertation, Jena, 1939). Although the wartime female work force had increased from 9.6 to 15 million, the percentages of women in the postwar labor market remained at about 36 percent.

59. Winkler, *Frauenarbeit,* 22–23, 25. 11.5 million women had entered the labor force, 7.8 million of them single (75 percent of the single category worked in family businesses). Of the 835,000 married women 80 percent said they worked only because of economic need. Elisabeth Lüdy, *Erwerbstätige Muetter* (Berlin: Müller, 1932), 8–15. "Alter und Familienstand der berufstätigen weiblichen Bevölkerung in Deutschland," *Jahrbuch der Frauenarbeit* 6 (March 1930), 31. Just under one-third of all married women worked full time in 1930, mainly between the ages of 25 and 50. 13 percent of all employed women were married, however, SB, 41:50 (15.12.1932), 1577.

60. *Mein Arbeitstag Mein Wochenende. 150 Berichte von Textilarbeiterinnen,* ed. deutschen Textilarbeiter-Verband (Berlin: Textilpraxis, 1930), 79. Cf. also the study, *Not und Kampf der Arbeiterinnen* (Berlin: n.d.), rare copy in the International Institute for Social History in Amsterdam.

61. Ehrenburg, *Memoirs,* 11.

62. Emil J. Gumbel, *Vier Jahre politischer Mord* (Berlin-Fichtenau: Neue Gesellschaft, 1922), 81. The average sentence of right-wing assassins was four months, compared to fifteen years' average prison term for left-wing assassins. Cf. *Denkschrift des Reichsjustizminister* (Berlin: Malik, 1924).

63. Joseph Schumpeter, quoted in Joachim Fest, *Hitler*, trans. Richard and Clara Winston (New York: Random House, 1974), p. 256.

3. Nazi Women and Their "Freedom Movement"

1. Heinrich Winkler, "German Social History and the Illusion of Restoration," *Journal of Contemporary History* (October 1976), 9. *Der Angriff*, quoted in Werner Maser, *Hitler's Letters and Notes* (New York: Harper & Row, 1974), 149.

2. Gottfried Feder, quoted by Kirkpatrick, *Nazi Germany*, 109.

3. Alfred Rosenberg, *Der Mythos des XX. Jahrhunderts* (Munich: Hoheneichen, 1938), 512. Until the end of World War II, Hitler was not as obsessed with the Woman Question as he was with the Jewish Question. Christine Wittrock, in *Weiblichkeitsmythen* (Frankfurt a.M.: Sendler, 1984), 193–230, analyzes the contradictions. Gisela Bock, " 'No Children at Any Cost': Perspectives on Compulsory Sterilization, Sexism and Racism in Nazi Germany," Judith Friedlander, et al, *Women in Culture and Politics: A Century of Change* (Bloomington: Indiana University, 1986), 286–299, investigates pragmatic and ideological consequences.

4. Quoted in Peter Engelmann, *Living Age*, 359 (October 1940), 112–116.

5. Quoted in "Der deutsche Frauenorden," *Nationalsozialistische Monatshefte* I:1 (April 1930), 43. The author, like virtually every Nazi who addressed the Woman Question, stressed the restoration of a natural or genuine woman.

6. Anon., "Die politische Frau," *Opferdienst der deutschen Frau* (August 24, 1930).

7. Gertrud Moldenhauer Michael, Abel no. 574, Bl. 2. This report comes from the extraordinary set of essays collected by sociologist Theodore Abel, which became the basis of his *Why Hitler Came to Power. An Answer Based on the Original Life Stories of 600 of His Followers* (New York: Prentice-Hall, 1938). Abel did not include women's responses, but he did deposit them along with the men's essays at the Hoover Institution on War, Revolution, and Peace, Stanford University (hereafter referred to as HI) where Agnes Peterson called them to my attention in 1974. Peter Merkl, *Violence Under the Swastika* (Princeton: Princeton University Press, 1975), analyzes the women's responses.

8. "The Battlecries of Hitlerism Modified as Election Nears," *The New York Times*, 8, 3:1 (July 10, 1932). Others suggested women's nostalgia for an agrarian past drove them to vote Nazi. Calvin B. Hooper, *Germany Enters the Third Reich* (New York: Macmillan, 1933), 165–167.

9. Miriam Beard, "The Tune Hitler Beats . . ." *The New York Times*, June 7, 1931. She described "a medley of disillusioned women, theological students, dispossessed . . . men, once the most stable and now the most insecure . . ."

10. Adolf Hitler, *Mein Kampf*, trans. Ralph Mannheim (Boston: Houghton-Mifflin, Sentry, 1962), 441.

11. Ibid., 231.

12. Ibid., 236–237 and 408. "Sins against the blood and racial mixing *[Rassenschande]* are the original sins." *Mein Kampf* (Munich: Eher, 1925) I, 263.

13. Ibid., 409.

14. Joseph Goebbels, *Michael: Ein deutsches Schicksal in Tagebuchblättern* (Munich: Eher, 1929), 41.

15. Speech at Nuremberg Rally, 1932, "NS Frauenschaft," *Hochschule für Politik-Berlin*, Schriftenreihe, Abt. 2, 12–20 (1937–1938). (Berlin: Junker & Dünnhaupt, 1937), 5–16. This account emphasizes musical evenings, sewing machine collectives and fund raising. Women took in 12,300 reichsmarks in 1932 and 61,000 reichsmarks in 1933. Hedwig Kruk, Berlin reported on the Weimar Party Rally in August 1924, BA Koblenz/NS22/vorläufig 239. Hitler's speech in translation appears in S. Bell and K. Offen, eds., *Women, the Family and Freedom: The Debate in Documents* (Stanford: Stanford University Press, 1983), II, 375–376. Henriette Schirach, *Frauen um Hitler* (Berlin: Herbig, 1983), 2nd ed., 1985, 8. For a survey of the legends about Hitler and his women admirers in Munich, cf. Werner Maser, *Hitler. Legend, Myth and Reality*, trans. Peter and Betty Ross (New York: Harper & Row, 1973), 194–209.

16. Heyen, Franz, *N. S. im Alltag* (Boppard: Boldt, 1967), 330–331. Georg Franz-Willing, *Die Hitlerbewegung. Der Ursprung 1919–1922* (Hamburg: Deker, 1962), 126, 193–198. The composition of the 230 Nazi Reichstag delegates after the July elections of 1932 was: 55 blue- and white-collar workers, 50 peasants, 43 independent businessmen, artisans, and industrial managers, 29 functionaries, 20 civil servants, 12 teachers, and 9 former army officers and 12 other. *Reichstags-Handbuch*, 6. Wahlperiode (Berlin, 1932), 270. Michael Kater, *The Nazi Party: A Social Profile of Members and Leaders, 1919–1945* (Cambridge: Harvard University Press, 1983), esp. 148–153. Thomas Childers, *The Nazi Voter*, (Chapel Hill: University of North Carolina, 1983), 215–225.

17. John Farquharson, "The NSDAP in Hannover and Lower Saxony, 1921–1926, *Journal of Contemporary History* 8:4 (October 1973), 106. John Farquharson and John Hidden, *Explaining Hitler's Germany: Historians and the Third Reich* (Totowa, N.J.: Barnes and Noble, 1983), 91.

18. Annette Kolb, *Das Exemplar* (Berlin: Fischer, 1922), 73.

19. William Sheridan Allen, ed., *The Infancy of Nazism. The Memoirs of Ex-Gauleiter Albert Krebs, 1923–1933* (New York, London: Franklin Watts, 1976), 59. Krebs also recalls a small group of career women and the leader of the auxiliary, Frieda Koenig, who owned a dress-making shop, Ibid., 83. Elsewhere, Krebs likened a labor organization itself to a mother, "provid[ing] for the daily needs of every single member." Ibid., 17.

20. These generalizations are born out by the records of new members in Hesse, which are remarkably complete. Hessisches Hauptstaatsarchiv, Wiesbaden (hereafter HHW), Rep. G 12/B, "Neuaufnahmen," 1931–1933, May 6, 1932 (Bl. 483–596); May 12, 1932, July 1, 1932 (Bl. 66–74); November 10, 1932 (Bl. 1–232); and March 20, 1933 (Bl. 232–259), 13. April, 1933 through May 15, 1933. Cf. Eberhard Schön, *Die Entstehung des Nationalsozialismus in Hessen* (Meisenheim am Glan: Hain, 1972), 100, 103. Except for one tiny

town (Bidenkopf) women comprised between 2 and 4 percent of the membership. Of women members in 1935, more had joined before 1933 than afterward, in contrast to the men.

21. This tallies with Thomas Childers, "The Social Bases of the National Socialist Vote," *Journal of Contemporary History* 11 (1976), 17–42. For a different interpretation, cf. Hamilton, *Who Voted for Hitler?* (Princeton: Princeton University Press, 1983), 9–36, 309–361. Alexander Weber, *Soziale Merkmale der NSDAP Wähler. Eine Zusammenfassung bisheriger empirischer Untersuchungen und eine Analyse in den Gemeinden der Länder Baden und Hessen.* (Ph.D. dissertation, Freiburg, 1969), esp. pp. 159–164, 176–177. Robert Ley, ed., *Parteistatistik* (Munich: Zentral Verlag, 1936), reports that 2,387 women who were leaders in 1935 had joined the party before 1933 and *Parteistatistik II*, that 5,536 women leaders in the NSF had joined prior to 1933, 146–147. See also the special issue of *Central European History* 17:1 (March 1984) devoted to the question of early support for National Socialism.

22. Donald Douglas, "The Parent Cell: Some Computer Notes on the Composition of the First Nazi Party Group in Munich, 1919–1921," *Central European History* 10 (1977), 60–61. Franz-Willing, *Die Hitler-Bewegung*, 120, 129. Interestingly and mistakenly, Michael Kater in *The Nazi Party* attributes women's deviation from the male norm to a shortage of men in the joiner cohort.

23. Gabrielle Bremme, *Die politische Rolle der Frau in Deutschland* (Göttingen: Van den Hoeck and Ruprecht, 1956), 47, 54–55, 73–75, 243–252. Bremme endorses Bäumer's explanation that women voted Nazi because they opposed the equality granted in 1919.

24. Maria M. Gehrke, "Frauenwahl," *Vossische Zeitung* (July 27, 1932).

25. Louis Lochner, *What About Germany?* (New York: Dodd, Mead, 1942), 22.

26. Katharine Thomas, *Women in Nazi Germany* (London: Gollancz, 1943), 31. Thomas recalls the appeal of Hitler praising women as the "Guardians of the Family."

27. Translated by Merkl, *Violence*, 129.

28. Isobardia Rogetski, Abel no. 305.

29. The first is Respondent Maria Wiebe, no. 456, the second, Hilde Boehm-Stoltz, Abel no. 44, Party no. 429,341, and the third Helene Radtke, no. 207, Party no. 218,054. Marlene Heder, Abel no. 41, barely remembered the war, but described vividly the deprivation caused by her father's death at the front, and respondent Maria Engelhardt, Abel no. 145, recalled the war as a "magnificent holy time." Karl Zacher, Abel no. 254, by contrast, discovered "a pronounced masculine consciousness."

30. Eiden, Abel no. 244, Party no. 1,400,825. Cf. also G. Michael and M. Schrimpf, Abel nos. 574 and 582.

31. Merkl, *Violence*, 123–124. Several essays contained passing references to Jews, usually as enemies. For example, Maria Engelhardt, Abel no. 145, recalled, "A Jew in our office jeered and said [after an electoral setback], 'Now it is all finished with your threat to destroy our government.'"

32. Sissy Schneider, Abel no. 107.

33. Helene Radtke, Abel no. 207. This fascination with Hitler's eyes from his earliest years as a politician became a routine part of many descriptions. For example, Frau Förster-Nietzsche (according to Harry Kessler), "chiefly, she said, noticed his eyes, which are fascinating and stare right through one. But he struck her as a religious rather than a political leader and she did not feel him to be an outstanding politician." Harry Kessler, *In the Twenties. The Diaries of Harry Kessler*, trans. Charles Kessler (New York: Holt, Rinehart & Winston, 1961), entry for Sunday, August 7, 1932, 426. Louis Lochner recalled, "Again and again I had heard women say, 'Once you look into Hitler's eyes, you are his devoted follower forever!'." *What About Germany?*, 121. The attraction was not limited to women. "I looked into his eyes, he looked into mine, and I was left with only one wish—to be at home and alone with the great, overwhelming experience." Hermann Rauschning, *The Revolution of Nihilism: A Warning to the West*, trans. E. W. Dickes (New York: Longmans Green, 1939), 131.

34.. Eva Maria Wisser Wellmann, *Kämpfen und Glauben: Aus dem Leben eines Hitler Mädels*, intro. Frau Dr. Goebbels (Berlin: Steuben, 1933), 96. The author continues to express her profound gratitude that God had sent this national savior. Of course, this is propaganda; but the point is that this sort of pseudoreligious verbiage pervades even the "spontaneous" statements.

35. Maria Engelhardt, Abel no. 145, Bl. 14. "*Mein Kampf* became our Bible."

36. E. Zander, *Opferdienst der deutschen Frau* II (September 1930 and June 1930), in BA Koblenz, NSD 47/2.

37. Maria Bauer, Abel no. 30 and Maria von Belli, Abel no. 212.

38. Isobardia Rogetski, Abel no. 305. Einem said she felt a "holy duty" to work for Hitler, Abel no. 244. Nazi women typically referred to their Nazi beliefs as a "deepest religion." For similar sentiments by an anonymous author, "Mein Kampf als Nationalsozialistin," HI, Reel 13.

39. Lusi Jost, Abel no. 153.

40. Helene Radtke, Abel no. 207, spoke of the "holy idea of our beloved Führer." Maria von Belli, Abel no. 212.

41. "Adolf Hitler, the Master Builder of the New Reich," had, she believed, researched and diagnosed the essence of the German people and constructed a new political structure that would strengthen the ancient *Volk*. *Geschichte, Blut und Boden* and *Der Baumeister des neuen Reiches*, pamphlets, BA Koblenz/NSD47/Bl. 37–39. "All great, world-shaking events have been brought about, not by written matter but by the spoken word," Hitler wrote in *Mein Kampf*. He spoke also of the "magic power of words," in arousing passion between speaker and audience.

42. Maria Engelhardt, Abel no. 145.

43. Joseph Goebbels, quoted in William Shirer, *The Rise and Fall of the Third Reich* (New York: Simon and Schuster, 1960), 127. "At that moment I was reborn." Joseph Goebbels, *Revolution der Deutschen* (Oldenbourg: Stalling, 1933). "We love this man. We know he has earned our absolute love . . ." 223. Himmler's adoration for Hitler was no less dramatic. On one occasion he declared, "a figure of the greatest brilliance has become incar-

nate in his person." Joachim Fest, *The Face of the Third Reich*, trans. M. Bullock (New York: Pantheon, 1970), 122.

44. Hermann Rauschning, *The Voice of Destruction* (New York: Putnam, 1940), 265. Despite his own enchantment with Hitler, the author believed that "Hitler was discovered by women," and asserted that wives converted before their husbands.

45. Quoted in Rudolph Binion, *Hitler Among the Germans* (New York: Elsevier, 1976), 124–126. Binion puts it succinctly: "The magic went with the message." 124.

46. Heinrich Hoffmann, *Hitler Was My Friend*, trans. R. H. Stevens (London: Burke, 1965), 56.

47. Louise Solmitz, "Diary," in Jeremy Noakes and Geoffrey Pridham, eds., *Documents of Nazism: 1919–1945* (New York: Viking, 1974), 165–166.

48. *Mein Kampf*, 475.

49. Quoted in Walter Charles Langer, *The Mind of Adolf Hitler* (New York: Signet, 1973), 72. He also said, "to convince women by reasoned argument is always impossible." Hugh Trevor-Roper, ed., *Hitler's Secret Conversations* (New York: Octagon, 1981), 393.

50. Hermann Rauschning, *The Voice of Destruction*, 265.

51. Quoted in Joachim Fest, trans. Clara and Richard Winston, *Hitler* (New York: Vintage, 1975), 203.

52. Gregor Strasser, January 9, 1927, quoted in Noakes and Pridham, *Documents of Nazism*, 84. Rauschning recalled times when Hitler "behaved like a combination of a small child and a hysterical woman. He scolded in high, shrill tones, stamped his feet, and banged his fist on tables and walls. . . . An alarming sight." Rauschning, *Voice*, 82.

53. Franz-Willing, *Die Hitler-Bewegung*, 190. Hidden and Farquharson, *Explaining*, 65–77. Schön, *Entstehung*, 100.

54. Gregor Strasser, "Auftreten und Verhalten des politischen Leiters," n.d. (probably 1932), BA Koblenz/NS22/vorläufig 110/1–2. Strasser circulated these views to the party leadership on August 12, 1932, BA Koblenz/NS 22/vorläufig 348. Others noted the confusion in the ranks. Hans Frank commented much later, "There were as many National Socialisms as there were leaders." Hans Frank, *Im Angesicht des Galgens* (Munich: Beck, 1953), 184. Joseph Goebbels was driven to despair by the chaos, but it was Strasser who left the Party. *Vom Kaiserhof zur Reichskanzelei* (Munich: Reichsdruckerei, 1934), 392.

55. Hitler, *Mein Kampf*, 472.

56. Waite, *Psychopathic God*, 346. Lochner, *What About Germany?*, also noted Hitler's refusal to speak from a written text, 73.

57. "Ordnung der Frauenschaft," BA Koblenz, NS 22/vorläufig 349. The author proposed the creation of a vast network of "cell mothers," political indoctrination units with identically dressed (not uniformed) women's cadres. Under no circumstances would this organization become a "*Frauenverein* or "ladies' club." But it pledged to work closely with the Nazi leadership to combat masculinization and despiritualization of women.

58. Hildegard Passow, in "Sozial oder Sozialistisch?" developed similar themes for a national propaganda campaign. BA Koblenz, NSD 47/37–39.

59. Maria von Belli, Abel no. 212.

60. Margarethe Schrimpff, Abel no. 582, Waldemar Theobald Groetschel, Abel no. 117, and Huhn, Abel no. 297, Bl. 4. In an unsigned report dated November 1931, one Nazi woman describes her joy at a Sport Palace meeting when many SA and SS men fainted. BA Koblenz/Sammlung Schumacher/230.

61. A. Weber, *Merkmale*, 176. William Sheridan Allen, *The Nazi Seizure of Power. The Experience of a a Single German Town* (New York: Watts, 1984), 29. One-third of the Abel contestants mentioned a meeting or rally as their first acquaintance with the Nazi movement, more than any other form of contact. Cf. Renate Wiggershaus, *Frauen unterm Nationalsozialismus*, (Wuppertal: Hammer, 1984), 5–34 on the early movement.

62. Erna Stoyke, Abel no. 363.

63. Helene Radtke, Abel no. 207. Cf. E. Frick, "Das Erholungsheim," *Völkischer Beobachter*, Munich, 59 (February 27, 1935) for a memoir of the days when the most trivial tasks took on deep meaning.

64. "Völkischer Frauenbund," Nuremburg, written 1924, HI Reel 13/255.

65. "Mein Kampf als Nationalsozialistin," HI reel 13, 254.

66. Frau Dornberg, Münster, interviewed by L. Koller, in 1940, Staatsarchiv Münster/Westfalen-Nord/NSF/128. Hereafter referred to as SAM/W-N/NSF/file number/and "Bl." if the individual pages have been numbered within the file.

67. M. Engelhardt, and M. von Belli, Abel nos. 145 and 212.

68. Trevor-Roper, *Conversations*, 87. For an account of the gossip surrounding Hitler and his women supporters in Munich, cf. Werner Maser, *Hitler: Legend, Myth and Reality*, trans. Peter and Betty Ross (New York: Harper Torch, 1973), 194–209. Originally published as *Adolf Hitler: Legende, Mythos, Wirklichkeit*, (Munich: Bechtle, 1971), 235.

69. Zander to Hitler, May 28, 1926, Sammlung Schumacher, 230. On March 24, 1925, Hitler invited women to join in this "most masculine of fighting movements." Dr. Hadlich's open letter to Zander accused her of "inability to provide leadership." Beilage (Supplement) to the *Völkischer Beobachter* 4 (January 23, 1926). Rules of the *Frauenorden* of 1924 were: to follow Hitler, Ludendorff and Streicher, to fight alien races, educate the young, support the youth organizations, and care for the needy. HI reel 13, no. 255. Kater, *The Nazi Party*, 148 ff. Theodor Eichhoff, "Frauenwirken am Wiederaufbau," *Soziale Praxis* 42:40 (December 7, 1933), 1426–1427.

70. Karl Dietrich Bracher, *Die deutsche Diktatur. Entstehung, Struktur, Folgen des Nationalsozialismus* (Cologne: Kiepenheuer & Witsch, 1969), 139. *Nationalsozialistische Frauenschaft* (Berlin: 1937), 10. "Der Reichs-Vertretertag des Deutsche Frauenordens," *Volkische Beobachter* no. 246, (October 25, 1927). HI Reel 89, #1865. Cf. Richtlinien des deutschen Frauenordens," January 2, 1931, BA Koblenz/Sammlung Schumacher/230.

71. Anna-Luise Kühn, "Der NS ist gleich einer religiösen Weltanschauung," *Hilfdienst der braunen Mädel*, Nr. 15 (September 1931), 1.

72. The author added, the Women's Movement had "rows of resplendent officers but very few corporals and no privates." Katherine Thomas, *Women in Nazi Germany* (London: Gollancz, 1943), 20.

73. "Zur Chronik," July 1, 1934, HI, Reel 14, no. 254.

74. Joachim Fest, *The Face of the Third Reich*, trans. Michael Bullock, (New York: Pantheon, 1970), noted the pervasive Nazi contempt for "ladies," by which they meant creatures with polished nails, fragile bodies, and cigarettes. Cf. also Kirkpatrick, *Nazi Germany*, 110 ff.

75. Zander, "Wir stellen die Frauen! Gibt uns den Staat!" speech to the 1931 women's leadership conference. BA Koblenz, NSD 47/2. Reprinted in *Opferdienst*.

76. Election appeal, "Die deutsche Frau," *Völkischer Beobachter*, Munich 212, Second Supplement (July 30, 1932).

77. Siber, *Lichterfelder Lokalanzeiger* 18, April 1934, quoted in Kirkpatrick, *Nazi Germany*, 207.

78. Hilde Browning, *Women under Fascism and Communism* (London: Lawrence, n.d. 1943?), 9.

79. Anna Zuhlke, *Frauenaufgabe und Frauenarbeit im dritten Reich. Bausteine zum neuen Staat und Volk* (Leipzig: Quelle und Meyer, 1934).

80. HI Reel 89, #1865. Cf. Dietrich Orlow, *The History of the Nazi Party 1919–1933* (Pittsburgh: University of Pittsburgh, 1969), 229 on the DFO.

81. "Unser Weg! Die nationalsozialistische Frauenarbeit von ihren Anfängen," BA Koblenz/Sammlung Schumacher/230. Women frequently called their "struggle" "our struggle," implicitly complementing Hitler's "My Struggle." Else Frobenius, *Die Frau im Dritten Reich* (Berlin: Nationaler, n.d. 1934?), 101.

82. Thomas, *Women*, 13.

83. History of the Steinfurth NSF, compiled on February 20, 1934, SAM/W-N/NSF 232. See also Boehm-Stoltz's (no. 46) and Engelhardt's Abel essays.

84. Fran Dornberg, interviewed by L. Koller, 1940, SAM/W-N/NSF/128. The autobiography of Helene Radtke, in the Abel Collection describes a similar spirit.

85. Compiled from biographies of Marlene Heder, no. 41; H. Huhn, no. 297 Grete Kirchner, no. 46, in the Abel Collection and *Mein Kampf als Nationalsozialistin* HI Reel 13, 254.

86. Helene Radtke, Abel no. 207. This woman also boasts of having carried a pistol in self-defense against hostile neighborhood. Gudrun Streiter, *Dem Tod so nah . . . Tagebuchblätter einer SA-Manns Braut* (privately published) related a similar story.

87. Fritz Kepner, Abel no. 408, trans. by Merkl, *Political Violence*, 124. Cf. also "Mein Kampf als Nationalsozialistin," HI Reel 13.

88. Huhn, Abel no. 297, B1.5. The author served for a time in the SA home in Steglitz with Zander. For an insightful analysis of the appeal to "roughness and respectability," cf. Richard Bessel, *Political Violence and the Rise of Nazism. The Storm Troopers in Eastern Germany* (New Haven: Yale University Press, 1984), 75–96. Bessell cautions us to take seriously the Nazi

exaltation of violence because, "It constituted a language and described an activity which many found attractive, and the willingness of the Nazi movement . . . to engage in this kind of politics was an important drawing card." 75.

89. Pridham and Noakes, eds., *Documents*, 122.

90. Marlene Heder, Abel No. 41. This woman noted that once they had converted the wife, the husband often followed into the movement.

91. Guida Diehl, *Christ sein heisst Kämpfer sein: Die Führung meines Lebens* (Eisenach: Brunnen, 1960), 123. Idem., *Studienkriese* (Eisenach: Neuland, 1919), 40–41.

92. Guida Diehl, *Die deutsche Frau und der Nationalsozialismus*, 5th Edition (Eisenach: Neuland, 1933), 54, 17, 19, and 129. Idem., *Was Wir wollen* (Eisenach: Neuland, n.d.), 9.

93. *Aufruf! Deutsche Zukunft in Gefahr?* November 23, 1928. The annual report stated that 200,000 announcements of the convention had been mailed and claimed that 15,000 people had attended their largest rally. Oberkirchenrat Vereine, Deutscher Frauen-Kampfbund, 4709 in Landeskirchl. Evangelischer Archiv, Karlsruhe (hereafter LAK).

94. Diehl, *Die deutsche Frau*, 74. Cf. Wittrock, *Weiblichkeits Mythen*, 115–148.

95. Diehl, *Die Deutsche Frau*, 42.

96. Hans Beyer, *Die Frau in der Politischen Entscheidung* (Stuttgart: Enke, 1933), 30–35.

97. Guida Diehl, *Erlösung vom Wirrwahn wider Dr. Mathilde Ludendorff und ihr Buch, Erlösung von Jesu Christo* (Eisenach: Neuland, 1931).

98. Childers, *The Nazi Voter*, 215–255. At the 1927 rally, Party leaders decided to organize special interest branches, although not for women.

99. Münster residents felt the impact of the Depression as the number of people registering for welfare increased from 2,200 in March 1930 to just over 5,000 in early 1933. Of 54,000 in the labor force, 2,500 in 1930 were out of work. The total grew to just over 5,000 in early 1933. The vote for the Nazi Party increased from 10 percent in 1930 to 24 percent in November 1932; while the Center Party attracted 50 percent in 1930 and 47 percent in November 1932, the Socialists and Communists together drew 20 percent in 1930 and 16 percent in November 1932. Participation remained relatively constant at about 77 percent. In the March 1933 election the Center vote fell to 42 percent and the Nazi vote rose to 36 percent—national percentages for each were respectively 14 percent and 43 percent. Doris Kaufmann, *Katholisches Milieu in Münster 1928–1933* (Düsseldorf: Schwann, 1984), 144, 167.

100. "Mutterhaus," report, March 4, 1933. NSF, cf. the report on her charitable work, Gelsenkirchen-Beur, September 27, 1932, BA Koblenz/NS22/355. For an account of the history of local groups in the area, cf. SAM/WSF/W-N/405 from 1924 and ibid., 128 includes a more comprehensive survey written in 1940. An excellent background on Catholic Münster is provided by Kaufmann, *Das katholisches Milieu in Münster*.

101. Polster, personnel file, Berlin Document Center, was born April 7, 1891, and joined the Party on October 1, 1931, and received Party member-

ship number 698,012. She listed her profession as *Ehefrau* (housewife). The file also contains an inquiry by Käthe Auerhahn, attempting to smear Polster, September 13, 1932. Auerhahn, born in 1901, joined the party on April 1, 1930 (Party no. 231,171), BDC. Profession Hausfrau. Her Gauleiter (district leader) wrote a glowing praise of her dedication but admitted she frequently had difficulties with her subordinates.

102. Memo, SAM/W-N/NSF/393/B1.78. Seydel was born on June 10, 1893, in Bielefeld and joined the Party in March 1931 (Party number 478,448). Her photo and "Beurteilungsbogen," (Evaluation) from the leadership training school at Coburg, are in BA Koblenz/NS 44/2.

103. "Frauenschicksal Männerschicksal," n.d.   SAM/W-N/NSF/268/1/ SAM.

104. Seydel, speech given April 17, 1935, "Verstand und Herz," 2. SAM/ W-N/NSF/313. Seydel to Polster, August 12, 1932 reports her activities, BA Koblenz/NS22/355.

105. In this passage she bitterly attacked anyone who would say, " 'The woman belongs at the stove and *basta.*' " Ibid., 3.

106. SAM/W-N/NSFS/393/80 and "Die Frau als Hüterin deutscher Volkskraft," n.d. For a variant on the same ideas, cf. SAM/W-N/NSFS/268/1–3.

107. Hitler, *Mein Kampf,* 471.

108. Hedwig Eggert, Abel No. 259, who joined the Party in 1928.

109. Hilde Böhm-Stoltz, Abel No. 44. Cf. Margarethe Berkel, no. 130.

110. Susan Sontag, "Fascinating Fascism," *Under the Sign of Saturn* (New York: Farrar, Straus, & Giroux, 1972) discusses the appeal of violence. Cf. also Richard Bessel, *Political Violence and the Rise of Nazism: The Storm Troopers in Eastern Germany, 1925–1934* (New Haven: Yale University Press, 1984), 75–96. Bessell reminds us to take seriously the Nazi exaltation of violence because, "It constituted a language and described an activity which many found attractive, and the willingness of the Nazi movement . . . to engage in this kind of politics was an important drawing card." In her classic *The Origins of Totalitarianism* Hannah Arendt suggested that beneath a prudish exterior, the bourgeoisie shares with "the mob" a longing for violence. Hermann Rauschning made a similar observation even earlier. *Voice of Destruction* (New York: Putnam, 1940), 83.

111. Strasser circulated these views to the party leadership on August 12, 1932, BA Koblenz/NS 22/vorläufig 348. Strasser told organizers, "There will be no nine to five. We must work until the job is done. . . . We are not some sort of business . . . in which people work according to their convenience. On the contrary, we are an organization that is full of motion, never resting, and always ready to fight." He railed against the "dullness and stiffness that rot out the heart of the movement" and launched a campaign against "unhealthy bureaucratism that erodes the soul." July 28, 1932. BA Koblenz/ NS22/356. Goebbels, by contrast, despaired at the discrepancy between the chaotic desperation of everyday life and the public image of order. Goebbels, *Vom Kaiserhof,* entries for November 18 and 20, 1932. However, it was Strasser and not Goebbels who left the Party.

112. H. Rauschning, *Men of Chaos* (New York: Putnam's, 1942). "It was

the seduction of liberation! . . . A world of great appetites and passions was spread before their eyes!" Rauschning commented.

4. Liberation and Depression

1. Irmgard Keun, *Gilgi. Eine von uns* (Düsseldorf: Claassen Verlag, 1979), 170. This extract was translated by Atina Grossmann, *The New Woman*, 37–38. Marie Diers, *Freiheit und Brot! Der Roman einer Arbeiterfamilie* (Berlin: Nationaler Freiheit, 1933). Another conservative best-seller about a young woman sold 130,000 copies in 1932, Kuni Tremel-Eggert, *Barb* (Munich: Eher, 1934).

2. Gustav Stresemann. *Vermächtnis. Der Nachlass* (Berlin: Ullstein, 1932–33), III, 128.

3. A. J. Ryder, *Twentieth Century Germany: From Bismarck to Brandt* (New York: Columbia University, 1973), 264.

4. Quoted in Koppel S. Pinson, *Modern Germany. Its History and Civilization* (New York: Macmillan, 1964), 411.

5. During the early years of the Republic, President Friedrich Ebert, a socialist, had utilized the provision precisely as its authors had intended.

6. The following chart summarizes Reichstag composition, 1928–1932

	May 1928	Sept 1930	July 1932	Nov 1932
Nazi	12	107	230	196
Nationalist	73	41	37	52
German People's	45	30	7	11
Bavarian People's	16	19	22	20
Catholic Center	62	68	75	70
Democratic	25	20	4	2
Social Democrat	153	143	133	121
Communist	54	77	89	100
Miscellaneous	51	72	11	12
Total	491	577	608	584

The variation in Reichstag size reflects the changes in voter turnout, which increased by 2.3 million between 1928 and 1932.

7. Karl Braunias, *Das Parlamentarische Wahlrecht* vol. I (Berlin and Leipzig: de Gruyter, 1932), 81–89. For an analysis of nonvoters by age and sex in Cologne, cf. "Alter und Wahl der Beteilung," *Die Frau* 40:5 (February 1933), 314. On the development of single issue parties, cf. Thomas Childers, "The Social Bases," *The Journal of Comtemporary History* 17–42; Walter Dean Burnham, "Political Immunization and Political Confessionalism: the United States and Weimar Germany," *Journal of Interdisciplinary History*, 3 (1772–1973), 1–30. Richard F. Hamilton, *Who Voted for Hitler?* (Princeton: Princeton University Press, 1982), 437–453.

8. Karl Dietrich Bracher notes that "88 percent of the National Socialist

and 53 percent of the Communist delegates were newcomers . . . to a parliament which they tried to obstruct with all their might." *The German Dictatorship*, trans. J. Steinberg (New York: Praeger, 1970), 183. Nazi delegates used their benefits (from free railway passes to immunity from libel suits) to promote their cause. The youthfulness of both Nazis and Communists has been widely commented on. It has also been remarked that the Communists and Nazis (along with the Democrats) found the least favor with women voters in the 1920s.

9. Stephen Spender, *World within World: The Autobiography of Stephen Spender* (London: Hamish Hamilton, 1951), 195–196.

10. David Abraham, *The Collapse of the Weimar Republic. Political Economy and Crisis* (Princeton: Princeton University Press, 1981), 229–255, 301.

11. Ilya Ehrenburg, *Memoirs: 1921–1941*, trans. Tatania Shebunina with Yvonne Kapp (Cleveland and New York: World, 1963), 176–177.

12. Erich Fromm, *Arbeiter und Angestellte am Vorabend des Dritten Reiches*, part of *Studien über Autorität* (Paris: Alcan, 1936) 80, 272, 925. English edition: *The Working Class in Weimar Germany. A Psychological and Sociological Study*, trans. Barbara Weinberger (Cambridge: Harvard University Press, 1984), 69–80, 150–180. The religious breakdown was as follows: 11 percent Catholic; 25 percent Protestant; 7 percent belonged to minorities, including Jewish; and 57 percent declared they were atheists. 74 percent said their parents had moved to the cities. In 66 percent of the cases, the respondents said their wives worked outside the homes, but only 47 women answered the questionnaire (and of these 7 were married). Two-thirds of the men were married, and only 17 percent had no children; the average number of children per family was 1.8. 31 percent said their mothers had been employed, and 58 percent had sisters in the work force. Only 16 percent of all respondents were unemployed. 17 belonged to the National Socialist Party; 150 to the Communists; 45 to left-wing Independent Socialists; and 262 to the Social Democratic Party (45 percent); 76 (or 11 percent) did not vote at all.

13. George Mosse, *Nationalism and Sexuality. Respectability and Abnormal Sexuality in Modern Europe* (New York: Fertig, 1984), 1.

14. Max Hirsch, review of Frank Thiess, "Wiedergeburt der Liebe!" *Archiv für Frauenkunde* 18:1–2 (1932), 131–132.

15. "Zu viel Zeit," *Frauenwelt* 8:11 (May 1931), cf. also Henny Schumacher series on marriage crisis. M. Lueckerath to A. Hopmann, July 12, 1930, Breslau Tagung of the Katholischer Deutscher Frauenbund (hereafter KDF). KDF Ordner, KDF National Headquarters, Cologne. Helene Weber called women's employment the "greatest inner revolution of the last historical epoch." "Vom Sinn des Berufes," *Frauenberufe und Frauen bewegung*, KDF, 1932. "Berufswahl ohne Beruf," *Frauenland* (February 1931), 42.

16. *Doppelverdiener, Stenographische Berichte*, vol. 424, Sessions 43–44, 57, and 63(1932); and vol. 428, sessions 177 and 178.

17. Richard Hofstätter, *Die Arbeitende Frau: Ihre wirtschaftliche Lage* (Vienna and Leipzig: Perles 1929), 1–15. "The wounds that battered the *Volk* body were made by the men and must be healed by the women," 23.

18. E. F. W. Eberhard, *Feminismus und Kulturuntergang: Die Erotische*

Grundlagen der Frauenemanzipation, 2nd ed. (Vienna and Leipzig: Braun-müller, 1927), 339 ff.

19. Anton Schücker, *Zur Psychopathologie der Frauenbewegung* (Leipzig: C. Kabitsch, 1931), 37 49. E. F. W. Eberhard, *Geschlechtscharakter und Volkskraft. Grundprobleme des Feminismus* (Darmstadt and Leipzig: Ernst Hoffmann, 1930); idem., *Feminismus und Kulturuntergang; Otto Helmut, Volk in Gefahr. Der Geburtenrückgang und seine Folgen für Deutschlands Zukunft* (Munich: Lehmanns, 1933); Hjelmar Kutzleb, *Mord an der Zukunft* (Berlin: Widerstandsverlag, 1930); J.A. Hamann, *Ein Wort gegen die überlässige Verehrlichung und Verweichlichung des weiblichen Geschlechts* (Riga: Privat, 1925); Edgar J. Jung, *Die Herrschaft der Minderwertigen* (Berlin: Verlag der Deutschen Rundschau, 1930). (Jung during these years wrote best-selling anti-capitalist books.) Hugh Wiley Puckett, *Germany's Women Go Forward* (New York: Columbia, 1930), 308–313 gives an excellent eyewitness survey in English.

20. Jeffrey Weeks, *Sex, Politics, and Society. The Regulation of Sexuality since 1800* (London: Longman, 1981), 214. Weeks cited "Purity, public decency and familialism" as the major social norms of the interwar period.

21. Mirette Rohde-von Vorries, "Ehe und Familie," *Evangelische Frauenzeitung* 32, 2–7 (September 1931).

22. Annemarie Niemeyer, *Zur Struktur der Familie. Statistische Materialen* (Berlin: Herbig, 1931). Women's suicide rates were 29 percent higher than in 1913, while men's dropped by 11 percent. "Schicksal des Frauenkriegsgeneration," *Frauenstimme* 46:15, 2 (August 8, 1929). About 13 percent of all births were out of wedlock; and the fertility rates among unmarried women grew faster than among married women. *Frauenwelt* 8:10 (May 1931), 219.

23. The German birthrates had been dropping for decades, but only in the twentieth century did working-class fertility decline, and even then it did not do so more rapidly than in other industrializing nations. Brian R. Mitchell, *European Historical Statistics* (New York: Facts on File, 1980), 92 ff.

24. "Richtlinien: Die Fragen des geschlechtlichen Sittlichkeit," *Evangelische Frauenzeitung* (February 1933), 34, 71.

25. Kläre Schuch, "Kapitalismus zerstört die Familie," *Frauenwelt* 20:4 (February 18, 1933), 83.

26. Sociologists reported that deep alienation separated family members. Maria Johoda, Paul F. Lazarsfeld, Hans Zeisel, *Marienthal. The Sociography of an Unemployed Community* (New York and Chicage: Aldine, 1971). 84–85, 93. First published in 1933, as *Die Arbeitslosen von Marienthal.* (Leipzig: S. Hirzel, 1933).

27. "Arbeiterfrauen Schreiben," *Frauenstimme* 46:15 (August 8, 1929).

28. *Die Ehe des arbeitslosen Martin Krug* (Oldenbourg: G. Stalling, 1932).

29. W. Kiaulehn, *Berlin: Schicksal einer Weltstadt* (Munich: Biederstein 1958), 559. As the Depression worsened, 20,000 such colonies were planned to house the homeless. E. Kramer, "Die Siedlung," *Frauenland* (1933), 202. Each house would be backed by 2,500 reichsmarks and inspected regularly by government officials to guarantee order and cleanliness.

30. BDF, Hirschberg Convention, September 1932.

31. Quoted in Elisabeth Lüdy, *Erwerbstätige Mütter in Vaterlosen Familien*, (Berlin: R. Mueller, 1932), 182. This was one volume of a massive twelve-volume study done by women social workers and social scientists on the "Decline and Fall of the German Family" between 1929 and 1932.

32. Gerard Bry, *Wages in Germany* (Princeton: Princeton University Press, 1960), 29. Wage differentials actually narrowed, as everyone's pay dropped to the subsistence levels at which women were typically paid. For a contemporaneous analysis, cf. 31. *Reichsarbeitsblatt* 13:3 (Berlin, January 25, 1932), 2, 24 ff.

33. Else Lüders, "Die Erhaltung der Familie in der Gegenwart," *Reichsarbeitsblatt II* (March 7, 1931), 108. Actually, the number of women in industrial jobs had dropped steadily during the 1920s from 2.9 million in 1925 to 1.1 million in 1933, and this decline occurred mainly among unmarried women workers. Cf. Stephenson, *The Nazi Organization of Women* (New York: Barnes and Noble, 1980), 88. Also "Alter and Familienstand der berufstätigen weiblichen Bevölkerung in Deutschland," *Jahrbuch der Frauenarbeit* 6 (March 1930) and Julius Silbermann, "Beseitigung der Frauenarbeit?" *Soziale Praxis* 41:50 (December 15, 1932), 1579.

34. Gertrud Hannah, "Alter and Familienstand der berufstätigen weiblichen Bevölkerung," 31, and idem., "Von Kampf gegen die Gleichberechtigung," *Die Genossin* 10:1 (January 1933); and Maria Juchacz, "Gefährdetes Frauenrecht," ibid.

35. Between 1895 and 1907, women's union membership increased by 2,000 percent, in marked contrast to developments after the war. In 1920 women workers had comprised 27 percent of union membership; this percentage dropped to 16 percent by 1931 despite higher employment rates. In left-wing unions, women's participation dropped to less than 5 percent. Catholic working women's associations complained that their organizations lost as much as a fifth of their members; in 1932 the Protestant Working Women's Union (with an unemployment rate among its members of 24 percent) reported only 10,000 members, a sharp decline compared to 1929. Women as a percentage of the Socialist Party increased relative to men only because hundreds of thousands of men deserted the party and joined the Communists. European socialist men pointed to declining women's participation in labor organizations and used these statistics to demonstrate their belief that women needed men leaders. Werner Thoennessen, *The Emancipation of Women: The Rise and Decline of the Women's Movement in German Social Democracy 1863–1933*, trans. Joris de Bres (London: Pluto, 1976), 56.

36. Hans-Jürgen Arendt, "Die 'Gleichschaltung' der bürgerliche Frauenorganisationen in Deutschland 1933/34," *Zeitschrift für Geschichtswissenschaft* (July 1979), 620. Jochen-Christoph Kaiser, *Frauen in der Kirche* (Düsseldorf: Schwann, 1985), 139–140. Charlotte von Hadlen, President of the Queen Louisa League to Adolf Hitler, April 6, 1933, claimed 130,000 members. BA Koblenz/R43II/823a.

37. Amy Hackett, "The Politics of Feminism in Wilhelmine Germany, 1848–1933," Ph.D. Dissertation, Columbia University 1976. Richard Evans,

The Feminist Movement in Germany 1848–1933, (London and Beverly Hills: Sage, 1976), 193, 239–242, 250–252; Fritz Mybes, *Die Geschichte der evangelischen Frauenhilfe in Quellen* (Gladbeck: Schriftenverlag, 1975); Marion Kaplan, *The Jewish Feminist Movement in Germany. The Campaigns of the Jüdischer Frauenbund, 1904–1938* (Westport, CT: Greenwood, 1979); Werner Thönnessen, *The Emancipation of Women in Germany. 1863–1933*, trans. Joris de Bres (London: Pluto, 1973), 57, 116, 119.

38. Clara Phillips, "Hausfrau und V*olk,*" in Clara Siebert, ed. *Frau und Volk* (Freiburg im B. Huber, 1929), 11.

39. Agnes von Zahn-Harnack, *Reden und Aufsätze.* (Stuttgart: C. Scheufele, 1928), 131.

40. Anna Heidenhaus, "Hausfrau, hilft mit!" *Frauenland* (1931), 29. These sentiments were ubiquitous among Protestants as well. Cf. lecture delivered in Hanover June 7, 1924, reprinted in *Der Deutsch-Evangelische Frauenbund im Kampf der Zeiten*, Heft 7 of *Schriften zur Frauenbildung*, n.d.

41. Anna Heidenhaus, "Arbeitslosigkeit und Wirtschaftskrise," *Frauenland* (January 1931), 17; and Leonore Kühn, *die Frau* (August 1932). Helene Düvert, in her popular book, *Die Frau von Heute, Ihr Weg und Ziel* (Berlin: Bartelsmann, 1933), 28–29, was more charitable: She blamed not average men, but Junker men.

42. Dr. Phil. Dorothea Klaje-Wenzel, *Die Frau in der Volksgemeinschaft* (Leipzig: Adolf Klein, 1934), 53.

43. Joseph Beeking, in *Die katholische Frau im Lebensraum von Familie, Volk, und Kirche* (Freiburg: Jugendwohl, 1934), 82.

44. This argument resembles Barbara Ehrenreich's thesis in *In the Hearts of Men* (Garden City: Anchor, 1983) and her May 20, 1984, *New York Times* Sunday Magazine article.

45. Gertrud Bäumer, *Die Frau in der Krisis der Kultur.* (Berlin: Klein, 1926), 12. Claudia Koonz, "Some Political Implications of Separatism: German Women between Democracy and Nazism, 1928–1934"; Judith Friedlander, Blanche Wiesen Cook, Alice Kessler-Harris, and Carroll Smith-Rosenberg, eds., *Women in Culture and Politics: A Century of Change.* (Bloomington: Indiana University Press, 1986), 269–286.

46. Gertrud Bäumer, *Die Frau im neuen Lebensraum* (Berlin: Herbig, 1931) and idem., *Deutsche Schulpolitik* (Karlsruhe: Braun, 1928). Male authors also used the term as a warning against an invasion of women, for example: Josef Rompel, *Die Frau im Lebensraum des Mannes* (Darmstadt, 1932). Beeking, in *Die katholische Frau im Lebensraum*, devoted a chapter to "Die Frau im Lebensraum des Mannes," warning men of impending danger. "Katholische Frauenbewegung und Frauenberufsarbeit," *Kölnische Volkszeitung* No. 349 (December 19, 1932). Gerta Krabbel and Dr. Amalie Lauer argued strongly for women professionals' right to work in their own *Lebensraum*. A Nazi writer, Emma Witte, adapted the popular theme, "Die Frau im Lebensraum des Mannes," *Nationalsozialistische Monatshefte* 3:22 (January 1932), 29–32.

47. This and the previous quotation are from Jost Hermand, "All Power to the Women: Nazi Concepts of Matriarchy," *Journal of Contemporary History*

19:4 (October 1984), 656 and 647. Helen Diner (Bertha Eckstein), *Mothers and Amazons: The First Feminine History of Culture* (New York: Julian, 1965).

48. Karin Hausen, "Mother's Day in the Weimar Republic," in Renate Bridenthal, Atina Grossmann, Marion Kaplan, eds., *When Biology Became Destiny* (New York: Monthly Review, 1984), 131, 148–149. The BDF and Catholic women's associations withheld support, for reasons that are not clear.

49. Jessica Benjamin, "Authority and the Family Revisited, or a World Without Fathers," *New German Critique*, 1977, 36–57.

50. *Die Ärztin* reported in February 1932 on a poll of 2,836 women physicians, which drew 2,761 responses. Only 7 percent of the respondents favored stronger punishment for participating in abortion.

51. "Wenn eine Proletarierin kein Kind will," *Die Rote Fahne* 13:29 (February 4, 1930). Cf. also Frau Arensee, S. B. 428, Session 178 (June 18, 1930), 5563 ff. Ellen Scheuner, memo to Social Workers, Gefährdetes Mädchen, January 12, 1931 and letter of December 1, 1930, ADW/F 300/30. I254/IM and ADW/GF/CA/571/6/6 IM. E. Kienle, *Frauen: aus dem Tagebuch einer Ärtzin* (Berlin: Kiepenheuer, 1932), 275 ff.

52. For the debate about *Cynakali* among leftist parties, cf. Atina Grossmann, "Abortion and Economic Crisis: the 1931 Campaign Against Paragraph 218," Bridenthal, Grossmann, and Kaplan, eds., *When Biology Became Destiny* (New York: Monthly Review, 1984), 66–86. The Catholics with one voice condemned its message. But Protestants agonized, sometimes even admitting they envied the Catholics whose Pope spared them from such doubt. Cf. correspondence between Ellen Scheuner and various social workers, 1930–1931. Circular F300/30 of December 1, 1930. The film raised the question of how to define "endangered." Was a young woman like Hedwig, living in an unmarried state with a man *(wilde Ehe)*, "endangered" or did only prostitutes deserve that label? ADW/I254/IM.

53. Jean-Paul Sartre, *Anti-Semite and Jew*, trans. George J. Becker (New York: Schocken, 1965), 23, 16, and 31. S. M. Lipset, "History and Sociology," in Lipset and Richard Hofstadter, eds., *Sociology and History: Methods* (New York: Basic, 1968), 23–24. S. M. Lipset, *Political Man* (Garden City: Doubleday, 1960), 140–145. H. A. Winkler, *Mittelstand, Demokratie und Nationalsozialismus* (Cologne, Kniepheuer & Witsch, 1972), 21–26. Recently this interpretation has been challenged by Merkl, Childers, Hamilton, and others. Cf. *Central European History*, Spring 1984 special issue on the Nazi vote.

54. The first round on March 13, 1932, produced 49.6 percent for Hindenburg with 30.1 percent, 13.2 percent, and 6.8 percent for Hitler, Ernst Thälmann (Communist), and Düsterberg (Conservative) respectively; in the runoff on April 10, it was 53 percent Hindenburg, 36.8 percent Hitler, and 10.2 percent Thälmann.

55. W. Phillips Shively, "Party Identification, Party Choice, and Voting Stability: The Weimar Case," *The American Political Science Review* 66 (December 1972), 1203–1225. Unfortunately, when women's Nazi vote increased

rapidly after 1929, only nine urban areas tabulated the vote separately by sex.

56. B. Brecht, "Song of the SA Man," translated by A. J. Ryder, *Twentieth Century Germany* (New York: Columbia University Press, 1973), 309–310.

57. Quoted in B. T. Reynolds, *Prelude to Hitler* (London: J. Cape, 1933), 236. Cf. also Richard Bessel, *Political Violence and the Rise of Nazism* (New Haven: Yale University Press, 1984), 90–91.

58. K. D. Bracher, *Die deutsche Diktatur*, 182–183, 256–258. Bessel, *Political Violence*, 90–91. Arnold Brecht, *Prelude to Silence. The End of the German Republic* (New York: Oxford University Press, 1944), 64–65. Originally published as *Vorspiel zum Schweigen* (Vienna: Europa, 1948). When Nazi criminals were found guilty and sentenced to jail, Hitler sent them a telegram, "My comrades! In the face of this most monstrous of blood judgments, I feel myself linked to you in unbounded loyalty. From this moment on your freedom is a matter of our honor." Elliot B. Wheaton, *The Nazi Revolution* (Garden City: Doubleday Anchor, 1968), 382. The fact that the elitist 130,000-member Queen Louisa League congratulated the murderers reminds us that men alone were not responsible for the escalating violence. Joachim Fest, *The Face of the Third Reich* (New York: Pantheon, 1970), 157.

59. Richard Hamilton, *Who Voted for Hitler?* (Princeton: Princeton University Press, 1982). BDM, ed., *Das war unser Angfang. Aus den Jahren des Kampfes und des Aufbaues des Berliner BDM* (n.d. 1933?). However, the boys' Hitler Youth claimed ten times that membership. Stephenson in *The Nazi Organization*, 25, points out that half the total lived in three areas: Berlin-Brandenburg, Saxony, and Bavaria. John Farquharson, "The NSDAP in Hanover and Lower Saxony, 1921–1926," *Journal of Contemporary History* 8:4 (October 1973), 106. Cf. also Eberhard Schön, *Die Entstehung des Nationalsozialismus in Hessen* (Meisenheim am Glan: Hamm, 1972), 100. Bracher, *Die deutsche Diktatur*, 182–183, 256–258. At its peak in 1941, 8 million Germans belonged to the Nazi Party and one third fell into the leadership category. For a sophisticated analysis of the social composition of the Party at both grassroots and elite levels, cf. Michael Kater, *The Nazi Party: A Social Profile of Members and Leaders, 1919–1945* (Cambridge: Harvard University Press, 1983), 51–71. While Kater demonstrates that Party support among workers was more significant than previously assumed, he emphasizes the lower-middle-class component in both membership and leadership categories, 74–97. Women "accounted for 7.8 percent of Nazi joiners; but in 1933 their contribution dropped sharply to 5.1 percent." But by 1937 the percentage had risen to just over 7 percent and the average of the joiners dropped below men's age at joining after 1933. 151–152.

60. For example, cf. report from Geislingen, "Gauenarbeitsgemeinschaft" (July 19, 1931), SAM/W- N/NSF.

61. Diehl, letter, Eisenach, June 6, 1931. EZV/B 3/440. Cf. also *Frauenkampfblatt des deutschen Frauen-Kampfbundes gegen die Entartung im Volksleben* (Eisenach, October 6, 1931).

62. Pia Sophie Rogge, *Zurück zum Mutterrecht? Studie zu Professor Ernst*

Bergmann, "Erkenntnisgeist und Muttergeist" (Leipzig: Klein, 1932), 41, 33, 36, 71–74. Cf. Hermand, "All Power to the Women," 658–659. Rogge-Börner's slogan was, "All power to the women!"

63. Pia Sophie Rogge, *Die deutschnationale Frau*, January 1, 1922.

64. Cf. Hanna Otto, review of Gottschewski, *Die Deutsche Kämpferin* II:1 (April 1934), 28.

65. Born in 1906, she received Party number 112,368. BDC.

66. Lydia Gottschewski, *Männerbund und Frauenfrage* (Munich: Eher, 1934), 8, 9. Robert Brady gives an excellent first-hand description, *The Spirit and Structure of German Fascism* (New York: Viking, 1937), 201 ff.

67. Gottschewski, *Männerbund*, esp. 14–78. George Mosse, *Nationalism and Sexuality. Respectability and Abnormal Sexuality in Modern Europe* (New York: Fertig, 1984), 161–162.

68. Illustrating the doctrinal fluidity are statements such as: "Grundsätze der Nationalsozialistischen Frauenschaft," BA Koblenz/NS22 vorläufig 349. "The woman's will comes from GOD, nature, family, *Volk*, and fatherland." "Grundsätze und organisatorische Richtlinien der NSF," a ten-page type-script, ibid., NS26/254/B1. 1–10.

69. Munich, September 8, 1931. BA Koblenz, NS 22/vorläufig 349.

70. H. Kelber (illegible), Bayreuth, November 16, 1931. Ibid.

71. DFO (Beyer) to Strasser (first page missing), ibid.

72. Gauleiterin, Lübeck, to Strasser, June 24, 1931, and to Hildebrandt, December 4, 1930. Ibid. This letter contains an excellent survey of complaints against Zander. BA Koblenz/NS22/vorläufig 349.

73. Letter to Strasser, Munich, April 7, 1931. NS22/vorläufig 349. Rumors circulated that the Gauleiter Wagner had ripped the armbands from the arms of marching Nazi women. From Austria came the complaint that women needed an official uniform and party symbol. Ibid. Other women, by contrast, deplored women in uniform.

74. Röpke to Strasser, Chemnitz, October 17, 1932. Ibid.

75. Lotte Rühlemann to Gregor Strasser, 8. August 1931, NS 22/vorläufig 349/BA Koblenz. "You would not believe how difficult it often was to be leader in the big cities, where you had to confront so much hostility."

76. Gregor Strasser, "Rundschreibung Nr. 26," notice, Berlin September 24, 1931, which officially dissolved both Frauenorden and Women's Working Committee *(Frauenarbeitsgemeinschaft)*, and founded a new *Frauenschaft*. "Organisations-Plan für die Arbeit der Frauenschaft, Berlin, October 1, 1931, by NSDAP Gau Berlin, Abt. I., responded to the change, noting that 90 percent of the funds collected went to Party headquarters. BA Koblenz/Sammlung Schumacher/230. Goebbels to Strasser, June 10, 1931, "Aufführungsbestimmung," ibid.

77. "Richtlinien des deutschen Frauenordens," January 2, 1931, BA Koblenz/Sammlung Schumacher/230. These guidelines contained provisions for expelling dishonorable, immoral, disorderly, and quarrelsome members. The *Völkischer Beobachter* repeated the official ban on women from Party office, November 26, 1930.

78. She pledged to concern herself with: education in nursing and wom-

en's health; support of families with many children; aid for prisoners; support for Germans living outside Germany; and racial education for girls. "Richlinien des deutschen Frauenordens," BA Koblenz. For the discussion of goals, cf. ibid., Sammlung Schumacher, 230, Zander, January 2, 1931, and letters from the Gauleiterin in Lübeck to Strasser June 24 and July 3, 1931, and to Hildebrandt (Strasser's colleague) December 4, 1931. Ibid., NS 22/vorläufig 349. For an excellent account of Strasser's activities at this time, cf. Peter Stachura, *Gregor Strasser and the Rise of Nazism* (London: Allen and Unwin, 1983), 89–95.

79. *(Eine gediegene, gehaltvolle, und vielseitige Zeitung).* Rogge-Börner to Zander, April 20, 1931, BA Koblenz/NS 22/vorläufig 349.

80. Frau Stütz (illegible), Party no. 6983, BA Koblenz/NS22/Vorläufig 349.

81. Dr. Conti to Strasser, June 3, 1931, BA Koblenz, Sammlung Schumacher 230/Bl. 79. February 19, 1931, letter from the Frauenorden and Frau Beyer, DFO, Breslau, 1931. BA ibid., NS 22/vorläufig 349/Bl.7.

82. "Ordnung der Frauenschaft," BA Koblenz, NS22/vorläufig 349. Cf. also Hildegard Passow to Gregor Strasser, "The woman places her faith absolutely where she sees an idea that most purely expresses her personality." Then she outlines a propaganda line designed especially for women, ibid., NS26/254. Gertrud Myska-Lindemann to Martschenke, August 11, 1931, and a ten-page letter from Maria Martschenke to Strasser, August 26, 1931, BA Koblenz/NS 22/vorläufig 349. This file contains an array of letters from 1930 to 1931.

83. Zander to Strasser, June 6, 1931, ibid., NS22/349. In the latter communication, Zander defends herself against various male officials who do not appreciate women's work and who slander her.

84. For a list of Zander and her staff, cf. "Rundschreibung" August 17, 1932, BA Koblenz/NS22/356. The national rally, "Tagung der NSFS-Deutsche Frauenorden," August 29–30, 1932, in Munich featured both Diehl and Zander. Cf. the printed program and the report, dated October 13, 1932, SAM/W- N/NSF/405. Stephenson, *Nazi Organization*, 42–45.

85. Lotte Rühlemann to G. Strasser, August 8, 1931, BA Koblenz, NS 22/vorläufig 349. A letter from a local leader in Munich to Zander dated October 11, 1932, complained about the "total lack of understanding on the part of political leaders" of the women's point of view. Official propaganda, she wrote, was written for men by men. BA Koblenz/NS22/355.

86. Rundschreiben 6 (November 9, 1931), Berlin. BA Koblenz/Sammlung Schumacher/230 and NS22/vorläufig 349. Cf. also the autobiographical account, "Mein Kampf als Nationalsozialistin," HI reel 13.

87. Anti-Nazi pamphlets: Dr. Amalie Lauer, MdL (Member of the Landtag), *Die Frau in der Auffassung des Nationalsozialismus* (Cologne: Görreshaus, 1932); Elisabeth Schwarzhaupt, *Was hat die Deutsche Frau vom Nationalsozialismus zu erwarten?* (Berlin: Erneuerung, 1932); and SPD, *Nationalsozialismus und Frauenfragen: Material zur Information und Bekämpfung* (Berlin: February 1932). *Die Frau im "Dritten Reich" Was die werktätige Frauen von den Nationalsozialismus zu wissen haben* (Berlin:

Interna, 1931) and *Frauen im Kampf für Freiheit und Brot!* (Berlin: Interna, 1931).

88. Maria Juchacz, "Gefährdetes Frauenrecht," *Die Genossin* 10 (January 1933), 5.

89. Dr. Frieda von Herwarth, Terramare Office, London, Hoover Institution Archives.

90 Emma Witte, "Die Frau im Lebensraume des Mannes," *Nationalsozialistische Monatshefte* IV (1933), 29. cf. C. Koonz, "The Competition for Women's *Lebensraum*, 1928–1934," in Bridenthal, Kaplan and Grossmann, eds., *When Biology Became Destiny*, 199–236.

91. Betty Friedan, *The Feminine Mystique* (New York: Dell, 1963), 34–35. Post-1945 American women's magazines, films, and television accomplished a more radical transformation of women's identity than Scholtz-Klink ever did (or cared to do) when they privatized women and defined their homes as the woman's world.

92. Marianne Weber, *Lebenserinnerungen* (Bremen: Storm, 1948), 235.

93. "Unsere Bundesbriefe," 1932, BDM, *Das war unser Angfang*, 37.

5. "Old-Timers" in the New State

1. "Grundsätze der Nationalsozialistischen Frauenschaft," BA Koblenz/ Sammlung Schumacher/230. On the genesis of the women's bureaucracy, cf. Jill Stephenson, *The Nazi Organization of Women* (New York: Barnes & Noble, 1980), 65–91, and Dietrich Orlow, *The History of the Nazi Party*, 2 vol. (Pittsburgh: University of Pittsburgh Press, 1969), 257, 273–274.

2. "Was Wollen die Nazis?" Election pamphlet, dated April 24, 1932, HI/ NSDAP/S. On the eve of the July elections the *Völkischer Beobachter* included election appeals to women by Strasser and Zander, *Völkischer Beobachter* 212 (July 30, 1932), Second Section. P. Germany. In connection with a change of attitude toward women followers, cf. Goebbels Diary entry of March 29, 1932. "The Führer developed a totally new notion about our position on women. . . . The woman is the sexual and work partner of the man. She has always been so and will remain. But in the current economic situation she must remain so. Earlier in the field and today in the office. The man is the organizer of life and the woman his helper and administrator," Joseph Goebbels, *Vom Kaiserhof zur Reichskanzlei* (Munich: Eher, 1937), March 29, 1932, 72.

3. Zander's proposal, NSF to Strasser, "Btr. Verleihung des Staatasbürgerrechts an Frauen," Munich, November 17, 1932. Zander noted the unpopularity of the NSDAP stand on the Woman Question and insisted that only a strong affirmation of women's equality (Ebenbürtigkeit) would appease critics. She added that she wanted proof of "Aryan" descent, as well. BA Koblenz/NS22/vorläufig 355. Strasser's rebuke came at once. "Rundschreiben No. 6," February 1933, ibid., NS25/75. Auerhahn and Rienhardt also exchanged letters on the same topic. Ibid., NS22/vorläufig 355. Zander had not been totally unrealistic about Strasser's views, for in 1926 he had written,

"The working woman has equality of status in the National Socialist state, and has the same right to security as the married woman and mother." Gregor Strasser, *Kampf um Deutschland* (Munich: Eher, 1932), 133.

4. "Anordnung," Käte Auerhahn and Elsbeth Zander, September 12, 1932, BA Koblenz/NS22/vorläufig 355. Memo of October 1, 1932, ibid., Sammlung Schumacher/230. Throughout months of strife, Strasser stood behind Zander, cf. for example the letter from Reinhardt to Elsbeth Unverricht, December 8, 1932, ibid., NS22/355. Ley complained about the lack of charity work, ibid., NS22/2002. Behind the scenes, several proposals circulated: Ley promised to emphasize women's employment; Auerhahn pledged to pay attention to peasant women; Zander worried about finding work for the unemployed; Boehm proposed new racial hygiene programs; Unverricht planned improved editorial work on the periodical *Frauenwart*. Report of August 29–30, 1932, NSF and Frauenorden Rally, dated October 13, 1932. SAM/W-N/NSF/405.

5. Lotte Rühlemann to Strasser, August 8, 1931, ibid., NS22/vorläufig 3 "Zur Chronik der N. S. Frauenschaft," unsigned history, dated July 1, 1934, HI reel 13/No. 254. For an excellent account of these events, cf. Stephenson, *The Nazi Organization*, 99–103.

6. The Nazi Reichstag representation declined by 34 seats, while the Communists gained 14 and the reactionary Nationalist Party picked up 11 additional seats.

7. *The New York Times* (December 18, 1932), editorial page.

8. W. P. Shively, "Party Identification," *American Political Science Review*, 66 (December 1972), 1203–1225.

9. Peter Stachura, "Der Fall Strasser," in Stachura, ed., *The Shaping of the Nazi State* (London: Allen & Unwin, 1983), 110–116. Gregor Strasser, *Kampf um Deutschland. Reden und Aufsätze* (Munich: Eher, 1932).

10. Joseph Goebbels, *Vom Kaiserhof zum Reichskanzlei. Eine historische Darstellung in Tagebuchblättern* (Munich: Zentralverlag der NSDAP, 1934), 78.

11. Hedwig Eggert, Berlin-Steglitz, Abel no. 459.

12. Gotthard Jasper, *Von Weimar zu Hitler* (Cologne: Kniepenheuer and Witsch, 1968), 236. "Hitler's Chances," *The New York Times* (February 4, 1933), II: 4 E. Foreign observers concurred. One of the most surprising (though hardly atypical) came from British Socialist Harold Laski in 1932. "Accident apart, it is not unlikely that Hitler will end his career as an old man in some Bavarian village, who in the tiergarten in the evening, tells his intimates how he nearly overturned the German Reich. . . . The old man, they will think, is entitled to his pipedreams." Lord Templewood (Samuel Hoare), *Nine Troubled Years* (London: Collins, 1954), 121.

13. General von Schleicher called Hitler an "unimportant but perfectly decent fellow." Quoted by Albert Wucher, *Die Fahne Hoch. das Ende der Republik und Hitlers Machtübernahme. Ein Dokumentarbericht.* (Freiburg: Herder, 1965).

14. Hermann Rauschning, *Revolution of Nihilism. A Warning to the West*, trans. E. W. Dickes (New York: Longmans Green, 1939), 218.

15. Vicki Baum, *Es war alles ganz anders. Erinnerungen* (Berlin: Ullstein, 1962), 355.

16. André François-Ponçet, *The Fateful Years*, trans. Jacques le Clercq (New York: Harcourt Brace, 1944), 66.

17. Melita Maschmann, *Account Rendered. A Dossier on My Former Self*, trans. Geoffrey Strachan (London, New York, Toronto: Abelard-Schuman, 1965), 9–12.

18. Renate Finckh, interviewed by Heike Mundzeck, "Gespräch," Charles Schüddekopf, ed. *Der alltägliche Faschismus. Frauen im Dritten Reich* (Berlin: Dietz, 1982), 69. After the war she recorded her transformation from faithful believer to cynic, *Mit uns zieht die Neue Zeit* (Baden: Braun, 1979).

19. Margarete Schrimff, Abel no. 582.

20. Louise Solmitz, "Diary," trans. and quoted in Jeremy Noakes and Geoffrey Pridham, eds., *Documents of Nazism 1919–1945* (New York: Viking, 1974), 161.

21. Quoted in Eliot Barculo Wheaton, *The Nazi Revolution 1933–1935. Prelude to Calamity* (Garden City, New York: Doubleday Anchor, 1969), 214. Wheaton points out that the *Völkisher Beobachter* in September 1932 did not dare to print such a tactless claim. On the sources of weakness among Hitler's opponents, cf. K. D. Bracher, *Die deutsche Diktatur* (Cologne: Kniepenheuer & Witsch, 1969), 215–281.

22. Dorothy Thompson, *I Saw Hitler!* (New York: Farrar and Reinhart, 1932), v, 16. "In intercourse he is shy, almost embarrassed . . . he gives the impression of a man in a trance." Louis Lochner, *What About Germany* (New York: Dodd, Mead, 1942), chastised Thompson's naiveté. A. R. Knickerbocker, *Germany. Fascist or Soviet?* (London: J. Lana, 1932), 142, also perceived the threat more clearly.

23. "The Battlecries of Hitlerism Modified as Election Nears," *The New York Times* (July 10, 1932), 8, 3:1. The author defined Hitlerism as "The political expression of the spiritual yearnings of a great epoch. The movement is a protest against making a machine of man; it is an agency with which to create an ideal state of pure-blooded Germans." The journalist concluded that Hitler was "more democratic than Ramsay MacDonald."

24. Joachim Fest, *Hitler*, trans. Richard and Clara Winston (New York: Vintage, 1975), 388. Cf. David Child, *Germany Since 1918* (New York: St. Martin's, 1980), 40 ff.

25. Joseph Goebbels, *Vom Kaiserhof zur Reichskanzlei* (Munich: Zentralverlag, 1934), 78.

26. Rudolf Diels, *Lucifer ante portas* (Zurich: Internaverlag, 1949), 142–143. Friedrich Zipfel, "Gestapo and SD" in Larsen, et al., *Who Were the Fascists?* (Bergen: Universitets-forlaget, 1980), 301–306.

27. Fest, *Hitler*, 392.

28. Göring at the Nuremberg Trials said the fire came too early. Legally, the law ought to have been revoked when the Supreme Court ruled that there had been no connection between the fire and plans for a Communist revolution. Hajo Holborn, *History of Modern Germany* (New York: Knopf, 1969), 724.

29. Quoted in *Die Frau*, "Bund deutscher Frauen," 40:6 (March 1933), 382.

30. With an 89 percent turnout, the results disappointed Nazi leaders. Despite severe harassment, the Communists lost only 27 percent of their support and retained 81 seats; Social Democrats increased their vote by 11 percent and won 120 seats; the Nationalists (DNVP) lost a stunning 39 percent and retained 52 seats. Despite access to unlimited state funds and control over the police, the Nazi Party increased its popularity by only 14 percent and won 288 seats. Looked at in another way, the Nazi Party in 1933 received a lower percentage of the vote than the Social Democrats had in the first election of the Weimar Republic, in 1919. For complete charts on electoral results, cf. Koppel S. Pinson, *Modern Germany, Its History and Its Civilization* (New York: Macmillan, 1964), 572–576.

31. Max Domarus, *Hitler. Reden und Proklamationen, 1932–1945* (Munich: Suddeutscher Verlag, 1965), May 17, 1933, I, 275.

32. *Le Temps*, February 1, 1933. As "Man of the People," the reporter asked, "Could he ever function well in 'a cabinet of big business and agriculture?' "

33. "Herr Hitler in Office," *The Times* (London: January 31, 1933), 9.

34. *The Times* (London: March 15, 1933), 11.

35. "Au Seuil," *Le Temps* (March 6, 1933), 1. Most dictators waited or staged a reign of terror before risking an election. "La dictature raciste" (March 11, 1933), called Hitler a "revolutionary" for the first time.

36. "Nazi Discipline," *The Times* (London, March 9, 1933), 11.

37. "Violence in Berlin," *The Times* (London, February 28, 1933), 13.

38. Frederik Böök, *An Eyewitness in Germany*, trans. E. Sprigge and C. Napier (London: Lovat Dicson, 1933), 41 ff.

39. "May Day," *The Times* (London, May 2, 1933), 14.

40. William Shirer, *The Rise and Fall of the Third Reich* (New York: Simon and Schuster, 1960), 209. Hitler criticized simpleminded nineteenth-century nationalists who attempted to "Germanize their neighbors" and thereby weakened their own cause.

41. D. Eiden, Abel no. 244.

42. H. Huhn, Abel no. 297. Cf. also Böhm-Stolz, no. 46; Heder, no. 41; and Radtke, no. 207. Nazi women had stepped outside traditional roles they themselves defended as the norm for women in order to participate in "out role" activities. Having had the experience in public life, they were loath to relinquish it and return to their homes. Nazi women from Berlin had already expressed misgivings about Party attention in 1931 when Strasser integrated women's associations. "Voluntary work ends now. This is a solution that we greet partly with joy and partly with scepticism." If, the report continued, men take over completely, women will leave in a "mass exodus."

43. Magda Goebbels, quoted *Vossische Zeitung* (July 6, 1933) Idem., *Die deutsche Mütter. Rede zum Muttertag. 14. Mai, 1933* (Heilbronn: E. Salzer, 1933).

44. Diehl claimed that Hitler promised her the position of National Cul-

tural Affairs director. Leipzig, August 27, 1940. Personnel file, BDC. Gertrud Scholtz-Klink, "Stellungsnahme," March 13, 1936, ibid.

45. At that point, Rudolf Hess assured her of a liberal pension as compensation for her early services to the movement. Stephenson, *The Nazi Organization of Women*, 100. Michael Kater, "Frauen in der NS Bewegung," *Vierteljahrsheft für Zeitgeschichte* 31:202–241 (1983), and Kater, *Party*, 148–153.

46. K. Thomas, *Women in Nazi Germany* (London: Gollancz, 1943), 26.

47. Quoted in Norman H. Baynes, *The Speeches of Adolf Hitler, April 1922–1939*, 2 vol. (New York: Fertig, 1969), I, 528.

48. Hermann Rauschning, *Revolution of Nihilism. A Warning to the West*, trans. E. W. Dickes (New York: Longmans, Green, 1939), 49. Fest, *Hitler*, 430.

49. Regierung von Oberfranken und Mittelfranken to Bürgermeister (mayor) of Ansbach, July 31, 1933. Hauptstaatsarchiv Nuremberg. Bestand: LRA Ansbach, Abg. 61/no. 4162.

50. Leonore Kühn, "Natürlicher Aristokratismus," in Irmgard Reichenau, ed., *Deutsche Frauen an Adolf Hitler*, 3rd ed. (Leipzig: A. Klein, 1933), 36–37.

51. Irmgard Reichenau, "Die begabte Frau," ibid., 12–34. She believed that the "heroic woman" must be allowed the freedom to develop her talents. A contributor to the same volume, Yella Erdmann, insisted that mothers needed total equality with fathers in order to raise a healthy Nazi generation.

52. Lydia Gottschewski, *Männerbund und Frauenfrage* (Munich: Eher, 1934), 81. Cf. also Theodor Eichdorff, "Frauenwirken am Wideraufbau," *Soziale Praxis* 42:49 (1933), 1426. "The German Women's Front took a strongly negative stance toward the 'old women's movement.' "

53. Ibid., 52, and "Deutsches Führertum: Die Eingliederung der Frau in den neuen Staat," *Amtliche Frauenkorrespondenz* 12:21.

54. Leonore Kühn, "Auflösung," *Die Deutsche Kämpferin. Stimmen zur Gestaltung der wahrhaftigen Volksgemeinschaft* I:40 (1933), 40–41.

55. Walter Buch to Gottfried Krummacher, September 29, 1933, BDC.

56. Hans-Jürgen Arendt, "Die 'Gleichschaltung' der bürgerlichen Frauenorganisationen in Deutschland 1933/1934," *Zeitschrift für Geschichtswissenschaft* (July 1979). Special thanks to Renate Bridenthal for bringing this excellent article to my attention. Alice Salomon's memoirs describe the process succinctly, in her autobiography, 257 ff. "Character Is Destiny," typewritten manuscript in the Leo Baeck Institute, New York (hereafter LBI), Alice Salomon Collection, AR3875.

57. G. Bäumer, "Die Frauen in der Volks- und Staatskrisis," *Die Frau*, 40:6 (March 1933), 321–325. In June Bäumer declared "the house has collapsed" (40:9), 513, but ironically the following article looked forward to the rebuilding of a new Lebensraum. Leonore Kühn, "Lebensraum für die Frau in Staat und Kultur," ibid., 515–526.

58. Quoted in Evans, *German Feminism*, 256. The BDF statement on the March elections did not speak out against the Nazis. "Bund deutscher Frauen," 40:6 (March, 1933), 380–381.

59. The initials in German were: ADLV, VDEL, and VkdL. Clifford Kirkpatrick, *Nazi Germany. Its Women and Family Life* (New York and Indianapolis: 1938), 62. H. J. Arendt, "Gleichschaltung," 615–625. E. Beckmann, "Die Auflösung des Allgemeinen Deutschen Lehrerinnen Vereins," *Die Frau* 40:8 (May 1933), 546–548. This organization alone included 40,000 members.

60. Circular to Altmitglieder des Verbands der Studentinnenvereine Deutschland, minutes of the October 29, 1933, meeting. Mailed January 1934, Deutsches Zentralinstitut fuer Sozialen Fragen, hereafter DZfSF/Lange Papers/Bo/folder, "Anti-Nazi und Nazi." The authors added, "Still we will have to deal with the exodus of many members."

61. Atina Grossmann, "The League of German Women Doctors: from Social Reform to Gleichschaltung," unpublished manuscript. Kirkpatrick gives the following figures: Three hundred Jewish women lost their practices; and 115 married physicians lost their panel practices. In 1935, 3,675 women physicians practiced, as compared to 3,405 in 1932, Kirkpatrick, *Nazi Germany*, 249.

62. Dörte Winkler, *Frauenarbeit im 'Dritten Reich,'* 38–68. Winkler points to the discrepancies of policy on the question of women in the labor force. For example, she notes that women on the job did not welcome the protective legislation passed by the Nazis. Women, however, received about 75 percent of men's wages in industry, a relatively high rate. Ultimately, contradictions damaged the effort to manage the Woman Question and labor needs. Cf. also Stefan Bajhor, *Die Hälfte der Fabrik. Geschichte der Frauenarbeit in Deutschland, 1914 bis 1945* (Marburg: Verlag Arbeiterbewegung und Gesellschaftswissenschaft, 1979), 251–254. Richard Grunberger, *The Twelve Year Reich* (New York: Ballantine, 1972), 190–192, 276; Jill Stephenson, *Women in Nazi Society* (New York: Barnes and Noble, 1975), 95–115; and Said, "Zur Situation," Frauengruppe, ed. *Mutterkreuz und Arbeitsbuch* (Frankfurt: Fischer, 1981), 105–130. Schoenbaum, *Hitler's Social Revolution* (New York: Norton, 1980), 182, 190–191. Schoenbaum and Winkler see modernization and not Nazi prejudices as the key variable in women's lives. Because women's status to a far greater degree than men's depended upon pre-modern and nonmonetary considerations, the interpretation remains too narrow. Paradoxically, however, the "status revolution" at the core of Schoenbaum's thesis may have affected women more than men. Proponents of modernization overlook the decline in women's political status, women's share of well-paid jobs, and the deformation of family life. For an evaluation of the modernization thesis, cf. Ian Kershaw, *The Nazi Dictatorship. Problems and Perspectives of Interpretation* (London: Edward Arnold, 1985), 130–148. J. Hidden and J. Farquharson, *Explaining Hitler's Germany*, (London: Batsford, 1983), 83 ff.

63. Dr. Nowack, Anwaltskammer, Geheimes Hauptstaatsarchiv Preussischer Kulturbesitz/Rep. 84a/580. Berlin-Dahlem. The participants in the debate referred frequently to law as a profession for the "male union" (Männerbund). The career prospects had never seemed bright in the profession devoted to justice: In 1933, for example, three percent of all applicants for the bar were women. Although 1.13 percent of women failed (compared with

22.4 percent of the men) and 10.5 percent of all women passed with high honors (compared with 6.5 percent of the men), women lawyers were considered "unfit" to practice and in 1936 officially banned. Martha Döhnhoff, "Von der parlamantarische Arbeit der Frau," 40:12 (September 1933), 730, and ibid., 42:12 (September 1935), and Kirkpatrick, *Nazi Germany*, 238–239.

64. Franz Seldte, *Sozialpolitik im Dritten Reich* (Berlin: Reichsdruckerei, 1935), 11–12. Jill Stephenson argues that women were discriminated against as members of politically "unreliable" groups rather than as women. *Women in Nazi Society*, 147–163. She insists that the Nazi bureaucracy always had room for talented and loyal professional women. For an excellent statement of the opposite thesis, cf. Claudia Hahn, "Der Öffentliche Dienst und die Frauen, Beamtinnen in der Weimarer Republik," and Erika Said, "Zur Situation der Lehrerinnen," *Mutterkreuz*, 72–78, 92–99.

65. Ursula von Gersdorff, ed., *Frauen im Kriegsdienst* (Stuttgart: Deutsche Verlags-Anstalt, 1969), Doc. 104, 178–179.

66. Agnes von Zahn-Harnack, "Frauenbewegung und Nationale Revolution" *Deutsche Allgemeine Zeitung* (April 30, 1933).

67. "Die Frau im Nationalsozialismus," *Vossische Zeitung* (June 22, 1933).

68. "Kein Abbau erwerbstätiger Frauen die Ernährerinnen sind," *Die Deutsche Kämpferin* I:12 (March 1934). Women, she wrote, must share a feeling of kinship, *Gebundenheit*.

69. Dr. Margarete Adam, "Eine Widerlegung," *Die Deutsche Kämpferin* I:9 (December 1933), 175–176. She cited two questionnaires returned by 9,000 and 4,000 Catholic women teachers in 1927 and 1932, respectively. Because most teachers supported mothers and sisters, they deserved their jobs.

70. "Doppelverdiener," *Reichsarbeitsblatt* 8:1, no. 25 (September 5, 1933), 224–226. For Seldte's proclamation, cf. ibid. September 9, 1933, and Franz Seldte, *Sozialpolitik*, 23. K. Amon, "Doppelverdienertum," *Soziale Praxis* 42:39 (1936). Bahor, *Die Hälfte*, 168–188.

71. Several dozen messages defended Bäumer, BA Koblenz, R18/7108. Bäumer's "Lebenslauf," ibid., R36/2379. Her invitation to become Referentin in the Education Ministry (April 21, 1933) is included in this file. Her earlier "Lebenslauf" (autobiography), dated June 27, 1928, is in ibid., R36/2379.

72. G. Bäumer, personnel file, BDC. Bäumer to Emmy Beckmann, January 14, 1933, BA Koblenz/ Kleine Erwerbungen/267/2. Cf. "Das Haus ist zerfallen," *Die Frau* 40:9 (June 1933), 513. Actually, her own "Haus" did not collapse as she retained her country castle. The phrase comes from a traditional poem, *"Das Haus ist zerfallen/ was hat's den für Not?/ Der Geist lebt in uns allen/ und unsere Burg ist Gott."* "The house has collapsed/ What do we need?/ The spirit lives in us all/ and our castle is God."

73. In several essays, Gertrud Bäumer made her acceptance of Nazism clear. "Unsere Nationalsoziale Bewegung und der Nationalsozialismus," *Die Hilfe* 39:6 (March 8, 1933). "Umwege und Schicksal der Frauenbewegung," ibid., 39:9 (June 1933), 385–387. "Zur Kanzlerrede," *Die Frau* 40:8 (June 1933), 526. "Spiessbürgertum in der Frauenfrage," *Die Frau* 41:6 (March 1934), 322. R. Evans, "German Women and the Triumph of Hitler," *Journal*

of Modern History (March 1976) and Jill Stephenson, *Women in Nazi Society* (New York, 1976), 194.

74. "Evolution nicht Reaktion," 40:11 (August 33), 658–663, *Die Frau* and "30 Jahre Frauenstudium," ibid., 45:11 (1937/8), 579–584.

75. Bäumer, "Spiessbürgertum in der Frauenfrage," *Die Frau* 41:6 (March 1934), 321.

76. BDC. Velsen was born in 1883 and worked as a social worker and organizer for the BDF and Democratic Party, with special concern for international affairs. Nachlass von Velsen, Kleine Erwerbung, BA Koblenz.

77. Else Ulich-Beil, *Ich ging meinen Weg* (Berlin-Grunewald: Herbig, 1961), 145–146. Gertrud Bäumer, *Des Lebens wie der Liebe Band. Briefe*, ed. E. Beckmann (Tübingen: Wunderlich, 1956); idem., *Der neue Weg der deutschen Frau* (Stuttgart: Deutsche-Verlags-Anstalt, 1946); M. E. Lüders, *Fürchte dich nicht. Persönliches und Politisches aus mehr als 80 Jahren* (Cologne and Opladen, West-deutscher Verlag, 1963); Agnes von Zahn-Harnack, *Schriften und Reden, 1914–1950* (Tübingen: Hopper, 1967).

78. Irene Stoehr, " 'Organisierte Mütterlichkeit,' zur Politik der deutschen Frauenbewegung um 1900," in Karin Hausen, ed., *Frauen suchen ihre Geschichte* (Munich: Beck, 1983), 221–223. This essay provides the ideological basis for treatments of motherliness in political life.

79. F. H. Hankins, "German Policies for Increasing Births," *American Journal of Sociology* 42:5 (March 1937), 630–646. In 1933, 631,000 couples married, 25 percent more than in the previous year. Friedrich Burgdörfer, *Bevölkerungsentwicklung im Dritten Reich* (Berlin and Heidelberg: Vorwinckel, 1935), 25–29. For the announcement of the program, cf. *Soziale Praxis* 42:27, 831.

80. Dr. Stähle, "Unfruchtbarmachung und Weltanschauung," *Ärzteblatt*, (Karlsruhe, May 4, 1935).

81. Richard Peikow, *Die soziale und wirtschaftliche Stellung der deutschen Frau in der Gegenwart* (Berlin: Hoffmann, 1937), 12 ff. The average loan was RM 500 and the total cost of the program during the first three years was RM 31 million.

82. Michaelis, Schräpler and Scheel, eds., *Innere Gleichschaltung des Staates und die Kirchen* (Berlin: Wendler, 1967); Peikow, *Stellung*, 19-20; Tim Mason, "Women in Germany, 1925–1940: Family, Welfare, and Work," *History Workshop Journal*, 1 and 2 (Summer and Autumn, 1976), esp. II:12 ff.; Rita Thalmann, *Être Femme dans le troisième Reich* (Paris: LaFont, 1982) 120–137; and Dorothee Klinksiek, *Die Frau im NS-Staat* (Stuttgart: Deutsche Verlags-Anstalt, 1982), 82–94.

83. Alice Platen Hallermund, *Die Tötung der Geisteskranken in Deutschland* (Frankfurt a.M., 1948); cf. also *Trials of War Criminals before the Nuremberg Military Tribunals*, Nuremberg, October 1946–April 1949, vol. 10. case 1, United States Government Printing Office.

84. "Kirche und Sterilization," *Der Alemane*. (Freiburg i. Br., January 26, 1934). François-Poncet, an ardent opponent of Nazi rule, described the sterilization laws without comment. *The Fateful Years*, 82.

85. Daniel J. Kelves, *In the Name of Science. Eugenics and the Uses of*

Human Heredity (New York: Knopf, 1985), 138–159. Loren R. Graham, "Science and Values: The Eugenics Movement in Germany and Russia in the 1920s," *American Historical Review* 82 (December 1977), 1133–1164.

86. Alice Salomon, "Character Is Destiny," 256. In *Mein Kampf*, trans. Ralph Mannheim (Boston, Sentry, 1962), Hitler wrote, "The demand that defective people be prevented from propagating equally defective offspring is a demand of the clearest reason and if systematically executed represents the most human act of mankind." 255.

87. Theodore Eichhoff, "Frauenwirken am Wiederaufbau," *Soziale Praxis*, 42:40 (December 7, 1933), 1426–1427. BDC personnel file. Memo, November 5, 1931, BA Koblenz/NS22/vorläufig 349.

88. Liselotte Flintermann, "Noch ein Wort über den Antisemitismus," *Informationsdienst*, 17 (July 1, 1933), quoted by Kirkpatrick, *Nazi Germany*, 46–47.

89. Paula Siber, lecture December 12, 1933, quoted by Kirkpatrick, *Nazi Germany*, 119.

90. Siber, "Plan für den Aufbau der Frauenschaft," SAM/W-N/NSF/326. These were the same plans she had drafted for Strasser before his departure from the Party in December 1932. Cf. Siber to Feder, August 21, 1933, BA Koblenz/R43II/823a.

91. USCHLA (Untersuchungs- und Schlichtungsausschuss der NSDAP). BDC.

92. 51 percent of all delegates and the entire leadership would be comprised of Nazis. Women's professional groups would be represented in subsections: housewives, servants, women without a profession, artisans and workers, professions, unemployed and teachers and state officials. Meta Mischka, woman district director NSDAP, Hannover South, to Gauleiter Schmalz. I am grateful to Dr. Gisela Bock, who forwarded to me a copy of this proposal.

93. Arnold and Veronica Toynbee, *Hitler's Europe* (London: Oxford, 1954), 21. Franz Neumann, *Behemoth. The Structure and Practice of National Socialism* (New York: Harper Torch, 1966). Originally published 1942. Hannah Arendt's *Origins of Totalitarianism* (New York and Cleveland: World, 1958), expanded on the theme of what Neumann termed "planned shapelessness."

94. Michael Kater, *The Nazi Party*, 151. Party membership expanded from 850,000 just before Hitler's takeover to 2,500,000 in 1934, and only 5 percent of that total were women (as compared to 8 percent in 1932). After 1933 the sex ratio narrowed slightly, partly for bureaucratic reasons. David Schoenbaum, *Hitler's Social Revolution*, 274 and 224 ff.

95. On the fate of male "old fighters" in the Nazi movement generally, cf. Schoenbaum, *Hitler's Social Revolution* 224 ff, 274, and Martin Broszat, *The Hitler State. The Foundation and Development of the Internal Structure of the Third Reich*, trans. John W. Hidden (London and New York: Longman, 1981), 193–241, and Kater, *Nazi Party*, 72–116 and 190–212.

96. Seydel to Polster, reporting comments of Baroness von Oeynhausen, September 29, 1933, Seydel to Koch (the Bielefeld woman leader) May 23,

1933, SAM/W-N/NSF 393/Bl. 38 and Seydel to Polster, December 22, 1933, SAM/W-N/NSF 525.

97. Initially, Seydel had written "no hysterical" but changed it to "not only."

98. Seydel to Hitler's sister, December 12, 1933, SAM/W-N/NSF/393.

99. Walter Buch to Gottfried Krummacher, September 29, 1933, Gottschewski file, BDC. Typical of middle-class women's responses was an essay by Gisela Gröning, "Jugend und die alte Frauenbewegung," *Die Frau* 41:10 (August 1934), 617. Her views justify the court's opinion. Käthe Miethe, "Haben die Frauen?" *Deutsche Allgemeine Zeitung* 142 (March 25, 1934).

100. Paula Siber, "Parteiamtliche Anordnungen und Bekanntmachungen betreffend Neugliederung der Frauenschaftsverbände," *Das deutsche Frauenwerk* 1:3 (October 1933).

101. "Dr. Gottfried Krummacher, Leiter der NSF," *Das Archiv* (September 13, 1933), 854. Cf. also notices in *Germania* (September 16, 1933), no. 255, and "Deutsches Frauenwerk," *Der Tag*, no. 233. He was born in 1892 and had belonged to the Nazi Party since April 1930 (Party no. 229, 473).

102. Wilhelm, "Geheimbericht," Munich, December 27, 1933, BDC.

103. *Amtliche Frauenkorrespondenz*. This sentiment was one of Hitler's favorites, and often repeated by his subordinates, cf. for example, Goebbels' statement at the 1934 Nuremberg Rally, quoted in Leni Riefenstahl's film *Triumph des Willens*. On his defense of the "Aryan" paragraph, cf. Krummacher's letter to the Lord Bishop of Chicester, October 28, 1932. EZA Berlin/C3/219.

104. Dr. Krummacher, "Die Organisation, Aufgaben, und Pflichten der Nationalsozialistischen Frauenschaft," *Amtliche Frauenkorrespondenz* no. 1 (October 25, 1933), 1. On the selection of Krummacher, cf. BA Koblenz/ R43II/823a.

105. Letter by Krummacher, dated Gummersbach, November 11, 1933. Krummacher statement in BDC personnel file. Krummacher had served as a Party speaker and also had in the past supported conservative local organizations (report of December 27, 1933). Cf. also the extensive debates about the organization of women, BA Koblenz/NS22/vorläufig 348. When faced with complaints that the Party failed to win women's support, Krummacher proposed selecting a few local women leaders to make a well-publicized visit to Hitler. "This will demonstrate the type of woman who can be validated in the new state." Ibid., R43II/823a/Bl. 16. Kirkpatrick, *Nazi Germany*, 60–61, and Mary Beard, *Woman as a Force in History* (New York: Collier, 1962), 17–30.

106. Krummacher, "1. Einführung," n.d. "Reglung des Ausgleichswesens," BA Koblenz/Sammlung Schumacher 230.

107. Sophie Diederichs, "Frauenarbeit ohne Frauen," *Die deutsche Kämpferin* Leipzig, 1:9 (December 1933), 179.

108. Seydel letter of November 25, 1933, to Krummacher, BDC, Krummacher personnel file.

109. Memo, Munich, January 15, 1933. BA Koblenz/Sammlung Schumacher/230.

110. Maria Jecker, born in 1874, joined the Party on May 1, 1933, in Cologne (Party no. 2,233,010), and had already joined the Labor Front, National Socialist Welfare and the Frauenschaft. Earlier she had belonged to the moderately conservative People's Party. She was raised Catholic. "Zum Feiertag der nationalen Arbeit," *Die Deutsche Hausfrau* 18:5 (May 1, 1933), 1. Cf. Renate Bridenthal, "Class Struggle Around the Hearth: Women and Domestic Service in the Weimar Republic," in Martin Dobkowski and Isidor Walliman, eds., *Towards the Holocaust: The Social and Economic Collapse of the Weimar Republic* (Westport, Connecticut: Greenwood, 1983).

111. Franziska Weimann to local chapter, Osnabruck, August 30, 1932. Niedersächsisches Hauptstaatsarchiv Hannover/Patensen, hereafter NHH. Hann. 320 I/70.

112. Bertha Hindenberg-Delbrück was born in August 1885 near Hannover and joined the Party on May 1, 1933 (Party no. 2,956,472); she had already joined the Frauenschaft. BDC personnel file. Dr. A. M. Wissdorff to M. Winkelmann, June 7, 1933, NHH Hann 320 I/72 II.

113. Dr. Anne-Marie Wissdorff, "Bevölkerungspolitik im neuen Staat," *Die Deutsche Hausfrau* 18:10 (October 1, 1933), 2.

114. Lydia Gottschewski had warned them, but did not follow up. Gottschewski, quoted in Dr. A. M. Wissdorff to M. Winkelmann, June 7, 1933. NHH Hann 320I/72II.

115. Hindenberg-Delbrück to Carius, September 21, 1933. NHH Hann 320 I/71. Frau Mischka looked down on the Housewives because for years she had worked for the Nazis. Fräulein? (illegible) to Äsch, 4. August, 1933, Hann 320 I/72 I.

116. Hindenberg-Delbrück to Wilhelm, September 14, 1933, NHH Hann 320I/72I.

117. Helene Nicker Nylhoff, "Erklärung," July 4, 1933, NHH Hann 320 I/72 II.

118. Renate Bridenthal, "Class Conflict Around the Hearth." *Towards the Holocaust*, 243–261. Showing considerable political flexibility, the reactionary leadership made the same demand of the Socialist government in 1919, and in fact did meet with the "economic parliament" during the early 1920s.

119. Maschmann, *Account Rendered*, 10.

120. Hindenberg-Delbrück to Staudacher, Bielefeld, November 17, 1933, NHH Hann 320 I/36.

121. Hindenberg-Delbrück to Carius, DAF, Hanover, October 19, 1933. NHH Hann 320 I/36.

122. October 19, 1933, NHH Hann 320 I/71.

123. Maria Dralle to Hindenberg-Delbrück, Hamlin, December 1, 1933, NHH Hann 320 I/36. Deutscher Heimarbeiter und Hausgehilfenverband, Hanover, 20 February, 1934, Hann 320 I/36. Jecker, November 6, 1933, Hann 320 I/36.

124. Robert Ley, Rundschreiben, circular, January 1934, SAM/W-N/NSF/327.

125. Edward N. Peterson, *The Limits of Hitler's Power*, 68.

126. Wilhelm Frick, "Die deutsche Frau im nationalsozialistischen

Staate," *Fr. Mann's Pädagog. Magazin* Heft 1400 (Langensalza: Beyer, 1934), 7–10.

127. Minutes of a hearing on March 29, 1934, taken by Hans Pfundtner, USCHLA file, BDC, 219ff. The pamphlet in question was "Um das Gewissen der deutschen Frau" ("On the Conscience of the German Woman"). Siber's office distributed 30,000 copies. Throughout the essay, Siber insisted that "Motherliness is the deepest core of women's essence." Cf. also "Die Frauenfrage," *N. S. Frauenwarte*, I:3 (1933).

128. "NS Frauenschaft in Breslau," Mittelschlesischer Gau. *Völkischer Beobachter*, March, 7, 1934. The Party chiefs were concerned about women's lack of support, as evidenced by their publication of an election supplement of *Das Dritte Reich* I:5 for women voters (November 4, 1933). The propaganda was extremely crude, "As the wife of an official you must vote Nazi." The December 6, 1933, issue featured women's responses to the question, "What can I do for my Germany?" Starting in 1933 the paper published a women's supplement.

129. Paula Siber, *Die Frauenfrage und ihre Lösung durch den Nationalsozialismus* (Wolfenbüttel-Berlin: G. Kallmeyer, 1933), 5–9. In this booklet, Siber blamed Marxism and Materialism for Germany's decay, and also for the widespread refusal to accept the purifying ideals of Nazism as a solution. "Now that the old ideals have failed," she wrote, the nation would have to look to the "most hated and scorned ideology" for salvation. She spoke of the women's *Lebensraum* and womb (*Schoss*) As the source of "Salvation for the German *Volk*."

130. Robert Wagner to Gertrud Scholtz, July 29, 1931, Gau Baden, "Freiheit und Brot," BA Koblenz, NS 22/1044. Scholtz-Klink, *Die Frau im Dritten Reich* (Tübingen: Grabert, 1979), 28–29. For an excellent survey of women's activities in Baden, cf. Johnpeter Horst Grill, *The Nazi Movement in Baden* (Chapel Hill: University of North Carolina Press, 1983), 221–225. Grill notes the complete discord in Baden on the subject of women's role in Nazi society, 311.

131. Dörte Winkler, *Frauenarbeit*, note 11, 212. Stephenson, *Nazi Organization*, 114–115.

132. "Vortrag," Spiewok, Berlin. February 1934. DCV-A/CAXX 62 C. Cf. Martin Bormann to Erich Hilgenfeldt, April 17, 1942, reprinted in *Der politische Soldat*, 12:10, 27 and "10 Jahre NS Volkswohlfahrt," in VB, (April 18, 1942).

133. Reichstagung der Gaufrauenschaftsleiterinnen," *Nachrichtendienst* no. 10 (March 15, 1934).

134. Margarete Unger, "Der Staat und wir Frauen," *Amtliche Frauenkorrespondenz* 11 (April 1934). Those obligations were: to "fight for Volk and honor and equal rights to *Lebensraum*, for Order and Morality, against poverty, misery, and pornography." Cf. Kirkpatrick, *Nazi Germany*, 125. Stephenson, *Nazi Organization*, 166–167.

135. Scholtz-Klink, *Die Frau im Dritten Reich*, 44–45.

136. Ibid., 493–494. In 1981, Scholtz-Klink, when asked if she has any regrets, responded wistfully that she had only one: "I am sorry I did not pay

more attention to ideology. Since 1945 I have been studying the intellectual origins and inspiration of the movement." Especially when appealing to middle-class educated women, Scholtz-Klink made every effort to speak in pragmatic and nonideological terms. For example, she attacked "Dogma and stupidity *(Dummneit)*" as women's greatest enemies in a speech published in *Die Frau* 46:1 (1938), 50.

137. Interview with the author.

138. Major Siber, January 27, 1935. BDC. Hilgenfeldt, significantly, bypassed both women in the controversy and appealed directly to Major Siber to intervene.

139. Hans Pfundtner, "Niederschrift" (minutes) of a conversation held on March 29, 1934. Cf. also Walter Buch to Martin Bormann, June 2, 1934, in USCHLA proceedings, BDC, 263. Siber kept writing proposals, however. "Kulturarbeit Sozialarbeit und Volkswirtschaft," Paula Siber to Hans Hinkel, February 16, 1934. Stephenson, *Nazi Organization*, 107–111.

140. Krummacher to Frick, April 25, 1934, 236–240, BDC. Edward N. Peterson, *The Limits of Hitler's Power*, 78. Cf. Stevenson, *Nazi Organization*, 498.

141. USCHLA, December 5, 1934. BDC.

142. Scholtz-Klink to Rudolf Hess, BDC file, Bl. 357.

143. Major Siber to Führer und Reichskanzler, August 5, 1935. USCHLA, BDC, Bl. 408–413.

144. Kirkpatrick, *Nazi Germany*, 232.

145. Kent, *I Married a German*, 111. Speer referred to the metaphor from Goethe's *Faust* of the Devil tapping him on the shoulder. Hjalmar Schacht said once, "I desire a great and strong Germany and to achieve it I would enter into an alliance with the Devil." Quoted in Fest, *Face of the Third Reich*, 162. Perhaps this suggests that men were opportunistic and women played it safe.

6. The Second Sex in the Third Reich

1. Gertrud Scholtz-Klink, *Die Frau im Dritten Reich* (Tübingen: Grabert, 1979), 501.

2. Walter Hofer, ed., *Der Nationalsozialismus. Dokumente. 1933–1945* (Frankfurt: Fischer, 1957), 89. A. Wucher, *Die Fahne Hoch* (Freiburg: Herder, 1965), 162–164.

3. Joachim C. Fest, *Hitler*, trans. Richard and Clara Winston (New York: Vintage, 1975), 418.

4. Hermann Rauschning, *Hitler Speaks. Political Conversations with Adolf Hitler on his Real Aims* (London: Gollancz, 1939), 27.

5. Quoted in Rauschning, *The Voice of Destruction* (New York: Putnam, 1940), 78. Years earlier, Zander paraphrased Hitler, "The cure does not lie in the creation of new parties, but in the creation of new people *(Menschen)*." "Werbeblatt Nr. 3," Election flyer, 1926. BA Koblenz/Sammlung Schumacher 230. Cf. Bernard Rust, *Völkischer Beobachter* (March 24, 1935). Scholtz-Klink, *Die Frau*.

6. Max Domarus, *Hitler. Reden und Proklamationen* (Munich: Süd-deutsche, 1965), I, 531. 531 ff.

7. David Schoenbaum, *Hitler's Social Revolution,* 182 ff. Michael Kater, *The Nazi Party* (Cambridge: Harvard University Press, 1983), 232–233, notes 66 and 72. Percentages of women in the Party averaged between 6 and 8 percent after 1934. Cf. HSAM/NSDAP/599 and Robert Ley, ed., *Parteistatistik* (Munich: Reich, 1935), I, 18, 28–30, 85, 157, II, 164 and III, 58. *Amtliche Frauenkorrespondenz.* October 1937. Stephenson, *Nazi Organization,* 148.

8. Adolf Wagner, Gauleiter, Munich, 22. August, 1935, HSAM/NSDAP/348.

9. Albert Speer, *Inside the Third Reich* (New York: Macmillan, 1970), 61. Hitler's first choice had been Fritz Lang who, upon receiving the invitation, left Germany for exile.

10. "Fragebogen," telegram to Hitler, letter to Julius Streicher dated July 7, 1937 in Riefenstahl's Party file, BDC. Riefenstahl also gave Streicher power of attorney to handle a dispute "with the Jew Bela Balacs."

11. BDC file, "Protocol," October 6, 1937, Rundschreiben 128/1937 for confusion about her status. Memo, November 14, 1940, for her family tree. SS men needed "Jew-free" family trees that dated back for more than the two generations required for most people.

12. Scholtz-Klink to Bormann, January 24, 1938, BA Koblenz/R/43II/427, reprinted in Ursula von Gersdorff, ed., *Frauen im Kriegsdienst, 1914–1945* (Stuttgart: Deutsche Verlags-Anstalt, 1969), 28–35. Key decision-making occurred far beyond her actual range of competence.

13. Interview with the author, 1981. Scholtz-Klink, "Das Geistes und der Hände Werk," *Amtliche Frauenkorrespondenz,* 1937.

14. *Organisationsbuch der NSDAP* (Munich: Eher, 1937), 625.

15. Clifford Kirkpatrick, *Nazi Germany: Its Women and Its Family Life* (New York and Indianapolis: Bobbs-Merrill, 1938), 73, 87. Jill Stephenson, *Nazi Organization,* 147–155.

16. "Beurteilungsbogen" (evaluations) of women leaders, BA Koblenz/NS/44/26. Stephenson, *Nazi Organization,* 154.

17. Karin Hausen, "Mother's Day," Renate Bridenthal, Atina Grossmann, and Marion Kaplan, *When Biology Became Destiny* (New York: Monthly Review, 1985).

18. In 1925, 28.4 percent of the total population was considered by census takers as "dependent." Ten years later (even with the increased age limit), only 26.5 percent were included in this category. *Statistik des deutschen Reiches, Vol. 453,* "*Berufszählung,*" Heft 2. "Die Erwerbstätigkeit der Reichsbevölkerung" (Berlin, 1936), based on census taken June 16, 1933. Jill Stephenson, *Women in Nazi Society* (New York: Barnes and Noble, 1975), 80–99.

19. "Die Reichsjustizministerium, "Abtreibungskriminalität der Heilspersonen," 1937–1939, BA Koblenz/R22/1157. The law against abortion itself was made more stringent only in 1943.

20. Between 1933 and 1938, fertility rose from 14.7 to 18 births per 1000 of the population. Had this rate been sustained, the results would indeed have been startling, but in fact fertility rates resumed the downward trend that

had begun before 1900. In 1934 2.7 million marriages had produced no children at all; 3.3 million had produced one child; and 2.8 million two children. In percentages, this translated into: 18.9 percent with one; 23.2 percent with two; 19.8 percent three; Richard Peikow, *Die soziale und wirtschaftliche Stellung der deutschen Frau in der Gegenwart* (Berlin: Hoffmann, 1937), 12–18; "Zur Lage," *Die Frau* 46:6 (June 1939), 499. Dorothee Klinksiek, *Die Frau im NS Staat* (Stuttgart: Deutsche Verlags-Anstalt, 1982), 124, Dörte Winkler, *Frauenarbeit* (Hamburg: Hoffmann und Campe, 1977), 49.

21. Friedrich Burgdorfer, *Bevölkerungsentwicklung im Dritten Reich* (Berlin: Vorwinckel, 1935), 103. Cf. Mason's intelligent and cautious analysis of the statistics, "Women in Germany, 1925–1940: Family, Welfare and Work," *History Workshop* I and II (Summer and Autumn 1976). Dorothee Klinksiek, *Die Frau im NS-Staat*, 127–131.

22. Letter dated June 31, 1940, IfZ microfilm/Fa 202, Bl. 47–48. The *Lebensborn* program, incidentally, cared for only 1,436 mothers (of whom 823 were unmarried) between 1936 and 1939. Klinksiek, *Die Frau*, 97. Cf. also the International Tribunal Nuremberg, 1948, 31:176 ff.

23. Tim Mason, "Women in Nazi Germany," *History Workshop*, II, 14.

24. Stefan Bajhor, *Die Hälfte der Fabrik* (Marburg, 1979), 183.

25. "Zur Lage der deutschen Frau," *Die Frau* 45:12 (September 1938), 663–670. Every day 90,000 German children received meals under the national lunch program.

26. Special Report on the NSV, *Deutschland Berichte der SOPADE* (7 vols), Paris, September 1937, 96–101. This is from a monthly series of reports on real conditions in Germany, edited by the Socialist Party in exile. Hereafter referred to as SOPADE.

27. Ilse Köhn, *Mischling, Second Degree: My Childhood in Nazi Germany* (New York: Greenwillow, 1977), 22–23.

28. 43,000 of these were from women and 41,700 from men. "Die gegenwärtige Lage," Report, December 31, 1934. EAF 48/18, 1,844. Lewy cites lower figures as follows: 32,000 in 1934; 73,000 in 1935, and 63,000 during 1936. Günter Lewy, *The Catholic Church and Nazi Germany* (New York: McGraw Hill, 1955), 258–262. Gisela Bock, "Frauen und ihre Arbeit im Nationalsozialismus," Annette Kuhn/Gerhard Schneider, eds., *Frauen in der Geschichte* (Düsseldorf: Schwann, 1979), 113 ff. and idem., " 'No Children at Any Cost,' " Judith Friedlander, et al, *Women in Culture and Politics. A Century of Change* (Bloomington, Indiana: Indiana University Press, 1986), 286–298.

29. Dr. Gross, *Nationalsozialistische Rassenpolitik. Eine Rede an die Deutschen Frauen* (Dessau: C. Dünnhaupt, 1934), 12. I want to express my gratitude to Rudolph Binion for giving me this rare pamphlet. Hitler on many occasions spoke disparagingly about the notion that people had rights to control their own bodies.

30. Else Frobenius, *Die Frau im Dritten Reich. Eine Schrift für das deutsche Volk* (Berlin: Nationaler, 1933), 12.

31. Notice sent by the Wolff News Service on the eve of the boycott, reprinted in Comité des Délégations Juives, Paris 1934, *Die Lage der Juden in Deutschland. 1933* (Frankfurt a.M.: Ullstein, 1983), 65–66.

32. Käte Auerbach, "Das Warenhaus," *N. S. Frauenwarte*, I:3, 56–57.

33. Kirkpatrick, *Nazi Germany*, 47.

34. Hanna Rees, *Frauenarbeit in der NS-Volkswohlfahrt* (Berlin: NSDAP, 1938), 8–9.

35. Kirkpatrick, *Nazi Germany*, 260 ff. Divorce rates were 29.7 per 10,000 in 1933 and 33.1 in 1935. Ibid., 258. Agnes Edelmann-Martens, "Das Gesetz über die Eheschliessung und Ehescheidung von 6. Juli, 1938," *Die Frau* 46:10 (July 1938), 349, and "Aus der Begrundung zum neuen Ehegesetz," ibid., 570.

36. Klinksiek, *Die Frau*, 82, notes that the post-1945 constitution adopted this divorce code without its racial components. Klinksiek incorrectly considers it anomalous that the Nazis had been so liberal. Several nations in the post-1945 world have "liberalized" divorce by making separation easier and equal for men and women, without recognizing women's endemic financial inequality. Cf. Dieter Petzina, Werner Abelshauser and Anselm Faust, eds., *Sozialgeschichtliches Arbeitsbuch* (Munich: Beck, 1978), III, 30, ff.

37. Christa Wolf, *A Model Childhood*, trans. Ursula Molinaro and Hedwig Rappolt (New York: Farrar, Straus & Giroux, 1980), 189–190, the poem song lyrics are quoted on 191. For an excellent summary of the conflicting loyalties of BDM members, cf. Renate Wiggershaus, *Frauen unterm Nationalsozialismus* (Wuppertal: Hammer, 1984), 35–62.

38. I express my gratitude to Mary Feldsteiner for giving me a copy of Ingeborg Drewitz, "The Education of Girls in the Third Reich," trans. D. C. G. Lorenz, typed manuscript.

39. Melita Maschmann, *Account Rendered. A Dossier on My Former Self*, trans. Geoffry Strachan (London, New York, Toronto: Abelard-Schuman, 1965), 9–12, 21.

40. Renate Finckh, "Im Gespräch mit Heike Mundzeck," Schüddekopf, ed., *Der alltägliche Faschismus. Frauen im Dritten Reich* (Berlin: Dietz, 1982), 70–71.

41. SOPADE, June 1936, 117.

42. Cf. Dagmar Reese's excellent history and analysis of the BDM "Bund Deutscher Mädel," in Frauengruppe Faschismus Forschung, ed., *Mutterkreuz und Arbeitsbuch*, (Frankfurt: Fischer, 1981), 163–184. Noakes and Pridham, eds., *Documents*, 335.

43. *Reichsgesetzblatt*, September 23, 1936.

44. Gerda Zorn, "Mein alltäglicher Faschismus," Schüddekopf, ed., *Der alltägliche Faschismus*, 45.

45. *Sei wahr, sei klar, sei deutsch; Treu leben, trotzend kämpfen, lachend sterben.* Boys also learned to be "fast as greyhounds, tough as leather, hard as Krupp steel."

46. In absolute terms, the number of wage-earning women increased during 1933–1936. Similarly, women's unemployment rates also dropped. *Statistik des deutschen Reiches* (1973), 344, 613.

47. From 1925 to 1939, the percentage of adult women who earned wages rose from 48.2 percent to 49.2 percent. In numbers this meant an increase from 4.24 million in 1933 to 4.52 million in 1936 and 5.2 million in 1938.

Mason, "Women in Germany," *History Workshop*, II, 6. D. Winkler's comparison with USA shows the Germans far ahead of the Americans on protective legislation. *Frauenarbeit* (Hamburg: Hoffmann und Campe, 1977), 154–163.

48. Dr. Hertha Siemering, "Schichtwechsel der Generationen," *Soziale Praxis*, 47.17 (September 1, 1938), 1079.

49. In the late 1930s, one civil servant in ten was female, about the same proportion as during the 1920s. 1933 and 1938 women white collar workers ("appropriate" employment for women) increased; while women's industrial employment dropped from 29.3 percent in 1933 to 25.2 percent in 1938. Bajhor, *Die Hälfte der Fabrik*; Winkler, *Frauenarbeit*, 196. Mason, *History Workshop*, II, 15–23. Renate Bridenthal, "Beyond *Kinder, Küche, Kirche*: Weimar Women at Work," *Central European History* 6:2 (1973), 148–166.

50. Margot Schmidt, "Krieg der Männer, Chance der Frauen?" in Lutz Niethammer, ed., *"Die Jahre weiss man nicht, wo man die Heute hinsetzen soll"* (Berlin and Bonn: Dietz, 1983), 133–161.

51. Cf. reports on wages and working conditions in Nuremberg Staatsarchiv/1978 Reg. MF/3967/1. Even wages of menial workers and servants rose dramatically as the pressure mounted. Grunberger, *Twelve Year Reich*, 207; Winkler, *Frauenarbeit*, 71 ff. and 164–171.

52. Cf. David Schoenbaum, *Hitler's Social Revolution*, has argued that government concern with women indicates an improvement in status. Jill Stephenson, Jacques Pauwels, and others have blamed the disadvantages some women suffered on long-range demographic trends and not on Nazi policy *per se*.

53. Alice Rilke and Dorothea Gödicke, "Die Freizeit der erwerbstätigen Frau, Ergebnisse einer Umfrage des Frauenamts," BA Koblenz/NS5I/3–4. 35 percent loved to read and 27 percent longed to go hiking, yet over a quarter of all respondents had no free time at all and about a fifth of single women reported having about two hours a week. "Astonishingly" the authors observed, 81 percent of the respondents "demonstrate a general need to have a part of their lives that they alone control." Under a quarter expressed any interest at all in the KdF (Strength through Joy) programs. Another report concluded that workers felt oppressed by contributions and dues they paid to Nazi causes. "Die Belastung . . . der Arbeitnehmerschaft," ibid., R43II/561/ Bl. 114–122. *Frau am Werk*, Frauenamt der DAF I:9 (1936). "Tagewerk und Feierabenden der schaffenden deutschen Frau" (Berlin: Beyer, 1937).

54. "Arbeitseinsatz der Frauen," *Frau am Werk, Zeitschrift für die Werktätige Frau der Arbeits Front*, January 1938, III:1, 23.

55. Kirkpatrick, *Nazi Germany*, 90. "About 97 percent of all teachers male and female belonged to the National Socialist Teachers Union, and 32 percent of those joined the Party. 700 had been made honorary members." Report from 1936, in Michaelis, Schräpler, and Scheel, eds., *Innere Gleichschaltung der Staat und die Kirchen in Ursache und Folgen vom deutschen Zusammenbruch 1918 & 1945*, XI (Berlin: Wendler, 1967), 83. Cf. SOPADE, April 1937, 108. In 1934 83,000 women teachers belonged to the NSLB, Schemm to Scholtz-Klink, October 20, 1934. BA Koblenz/NS12/1315.

56. Erika Said, "Zur Situation der Lehrerinnen in der Zeit des National-sozialismus," in *Mutterkreuz*, 113–114. Said, unlike Pauwels, understands the importance of mobility within the role of student or teacher as a measure of discrimination. Neither author takes into account the relative failure of Nazi women students' organizations to challenge the predominating influence of Catholic and Protestant women students' organizations.

57. Demographic calculations have led Pauwels to clear Nazi policy of responsibility for declining women's enrollments. By defining "policy" as only official proclamations, he neglects the possibility that pervasive misogyny dampened young women's ambitions to excel in "masculine" spheres. Jacques Pauwels, *Women, Nazis and Universities. Female University Students in the Third Reich, 1933–1945* (Westport, Connecticut, and London: Greenwood, 1984) 33, 36–38; cf. his excellent charts, 34–35, 102–103, 150–151.

58. Before 1933, only 704 of 1900 female students were in the National Socialist Students League (ANST). Pauwels, *Women, Nazis and Universities*, 55–61, 66–70.

59. "Tätigkeitsberichte," 1937. BA Koblenz/NS12/844.

60. Magda von Tiling und Konrad Jarausch, eds., *Grundfragen pädagogischen Handelns. Beiträge zue neuen Erziehung*, (Stuttgart, 1934), 101–102, and BA Koblenz/NS12/831. Gilmer W. Blackburn, *Education in the Third Reich*, (Albany, New York: SUNY Press, 1985), 93–115, provides an ideological overview. Rolf Eilers, *Die nationalsozialistische Schulpolitik* (Cologne: Westdeutscher, 1963), 54–61, 74–83.

61. Dr. Stölten, "Denkschrift über die Neugestaltung der Lehrerinnenbildung," and commentary by Dr. Böde, ibid.

62. Dr. Marie Tscherning, "Anforderungen an die Arbeit der Frauen," *N.S. Mädchen Erziehung* (Esslingen a. N.: Burg, 1933), 2–26.

63. Frederika Matthias, "Vorschläge für die Mädchenbildung der höheren Schule," report, BA Koblenz/NS12/86.

64. Matthias, "Grundsätzliches zur Reform der Höheren Mädchenschule," Reber-Gruber, *Weibliche Erziehung im NSLB* (Leipzig: Teubner, 1934), 27.

65. Reber-Gruber had earned a Ph.D. in pedagogy and taught at the School for Physical Training. Her brief biography tells us that she was born in 1892, and was a "Professor an der Hochschule für Leibeserziehung, Munich-Pasing," NSDAP Findbuch, HSAM. Her BDC file gives her Party no. 1,117,347—joining date May 1932. Her views on education appear in Reber-Gruber, *Weibliche Erziehung im NSLB* (Leipzig and Berlin: Teubner, 1934). For a census of her core of teachers in higher education, cf. "Liste" HSAM/NSDAP/1000.

66. Ibid, 9. Cf. also best-selling Kuni Tremel-Eggert, *Barb* (Munich, Eher, 1934).

67. Hans Schemm, *Mutter oder Genossin? Der Rote Krieg* (Bayreuth: NS Kultur, 1931), 69. Michael Kater, *The Nazi Party* (Cambridge: Harvard, 1983), 186–187. It should be noted that Bernard Rust, not Schemm, became the Minister, even though Schemm founded the NSLB in 1927.

68. Reber-Gruber to Schemm, October 1, 1934, and October 13, 1934, meeting with Scholtz-Klink, BA Koblenz/NS12/1315.

69. Reber-Gruber became "Referentin" (consultant). Although she insisted on the title *Leiterin*, or "leader," she lost the debate. Reber-Gruber to Georg Roder, November 19, 1934, BA Koblenz/NS12/1315.

70. Reber-Gruber to Adolf Wagner, April 5, 1937, HSAM/NSDAP 944.

71. Reber-Gruber and Scholtz-Klink met on October 12, 1934. "Scholtz-Klink's power is not to be underestimated. We must be careful to avoid any conflict," Reber-Gruber told Schemm.

72. Schemm to Scholtz-Klink, October 20, 1934, BA Koblenz/NS12/1315; Reber-Gruber to Else Schuberth (BDM), July 14, 1934; Reber-Gruber to Deniselle, July 17, 1934. Ibid.

73. Reber-Gruber to Roder, November 30, 1934; and Reber-Gruber to Schemm, October 20, 1934.

74. Agreement, April 22, 1937, 230 Schumacher series, BA Koblenz on Reber-Gruber's views of Scholtz-Klink cf. Bürkner to Reber-Gruber May 11, 1934 and Bürkner to Reber-Gruber June 9, 1937, HSAM/NSDAP 948.

75. Reber-Gruber to Roder, June 29, 1934, BA Koblenz/NS12/1315; and exchange between Mohr and Reber-Gruber, July and August 1934, NS12/1934.

76. Reber-Gruber to Kolb, April 4, 1934, BA Koblenz/NS12/1315.

77. Reber-Gruber to Georg Roder, February 1, 1935, BA Koblenz/NS12/1315.

78. Reber-Gruber to Roder, November 30, 1934, and January 4, 1935, BA Koblenz/NS12/1513.

79. Reber-Gruber to Hilde Zehnke, December 15, 1937, HSAM/NSDAP 944.

80. Christine Wittrock, *Weiblichkeits Mythen* (Frankfurt a. M.: Sendler, 1984), 230–324.

81. Reber-Gruber, *Weibliche Erziehung im National-sozialistischen Lehrerbund* (Leipzig and Berlin: Klein, 1934), 1–6.

82. Reber-Gruber to J. Bente, July 22, 1937, HSAM/NSDAP 998. Cf. also Reber-Gruber to Sartorius, November 17, 1937, ibid., and Reber-Gruber to Röpke, May 11, 1937, NSDAP/ 998. Reber-Gruber to Anna Frank, November 11, 1938, NSDAP/1000.

83. September 27, 1938, Guida Diehl to Reber-Gruber, complaining that Bäumer had recently addressed a foreign audience in Paris, and spoke French! Diehl speculated that Jewish intellectualism had damaged Scholtz-Klink's Frauenwerk. HSAM/NSDAP 1000. Since in 1933 the editors of *Die Frau* had decided not to celebrate Bäumer's sixtieth birthday, this turnaround is dramatic indeed. *Die Frau*, 40:12 (September 1933), 705. By 1939, the women's press had begun to honor the "old" women's movement because it promoted female pride. One author even called Luise Otto-Peters a *Stammother*, Klara Fassbinder, letter of November 5, 1940, to Reichsschriftkammer, BDC personnel file. The foremothers for the first time were viewed as political, "Der Weg zur politisch denkenden Frau," *National-Zeitung* Essen 55 (February 24, 1939), clippings collection, DCV-A/CA 8/a/bl3, Bl. 51052. *Rundschreiben*, 1941, HI/13/253.

84. *Völkischer Beobachter* 27 (September 1935). On the subject of the liberal women's movement, and Scholtz-Klink, Reber-Gruber to Bürkner, May 11, 1937, and June 7, 1937, HSAM/NSDAP 998. Reber-Gruber to Mia Zarnitz, July 14, 1937, HSAM/NSDAP/944. and to Schickendanz, November 28, 1939, HSAM/NSDAP/1003.

85. Luise Linkmann, September 16, 1934, SAM/W- N/NSF 151.

86. "Monatsbericht" (monthly report), Gelsenkirchen, December 14, 1934, SAM/W-N/NSF 151.

87. Paula Werth, ibid. In Munich. One husband complained about his wife's "greedy materialism" and newfound "arrogance" after she became district leader. Tittmoning, 11. July 1935, HSAM/NSDAP 351.

88. "Bericht," (report), Hervest-Dorsten, SAM/W-N/NSF 265. For examples of women's low morale in NSV, cf. BA Koblenz/R43II/561a and 562a. From Baden came reports of failure. Zehringer/NS12/vorläufig 844.

89. "Monatsbericht," SAM/W- N/NSF 151.

90. L. Linkmann to Polster, September 16, 1934, SAM/W-N/NSF 151. Irene Seydel to Hildegard Passow, September 15, 1933. SAM/W-N/NSF 393/60.

91. References for these quotations are found in SAM/W-N/NSF 393. Seydel to Meta Bottke, Munich, Reichsleitung der NSDAP, March 2, 1934, 69; Bottke to Polster, March 15, 1934, ibid.; Gauschulungsamt to Polster, March 29, 1934, ibid.; Else Paul to Polster, April 25, 1934, ibid., 49.

92. Seydel to Polster, May 3, 1934, and "Beschwerde (complaint) I. Seydel gegen E. Polster," May 22, 1934, SAM/W-N/NSF 393/Bl. 39–48.

93. November 1–19, 1934, BA Koblenz/NS 44/2.

94. Countess Marie-Amthilde Mehrveldt to Polster, 29. August 1934. Rosenbaum, "Weltanschauliche Schule," SAM/W-N/NSF 4. Polster rallied "her" women under the motto: "I can fight for that which I love; I can love only that which I respect; and I can respect only that which I at least know," in "Wichtiges Rundschreiben," *Volkswirtschaft-Hauswirtschaft*, October 29, 1935, ibid.

95. F. Steinbrück, Kassel to Polster, September 13, 1934. SAM/W-N/NSF 393/Bl. 151.

96. Maria Cordes to Seydel, Minden, January 31, 1935. SAM/W-N/NSF 393/15.

97. DFW to Polster to Seydel, May 2, 1935, NSF 393, 9.

98. Polster, July 19, 1935. SAM/W-N/NSF 313.

99. Hess, "Rundschreiben" 21/34 (May 4, 1934), SAM/W-N/NSF 327.

100. Beyer to Münster and Polster, January 12, 1934, SAM/W-N/NSF 327; July 19, 1935, SAM/W-N/NSF 313.

101. Seydel to Polster, n.d. (1935), SAM/W-N/NSF 393/Bl. 72. Seydel wished Polster well in her "restless, agitated life."

102. "Tätigkeitsbericht" (activity report), Polster, July and August, 1935. A visit by Scholtz-Klink improved morale, "Stimmungsbericht," Dec./Jan. 1935/6. SAM/W-N/NSF 122.

103. Helma Schmuck, "Geschichte der NSF, 1930–1940," December 12, 1940, SAM/W-N/NSF 122. "Tagung der NSFS-Deutschen Frauenorden," September 1932. Ibid., 405.

104. "The greatest confusion prevails here," "Hinweis," June 12 and July 25, 1935, NSF and Polster to Gauleiterinnen, February 1935, NSF 231, and "Rundschreiben," December 3, 1935, SAM/W-N/NSF 545. For the answer to these organizational questions, cf. Erich Stockhorst, *Fünf Tausand Köpfe. Wer war Was im Dritten Reich* (Bruchsal: Blick und Bild, 1967), 13 ff. Significantly, none of his "heads" were women except Scholtz-Klink.

105. Countess Mehrveldt to Polster, September 14, 1934, SAM/W-N/NSF 315.

106. Polster to district leaders, February 1935/SAM/W-N/NSF 231.

107. "Stimmungsbericht" (report on morale), Rotes Kreuz, Detmold, 25. July, 1937, SAM/W-F/NSF 545. "Stimmungsbericht," Kreis Büren and Paderborn, May 16, 1935, ibid., NSFS/W-N/313.

108. Scholtz-Klink to Zimmermann and Warnecke, April 9, 1937, NSF 545.

109. Luise Bierling to Polster, November 20, 1935, NSF 139, 4–5; L. Dornemann to Polster, November 20, 1935, 1239, 28–29; Polster, "Meine Stellungsnahme," November 23, 1935, SAM/W-N/NSF, 8–9.

110. Luise Dornemann to Gertrud Scholtz-Klink, copy to Polster, November 18, 1935; November 25, 1935, NSF 139, SAM/W-N/NSF 139/Bl. 18 and 41–47.

111. Kirkpatrick, *Nazi Germany*, 89–90, 71.

112. Scholtz-Klink, speech given in Baden, June 21, 1933, *Die Frau im Dritten Reich*, 486, 489.

113. Hitler at 1934 *Parteitag*, September 8, 1934, Domarus I, *Reden*, 450.

114. Scholtz-Klink, *Die Frau im Dritten Reich* (Tübingen: Grabert, 1981), 493.

115. Stephenson, *Nazi Organization*, 152–155. Scholtz-Klink, *Die Frau*, 74–80.

116. Gerber to Ortsgruppe, May 25, 1939. Hann 310/I/041.

117. Max Horkheimer, "Allgemeiner Teil," in Horkheimer, Fromm, Adorno, eds., *Autorität und Familie*, I (Paris: Félix Alcan, 1936), 63–67. William J. Goode. *World Revolution and Family Patterns* (New York: Free Press, 1963). Tables 11-7 and 11-8 show that marriage rates in Germany were higher than other western nations.

7. Protestant Women for Fatherland and Führer

1. William Shirer, *20th Century Journey. The Nightmare Years* (Boston: Little, Brown, 1984), 137.

2. R. Waite, *Psychopathic God*, (New York: Basic, 1977), 362.

3. Albert Speer, *Inside the Third Reich*, 110 and Hugh Trevor-Roper, ed., *Secret Conversations* (New York: Octagon, 1981), 247.

4. Max Domarus, ed., *Hitler Reden und Proklamationen* (Munich: Suddeutsch, 1965), I, 641.

5. André François-Poncet, *The Fateful Years* (New York: Harcourt Brace, 1949), 209. A. R. Knickerbocker, *Germany* (London: Lana, 1932), called Hitler "an evangelist speaking to a camp meeting, the Billy Sunday of German politics," 242.

6. William L. Shirer, *Berlin Diary. The Journal of a Foreign Correspondent, 1934–1939* (New York: Knopf, 1941), 16–18.

7. Domarus, *Hitler Reden* I speech of February 10, 1933, I: 538.

8. Shirer, *Nightmare*, 121.

9. Domarus, *Hitler Reden* I, 641, speech of September 11, 1936, to the political leadership, 641. "Reich," it should be noted, means "kingdom" or "realm" with the same heavenly/earthly ambiguity as in English. In this context, cf. the "Sleepwalker" speech. Hitler, speech on March 14, 1936, Munich. Ibid., 606. Bullock, *Study in Tyranny*, revised edition (New York: Harper Torchbooks, 1962), 279.

10. Domarus, *Reden* speech on June 27, 1937, Würzburg, I, 704; cf. also Hans Müller, "Der pseudoreligiöse Charakter der nationalsozialistischen Weltanschauung," *Geschichte in Wissenschaft und Unterricht*, Heft 6 (1961), 339, 349.

11. A. Hitler, *Mein Kampf*, 87.

12. Klaus Scholder, *Die Kirchen und das Dritte Reich. 1918–1934* (Frankfurt a. M.: Ullstein, 1977), 701–742; and J. R. C. Wright, *"Above Parties": The Political Attitudes of the German Protestant Church Leadership. 1918–1933* (Oxford: Historical Monograph, 1974), 77 ff.

13. John Conway, *The Nazi Persecution of the Churches, 1933–1945* (New York: Basic, 1968), 2–4; R. Binion, *Hitler Among the Germans* (New York: Elsevier, 1976), 21–23 on the psychological origins of his sense of mission; J. Fest, *Hitler*, 443–445; R. Waite, *Psychopathic God*, 28–32; Konrad Heiden, *Der Führer, Hitler's Rise to Power* (Boston: Beacon, 1969), 410–412. From a political standpoint, Hitler's revelation of his racial-revolutionary and messiah-like ambitions may have been calculated to appease Nazi fanatics who felt cheated by Hitler's moderate treatment of the state apparatus (including the military).

14. Hildegard von Kotze and Helmut Krausnick, eds., with aid from F. A. Krummacher, *Es Spricht der Führer* (Gütersloh: Mohn, 1966), 147–148. These excerpts are from a speech to the *Kreisleiter* at Ordensburg Vogelsang on April 29, 1937. My thanks to Saul K. Friedländer for calling my attention to this speech.

15. This meant financial health for organized religion even in times of economic hardship. Each citizen who did not register as an atheist with local authorities paid a percentage of his annual taxes to support the faith of his choice; and the government distributed the proceeds proportionately to priests, pastors, and rabbis, according to membership. Clergymen commonly read out the names of atheists during religious services—a practice that to this day discourages all but the most committed atheists from declaring themselves.

16. Richard Hamilton, *Who Voted for Hitler* (Princeton: Princeton University Press, 1982), 40–44 and 382–383.

17. Wright, *"Above Parties": The Political Attitudes of the German Protestant Church Leadership 1918–1933* (Oxford: Historical Monograph, 1974), 34–39.

18. Speech at Königsberg, March 4, 1933, cited by Scholder, *Die Kirchen*, 283. Hitler's first speech as Chancellor, 191–194, contains similar references.

"May the Almighty God protect our work by his grace. . . ." Domarus, *Hitler Reden* I, 191–194.

19. On the attempt to unify all Protestants, cf. James Zabel, *Nazism and the Pastors* (Missoula, Montana: Scholars Press, 1976); Peter Matheson, *The Third Reich and the Christian Churches* (Grand Rapids, Michigan: Eardmanns, 1981). Leonore Siegele-Wenschkewitz, *Nationalsozialismus und Kirchen. Religionspolitik von Partei und Staat bis 1935* (Düsseldorf: Droste, 1974).

20. Quoted in *Deutsch-Evangelische Frauenzeitung* (June 1933), 34:6, 133.

21. Wilhelm Niemöller, *Die Evangelische Kirche im Dritten Reich* (Bielefeld: Bechauf, 1956), 63–64.

22. Conway, *Persecution* 51; cf. also Hofer, doc. 65, "Entkonfessionalisierung."

23. "Wille und Macht," April 15, 1935, quoted in Hofer.

24. Quoted in Scholder, *Die Kirchen*, I:369.

25. "Die deutsche evangelische Kirche und ihr Verhältnis zum Nationalsozialismus seit seiner Machtübernahme," hectograph SD Bericht, June 9, 1937, BA Koblenz/Schumacher series/245/1/91.

26. Conway, *Persecution*, 73.

27. Quoted in Rudolf Weckerling and Wolfgang See, *Frauen im Kirchenkampf* (Berlin: Wichern, 1984), 94. Conway, *Persecution*, 26–27.

28. Paula Müller-Otfried, "Was Nun?" *Evangelische Frauenzeitung* (1918/1919), 19:17. Jochen-Christoph Kaiser, *Frauen in der Kirche* (Düsseldorf: Schwann, 1985), 166–175.

29. Paula Müller-Otfried, "Vorüber," ibid., (1918/1919), 19:89 ff.

30. W. Richter, "Ins neue Jahr," *Frauenhilfe* (1919), 19:1–3.

31. Wright, "*Above Parties*," 81; Müller-Otfried, *Evangelische Frauenzeitung* (March 23, 1933), 24:81.

32. "Rückblick und Ausblick," *Evangelische Frauenzeitung*, (January 1934), 35:49.

33. Dr. Annerose Frölich, "Erkenntnisgeist und Muttergeist," *Evangelische Frauenzeitung*, 34:23. "Rationality," she insisted, was masculine, while motherliness remained exclusively a female emotion. Each sex ought to refine the capacity which God gave it. Ilse Hamel, "Das erste Jahr der Ehetandsdarlehnen," *Evangelische Frauenzeitung* 36 (1934/35), 5–6.

34. She declared her intention to retire from public life. Cf. her articles in the *Evangelische Frauenzeitung*, especially, "Die Lage" (1932–1933), 34:18.

35. Ibid., 50–51.

36. Evangelische Pressedienst, June 21, 1933. EZA/C3/441. Cf. also ibid., "Niederschrift" (minutes) of meeting on May 5, 1933, which planned work under the slogan "Man and Woman in *Volk* and State" and requested increased attention to women's theological education.

37. Magdalene von Tiling, "Rundschreibung," circular, May 15, 1933. 4/1933 EZA/B3/441.

38. Ibid., and documents cited in Kaiser, *Frauen in der Kirche*, 185–187.

39. "Bericht," Gau Sachsen, February 21, 1934. EZA/C3/183/Bl. 161.

40. Meta Eyl, "Das Gebot der Stunde," *Evangelische Frauenzeitung*.

(April 1934), 35:98–102. She cited *Mein Kampf* (1933 ed., p. 270) as her inspiration.

41. Fritz Mybes, *Agnes von Grone und das Frauenwerk der Deutschen Evangelischen Kirche* (Düsseldorf: Presseverband der Evangelischen Kirche, 1981), 14–15.

42. Protest petition defending Tiling, July 29, 1933. EZA/B3/441 and May 23, 1936 EZA/EKDC/3/186.

43. Meta Eyl, "Vom Evangelischen Frauenwerk," *Evangelische Frauenzeitung* (February 1934), 35:67 and "Das Frauenwerk"(October 1933), 24:9.

44. "Richtlinien," August 7, 1933. Guidelines issued by Siber and Frick.

45. Siber to Reichsverband Evangelisches Frauenwerkes, September 26, 1933. Rundschreiben no. 10, Siber, April 6, 1934.

46. "Niederschrift" (notes) January 23, 1934. Archiv des Diakonischen Werkes der EKD, Berlin. (Hereafter referred to as ADW.) BP 50, P1 (I 249) B-1C. "Aufruf" (proclamation), June 21, 1933, calling women to join the state. Cf. also von Grone to Landesgerichtspräsident, August 13, 1935, BDC personnel file.

47. "Richtlinien," August 7, 1933, and "Übereinkunft" (agreement), n.d., EZA/C3/441.

48. *Deutsche Allgemeine Zeitung*, no. 27 (January 17, 1934).

49. *Völkisher Beobachter* (July 22, 1933).

50. Report of the meeting reprinted in Mybes, *Geschichte*, 64.

51. A. Jorns, "Zur Frage des Doppel-Verdienertums," *Evangelische Frauenzeitung* (January 1934), 35:55–7.

52. Bavarian women Protestants, for example, welcomed the Nazi centralization of their 26 local groups and 37 member associations; in September, over 6,000 women gathered to reorganize and exchange information. Cf. memos from September 8 and Spring 1933, appended to "Bericht," March 28, 1936. EZA/B3/186.

53. M. L. zur Nedden, "Freiwilliger Arbeitsdienst," *Evangelische Frauenzeitung* (January 1934), 35:55.

54. David Schoenbaum, *Hitler's Social Revolution* (New York: Norton, 1981), 180–184; Bajohr, *Die Hälfte der Fabrik*, 191; Dr. V. Flincke, "Frauenarbeitsdienst," *Reichsarbeitblatt* 13:36 (December 25, 1933), 490. "Die Zukunft," *Soziale Praxis* 44:17 (1935), 1027; Jill Stephenson, "Nationalsozialistischen Dienstgedanke." Else Lüders, "Die Dienstpflicht der Frau," *Soziale Praxis* 47:22 (November 15, 1938), 1347.

55. She had been born in 1898 in the countryside east of Berlin; worked for the war effort; studied social-work education; and married Georg Schlossmann, a wounded veteran of the World War, in 1923. BDC personnel file; and data brought up in an investigation of Schlossmann-Lönnies in 1936, EZA/C3/185, Bl. 431–443; and C3/183, Bl. 289, 345; and C3/185, Bl. 122 ff. During the Depression she agitated in favor of laws that made it financially possible to employ domestics; cf. her pamphlet "Stand und Aussichten der Müttererholungsfürsorge," 1932, in Landesarchiv Berlin, PrBr/57/852. Cf. RKA to "Mutter und Volk," Berlin, December 3, 1936, 257–259, EZA/C3/186.

56. Hans Harmsen, *Praktische Bevölkerungspolitik* (Berlin: Junker und

Dünnhaupt, 1931), 37. Harmsen supported a "social wage" for parents who could not afford children. In the same book he advocated liberalizing abortion laws, praised Margaret Sanger, and defended "positive" eugenics.

57. Barbara Wenzel, June 18, 1933, ADW/I 255.

58. "Lex Zwickau," a sterilization bill, was the primary example. Otto Kleinschmidt, *Blut und Rasse. Die Stellung des evangelischen Christen zu den Forderungen der Eugenik* (Berlin: Warnecke, 1933); Hans Harmsen, *Praktische Bevölkerungspolitik.* For an excellent survey of eugenics and religion, cf. Kurt Nowak, *"Euthanasie" und Sterilisierung im Dritten Reich. Die Konfrontation der evangelischen und katholischen Kirche mit dem Gesetz zur Verhütung erbkranken Nachwuchses* (Göttingen: Vandenhoeck and Ruprecht, 1978), 39–64.

59. Hermine Bäcker to Fachgruppe der Gefährdetenfürsorgerinnen, June 27, 1933, ADW/I 255.

60. Only "Aryan" parents were permitted to join. Hans Harmsen EZA/ Innere Mission/Gafährdetenfürsorge/A/GF 200/II. The most effective argument seemed to be "the considerations of sacrifice for the good of the *Volk* community." "Rundschreiben" 7, letter of August 2, 1934, to Conference for Gefährdetenfürsorge praising Baden as the most progressive state. For an excellent overview, cf. Gisela Bock, "Racism and Sexism in Nazi Germany: Motherhood, Compulsory Sterilization, and the State," *Signs* (Spring 1983) 8:3, 400–421. Nowak *Euthanasie*, 91–93.

61. The Weimar Republic granted to women the right of entering into the party life, which many thought served only to shatter German loyalty; now Protestant women could come into their own in a vast eugenics program which, they foolishly believed, would reunify the *Volk* and enhance their status.

62. "Bund Evangelischer Frauen im Sozialen Dienst, 1933–1934." Typed manuscript, ADW/ADN/CA/GF 1352/1/III, 42 ff. This report was issued by 26 regional groups (with 1,500 members) of social workers.

63. Minutes, Evangelisches Frauenwerk, January 23, 1934, Berlin. ADW Bl. 50/(I 249) B IC/3/1–3/5. Evangelisches Frauenwerk, Mark Brandenburg.

64. Eitner to Müller, February 6, 1934, EZA/C3/183/Bl. 46.

65. Martha Messdorff, Neumünster, February 22, 1934, ibid., 113.

66. Peller-Schlomke, "Bericht," July 2, 3, 1934, ibid., Bl. 366.

67. Fritsch to Klein, Kassel, February 12, 1934. EZB/C3/183, 80. This file contains over one hundred letters voicing similar complaints.

68. Glässer to Landesverband, March 3, 1934, EZA/C3/183/Bl. 186.

69. "Einheit und Geschlossenheit der deutschen Volksgemeinschaft," 1934, DCV-A/R580/Bl. 20–30. Observers noted, however, that traditional antipathy between Catholics and Protestants diminished in the face of a common threat.

70. Pfarrer Schräpler, Schenkenberg to headquarters, Magdeburg, February 22, 1934, EZA/C3/183, Bl. 86.

71. Nonetheless, many of these organizations continued to maintain some semblance of solidarity as late as 1938–1939. The women in social work, for example, were allowed to meet despite their ties with the Confessing Church.

DCA-V/GF 1353/1/III. For an excellent character evaluation of Klara Lönnies, cf. Kaiser, *Frauen in der Kirche*, 196–206.

72. Müller to Siber, February 10, 1934. DCV-A/R 280, also Pfarrer Klein, Charlottenburg, to Chancellor Hitler, EZA/C3/183/Bl. 68.

73. Quoted in Fritz Mybes, *Die Geschichte der Evangelische Frauenhilfe* (Gladbeck: Schriften-Mission, 1975), 66–67, 85–86.

74. Von Grone to Berlin Church Headquarters, August 20, 1934.

75. The author did not specifically mention modern Jewish women, but did criticize the Catholic tradition on the Woman Question. "Die Frau nach christlichem Glauben," *Evangelische Frauenzeitung* (July 1934), 35:129–134.

76. Evangelisches Frauenwerk, ADW/Bl. 50, 1 (I 249), BIC.

77. Ida Günther, Danzig District Leader, February 24, 1934, EZA/C3/183, 125.

78. "Tatsachenmaterial" information on membership, June 30, 1936, EZA/C3/190. Krummacher to von Grone, December 14, 1933, EZA/C3/183, p. 132. Scholtz-Klink, "Rundschreiben" no. 10, March 16, 1934. LAK, 4705.

79. Geschäftsführer (manager) Jeep, Potsdam, February 8, 1934, EZA/C3/183, Bl. 63 ff. Jeep only held that office for a few months before he sided openly with the Confessing Church. Conway, *Persecution*, 72–74.

80. "Rundschreiben 1," Westerbrack, November 5, 1934. Baden Landeskirchliches Archiv/4705. Her regional suborganizations supported her position; as the Bavarian women put it, "We welcome the coordination of vital Protestant powers into one unified Protestant Church. However, we see that this unification effort is seriously impaired." Quoted in Mybes, 77.

81. Dagmar von Bismarck and Meta Eyl to Müller, Hanover. Karlsruhe Landeskirchliches Archiv/4705. Mybes, 72, quotes their direct attacks on Hermenau, the fanatical German Christian who later became director of the Protestant Frauenhilfe.

82. "Was ist der DEF?" (October). Emma Westare, "vom Frauenwerk der Deutschen Evangelischen Kirche" (April). D. von Bodelschwing, "Der gegenwärtige Auftrag der diehenden Kirche," in *Evangelische Frauenzeitung* 36 (1934/35), (February). 6, 32 and 98.

83. Freifrau von Marschall, Freiburg i. Br., October 11, 1934, to Kirchenrat, Baden, Baden Landeskirchliches Archiv/4705.

84. Westerbrack, November 5, 1934, to the leaders of the Evangelische Frauenwerk. "Rundschreiben 2," Frauenwerk/Baden/4705. Von Grone defended the "reputation of Protestant women's work," and told Scholtz-Klink, "We Protestant women want to work in closest sisterly cooperation in your programs . . . just as our great *Volk* Chancellor wants us to." Von Grone to Scholtz-Klink, November 2, 1934, BDC USCHLA records.

85. "Rundschreiben" 50/35, circular, December 20, 1934. ADW/I/242; Scholtz-Klink, memo, August 16, 1935. EZA/C3/187.

86. Hermenau was born on July 17, 1894, in eastern Germany and joined the Nazi Party in May 1933 (Party no. 2,279,886). BDC file.

87. *Aufwärts* (October 8, 1932). In a radio sermon on June 18, 1933, he spoke of women's "priest-like" nature.

88. Hermenau, *Vom Werk zum Ziel*, pamphlet, n.d., n.p. (1933), 5.

89. Hermenau, *Bausteine*, 8. *Mutter, du Wachterin still in der Nacht/ Mutter, wer hat dich so stark gemacht?/Mutter, du Kelch voll Leid,/Mutter, du Ewigkeit!*

90. Hermenau, *Frau und Volk*, n.d., 7. Cf. also his periodical *Frauenhilfe* (1933), 274. "Purity and truthfulness are the fundamental characteristics of woman's incorruptible nature." For Mother's Day, 1933, Hermenau wrote, "He [God] teaches us to believe in mothers and the victory of Life. The word *mother* is a great rejoicing peal of bells, like eternal music. Mother, she has ever new life that is the future. As long as we have mothers, death has no power. She defies him by bringing forth life."

91. Frau Pfarrer Lüttich, Obermehl, to Eitner, January 16, 1934, and to Thea Lüttich, February 1, 1934, EZA/C3/183, 59. For an enthusiastic contemporaneous account, cf. Charles S. MacFarland, *The New Church and the New Germany* (New York: Macmillan, 1934).

92. Scholtz-Klink, *Die Frau im Dritten Reich*, speech at Nuremburg; cf. also Hilde Lösser (for Scholtz-Klink) to Klein, April 7, 1934, which permits dual membership but outlaws expansion. EZA/C3/183, Bl. 224. Krummacher to Hermenau, September 22, 1933, promised to lift all bans on double membership. EZA/B3/441.

93. Quoted in Heinz Boberach, *Berichte der S.D. und der Gestapo* (Mainz: Mathias-Grünewald, 1971), Doc. 4, 111–116.

94. These women represented 25 major Protestant federations and 107 individual nationwide organizations. "Tagung des evangelischen Frauenwerkes," *Thüringer Allgemeine Zeitung* (January 30, 1935).

95. Hermenau, "Rundschreiben," March 15, 1935. Quoted in Mybes, 102. Countess Hochberg, Erika Kliesch, Thea Zimmermann. "Rundbrief" 2, March 22, 1935, Schlesien, EZA/C3/191.

96. Von Grone letter of March 18, 1935. BDC, USCHLA file. News of von Grone's protest never appeared in the Protestant women's press.

97. Boberach, *Berichte*, 59. By March 1935, 480 Protestant clergymen had been imprisoned and dozens had been sent to concentration camps. On March 4–5, 1935, 715 additional ministers were arrested. Niemöller, *Evangelische Kirche*, 53. Conway, *Persecution*, 202–208.

98. Eyl and Bismarck to Müller, October 19, 1934. Mybes, *Geschichte*, 72–73. Source: ADW/CA/401/111/3.

99. Schlesische Frauenhilfe, March 3, 1935, in support of von Grone, Bodelschwingh, and Koch, EZA/C3/191, 9.

100. Arbeitsgemeinschaft to Kerrl, March 23, 1935, Mybes, 83.

101. Von Grone "Rundschreiben" of November, quoted by Scholtz-Klink, May 20, 1935, BDC, USCHLA proceedings file, 188–192. Ernst Christian Helmreich, *The German Churches under Hitler* (Detroit: Wayne State, 1979), 345.

102. Eyl and Bismarck to Scholtz-Klink, August 10, 1935, EZA/C3/186. Cf. also letter of May 14, 1935, LAK/A 9806.

103. Letter of August 16, 1935, EZB/C3/192.

104. Frauenwerk, GSK, August 16, 1935. Ibid., 187, 206. Some pastors

agreed, for example, Landeskirchenamt Hannover to RKA Berlin. March 8, 1934. EZA/C3/183.

105. Pfarrer Tobias, 191. Kleindöbbern Cottbus, November 23, 1935, EZA/C3/185/Bl. 81 and 191.

106. Hermenau, "Rundschreiben," 4/35, May 2, 1935, EZA/C3/191.

107. Tobias, November 23, 1935. EZA/C3/185/Bl. 81.

108. Several groups, however, seceded from the Protestant Women's Bureau and were not counted in this official tally. For example, in the Rhineland, 25,000 women formed 180 local groups with informal ties to the local Nazi organizations. Mybes, *Geschichte*, 110. Various reports in EZA/C3/219. Throughout Germany, the cause of the German Christians appeared to be lost. In Nuremberg, the very heart of Nazi society, only 6,000 of 133,000 Protestants had joined the German Christians by 1935. Hermann Schirmer, *Das andere Nürnberg. Antifaschistischer Widerstand in der Stadt der Reichsparteitage* (Frankfurt: Röderberg, 1974), 179.

109. The other side of this arrangement, however, held the implicit threat that at any moment she might strengthen her ties with Pastor Niemöller. In this regard, her tactics strongly resembled Hitler's own strategy in the last months of 1932.

110. Ibid., EZA/C3/187/B. 206. "We must bring the church leadership into harmony with our total claim." Meanwhile, Protestant women carried on without von Grone, "Verbände," *Die Frau*, 45:3 (December 1937), 157–158. By 1938 all Protestant groups were dissolved.

111. Munich, October 11, 1935, to January 30, 1936, *Parteigericht* (Party courts). For records of her trial, cf. EZA/C3/186, 361 ff.

112. Scholtz-Klink, November 23, 1936, EZA/C3/187/Bl. 314.

113. Hilgenfeldt to DFW, January 6, 1936, Zöllner. EZA/C3/18 185, Bl. 32–33.

114. Kaiser, *Frauen in der Kirche*, 234.

115. "Denkschrift," May 28, 1936. Doc. 2531, *Innere Gleichschaltung* 9:260. The committee appointed to reconcile differences among the clergy resigned in despair. They registered their protest directly with Hitler (although there is no evidence to suggest he ever saw their letter). "No power on earth, no matter what its name, can destroy the Church of God against His will; only God can decide that."

116. November 23, 1936. Two months before, von Grone had called a meeting in her home to organize a committee for her defense.

117. Eight-page justification, Z/28/336/HS, handed down on November 28, 1938, in BDC USCHLA file.

118. Party no. 2,371,633; BDC personnel file. Fritz Mybes, *Agnes von Grone*, 12. EZA/C3/191 contains many letters from women who, like von Grone, believed deeply in Hitler and the Bible.

119. Von Grone to the District Court, Hannover, October 10, 1935, BDC, USCHLA file, 7–9.

120. Agnes von Grone to Major Buch, Director of the Highest Party Court, June 1, 1935. BDC, USCHLA file, 7–8. Daumüller, September 11, 1936. LAK/Vereine/4705.

121. Letter, October 19, 1936 RKA to Minister of the Interior reports von Grone's sentence. EZA/C3/187/Bl. 183. This file contains an excellent record of protests on von Grone's behalf from 1934 through 1938. Cf. also the records of the Nazi Party Secret Court proceedings in the BDC. Müller claimed von Grone lost her status because she supported the Confessing Church. 26.4.36 *Gesetzblatt*, LAK 705.

122. Women's complaints concerned education, marriage, and charity. Boberach, *Berichte*, 322.

123. E. Liebe-Harcourt to Kerrl, EZA/C3/185, 11–13. Jochen-Christoph Kaiser, "Kirchliche Frauenarbeit in Westfalen," *Jahrbuch für Westfälische Kirchengeschichte* 74 (1981), 159–190. Special thanks to the author for forwarding this valuable study to me. Liebe-Harcourt was born in 1884 and died in 1958. In 1934 she broke with von Grone; letter, November 14, 1934, ADW/ I242.

124. Letter, September 27, 1935, EZA/C3/191.

125. Koch to Frauendienst, Westphalia, EZA/C3/185, Bl. 366.

126. Else Lehbrink to Kerrl, Gelsenkirchen, February 7, 1936 and Widmann, February 7, 1936, EZA/C3/185, Bl. 394.

127. *"Willst Du nicht mein Bruder sein, schlag' ich Dir den Schädel ein."* Willibald Liebe-Harcourt, August 8, 1935, EZA/C3/185/Bl. 12–17. ADW, CA/GF 2000/II.9.

128. "Rechtsprechung," *Deutsche Justiz*, Heft 42, 1514.

129. These complaints run through a series of letters in ADW/IM/CA/GF 2000/11, 12.

130. Dagmar Reese-Nübel, interviewing Frau S., 1981. I want to thank the interviewer for sending me the typescript of this conversation.

131. Salomon, "Character," 234 or 243. Cf. Marion Kaplan, "Schwesterlichkeit auf dem Prüfstand: Feminismus und Antisemitismus," and Marlis Dürkop, "Erscheinungsformen des Anti-Semitismus in BDF," *Femistische Studien* 3:1 (May 1984), 140–150. Marion Kaplan, *The Jewish Feminist Movement in Germany* (Westport, Ct., Greenwood: 1979), 81–85.

132. Salomon, "Character," LBI. 245.

133. Ibid., 237.

134. Ibid., 248.

135. Ibid., 253. Kurt Meier, *Kirche und Judentum* (Göttingen: Van den Hoeck and Ruprecht, 1968), 21–39.

136. Von Grone, October 11, 1935, ADW/I 241, Bund dt. Frauen im soz. Dienst.

137. For example, Käthe Klamroth, "Die Neugestaltung der Evangelische Kirche Deutschlands," 34: 133–135; and anon. "Von der Bewegung für einen 'Deutschen Glauben,'" 35:60–62. *Evangelische Frauenzeitung*. Klamroth belonged to the old guard of women who had actively participated in religious leadership for several decades.

138. Letters exchanged between Friedenthal and Bodelschwingh, Albertz, Lucas, and Anna von Gierke, ADW, Berlin. I 249, PB I 249. Cf. Christine Karl, *Diakonische Hilfe für den Bedrängten Nächsten im Nationalsozialismus* (Heidelberg: Diplomarbeit, 1982), 69–90. On anti-Semitism, cf. the material in EZA/C3/170–172, and case of Charlotte Herz, EZA/C3/219.

139. Margarete Grüber's and Helge Weckerling's recollections in, Weckerling and See, eds., *Frauen im Kirchenkampf*, 66. Heinrich Grüber, *Erinnerungen an sieben Jahrzehnten* (Cologne: Kiepenheuer & Witsch, 1968), 221–224. Meier, *Kirche*, 27–39.

140. Katarina Staritz, *Des grossen Lichtes Widerschein* (Berlin, 1947), 20–31; Leuner, *Compassion*, 102.

141. *Grösse und Verhängnis deutsch-Jüdischen Existenz. Zeugnisse* (Heidelberg: Schneider, 1974), 167.

142. Kotze and Krausnick, eds., *Es Spricht der Führer*, 147–148.

143. Quoted in Boberach, *S.D. Berichte*, 53. Hitler quelled political party disunity and opened up a divisive and abrasive debate on the religious front.

144. SOPADE, November 26, 1934, B10–36. The church defended itself on theological and administrative issues without defending "non-Aryans'" lives.

145. Quoted Weckerling and See, *Frauen im Kirchenkampf*, 96. The editors note in this context that they ought to have grown alarmed as soon as they heard Hans Schemm declare in 1933, "Religion and *Volk* remain forever merged."

146. Weckerling and See, *Frauen im Kirchenkampf*, 67.

8. Catholic Women Between Pope and Führer

1. Dr. Stähle, "Unfruchtbarbachung und Weltanschauung," *Ärzteblatt*, May 4, 1935, LAK. The guidelines announced by the Office of Racial Science in Berlin make it clear that the authority for racial legislation came from "above," by implication from Providence or science. Dr. Gross, *Nationalsozialistische Rassenpolitik. Eine Rede an die deutschen Frauen*, pamphlet of a speech given on October 18, 1934.

2. Friedrich Heer, *Der Glaube des Adolf Hitler. Anatomie einer politischen Religiösität* (Munich and Esslingen: Bechtle, 1968), and Hans Müller, "Der pseudoreligiöse Charakter der nationalsozialistischen Weltanschauung, "*Geschichte in Wissenschaft und Unterricht* (1961), 6:339, 349 f.

3. Albert Speer, *Inside the Third Reich*, trans. Richard and Clara Winston (New York: Macmillan, 1970); Joachim C. Fest, *Hitler* (New York: Vintage, 1975) 513–516, 523–524.

4. Robert Waite, *The Psychopathic God* (New York: Basic, 1977), 29. Göring told his audience in Franconia, "Never has a greater miracle happened than in our time. The Almighty made this miracle through Adolf Hitler!" Konrad Heiden, *Der Führer: Hitler's Rise to Power* (London: Beacon, 1969), 758–759. For a thorough examination of the origins of Hitler's hatred of the forged *Protocols of the Elders of Zion*, cf. Normal Cohn, *Warrant for Genocide* (Chico, California: Judaic Studies, 1981). A major source of his political genius lay in Hitler's uncanny skill at converting his enemies' slogans to his own. In psychological terms, Hitler projected his own worst fears about himself onto his enemies, and simultaneously incorporated their strengths.

5. Quoted by Waite, *Hitler*, 30. Hitler in *Mein Kampf* praised celibacy.

"(T)he Catholic church can be regarded as a model. The celibacy of its priests is a force compelling it to draw the future generation again and again from the masses . . . instead from their own ranks." 432.

6. Waite, *Hitler*, 30. The parallels by no means meant cooperation. On the contrary, the Jesuit Order was regarded as the most dangerous. John Conway, *The Nazi Persecution of the Churches 1933–1945* (New York: Basic, 1968), 145–155.

7. Günter Lewy, *The Catholic Church and Nazi Germany* (London: Weidenfeld and Nicolson, 1964), 18. Ernst Christian Helmreich, *The German Churches under Hitler: Background, Struggle and Epilogue* (Detroit: Wayne State, 1979).

8. Ryder, *Twentieth Century Germany* (New York: Columbia, 1973), 371.

9. The Nazi vote in his district climbed from under 1 percent in 1928 to over 24 percent in 1930. Lewy, *The Catholic Church*, 10 ff.

10. When Hitler sent his congratulations to the men found guilty of brutally murdering a worker in his home in Potempa, one prelate called him the "incarnation of evil." Ibid., 21. Helmreich, *The German Churches*, 86–87.

11. The Catholic Center Party launched anti-Nazi campaigns at election time. For example, cf. the pamphlet, *Der nationalsozialismus und die deutschen Katholiken* (Munchen-Gladbach: Volksverein fur d. kath. Dt., 1931), 7–8, in which Catholics were warned that voting for Nazis "endangered their lives." Particularly, the authors assailed racial teachings and the Nazis' psychological attack on the "weak and helpless." The ecclesiastical leaders said little. As Hitler became more popular, the attacks became less strident. Lewy, *Catholic Church*, 27, 99.

12. Lewy, *Catholic Church*, 4. Before 1914, about 80 percent of all Catholics voted for the Catholic Center Party; after the war, only about 60 percent did so, and those who did were largely women. On the Catholic vote generally, Lewy, *Catholic Church*, 19–22. Conway, *Persecution*, 17–18. Helmreich, 95–102.

13. Norman Baynes, ed. and trans., *The Speeches of Adolf Hitler* I (New York: Fertig, 1969), 369–70.

14. Lewy, *Catholic Church*, 63ff. Cf. Conway, *Persecution*, 25–33 on Papen's role as go-between, and subsequent cowardice.

15. Joseph Lortz, *Katholischer Zugang zum Nationalsozialismus, kirchlich-geschichtlich gesehen* (Münster: Herder, 1933), 9–15. On May 1, 1933, Lortz became a member of the National Socialist Party. Conway, *Persecution*, 26–29.

16. C. Gröber, *Handbuch der religiösen Gegenwartsfragen* (Freiburg i. Br., Herder, 1937), 362. Gröber already had been an honorary SA man. Lewy, *Catholic Church*, 45, 107, 167.

17. Gerta Krabbel, "Wege der Persönlichkeitsbildung durch die katholische Frauenbewegung," in Gertrud Ehrle, ed., *Licht über dem Abgrund. Zeichnungen und Erlebnisse christlicher Frauen, 1933–1945* (Freiburg i.B.: Herder, 1951), 12.

18. Erster Nationalsozialistische Frauen-Kongress," *Völkischer Beobachter* (Düsseldorf, July 18, 1933). The rally began with a *Feldgottesdienst* (outdoor mass).

19. "Der KDF in der Zeit," *Nachrichtenblatt* (May, 1933) 17:5.

20. A. Bertram, Fulda Bishops Conference, Breslau, memo April 20, 1933, Erzbischöfliches Archiv Freiburg im Breisgau (hereafter EAF)/EQ 1. Gen. Vereine, Lehrerseelensorge, 55/106A, 5017.

21. Kreutz to Zilliken, May 11, 1934, Deutscher Caritas Verein-Archiv (hereafter DCVA), Freiburg/R218IV.

22. Lewy, *Catholic Church*, 50–52. For parallels with Catholic doctrine, cf. Raul Hilberg, *The Destruction of the European Jews* (Chicago: Quadrangle, 1961), 1–27.

23. Lewy, *Catholic Church*, 25–27, 89–93. Hitler thought he had manipulated his clerical rivals "into the corner," from which they could not emerge. H. Rauschning, *Voice of Destruction* (New York: Putnam's, 1940), 49–52.

24. Quoted in Lewy, *Catholic Church*, 165. A local study of the heart of Catholic Germany illustrates the impact of this period of uncertainty. Ulrich von Hehl, *Katholische Kirche und Nationalsozialismus im Erzbistum Köln* (Mainz: Grünewald, 1977), 22–45.

25. Lewy, *Catholic Church*, 166. Heinz Boberach, *Berichte des S.D. und der Gestapo über Kirchen und Kirchenvolk* (Mainz: Grünewald, 1971) Doc. 1, May/June 1934, 29 ff, and report from June 1936, 212–217.

26. John Wheeler-Bennett, ed., *Documents on International Affairs* (London: Oxford University Press, 1934), 405.

27. A. Hopmann, *Nachrichtenblatt* no. 8 (August 1933), 16 (newsletter). It ought to be noted that on the eve of Hitler's takeover, many Catholic women expressed a vague desire for an undefined "authoritarian democracy" that cannot be read as a pro-Nazi sentiment, but indicates their fear the Republic would not prove strong enough to protect their freedoms. Krabbel in November 1934 outlined her position—endorsing enthusiastically the "Stew Day" program, the anti-pornography drive, the appeal to end class conflict, and the Concordat. "The Catholic women's movement has always seen itself as a protective dike against waves of liberalism," "Frauenbund," *Freiburger Tagespost* (November 21, 1934). She concluded that "We endorse the new state, not because of opportunism, but because of the belief it represents God's holy order [Ordnung] and despite great personal sacrifices on the part of Catholic women."

28. A. Hopmann, "Doppelmitgliedschaft," *Nachrichtenblatt* newsletter (November 1933), 39.

29. "Ringen der Zeit," *Die Christliche Frau* (September 1933), 31:9, 225–228.

30. "Das Jahr des Herrn 1933," *Frauenland* (February 1934), 1.

31. "Mädchenschutzverein," memo October 11, 1933, EAF 55/112.

32. Max Horst and Richard Hebing, eds., *Volk im Glauben. En Buch vom Katholischen Deutschen* (Berlin: Schmid, 1933), 14. NA 836:59/391, DCA.

33. Elisabeth Denis, "Aus der Erfahrung des katholischen Mädchenschutzes" in Ehrle, ed., *Licht*, 88–96.

34. Ryder, *Twentieth Century Germany*, 379.

35. Report from Penzburg, NSF, Haupt Staatsarchiv München, NSDAP/655 (hereafter HSAM).

36. "Winterhilfe" (winter aid), EAF/55/112. Krabbel greeted the Concordat "with thankful joy" and added her conditions.

37. "Streng Vertraulich!" (Strictly confidential.) Krabbel to KDF central, August 1933, EAF/55/, 134.

38. "Sitzung" (meeting), October 30, 1933, Baden, DCV- A R/580. Judging by what we know about Scholtz-Klink's future career, we can interpret her closing comment as an overt job offer to opportunists. The records do not reveal any takers. Many women teachers who lost their jobs under the Nazi regime found employment in the ranks of the rapidly expanding women's bureaucracy. By 1936, 60,000 women were defined as leaders; 25,000 as lawyers with the Labor Front and 800 leaders worked for the Frauendienst. E. Said, "Zur Lage," *Mutterkreuz* (Frankfurt: Fischer, 1981), 118. *Die Frau*, 43:7 (April 1936), 432; and 45:1 (October 1937), 1–4.

39. Gerta Krabbel, Heinich Klenz, Elisabeth Zilliken, "Richtlinien für die Teilnahme," EAF/55/69.

40. Bischöfliches Ordinariat to Reichsstatthalter (hereafter EZR), July 5, 1933, Bl. 8868, EAF/G1a/NS81.

41. Oftersheim report, August 4, 1933, ibid., Bl. 10,336. Similar reports came in from southeastern Germany, cf. the Bishopric of Rebensburg's archives, letter of the Dioezensansek. fu. weib. Jugendpflege, May 5, 1934, to the bishop, folio number OA/161. It used, incidentally, the newsletter *The White Rose* as its means of communicating with other oppositional groups.

42. "Aufgaben des KDF in der Zeit," September 8, 1933, EAF 55/69. Cf. also Krabbel to Caritasverband, December 11, 1933, DCV-A, R 582.

43. "Bericht," December 13, 1933, EAF 55/69. Doris Kaufmann, *Das Katholische Milieu* in Münster (Düsseldorf: Schwann, 1984), 160–182. "Healthy Core," Lewy, *Catholic Church*, 99.

44. R.J. O'Neill, *The German Army and the Nazi Party. 1933–1939* (London: Cassell, 1966), 38. Conway, *Persecution*, 44.

45. According to Nazi reports, the victims had either been shot while escaping or committed suicide in their cells. Lewy, *Catholic Church*, 124, 169–172. Fest, *Hitler*, 464–480. Conway, *Persecution*, 93–94. Helmreich, *German Churches*, 270.

46. Conway, *Persecution*, 94. Hugh Trevor-Roper, British historian, commented, "The blood bath of June 30 set the tune for Adolf Hitler's rule. It showed that it was not only a dictatorship, but a criminal dictatorship." The Vice-Chancellor, himself a Catholic, thanked the Führer even though two of his closest associates had been murdered. The German Army obediently swore an illegal oath . . . to its bloodstained master. The German people . . . emphatically confirmed the regime." Intro. to Terrence Prittie. *Germans Against Hitler*. (Boston: Little, Brown, 1964).

47. Fest, *Hitler*, 469.

48. Fulda bishops to Reich Ministry, September 12, 1933, signed Bertram, EAF 48/18, 1,3267. This response was based on Pius XI's *Casti Connubii* of 1930. Gröber expressed support for voluntary sterilization.

49. Lewy, *Catholic Church*, 259–261.

50. The *Osservatore Romano* on July 9–10, 1934, reasserted its stance

against sterilization, and still government officials issued press releases to the contrary. EAF- EDA Gen Sittlichkeit-Sterilization 48/18.

51. Archbishop Gröber of Freiburg led the way. "Aussprache," *Freiburger Tagespost*, no. 1446 (January 26, 1934). Catholics could, Gröber said, comply without "conflict of conscience." He threatened to dismiss protesting priests. Lewy, *Catholic Church*, 162–164, 263.

52. Estimates from 1931–1933 showed that 75 percent asked legal questions and 25 percent eugenics-related questions. "Katholische Eheberatung," *Märkische-Volkszeitung*, no. 22 (January 22, 1933). Further, between 60 and 80 percent of all clients came from "mixed" marriages—i.e., between Protestants and Catholics.

53. Correspondence between Zilliken and Kreutz ordering women to report genetic defects in children. Dortmund, March 27, 1934, DCV-A R 218/IV. For more protests, cf. 1934–1935, DCV-A/R332. Lewy, *Catholic Church*, all but ignores women, 42–43.

54. Letter of April 27, 1935, Würzburg Caritasverband, Paderborn Caritas, to the national headquarters in Freiburg. DCV-A R 332.

55. SOPADE, September 1937, 98. On Brown Sisters, cf. Franz Heyen, *N.S. im Alltag* (Boppard: Boldt, 1967), doc. 101, 196–197.

56. Kreutz to Zilliken, May 11, 1934, DCV-A/R 218/IV. He rebuked her lack of political sense. His brusque treatment of Zilliken did not prevent him from appealing to her for a job after the war for an old friend who had been an SA doctor. DCV-A/R218/IV.

57. Bezirksartzt Emmendingen to Riegel, April 4, 1934, EAF 48/18.

58. Gerta Krabbel, "Wege," in Ehrle, *Licht*, 10–14.

59. "Verhandlung" (conference), October 14, 1935, EAF 48/18.

60. "Böswillige Äusserungen aus den Erbgesundheitsgerichten," EAF 48/18.

61. Alice Platen Hallermund, *Die Tötung der Geisteskranken in Deutschland.* (Frankfurt a. M. 1948); cf. also the Nuremberg Trials, vol. 10, case 1. Kurt Nowak *"Euthanasie" und Sterilisierung im Dritten Reich* (Göttingen: Vandenhoeck and Ruprecht, 1978), 107–131. Gisela Bock, *Zwangssterilization.* (Berlin: Zentralinstitut, 1985).

62. DCV-A/580.

63. Gestapo Baden to Gröber, January 7, 1935, EAF 48/18.

64. Conway, *Persecution*, 263, 272–276. Franklin H. Littell and Hubert G. Locke, *The German Church Struggle and the Holocaust* (Detroit: Wayne State, 1974).

65. "Anhang 1," which also noted that 8,000 official protests had been launched against individual orders *for* sterilization; 92.8 percent of all cases were not successful. 428 citizens protested *against* the court *rejections* of their application for sterilization, and as of December 31, 1934, 179 had succeeded, while 108 had been turned down. The remainder had not been decided. Ibid.

66. Exchange between Reichs Ministry of the Interior and Archbishop Gröber, June 1934, EAF 48/18–21, and Lewy, *Catholic Church*, 259–261. Kreutz to Teusch, February 12, 1935 re compromise on sterilization. Allen

Chase, *The Legacy of Malthus* (New York: Knopf, 1977), 347–351, and Daniel Gasman, *The Scientific Origins of National Socialism* (New York: Elsevier, 1972), 147–173.

67. Robert Ley, ed., *Partei-Statistik* (Berlin: Reichsdruckerei, 1935), 45.

68. "Die Atmosphäre des Elternhauses," Ehrle, *Licht*, 24–26. Heyen, *Alltag*, 226–231.

69. Waite, *Psychopathic God*, 31.

70. Maria Deku, in Ehrle, *Licht*, 35–38.

71. "If one later looked back—one could say to oneself: Even X, with his passion for Greek philosophy, or Y, who considered the Sermon on the Mount to be the supreme revelation granted to mankind, were ready to enter the Party. It was an alibi which they could use as a cover if doubts arose." Melita Maschmann, *Account Rendered. A Dossier of My Former Self* (London: Abelard, 1965), 31.

72. Kershaw, *Public Opinion*, 211.

73. Langer, *Josephine Herbst*, 213.

74. Kershaw, *Public Opinion*, 351.

75. Ibid., 219.

76. Zilliken to Kreutz, April 30, 1934, DCV-A/R/218 IV.

77. Conway, *Persecution*, 188.

78. Dekanat Säckingen, Seflingen, July 3, 1933, Bl. 8999 EAF/G1a/NS.

79. Lewy, *Catholic Church*, 174.

80. Report from Breslau, November 23, 1934, EAF 48/18.

81. Gertrud Scholz to Bertram, the Fulda Bishops Conference, Krolewska Huta, KDF, April 10, 1934, DCV-A, R 582. The author in this case asked for the bishops' intervention in a program that brought ethnic German children from non-German territories to live with families in Germany for the summer.

82. E. Denis, June 16, 1934, EAF 55/112.

83. Dingolfing, Regensburg, July 26, 1934, BZR OA 613. Christine Teusch, formerly a member of the Reichstag and for decades a leader in Catholic politics, appealed directly to Bishop Gröber for more funding, and more support. Teusch to Gröber, May 23, 1934. Ibid. Lewy, *Catholic Church*, 315.

84. Penzburg, June 4, 1934.

85. Elisabeth Böhmer to Zilliken, Heidelberg, July 4, 1934, DCV-A R 218, HASK/1187/k26, esp. E. Denis, letter to Schmitt, Berlin, February 13, 1939.

86. Walter Buch, "Gedanken um das Familienrecht," *Deutsches Recht* Heft 7 (1934), 145–151. Fulda bishop's protest, "Against the Attack on Marriage," November 23, 1934, Breslau, EAF 48/18. Dr. Gürther from the Justice Ministry apologized on January 24, 1935, EAF 48118.

87. Erlass des Reichs- und Preussischen Ministers des Innern vom July 3, 1935, DCV-A/172/m/1 "Begründung für die konfessionelle und Ablehnung einer allgemein interkonfessionell durchgeführten Mütterschulung," Referate Kinder- und Jugendfürsorge im Deutschen Caritasverband, Freiburg, November 2, 1934, DCA/R 580.

88. DCV to Krabbel, December 21, 1934, DCV-A/R 580.

89. Dr. Maria Bornitz, Berlin, January 28, 1937, to Kreutz, St. Elizabeth Verein, DCV-A, DK3.49.3. Cf. Michael Gosteiger, *Der St. Elisabethenverein in München*, typed manuscript, Munich, 1942. DCV-A/DK3/49K/og1.

90. Emma Haas and Maria Kuenzer, Freiburg, November 17, 1934, EAF 55/69.

91. "Mütterschulung," 1935, typed document, DCV-A/R 580. The KDF set out its goals: 1) deepen personal faith; 2) strengthen family life and reach out to unmarried women; 3) "as our efforts become less visible, they become fiercer."

92. Conway, *Persecution*, 177.

93. Statistically this meant that of 9.656 million eligible youths, only 5.4 million actually joined. After 1933 the increase among girls had been more rapid than among boys; but by 1935 those increases, as well, diminished. On the other hand, about 90 percent of the youth born in 1926 joined the Hitler youth. Dagmar Reese, "Bund deutscher Mädel: Zur Geschichte der weiblichen deutschen Jugend im Dritten Reich," *Mutterkreuz*, 173–174. Membership among private school students lagged far behind public school rates: 59 percent of private school students joined in 1935, as compared to nearly 90 percent of students in public institutions.

94. Michael Kater, *The Nazi Party* (Cambridge: Harvard, 1983). Figures 7–12, 139–148, 150–153, and 200–203.

95. Three percent declared themselves as "believers in God," while 1.5 percent said they were atheists. Conway, *Persecution*, 232. Kershaw, *Hitler-Mythos*, 363.

96. Arno Klönne, *Gegen den Strom. Bericht über den Jugendwiderstand im Dritten Reich* (Hanover and Frankfurt a. M.: Gödel, 1957), 50.

97. Heinz Boberach, ed., *Meldungen aus dem Reich*, and Martin Broszat, Elke Frölich, and Falk Wiesemann, *Bayern in der NS-Zeit*, 2 vols. (Munich: Oldenbourg, 1977), provide extensive evidence of this. Heyen, *Alltag*, 290–293.

98. Baroness O'Bryn, addressing the "Generalversammlung des KDF," *Volkszeitung* (January 10, 1935).

99. For example, Scholtz-Klink speech of November 2 and 3, 1935, EZB/C3/184/Bl. 381–382. Hilgenfeldt did not bother (or dare) to withdraw officially from the Protestant Church until May 1940. On his 1933 personnel file he listed "Protestant" rather than "believing in God." BDC, personnel file.

100. Quoted by Hermann Rauschning, *The Voice of Destruction* (New York: Putnam's, 1941), 52, 53. Hitler despised the "Jewish Christian creed with its effeminate pity-ethics," 49.

101. Hildegard von Klotze and Helmut Krausnick, eds., with aid from F. A. Krummacher, *So Spricht der Führer* (Gütersloh: Mohn, 1966), 147–148. For a comprehensive summary of medical opinion on Hitler's health, cf. Waite, *The Psychopathic God*, 348–362; and 396–397. Waite perceptively notes the unstable equilibrium in Hitler's personality. "He felt compelled to give opposing orders; to destroy and to preserve; to demand victory, but to invite defeat." Ibid., 397. Paradoxically, Hitler, who expressed a monomaniacal faith in his own destiny, did not completely trust Providence to grant

him a sufficiently long life in which to accomplish his mission. Throughout his twelve-year reign, he became increasingly dependent upon his physician Dr. Morell's prescriptions and grew to be a vegetarian food fanatic.

102. Other members of the section were: Adolf Eichmann, three ex-priests, and one Protestant pastor. Conway, *Persecution*, 168–169, 218.

103. Lewy, *Catholic Church*, 167.

104. Conway, *Persecution*, 95, 161, 188–189.

105. Ian Kershaw, *Popular Opinion and Political Dissent in the Third Reich. Bavaria* (New York: Oxford University Press, 1983), 197. Idem, *Hitler-Mythos*, 109–110.

106. Hitler, quoted in Kotze and Krausnick, *So Spricht*, 161.

107. Between 1937 and 1939, 286,000 Catholics severed ties with the church. Lewy, *Catholic Church*, 373.

108. Herr Krummacher had in the fall of 1933 attempted to enforce a ban against double membership, but failed. Kershaw, *Hitler-Mythos*, 90–96, 109–110. Conway, *Persecution*, 129–132.

109. *Stellenvermittlung* (employment referrals), HASK/1187/K26/5.

110. Elisabeth Denis and Bishop von Ermland, correspondence from 1939, HASK 1187/K 26.

111. *Frauenland* files, HSAD File 52, 792.

112. Zilliken to Kreutz, March 15, 1937. DCA-V/R218/IV.

113. Ehrle, *Licht*, 22–23.

114. SOPADE, February 1937, A-19. Heyen, *Alltag*, Doc. 136, 259–260.

115. RMdI to Stellv. d.F., March 10, 1939, BA Koblenz/R43II/561a/Bl. 83.

116. RMdI memo, 147–150, June 16, 1939. 80,000 nuns worked for charitable causes, 40,000 Catholic professionals staffed Catholic agencies, and untold hundreds of thousands of volunteers contributed to civic organizations. Bertram, "Grundsätzliche Erklärung," (after 1939), BA Koblenz/R43II/526b/Bl. 112.

117. Conrad Gröber, March 29, 1940. EAF/55/69/KDF. Gerta König, "Wachsen," November 30, 1939, ibid.

118. I would like to express my gratitude to Frau Dr. Pflug and Frau Emmench for making those archives available to me. Cf. "Zur Lage," HSAK/1187/K26/2.

119. HSAK/1187/K26/2.

120. Variations on this letter were ubiquitous, this one is from Kalkum/1004/1375. Louis Lochner, ed., *The Goebbels Diaries*, trans. Fred Taylor (New York: Penguin, 1984), March 3, 1942, 110. Conway, *Persecution*, 288; Lewy, *Catholic Church*, 255.

121. Collection of letters circulated by KDF, Geheime Staatspolizei. HSAD, RW 58/ This excerpt is dated September 28, 1942.

122. Interview with the author, 1982. Geheime Staatspolizei, HSAD/RW58/66, 035. Report dated Autumn 1942.

123. Gestapo Düss. RW58/49, 539. Friedrich Werksage, Duisberg, born January 13, 1892.

124. I. Kershaw, *Popular Opinion*, 337.

125. Maria Kubasec, *Sterne über dem Abgrund. Aus dem Leben der Antifascisten Dr. Maria Grollmuss* (Bautzan: VEB Domowina, 1961), 44, 81, 100–102.

126. Kurt R. Grossmann, *Die unbesungenen Helden*, 100. In 1940 Dr. Margarete Sommer began to work with the Bishop of Berlin at an "aid station" for Jews. H. D. Leuner, *Compassion*, 141. Lewy, *Catholic Church*, 295, 397. Gröber by 1937 reversed his earlier support for Nazism and began to rescue victims. Krabbel, June 24, 1937, EAF/55/70.

127. Erna Becker-Cohen, "Tagebuch," LBI.

128. Else Sara Müller (nee Cohen), born November 22, 1886, divorced, with Jewish parents and Catholic faith. HSAD/RW/9, 320. Bl. 1–36.

129. Stein was killed as part of a retaliatory action after Catholics in Holland spoke out against the Nazi deportations. Occupation officials declared they would then deport all Catholics with Jewish parentage. A. Leber, *Conscience in Revolt* (London: Valentine, 1954), 203–206. Waltraud Herbstrith, *Edith Stein: A Biography* (San Francisco: Harper, 1985).

9. Courage and Choice: Women Who Said No

1. One can, and many have, explained Hitler's success by using electoral or economic analyses. His personality has been fair game for psycho-historians since the OSS commissioned an in-depth study of the Führer in 1944. Diplomatic negotiations, similarly, have been exhaustively examined by those who explain Hitler's expansionist vision. Students of Hitler's personality delve into the buried motivations or twisted values, and sociologists cross-reference shared traits of Nazi leaders as if they were the "abnormal" that needed explanation. Until recently the psychology of courage has been overlooked.

2. H. G. Wells, *Experiment on Autobiography* (New York: Macmillan, 1934), 486.

3. Detlev Peukert, *Die Edelweispiraten, Protestbewegung jugendlichen Arbeiter im Dritten Reich* (Cologne: Bund-Verlag, 1983).

4. Christine E. King, "Strategies for Survival: An Examination of the History of Five Christian Sects in Germany, 1933–1945," *Journal of Contemporary History* 14 (1979), 211–234. Michael Kater, "Die ernsten Bibelforscher im Dritten Reich," *Vierteljahresheft für Zeitgeschichte* 17 (1969), 181–218.

5. "La Crise," *Le Temps*, (February 21, 1933), 1.

6. Klaus Mann, *Turning Point. 25 Years in the Century* (London: Fischer, 1942), 27.

7. Gisela Kraus, "Frauen vor dem Sondergericht München von 1933 bis 1939," unpublished article, IfZ. The trial rate was highest during the first three years of the pre-war period, suggesting that people became more cautious after 1934.

8. *Frauen unter Faschisten Terror! Frauen in der solidaritäts- und Kampffront* (Zurich and Paris: MOPR, 1934), 4.

9. Günther Weisenborn, *Der lautlose Aufstand, Bericht über die Wider-

standsbewegung des deutschen Volkes, 1933–1945 (Hamburg: Rowohlt, 1953), 263.

10. Interview by Christa Randizo-Plath, in *Der alltägliche Faschismus*, 21–22.

11. Hannah Tillich, *From Time to Time* (New York: Stein and Day, 1973), 151.

12. "German Political Violence," *The Times* (London, February 4, 1933), 9.

13. Ursel Hochmuth and Gertrud Meyer, *Streiflichter aus dem Hamburger Widerstand, 1933–1945* (Frankfurt: Röderberg, 1969), 154.

14. Martin Broszat, *The Hitler State* (New York: Longman, 1981), 79, and Rudolf Diels, *Lucifer ante Portas zwischen Severing und Heydrich* (first written in 1935), (Zurich: Internaverlag, 1949), 23–24, 150–152.

15. Peter Hoffmann, *The History of the German Resistance, 1933–1945*, trans. Richard Barry (Cambridge, Massachusetts: MIT, 1977), 15, and Günther Weisenborn, *Der Lautlose Aufstand*, 175; and Walter Hammer, *Hohes Haus in Henkers Hand. Rückschau auf die Hitlerzeit auf Leidensweg und Opfergang deutscher Parlamentarier* (Frankfurt: Europäische Verlagsanstalt, 1956), and *Deutsche Widerstandskämpfer. 1933–1945. Biographien und Briefe*, 2 vols. (Berlin: Dietz, 1970).

16. Hochmuth and Meyer, *Streiflichter*, 239–246. They hiked, discussed books, and very occasionally distributed illegal pamphlets. 97, 100, 117–120.

17. Christabel Bielenberg, *The Past Is Myself* (London: Chatto and Windus, 1968), 28.

18. Annette Kuhn and Valentine Rothe, ed., *Frauen in deutschen Faschismus* (Düsseldorf: Schwann, 1982), II, 173–175.

19. Margaret Boveri, *Treason in the Twentieth Century*, trans. Jon Steinberg (New York: Putnam's, 1963), 250. Greta Kuckhoff, *Vom Rosenkranz zur Roten Kapelle: ein Lebensbericht* (Berlin: Neues Leben, 1972), 191.

20. W. W. Schütz, *Pens under the Swastika. A Study in Recent German Writing* (Port Washington, New York, and London: Kennikat, 1971), 21. First published in 1946.

21. Käthe Kollwitz was born July 8, 1867. When the Prussian Academy of Art voted to cooperate with Hitler, she withdrew her membership. Cf. Huch Personnel Files, BDC. Memo by Der Chef der Sicherheitspolizei, February 19, 1942. Huch, Personnel File, BDC. Huch resigned from the Academy of Arts, saying that her idea of German was not the same as that of the government. Ingeborg Drewitz. *Die zestörte Kontinuität. Exilliteratur und Literatur des Widerstandes* (Vienna and Munich: Europa Verlag, 1981), 52.

22. Paul Westheim, "Käthe Kollwitz," *Women under the Swastika* (London: German League of Culture, December 1942), 25–26.

23. Kaye Boyle, "Decision," *Three Short Novels* (New York: Penguin, 1982), 258.

24. Quoted in Erika Mann and Klaus Mann, *Escape to Life* (Boston: Houghton-Mifflin, 1939), 58.

25. Heymann and Augspurg, *Erlebtes-Erschautes. Heymann Memoiren*, ed. Margit Twellmann (Meisenheim am Glan: Hain, 1972), 290 ff. Both women were over 60 at the time.

26. Amy Hackett, "Helene Stöcker," Bridenthal, Grossmann, and Kaplan, *When Biology Became Destiny*, and Hans-Jürgen Arendt, "Die 'Gleichschaltung,' der bürgerliche Frauenorganisationen in Deutschland 1933/34," *Zeitschrift für Geschichtswissenschaft* (July 1979).

27. Interview with the author, February 27, 1983. I want to express my special thanks to Joan DuPont for arranging this meeting. Gilbert Badia, intro., *Exilés en France. Souveniers d'antifascistes allemands émigrés (1933–1945)* (Paris: Maspero, 1982), 279–312.

28. Max Oppenheimer, *Das kämpferische Leben der Johanna Kirchner. Portrait einer anti-fasischisten Widerstandskämpfer* (Frankfurt: Röderberg, 1974), 81, and Annemarie Leber, ed. *Conscience in Revolt* (London: Valentine, Mitchell, 1954), 100–103.

29. Friesler, "Todesurteil gegen Johanna Kirchner," Oppenheimer, *Das kämpferische Leben*, 42–43. Leber, ed., *Conscience in Revolt*, 100 ff.

30. . . . *Besonders jetzt tu Deine Pflicht! Briefe Anti-faschisten geschrieben vor ihrer Hinrichtung* (Potsdam: WUN, 1949), 145; Lya Kralik, "Als Antifaschisten in Frankreich," in Schabrod, *Widerstand*, 169–170; and Dora Schaul, *Resistance: Erinnerung deutscher Anti-faschisten* (Berlin: Dietz, 1973), and Heinz Gollwitzer, Käthe Kuhn and Reinhold Schneider, eds., trans. R. C. Kuhn, *Dying We Live. The Last Messages of the Men and Women Who Resisted Hitler and Were Martyred* (New York: Pantheon, 1956).

31. . . . *Besonders*, 132–133.

32. Foreword to Weisenborn, *Lautlose*, 14. "They were not given the chance to save Germany; they had only the opportunity of dying."

33. Quoted in *Frauen unter Faschisten Terror! Frauen in der Solidaritäts- und Kampffront* (Zurich and Paris: MOPR, 1934), 2.

34. Lore Wolf, *Ein Leben ist viel zu wenig* (Frankfurt: Röderberg, 1974), 28 ff.

35. Hammer, *Hohes Haus*, 10, 30, 73. Three of the 112 women in the Reichstags committed suicide (Pfülf, Bollmann, and Wurm). Of about 1500 men in the Reichstag, 3 took their own lives.

36. Valentin Senger, *No. 12 Kaiserhofstrasse. The Story of an Invisible Jew in Nazi Germany*, trans. Ralph Mannheim (New York: Dutton, 1980), 56.

37. Maria Deeg, "Bericht," Elling, *Frauen*, 89–90.

38. "Jenny," *Neue Deutsche Literatur* (Heft 9/1968).

39. Heike Bretschneider, *Der Widerstand gegen den Nazismus in München, 1933–1945* (Munich: Neue Schriftenreihe des Stadtarchivs München, 1968), 50–51.

40. Arno Kloenne. *Gegen den Strom. Der Widerstand der Jugend gegen Hitler* (Hanover and Frankfurt: Gödel, 1957), 37.

41. Lina Haag, *Eine Handvoll Staub* (Halle Saale: Mitteldeutscher, 1948), 93.

42. Hannah Elling, *Frauen im deutschen Widerstand 1933–1945* (Frankfurt: Röderberg, 1981), 54. More is not known about her life.

43. Ellen Wilkinson, *The Terror in Germany* (London: British Committee for the Relief of the Victims of German Fascism: 1934). The committee was chaired by Albert Einstein, 18, and *The Times* (London) reported the incident without details on April 3, 1933, 14. The woman's name was Frau

Janowsky and the town was Koepnick, located in what became after 1945 Poland.

44. Irma Keilhack, interviewed by Ingrid Fischer, Charles Schuddekopf, ed., *Der alltägliche Faschismus* (Berlin: Dietz, 1982), 134.

45. Ellen Wilkinson, *The Terror in Germany*, 11. Simone Weil, only six months prior to Hitler's takeover, reported that "in the trams and busses," politics had already become too explosive to discuss. *Ecrits historiques et politiques* (Paris: Gallimard, 1960), "Premieres impressions," 25. August, 1932, 124–125. Toni Sender reported that her socialist neighbors witnessed a brawl between police and socialists and decided to fly the swastikas. *The Autobiography of a German Rebel* (New York: Vanguard, 1939), 294.

46. Madeline Kent, *I Married a German* (London: Allen and Unwin, n.d.), 173.

47. Karl Schabrod, *Widerstand gegen Flick und Florian* (Frankfurt: Röderberg, 1978) 1136 and Weisenborn, *Der Lautlose Aufstand*, 158–159.

48. Hannah Elling, *Frauen im Widerstand*, 85.

49. Annette Kuhn and Valentine Rothe, *Frauen in deutschen Fascismus*, (Düsseldorf: Schwann, 1982), II, 89.

50. "Widerstandskämpferin im Dritten Reich," Angelika Schmidt-Biesalski, *Lust, Liebe und Verstand* (Gelnhausen: Burckhardthaus, 1981), 87–88.

51. Greta Kuckhoff, *Vom Rosenkranz zur Rote Kapelle: eine Lebensbericht* (Berlin: Neues Leben, 1972), 220–284.

52. Weisenborn, *Der Lautlose Aufstand*, 158.

53. Maria von Maltzan, quoted in Gerda Szepansky, *Frauen leisten Widerstand*, (Frankfurt: Fischer, 1983), 121.

54. Quoted in ibid., 120. Cf. Leonard Gross, *The Last Jews in Berlin* (New York: Simon and Schuster, 1982). 126ff. for the extraordinary underground life of Hans Hirschel.

55. Detlev Peukert. *Ruhr Arbeiter gegen den Faschismus: Dokumentationen* (Frankfurt: Röderberg, 1977), 245–246. Kuhn and Rothe, *Frauen in deutschen Faschismus* II, 181–182.

56. W. S. Allen, *The Nazi Seizure of Power. The Experience of a Single German Town* (New York: Watts, 1984), 266–279. The SOPADE reports reinforce the importance of economic well-being as a major source of acquiescence.

57. Elisabeth Ostermeier, in Schüddekopf, ed., *Der alltägliche Faschismus*, 86–87.

58. Gudrun Schwarz, unpublished lecture. My thanks to the author for sharing this account with me.

59. Christine King, "Strategies," 214. In 1933, the author notes, 90 branches of the Christian Scientist Church existed in Germany; but because its members did not resist military service, repression was not as severe as with Jehovah's Witnesses. The Mormon Church escaped repression altogether. 37,000 Seventh Day Adventists swore allegiance to Hitler.

60. Interview with the author, Brookline, December 1982.

61. Ibid.

62. Franz Züricher, *Kreuzzug gegen Christendom. Moderne Christenverfolgung. Eine Dokumentatensammlung* (Zurich: Interna, 1938), 60.

63. Martin Broszat, Elke Frölich, and Falk Wiesemann, eds., *Bayern in der NS Zeit* (Munich: Oldenbourg, 1977), 364.

64. Albert Camus, *The Rebel. An Essay on Man in Revolt* (New York: Vintage, 1956), 13.

65. M. D. R. Foot, *European Resistance to Nazism, 1940–1945* (New York: McGraw, 1977), 10. This set up categories: gathering intelligence, escape, subversion. The last is divided into sabotage, attacks on troops and individuals, politics, and insurrection.

66. Rita Thalmann, *Être Femme dans troisième Reich* (Paris: Lafont, 1983); Angelika Reuter and Barbara Poneleit, *Seit 1848. Frauen im Widerstand* (Münster: Frauenpolitik, 1977); Hannah Elling, *Frauen*; Vera Laska, "Nazism, Resistance and Holocaust in W. W. II, a bibliography of over 1,300 entries," mimeograph (Westport, Connecticut: Greenwood, 1983); idem, *Women in the Resistance and the Holocaust* (Westport, Connecticut: Greenwood, 1983); Maruta Schmidt and Gabi Dietz, eds. *Frauen unterm Hakenkreuz* (Berlin: Elfanten, 1983); Marie-Therese Kerschbaumer's strangely fictionalized *Der weibliche Name des Widerstands. Sieben Berichte* (Munich: DTV, 1980); Gerda Szepansky, *Frauen leisten Widerstand: 1933–1945* (Frankfurt: Fischer, 1983); and Gerda Zorn and Gertrud Meyer, *Frauen Gegen Hitler. Berichte aus dem Widerstand* (Frankfurt: Röderberg, 1974).

67. Gisela Kraus, "Frauen vor dem Sondergericht München von 1933 bis 1939," unpublished paper. Cf. also Ilse Staff, *Justiz im Dritten Reich. Eine Dokumentation* (Frankfurt: Fischer, 1964) and *Frauenschicksale*, 195–209.

68. Else (Wibeck) Breuer, born July 26, 1882, in Braunschweig. Gestapo Archives, HSAD/28,555.

69. That depends on how one defines "camp." Contemporary sources claimed three. *Frauen unter Faschistischen Terror*, 2. A study conducted by a Marxist underground information service centered in Prague counted ten women's camps, detention centers and prisons. *Frauenschicksale* (London: Malik, 1938), 46–54. I would like to thank Meaghan Sheedy for making this source available to me.

70. Elling, *Frauen*, 71–73. The Munich Sondergericht records suggest that women's arrest rates for "gossip" decreased faster than female criminality. Kraus, "Sondergericht," 15. Cf. St.d.d.R. 59 (1941–1942), 659.

71. Weisenborn, *Der lautlose Aufstand*, 38, classified Germans who served time or were killed for anti-Nazi activities as 66 percent peasants, civil servants, or middle class; 11 percent youthful. H. D. Leuner, *Germany's Silent Heros 1933–1945* (London: Wolff, 1978), 31. The editors of *Frauenschicksale* published the names of 190 women prisoners, their ages, crimes, and sentences for 1935–1936. Thirty-two were charged with high treason, 33 had been arrested for Communist activities. Other crimes included being a Jehovah's Witness, spreading malicious gossip, smuggling, and cooperating with foreign enemies. *Frauenschicksale*, 195–209. In just one month after the war began (October 1941), 1,518 people were arrested in Germany for "op-

position." 7,729 were guilty of not working. Only 544 were arrested for Marxist activities. Helmut Krausnick and Martin Broszat, *Anatomy of the SS State*, trans. Dorothy Long and Marian Jackson (London: Granada, 1968), 215.

72. Christian Bernadac, *Le Camp des Femmes. Ravensbruck* (Paris, 1972).

73. Detlev Peukert, *Die KPD im Widerstand, Verfolvung und Untergrundarbeit an Rhein und Ruhr* (Wuppertal: Hammer, 1980), 76–80, 92, 127–130.

74. Sarah Gordon, *Hitler, Germans, and the "Jewish Question"* (Princeton: Princeton University Press, 1984), 242. Before 1939 the most common crime was *Rassenschande* (sexual relations with Jews); after that date it changed to being a *Judenfreund*, or aiding Jews. The fact that more Germans in the middle and upper classes than workers or peasants aided Jews comes as no surprise, since they would have been more likely to have developed personal ties to Jews. Only one prisoner among the 290 cited in *Frauenschicksale* was charged with "Rassenschande," Gordon concluded. "Women outnumber men at the time of writing."

75. H. D. Leuner, *When Compassion Was a Crime*, 81. 1,500 Jews lived from 1940–1945 underground in Berlin; ibid., 80.

76. These files formed the basis of Kurt Grossmann's *Unbesungenen Helden*. Unfortunately, he did not compile a master list and in the intervening years the government has passed a rigorous law that prevents any personal file from becoming public. Thus, *Aktion Unbesungenen Helden* records were not available. I used the newspaper files to survey 63 cases, but cannot assess how representative they were. Women figure prominently because they performed acts of kindness that often meant a life saved. Since they were so successful, the Senate had no Gestapo records and relied upon testimonials of the people they saved.

77. Sybil Milton, "Women and the Holocaust: The Case of German and German-Jewish Women," in Bridenthal, Grossmann, and Kaplan, eds., *When Biology Became Destiny. Women in Weimar and Nazi Germany* (New York: Monthly Review, 1984), 297. Cf. illustration.

78. Barbara Beuys, *Familienleben in Deutschland. Neue Bilder aus der deutschen Vergangenheit* (Reinbek bei Hamburg: Rowohlt, 1980), 486–487. Additional sources, Heinz Boberach, *Meldungen aus dem Reich* (Düsseldorf: Luchterhand, 1965) and Broszat, Frölich, and Wiesemann, eds., *Bayern in der NS Zeit*.

79. Henry Picker, *Hitlers Tischgespräche im Führerhauptquartier* (Stuttgart: Seewald, 1976), 3rd edition, 124 and 145.

80. Annie Kienast, in Schüddekopf, ed., *Alltäglich*, 28.

81. Kuhn and Rothe, *Frauen in deutschen Faschismus*, II, 178. Quoted from Willi Bohn, *Stuttgart: Geheim! Ein dokumentarische Bericht* (Frankfurt: Röderberg, 1969), 125, 131–140.

82. Elling, *Frauen*, 225. Until 1940, relatively few (less than 100 per year) Germans were tried and executed; we have no reliable estimates of the number killed unofficially, by "suicides," disease or torture. In 1940 the total rose to 306 and climbed to 5,684 in 1943. These statistics, however, were not

broken down by sex. Between 1933 and 1939, about 225,000 men and women were formally brought to trial and received average sentences of three years each. Weisenborn, *Aufstand*, 175.

83. Elling, *Frauen*, 213.

84. "Ich war verfügbar," in Jochen Köhler, *Klettern in der Grossstadt. Geschichten vom Überleben zwischen 1933–1945* (Berlin: Wagenbach, 1981), 137.

85. H. G. Adler, *Der verwaltete Mensch* (Tübingen: Mohr, 1979), 307. Milton, "Holocaust," 37, notes that, "protests at a Jewish old-age home on March 6, 1943, resulted in temporary cessation of deportation." Moritz Henschel, in K. J. Ball-Kaduri, "Berlin is 'purged' of Jews: The Jews of Berlin in 1943," *Yad Vashem Studies* 5 (1963), 274–275. Louis P. Lochner, ed., *The Goebbels Diaries, 1942–1943* (New York: Doubleday, 1948), 276. Hans Adolf Jacobson, *Germans against Hitler* (London: Huchinson, 1964), 13.

86. Lochner, *Goebbels Diaries*, 294.

87. Schüddekopf, ed., *Der alltägliche Faschismus*, 122.

88. Elling, *Frauen*, "Totenliste," 172–211.

89. On Edith Stein, cf. Robert M. E. Kempner, *Edith Stein und Anne Frank. Zwei von Hunderttausend. Die Enthüllungen über die N. S. Verbrechen in Holland vor dem Schwurgericht in München* (Freiburg: Herder, 1968). Waltraud Herbstrith, *Edith Stein. A Biography*. Trans. Bernard Bonowitz (San Francisco: Harper & Row, 1985).

90. "Bericht Luise Rinser," Elling, *Frauen*, 159. Luise Rinser, *Gefängnis Tagebuch* (Munich: Zinnen, 1946).

91. Elling, *Frauen im Widerstand*, 45.

92. Vera Laska, *Women in the Resistance and in the Holocaust, The Voices of Eyewitnesses* (Westport, Connecticut: Greenwood, 1983), xiv. Most of her eyewitnesses came from outside Germany and resisted after the war began; German women who resisted before 1939 are much more difficult to trace because fewer of them survived; by 1937, most had already been arrested. Because they rebelled against tyranny in their own land, and not against foreign aggression, they remain in a special category.

93. Statement, June 21, 1983, AFI meeting, Paris, recorded by the author.

94. "Bericht Käthe Popall," in Elling, *Frauen*, 150–151. Many books on women in the Nazi state overlook women resisters entirely, for example, Jill Stephenson, *Women in Nazi Society* and *Nazi Organization*, Dorothee Klinksiek, *Die Frau im NS-Staat* (Stuttgart: Deutsche, 1982), and Georg Tidl, *Die Frau im Nationalsozialismus* (Vienna: Europa, 1984).

95. Bouglé collection, at the Bibliothèque historique de la Ville de Paris, "Coupures de Presse," Box 6, F-L, esp. essays by Denise Morgan. Cf. Wilhelm Florin, "Die Faschistische Knechtung der Frau," in Kuhn and Rothe, *Frauen in deutschen Faschismus*, II, 166–167.

96. Peukert, *Ruhr Arbeiter*, 247.

97. Jacobs, Annemarie, *Hinter den Zeilen* (Halle a.d. Saale: Mitteldeutscher Verlag, 1959), 67.

98. Already in 1935 the Gestapo investigated "Fliessbandhetze bei Osram" in Berlin where women workers protested the increasing tempo. Altrichter,

ed., *Unser Kampf. 200 Beispiele aus dem antifaschistischen Kampf in Deutschland* (Prague: n.p., n.d.), 51. Cf. Margot Pikarski's collection of hand bills and posters, *Die KPD lebt! Flugblätter aus dem antifaschistischen Widerstandskampf der KPD, 1933–1945* (Berlin: Dietz, 1980), and Broszat, Frölich, Wiesemann, eds., *Bayern in der NS-Zeit* I, 210.

99. Interview with the author.

100. As told to Erich Klausener. *Frauen in Fesseln. Erinnerungen einer Berliner Gefängnisfürsorgerin. 1933–1945* (Berlin: Morus, 1962), 2.

101. Helene Jacobs, quoted in Szepansky, *Frauen*, 63.

102. Kurt R. Grossman, *Unbesungenen Helden* (Berlin: Arani, 1961), 121.

103. Interview with Ilse Rothschild, Worcester, Massachusetts, January 1984.

104. Maria von Maltzan, Szepansky, *Frauen*, 119, 122.

105. Doris Masse, interviewed by Erika Runge, "Statt eines Nachworts: Gespräch," Elling, *Frauen*, 212–213.

106. Maria Agnes Gräfin zu Dohna, quoted in Szepanski, *Frauen*, 52, who looked back and decided that her identity as a "Christian and as a mother" left her no alternative to resistance, provides an exception.

107. Szepansky, *Frauen*, 121.

108. . . . *Besonders*, 48–49.

109. Quoted in Gollwitzer, Kuhn, and Schneider, *Dying We Live*, trans. R. Kuhn (New York: Pantheon, 1957), 194–195.

10. Jewish Women Between Survival and Death

1. Madeline Kent, *I Married a German* (London: Allen and Unwin, n.d.), 216.

2. Annette Kuhn and Valentine Rothe, eds., *Frauen im deutschen Faschismus* (Düsseldorf: Schwann, 1983). David Schoenbaum, *Hitler's Social Revolution. Class and Status in Nazi Germany* (New York and London: W. W. Norton, 1980). Dorothee Klinksiek, *Die Frau im NS Staat* (Stuttgart: Deutsche, 1982). *Mutterkreuz und Arbeitsbuch* likewise includes nothing on Jews. The single and outstanding book in English is Karl Schleuenes, *The Twisted Road to Auschwitz* (Urbana, Chicago and London, University of Illinois, 1970). Of course, biographies and scholarly examinations of specific organizations and aspects of Jewish life exist (as do stories of underground survival and deportation after 1941). Leonard Baker, *Days of Sorrow and Pain* (New York: Oxford University Press, 1978) brilliantly recreated the milieu around Leo Baeck. Thus, we have general histories of Germany that omit Jews and careful examination of many aspects of Jewish life written, one assumes, with a Jewish audience in mind.

3. For example, of 66 memoirs at the Leo Baeck Institute, 22 are by women; and of 68 accounts of concentration camps, 26 were written by women. Special thanks to Marion Kaplan for this information. On this general topic, cf. my brief essay, "Courage and Choice among Jewish German Women and Men," in the collection of papers presented at the Leo Baeck Conference on Jews in Germany, Berlin 1985. Arnold Pauker, ed., *Self-*

Assertion in Adversity. The Jews in National Socialist Germany, 1933–1945, *Leo Baeck Yearbook*, Autumn 1986.

4. Lucy Maas-Friedmann, "Memoirs," 10. LBI.

5. In this regard, two facets of Hitler's personality stood in opposition: his passionate hatred of Jews and his political savoir faire that cautioned gradualism. Schleuenes, *Twisted Road*, 60–65.

6. Schleuenes, *Twisted Road*, 70–71. H. G. Adler, *Der verwaltete Mensch. Studien zur Deportation der Juden aus Deutschland* (Tübingen: J. C. B. Mohr, 1974), 278–281. Adler notes that the word "Jew" did not even appear in the 1935 revision of the Law Code.

7. Edward Peterson, *The Limits of Hitler's Power* (Princeton: Princeton University Press, 1967), 265, and Comité des Délégations Juives, Paris 1934, ed., *Die Lage der Juden in Deutschland. Das Schwarzbuch-Tatsachen und Dokumente* (Frankfurt a. M.: Ullstein, 1983), originally published in 1934, 93–119.

8. Maas-Friedmann, "Memoirs," 4. LBI.

9. Gerda Szepansky, *Frauen leisten Widerstand, 1933–1945* (Frankfurt: Fischer, 1983), 150–151. This account neglects to point out how very rare such instinctive courage was. As Donald Niewyk has demonstrated, while most Germans were not anti-Semites, pervasive prejudice dampened their concern for Jewish victims. In other words, "the Nazis were able to attract hard-core anti-Semites with racialist appeals without having to fear that this would drive away an equal or greater number of potential followers." *The Jews in Weimar Germany* (Baton Rouge, Louisiana: Louisiana University Press, 1980), 81. Ian Kershaw summed up a later stage of this reality: "The road to Auschwitz was built by hate, but paved with indifference." *Political Opinion and Political Dissent* (New York: Oxford, 1983), 277.

10. Jews decreased from 1.2 percent in 1871 to .9 percent of the German population in 1925. During the 1920s, Jews comprised 4.29 percent of the population in Berlin, 6.3 percent in Frankfurt, and 4.17 percent in Breslau. About half of all Jewish Germans worked in trade and banking, as compared to 12 percent of non-Jews. But when we compare urban populations the difference diminishes: 23 percent non-Jews in banking and commerce in the large cities. About 26 percent of all Jews worked as artisans and small shopkeepers, as compared to 52 percent of all non-Jews in urban areas. Six percent of employed Jews were in the civil service and professions, as compared to 8 percent of non-Jews. These statistics are compiled from Schleuenes, *Twisted Road*, Frances Henry, *Victims and Neighbors* (Northampton, Massachusetts: Bergin and Garvey, 1983), and Rosenstock, "Exodus. 1933–1939," *Leo Baeck Yearbook* I:1 (1956), 373–393.

11. Interviews with Ilse Wischnia, Worcester, Massachusetts, 1983, and with Charlotte Blaschke, North Easton, Massachusetts, 1986.

12. Henry, *Victims and Neighbors*, 62. The number of Jews who married non-Jews rose from 8 percent in 1910 to 23 percent in 1929. In urban areas, one out of every three Jews married outside the faith.

13. *Die Lage der Juden in Deutschland*, 75. While this marked a dramatic increase from the 200 "mixed marriages" of 1831–1840, it hardly "threatened"

most Christians. The authors of this report note that half of all mixed marriages produced no children, so the Jewish Question might eventually die out altogether. The numbers of people who formally left the Jewish faith rose from 1500 per year in 1831–1840 to 8,000 in 1921–1930.

14. *The Times* (London, April 3, 1933).

15. "Reisebeobachtungen," 1, EZA, EKD, C 3/170.

16. Ian Kershaw, "Antisemitism and Volksreinung" 296. L. T. Stokes, "The German People and the Destruction of the European Jews," *Central European History* 6 (1973), 173. Sarah Gordon, *Hitler, Germans, and the "Jewish Question"* (Princeton: Princeton University Press, 1984), 168–170.

17. *LBI News* 45 (Winter 1983), 3.

18. Marta Appel (née Insel), "Memoirs," in Monika Richarz, ed., *Jüdisches Leben in Deutschland. 1918–1945* (Stuttgart: Deutsche, 1982), 232.

19. Toni Lessler, "Vor und Nach 30.1.33," M. E. 593, L.B.I.

20. Quoted in Leonard Baker, *Days of Sorrow and Pain. Leo Baeck and the Berlin Jews* (New York: Oxford University Press, 1978), 156. Gordon Zahn, *German Catholics and Hitler's Wars: A Study in Social Control* (New York: Sheed and Ward, 1962), demonstrates forcefully the contrast between brave individuals and craven institutions during the Second World War.

21. Rahel Straus, "Moderne Frauenprobleme," *Blätter des jüdischen Frauenbundes* VI:2 (February 1930), 1 (hereafter BJF). Cf. Rahel Straus, *Wir lebten in Deutschland: Erinnerungen einer deutschen Jüdin. 1880–1933* (Stuttgart: Deutsche Verlags-Anstalt, 1962).

22. Dr. Else Rabin, "Was sollen wir tun?" *BJF*.

23. Lucy Dawidowicz, *The War Against the Jews* (New York: Bantam, 1975), 231.

24. "Unsere Pflicht!" BJF, IX:5 (May 1933), 2–3.

25. "Neue Mitarbeiterinnen," BJF 9:7 (July 1933), 1.

26. Ibid.

27. Bertha Pappenheim, Bettina Brenner, Paula Ollendorff, Dr. Margarete Berent, and Hannah Karminski, letter dated May 20, 1933, BJF, 9:6 (June 1933), 12.

28. Hedwig Muschkatblatt, quoting Caro's address in Cologne on May 2, 1933, BJF 9:6 (June 1933), 12–13.

29. Bertha Pappenheim, "Der Einzelne und die Gemeinschaft," BJF IV:6 (June 1933), 1.

30. Lotte Paepke, *Ich wurde Vergessen. Bericht einer Jüdin, die das Dritte Reich überlebte* (Freiburg I. B.: Herder, 1979), 24.

31. In this early legislation the term "Jew" did not appear, but was vaguely couched in legalistic terminology about "non-Aryans." Joseph Walk, *Das Sonderrecht für Jüden im NS Staat* (Heidelberg: D. F. Mueller, 1981), 127ff. Lothar Gruchmann, " 'Blutschutzgesetz' und Justiz. Zur Entstehung und Auswirkung des Nürnberger Gesetzes vom 15. Sept. 1935," *Vierteljahrshefte für Zeitgeschichte*, 31:3 (July 1983).

32. Schleuenes, *The Twisted Road*, 109.

33. Mary Feldsteiner, lecture and slide presentation made at the 1984 Berkshire Conference on Women's History, Smith College.

34. Alice Salomon, "Character Is Destiny," manuscript, LBI.

35. Klaus Mann, *Turning Point. 25 Years in the Century* (London: Fischer, 1942), 270.

36. Interview with the author, Worcester, Massachusetts, 1983.

37. Bruno Blau, "The Last Days of German Jewry," *YIVO Annual of Jewish Social Science* 8, 197–204. 63 percent worked in communication and commerce; and 13 percent in private and public service. In 1933, 23 percent of all Jews were artisans.

38. Kurt Grossmann, *Die unbesungenen Helden.* (Berlin: Arani, 1961), 10.

39. Jochen Köhler, *Klettern in der Grosstadt. Geschichte vom Überleben zwischen 1933 und 1945* (Berlin: Wagenbach, 1981), 77.

40. Dr. Hanns Reissner, "Die polnische Jüdin zwischen Gestern und Morgen," BJF, 7:1 (January 1931), 1. Hugo Rosenthal, "Zur Psychologie der jüdischen Frau," BJF, 8:7 (July 1932). The author accused Eastern European Jews of avoiding the real world by escape into religion *(Flucht in die Religion).*

41. Joseph Goebbels, *Revolution der Deutschen* (Oldenburg: Stalling, 1933), 158.

42. Schleuenes, *Twisted Road,* 114.

43. Ian Kershaw, *Popular Opinion,* 36–55. *Die Lage der Juden,* 294 ff.

44. Interview with the author, 1967.

45. Interview with the author, July 1983.

46. I expressed my astonishment to Marion Berghan, author of *German Jewish Refugees in England: The Ambiguities of Assimilation* (London: Macmillan, 1984). She said that the Jews in her study normally received their property because they had left it in the hands of trusted "Aryan" friends. Only the official government transactions, she told me, could not be reversed because they had been legal even though they had been Nazi.

47. Salomon, "Character Is Destiny," 256. Ruth Gay, "What I Learned About German Jews," *American Scholar* (Autumn 1985), 467–484.

48. The World War already created a slight asymmetry between men and women. Milton, "Holocaust," 8.

49. Schleuenes, *Twisted Road,* 186. In numbers, this meant a rise from 52,000 to 74,000 in the over-65 category.

50. Monika Richarcz, *Jüdisches Leben in Deutschland,* III, *Selbstzeugungnisse zur Sozialgeschichte 1918–1945* (Stuttgart: Deutsche, 1982), 237. Anthropologists have noted the increased salience of women's concerns and skills in conditions of racial oppression. Cf. Shirley Ardner, *Women and Space: Ground Rules and Social Maps* (New York: St. Martin's, 1981), especially Rosemary Ridd's essay on South African colored women.

51. Henry, *Victims,* 110.

52. Maas-Friedmann, *Memoirs,* LBI.

53. Ruth Nebel, "The Story of Ruth," Bridenthal, Grossmann, and Kaplan, eds., *When Biology Became Destiny,* 334.

54. Quoted in Schleuenes, *Twisted Road,* 107–108. Cf. the photos of a children's board game and story book in the photo section of this book. To offset this pollution of public education, Jewish teachers did their best (in

the words of one report from a Nuremburg school board), "to entirely fill our children with a Jewish spirit that they understand. The growing child should become more secure in his Jewish identity . . . he should learn to rejoice in his [Jewish] name, along with all the suffering it brings." November 22, 1937, Staatsarchiv Nuremburg, Reg. v. M. F./K1388/4815 [old code 1183bc].

55. Inge Deutschkron, *Ich trug den gelben Stern*. (Cologne: Wissenschaft und Politik, 1978), 7.

56. Margarete Buber-Neumann, *Milena, Kafkas Freundin* (München: Heyne, 1977), 123–125.

57. Henry, *Victims and Neighbors*, 69. Berghahn, *German-Jewish Refugees*, 74.

58. Paepke, *Ich wurde vergessen*, 60–61. The author discusses the situation of Jewish-Christian marriages and notes. "The ['Aryan'] man felt his masculinity was wounded," and "The very core of his being [*Lebensnerv*] suffered, . . . when he was insulted, professionally demoted, and had to look on enviously as his colleagues received their new uniforms. . . .", 32.

59. Henry, *Victims and Neighbors*, 92.

60. Werner Rosenstock, "Exodus, 1933–1939. A Survey of Jewish Emigration from Germany," *Leo Baeck Yearbook*, I:1 (1956), 373–393, and Dietrich Uwe Adam, *Die Judenpolitik im Dritten Reich* (Düsseldorf: Droste, 1972), 122–123.

61. Comité des Délégations Juives, ed., *Die Lage der Juden in Deutschland*, 82–83, and H. G. Adler, *Der verwaltete Mensch*, 281.

62. Ilse Blumenthal-Weiss, "Erinnerungen," 1979. Typed manuscript, MAN E, 128, LBI.

63. Kurt Meier, *Kirche und Judentum. Die Haltung der evangelischen Kirche zur Judenpolitik des dritten Reiches* (Göttingen: Vandenhoeck and Ruprecht, 1968), 13. G. Lewy, *The Catholic Church* (New York: McGraw-Hill, 1965), 268–308.

64. Rita Thalman and Emmanuel Feinermann, *Crystal Night* (New York: Holocaust, 1974). Originally published as *La Nuit de Cristal* (Paris: Lafont, 1972), 56 ff. Max Auwerbuch, former member of a German Jewish youth organization and later an engineer in Israel, told me that the "Crystal Night" was just another Nazi euphemism, probably modeled on the "Crystal Night" when anarchists blew up the World Exhibition palace in London.

65. Frances Henry, *Victims and Neighbors*, 117.

66. Louis Lochner, ed. *The Goebbels Diaries*, trans. Fred Taylor (London and New York: Penguin, 1984), 171.

67. Hitler, *Hitlers politisches Testament* (Hamburg: A. Knaus, 1981), 64–70, 110–111.

68. Rosalyn Mannowitz, *Reflections on the Holocaust* (New York: Hebrew Tabernacle, 1978), 98.

69. The national figures were 193, but if one discounts Jews arrested before 1933, the number drops to 118. Lucien Steinberg, *Jews Against Hitler*, trans. Marion Hunter (London: Gordon and Cremonesi, 1974), 22. Jizchak Schwersenz and Edith Wolf, "Jüdische Jugend im Untergrund: eine Zionistische Gruppe in Berlin," *Parlament* 31:15–16 (1981), 16–38.

70. Claude Lanzmann, *Shoah*, foreword by Simone de Beauvoir (New York: Pantheon, 1986), 51. Leonard Gross, *The Last Jews in Berlin* (New York: Simon and Schuster, 1982), 17–18. The pre-Nazi Berlin population had numbered 160,000 and by 1940 it had fallen to 40,000.

71. Ida Jausson-Frank, "Rückblick, Erinnerungen," 30, LBI.

72. Henry, *Victims and Neighbors*, 78.

73. Mixed marriage statistics: A total of 160,000 Jews (by ethnicity) had left the Jewish religion since the 1830s when statistics began to be collected.

74. My thanks to Marion Kaplan for calling my attention to this source; Joseph Walk. *Das Sonderrecht fur Juden im NS Staat*, 1981. The case of Else Sara Mueller (née Cohnen), divorced and unemployed, but since 1933 a member of the Frauenschaft and officer of the local Welfare organization (NSV), provides an example of someone who believed that her deep devotion to Nazism exempted her from suspicion. HSAD/Gestapo/RW/9,320.

75. This sex-typed pair of expressions indicates racial contempt for "inferior" passive males and sexual scorn for women. The term *Schmuckstück* itself plays on the double meaning of *Schmuck*, i.e. jewelry and penis.

76. Videotaped interview with Yale University Oral History of the Holocaust Project.

77. Hannah Levy-Hass, *Inside Belsen*, trans. Ronald Taylor, intro. Jane Caplan (Totowa, New Jersey: Barnes & Noble, 1982), 15.

78. Karminski to Schäffler, June 25, 1942. Reprinted in "Documents," *Year Book II*, Leo Baeck Institute of Jews from Germany (London: East and West, 1957), 310–311. Marion A. Kaplan, *The Jewish Feminist Movement in Germany* (Westport, Connecticut: Greenwood, 1979), concluded her book with this passage, 205.

79. Gertrud Staewen, Angelika Schmidt-Biesalski, *Lust, Liebe, und Verstand* (Gelnhausen: Burckhardthaus, 1981), 88. *Genesis* 26:2—"Dwell in the land which I shall tell thee of."

80. Vera Friedländer, *Späte Notizen* (Berlin: Neues Leben, 1982). Special thanks to Marion Kaplan for telling me about this book.

11. Consequences: Women, Nazis, and Moral Choice

1. Raul Hilberg, "The Significance of the Holocaust," Friedlander and Milton, eds., *The Holocaust: Ideology, Bureaucracy, and Genocide* (Millwood, New York: Kraus, 1980), 99. Karl Jaspers, in *The Question of German Guilt*, trans. E. B. Ashton (New York: Dial, 1947), distinguished between criminal, political, and metaphysical guilt, 31. But elsewhere he blamed foreign complicity and Hitler's hypnotic power, 94–95.

2. Peter Drucker, "The Monster and the Lamb," *The Atlantic Monthly* (December 1978), 82–87.

3. Warren I. Susman, in *Culture as History* (New York: Pantheon, 1984), brilliantly draws the contrast between personality and character, and examines the historical evolution of both.

4. *The New York Times*, (November 18, 1949) 12; *New York Herald Tribune*, (February 3, 1948). This was a longer sentence, incidently, than Hitler

had served after his conviction of treason following the Beer Hall putsch in 1923.

5. Scholtz-Klink to Rosenberg, Annual Report, April 25, 1941. IfZ/MA253/647.

6. *Deutschland-Berichte der SOPADE*, 4:1 (January 1937), A–37, and 4:2 (February 1937), A–26.

7. William Shirer, *20th Century Journey. The Nightmare Years.* (Boston: Little, Brown, 1984).

8. Franz Heyen, *Nationalsozialismus im Alltag* (Boppart: Boldt, 1967), 335–351.

9. These cases are from respectively: RW 58/97, and RW 58/9904, Nordrhein-westfälisches Hauptstaatsarchiv. Geheimstaatspolizei–Staatspolizeileitstelle/HSAD. Auguste Fink Henke was born in Cologne on January 21, 1904.

10. Robert A. Brady, *The Spirit and Structure of German Fascism* (New York: Viking, 1937), 194, 200.

11. BA Koblenz/R41/69/B. 17. Else Lüders, "Die Frau in der deutschen Landwirtschaft," *Soziale Praxis* 49:12 (June 15, 1940), 379, specifically urged *"Doppelverdienertum"* as a necessity.

12. Suzanne Charlotte Englemann, *German Education and Re-Education* (New York: International University Press, 1945), 113.

13. Leila J. Rupp, *Mobilizing Women for War. German and American Propaganda* (Princeton: Princeton University Press, 1978), 115. Policymakers left no doubt about long-range goals. "Wage work for married women must in the future be reduced. Women's employment is mandated by the war. It must not become permanent." Dr. Stittler, "Alle Kräfte für den Endziel!" *Sociale Praxis* 49:13 (July 1, 1940), 385. Statement, signed Butz, February 28, 1940, "There can be no question of equality with men." BA Koblenz/R41/69, Bl. 4 & 5. Cf. Von Riedebach, to Rüst[ungsamt] (Armaments), June 3, 1940, discusses how to clean up the image of women munition workers. BA Freiburg/Wi/If5.1220.UI.10. Jill Stephenson, *Women in Nazi Society* (New York: Barnes & Noble, 1975), 127–128, 171–181, and 194–197. Tim Mason, "Women in Germany, 1925–1940," *History Workshop*, II (Autumn 1976), 10–25. Annemarie Troeger, "The Creation of a Female Assembly-Line Proletariat," in Bridenthal, Grossmann, Kaplan, eds., *When Biology Became Destiny* (New York: Monthly Review, 1984), 246–165.

14. Ilse Buresch-Riebe, *Frauenleistung im Kriege* (Berlin: Eher, 1941), 6, 76, 38–39. The author pointed out that 800,000 women had become the sole proprietors of small businesses because of the war. Probably the most frequently cited study was Angela Meister's "Die deutsche Industriearbeiterinnen" (Jena: Dissertation, 1939).

15. On race, cf. Reber-Gruber to Hans Behrens, 18. October 1938 HSAM/NSDAP/1000, as always, she wanted to use non-Jewish psychology to mobilize her women. On Sudetenland, Reber-Gruber letter of October 18, 1938, ibid., NSDAP/1001. On the bureaucratic system and incentives for women, cf. Reber-Gruber to Maria Zillig, July 24, 1940, ibid., NSDAP 1008. No. 1676/40, Reber-Gruber to Else Maas, September 2, 1940, ibid., and Reber-

Gruber letters to Martha Engelbert, May 7, 22, May 17, 1940, ibid., NSDAP/ 1005.

16. "Zur Frage der verstärketen Frauenstudium," IfZ/MA 441/80/ frames 760480-760848. "Arbeitseinsatz im Krieg," Report dated February 2, 1937, IfZ/MA 468/5717, 5721, and 5723. "Kriegshilfsdienst," *Soziale Praxis* 50:16 (August 15, 1941), 625. *Frau am Werk*, a publication in the series *Schönheit der Arbeit* (Berlin: DAF, 1940). On August 26, 1940, Keitel urgently asked Göring to recruit 400,000 women for arms production, BA Freiburg/RüIVd.

17. Hilde Munske, ed. *Das bunte Jungmädelbuch* (Berlin, n.d.), 230–234. Magda Menzerath, *Kampffeld Heimat: Deutsche Frauenleistung im Kriege* (Stuttgart: Allemannen: 1941), 70–71. "It will always be exceptional for a woman to be so important at the front; but more and more women are stepping into important responsibilities." Reitsch also wrote about the necessity for duty to repress the passion for flying. Hanna Reitsch, born in 1912, does not seem to have joined the party, even though she received the Iron Cross second class in March 1941. BDC.

18. Annemarie Tröger, "Assembly Line," *Biology*, 252.

19. When all women between 17 and 45 were conscripted in 1943, authorities did not stringently enforce the decree and few women entered the labor force. Cf. Oberkommando der Wehrmacht to Oberkommando des Heeres, Rüst[ungsamt], (Armaments Office), March 5, 1940, BA Freiburg, Militärarchiv, Wi/IF5.103.1, and Thomas to Syrup, February 22, 1940, ibid. Wi/IF 5.103a. Report on the Rhineland, April 20, 1943, Düsseldorf/Kalkum/BR/ 1015/114/Bl. 7–11. Berenice Carroll, *Design for Total War: Arms and Economics in the Third Reich* (The Hague and Paris, Mouton: 1968). Burton H. Klein, *German Economic Preparation for War* (Cambridge: Harvard, 1959), Chapter 11. *U. S. Strategic Bombing Survey. Economic Report*, Appendix, Table 15. Albert Speer, *Inside the Third Reich*, 211–212, noted 1939 German production was only one-fourth of what it had been in 1918.

20. "Betriebsgewinn aus Frauenarbeit?" *Soziale Praxis* 50:19 (October 1, 1941), 753–754. Cf. "Frauenlöhne," BA Koblenz/R41/69, which pegged women's wages at 75 percent of men's for the same jobs. Ludwig Eibner, "Frauen in der Kriegsindustrie," Broszat, et al. *Bayern* vol. 3, 569–581.

21. Women in their twenties made ideal workers, and 90 percent of all unmarried women in this age bracket were in the labor market; but only a third of all married women at this age worked outside their homes. Tim Mason, *History Workshop*, II, 11–12. On the irrationality of Nazi priorities, cf. also Dörte Winkler, *Frauenarbeit im 'Dritten Reich'* (Hamburg: Hoffmann and Campe, 1977), 154–175. Policymakers in general never decided between the social Darwinist principle, which encouraged the most productivity, or the social solidarity principle, which keyed wages to status.

22. Burton H. Klein, *Economic Preparation*, 173–205.

23. Der Reichsleiter, Die Deutsche Arbeitsfront, to Reichsfrauenführerin Parteigenossin Scholtz-Klink, DAF, May 13, 1942, BA Koblenz, NS 5 I/ NSDAP 202. In tortured "logic" Ley contrasted the healthy NSDAP with Weimar and American decadence. The devastating impact of wartime policy on women is demonstrated by the morale report, "Das Zeitgeschehen," No-

vember 18, 1943, Boberach, *Meldungen aus dem Reich* (Berlin: Luchterhand, 1965), 445–455.

24. "Soziale Fragen," Press Conference, September 20, 1940, BA Freiburg/Wi/VIII/a 2. In the same file is an excellent example of the debate about social Darwinist vs. fairness wage policies. This vacillation sprang, in turn, from Nazi chiefs' more fundamental indecision when it came to organizing. Even within its own institutions, the Nazi Party encouraged vicious infighting. Reinhard Bollmus, *Das Amt Rosenberg und seine Gegner* (Stuttgart: Deutsche, 1970), 244–250.

25. Bäumer to Beckmann, October 17, 1940, BA Koblenz/Kleine Erwerbungen, 267–272.

26. *Frauen im Wehrdienst. Erinnerungen von Ingeborg Hecht, Ruth Henry, Crista Meves*, intro. Cordula Koepcke, (Freiburg, i. Br.: Herder, 1982), 9. The women referred to themselves as "70 men strong." Keitel, "Bereitstellung von Wehrmachthelferinnen," 1944, estimated that 80,000 women in uniform had replaced male soldiers to compensate for the "catastrophic decline of the army." BA Freiburg/RW4/V. 865/Bl. 80–104. Women in early 1945 had taken over air defense work, memo from the Interior Ministry to Civil Defense, March 14, 1945, BA Koblenz/Sammlung Schumacher/ 262/B, 118.

27. The military employed women in various capacities. Ursula von Gersdorff, ed. *Frauen im Kriegedienst* (Stuttgart: Deutsche-Verlagsanstalt, 1969), documents 220, 223, 228, and 236, pages, 446, 447, 451, 457, and 46, respectively. 80,000 women leaders from the BDF were drafted into the army and 100,000 women spotlight operators replaced men in 1944. By 1944 women had received war medals for bravery, "Verleihung der Kriegsverdienstmedaille an Frauen," Meissner, August 4, 1944, IfZ/MA356.

28. Reber-Gruber to Anni Hausner, April 1, 1940, HSAM/NSDAP/1007. Her mood grew steadily worse. She complained that women were not allowed to work on the frontier in the Ukraine, Poller and Reber-Gruber exchange, March 1942, ibid., NSDAP/1009. On occasion, too, she worried about women being encouraged to engage in prostitution in order to prevent male homosexuality, especially in the army. In addition to deploring the moral consequences, she worried about VD epidemics. Letter (marked Secret), February 29, 1940. Ibid., NSDAP/1008. Braunes Haus to NSLB, August 11, 1940. Ibid., NSDAP/1004.

29. Letters exchanged between Reber-Gruber and NSLB, Beyreuth, 1940. On July 17, 1940, the NSLB rebuked Reber-Gruber's concern for order. "You can organize as much as you want, but organization will never master life because it must remain artificial . . . and dead . . . willing people will work in any conditions."

30. Pridham and Noakes, eds., *Documents in Nazism, 1919–1945* (New York: Viking, 1974), 615. Himmler order of October 28, 1939. Stephenson, *Women in Nazi Society*, 57–71. Felix Kersten, *Totenkopf und Treue* (Hamburg: Robert Moelich Verlag, 1952), 180, said 50 percent of the mothers were unmarried. Heinrich Manvell and Roger Frankel, *Himmler* (New York: Putnam's, 1965), 89–94.

31. Hans Straudiger, "Germany's Population Miracle," *Social Research* (May 1938), 125, 140.

32. "Eine Frau hat das Wort," and "Der Sieg der Frauen" in *Das Schwarze Korps* (April 11 and January 4, 1940, respectively). Himmler proposed calling unwed parents "wartime mother" and "wartime father" to destigmatize their relationship. Peter Bleuel, *Sex and Society in Nazi Germany*, trans. J. M. Brownjohn (Philadelphia: Lippencott, 1973), 156. Ernst Bergmann (archrival of Sophie Rogge-Börner in the 1920s) proposed that 20 women for one man would provide an ideal ratio. Quoted in Thomas, *Women*, 46. Gertrud Bäumer decided not to criticize the program in the pages of *Die Frau*. Cf. the correspondence among Bäumer, Beckmann, and von Velsen in 1940, BA Koblenz/Kleine Erwerbung, 296–301.

33. Auguste Reber-Gruber, "Arbeit in den Gauen und Kreisen," June 14, 1941, HSAM/NSDAP 10004. Confidential letter to Else Mass, December 5, 1940, ibid., NSDAP/1005; protest to Reichsverwaltung (National Administration), December 16, 1940; and "Stellungshahme," November 8, 1945. In the latter memo she noted that while married women teachers still suffered the same disadvantages they had under Weimar, unmarried women teachers seemed to be having a field day. Morale among Reber-Gruber's teachers dropped when they heard the outcome of several controversial decisions. For example, a male teacher who had fathered three babies (each with a different mother) without marrying the mothers won the right to continue teaching. "Zur Lage," *Die Frau*, 46:9 (June 1939), 499. Peter Bleuel, *Sex and Society*, 156. Melita Maschmann, *Account Rendered: A Dossier of My Former Self*, trans. G. Strachan (London: Abelard-Schuman, 1965), 141.

34. EZA/C3/183, February 12, 1934, Bl. 152–154; February 3, 1934, Bl. 304; and Diehl to Reichsbishof, June 23, 1934 (opposing von Grone), Bl. 420. Regarding her trial, cf. July 10, 1940, letter from Rembe to Parteigericht, *Akten des obersten Parteigerichts*, I Kammer, 1941. BDC. Lecture, "Polizeiliche Massnahmen," March 9, 1940. HSAM/NSDAP/1004.

35. The publication to which she objected was Friedrich Hoffmann, "Sittliche Entartung und Geburtenschwund," copied by Diehl without identification, BDC. The phrase that upset her was, "He who scorns an unwed mother is just as "asocial" [*widernatürlich*] as those who scorn the brave soldier." Diehl was also declared guilty of loyalty to the Kaiser. Cf. Gruber to Diehl, July 6, 1940, and letters to "Mutter Guida," BDC.

36. Guida Diehl, *Christ sein heisst Kämpfer sein: Die Führung meines Lebens* (Eisenach: Brunnen, 1960), 166, 219–220.

37. Stephenson, *Women in Nazi Society*, 169. The nursing "order" included only 6,000 sisters in 1939, when the overall shortage of nurses was 30,000.

38. Lewy, *Catholic Church*, 292–293; Leuner, *Compassion*, 138–140. Wilhelm Frick (who was dismissed in 1943) had been in charge of the euthanasia program. At Nuremberg, Frick said he "felt he had worked long hours, given the best of his talents to the ordained authorities, and always done his duty for them and for his people." Eugene Davidson, *The Trial of the Germans* (New York: Collier, 1966), 281. By 1941, most people targeted for death had

been killed, and Hitler ordered smaller scale operations, which were moved to Poland. Sittengesetz 1940, EAF/48/21.

39. Fred Taylor, ed., *The Goebbels Diaries: 1939–1941* (New York: Penguin, 1984), 296. Speer, *Inside*, 220–221. Ministry of Economics to Ley, April 2, 1942, acknowledges failure of Party to impose hierarchy on the Frauenwerk/BA Koblenz. In 1943, Hitler ordered the importation of between 400,000 and 500,000 "girls" from conquered territories in the east to work as servants. But he refused to conscript mothers.

40. Report from Schleswig-Holstein to Himmler, April 2, 1942, IfZ/MA341, Scholtz-Klink, Rundschreiben, Circular, 118/40, HSAM/NSDAP/1004, and ibid. Letters from Reber-Gruber to Stricker and to Seybel, 1940. For an analysis of bureaucratic failure, cf. "Eindrücke," *Die Frau* 45:12 (September 1938), 663. "Overorganization" resulted in "the destruction of the personality."

41. Hitler, *Mein Kampf* (Boston: Houghton-Mifflin, 1962), 285.

42. Trevor-Roper, *The Last Days of Hitler* (New York: Collier, 1970), 239. Cf. also "Btr. Frauenueberschusses n.d. Kriege," typed report, March 10, 1940, Himmler Files No. 1302, Drawer 5, Folders 182–200, IfZ/MA 3/13. This report predicted a shortage of 2 million men. On November 10, 1944, Dr. Leonardo Conti (who in 1931 had inspected Zander's SA rest home for the Party headquarters), reported on the problem in alarmist terms and proposed a sperm bank. H. von Schirach, *Frauen*, 249.

43. Rudolf Hess, "An eine uneheliche Mutter," (n.d., June 1940?), National Archives microfilm, T-175/roll 128, frame 4115. By the end of the war research on artificial insemination had begun in earnest, secret letter, February 1944, IfZ/MA3/13/Folder 200/13. Himmler spoke of an "inner transformation" of attitudes toward children, and possible only when the Volk becomes reunified with natural law. Agnes F. Peterson and Bradley F. Smith, eds., *Heinrich Himmler. Geheimreden, 1933 bis 1945* (Frankfurt: Propyläen, 1924), 85.

44. Erna Segal, "You Shall Never Forget," unpublished manuscript, LBI, Box No. 59, 99–100.

45. H. G. Adler, *Der verwaltete Mensch. Studien zur Deportation der Juden aus Deutschland* (Tübingen: J. C. B. Mohr, 1974), 594. Reber-Gruber to Frau von Hutten, June 28, 1940. HSAM/NSDAP/Munich/1007.

46. Eugene Davidson, *The Trial of the Germans*, 434.

47. Ibid., 91–92. Emmy Göring, *An der Seite meines Mannes* (Göttingen: Schueltz, 1967), 64, 67, 70, 78.

48. Davidson, *Trial*, 102. Bormann had played a decisive role in the euthanasia program. *The Bormann Letters. January 1943–April 1945*. Intro. H. Trevor-Roper (London: Weidenfeld and Nicolson, 1954).

49. Cernyak-Spatz's remarks in Esther Katz and Joan Ringelheim, eds., *Proceedings of the Conference Women Surviving the Holocaust* (New York: Institute for Research on History, 1983), 147. Kaufmann-Krasowksi's comments in the biography of an SS woman guard, *Die Frauen von Majdanek. Vom zerstörten Leben der Opfer und der Mörderinnen*, ed. Ingrid Müller-Münch (Hamburg: RoRoRo, 1982), 115.

50. "Bericht Margarete Armbruster," Elling, *Frauen*, 75.

51. Olga Lengyel, *Five Chimneys: The Story of Auschwitz*, trans. Paul P. Weiss (London: Mayflower, 1972). Fania Fénélon, *Playing for Time*, trans. J. Landry (New York: Berkley, 1979), 147, 194–212, 244–250.

52. Elie Wiesel, *Night* (New York: Avon, 1969), 39.

53. Viktor Frankl, *Man's Search for Meaning*, trans. Ilse Lasch, preface by Gordon W. Allport (New York: Simon and Schuster, 1962), first published in 1946, 9.

54. Gitta Sereny, *Into That Darkness. An Examination of Conscience* (New York: Viking, 1983). First printed 1974, 176.

55. Miklos Nyiszli, *Auschwitz: A Doctor's Eyewitness Account*, trans. T. Kremer and R. Seaver, foreword Bruno Bettelheim (Greenwich, Connecticut: Fawcett Crest, 1960), 23. This division seemed so natural that orders rarely even mention it. On occasion, however, an official would comment, "It goes without saying that the men are to be separated from the women." Order from the Reich Minister for the Occupied Eastern territories, 1941, quoted in Helmut Krausnick and Martin Broszat, *Anatomy of the SS State*, trans. Dorothy Long and Marian Jackson (London, Toronto, Sydney, New York: Granada, 1982), 115.

56. Blumenthal-Weiss memoirs, 42 and 76, at the Leo Baeck Institute, New York.

57. In Esther Katz and Joan M. Ringelheim, eds., *Proceedings*, 79. She added, "Men were separated and we did not know what to do." Vladka Meed, *On Both Sides of the Wall: Memoirs from the Warsaw Ghetto* (Ghetto Fighters, 1972).

58. Lothar Gall, ed., *Fragen an die deutsche Geschichte*, 9th ed. (Stuttgart: Bundestag, 1983), 317.

59. The stages in every camp proceeded according to the following plan: "The killings were organized systematically to achieve the maximum humiliation and dehumanization of the victims before they died. This pattern was dictated by a distinct and careful purpose, not by 'mere' cruelty or indifference: the crammed airless freight-cars without sanitary provisions, food or drink, far worse than any cattle-transport; the whipped-up (literally so) hysteria of arrival; the immediate and always violent separation of men, women and children; the public undressing; the incredibly crude internal physical examinations for hidden valuables; and hair-cutting and shaving of the women; and finally the naked run to the gas chamber, under the lash of whips." Sereny, *Darkness*, 100–101. Since prisoners reported the immediate loss of sexual desire soon after arriving in the camps, it seems unlikely that Nazis separated men from women only to prevent sexual encounters.

60. Ibid., 237–238.

61. Jozef Garlinski, *Fighting Auschwitz* (New York: Fawcett, 1975), 150–151.

62. Sereny, *Darkness*, 165.

63. Eugene Weinstock, *Beyond the Last Path*, trans. C. Ryan (New York: Boni and Gaer, 1947), 74.

64. Kitty Hart, *I Am Alive* (London and New York: Abelard-Schumann,

1962), 63. Fénélon told new arrivals they depended on cooperation, otherwise "You may get out of here alive, but inwardly you'll be deader than any of those poor things they burn every day." *Playing*, 142. Camp policy fostered rivalry, 172.

65. William L. Shirer, *End of a Berlin Diary* (New York: Knopf, 1947), 317.

66. Former SS man Victor Brack at Nuremberg testified that he had "no idea" he would be ordered to direct mass killing operations. When he found out, he protested that men who worked on *"such an inconceivable assignment"* would "no longer be fit to be employed subsequently in mercy-killing." Sereny, *Darkness*, 105.

67. Nuremberg Doc. vol. 32, 385. Hilberg counts this as the first of five rationalizations. *The Destruction of the European Jews* (New York: New Viewpoints, 1973). Hannah Arendt, *Eichmann in Jerusalem. A Report on the Banality of Evil* (New York: Viking, 1964), 120–122, notes distinction between an order (limited in time and space) and a law (Hitler's wish, which had no temporal or spatial limitation at all). This demanded total loyalty to the *spirit* of the law, not the letter of the order. Eichmann says he felt like Pontius Pilate, but he did his *duty* and did not merely "obey orders." Göring often said, "I have no conscience. My conscience is Adolf Hitler," Hermann Rauschning, *Voice of Destruction* (New York: Putnam's, 1940), 78.

68. Helmut Krausnick and Martin Broszat, *Anatomie des SS-Staats* (Freiburg i. Br.: Walters, 1965), 265–266.

69. This often-quoted speech appears in Fest, *The Face of the Third Reich*, 115. Karl Dietrich Bracher, *Die deutsche Diktatur, Enstehung, Struktur, Folgen des Nationalsozialismus* (Cologne: Kiepenheuer Witsch, 1969), 422. *Trials of War Criminals before the Nuremberg Military Tribunals*, Nuremberg. United States Government Printing Office, 1946–1949, Vol. 29, PS-1919, 122. Roger Manvell and Heinrich Fränkel, *Himmler* (Frankfurt: Ullstein, 1965), 131. "These animals . . . must not be treated as decent people," Himmler told his men. Peterson and Smith, eds., *Himmler*, 185. Cf. Goebbels, *Diary*, February 14, 1942.

70. Susan Griffin, *Pornography and Silence* (New York: Pantheon, 1980), 195.

71. Sereny, *Darkness*, 101. By making victims look pathetic, euthanasia could seem ethical. In German, those who suffered could have "help in dying."

72. Quoted in Katz and Ringelheim, *Proceedings*, 140.

73. Sereny, *Darkness*, 203.

74. Quoted in Hilberg, *Destruction*, 218; Arendt, *Eichmann*, 83–84. Himmler behaved no differently on the one occasion when he witnessed a model execution. "At the first salvo . . . he almost fainted, and he screamed when the execution squad failed to kill two women outright." Fest, *The Face of the Third Reich*, 121.

75. Irmgard Litten, *A Mother Fights Hitler* (London: Allen and Unwin, 1940), 250.

76. Fania Fénélon, "Ensemble der Hölle," *Die Zeit*, no. 41 (October 3, 1980), 64. Idem., *Playing*, 194–212, 132–142.

77. Albert Speer, *Inside*, 112. Fénélon said of Mandel, the woman commandant who took the baby she had adopted to the gas chambers, her brain was "compartmentalized like a submarine, made of watertight sections." *Playing*, 248.

78. Sereny, *Darkness*, 162, 229.

79. Ibid., 200.

80. Although Himmler supported divorce, especially for childless couples, he insisted that husbands (and not the SS or the state) must control their own wives. "Even the wife belongs to the SS. She is the part of the SS that shows we are not only a soldierly union but a community, an order. The wife, too, must obey. . . . For her, you are the highest Führer." Peterson and Smith, eds., *Himmler*, 84.

81. Memo, Führerhauptquartier, February 4, 1944, Anordnung 22/44. Reprinted in Gersdorff, *Frauen im Kriegsdienst*, Doc. 213, 435. Michael Kater, *The Nazi Party* (Cambridge, Mass: Harvard, 1983), 148, from Göttingen, SF 6815. GA/6. Davidson, *The Trial*, 317. Thus, policy toward women resembled the directives to Germans, which urged them to treat foreign workers kindly, but not to befriend them.

82. Hermann Langbein, H. A. Adler, and Ella Lingens-Reiner, eds., *Menschen in Auschwitz* (Vienna: Europa Verlag, 1972). My thanks to Amy Hackett for bringing this example to my attention. Robert Jay Lifton, *Doctors in Auschwitz* (New York: Basic Books, 1986). Hermann Langbein and Ella Lingens-Reiner, eds., *Auschwitz: Zeugnisse und Berichte*, 2nd ed. (Cologne: Europäische, 1979).

83. Speer, *Inside*, 147. Eva Braun, he reports, was the only person in the bunker who remained calm during the last days and hours. " 'Why do so many more people have to be killed? And it's all for nothing.' " 484–485. Cf. Erich Ebermayer, *Gefährtin des Teufels* (Hamburg: Hoffmann & Campe, 1952); H. von Schirach, *Frauen*.

84. Rudolf Höss, *Commandant at Auschwitz. Autobiography of Rudolf Höss* (New York: Popular Library, 1964), 34.

85. Joel Dimsdale, *Survivors and Perpetrators* (Washington and New York: Hemisphere, 1980), Part III, which analyzes Rorschach data.

86. Hermann Langbein, *Liquidiert Sie Selber!* . . . *Wir haben es getan. Selbstporträts 1939–1945* (Vienna and Cologne: Europa, 1961), 49, 51.

87. Ibid., 51.

88. Sereny, *Darkness*, 361. Fénelon, *Playing*, decribes Kramer's happy home life at Auschwitz, 196–198.

89. Ibid., 235. The one woman with whom Therese Stangl spoke assured Frau Stangl that her husband must be innocent, and helped her to deny reality. Although Stangl's first name was Franz, his wife called him Paul.

90. Sociologists have examined the ways in which "amoral familialism" skews people's ethical thinking in other national settings. Edward C. Banfield, *The Moral Basis of a Backward Society* (Glencoe: Free Press, 1958). Renate Mayntz, "Role Distance Role Idenification, and Amoral Role Behavior," *European Journal of Sociology* II, 2:368–378, also *Social Research* 37: 3 (Autumn) 428–446.

91. Langbein, *Liquidiert*, 53, 57–65. The author describes with great sensitivity how nervous his dog has become.

92. 5.7.41, "Wunderbare Musik," ibid., 61.

93. Ibid., 62–63.

94. Emphasis in the original. Max Weber to his mother, quoted by Wolfgang J. Mommsen, *Max Weber und die deutsche Politik* (Tübingen: Mohr, 1974), 207.

95. Joseph Conrad, *Heart of Darkness* (London: Penguin, 1973), 69.

96. Sereny, *Darkness*, 350. In her conclusion, the author discusses the relationship between one's identity and his or her perception of guilt.

BIBLIOGRAPHY

Archival Sources

Archiv des Vereins Katholischen Deutschen Lehreinnen, Essen

Autobiographies of Catholic teachers, periodical and newspaper collection related to teaching

Archives Marie-Louise Bouglé, Bibliotheque historique de la Ville de Paris

Fonds Mme. Leo Wanner, 2, 5; Groupes et Associations, 1, 2, 6; Coupures de Presse, Biographies, étranger, Revues

Berlin Document Center (BDC)

Personnel records of members of Nazi Party affiliated organizations

Bishöfliches Zentralarchiv, Regensburg

OA 613–615, OA 618, OA 588, OA 619, OA 609, OA 616–619, OA 653–654, OA 664–670

Bundesarchiv Koblenz (BA Koblenz)

Kleine Erwerbung, 196–2, 258/2, 267/1–4, 296/1, 296/2
NS 4/10, 41, 99, 108–109
NS 5/ 3, 4, 242, 280–283
NS 10/ 31, 34, 48–49, 66–67, 73, 112–113, 141, 378, 463–469, 487
NS 12/9, 14, 22, 31, 264, 269, 277, 366, 381, 396, 416, 480, 539, 545, 554, 609, 637, 800, 803, 831–836, 844, 959, 1204, 1222, 1315, 1356, 1393–1399,
NS 26/254
NS22/ vorläufig 110, 121, 251, 262, 318–319, 342, 348–349, 354–357, 926, 1044
NS 22/ 2002, 2032, NS 44/1–38, 42
NSD 3/5 64/4
NSD 17/RAK
R 18/7108
R 22/ 41, 492, 964, 970, 1157, 3062, 4209, 5005
R36/ 515, 518, 994, 1146, 1148, 1159, 1386, 1397, 2000, 2746, 13k97f, 1394–1395, 2379

R 41/ 69, 161
R43 II/ 427, 443, 823a, 889, 561a–562b, 567, 1,523
R45 II/ 30, 62, 64,
R 45 III/ 14, 43
R 45 IV/ 10
R 45/ vorläufig 110, R45, II/
R 58/ 147
Nachlass Adele Schreiber, 15, 52–53, 64, 83–84
Plakatensammlung
Schumacher Sammlung 9, 16, 230, 239, 245, 249, 251, 257, 262, 494

Bundesarchiv Freiburg (BA Freiburg)

RW4 474–475, 488, 505, 709, 721, 748, 844, 865
RW6/ 10, 156, 491
RM7/ 95 (folio 226).
Wi/IF 5/ 103.c, 1123, 1189, 1215, 1217, 1220, 1222, 1234, 1543, 3139, 3186, 3475, 3690,
Wi/VI, 48

Deutscher Caritasverband Archiv, Freiburg i. Br. (DCV-A)

C.A. VII/ 3–4, 9, 15–16, 64, 70, 71, 84, 91–92, 117, 134–142, 150–151, 155–156, 161–162, R 218, 580–582,
R 332, 490–493, 586, 58–82,
DK 3) 51.2.1.; 3) 51.12.1.; 3.49K.091; 3. 49.o9.01–.93;
Temporary signature 172
CA LXX.62–a, c, d

Diakonisches Werk der evangelischen Kirche Berlin (DWK)

I 222, I 240–255, EI c5, CA/GF, various folios

Deutsches Zentralarchiv für soziale Fragen Berlin (DZFS)

Helene Lange Nachlass, periodical clippings file, correspondence, and library

Erzbischöfliches Archiv Freiburg (EAF)

Sittlichkeit 48/ 14, 18–21. Versammlungen 56/ 19,
Wohlfahrtspflege 59/52–53, NSDAP/36, 43, 51, 53A, 81–84, 161, and Dr. Conrad Gröber/ 44–49, 96

Evang. Oberkirchenrat Landeskirchliches Archiv, Karlsruhe (LAK)

4703–4709, 6037

Evangelisches Zentralarchiv Berlin (EZA)

C3/170–174, 183–191, 192, 201, 440–441,
A2/162, 436, 163–165, 187, 158–161, B3/66, 68

Historisches Archiv der Stadt Köln (HASK)

Bst. 1187 Nachlass Christine Teusch
124–125, 129, 382, 243, 253, 262, 326, 333, 338, 223 K26/2, K26/5
Bst. 1138/6, 12–17, 23–4, 31, 34, 43, 48, 60–63

The Hoover Institution on War, Revolution and Peace (HI)
Stanford, California

The Abel Collection
Hauptarchiv der NSDAP microfilms 254–257

Geheimes Staatsarchiv Preussischer Kulturbesitz Dahlem, Berlin

Rep 84a/570–581, and 135/10927

Niedersächisches Hauptstaatsarchiv Hannover Pattensen (NHH)

Hann 320/47–8, 50, 65–68
Hann 320 I/ 3–5, 7, 9–10, 12, 14–15, 36, 40, 55–59, 69–72 (I & II), 85
Hann 320 IV/ 14–15, 50, 55, 59, 85, 95. Hann 310/I/52
Hann 310/I/Q
Hann XX/61, 374/ a, b/ 374a–375a, Hann 80/ 245

Hauptstaatsarchiv Düsseldorf (HSAD)
Nordrhein-westfälisches Hauptstaatsarchiv, Geheimestaatspolitzei-
Staatspolizeileitstelle Düsseldorf

97, 2,195, 2,743, 6,330, 8,746, 9,320, 9,904, 11,950, 12,640, 13,523,
14,995, 15,201, 16,393, 16,613, 19,991, 21,670, 17,683, 26,394, 28,555,
28,373, 29,104, 29,461, 29,520, 31,343, 32,059, 33,219, 35,102, 38,681,
39,464, 39,585, 40,595, 41,073, 45,338, 46,884, 47,160, 48,159, 49,539,
49,713, 52,298, 52,334, 52,670, 52,792, 54,524, 54,524, 55,389, 51,810,
54,058, 55,249, 58,370, 63,758, 65,711, 66,035

(and Branch Archive Kalkum)

Hauptstaatsarchiv München, NSDAP und Gestapo-Leitstelle (HSAM)

NSDAP 74, 102, 144, 147, 225, 348, 350–354, 477, 548, 655, 773–774,
996–1009, 1052

Hessisches Staatsarchiv, Marburg

3943, 3907, 3936

Institut für Zeitgeschichte (IfZ) Munich

Microfilms photographed by the U.S. government, and catalogued by the IfZ:
F 37/3, Fa 195/2, Fa 202, 5–8, Fa 506/14, MA 387, MA 3/13, 47, 128/3, 129/9, 135, 138/1, 144/3, 145/20, 180, 225/8,9, 389/7, 253/, 254/, 259/0, 285/ 3, 286/8, 292/8, 293/0, 312/2, 330/4, 389/7–8, 391/0, 400/2, 413, 423/5, 434/ 2, 441/1, 4–8, 468/5, 470/4, 485/2, 540, 666/2, 697/1, 1159/7

Landesarchiv Berlin

Pr. Bro. Rep 57 folios 845–849, 850–859, 127, 129, 211–212
Aktion unbesungenene Helden

Leo Baeck Institute, New York

Manuscript memoirs: Erna Becker-Cohen, "Tagebuch"; Ilse Blumenthal-Weiss, "Memoirs"; Klara Caro, "Stärker als der Schwert"; Rosy Geiger-Kullmann, "'Memoirs"; Ida Jauffon-Frank, "Rückblick"; Marianne Joseph, "Erziehung,"; Liselotte Kahn, "Memoirs"; Bertha Katz, autobiography; Thekla Kauffmann, "Erinnerungen"; Nora Keizer, "Danse Macabre"; Gerty Spies, "Ein Stück Weges"; Toni Lessler, "Mein Leben in Deutschland"; Dodo Liebmann, "We Kept Our Heads"; Lucy Maas-Friedmann, "Memoirs"; Rosalyn Manowitz, "Krystalnacht"; Adele von Mises, "Tante Adele"; C. Neumann, "Hitlerzeit"; Hertha Pineas, "Meine Illegale Zeit"; Ottilie Schoenwald, "Lebenserinnerungen"; Erna Segal, "You Shall Never Forget"; Ilse Strauss, "Tagebuch"

Staatsarchiv des Landes Hessen, Wiesbaden (HHW)

Abt 483: 287, 588, 290, 591, 653, 685, 636, 822, 1180, 1631, 1746, 2088, 2090–2099, 2695, 2910, 3229, 3967, 2593–2596, 2793, 2923, 2932, 2993, 3099, 3145, 3197, 3279, 3937–3938, 4119, 4642, 4645, 5536, 5607–5610, 6501, 6118, 6158–6163, 6500, 6489, 6507, 6530, 10,113, 10,118–10, 119, 10,148

Staatsarchiv Münster (SAM)

NS-Frauenschaft/Westfalen-Nord
2, 4, 16–17, 25, 40, 60, 68, 70, 74, 80, 87–88, 90, 102, 117, 122, 126–129, 139, 148, 151, 173, 193, 206, 210, 213, 208, 216, 229, 230–231, 232–233, 240, 245, 257, 264–265, 268, 282, 303, 313, 315, 319–320, 325–327, 368, 375, 378, 393–394, 397–399, 405, 446, 459–460, 472, 483, 524–525, 538, 541, 543, 544–547

Staatsarchiv Nürnberg

k21/591, k24/59n, k68/698, k94/1089, k266/1737, k269/1760–1770, k272/ 1773–6, k318/1878. k332/1984, k374/2329/ k375/2331, k6923432, k6923433, k777/3690–3, k1080/1 3967, k 1326 4491 1076a–1092d, k1329 4515–4559,

k1386 4784/1169a–f, k1388/4814/1183a–bc, k1389 4824/1185b, k1393/4843/
1190–1, k1399/4860/1191h, k1478/6328/1702g, 1489/6436/503x, k1493/
6468/507g, k 1495/6497/520b, k1496/6513/530b, k1497/6526/544, k1508/
6648/1027d

Landesamt Ansbach, Verzeichnis, 212/1/III at the Staatsarchiv

153/28–33, 1676/167/1, 28, 30, 32–33, 1755/191/11, 1937/215/11, 2003/221/
1, 11, 2017/224/32, 2146/246/26, 2211/253/1–11, 2212/254/1–9, 2213/255/1–
7, 2214/256/1–17, 2221/253, 2316/269, 2321/271/1, 3208/364/2, 3214/364/
10, 3215/364/10, 3220/368/2,4184/428/2, 4162/426/30, 4409/455/29, 4415/
455

Staatliches Archiv Göttingen

Staatsarchiv Würzburg

Reg. von Unterfranken, 2950, 13353, 13384, 13388

Stadtarchiv Nürnberg

Verwaltungsberichte der Stadt Nürnberg, "Chronik der Stadt Nürnberg,
1930–1932," Frauenorden, N.S. Frauenschaft, Muttertag, Juden, and
"Kongress des Sieges" (1933)

Stadtarchiv München

Soziale Vereine, 470, 898, 1070, 1103, 1105, 1498, 1612, 710/5–6

Libraries

Bibliothèque de documentation internationale contemporaine, Nanterre
(BDIC)
Bobst Library, New York University
Centre de documentation Juives, Paris
Deutsches Zentralarchiv für soziale Fragen, Berlin
Erzbischöfliches Ordinariat Archiv, i.d. Carmiliten Kirche, Munich
Fachhochschule Caritas-Bibliothek, Freiburg, i.Br.
Germanica Judaica, Cologne
Historische Kommission, Berlin
Institute of Social History, Amsterdam
Institut für Zeitgeschichte, Munich
Leo Baeck Institute Library, New York
New York Public Library
Staatsbibliothek, Munich
Staatsbibliothek, Berlin
Verband Weibliche Angestellte, e.V. Library, Berlin
Weidener Library, Harvard University

Primary Sources
Books Published Before 1945, Memoirs, Oral Histories,
Document Collections

Abel, Theodore. *Why Hitler Came to Power: An Answer Based on the Original Life Stories of 600 of his Followers.* New York: Prentice-Hall, 1938.

Allen, William Sheridan, ed. *The Infancy of Nazism. The Memoirs of ex-Gauleiter Albert Krebs, 1923–1933.* New York and London: Franklin Watts, 1976.

Andreas-Friedrich, Ruth. *The Berlin Underground, 1938–1945,* trans. Barrows-Mussey. New York: Holt, 1947. Originally published as *Der Schattenmann. Tagebuch.* Berlin: Suhrkamp, 1947.

Augspurg, Anita, and Lida Gustava Heymann. *Erlebtes Erschautes. Heymann Memoiren,* ed. Margit Tellmann. Meisenheim am Glan, 1972.

Barrett, Michele, ed. *Virginia Woolf, Women and Writing.* New York: Harcourt, Brace and Jovanovich, 1979.

Baum, Marie. *Rückblick auf mein Leben.* Heidelberg: Kerle, 1950.

Baum, Vicki. *Es war alles ganz anders. Erinnerungen.* Berlin: Ullstein, 1962.

Bäumer, Gertrud. *Die Frau im deutschen Staat.* Berlin: Junker und Dünnhaupt, 1932.

———. "Die Frau in der Gemeinde," *Die Frau* 55:1. January 15, 1920.

———. *Der neue Weg der deutschen Frau.* Stuttgart: Deutsche Verlags-Anstalt, 1946.

———. *Des Lebens wie der liebe Band.* Tübingen: Wunderlich, 1956.

Baumgart, Gertrud. *Frauenbewegung: Gestern und Heute.* Heidelberg, 1933.

Baynes, Norman. ed. *The Speeches of Adolf Hitler.* 2 vols. New York: Fertig, 1969.

BDM, ed. *Das war unser Anfang. Aus den Jahren des Kampfes und des Aufbaues des Berliner BDM.* Berlin: Obergau Berlin, n.d.

Beeking, Joseph. *Die katholische Frau im Lebensraum von Familie, Volk und Kirche.* Freiburg i.Br.: Jugendwohl, 1934.

Behrend-Rosenfeld, Else. *Ich stand nicht allein: Erlebine einer Jüdin in Deutschland.* Hamburg: Europäische, 1945.

Beyer, Hans. *Die Frau in der politischen Entscheidung.* Stuttgart: Enke, 1933.

Beyer, Hans. *Die Ebenbürtigkeit der Frau im Nationalsozialistische Deutschland.* Leipzig: Armanen, 1932.

Bielenberg, Cristabel. *The Past Is Myself.* London: Chatto and Windus, 1968.

Boberach, Heinz, ed. *Meldungen aus dem Reich. Auswahl aus der Geheimen Lageberichten des Sicherheitsdienst der SS.* Neuwied and Düsseldorf: Luchterhand, 1965.

Boberach, Heinz. *Berichte des S.D. und der Gestapo über Kirchen und Kirchenvolk in Deutschland. 1933–1944.* Mainz: Grünewald, 1971.

Boehm, Eric. *We Survived. The Stories of the Hidden and the Hunted.* New Haven: Yale University Press, 1949.

Bohn, Willi, ed. *Stuttgart geheim! Ein dokumentarischer Bericht.* Frankfurt: Röderberg, 1969.

Böök, Frederik. *An Eyewitness in Germany*, trans. E. Sprigge and C. Napier. London: Lovat Dicson, 1933.

Bosch, Elisabeth. *Die Katholiken und das Hakenkreuz*. Stuttgart: Allemann, 1938.

Braunias, Karl. *Das parlamentarische Wahlrecht*. I. Berlin and Leipzig: de Gruyter, 1932.

Braun, Bertha. *Die Frauenbewegung am Scheidewege*. Munich, 1932.

Brecht, Arnold. *Prelude to Silence. The End of the German Republic*. New York: Oxford University Press, 1944.

Breit, Ernst. *Das sittliche Verhältnis der Frau zur Eugenik*. Münster: Helios, 1932.

Browning, Hilde. *Women Under Fascism and Communism*. London: Lawrence, n.d.

Broszat, Martin, Elke Frölich and Falk Wiesemann, eds. *Bayern in der NS Zeit. Soziale Lage und politisches Verhalten der Bevölkerung im Spiegel vertraulichen Berichte*. 2 vols. Munich: Oldenbourg, 1977.

Buber-Neumann, Margarete. *Die erloschende Flamme. Schicksale meiner Zeit*. Munich: Müller, 1976.

———. *Milena. Kafkas Freundin*. Munich: Wilhelm Heyne, 1977.

Buch, Walter. *Niedergang und Aufsteig der deutschen Familie*. Munich: Eher, 1934.

Buck, Pearl. *How It Happens. A Talk About the German People. 1914–1933*. New York: Doubleday, 1947.

Bürkner, Trude. *Der BDM in der HJ*. Berlin: Juncker and Dünnhaupt, 1937.

Buresch-Riebe, Ilse. *Frauenleistung im Krieg*. Berlin: Eher, 1941.

Burgdorfer, Friedrich. *Bevölkerungsentwicklung im Dritten Reich*. Berlin and Heidelberg: Vowinckel, 1935.

Camus, Albert. *The Rebel. An Essay on Man in Revolt*. New York: Vintage, 1956.

Comité des Délégations Juives, Paris 1934. *Die Lage der Juden in Deutschland. 1933. Das Schwarzbuch—Tatsachen und Dokumente*. Reprint. Frankfurt: Ullstein, 1983.

Deutsch, Regine. ed. *Politische Frauenarbeit*. 2nd ed. Gotha: Perthes, 1924.

Deutscher Textilarbeiter-Verband. *Mein Arbeitstag. Mein Wochenende. 150 Berichte von Textilarbeiterinnen*. Berlin: Textilpraxis, 1930.

Deutschland Berichte der SOPADE. Mimeographed reports. Social Democratic Party in Paris, 1933–1939.

Diehl, Guida. *Christ sein heisst Kämpfer sein: Die Führung meines Lebens*. Giessen: Brunnen, 1960.

———. *Die deutsche Frau und der Nationalsozialismus*. 5th ed. Eisenach: Neuland, 1933.

———. *Erlösung vom Wirrwahn wider Dr. Mathilde Ludendorff und Ihr Buch, Erlösung von Jesu Christo*. Eisenach: Neuland, 1931.

Diehls, Rudolf. *Lucifer ante portas*. Zurich: Internaverlag, 1969.

Diers, Marie. *Die deutsche Frauenfrage in ihrem Zusammenhang mit Geschichte, Volkswirtschaft, und Politik*. Potsdam: Stiftungs-Verlag, 1920.

————. *Freiheit und Brot! Der Roman einer Arbeiterfamilie.* Berlin: Nationaler Freiheits Verlag, 1933.

Deutschkron, Inge. *Ich trug den gelben Stern.* Cologne: Verlag Wissenschaft und Politik, 1980.

Diner, Helen (E. Eckstein). *Mothers and Amazons. The First Feminine History of Culture.* New York: Julian, 1965.

Domarus, Max, ed. *Hitler. Reden und Prolkamationen. 1932–1945.* Munich: Süddeutscher Verlag, 1965.

Dornemann, Louise. *German Women under Fascism: A Brief Survey of the Position of German Women up to the Present Day.* London: Allies Inside Germany, 1943, mimeograph.

Dransfeld, Helene. *Eintritt der katholischen Frau in die Politik.* Freiburg: Caritas, 1919.

Duel, Wallace R. *People Under Hitler.* New York: Harcourt, Brace & Co., 1942.

Düvert, Helene. *Die Frau von Heute. Ihr Weg und Ziel.* Berlin and Gütersloh: C. Bartelsmann, 1933.

Eberhard, E. F. W. *Feminismus und Kulturuntergang: Die Erotische Grundlagen der Frauenemanzipation.* 2nd ed. Vienna and Leipzig: Braunmüller, 1927.

Ehrenburg, Ilya. *Memoirs: 1921–1941,* trans. Tatiana Shebunina with Yvonne Kapp. Cleveland and New York: World, 1963.

Ehrle, Gertrud. *Leben spricht zu Leben. Wirklichkeitsbilder aus dem Alltag der Frau.* Freiburg: Herder, 1937.

————, ed. *Licht über dem Abgrund. Zeichnungen und Erlebnisse Christlicher Frauen. 1933–1945.* Freiburg: Herder, 1951.

Engfer, Hermann, ed., *Das Bistum Hildesheim. 1933–1945. Eine Dokumentation.* Hildesheim: A. Lax, 1971.

Faulhaber, Michael. *Judentum, Christentum, Germanentum.* Munich: Huber, 1934. English ed. *Judaism, Christianity and Germany,* trans. George D. Smith. New York: Macmillan, 1934.

Fénélon, Fania. *Playing for Time.* New York: Atheneum, 1977.

Finckh, Renate. *Mit uns zieht die neue Zeit.* Baden: Braun, 1979.

François-Poncet. *The Fateful Years. Memoirs of a French Ambassador, 1931–1938,* trans. Jacques le Clercq. New York: Harcourt Brace, 1949.

Frank, Hans. *Im Angesicht des Galgens* Munich: Beck, 1953.

Frankel, Viktor. *Man's Search for Meaning,* trans. Ilse Lasch, Preface by Gordon W. Allport. New York: Simon and Schuster, 1962.

Frauen unter Faschisten Terror! Frauen in der solidaritäts und Kampffront. Zurich and Paris: MOPR, 1934.

Friedländer, Vera. *Späte Notizen.* Berlin: Neues Leben, 1982.

Fromm, Bella. *Blood and Banquets. A Berlin Social Diary.* New York and London: Harper and Row, 1942.

Fromm, Erich. *Arbeiter und Angestellte am Vorabend des Dritten Reiches.* Part of the series edited by Max Horkheimer, Institut für Sozialforschung, *Studien über Autorität.* Paris: Alcan, 1936. English: *The Working Class in Weimar Germany: A Psychological and Sociological Study.* Trans. Barbara

Weinberger, ed. Wolfang Bonss. Cambridge, Massachusetts: Harvard University Press, 1984.

Frühauf, Ludwig. *Deutsches Frauentum. Deutsche Mütter.* Hamburg: Hanseatisch, 1935.

Garlinski, Joseph. *Fighting Auschwitz.* New York: Fawcett, 1975.

German League of Culture. *Women under the Swastika.* London: December 1942.

Gersdorff, Ursula von, ed. *Frauen im Kriegsdienst.* Stuttgart: Deutsche, 1969.

Glass-Lasson, Margarete. *Ich Will Reden.* Vienna: Molden, 1982.

Goebbels, Joseph. *Der Angriff: Aufsätze aus der Kampfzeit.* Munich: Zentralverlag der NSDAP, 1933. 2 vols.

————. *Michael: Ein deutsches Schicksal in Tagebuchblättern.* Munich: Eher, 1929.

————. *Revolution der Deutschen. 14 Jahre Nationalsozialismus.* Oldenbourg: Stalling, 1933.

Goebbels, Magda Ritschel. *Die Deutsche Mütter. Rede zum Muttertag.* May 14, 1933. Heilbronn: E. Salzer, 1933.

Gollwitzer, Heinz, Käthe Kuhn, and Reinhold Schneider, eds. *Dying We Live. The Last Messages of the Men and Women Who Resisted Hitler and Were Martyred.* New York: Seabury, 1968.

Göring, Emmy. *An der Seite meines Mannes. Begebenheiten und Bekenntnisse.* Göttingen: Stütz, 1974. English ed., *My Life with Goering.* London: David Bruce and Watson, 1972.

Gottschewski, Lydia. "Die Frauenbewegung und Wir," Hectograph. n.d.

————. *Männerbund und Frauenfrage.* Munich: Lehmann, 1934.

Gröber, Conrad. *Chrisus und die Frauen. Alte Wahrheiten für die neue Zeit.* Freiburg i.Br.: Herde, 1935.

————. *Handbuch der Religiösen Gegenwartsfragen.* Freiburg i.B., 1937.

Grosz, Georg. *A Little Yes and a Big NO,* trans. L. S. Dorin. New York: Dial, 1946.

Gross, Walter. *Nationalsozialistische Rassenpolitik. Eine Rede an die deutschen Frauen.* Dessau: Dünnhaupt, n.d. (1934?).

Grotjahn, Albert. *Erlebtes und Erstrebtes. Erinnerung eines sozialistischen Arztes.* Berlin: Herbig, 1932.

Grüber, Heinrich. *Erinnerungen an sieben Jahrzehnten.* Cologne: Kiepenheuer & Witsch, 1968.

Guirdham, A. *Revolt Against Pity: An Indictment of the Nazi Martyrdom of Women.* London: Crowther, 1943.

Gumbel, Emil J. *Vier Jahre politischer Mord.* Berlin-Fichtenau: Neue Gesellschaft, 1922.

Haag, Lina. *Ein Handvoll Staub.* Halle Saale: Mitteldeutscher, 1948.

Haas, Hilde. *Ich war Arbeitsmaid im Kriege.* Leipzig: Aufbau/Heinig, 1941.

Hadeln, Charlotte von. *Deutsche Frauen. Deutsche Treue.* Berlin: KdK, 1935.

Hagemeyer, Hans. *Frau und Mutter. Lebensquelle des Volkes.* Munich: Hoheneichen, 1942.

Hamann, J. A. *Ein Wort gegen die überlässige Verehrlichung und Verweichlichung des weiblichen Geschlechts.* Riga: Privat, 1925.

Handke, Peter. *Wunschloses Ungluck.* Frankfurt: Suhrkamp, 1972.

Harmsen, Hans. *Die uneheliche Mutter als beschränkte einsatzfänhige Arbeitskraft.* n.p., 1938.

———. *Praktische Bevölkerungspolitik.* Berlin: Juncker & Dünnhaupt, 1931.

Hasselblatt, Dora, ed. *Wir Frauen und die nationale Bewegung.* Hamburg, 1934.

Helmut, Otto. *Volk in Gefahr. Der Geburtneruckgang und seine Folgen dür Deutschlands Zukunft.* Munich: Lehmanns, 1933.

Hermenau, Hans. *Vom Werk zum Ziel.* Pamphlet. 1933.

Herz, Heinz. *Über das Wesen und die Aufgaben der politischen Statistik.* Waldenburg/Saxony: E. Kastner, 1932.

Heuss-Knapp, Elly. *Ein Leben in Briefen und Aufzeichnungen,* ed. M. Vater. Tübingen: Rainer Wunderlich, 1961.

Hieber, Helmut, ed. *The Early Goebbels Diaries,* trans. Oliver Watson. London: Weidenfeld and Nicolson, 1962.

Hierl, Konstantin. *Im Dienst für Deutschland. 1918–1945.* Heidelberg: Vowinckel, 1954.

Himmler, Heinrich. Bradley Smith and Agnes Peterson, eds. *Himmler. Geheimreden, 1933 bis 1945.* Frankfurt, Propyläen, 1974.

Hitler, Adolf. *Mein Kampf,* trans. Ralph Mannheim. Boston: Houghton-Mifflin, 1962.

Hoess, Rudolf, *Commandant of Auschwitz: Autobiography of Rudolf Hoess.* New York: Popular Library. 1964.

Hofer, Walter, ed. *Der Nationalsozialismus. Dokumente. 1933–1945.* Frankfurt: Fischer, 1957.

Hoffmann, Heinrich. *Hitler Was My Friend,* trans. R. H. Stevens. London: Burke, 1955.

Hofstätter, Richard. *Die Arbeitende Frau. Ihre wirtschaftliche Lage.* Vienna and Leipzig: Perles, 1929.

Hoover, Calvin B. *Germany Enters the Third Reich.* New York: n.p., 1933.

Hopmann, Antonie, Luise Bardewer and Anne Franken. *Die katholische Frau der Zeit.* Düsseldorf: Schwann, 1931.

Horst, Max und Richard Hebig, eds., *Volk im Glauben. Ein Buch vom deutschen Christen.* Berlin: Schmid, 1933.

Howe, Hans Ulrich. *Die berufstätige Frau als Verkaufsangestellte: Ein Beitrag zur Handelsgewerblichen Frauenarbeitsfrage.* Ph. D. dissertation. Kiel, 1930.

Hussong, Friedrich. *Kurfürstendammn. Zur Kulturgeschichte des Zwischenreiches.* Berlin: Scherl, 1933.

Imsel, Hans Ulrich. "Indikation und Technik der Sterilisierung des Weibes." Giesen: Ph.D. Dissertation, 1933.

Isherwood, Christopher. *Down There on a Visit.* New York: Simon and Schuster, 1962.

Jacobs, Annemarie. *Hinter den Zeilen.* Halle Saale: Mitteldeutscher, 1959.

Jahoda, Maria, Paul F. Lazarsfeld, Hans Zeisel. *Marienthal. The Sociography of an Unemployed Community.* New York and Chicago: Aldine, 1971. Originally published as *Die Arbeitslosen von Marienthal.* Leipzig: S. Hirzel, 1933.

Jaspers, Karl, *The Question of German Guilt*, trans. E. B. Ashton. New York: Dial, 1947.

Jung, Edgar. *Die Herrschaft der Minderwertigen.* Berlin: Verlag der deutschen Rundschau, 1930.

Jünger, Ernst. *Storm of Steel. From the Diary of a German Storm-Troop Officer on the Western Front*, intro. R. H. Mottram. New York: Fertig, 1975.

Karminski, Hannah. "Zum 30. Jährigen Bestehen des Isenburger Heims." n.p., 1937.

Kent, Madeline. *I Married a German.* London: Allen and Unwin, n.d.

Kessler, Harry. *The Diaries of a Cosmopolitan*, trans. Charles Kessler. London: Weidenfeld and Nicolson, 1971.

————. *In the Twenties. The Diaries of Harry Kessler.* Trans. Charles Kessler. New York: Holt, Rinehart & Winston, 1961.

Kerschbaumer, Marie-Therese. *Der weibliche Name des Widerstands. Sieben Berichte.* Munich: Deutscher Taschenbuch, 1982.

Keun, Irmgard. *Gilgi. Eine von uns.* Berlin: Claassen, 1979. Originally printed in 1931.

————. *Das Kunstseidene Mädchen.* Düsseldorf: Claassen, 1979.

————. *Nach Mitternacht.* Düsseldorf: Claassen, 1980.

Kiaulehn, W. *Berlin: Schicksal einer Weltstadt.* Munich: Biederstein, 1958.

Kirkpatrick, Clifford. *Nazi Germany: Its Women and Its Family Life.* New York and Indianapolis: Bobbs-Merrill, 1938.

Klaje-Wenzel, Dorothea. *Die Frau in der Volksgemeinschaft.* Leipzig: A. Klein, 1934.

Klucsarits, Richard and Friedrich Kürbisch, eds. *Arbeiterinnen kämpfen um ihre Rechte. Autobiographische Texte zum Kampf.* Wuppertal: Peter Hammer, 1981.

Klausener, Erich. *Frauen im Fesseln. Erinnerungen einer Berliner Gefängnisfürsorgerin. 1933–1945.* Berlin: Morus, 1962.

Kleinschmidt, Otto. *Blut und Rasse. Die Stellung des evangelischen Christen zu den Forderungen der Eugenik.* Berlin: Warnecke, 1933.

Knickerbocker, H. R. *The German Crisis.* New York: Farrar and Rinehart, 1932.

Koepcke, Cordula, ed. *Frauen im Wehrdienst. Erinnerungen von Ingeborg Hecht, Ruth Henry, Christa Meves.* Freiburg im Br.: Herder, 1982.

Köhler-Irgang, Ruth. *Die Sendung der Frau in der deutschen Geschichte.* Leipzig: Hase & Koehler, 1942.

Köhn, Ilse. *Mischling, Second Degree: My Childhood in Nazi Germany.* New York: Greenwillow, 1977.

Kolb, Annette. *Das Exemplar.* Frankfurt: Fischer, 1922.

Krausnick, Helmut and Hildegard von Kotze, eds. aided by F. A. Krummacher. *Es spricht der Führer.* Gütersloh: Mohn, 1966.

Krieger, Ruth. *Deutsche Mädel im Osten*. Berlin-Lichterfelde: Junge Generation, 1940.

Krineger-Fischer, Eva. *Die Frau als Richterin über Leben und Tod ihres Volkes*. Berlin: Reichsausschusses für Volksgesundheit, 1935.

Kuhn, Annette, and Gerhard Schneider, eds. *Frauen in der Geschichte*. Düsseldorf: Schwann, 1979.

Kuhn, Annette and Valentine Rothe, eds. *Frauen in deutschen Faschismus*. 2 vols. Düsseldorf: Schwann, 1982.

Kuckhoff, Greta. *Von Rosenkranz zur Roten Kapelle: Ein Lebensbericht*. Berlin: Neues Leben, 1972.

Kutzleb, Juelmar. *Mord an der Zukunft*. Berlin: Widerstandsverlag, 1930.

Lane, Ann, ed. *Mary Ritter Beard: A Source Book*. New York: Schocken, 1967.

Lauer, Amalie. *Die Frau in der Auffassung des Nationalsozialismus*. Cologne: Görreshaus, 1932.

Lanzmann, Claude, *Shoah: An Oral History of the Holocaust*, intro. S. de Beauvoir, New York: Pantheon, 1986.

Laska, Vera. *Nazism, Resistance, and Holocaust in W. W. II. A Bibliography*. Westport: Greenwood, 1982.

———. *Women in the Resistance and Holocaust*. Westport: Greenwood, 1983.

Lengyel, Olga. *Five Chimneys: The Story of Auschwitz*. trans. Paul P. Weiss. London: Mayflower, 1972.

Levy-Haas, Hannah. *Inside Belsen*, trans. Ronald Taylor, intro. Jane Caplan. Totowa, New Jersey: Barnes & Noble, 1982.

Ley, Robert. *Parteistatistik. Nationalsozialistisches Jahrbuch*. Annual statistical summary, 1927–1944. Munich: Zentralverlag der NSDAP.

Litten, Irmgard. *A Mother Fights Hitler*. London: Allen and Unwin, 1940.

Lochner, Louis. *What About Germany?*. New York: Dodd, Mead, 1942.

Lochner, Louis, ed. *The Goebbels Diaries, 1939–1941*, trans. Fred Taylor New York: Penguin, 1984.

Loos, Anita. *A Girl Like I*. New York: Viking, 1956.

Lorenz, Charlotte. *Die Gewerbliche Während des Krieges*. Vol. 6, James Shotwell, ed. *Wirtschaft- und Sozialgeschichte*. Stuttgart & Berlin: Deutsche, 1928.

Lortz, Joseph. *Katholischer Zugang zum Nationalsozialismus, kirchlichgeschichtlich gesehen*. Munich: Aschendorff, 1934.

Lüders, Marie-Elisabeth. *Fürchte Dich Nicht. Persönliches und Politisches aus mehr als 80 Jahren, 1878–1962*. Cologne: Westdeutscher Verlag, 1963.

Lüdy, Elisabeth. *Erwerbstätige Mütter in Vaterlosen Familien*. Berlin: Müller, 1932.

MacFarland, Charles S. *The New Church and the New Germany*. New York: Macmillan, 1934.

Mann, Erika. *School for Barbarians*. New York: Putnam's, 1938.

——— and Klaus Mann. *Escape to Life*. Boston: Houghton-Mifflin, 1939.

Mann, Klaus. *Mephisto*, trans. Robin Smyth. New York: Penguin, 1983.

———. *Turning Point. 25 Years in the Century*. London: Fischer, 1942.

Manowitz, Rosalyn. *Reflections on the Holocaust*. Washington Heights, New York: Hebrew Tabernacle, 1978.

Maschmann, Melita. *Account Rendered. A Dossier of My Former Self*, trans. Geoffrey Strachan. London: Abelard-Schumann, 1965.

Maser, Werner, ed. *Hitler's Letters and Notes*. New York: Harper & Row, 1974.

Mayer, A. *Gedanken zur modernen Sexual Moral*. Stuttgart: F. Enke, 1930.

Meed, Vlada. *On Both Sides of the Wall. Memoirs from the Warsaw Ghetto*. New York: Ghetto Fighters, 1972.

Meister, Angela. *Die deutschen Industriearbeiterinnen*. Ph.D. dissertation. Jena, 1939.

Menzerath, Magda. *Kampffeld Heimat. Deutsche Frauenleistung im Kriege*. Stuttgart: Allemann, 1941.

Moeckl, Marka. *Hitlermädel kämpfen um Berlin. Eine Erzählung aus der Kampfzeit*. Stuttgart: Union, 1936.

Moers, Martha. *Der Fraueneinsatz in der Industrie*. Berlin: Duncker und Humblot, 1943.

Munske, Hilde, ed., *Mädel. Eure Welt! das Jahrbuch der deutschen Mädel*. Munich: Eher, 1944.

Niemeyer, Annemarie. *Zur Struktur der Familie. Statistische Materialen*. Berlin: Herbig, 1931.

Noakes, Jeremy and Geoffrey Pridham, eds. *Documents of Nazism: 1919–1945*. New York: Viking, 1974.

Nyiszli, Miklos. *Auschwitz: A Doctor's Eyewitness Account*. Trans. T. Kremer and R. Seaver, Foreword by Bruno Bettelheim. Greenwich, Connecticut: Fawcett Crest, 1960.

Orlow, Dietrich. *The History of the Nazi Party. 1919–1933*. Pittsburgh: University of Pittsburgh Press, 1969.

Paepke, Lotte. *Ich wurde vergessen. Bericht einer Judin, die das Dritte Reich überlebte*. Freiburg I. Br.: Herder, 1979.

Papen, Franz. *Appell an das deutsche Gewissen. Reden zur nationalen Revolution*. Oldenbourg: Stalling, 1933.

Passow, Hildegard. *Der Baumeister des neuen Reiches*. Pamphlet.

———. *Geschichte, Blut und Boden*. Pamphlet.

Picker, Henry, *Hitlers Tischgespräche im Führerhauptquartier*. Stuttgart: Seewald, 1976.

Peikow, Richard. *Die soziale und wirtschaftliche Stellung der deutschen Frau in der Gegenwart*. Berlin: Hoffmann, 1937.

Pfaume, Eberhard, et al. *Frauen im Industriebetrieb. Einsatz-Schulung-Leistung*. Berlin: Elsner, 1941. Part of a Series: Reichsausschusses für Leistungssteigerung.

Pikarski, Margot. *Der Antifascischistische Widerstandskampf der KPD im Spiegel des Flugblattes. 1933–1945*. Berlin: Dietz, 1978.

———. *Die KPD lebt! Flugblätter aus dem antifaschistischen Widerstandskampf der KPD*. Berlin: Cietz, 1980.

———. *Jugend im Berliner Widerstand: Herbert Baum und Kampfgefahrten*. Berlin: VEB, 1978.

———. *Sie bleiben unvergessen*. n.p., n.d.

Protokol der Reichs-Frauen-Konferenz der USPD Berlin. Berlin: "Freiheit," n.d.

Puckett, Hugh Wiley. *Germany's Women Go Forward*. New York: Columbia University, 1930.

Rauschning, Hermann. *The Voice of Destruction*. New York: Putnam, 1940.

———. *Hitler Speaks*. London: Thornton Butterworth, 1939.

———. *Political Conversations with Adolf Hitler on His Real Aims*. London: Gollancz, 1939.

Reber-Gruber, Auguste. *Weibliche Erziehung im NSLB*. Leipzig and Berlin: Teubner, 1934.

Rees, Hanna. *Frauenarbeit in der NS-Volkswohlfart*. Berlin: NSDAP, 1938.

Reichenau, Irmgard, ed. *Deutsche Frauen an Adolf Hitler*. 3rd edition. Leipzig: A. Klein, 1933.

Reinhardt, Lore. *Die deutsche Frau als Quelle völkischer Kraft und sittliche Gesundung. Ein Beitrag zur Prägung eines neuen Frauentypes*. Leipzig: Klein, 1934.

Reichorganisationsleiter der NSDAP. *Die Front der Frauen*. Munich: Reichsdruckerei, 1942.

Remarque, Erich Maria. *All Quiet on the Western Front*. New York: Fawcett Crest, 1956.

Richarcz, Monika. *Jüdisches Leben in Deutschland III, Selbstzeugnisse zur Sozialgeschichte 1918–1945*. Stuttgart: Deutsches, 1982.

Ringelheim, Joan and Esther Katz, eds. *Women Surviving the Holocaust*. New York: Institute for Research in History, 1983.

Rinser, Luise. *Gefängnis Tagebuch*. Munich: Zinnen, 1946.

Ritter, Reinhard. *Die geschlechtliche Frage in der deutschen Volkserziehung*. Berlin and Cologne: A. Marcus und E. Weber, 1936.

Rogge, Pia Sophie. *Die deutschnationale Frau*. Pamphlet. January 1922.

———. *An geweihten Brunnen. Die deutsche Frauenbewegung im Lichte des Rassegedankens*. Munich: n.p., 1933.

Rogge-Börner, Pia Sophie. *Zurück zum Mutterrecht? Studie zu Professor Ernst Bergmann, "Erkenntnisgeist und Muttergeist."* Leipzig: Klein, 1932.

Rompel, Josef. *Die Frau im Lebensraum des Mannes*. Darmstadt: Hofman, n.d.

Rosenberg, Alfred. *Das Mythus des 20. Jahrhunderts. Eine Wertung der seelisch-geistigen Gestalten und Kämpfe unsere Zeit*. 4th ed. Munich: Hoheneichen, 1934.

Rühle-Gerstel, Alice. *Das Frauenproblem der Gegenwart*. Leipzig: Hirzel, 1932.

Salomon, Alice. "Character Is Destiny." Undated, typed manuscript in the Leo Baeck Institute, Alice Salomon Collection, AR 3875.

Salomon, Charlotte. *A Diary in Pictures*. New York: Harcourt Brace, 1983.

Scheffen-Döring, Luise. *Die Frau von Heute. Frauengedanken zur Sexualethik und Bevölkerungspolitik*. Leipzig: Quelle und Meyer, 1929.

Schemm, Hans. *Mutter oder Genossin? Der rote Krieg*. Bayreuth: NS Kultur, 1931.

Schickedanz, Margarethe. *Deutsche Frau und Deutsche Not im Weltkrieg*. Leipzig and Berlin: Teubner, 1938.

Schirach, Henriette. *Frauen um Hitler*. Berlin: Herbig, 1983.

Schmidt, Werner. *Die Erwerbstätigkeit der verheiraten Frau*, Ph.D. Dissertation. Giessen, 1933.

Scholtz-Klink, Gertrud. *Die Frau im Dritten Reich*. Tübingen: Grabert, 1978.

———. Preface. *Frauen Helfen Siegen: Bilddokumente*. Berlin: Zeitgseschichte, n.d.

———, and Adolf Hitler. *Reden an die Deutsche Frau*. Reichsparteitag, Nuremberg, September 8, 1934.

Schücker, Anton. *Zur Psychopathologie der Frauenbewegung*. Leipzig: C. Kabitsch, 1931.

Schwartzhaupt, Elisabeth. *Was hat die Frau vom Nationalsozialismus zu erwarten?* Berlin: Erneuerung, 1932.

Schwelwitz-Ültzen, Anna-Lise. *Die Frau im neuen Deutschland*. Berlin: Staatspol, 1920. *Stenographische Berichte der Verhandlungen des Reichstages*.

Seldte, Franz. *Sozialpolitik im Dritten Reich*. Berlin: Reichsdruckerei, 1935.

Semmelroth, Ellen and Renate von Stieder, eds. *N. S. Frauenbuch*. Munich: Lehmann, 1934.

Sender, Toni. *The Autobiography of a German Rebel*. New York: Vanguard, 1939.

Senger, Valentin. *No. 12 Kaiserhofstrasse. The Story of an Invisible Jew in Nazi Germany*, trans. Ralph Mannheim, New York: Dutton, 1980.

Seydewitz, Max. *Civil Life in Wartime Germany: The Story of the Homefront*. New York: Knopf, 1961.

Shirer, William. *Berlin Diary. The Journal of a Foreign Correspondent. 1934–1939*. New York: Knopf, 1961.

———. *The End of a Berlin Diary*. New York: Knopf, 1947.

Siber, Paula. *Die Frauenfrage und ihre Lösung durch den Nationalsozialismus*. Wolfenbüttel-Berlin: Kallmeyer, 1933.

———. *Um das Gewissen der deutschen Frau*. Munich: NSFS, Huber, n.d. (193?).

Smith, Bradley and Agnes Peterson, eds. *Himmler. Geheim Reden, 1933–1945*. Frankfurt: Propyläen, 1974.

SPD. *Nationalsozialismus und Frauenfragen: Material zur Information und Bekämpfung*. Berlin: February 1932. Pamphlet.

Speer, Albert. *Inside the Third Reich. Memoirs*. Trans. Richard and Clara Winston. New York: Macmillan, 1970.

Spender, Stephen. *World Within World. The Autobiography of Stephen Spender*. London: Hamish Hamilton, 1951.

Staritz, Katarina. *Das Grossen Lichtes Widerschein*. Berlin: Schmidt, 1967.

Stenographische Berichte der Verhandlungen des Reichstages.

Stockhorst, Erich. *Fünf Tausend Köpfe. Wer War Was im Dritten Reich*. Bruchsal: Blick und Bild, 1967.

Strasser, Gregor. *Kampf um Deutschland. Reden und Aufsätze eines Nationalsozialisten*. Munich: Eher Nachfolger, 1932.

———. *Der letzte Abwehrkampf des Systems. Drei aktuelle Aufsätze*. Munich: Eher, n.d.

Straus, Rachel. *Wir lebten in Deutschland: Erinnerungen einer Deutscher Judin, 1880–1933*. Stuttgart: Deutsche Verlags-Anstalt, 1962.

Streiter, Gudrun. *Dem Tod so nah . . . Tagebuchblätter einer SA-Manns Braut*. Private, n.d.

Templewood, Lord Samuel (Hoare, J. G.), *Nine Troubled Years*. London: Collins, 1954.

Thomas, Katharine. *Women in Nazi Germany*. London: Gollancz, 1943.

Thompson, Dorothy. *I Saw Hitler*. New York: Farrar and Reinhart, 1932.

Tiling, Magda von, and Konrad Jarausch, eds. *Grundfragen pädagogischen Handelns. Beiträge zur neuen Erziehung*. Stuttgart: 1934.

Tillich, Hannah. *From Time to Time*. New York: Stein and Day, 1973.

Toynbee, Arnold and Veronica. *Hitler's Europe*. London: Oxford University Press, 1954.

Trevor-Roper, Hugh, ed. *The Bormann Letters*, trans. R. H. Stevens. London: Weidenfeld and Nicolson, 1954.

———., ed. *Hitler's Secret Conversations*. New York: Octagon, 1961.

Tremel-Eggert, Kuni. *Barb*. Munich: Eher, 1934.

Trials of War Criminals before the Nürnberg Military Tribunals. Nuremberg, October 1946–April 1949. 15 vols. United States Government Printing Office.

Ulich-Beil, Else. *Ich ging mein Weg*. Berlin-Grünewald: Herbig, 1961.

Union für Recht und Freiheit. *Deutsche Frauenschicksale*. London: Malik, 1937.

Unser Kampf. 200 Beispiele aus dem anti-Faschistischen Kampf in Deutschland. Prague: Altricht, n.d.

Unverricht, Elizabeth. *Unsere Zeit und Wir. Das Buch der deutschen Frau*. Munich: Berg, 1932.

Vaerting, Mathilde. *Die weibliche Eigenart in Männerstadt und die männliche Eigenart im Frauenstaat*. Karlsruhe: Braun, 1921.

Vonschott, Hedwig, ed. *Frauenbildung, Frauenberufe*. Freiburg i. Br.: Herder, 1933.

Weber, Marianne. *Lebenserinnerungen*. Bremen: Storm, 1948.

Weil, Simone. *Ecrits historiques et politiques*. Paris: Gallimard, 1960.

Weinstock, Eugene. *Beyond the Last Path*. Foreword by Emil Lengyel. New York: Boni and Gaer, 1967.

Wellmann, Eva Maria Wisser. *Kämpfen und Glauben: aus dem Leben eines Hitler Mädels*. Berlin: Steuben, 1933.

Wells, H. G. *Experiment on Autobiography*. New York: Macmillan, 1934.

Wheeler-Bennett, ed. *Documents on International Affairs*. London: Oxford University Press, 1934.

Wilkinson, Ellen. *The Terror in Germany*. London: British Committee for the Relief of the Victims of German Fascism, 1934.

Wippermann, Wolfgang. *Die Berliner Gruppe Baum und der jüdische Widerstand*. Berlin, n.p., n.d.

Wolf, Christa. *A Model Childhood*. Trans. Ursula Molinaro and Hedwig Rappolt. New York: Farrar, Straus and Giroux, 1980.

Wolf, Lore. *Ein Leben ist viel zu wenig*. Frankfurt: Röderberg, 1974.

Wolff, Klara. *Die deutsche Frau im Wandel der Zeiten.* Halle: Schröder, 1936.

Zahn-Harnack, Agnes von. *Die Frauenbewegung: Geschichte, Probleme, Ziele.* Berlin: Das Deutsche Buch, 1928.

———. *Reden und Aufsätze.* Stuttgart: C. Scheufle, Universität Stuttgart.

———. *Wandlungen des Frauenlebens vom 18. Jahrhundert bis zur Gegenwart.* Berlin and Hannover: Schulz, 1951.

Zepler, Wally. ed. *Sozialismus und Frauenfrage.* Berlin: Cassirer, 1919.

Zuckmeyer, Carl. *Als wär's ein Stück von mir. Horen der Freundschaft.* Hamburg: S. Fischer, 1977.

Zuhlke, Anna. *Frauenaufgabe und Frauenarbeit im Dritten Reich. Bausteine zum neuen Staat und Volk.* Leipzig: Quelle and Meyer, 1934.

Züricher, Franz. *Kreuzzeug gegen des Christentums. Eine Dokumentensammlung.* Zurich: Internaverlag, 1938.

Secondary Sources
Books Published After 1945

Abraham, David. *The Collapse of the Weimar Republic. Political Economy in Crisis.* Princeton: Princeton University Press, 1981.

Adam, Dietrich Uwe. *Der Judenpolitik im Dritten Reich.* Düsseldorf: Droste, 1972.

Adler, H. G., *Theresienstadt. 1941–1945: Das Anlitz einer Zwangsgemeinschaft.* Tübingen: J. C. B. Mohr, 1955.

Adler, H. G., *Der Verwaltete Mensch. Studien zur Deportation der Juden aus Deutschland.* Tübingen: J. C. B. Mohr, 1979.

Ainsztein, Reuben. *Jewish Resistance in Nazi-Occupied Eastern Europe.* London: Paul Elek, 1974.

Allen, Ann Taylor. "Mothers of the New Generation: Adele Schreiber, Helene Stöcker, and the Evolution of a German Idea of Motherhood," *Signs* 20:3 (Spring 1985).

Allen, William Sheridan. *The Nazi Seizure of Power. The Experience of a Single German Town.* New York: Watts, 1984.

Arbeitsgemeinschaft sozialdemokratischer Frauen Karlsruhe. *Frauen berichten aus der Zeit des Nationalsozialismus.* Karlsruhe, n.p., 1983.

Ardner, Shirley. *Women and Space: Ground Rules and Social Maps.* New York: St. Martin's, 1981.

Arendt, Hannah. *Eichmann in Jerusalem. A Report on the Banality of Evil.* New York: Viking, 1964.

———. *The Origins of Totalitarianism.* New York and Cleveland: World, 1958.

Arendt, Hans Jürgen. "Die 'Gleichschaltung' der bürgerliche Frauenorganisationen in Deutschland 1933/34," *Zeitschrift für Geschichtswissenschaft.* 17 (July 1979), 615–627.

Ayçoberry, Pierre, *The Nazi Question* (New York: Pantheon, 1981).

Badia, Gilbert. *Exilés en France. Souvenirs d'antifascistes allemands émigrés.* *(1933–1945).* Paris: Maspero, 1982.

Baker, Leonard. *Days of Sorrow and Pain: Leo Baeck and Berlin Jews.* New York: Oxford University Press, 1978.

Bajohr, Stephen. *Die Hälfte der Fabrik.* Marburg: Verlag Arbeiterbewegung und Gesellschaftswissenschaften, 1979.

Banfield, Edward. *The Moral Basis of Backward Society.* Glencoe, Illinois: The Free Press, 1958.

Bauer, Jehuda. *The Holocaust in Historical Perspective.* Seattle: University of Washington, 1978.

Beard, Mary Ritter. *Woman as a Force in History. A Study in Traditions and Realities.* New York and London: Collier, 1971.

Benjamin, Jessica. "Authority and the Family Revisited. Or a World without Fathers," *New German Critique.* 1977, 36–57.

Berger, Peter. "On the Obsolescence of the Concept of Honor," *European Journal of Sociology* 11:2, 339–347.

Berghahn, Marion. *German-Jewish Refugees in England: The Ambiguities of Assimilation.* London: Macmillan, 1984.

Beyerchen, Alan D. *Scientists Under Hitler: Politics and the Physics Community.* New Haven: Yale, 1977.

Beuys, Barbara. *Familienleben in Deutschland.* Reinbeck bei Hamburg: Rowohlt, 1980.

Bernadac, Christian. *Le camp des femmes. Ravensbruck.* Paris: n.p., 1973.

Binion, Rudolph. *Hitler Among the Germans.* New York: Elsevier, 1976.

Bleuel, Hans Peter. *Sex and Society in Nazi Germany,* trans. J. M. Brownjohn. Philadelphia: Lippincott, 1973.

Bock, Gisela. *Zwangsterilisation in Nationalsozialismus. Untersuchungen zur Rassenpolitik und Frauenpolitik.* Berlin: Zentralinstitut für Sozialenwissenschaft, Freie Universität, 1985.

Bokolsky, Sidney. *The Distorted Image: German Jewish Perceptions and Germany.* New York: Elsevier, 1975.

Boveri, Margaret. *Treason in the Twentieth Century,* trans. Jon Steinberg. New York: Putnam's, 1963.

Bracher, Karl Dietrich. *Die deutsche Diktatur. Entstehung. Struktur. Folgen des Nationalsozialismus.* Cologne: Kiepenheuer & Witsch, 1969. English edition: *The German Dictatorship,* trans. Jean Steinberg, introduction Peter Gay. New York: Praeger, 1970.

Bremme, Gabrielle. *Die politische Rolle der Frau in Deutschland.* Göttingen: Van den Hoeck and Rüprecht, 1956.

Bretschneider, Heike. *Der Widerstand gegen den Nazismus in München, 1933–1945.* Munich: Neue Schriftenreihe des Stadtarchivs München. 1968.

Bridenthal, Renate, Atina Grossmann and Marion Kaplan, eds. *When Biology Became Destiny. Women in Weimar and Nazi Germany.* New York: Monthly Review, 1984.

Broszat, Martin. *The Hitler State. The Foundation and Development of the Internal Structure of the Third Reich,* trans. John W. Hidden. New York and London: Longman, 1981. Originally published as *Der Staat Hitlers*. Berlin: Deutscher Taschenbuch Verlag, 1980.

Bry, Gerard. *Wages in Germany*. Princeton: Princeton University Press, 1969.

Buchmann, Erika. "Frauen im Konzentrationslager." Stuttgart: Das Neue Wort, 1946. Mimeograph.

Bullock, Alan, *Hitler. A Study in Tyranny*. New York: Harper Torch, 1962.

Carroll, Bernice A. *Design for Total War: Arms and Economics in the Third Reich*. The Hague: Mouton, 1968.

——, ed. *Liberating Women's History*. Urbana: University of Illinois, 1976.

Chase, Allen, *The Legacy of Malthus. The Social Costs of the New Scientific Racism*. New York: Knopf, 1977.

Child, David. *Germany Since 1918*. New York: St. Martin's, 1980.

Childers, Thomas. *The Nazi Voter. The Social Foundations of Fascism in Germany, 1919–1933*. Chapel Hill: North Carolina University Press, 1983.

Cohn, Norman. *Warrant for Genocide. The Myth of the Jewish World Conspiracy*. Chico, California: Judaic Studies, 1981.

Conway, John. *The Nazi Persecution of the Churches, 1933–1945*. New York: Basic, 1968.

Davidowitz, Lucy. *The War Against the Jews*. New York: Bantam, 1975.

Davidson, Eugene. *The Trial of the Germans*. New York: Collier, 1966.

Deak, Istvan. *Weimar Germany's Left-Wing Intellectuals. A Political History of the "Weltbühne" and Its Critics*. Berkeley: University of California, 1968.

de Beauvoir, Simone. *The Second Sex*, trans. H. M. Parshley. New York: Bantam, 1961.

de Jonge, Alex. *The Weimar Chronicle*. New York: NAL, 1978.

Des Pres, Terrence. *The Survivor. An Anatomy of Life in the Death Camps*. New York: Oxford, 1976.

Dimsdale, Joel, *Survivors and Perpetrators*. Washington and London: Hemisphere, 1980.

Dobkowski, Martin and Isidor Walliman, eds, *Towards the Holocaust: The Social and Economic Collapse of the Weimar Republic*. Westport, Connecticut: Greenwood, 1983.

Drewitz, Ingeborg. *Die zestörte Kontinuität. Exilliteratur und Literatur des Widerstandes*. Vienna and Munich: Europa, 1981.

Ebermayer, Erich. *Die Gefährtin des Teufels*. Hamburg: Hoffman & Campe, 1952.

Eilerts, Rolf. *Die nationalpolitische Schulpolitik*. Cologne/Opladen: Westdeutscher Verlag, 1963.

Eley, Geoff, "What Produces Fascism: Preindustrial Traditions or a Crisis of the Capitalist State?" *Politics and Society* 12 (1983), 53–82.

Elling, Hannah. *Frauen im deutschen Widerstand. 1933–1945*. Frankfurt: Röderberg, 1981.

Engelmann, Suzanne Charlotte. *German Education and Re-Education*. New York: International University Press, 1945.

Evans, Richard. *The Feminist Movement in Germany, 1848–1933.* London and Beverly Hills: Sage, 1976.

Evans, Richard. "German Women and the Triumph of Hitler." *Journal of Modern History,* March 1976.

Fest, Joachim C. *Hitler,* trans. Richard and Clara Winston. New York: Vintage, 1975.

Fest, Joachim. *Das Gesicht des Dritten Reiches. Profile einer totalitären Herrschaft.* Munich: Piper, 1963. English trans. London: Weidenfeld and Nicolson, 1970.

Foot, M.D.R. *European Resistance to Nazism. 1940–1945.* New York: McGraw-Hill, 1977.

Frankel, Heinrich and Roger Manvell. *Himmler.* Frankfurt: Ullstein, 1965.

Franz-Willing, Georg. *Die Hitlerbewegung. Der Ursprung. 1919–1922.* Hamburg and Berlin: R. von Decker, 1962.

Frauengruppe Faschismus Forschung, ed. *Mutterkreuz und Arbeitsbuch.* Frankfurt: Fischer, 1981.

Friedländer, Saul. *Reflections on Nazism: An Essay on Kitsch and Death,* trans. Thomas Weyer. New York: Harper and Row, 1984.

Friedlander, Henry and Sybil Milton, *The Holocaust: Ideology, Bureaucracy, Genocide.* Millwood, New York: Kraus, 1980.

Friedlander, Judith, et al. *Women in Culture and Politics. A Century of Change.* Bloomington: Indiana University Press, 1986.

Friedrich, Otto. *Before the Deluge. A Portrait of Berlin in the 1920s.* New York: Harper & Row, 1972.

Gasman, Daniel. *The Scientific Origins of National Socialism.* New York: Elsevier, 1972.

Gay, Peter. *Weimar Culture.* New York: Harper & Row, 1968.

Gerhard, Ute. " 'Bis an die Wurzeln des Übels,' Rechtsgeschichte und Rechtskämpfe der Radikalen," *Feministische Studien* 1 (1984).

Gilbert, Sandra. "Soldier's Heart: Literary Men, Literary Women and the Great War," *Signs* 8:3 (Spring 1983).

Goode, William. *World Revolution in Family Patterns.* New York: Free Press, 1963.

Gordon, Sarah. *Hitler, Germans and the "Jewish Question."* Princeton: Princeton University Press, 1984.

Greven-Aschoff, Barbara. *Die bürgerliche Frauenbewegung in Deutschland. 1894–1933.* Göttingen: Van den Hoeck and Rüprecht, 1981.

Griffin, Susan. *Pornography and Silence.* New York: Harper and Row, 1981.

Grill, Johnpeter Horst. *The Nazi Movement in Baden.* Chapel Hill: University of North Carolina, 1983.

Gross, Leonard. *The Last Jews in Berlin.* New York: Simon and Schuster, 1982.

Grossmann, Atina. " 'The New Woman,' the New Family and the Rationalization of Sexuality." Ph.D. dissertation. Rutgers University. 1983.

Grossmann, Kurt R. *Die unbesungen Helden.* Berlin: Arani, 1961.

Grunberger, Richard. *The Twelve Year Reich.* New York: Ballantine, 1972.

Hackett, Amy Kathleen. "The Politics of Feminism in Wilhelmine Germany, 1890–1918," Ph.D. Dissertation, Columbia University, 1976.

Hallermund, Alice Platen. *Die Tötung der Geisteskranken in Deutschland.* Frankfurt a.M. 1948.

Hamilton, Richard. *Who Voted for Hitler?* Princeton: Princeton University Press, 1982.

Hammer, Walter. *Hohes Haus in Henkers Hand. Rückschau auf die Hitlerzeit auf Leidensweg und Opfergang deutscher Parlamentarier.* Frankfurt a.M.: Europäische, 1956.

Hausen, Karin, ed. *Frauen suchen ihre Geschichte. Historische Studien zum 19. und 20. Jahrhundert.* Munich: Beck, 1983.

Heer, Friedrich. *Der Glaube des Adolf Hitlers. Anatomie einer politischen Religiosität.* Munich and Esslingen: Bechtle, 1968.

Hehl, Ulrich von. *Katholische Kirche und Nationalsozialismus im Erzbistum Köln. 1933–1945.* Mainz: Grünewald, 1977.

Heiden, Konrad. *Der Führer: Hitler's Rise to Power.* Boston: Beacon, 1969.

Helmreich, Ernst Christian. *The German Churches under Hitler: Background, Struggle and Epilogue.* Detroit: Wayne State, 1979.

Henry, Frances. *Victims and Neighbors. A Small Town Remembered in Nazi Germany.* Northampton: Bergen and Garvey, 1984.

Herbstrith, Waltraud. *Edith Stein: A Biography.* Trans. Bernard Bonowitz. San Francisco: Harper and Row, 1985.

Hermand, Jost, "All Power to the Women: Nazi Concepts of Matriarchy," *Journal of Contemporary History.* 19:4 (October 1984).

Heyen, Franz. *Nationalsozialismus in Alltag.* Boppard: Bolt, 1967.

Hidden, John and John Farquharson. *Explaining Hitler's Germany. Historians and the Third Reich.* Totowa, New Jersey: Barnes & Noble, 1983.

Hilberg, Raul. *The Destruction of the European Jews.* Chicago: Quadrangle, 1961.

Hochmuth, Ursel and Gertrud Meyer. *Streiflichter aus dem Hamburger Widerstand, 1933–1945.* Frankfurt: M. Röderberg Verlag, 1969.

Hoffmann, Peter. *The History of the German Resistance, 1933–1945,* trans. Richard Barry. Cambridge, Massachusetts: MIT, 1977.

Höhne, Heinz. *Der Orden under dem Totenkopf.* Gütersloh: Mohn, 1963.

Holborn, Hajo. *A History of Modern Germany, 1840–1945.* New York: Knopf, 1969.

Jacobson, Hans Adolf. *Germans Against Hitler.* London: Huchinson, 1964.

Jasper, Gotthard. *Von Weimar zu Hitler.* Cologne: Kiepenheuer and Witsch, 1968.

Kaiser, Jochen-Christoph. *Frauen in der Kirche. Evangelische Frauenverbände in Spannungsfeld von Kirche und Gesellschaft 1890–1945.* Düsseldorf: Schwann, 1985.

Kaplan, Marion. *The Jewish Feminist Movement in Germany.* Westport, Connecticut: Greenwood, 1979.

Karl, Christine. "Diakonische Hilfe für den Bedrängten Nächsten im Nationalsozialismus." Heidelberg: Diplomarbeit, 1982.

Kater, Michael, "Frauen in der NS Bewegung," *Vierteljahrshefte für Zeitgeschichte.* 31:202–241, April 1983.

———. *The Nazi Party. A Social Profile of Members and Leaders, 1919–1945.* Cambridge: Harvard University Press, 1983.

Kaufmann, Doris. *Das katholische Milieu in Münster. Politische Aktionsformen und geschlechtsspezifische Verhaltensräume*. Düsseldorf: Schwann, 1984.

Kevles, Daniel J. *In the Name of Science: Eugenics and the Uses of Human Heredity*. New York: Knopf, 1985.

Kempner, Robert. *Edith Stein und Anne Frank zwei von Hunderttausand*. Freiburg im Br.: Herder, 1968.

Keneally, Thomas. *Schindler's List*. New York: Penguin, 1983.

Kershaw, Ian. *The Nazi Dictatorship. Problems and Perspectives of Interpretation*. London: Edward Arnold, 1985.

———. *Public Opinion and Political Dissent in the Third Reich. Bavaria, 1933–1945*. New York: Oxford University Press, 1983.

Klein, Burton H. *Germany's Economic Preparations for War*. Cambridge: Harvard University Press, 1959.

Klinksiek, Dorothee. *Die Frau im NS-Staat*. Stuttgart: Deutsche Verlags-Anstalt, 1982.

Kocka, Jürgen. *Facing Total War: German Society 1914–1918*, trans. B. Weinberger. Cambridge: Harvard University Press, 1984.

Köhler, Jochen. *Klettern in der Grosstadt. Geschichte vom Überleben zwischen 1933 und 1945*. Berlin: Wagenbach, 1981.

Klönne, Arno. *Gegen den Strom. Bericht über den Jugendwiderstand im Dritten Reich*. Hannover and Frankfurt: Gödel, 1957.

Kraus, Gisela. "Frauen vor dem Sondergericht München von 1933 bis 1945." Unpublished manuscript, 1982.

Krausnick, Helmut and Martin Broszat. *Anatomy of the SS State*. Trans. Dorothy Long and Marian Jackson. London: Granada, 1982.

Krummacher, F. A. *Die Kontroverse Hannah Arendt, Eichmann und die Juden*. Munich: Nymphenburger, 1964.

Kubasec, Maria. *Sterne über dem Abgrund. Aus dem Leben der Antifascisten Dr. Maria Grollmuss*. Bautzen: VEB, Domowina, 1961.

Kuczynski, Jürgen. *Die Lage der Arbeiterin in Deutschland vom 1700 bis zur Gegenwart*. Berlin: Akademie, 1963.

Langbein, Hermann. *Menschen in Auschwitz*. Vienna: Europa Verlag, 1972.

———. *Wir Haben es getan. Selbst-porträts, 1939–1945*. Vienna and Cologne: Europa, 1961.

Langer, Elinor. *Josephine Herbst. The Story She Could Never Tell*. Boston: Little, Brown, 1984.

Langer, W. L. *The Mind of Adolf Hitler*. New York: Signet, 1972.

Larsen, Stein U., Bernt Hagtvet, and Jan Peter Mykelbust, assisted by G. Gotz. *Who Were the Fascists? The Social Roots of European Fascism*. Bergen: Universitetsforlaget, 1980.

Leber, Annemarie. *Conscience in Revolt*. London: Valentine, Mitchell, 1954.

Leuner, H. D. *When Compassion Was a Crime*. London: Wolff, 1978.

Lewy, Günter, *The Catholic Church and Nazi Germany*, London: Weidenfeld and Nicolson, 1966.

Littell, Franklin H., and Hubert G. Locke. *The German Church Struggle and the Holocaust*. Detroit: Wayne State, 1974.

Manvell, Roger and Heinrich Frankel. *Dr. Goebbels: His Life and Death*. London: Heinemann, 1960.

———. *Himmler*. New York: Putnam's, 1945.

Matheson, Peter. *The Third Reich and the Christian Churches*. Grand Rapids, Michigan: Eardmanns, 1981.

Maser, Werner. *Hitlers Briefe und Notizen. Sein Weltsbild in handschriftlichen Dokumenten*. Düsseldorf and Vienna: Econ, 1973.

Mason, Tim. Sozialpolitik im Dritten Reich: Arbeiterklasse, Volksgemeinschaft Opladen: Westdeutscher, 1977.

———. "Women in Germany, 1925–1940: Family, Welfare, and Work," *History Workshop* I and II (Summer and Autumn 1976).

Meier, Kurt. *Kirchen und Judentum. Die Haltung der evangelischen Kirche zur Judenpolitik des Dritten Reiches*. Düsseldorf: Droste, 1972

Merkl, Peter. *Violence Under the Swastika*. Princeton: Princeton University Press, 1975.

Meybes, Fritz. *Agnes von Grone und das Frauenwerk*. Düsseldorf: Presseverband der evangelischen Kirche, 1981.

———, ed. *Geschichte der Evangelischen Frauenhilfe in Quellen*. Gladbeck: Schriftenverlag, 1975.

Michaelis, Schräpler and Scheel, eds. *Innere Gleichschaltung der Staat und die Kirchen* in *Ursache und Folgen des deutschen Zusammenbruches. 1918 & 1945*, vol. 11. Berlin: Wendler, 1967.

Milatz, Alfred. *Wähler und Wahlen in der Weimarer Republik*. Bonn: Bundeszentrale für Politische Bildung, 1965.

Mommsen, Wolfgang J. *Beamtentum im Dritten Reich*. Stuttgart: Deutsche Verlags-Anstalt, 1966.

Mosse, George. *Nationalism and Sexuality. Respectability and Abnormal Sexuality in Modern Europe*. New York: Fertig, 1984.

———. *Germans and Jews*. New York: Fertig, 1970.

———. *The Nationalization of the Masses*. New York: Fertig, 1975.

———. *Toward the Final Solution. A History of European Racism*. New York: Fertig, 1978.

Müller-Münch, Ingrid, *Die Frauen von Majdanek. Vom zerstörten Leben der Opfer und mörderinnen*. Hamburg: Rowohlt, 1982.

Musmanno, Michael. *The Eichmann Kommandos*. Philadelphia: Macrae Smith, 1961.

Neumann, Franz. *Behemoth. The Structure and Practice of National Socialism, 1933–1944*. (1942). New York: Harper Torch, 1966.

Niethammer, Lutz, ed. *"Die Jahre weiss mann nicht, wo man die heute hinsetzen soll."* Berlin and Bonn: Dietz, 1983.

Niemöller, Wilhelm. *Die Evangelische Kirche im Dritten Reich*. Bielefeld: Bechauf, 1956.

Niewyk, Donald. *The Jews in Weimar Germany*. Baton Rouge, Louisiana: Louisiana State University Press, 1980.

Nowak, Kurt. *"Euthanasie," und Sterilisierung im Dritten Reich. Die Konfrontation der evangelischen und katholischen Kirche mit dem Gesetz zur Verhütung erbkranken Nachwuchses*. Göttingen: Van den Hoeck and Rüprecht, 1978.

Nolte, Ernst. *The Three Faces of Fascism*. New York: NAL, 1965.

Orlow, Dietrich. *The History of the Nazi Party*. Pittsburgh: University of Pittsburgh Press, 1969.

Oppenheimer, Max. *Das kämpferische Leben der Johanna Kirchner. Portrait einer anti-faschischisten Widerstandskämpfer*. Frankfurt: Röderberg, 1974.

Paucker, Arnold. *Jüdischer Abwehrkampf in der Weimaren Republik*. 1968.

Pauwels, Jacques. *Women, Nazis and Universities. Female University Students in the Third Reich, 1933–1945*. Westport, Connecticut: Greenwood, 1984.

Pawelczynska, Anna. *Values and Violence in Auschwitz. A Sociological Analysis*. Trans. Catherine S. Leach. Berkeley: University of California Press, 1979.

Peterson, Edward. *The Limits of Hitler's Power*. Princeton: Princeton University Press, 1969.

Petzina, Dieter, Werner Abelshausen, and Anselm Faust, *Sozialgeschichtliches statistiches Arbeitsbuch des deutschen Reiches, 1914–1949*. Munich: Beck, 1978.

Peukert, Detlev. *Edelweisspiraten. Protestbewegung jugendlicher Arbeiter im Dritten Reich*. Cologne: Bund-Verlag, 1983. 2nd ed.

———. *Ruhr Arbeiter gegen den Fascismus: Dokumentationen*. Frankfurt: Röderberg, 1976.

———. *Volksgenossen und Gemeinschaftsfeinde: Anpassung, Ausmerze, und Aufbegehren*. Cologne: Bund, 1982.

Pinson, Koppel S. *Modern Germany. Its History and Civilization*. New York: Macmillan, 1954.

Poor, Harold. *Tucholsky*. New York: Scribner's, 1968.

Plath, Sylvia. *The Collected Poems*, ed. Ted Hughes. New York: Harper & Row, 1981.

Preller, Ludwig. *Sozialpolitik in der Weimarer Republik*. Stuttgart: Mittelbach, 1949.

Pridham, Geoffrey. *Hitler's Rise to Power. The Nazi Movement in Bavaria, 1923–1933*. New York: Harper Torch, 1973.

Prittie, Terrence. *Germans Against Hitler*. Boston: Little, Brown, 1964.

Pulzer, Peter. *The Rise of Political Anti-Semitism in Germany and Austria*. New York: Wiley, 1964.

Quataert, Jean. *Reluctant Feminists in German Social Democracy, 1885–1917*. Princeton: Princeton University Press, 1979.

Reichmann, Eva G., *Hostages of Civilization: The Social Sources of National Socialist Anti-Semitism*. Boston: Houghton-Mifflin, 1951.

Reuter, Angelika and Barbara Poneleit, *Seit 1848. Frauen im Widerstand und im Faschismus*. Munich: Frauenpolitik, 1977.

Rosenfeld, Alvin H. *Imagining Hitler*. Bloomington, Indiana: Indiana University Press, 1985.

Ryder, A. J. *Twentieth Century Germany: From Bismarck to Brandt*. New York: Columbia University, 1973.

Sartre, Jean-Paul. *Anti-Semite and Jew*, trans. George J. Becker, New York: Schocken, 1965.

Schaul, Dora. *Dying We Live.* New York: Pantheon, 1956.

Schabrod, Carl. *Widerstand gegen Flick und Florian.* Frankfurt: Röderburg, 1976.

Schirmer, Hermann. *Das andere Nürnberg. Antifaschistischer Widerstand in der Stadt der Reichsparteitage.* Frankfurt: Röderberg, 1974.

Schleuenes, Carl. *The Twisted Road to Auschwitz.* Urbana: University of Illinois Press, 1970.

Schmidt, Maruta and Gabi Dietz, eds. *Frauen unterm Hakenkreuz.* Berlin: Elefanten, 1983.

Schmidt-Biesalski. *Lust, Liebe und Verstand: Protestantische Frauen aus fünf Jahrhunderten.* Gelnhausen: Burckhardthaus, 1981.

Schön, Eberhard. *Die Entstehung des Nationalsozialismus in Hessen.* Meisenheim am Glan: Hamm, 1972.

Schoenbaum, David. *Hitler's Social Revolution. Class and Status in Nazi Germany.* New York: Norton, 1981.

Scholder, Klaus. *Die Kirchen und das Dritte Reich. 1918–1943.* Berlin, Vienna and Frankfurt: Ullstein, 1977.

Schüddekopf, Charles, ed. *Der alltägliche Faschismus. Frauen im Dritten Reich.* Berlin: Dietz, 1982.

Schuetz, W. W. *Pens under the Swastika. A Study in Recent German Writing.* Port Washington, New York, and London: Kennikat, 1971.

Schwersenz, Jizchak, and Edith Wolfe, "Jüdische Jugend im Untergrund," *Parlament* 31:15–16 (1981), 15–34.

See, Wolfgang and Rudolf Weckerling. *Frauen im Kirchenkampf. Beispiele aus der Bekennenden Kirche Berlin-Brandenburg 1933 bis 1945.* Foreword by Renate Scharf. Berlin: Wichern, 1984.

Sereny, Gitta. *Into that Darkness: An Examination of Conscience.* New York: Viking, 1985. First printed 1974.

Shirer, William. *20th Century Journey. The Nightmare Years.* Boston: Little, Brown, 1984.

———. *The Rise and Fall of the Third Reich.* New York: Simon and Schuster, 1960.

———. *Berlin Diary. The Journal of a Foreign Correspondent. 1934–1939.* New York, 1941.

———. *The End of a Berlin Diary.* New York: Knopf, 1947.

Shiveley, W. Phillips. "Party Identification, Party Choice and Voting Stability, The Weimar Case," *American Political Science Review* 66: (December 1972).

Siegle-Wenschkewitz, Leonore. *Nationalsozialismus und Kirchen. Religions politik von Partei und Staat bis 1935.* Düsseldorf: Droste, 1974.

Snitow, Ann, Christine Stansel, and Sharon Thompson, eds., *Power of Desire. The Politics of Sexuality.* New York: Monthly Review, 1983.

Sontag, Susan. *Under the Sign of Saturn.* New York: Farrar, Straus, & Giroux, 1972.

Stachura, Peter, ed. *The Shaping of the Nazi State.* London: Croom, Helm, 1978.

————. *Gregor Strasser and the Rise of Nazism*. London: Allen and Unwin, 1983.

Steinberg, Lucien. *Jews Against Hitler*, trans. Marion Hunter. London: Gordon and Cremonesi, 1974.

Steinert, Marlis G. *Hitler's War and the Germans*. Athens, Ohio: Ohio University Press, 1977.

Stephenson, Jill. *Women in Nazi Society*. New York: Barnes & Noble, 1975.

————. *The Nazi Organization of Women*. New York: Barnes & Noble, 1980.

Stoeffler, Erika, ed. *Initiativen und Lebensbilder Evangelischen Frauen*. Stuttgart: Quelle, 1984.

Stokes, L. D. "The German People and the Destruction of the European Jews," *Central European History* 6 (1973).

Susman, Warren I. *Culture as History*. New York: Pantheon, 1984.

Szepansky, Gerda. *Frauen leisten Widerstand*. Frankfurt: Fischer, 1983.

Thalmann, Rita. *Être Femme dans le Troisième Reich*. Paris: Lafont, 1981.

————, and Emmanuel Feinermann. *Crystal Night*, trans. Gilles Gremonesi. New York: Holocaust Library, 1974.

Theweleit, Klaus. *Männerphantasier*. Frankfurt: Roterstern, 1978.

Thönessen, Werner. *The Emancipation of Women in Germany*, trans. Joris de Bres. London: Pluto, 1976.

Tidl, Georg. *Die Frau im Nationalisozialismus*. Vienna: Europa, 1984.

Todd, Emmanuel. *La troisième planète. Structures familiales et systèmes idéologiques* (Paris: Seuil, 1983).

Toynbee, Arnold and Veronica. *Hitler's Europe*. London: Oxford University Press, 1954.

United States Strategic Bombing Survey. Economic Report, 1945.

Waite, Robert. *Hitler: The Psychopathic God*. New York: Basic, 1977.

Walk, Joseph. *Das Sonderrecht für Juden im NS Staat*. Heidelberg: D. F. Müller, 1981.

Weber, Alexander. *Soziale Merkmale der NSDAP Wähler. Eine Zusammenfassung bisheriger empirischer Untersuchungen und eine Analyse in den Gemeinden der Länder Baden und Hessen*. Dissertation. Freiburg. 1969.

Weeks, Jeffrey. *Sex, Politics, and Society. The Regulation of Sexuality Since 1800*. London: Longman, 1981.

Weisenborn, Günter. *Der lautlose Aufstand, Bericht über die Widerstandsbewegung des deutschen Volkes, 1933–1945*. Hamburg: Rowohlt, 1953.

————. *Deutsche Widerstandskämpfer. 1933–1945. Biographien und Briefe*. 2 vols. Berlin: Dietz, 1970.

Weil, Simone. *Ecrits historiques et politiques*. Paris: Gallimard, 1960.

Wiggershaus, Renate. *Frauen unterm Nationalsozialismus*. Wuppertal: Hammer, 1984.

Winkler, Dörte. *Frauenarbeit im "Dritten Reich."* Hamburg: Hoffmann und Campe, 1977.

Winkler, H. A. *Mittelstand, Demokratie und Nationalsozialismus*. Cologne, Kniephauer & Witsch, 1972.

Wischermann, Ulla. "Die Presse der radikalen Frauenbewegung," *Feministische Studien* 3:1 (May 1984).

Wittrock, Christine. *Weiblichkeits Mythen*. Frankfurt a.M.: Sendler, 1984.

Wright, J. R. C. *"Above Parties": The Political Attitudes of the German Protestant Church Leadership. 1918–1933*. Oxford: Historical Monograph, 1974.

Wucher, Albert. *Die Fahne Hoch. Das Ende der Republik und Hitlers Machtübernahme. Ein Dokumentarbericht*. Freiburg: Herder, 1965.

Zabel, James. *Nazism and the Pastors*. Missoula, Montana: Scholars, 1976.

Zahn, Gordon. *German Catholics and Hitler's Wars: A Study in Social Control*. New York: Sheed and Ward, 1962.

Zipfel, Friedrich. *Kirchenkampf in Deutschland. 1933–1945*. 2 vols. Berlin: Historische Kommission, 1965.

Zorn, Gerda and Gertrud Meyer. *Frauen gegen Hitler: Berichte aus dem Widerstand*. Frankfurt: Röderberg, 1974.

INDEX